Psy...

R 15    ☑ O9-BHJ-016

# PSYCHOLOGY BASICS

# PSYCHOLOGY BASICS

**Volume 2**

Logic and Reasoning—
Women's Psychology: Sigmund Freud
Index

*Editor*
**Nancy A. Piotrowski, Ph.D.**
University of California, Berkeley

SALEM PRESS
Pasadena, California
Hackensack, New Jersey

The essays in this work originally appeared in *Magill's Encyclopedia of Social Science: Psychology,* 2003; new material has been added.

**Library of Congress Cataloging-in-Publication Data**
Psychology basics / editor, Nancy A. Piotrowski.— Rev. ed.
    p.  cm. — (Magill's choice)
    Includes bibliographical references and index.
    ISBN 1-58765-199-8 (set : alk. paper) — ISBN 1-58765-200-5 (v. 1 : alk. paper) — ISBN 1-58765-201-3 (v. 2 : alk. paper)
    1. Psychology—Encyclopedias.  I. Piotrowski, Nancy A.  II. Series
BF31.P765  2004
150′.3—dc22

2004016637

Second Printing

PRINTED IN THE UNITED STATES OF AMERICA

# TABLE OF CONTENTS

# PSYCHOLOGY BASICS

# LOGIC AND REASONING

TYPE OF PSYCHOLOGY: Cognition
FIELDS OF STUDY: Cognitive processes; thought

*Logic and reasoning are essential elements of the human mind and underlie many daily activities. Although humans may not follow the prescriptions of formal logic precisely, human reasoning is nevertheless often systematic. Study of the structures and processes involved in the use of logic and reasoning provides insight into both the human mind and the possible creation of intelligent machines.*

KEY CONCEPTS
- atmosphere hypothesis
- availability
- belief-bias effect
- confirmation bias
- deductive reasoning
- gambler's fallacy
- heuristic
- inductive reasoning
- representativeness
- syllogism

Logical and reasoning tasks are typically classified as either deductive or inductive. In deductive reasoning, if the premises are true and a valid rule of inference is used, the conclusion must be true. In inductive reasoning, in contrast, the conclusion can be false even if the premises are true. In many cases, deductive reasoning also involves moving from general principles to specific conclusions, while inductive reasoning involves moving from specific examples to general conclusions.

Cognitive psychologists study deductive reasoning by examining how people reason using syllogisms, logical arguments comprising a major and a minor premise that lead to a conclusion. The premises are assumed to be true; the validity of the conclusion depends upon whether a proper rule of inference is used. The classic example of deduction is:

All men are mortal.
*Socrates is a man.*
Socrates is a mortal.

A more modern example of deduction might be:

All dinosaurs are animals.
*All animals are in zoos.*
All dinosaurs are in zoos.

The conclusion is valid but is not true, because one of the premises (all animals are in zoos) is not true. Broadly speaking, truth refers to content (that is, applicability of the conclusion to the real world), and validity refers to form (that is, whether the conclusion is drawn logically). It is thus possible to have a valid argument that is nevertheless untrue. Even if a valid rule of inference is applied and a valid conclusion is drawn, the conclusion may not be true. If a valid conclusion has been drawn from true premises, however, the argument is called "sound."

With inductive reasoning, the validity of the conclusion is less certain. The classic example of induction is:

> *Every crow I have seen in my life up to this time has been black.*
> All crows are black.

Other examples of induction include a child who begins to say "goed" (from "go") instead of "went," a detective piecing together evidence at the scene of a crime, and a stock analyst who, after observing that prices have fallen during the past two Septembers, urges clients to sell in August. In all these cases, a conclusion is drawn based on evidence observed prior to the conclusion. There remains the possibility, however, that additional evidence may render the conclusion incorrect. It does not matter how many positive instances (for example, black crows, September stock declines) have been observed; if one counterexample can be found (a white crow, a September stock rise), the conclusion is incorrect.

## HEURISTICS

The study of induction spans a variety of methods and topics. In this article, most of the consideration of induction involves cases in which people rely on heuristics in their reasoning. Heuristics involve "rules of thumb" that yield "ballpark" solutions that are approximately correct and can be applied across a wide range of problems.

One common heuristic is representativeness, which is invoked in answering the following questions: What is the probability that object A belongs to class B, event A originates from process B, or that process B will generate event A? The representativeness heuristic suggests that probabilities are evaluated by the degree to which A is representative of B, that is, by the degree to which A resembles B. If A is representative of B, the probability that A originates from B is judged to be high; if A does not resemble B or is not similar to B, the probability that A originates from B is judged to be low.

A second heuristic is availability, which is invoked in judgments of frequency. Specifically, people assess the frequency of a class by the ease with which instances of that class can be brought to mind. Factors that influence the ability to think of instances of a class, such as recency, salience, number of associations, and so forth, influence availability in such a way that certain types of events (such as recent and salient) are more available. For example, if several people one knows have been involved in car crashes recently, one's subjective probability of being in a car crash is increased.

### RULES OF INFERENCE

Before examining how people reason deductively, two rules of inference must be considered: *modus ponens* (the "method of putting," which involves affirming a premise) and *modus tollens* (the "method of taking," which involves negating a premise). Considering $P$ and $Q$ as content-free abstract variables (much like algebraic variables), *modus ponens* states that given "$P$ implies $Q$" and given $P$, one can infer $Q$. In the following example, applying *modus ponens* to 1 and 2 (in which $P$ is "it rained last night" and $Q$ is "the game was canceled"), one can infer 3.

1. If it rained last night, then the game was canceled.
2. It rained last night.
3. The game was canceled.

*Modus tollens* states that given "$P$ implies $Q$" and $\sim Q$ (read "not $Q$"; "$\sim$" is a symbol for negation), one can infer "$\sim P$." Applying *modus tollens* to 1 and 4, one can infer 5.

4. The game was not canceled.
5. It did not rain last night.

In general, people apply *modus ponens* properly but do not apply *modus tollens* properly. In one experiment, four cards showing the following letters or numbers were placed in front of subjects:

E K 4 7

Subjects saw only one side of each card but were told that a letter appeared on one side and a number on the other side. Subjects were asked to judge the validity of the following rule by turning over only those cards that provided a valid test of the following statement: If a card has a vowel on one side, then it has an even number on the other side. Turning over E is a correct application of *modus ponens*, and turning over 7 is a correct application of *modus tollens* (consider $P$ as "vowel on one side" and $Q$ as "even number on the other side"). Almost 80 percent of subjects turned over E only or E and 4, while only 4 percent of subjects chose the correct answer, turning over E and 7. While many subjects correctly applied *modus ponens*, far fewer correctly applied *modus tollens*. Additionally, many subjects turned over 4, an error called affirmation of the consequent.

When stimuli are concrete, reasoning improves. In an analogous experiment, four cards with the following information were placed before subjects:

beer Coke 16 22

One side of each card showed a person's drink; the other side showed a person's age. Subjects evaluated this rule: If a person is drinking beer, that person must be at least nineteen. In this experiment, nearly 75 percent of the subjects made the correct selections, showing that in some contexts people are more likely to apply *modus tollens* properly.

When quantifiers such as "all," "some," and "none" are used within syllogisms, additional errors in reasoning occur. People are more likely to accept positive conclusions to positive premises and negative conclusions to negative premises, negative conclusions if premises are mixed, a universal conclusion if premises are universal (all or none), a particular conclusion if premises are particular (some), and a particular conclusion if one premise is general and the other is particular. These observations led to the atmosphere hypothesis, which suggests that the quantifiers within the premises create an "atmosphere" predisposing subjects to accept as valid conclusions that use the same quantifiers.

### INFLUENCE OF KNOWLEDGE AND BELIEFS

Prior knowledge or beliefs can influence reasoning if people neglect the form of the argument and concentrate on the content; this is referred to as the belief-bias effect. If a valid conclusion appears unbelievable, people reject it, while a conclusion that is invalid but appears believable is accepted as valid. Many people accept this syllogism as valid:

All oak trees have acorns.
*This tree has acorns.*
This tree is an oak tree.

Consider, however, this logically equivalent syllogism:

All oak trees have leaves.
*This tree has leaves.*
This tree is an oak tree.

In the first syllogism, people's knowledge that only oak trees have acorns leads them to accept the conclusion as valid. In the second syllogism, people's knowledge that many types of trees have leaves leads them to reject the conclusion as invalid.

### BIASES IN REASONING

A common bias in inductive reasoning is the confirmation bias, the tendency to seek confirming evidence and not to seek disconfirming evidence. In one study, subjects who were presented with the numbers (2, 4, 6) determined what rule (concept) would allow them to generate additional numbers in the series. In testing their hypotheses, many subjects produced series to confirm their hypotheses—for example, (20, 22, 24) or (100, 102, 104)—of "even numbers ascending by 2," but few produced series to disconfirm their hypotheses—for example, (1, 3, 5) or (20, 50, 187). In fact, any ascending series (such as 32, 69, 100,005) would have satisfied the general rule, but because subjects did not seek to disconfirm their more specific rules, they did not discover the more general rule.

Heuristics also lead to biases in reasoning. In one study, subjects were told that bag A contained ten blue and twenty red chips, while bag B contained twenty blue and ten red chips. On each trial, the experimenter selected one bag; subjects knew that bag A would be selected on 80 percent of the trials. The subject drew three chips from the bag and reasoned whether A or B had been selected. When subjects drew two blues and one red, all were confident that B had been selected. If the probability for that sample is actually calculated, however, the odds are 2:1 that it comes from A. People chose B because the sample of chips resembles (represents) B more than A, and ignored the prior probability of 80 percent that the bag was A.

In another experiment, subjects were shown descriptions of "Linda" that made her appear to be a feminist. Subjects rated the probability that Linda was a bank teller and a feminist higher than the probability that Linda was a bank teller. Whenever there is a conjunction of events, however, the probability of both events is less than the probability of either event alone, so the probability that Linda was a bank teller and a feminist was actually lower than the probability that she was only a bank teller. Reliance on representativeness leads to overestimation of the probability of a conjunction of events.

Reliance on representativeness also leads to the "gambler's fallacy." This fallacy can be defined as the belief that if a small sample is drawn from an infinite and randomly distributed population, that sample must also appear randomly distributed.

Consider a chance event such as flipping a coin. (H represents "heads"; T represents "tails.") Which sequence is more probable: HTHTTH or HHHHHH? Subjects judge that the first sequence is more probable, but both are equally probable. The second sequence, HHHHHH, does not appear to be random, however, and so is believed to be less probable. After a long run of H, people judge T as more probable than H because the coin is "due" for T. A problem with the idea of "due," though, is that the coin itself has no memory of a run of H or T. As far as the coin is concerned, on the next toss there is .5 probability of H and .5 probability of T. The fallacy arises because subjects expect a small sample from an infinitely large random distribution to appear random. The same misconceptions are often extended beyond coin-flipping to all games of chance.

In fallacies of reasoning resulting from availability, subjects misestimate frequencies. When subjects estimated the proportion of English words beginning with R versus words with R as the third letter, they estimated that more words begin with R, but, in fact, more than three times as many words have R as their third letter. For another example, consider the following problem. Ten people are available and need to be organized into committees. Can more committees of two or more committees of eight be organized? Subjects claimed that more committees of two could be organized, probably because it is easier to visualize a larger number of committees of two, but equal numbers of committees could be made in both cases. In both examples, the class for which it is easier to generate examples is judged to be the most frequent or numerous. An additional aspect of availability involves causal scenarios (sometimes referred to as the simulation heuristic), stories or narratives in which one event causes another and which lead from an original situation to an outcome. If a causal scenario linking an original situation and outcome is easily available, that outcome is judged to be more likely.

### EVOLUTION OF STUDY

Until the twentieth century, deductive logic and the psychology of human thought were considered to be the same topic. The mathematician George Boole titled his 1854 book on logical calculus *An Investigation of the Laws of Human Thought*. This book was designed "to investigate the fundamental laws of those operations of the mind by which reasoning is performed." Humans did not always seem to operate according to the prescriptions of logic, but such lapses were seen as the malfunctioning of the mental machinery. When the mental machinery functioned properly, humans were logical. Indeed, it is human rationality, the ability to think logically, that for many thinkers throughout time has separated humans from other animals (for example, Aristotle's man as rational animal) and defined the human essence (for example, René Descartes's "I think, therefore I am").

As a quintessential mental process, the study of reasoning is an integral part of modern cognitive psychology. In the mid-twentieth century, however, when psychology was in the grip of the behaviorist movement, little attention was given to such "mentalistic" conceptions, with the exception of isolated works such as Frederic C. Bartlett's studies of memory and Jerome S. Bruner, Jacqueline J. Goodnow, and George A. Austin's landmark publication *A Study of Thinking* (1956), dealing with, among other topics, induction and concept formation. The development of the digital computer and the subsequent application of the computer as a metaphor for the human mind suggested new methods and vocabularies for investigating mental processes such as reasoning, and with the ascendancy of the cognitive approach within experimental psychology and the emergence of cognitive science, research on human reasoning has become central in attempts both to understand the human mind and to build machines that are capable of independent, intelligent action.

### INVOLVEMENT OF COMPUTERS

In the latter part of the twentieth century, there were attempts to simulate human reasoning with computers and to develop computers capable of humanlike reasoning. One notable attempt involved the work of Allen Newell and Herbert Simon, who provided human subjects with various sorts of problems to solve. Their human subjects would "think out loud," and transcripts of what they said became the basis of computer programs designed to mimic human problem solving and reasoning. Thus, the study of human logic and reasoning not only furthered the understanding of human cognitive processes but also gave guidance to those working in artificial intelligence. One caveat, however, is that even though such transcripts may serve as a model for computer intelligence, there remain important differences between human and machine "reasoning." For example, in humans, the correct application of some inference rules (for example, *modus tollens*) depends upon the context (for example, the atmosphere hypothesis or the belief-bias effect). Furthermore, not all human reasoning may be strictly verbalizable, and to the extent that human reasoning relies on nonlinguistic processes (such as imagery), it might not be possible to mimic or re-create it on a computer.

After being assumed to be logical, or even being ignored by science, human reasoning is finally being studied for what it is. In solving logical problems, humans do not always comply with the dictates of logical theory; the solutions reached may be influenced by the context of the problem, previous knowledge or belief, and the particular heuristics used in reaching a solution. Discovery of the structures, processes, and strategies involved in reasoning promises to increase the understanding not only of how the human mind works but also of how to develop artificially intelligent machines.

## SOURCES FOR FURTHER STUDY

Halpern, Diane F. *Thought and Knowledge: An Introduction to Critical Thinking.* 4th ed. Mahwah, N.J.: Lawrence Erlbaum, 2003. Presents a brief overview of memory and language, then presents data and theory on performance with different types of deductive arguments, analyzing arguments, fallacies, reasoning with probabilities, and hypothesis testing. The author provides numerous examples and exercises, and the text can be understood by high school or college students.

Holland, John H., et al. *Induction: Processes of Inference, Learning, and Discovery.* Reprint. Cambridge, Mass.: MIT Press, 1989. Presents a broad cross-disciplinary account of induction and examines the role of inferential rules in induction, people's mental models of the world, concept formation, problem solving, and the role of induction in discovery. The authors provide an extensive bibliography of scholarly research on induction.

Johnson-Laird, Philip Nicholas. *Mental Models.* Cambridge, Mass.: Harvard University Press, 1983. Presents an extensive review of data and theory on syllogistic reasoning. The author presents a unified theory of the mind based on recursive procedures, propositional representations, and mental models. The text is very thorough and detailed, and many readers may find it daunting.

Kahneman, Daniel, Paul Slovic, and Amos Tversky, eds. *Judgment Under Uncertainty: Heuristics and Biases.* New York: Cambridge University Press, 1987. Presents a collection of many of the important papers on heuristics, including several papers each on representativeness, availability, causality and attribution, and corrective procedures. Many of the papers are thorough and present detailed information on experiments or theory.

Kelley, David. *The Art of Reasoning.* 3d ed. New York: W. W. Norton, 1998. A well-regarded introduction to classic logic. Thorough and accessible.

Sternberg, Robert J., and Talia Ben-Zeev. *Complex Cognition: The Psychology of Human Thought.* New York: Oxford University Press, 2001. An introduction to cognitive psychology, including explanations of the types of reasoning in theory and in practice. Synthesizes the "normative reference" and "bounded rationality" approaches to understanding human thought.

Weizenbaum, Joseph. *Computer Power and Human Reason II.* New York: W. H. Freeman, 1997. Provides many examples of "computer reason" and argues that some aspects of the mind cannot be explained in information-processing (computational) terms. Makes the case that computers should not be given tasks that demand human reason or wisdom. Written in an accessible and easy-to-read style.

*Timothy L. Hubbard*

SEE ALSO: Thought: Study and Measurement.

# Madness

## Historical Concepts

Type of psychology: Psychopathology
Fields of study: General constructs and issues; models of abnormality

*Throughout history, humans have tried to explain the abnormal behavior of people with mental disorders. From the ancient concept of demoniacal possession to modern biopsychosocial models, beliefs regarding the cause of mental disorders have influenced the way communities treat those variously labeled mad, insane, or mentally ill.*

### Key concepts

- asylum
- biopsychosocial model of mental disorders
- deinstitutionalization
- demoniacal possession
- humoral imbalance
- lobotomy
- madness
- moral treatment
- phenothiazines

People are social creatures who learn how to behave appropriately in families and communities. What is considered appropriate, however, depends on a host of factors, including historical period, culture, geography, and religion. Thus, what is valued and respected changes over time, as do sociocultural perceptions of aberrant or deviant behavior. How deviancy is treated depends a great deal on the extent of the deviancy—is the person dangerous, a threat to self or to the community, in flagrant opposition to community norms, or is the person just a little odd? How the community responds also depends on its beliefs as to what causes aberrant behavior. Supernatural beliefs in demons, spirits, and magic were common in preliterate societies. In the medieval Western world, Christians believed that the devil was in possession of deranged souls. Hence, the mentally ill were subjected to cruel treatments justified by the idea of routing out demons or the devil. For centuries, the prevailing explanation for madness was demoniacal possession. Prior to the nineteenth century, families and communities cared for the mad. If they were unmanageable or violent, the mad were incarcerated in houses of correction or dungeons, where they were manacled or put into straitjackets. If a physician ever attended someone who was deemed mad by the community, it was to purge or bleed the patient to redress a supposed humoral imbalance.

Most medical explanations prior to the advent of scientific medicine were expressed in terms of the four humors: black bile, yellow bile, blood, and phlegm. Imbalances usually were treated with laxatives, purgatives, astringents, emetics, and bleeding. Understanding moved from the holistic and humoral to the anatomical, chemical, and physiological. Also, views of humans and their rights changed enormously as a consequence of the eighteenth century American and French Revolutions.

During the nineteenth and twentieth centuries, madhouses were first replaced by more progressive lunatic asylums and then by mental hospitals and community mental health centers. In parallel fashion, custodians and superintendents of madhouses became mad-doctors or alienists in the nineteenth century and psychiatrists, psychologists, and counselors of various kinds in the twentieth century. Similarly, the language changed: Madness was variously called lunacy, insanity, derangement, or alienation. The term currently used is mental disorder. These changes reflect the rejection of supernatural and humoral explanations of madness in favor of a disease model with varying emphases on organic or psychic causes.

### EARLY VIEWS OF MADNESS

One of the terrible consequences of the belief in supernatural possession by demons was the inhumane treatment in which it often resulted. An example is found in the book of Leviticus in the Bible, which many scholars believe is a compilation of laws which had been handed down orally in the Jewish community for as long as a thousand years until they were written down, perhaps about 700 B.C.E. Leviticus 20:27, in the King James version, reads, "A man or a woman that hath a familiar spirit . . . shall surely be put to death: they shall stone him with stones." The term "familiar spirit" suggests demoniacal possession.

There were exceptions to the possession theory and the inhumane treatment to which it often led. Hippocrates, who lived around 300 B.C.E. in Greece and who is regarded as the father of medicine, believed that mental illness had biological causes and could be explained by human reason through empirical study. Although Hippocrates found no cure, he did recommend that the mentally ill be treated humanely, as other ill people would be treated. Humane treatment of the mentally ill was often the best that physicians and others could do.

The period of Western history that is sometimes known as the Dark Ages was particularly dark for the mad. Folk belief, theology, and occult beliefs and practices of all kinds often led to terrible treatment. Although some educated and thoughtful people, even in that period, held humane views, they were in the minority regarding madness.

### EIGHTEENTH AND NINETEENTH CENTURY VIEWS

It was not until what could be considered the modern historical period, beginning at the end of the eighteenth century—the time of the American and French Revolutions—that major changes took place in the treatment of the mentally ill. Additionally, there was a change in attitudes toward such persons, in approaches to their treatment and in beliefs regarding the causes of their strange behaviors. The man who, because of his courage, became a symbol of this new attitude was the French physician Philippe Pinel (1745-1826), appointed physician-in-chief of the Bictre Hospital in Paris in 1792. The Bictre was one of a number of "asylums" which had developed in Europe and in Latin America over several hundred years to house the insane. Often started with the best of intentions, most of the asylums became hellish places of incarceration.

In the Bictre, patients were often chained to the walls of their cells and lacked even the most elementary amenities. Pinel insisted to a skeptical committee of the Revolution that he be permitted to remove the chains from some of the patients. In one of the great, heroic acts in human history, Pinel introduced "moral treatment" of the insane, risking grave personal consequences if his humane experiment had failed.

This change was occurring in other places at about the same time. After the death of a Quaker in Britain's York Asylum, the local Quaker community founded the York Retreat, where neither chains nor corporal punishment were allowed. In the United States, Benjamin Rush, a founder of the Ameri-

*Benjamin Rush invented this "tranquillizing chair" in 1811.* (National Library of Medicine)

*A "centrifugal bed" was used to spin mental patients in the early nineteenth century.* (National Library of Medicine)

can Psychiatric Association, applied his version of moral treatment, which was not entirely humane as it involved physical restraints and fear as therapeutic agents. Toward the middle of the nineteenth century, American crusader Dorothea Lynde Dix fought for the establishment of state hospitals for the insane. As a result of her activism, thirty-two states established at least one mental hospital. Dix had been influenced by the moral model as well as by the medical sciences, which were rapidly developing in the nineteenth century. Unfortunately, the state mental hospital often lost its character as a "retreat" for the insane.

The nineteenth century was the first time in Western history (with some exceptions) that a number of scientists turned their attention to abnormal behavior. For example, the German psychiatrist Emil Kraepelin spent much of his life trying to develop a scientific classification system for psychopathology. Sigmund Freud attempted to develop a science of mental illness. Although many of Freud's ideas have not withstood empirical investigation, perhaps his greatest contribution was his insistence that scientific principles apply to mental illness. He believed that abnormal behavior is not caused by supernatural forces and does not arise in a chaotic, random way, but that it can be understood as serving some psychological purpose.

### MODERN MEDICINES

Many of the medical/biological treatments for mental illness in the first half of the twentieth century were frantic attempts to deal with very serious problems—attempts made by clinicians who had few effective therapies available. The attempt to produce convulsions (which often did seem to make people "better," at least temporarily) was popular for a decade or two. One example was insulin shock therapy, in which convulsions were induced in mentally ill people by insulin injection. Electroconvulsive (electric shock) therapy was also used. Originally it was primarily used with patients who had schizophrenia, a severe form of psychosis. Although it was not very effective with schizophrenia, it was found to be useful with patients who had resistant forms of depressive psychosis. Another treatment sometimes used, beginning in the 1930's, was prefrontal lobotomy. Many professionals today would point out that the use of lobotomy indicates the almost desperate search for an effective treatment for the most aggressive or the most difficult psychotic patients. As originally used, lobotomy was an imprecise slashing of the frontal lobe of the brain.

The real medical breakthrough in the treatment of psychotic patients was associated with the use of certain drugs from a chemical family known as phenothiazines. Originally used in France as tranquilizers for surgery patients, their potent calming effect attracted the interest of psychiatrists and other mental health workers. One drug of this group, chlorpromazine, was found to reduce or eliminate psychotic symptoms in many patients. This and similar medications came to be referred to as antipsychotic drugs. Although their mechanism of action is still not completely understood, they improved the condition of many severely ill patients while causing severe side effects for others. The drugs allowed patients to function outside the hospital and often to lead normal lives. They enabled many patients to benefit from psychotherapy. The approval of the use of chlorpromazine as an antipsychotic drug in the United States in 1955 revolutionized the treatment of many mental patients. Individuals who, prior to 1955, might have spent much of their lives in a hospital could instead control their illness effectively enough to live in the community, work at a job, attend school, and be a functioning member of a family.

In 1955, the United States had approximately 559,000 patients in state mental hospitals; seventeen years later, in 1972, the population of the state mental hospitals had decreased almost by half, to approximately 276,000. Although all of this cannot be attributed to the advent of the psychoactive drugs, they undoubtedly played a major role. The phenothiazines had finally given medicine a real tool in the battle with psychosis. One might believe that the antipsychotic drugs, combined with a modern version of the moral treatment, would enable society to eliminate mental illness as a major human problem. Unfortunately, good intentions go awry. The "major tranquilizers" can easily become chemical straitjackets; those who prescribe the drugs are sometimes minimally involved with future treatment. In the early 1980's, policy makers saw what appeared to be the economic benefits of reducing the role of the mental hospital, by discharging patients and closing some facilities. However, they did not foresee that large numbers of homeless psychotics would live in the streets as a consequence of "deinstitutionalization." The plight of the homeless continues in the early part of the twenty-first century to be a serious problem throughout the United States.

## DISORDER AND DYSFUNCTION

The twentieth century saw the exploration of many avenues in the treatment of mental disorders. Treatments ranging from classical psychoanalysis to cognitive and humanistic therapies to the use of therapeutic drugs were applied. Psychologists examined the effects of mental disorders on many aspects of life, including cognition and personality. These disorders affect the most essential of human functions, including cognition, which has to do with the way in which the mind thinks and makes decisions. Cognition does not work in "ordinary" ways in the person with a serious mental illness, making his or her behavior very difficult for family, friends, and others to understand. Another aspect of cognition is perception. Perception has to do with the way that the mind, or brain, interprets and understands the information which comes to a person through the senses. There is a general consensus among most human beings about what they see and hear, and perhaps to a lesser extent about what they touch, taste, and smell. The victim of mental illness, however, often perceives the world in a much different way. This person may see objects or events that no one else sees, phenomena called hallucinations. The hallucinations may be visual—for example, the person may see a frightening wild animal that no one else sees—or aural—for example, the person may hear a voice that no one else hears, accusing him or her of terrible crimes or behaviors.

A different kind of cognitive disorder is delusions. Delusions are untrue and often strange ideas, usually growing out of psychological needs or problems of a person who may have only tenuous contact with reality. A person, for example, may believe that other employees are plotting to harm her in some way when, in fact, they are merely telling innocuous stories around the water cooler. Sometimes people with mental illness will be disoriented, which means that they do not know where they are in time (what year, what season, or what time of day) or in space (where they live, where they are at the present moment, or where they are going).

In addition to experiencing cognitive dysfunction that creates havoc, mentally ill persons may have emotional problems that go beyond the ordinary. For example, they may live on such an emotional "high" for weeks or months at a time that their behavior is exhausting both to themselves and to those around them. They may exhibit bizarre behavior; for example, they may talk about giving away vast amounts of money (which they do not have), or they may go without sleep for days until they drop from exhaustion. This emotional "excitement" seems to dominate their lives and is called mania. The word "maniac" comes from this terrible emotional extreme.

At the other end of the emotional spectrum is clinical depression. This does not refer to the "blues" of ordinary daily life, with all its ups and downs, but to an emotional emptiness in which the individual seems to have lost all emotional energy. The individual often seems completely apathetic. The person may feel life is not life worth living and may have anhedonia, which refers to an inability to experience pleasure of almost any kind.

## TREATMENT APPROACHES

Anyone interacting with a person suffering from a severe mental disorder comes to think of him or her as being different from normal human beings. The behavior of those with mental illness is regarded, with some justification, as bizarre and unpredictable. They are often labeled with a term that sets them apart, such as "crazy" or "mad." There are many words in the English language that have been, or are, used to describe these persons—many of them quite cruel and derogatory. Since the nineteenth century, professionals have used the term "psychotic" to denote severe mental illness or disorders. Interestingly, one translation of psychotic is "of a sickness of the soul" and reflects the earlier belief regarding the etiology or cause of mental illness. This belief is still held by some therapists and pastoral counselors in the twenty-first century. Until the end of the twentieth century, the term "neurosis" connoted more moderate dysfunction than the term "psychosis." However, whether neurosis is always less disabling or disturbing than psychosis has been an open question. An attempt was made to deal with this dilemma in 1980, when the American Psychiatric Association's *Diagnostic and Statistical Manual of Mental Disorders* (3d ed., 1980, DSM-III) officially dropped the term "neurosis" from the diagnostic terms.

The current approach to mental disorders, at its best, offers hope and healing to patients and their families. However, much about the etiology of mental disorders remains unknown to social scientists and physicians. In 1963, President John F. Kennedy signed the Community Mental Health and Retardation Act. Its goal was to set up centers throughout the United States offering services to mentally and emotionally disturbed citizens and their families, incorporating the best that had been learned and that would be learned from science and from medicine. Outpatient services in the community, emergency services, "partial" hospitalizations (adult day care), consultation, education, and research were among the programs supported by the act. Although imperfect, it nevertheless demonstrated how far science had come from the days when witches were burned at the stake and the possessed were stoned to death.

When one deals with mental disorders, one is dealing with human behavior—both the behavior of the individual identified as having the problem and the behavior of the community. The response of the community is critical for the successful treatment of disorders. For example, D. L. Rosenhan, in a well-known 1973 study titled "On Being Sane in Insane Places," showed how easy it is to be labeled "crazy" and how difficult it is to get rid of the label. He demonstrated how one's behavior is interpreted and understood on the basis of the labels that have been applied. (The "pseudopatients" in the study had been admitted to a mental hospital and given a diagnosis—a label—of schizophrenia. Consequently, even their writing of notes in a notebook was regarded as evidence of their illness.) To understand mental disorders is not merely to understand personal dysfunction or distress but also to understand social and cultural biases of the community, from the family to the federal government. The prognosis for eventual mental and emotional health depends not only on appropriate therapy but also on the reasonable and humane response of the relevant communities.

## Sources for Further Study

American Psychiatric Association. *Diagnostic and Statistical Manual of Disorders: DSM-IV-TR.* Rev. 4th ed. Washington, D.C.: Author, 2000. This is the official manual for the classification of mental disorders used by clinicians and researchers in a variety of settings. The manual also is used for educational purposes as disorders are described with respect to diagnostic features, cultural and age considerations, prevalence, course, and familial patterns. The language is accessible to advanced students.

Berrios, German E., and Roy Porter. *A History of Clinical Psychiatry: The Origin and History of Psychiatric Disorders.* Washington Square: New York University Press, 1995. This book addresses the clinical and social history of mental disorders and is a good follow-up for readers interested in studying a particular type of disorder. A major theme throughout involves tracking the interaction between clinical signals of disorder, successive historical periods, and psychosocial contexts. For advanced students.

Frankl, Viktor Emil. *Man's Search for Meaning: An Introduction to Logotherapy.* New York: Insight Books, 1997. A powerful book which serves as an example of many publications that emphasize what has been called "moral treatment." Frankl's book is partly autobiographical, based on his experiences as a Jew in a German concentration camp. The book then goes on to develop some ideas related to abnormal behavior.

Freud, Sigmund. *The Freud Reader.* Edited by Peter Gay. 1989. Reprint. New York: W. W. Norton, 1995. This book offers a selection of essays and excerpts meant to give the reader an understanding of the breadth of Freud's seminal work. Topics include Freud's psychosexual theory of human development, his theory of mind, psychoanalysis, and his ideas on the arts, religion, and culture. The editor offers introductions for each selection. Good overview of a historically important thinker.

Grob, Gerald N. *The Mad Among Us: A History of the Care of America's Mentally Ill.* New York: Free Press, 1994. This history of the care and treatment of the mentally ill in America begins with the colonial period and ends with the modern period. It is a thoughtful analysis of changing societal perceptions of moral obligation and of the historically varying policies regarding presumed effective care. Documents the contradictory policies of confinement versus community living for the disordered. Also looks at the question of whether the public need for protection overrides the needs of the individual. Written for the general reader.

Porter, Roy. *The Greatest Benefit to Mankind: A Medical History of Humanity.* New York: W. W. Norton, 1997. An engaging book that includes a chapter on psychiatry, a short history of mental disorders covering the eighteenth through the twentieth centuries in Britain, Europe, and North America. Good discussions of the asylum movement, degeneration theory and Nazi psychiatry, psychoanalysis, and modern developments. Porter was a social historian of medicine whose scholarship is accessible to the general reader. There is an extensive list of sources for further reading. Highly recommended.

_____. *Madness: A Brief History.* New York: Oxford University Press, 2002. A history of Western ideas about mental illness by one of the most respected historians of medicine. Changing ideas about "madness" help trace the evolution of psychology.

Robinson, Daniel N. *An Intellectual History of Psychology.* 3d ed. Madison: University of Wisconsin Press, 1995. Although mental illness as such occupies a small part of this book, it is a genuinely important book in helping to understand the philosophical and intellectual currents which have played such a major role in the psychological and scientific understanding of mental illness. A sometimes demanding book to read, it is well worth the intellectual energy for one who wants to understand various intellectual disciplines.

Rosenhan, David L. "On Being Sane in Insane Places." *Science* 179 (January 19, 1973): 250-258. More of a "naturalistic illustration" than a scientific experiment, this article raises provocative questions and puts forth some controversial conclusions. Enjoyable reading that does not require much psychological background on the part of the reader.

*James Taylor Henderson; updated by Tanja Bekhuis*

SEE ALSO: Psychology: Fields of Specialization; Psychosurgery; Schizophrenia: Background, Types, and Symptoms; Schizophrenia: Theoretical Explanations; Thought: Study and Measurement.

# MEMORY

TYPE OF PSYCHOLOGY: Memory
FIELD OF STUDY: Cognitive processes

*Theories of memory attempt to identify the structures and explain the processes underlying the human memory system. These theories give coherence to an understanding of memory and suggest new research needed to extend knowledge about learning and memory.*

KEY CONCEPTS
- episodic memory
- iconic memory
- long-term memory
- memory trace
- schemas
- semantic memory
- sensory memory
- short-term memory

Human memory is among the most complex phenomena in the universe. A Russian newspaper reporter once flawlessly recalled a list of fifty unrelated words he had studied for only three minutes fifteen years earlier. On the other hand, as everyone knows from personal experience, the memory system is also capable of losing information presented only seconds before. Errors in memory create so many problems that it seems imperative to know all that is possible about human memory. For that, a theory is needed.

A scientific theory is a systematic way to understand complex phenomena that occur in nature. A theory is judged to be useful insofar as its claims can be supported by the findings of empirical tests, especially experimentation, and insofar as it leads to further research studies. A theory is not right or wrong; it is simply a tool to describe what is known and to suggest what needs further study.

Three major forms of memory are generally described: short-term, long-term, and sensory memory. Short-term memory represents the temporary retention of newly acquired information. Generally, short-term memory lasts no longer than about twenty seconds. This is useful for short-term tasks, such as the recall of speech during discussions or discourse with another person. Short-term memory is rapidly lost, sometimes referred to as a process of decaying. Alan Baddeley, a major researcher in the field of memory, has suggested a concept of "working memory" may be substituted for short-term. Repeat stimulation, or rehearsal, may transfer short-term memory into that of long-term.

Long-term memory involves storage of information over longer periods of time, potentially as long as the life of the individual. Some researchers into the subject consider long-term memory to include two major areas: episodic and semantic. Episodic memory addresses events that have a temporal relationship with a person's life. This may include recall of when events or information appeared. Semantic memory represents the concepts or skills, represented in part by learning, that people acquire through the course of their lives.

Sensory memories are those which can be retrieved as a result of sensory stimuli. For example, a particular odor may result in recall of events from the past. The unusual smell of a cleaning solution may cause recall of a college dormitory from years past. This form of recall has been called olfactory memory. The image of a flower may result in the memory of a teenage boyfriend. Such a visual stimulus is sometimes referred to as iconic memory.

Theories of memory have been important to psychology for a long time, often occupying the time and interest of researchers throughout their careers. Memory, which is always connected to learning, is defined as the mental process of preserving information acquired through the senses for later use. The cognitive approach to memory places emphasis on mental processes, which result in the ability to comprehend or recall what is learned. The basis is found in changes that occur in the regions of the brain, such as the hippocampus, associated with memory. In a sense, memory is the record of the experiences of a lifetime. Without it, a person could not reexperience the past; everything at every moment would be brand-new. A person could not recognize the face of a loved one or learn from any experience. A person would thus have a greatly reduced chance for survival and would have no sense of personal identity. Memory is, in short, critical to functioning as a human being.

### ASSOCIATIONISM, COGNITIVE THEORY, AND NEUROPSYCHOLOGY

The goal of a theory of memory is to explain the structures (analogous to hardware) and the processes (analogous to software) that make the system work. Explaining how such a complex system works is a massive undertaking. Many attempts have taken the form of large-scale theories, which seek to deal with all major operations of the memory systems. The major theories of memory are associationism and theories from cognitive psychology and neuropsychology. The theories differ primarily in views of the retention and retrieval functions of memory. They also differ in terms of their conception of memory as active or passive.

Associationism, is the theory that memory relies on forming links or bonds between two unrelated things. This theory stems from the work of Hermann Ebbinghaus, who started the use of laboratory methods in the study of memory in the late nineteenth century. According to this theory, the ability to remember depends on establishing associations between stimuli and responses (S-R). Establishing associations depends on the frequency, recency, and saliency of their pairing. If these bonds become very strong, the subject is said to have developed a habit. Associationism also assumes the existence of internal stimuli that produce behavioral responses. These responses then become stimuli for other unobservable internal responses, thus forming chains. In this way, complex physical behaviors and mental associations can be achieved. Associationists tend to view the memory system as essentially passive, responding to environmental stimuli.

Cognitive theory emphasizes studying complex memory in the real world; it is concerned with the ecological validity of memory studies. Most of this work stems from the research of Sir Frederic C. Bartlett, who was not satisfied with laboratory emphasis on "artificial memory," but rather chose to study what he called meaningful memory. Meaningful memory, he said in his book *Remembering: A Study in Experimental and Social Psychology* (1932), is a person's effort to make sense of the world and to function effectively in it. Cognitive psychology recognizes subjective experiences as inescapably linked to human behavior. It centers on internal representation of past experiences and assumes that intentions, goals, and plans make a difference in what is remembered and how well it is remembered. The focus in memory research is on semantic memory—the knowledge of words, categories, concepts, and meanings located in long-term memory. People have highly complex networks of concepts, which helps account for their behavior in the real world. These networks are called schemas. New experiences and new information are viewed in light of old schemas so that they are easier to remember. Cognitive theory emphasizes how the individual processes information, and it uses the computer as its working model of memory.

Neuropsychology has contributed the third major theory of memory. Although psychology has always recognized the connection between its concerns and those of biology and medicine, the technology now available has made neuropsychological analysis of brain structure and functioning possible. Karl Lashley was an early researcher who sought to find the location of memory in the brain. He ran rats through mazes until they had learned the correct pathway. His subsequent surgical operations on experimental rats' brains failed to show localization of memory.

The search for the memory trace, the physiological change that presumably occurs as a result of learning, continued with Donald Hebb, who had assisted Lashley. The brain consists of billions of nerve cells, which are connected to thousands of other neurons. Hebb measured the electrical activity of the brain during learning, and he discovered that nerve cells fire repeatedly. He was able to show that an incoming stimulus causes patterns of neurons to become active. These cell assemblies discovered by Hebb constitute a structure for the reverberating circuits, a set of neurons firing repeatedly when information enters short-term memory. This firing seems to echo the information until it is consolidated in long-term memory. Other researchers have found chemical and physical changes associated with the synapses and in the neurons themselves during learning and when the learning is consolidated into long-term memory. The discovery of the memory trace, a dream of researchers for a long time, may become a reality. Neuropsychology sees memory as a neural function controlled by electrical and chemical activity.

### CLINICAL APPROACHES TO MEMORY DISORDERS

Human memory is so important to daily life that any theory that could explain its structures and processes and thus potentially improve its functioning would be invaluable. Memory is inextricably tied to learning, planning, reasoning, and problem solving; it lies at the core of human intelligence.

None of the three theories is by itself sufficient to explain all the phenomena associated with memory. Over the years, a number of ideas have been developed in the attempt to improve memory functioning through passive means. Efforts to induce learning during sleep and to assess memory of patients for events taking place while under anesthesia have had mixed results, but on the whole have not succeeded. Memory enhancement through hypnosis has been attempted but has not been shown to be very effective or reliable. Pills to improve memory and thereby intelligence have been marketed

*Although memory does decline with age, most older people do not experience significant impairment.*
(PhotoDisc)

but so far have not been shown to be the answer to memory problems. Research has begun on the possibility that certain drugs (such as tacrine) may interactively inhibit memory loss in people afflicted with certain kinds of dementia (for example, Alzheimer's disease). Work in neuropsychology has shown the influence of emotion-triggered hormonal changes in promoting the memory of exciting or shocking events (such as one's first kiss or an earthquake). This has led to an understanding of state-dependent memory: Things learned in a particular physical or emotional state are more easily remembered when the person is in that state again. This helps explain the difficulties in remembering events that took place when a person was intoxicated or depressed. In fact, heavy use of alcohol may result in significant memory loss. A person may not even remember having injured someone in a car crash. Although not fully researched, it may be that certain kinds of memory are mood-congruent. Perhaps memories of events that occurred when a person was in a certain mood may become available to the person only when that mood is again induced.

More active means for memory improvement have met with greater success. Associationist theory has demonstrated the value of the use of mnemonics, devices or procedures intentionally designed to facilitate encoding and subsequent recall. The use of rhymes, acronyms, pegwords, and the like enables people to recall factual information such as the number of days in each month ("Thirty days have September . . . "), the names of the Great Lakes (the acronym HOMES), and the colors of the visible spectrum (ROY G. BIV). Visual cues, such as tying a string around one's finger or knotting one's handkerchief, are traditional and effective ways to improve prospective memory. Cognitive psychology has demonstrated the importance of emotional factors—how and why something is learned—to the effectiveness of memory. It has provided the research base to demonstrate the effectiveness of study strategies such as the SQ3R (survey, question, read, recite, review) technique. Cognitive theory has also shown that metamemory, a person's knowledge about how his or her memory works, may be important for the improvement of memory.

In clinical settings, much research has been concerned with memory impairment as a means to test the applicability of theories of memory. Head injuries are a common cause of amnesia in which events immediately prior to an accident cannot be recalled. Damage to the hippocampus, a part of the brain that is vital to memory, breaks down the transfer of information from short-term to long-term memory. One dramatic case concerns "H. M.," a patient who had brain surgery to control epileptic seizures. After surgery, H. M.'s short-term memory was intact, but if he was momentarily distracted from a task, he could not remember anything about what he had just been doing. The information was never transferred to long-term memory. Such patients still remember information that was stored in long-term memory before their operation, but to them everyday experiences are always strangely new. They can read the same paragraph over and over, but each time the material will be brand-new. In H. M.'s case, it was discovered that his intelligence as measured by standardized tests actually improved, yet he was continually disoriented and unable to learn even the simplest new associations. Intelligence tests are made to measure general information, vocabulary, and grammatical associations; these things were stored in H. M.'s long-term memory and were apparently not affected by brain surgery. In cases less dramatic than H. M.'s, damage to particular areas of the brain can still have devastating effects on the memory. Damage can be caused by accidents, violent sports activity, strokes, tumors, and alcoholism. Alzheimer's disease is another area to which research findings on memory may be applied. In this fatal disease a patient's forgetfulness increases from normal forgetting to the point that the patient cannot remember how to communicate, cannot recognize loved ones, and cannot care for his or her own safety needs.

Associationism, cognitive psychology, and neuropsychology can each explain some of the structures and processes involved in these and other real-world problems, but it seems as though none of the theories is sufficient by itself. Memory is such a complex phenomenon that it takes all the large-scale theories and a number of smaller-scale ones to comprehend it. The truth probably is that the theories are not mutually exclusive, but rather are complementary to one another.

### PHYSIOLOGICAL BASIS OF MEMORY

Theories of learning and memory have been of great concern to philosophers and psychologists for a long time. They have formed a major part of the history of psychology. Each of the theories has been ascendant for a time, but the nature of theory building requires new conceptions to compensate for perceived weaknesses in currently accepted theories and models. Associationism was the principal theory of memory of stimulus-response psychology, which was dominant in the United States until the mid-1950's. Cognitive psychology evolved from Gestalt psychology, from Jean Piaget's work on developmental psychology, and from information-processing theory associated with the computer, and was extremely important during the 1970's and 1980's. Neuropsychology developed concurrently with advanced technology that permits microanalysis of brain functioning. It has resulted in an explosion of knowledge about how the brain and its systems operate.

Formation of memory seems to involve two individual events. Short-term memory develops first. Repeated rehearsal transfers this form of memory into long-term storage. At one time, it was believed both these forms of memory involved similar events in the brain. However, experimental models have shown such a theory to be incorrect. Two experimental approaches have addressed this issue: the separation of memory formation involving "accidental" or intentional interference with brain function, and development of an animal model for the study of memory.

Electroshock treatment of depression in humans has been shown to interfere with short-term memory formation. However, these persons are still perfectly able to recall the memory of earlier events stored within long-term memory. Accidental damage to temporal lobes of the brain does not appear to interfere with short-term memory, but may inhibit the ability to recall events from the past.

The experimental use of an animal model in the study of memory formation was developed by Eric Kandel at Columbia University. Kandel has utilized the sea slug *Aplysia* in his study of memory. The advantage of such a model is its simplicity—instead of approximately one trillion neurons which make up the nervous system of humans, *Aplysia* contains a "mere" twenty thousand.

Using a variety of stimuli on the animal, and observing its response, Kandel has shown that the physiological basis for short-term memory differs from that of long-term. Specifically, short-term memory involves stimulus to only a small number of individual neurons. Long-term memory involves *de novo* (new) protein synthesis in the affected cells, and formation of extensive neural circuits. Kandel was awarded the Nobel Prize in Physiology or Medicine in 2000 for this work.

## MEMORY RETRIEVAL

The basis for memory recall remains an active area of study. Memory retrieval can be of two types: recognition and recall. In recognition, the individual is presented with information that had been previously learned. The subject remembers he or she has already observed or learned that information. In effect, it is analogous to seeing a movie or book for the second time. In recall, information is reproduced from memory, as in response to a question. The physiological basis for retrieval probably involves the activation of regions of the brain which were involved in the initial encoding.

## SOURCES FOR FURTHER STUDY

Baddeley, Alan D. *Human Memory: Theory and Practice.* Rev. ed. Boston: Allyn and Bacon, 1998. Updated edition of a classic text. The original emphasis on history of memory research continues, along with experimental views of consciousness and implicit memory.

Collins, Alan, ed. *Theories of Memory.* Mahwah, N.J.: Lawrence Erlbaum, 1993. Emphasis of the book is on research into theories of memory, particularly that of a cognitive approach. Various explanations are presented.

Hunt, R. Reed, and Henry Ellis. *Fundamentals of Cognitive Psychology.* 6th ed. Boston: McGraw-Hill, 1999. The authors approach the role of cognitive psychology in memory using an experimental problem-solving approach. Updated theories explaining both long-term and short-term memory, as well as retrieval, are included.

Kandel, Eric. "The Molecular Biology of Memory Storage: A Dialogue Between Genes and Synapses." *Science* 294 (2001): 1030-1038. A summary of the Nobel Prize-winning research into the physiological basis of memory. The author provides an experimental approach in differentiating short-term and long-term memory at the molecular level. The article requires some knowledge of neural function.

Neisser, Ulric. *Cognition and Reality: Principles and Implications of Cognitive Psychology.* San Francisco: W. H. Freeman, 1981. This book marked the acceptance of cognitive psychology as a major component within the approach to the study and understanding of memory. The major goals of the approach are described. Many of the author's suggestions as to an experimental approach using real-world models have been applied in subsequent years.

Norman, Donald A. *The Psychology of Everyday Things.* 1988. Reprint. New York: Basic Books, 2002. An enjoyable approach to the subject. The author emphasizes the cognitive approach in dealing with problems. Topics include recognition of both good and bad design as well as ways to improve design based upon psychology of the consumer.

Nyberg, Lars, et al. "Reactivation of Encoding-Related Brain Activity During Memory Retrieval." *Proceedings of the National Academy of Sciences of the United States of America* 97 (September 26, 2000): 11, 120-121, 124. Description of positron emission tomography (PET) studies which monitor brain activity during memory recall. The authors demonstrate, through linkage of visual and auditory recall, that recall involves regions of the brain initially involved in memory formation.

*R. G. Gaddis; updated by Richard Adler*

SEE ALSO: Brain Structure; Memory: Animal Research.

# MEMORY
## ANIMAL RESEARCH

TYPE OF PSYCHOLOGY: Biological bases of behavior; memory
FIELDS OF STUDY: Biological influences on learning; nervous system;
  Pavlovian conditioning

*Research with nonhuman animals has significantly contributed to an understanding of the basic processes of memory, including its anatomy and physiology. Important brain regions, neurotransmitters, and genes have been identified, and this information is now being used to understand further and treat human memory disorders.*

KEY CONCEPTS
- anterograde amnesia
- engram
- experimental brain damage
- genetic engineering
- hippocampus
- prefrontal cortex
- retrograde amnesia
- stroke

Nonhuman animals have been used as subjects in memory research since the earliest days of psychology, and much of what is known about the fundamental processes of memory is largely based on work with animals. Rats, mice, pigeons, rabbits, monkeys, sea slugs, flatworms, and fruit flies are among the most commonly used species. The widespread use of animals in memory research can be attributed to the ability systematically to manipulate and control their environments under strict laboratory conditions and to use procedures and invasive techniques, such as surgery and drugs, that cannot ethically be used with humans. A typical research protocol involves training animals on any of a variety of learning paradigms and concurrently measuring or manipulating some aspect of the nervous system to examine its relationship to memory.

Although learning and memory are closely related, a distinction should be drawn between learning and memory. Learning is defined as a relatively permanent change in behavior as a result of experience. Memory is the underlying process by which information is encoded, stored, and retrieved by the nervous system. Modern learning and memory paradigms are based on the principles of classical and operant conditioning first established by the early behaviorists: Ivan Pavlov, Edward L. Thorndike, John B. Watson, and B. F. Skinner. These learning paradigms can be used to examine different types of memory and to explore the underlying brain mechanisms that may mediate them. For classical conditioning, widely used paradigms include eyeblink conditioning, taste aversion learning, and fear conditioning. For operant conditioning, memory for objects, spatial memory, context discrimination, and maze learning are among the most frequently used procedures. Two other very simple forms of learning, habituation (the gradual decrease in response to a stimulus as a result of repeated exposure to it) and sensitization (the gradual increase in response to a stimulus after repeated exposure to it) are both simple forms of nonassociative learning also extensively used in animal memory research.

Researchers have at their disposal a number of techniques that allow them to manipulate the nervous system and assess its functions. Historically, experimental brain damage has been one of the most widely used procedures. This technique involves surgically destroying (known as lesioning) various parts of the brain and assessing the effects of the lesion on memory processes. Pharmacological manipulations are also frequently used and involve administering a drug known to affect a specific neurotransmitter or hormonal system thought to play a role in memory. Functional studies involve measuring brain activity while an animal is actually engaged in learning. Recordings can be made from individual brain cells (neurons), groups of neurons, or entire anatomical regions. Beginning in the late 1990's, genetic engineering began to be applied to the study of animal memory. These procedures involve the direct manipulation of genes that produce proteins suspected to be important for memory.

By combining a wide variety of memory paradigms with an increasing number of ways to manipulate or measure the nervous system, animal research has been extremely useful in addressing several fundamental questions about memory. These issues include the important brain structures involved in memory, the manner in which information is stored in the nervous system, and the causes and potential treatments for human memory disorders.

## THE ANATOMY OF MEMORY

One of the first questions about memory to be addressed using animals was its relationship to the underlying structure of the nervous system. American psychologist Karl Lashley (1890-1958) was an early pioneer in this field. His main interest was in finding what was then referred to as the engram, the physical location in the brain where memories are stored. Lashley trained rats on a variety of tasks, such as the ability to learn mazes or perform simple discriminations, and then lesioned various parts of the cerebral cortex (the convoluted outer covering of the brain) in an attempt to erase the memory trace. Despite years of effort, he found that he could not completely abolish a memory, no matter what part of the cortex he lesioned. Lashley summed up his puzzlement and frustration at these findings in this now well-known quote: "I sometimes feel, in reviewing the evidence on the localization of the engram, that the necessary conclusion is that learning just is not possible."

While the specific location of the brain lesion did not appear important, Lashley found that the total amount of brain tissue removed was critical. When large lesions were produced, as compared to smaller ones, he found that memories could be abolished, regardless of the location in the cortex where they were made. This led Lashley to propose the concepts of mass action and equipotentiality, which state that the cortex works as a whole and that all parts contribute equally to complex behaviors.

Further research has generally supported Lashley's original conclusions about the localization of the engram. However, better memory tests and more sophisticated techniques for inducing brain damage have revealed that certain brain regions are more involved in memory than others and that different brain regions are actually responsible for different types of memory. For example, classical conditioning, which is the modification of a reflex through learning, appears primarily to involve the brain stem or cerebellum, which are two evolutionarily old brain structures. Specific circuitry within these structures that underlies a number of forms of classical conditioning has been identified.

In the rabbit, a puff of air blown into the eye produces a reflexive blinking response. When researchers repeatedly pair the air puff with a tone, the tone itself will eventually elicit the response. The memory for this response involves a very specific circuit of neurons, primarily in the cerebellum. Once the response is well learned, it can be abolished by lesions in this circuit. Importantly, these lesions do not affect other forms of memory. Similarly, taste aversion learning, a process by which animals learn not to consume a food or liquid that has previously made them ill, has been shown to be mediated by a very specific circuit in the brain stem, specifically the pons and medulla. Animals with lesions to the nucleus of the solitary tract, a portion of this circuit in the medulla where taste, olfactory, and illness-related information converge, will not readily learn taste aversions.

More complex forms of learning and memory have been shown to involve more recently evolved brain structures. Many of these are located in either the cortex or the limbic system, an area of the brain located between the newer cortex and the older brain stem. One component of the limbic system believed to be heavily involved in memory is the hippocampus. One of its primary functions appears to be spatial memory. Rats and monkeys with damage limited to the hippocampus are impaired in maze learning and locating objects in space but have normal memory for nonspatial tasks. Animals that require spatial navigation for their survival, such as homing pigeons and food-storing rodents (which must remember the location of the food that they have stored) have disproportionately large hippocampi. Moreover, damage to the hippocampus in these species leads to a disruption in their ability to navigate and find stored food.

One area of the cortex that has been shown to be involved in memory is the prefrontal cortex. This area has been implicated in short-term memory, which is the ability to hold temporarily a mental representation of an object or event. Monkeys and rats that received lesions to the prefrontal cortex were impaired in learning tasks that required them to remember briefly the location of an object or to learn tasks that require them to switch back and forth between strategies for solving the task. Studies involving the measurement of brain function have also demonstrated that this area of the brain is active during periods when animals are thought to be holding information in short-term memory.

While experimental brain damage has been one of the predominant techniques used to study structure/function relationships in the nervous system, difficulty in interpretation, an increased concern for animal welfare, and the advent of more sophisticated physiological and molecular techniques have led to an overall decline in their use.

## THE MOLECULES OF MEMORY

While lesion studies have been useful in determining the brain structures involved in memory, pharmacological techniques have been used to address its underlying chemistry. Pharmacological manipulations have a long history in memory research with animals, dating back to the early 1900's and the discovery of neurotransmitters. Neurotransmitters are chemical messengers secreted by neurons and are essential to communication within the nervous system. Each neurotransmitter, of which there are more than one hundred, has its own specific receptor to which it can attach and alter cellular functioning. By administering drugs that either increase or decrease the activity of specific neurotransmitters, researchers have been able to investigate their role in memory formation.

One neurotransmitter that has been strongly implicated in memory is glutamate. This transmitter is found throughout the brain but is most highly concentrated in the cerebral cortex and the hippocampus. Drugs that increase the activity of glutamate facilitate learning and improve memory, while drugs that reduce glutamate activity have the opposite effect. The neurotransmitter dopamine has also been implicated in memory formation. In small doses, drugs such as cocaine and amphetamine, which increase dopamine activity, have been found to improve memory in both humans and lower animals. Moderate doses of caffeine can also facilitate memory storage, albeit by a less understood mechanism. Other neurotransmitters believed to be involved in memory include acetylcholine, serotonin, norepinephrine, and the endorphins.

Research with simpler organisms has been directed at understanding the chemical events at the molecular level that may be involved in memory. One animal in particular, the marine invertebrate *Aplysia californica*, has played a pivotal role in this research. *Aplysia* have very simple nervous systems with large, easily identifiable neurons and are capable of many forms of learning, including habituation, sensitization, and classical conditioning. Canadian psychologist Donald Hebb (1904-1985), a former student of Lashley, proposed that memories are stored in the nervous system as a result of the strengthening of connections between neurons as a result of their repeated activation during learning. With the *Aplysia*, it is possible indirectly to observe and manipulate the connections between neurons while learning is taking place. Eric Kandel of Columbia University has used the *Aplysia* as a model system to study the molecular biology of memory for more than thirty years. He demonstrated that when a short-term memory is formed in the *Aplysia*, the connections between the neurons involved in the learning process are strengthened by gradually coming to release more neurotransmitters, particularly serotonin. When long-term memories are formed, new connections between nerve cells actually grow. With repeated disuse, these processes appear to reverse themselves. Kandel's work has suggested that memory (what Lashley referred to as the engram) is represented in the nervous system in the form of a chemical or structural change, depending on the nature and duration of the memory itself. For these discoveries, Kandel was awarded the Nobel Prize in 2000.

Modern genetic engineering techniques have made it possible to address the molecular biology of memory in mammals (predominantly mice) as well as invertebrates. Two related techniques, genetic knockouts and transgenics, have been applied to the problem. Genetic knockouts involve removing, or "knocking out," a gene that produces a specific protein thought to be involved in memory. Frequently targeted genes include those for neurotransmitters or their receptors. Transgenics involves the insertion of a new gene into the genome of an organism with the goal of either overproducing a specific protein or inserting a completely foreign protein into the animal. Neurotransmitters and their receptors are again the most frequently targeted sites. A remarkable number of knockout mice have been produced with a variety of short- and long-term memory deficits. In many ways, this technique is analogous to those used in earlier brain lesion studies but is applied at the molecular level. Dopamine, serotonin, glutamate, and acetylcholine systems have all been implicated in memory formation as a result of genetic knockout studies. Significantly, researchers have also been able to improve memory in mice through genetic engineering. Transgenic mice that overproduce glutamate receptors actually learn mazes faster and have better retention than normal mice. It is hoped that in the future gene therapy for human memory disorders may be developed based on this technique.

## ANIMAL MODELS OF HUMAN MEMORY DISORDERS

Animal research has many practical applications to the study and treatment of human memory dysfunction. Many types of neurological disorder and brain damage can produce memory impairments in humans, and it has been possible to model some of these in animals. The first successful attempt at this was production of an animal model of brain-damaged-induced amnesia. It had been known since the 1950's that damage to the temporal lobes, as a result of disease, traumatic injury, epilepsy, or infection, could produce a disorder known as anterograde amnesia, the inability to form new long-term memories. This is in contrast to the better-known retrograde amnesia, which is an inability to remember previously stored information. Beginning in the late 1970's, work with monkeys, and later rats, began to identify the critical temporal lobe structures that, when damaged, produce anterograde amnesia. These structures include the hippocampus and, perhaps more important, the adjacent, overlying cortex, which is known as the rhinal cortex. As a result of this work, this brain region is now believed to be critical in the formation of new long-term memories.

Memory disorders also frequently develop after an interruption of oxygen flow to the brain (known as hypoxia), which can be caused by events such as stroke, cardiac arrest, or carbon monoxide poisoning. There are a variety of animal models of stroke and resultant memory disorders. Significantly, oxygen deprivation produces brain damage that is most severe in the temporal lobe, particularly the hippocampus and the rhinal cortex. Using animal models, the mechanisms underlying hypoxic injury have been investigated, and potential therapeutic drugs designed to minimize the brain damage and lessen the memory impairments have been tested. One potentially damaging event that has been identified is a massive influx of calcium into neurons during a hypoxic episode. This has led to the development of calcium blockers and their widespread use in the clinical treatment of complications arising from stroke.

Alzheimer's disease is probably the best-known human memory disorder. It is characterized by gradual memory loss over a period of five to fifteen years. It typically begins as a mild forgetfulness and progresses to anterograde amnesia, retrograde amnesia, and eventually complete cognitive dysfunction and physical incapacitation. One pathological event that has been implicated in the development of Alzheimer's disease is the overproduction of a protein known as the amyloid-beta protein. The normal biological function of this protein is not known, but at high levels it appears to be toxic to neurons. Amyloid-beta deposits are most pronounced and develop first in the temporal and frontal lobes, a fact that corresponds well with the memory functions ascribed to these areas and the types of deficits seen in people with Alzheimer's disease. The development of an animal model has marked a major milestone in understanding the disorder and developing a potential treatment. Mice have been genetically engineered to overproduce the amyloid-beta protein. As a result, they develop patterns of brain damage and memory deficits similar to those in humans with Alzheimer's disease. The development of the Alzheimer's mouse has allowed for a comprehensive investigation of the genetics of the disorder as well as providing a model on which to test potential therapeutic treatments. Limited success for potential treatments has been obtained with an experimental vaccine in animals. This vaccine has been shown to reduce both brain damage and memory deficits. Application to the treatment of human Alzheimer's disease is many years away.

**SOURCES FOR FURTHER STUDY**

Anagnostopoulos, Anna V., Larry E. Mobraaten, John J. Sharp, and Muriel T. Davisson. "Transgenic and Knockout Databases: Behavioral Profiles of Mouse Mutants." *Physiology and Behavior* 73 (2001): 675-689. A summary of an ongoing project to construct a database of genetically engineered mice designed to facilitate the dissemination of findings among researchers. The article contains an exhaustive reference section on mutant mice and their behavioral and physiological profiles.

Cohen, Neil J., and Howard Eichenbaum. *Memory, Amnesia, and the Hippocampal System.* Cambridge, Mass.: MIT Press, 1993. A discussion of memory impairments resulting from damage the hippocampus and adjacent brain regions.

Duva, Christopher A., Thomas J. Kornecook, and John P. J. Pinel. "Animal Models of Medial Temporal Lobe Amnesia: The Myth of the Hippocampus." In *Animal Models of Human Emotion and Cognition,* edited by Mark Haug and Richard E Whalen. Washington, D.C.: American Psychological Association, 1999. A critical evaluation of the role of the hippocampus in memory for objects. The article includes a historical description of human amnesia and attempts to model it in monkeys and rats.

Kiefer, Steven W. "Neural Mediation of Conditioned Food Aversions." *Annals of the New York Academy of Sciences* 443 (1985): 100-109. A comprehensive review of the brain areas and neural systems involved in food aversion learning.

Martinez, Joe L., and Raymond P. Kesner. *Neurobiology of Learning and Memory.* New York: Academic Press, 1998. An overview of information on the neurobiology of learning and memory from developmental, pharmacological, and psychobiological perspectives. A good introductory source.

Morgan, Dave, et al. "A Peptide Vaccination Prevents Memory Loss in an Animal Model of Alzheimer's Disease." *Nature* 408 (2000): 982-985. This original research report describes a successful attempt to vaccinate Alzheimer's mice against the disorder and prevent memory loss.

Squire, Larry R., and Eric Kandel. *Memory: From Mind to Molecules.* New York: Scientific American Library, 1999. An approachable volume summarizing the major developments in understanding the anatomy and physiology of vertebrate and invertebrate learning. This text contains an extensive discussion of Kandel's work with the molecular biology of memory in *Aplysia* and Squires's work on the neuroanatomy of memory with monkeys. An excellent source for people with a limited background in biology and chemistry.

Tang, Ya-Ping, et al. "Genetic Enhancement of Learning and Memory in Mice." *Nature* 401 (1999): 63-69. An original research report that describes how memory was improved in a strain of mice by genetically engineering them to contain an overabundance of glutamate receptors in the hippocampus.

Thompson, Richard F. "The Neurobiology of Learning and Memory." *Science* 233, no. 13 (1986): 941-947. The author summarizes his work on the brain mechanisms involved in classical conditioning of the eyeblink reflex in rabbits.

Tulving, Endel, and Fergus I. M. Craik. *The Oxford Handbook of Memory.* New York: Oxford University Press, 2000. A comprehensive volume dealing with a wide variety of topics related to both animal and human memory. An excellent general reference source.

*Christopher A. Duva*

SEE ALSO: Animal Experimentation; Brain Structure; Habituation and Sensitization; Memory.

# MENTAL RETARDATION

TYPE OF PSYCHOLOGY: Developmental psychology
FIELDS OF STUDY: Childhood and adolescent disorders; organic disorders

*Mental retardation occurs about three times per thousand births and usually indicates an intelligence quotient (IQ) of less than 70. Variations in severity may allow some individuals to be virtually independent and capable of retaining simple jobs, whereas more severely affected persons may require lifetime institutional care. The causes of mental retardation are numerous, with many having a clear-cut underlying genetic basis, others implicating environmental factors, and still others with no known cause.*

KEY CONCEPTS
- congenital
- Down syndrome
- fetal alcohol syndrome
- fragile X syndrome
- idiopathic
- intelligence quotient (IQ)
- mental retardation
- phenylketonuria
- teratogens

The term "mental retardation" conjures up different meanings for different people. A useful definition is provided by the American Association on Mental Retardation: "Mental retardation is a particular state of functioning that begins in childhood and is characterized by limitation in both intelligence and adaptive skills." Mental retardation reflects the "fit" between the capabilities of individuals and the structure and expectations of their environment. It is characterized by significantly subaverage intellectual functioning, existing concurrently with related limitations in two or more of the following skill areas: communication, home living, community use, health and safety, leisure, self-care, social skills, self-direction, functional academics, and work. It is evident that deficits in intelligence and adaptive skills will be related to the complexity of the society in which the individual lives.

Categorizations of the severity of mental retardation have been established based on IQ scores. The four levels of severity are mild retardation (IQ range 50-70), moderate retardation (IQ range 35-50), severe retardation (IQ range 20-35), and profound (IQ range less than 20). Rather than use a classification based on the severity level, a classification based on the type and intensity of support needed also is now in practice: intermittent, limited, extensive, or pervasive. Persons with mild retardation usually are capable of living with some degree of independence in the community and can usually work successfully at simple jobs. The great majority—85 percent—of cases of mental retardation fall into this category. The remaining 15 percent of cases are at the moderate, severe, and profound levels, with only approximately 1 percent to 2 percent at the profound level. These last three levels are sometimes grouped together as severe. Profoundly affected individuals require constant care and supervision.

Several causes of mental retardation are becoming known, although in many cases it may not be possible to ascribe mental retardation to a specific cause. Just because a disorder is congenital (present at birth) does not necessarily imply that the disorder is genetic. Agents that are capable of affecting the developing fetus such as alcohol, mercury, infections, maternal phenylketonuria, and many other substances may lead to mental retardation. Many single-gene disorders and chromosomal abnormalities produce mental retardation as part of their syndromes, or disorders characterized by multiple effects. A large-scale study of severely mentally retarded patients institutionalized in Wisconsin, summarized by Sarah Bundey in 1997, indicated that 11.8 percent of the cases were caused by chromosomal abnormality, 6.5 percent by single-gene defects, 16.3 percent by multiple congenital anomaly syndromes, 14.7 percent by central nervous system malformations such as hydrocephalus, 32.1 percent by central nervous system dysfunction due to perinatal or unidentified prenatal causes including cerebral palsy, 8.5 percent by infectious disease, 3.9 percent by postnatal brain damage, and 1.2 percent by infantile psychosis; 4.3 percent were unclassified. It was noted that the number of patients with Down syndrome was low because they were admitted less frequently. Other surveys have shown that Down syndrome accounts for about one-third of mentally retarded patients.

### ETIOLOGY

Although some cases of mental retardation are idiopathic (without a specific known cause), many known causes account for many of the cases of mental retardation. The difficulties in teasing out factors involved in mental and behavioral disorders are seen clearly in the study of children exposed prenatally to radiation following the Chernobyl nuclear plant disaster in 1986, as reported by S. Igumnov and V. Drozdovitch. The children who had been exposed to radiation displayed borderline intellectual functioning and emotional disorders to a greater degree than those in a control group. Other unfavorable social-psychological and sociocultural factors included a low educational level of the parents and problems associated with relocation from the contaminated areas.

Similar complications are seen in the work of M. S. Durkin and colleagues on prenatal and postnatal risk factors among children in Bangladesh. The study screened more than ten thousand children from both rural and urban areas. Significant predictors of serious mental retardation included maternal goiter and postnatal brain infections. Consanguinity (having ancestors who were closely related) also was a significant factor in the rural areas. For less severe mental retardation, maternal illiteracy, maternal history of pregnancy loss, and small size for gestational age at birth were significant independent risk factors.

It is convenient to separate the known causes of mental retardation into

## DSM-IV-TR Criteria for Mental Retardation

Significantly subaverage intellectual functioning:

- for children and adults, IQ of approximately 70 or below
- for infants, clinical judgment of significantly subaverage intellectual functioning

Concurrent deficits or impairments in adaptive functioning (effectiveness in meeting standards expected for age and cultural group) in at least two of the following areas:

- communication
- self-care
- home living
- social/interpersonal skills
- use of community resources
- self-direction
- functional academic skills
- work
- leisure
- health
- safety

Onset before age eighteen

DSM code based on degree of severity reflecting level of intellectual impairment:

- Mild Mental Retardation (DSM code 317): IQ level of 50-55 to approx. 70
- Moderate Mental Retardation (DSM code 318.0): IQ level of 35-40 to 50-55
- Severe Mental Retardation (DSM code 318.1): IQ level of 20-25 to 35-40
- Profound Mental Retardation (DSM code 318.2): IQ level below 20 or 25
- Mental Retardation, Severity Unspecified (DSM code 319): IQ level Untestable

the two categories of genetic and acquired or environmental. However, many cases of mental retardation may be a result of the interaction of several genes and the environment, in which case the disorder is said to be multifactorial.

### Genetic Causes

Approximately one thousand genetic disorders are associated with mental retardation, and the number increases regularly. If mental retardation is associated with other conditions or features, it is syndromic; if it is the only primary symptom, it is said to be nonspecific. In general, a genetic involvement is more likely to be found in severe forms of mental retardation than it is in milder forms. A few examples of chromosomal and single-gene disorders leading to mental retardation will be discussed as representative examples.

**CHROMOSOMAL DISORDERS.** Down syndrome was first described by John Langdon Down in 1866, and although heredity was suspected in its etiology, it was not until 1959 that it was discovered that Down syndrome patients had one extra chromosome, for a total of forty-seven instead of the normal forty-six. Down syndrome occurs at a frequency of about one in one thousand births and is the single most prevalent cause of mental retardation. The great majority of Down syndrome patients have three chromosomes number 21 instead of two (a condition called trisomy 21). The physical features associated with Down syndrome are easily recognizable: short stature, a short neck with excessive loose skin, thick lips, epicanthal folds of the eye, malformed ears, poor muscle tone, and a flattened facial profile. Major physical problems include heart and kidney defects, deafness, and gastrointestinal blockages. Developmental milestones are delayed, and mental retardation is common. Intelligence varies considerably, with an average IQ of 50 and only a small percentage of patients approaching the normal range. It is essential that parents and educators assess the capabilities of each child and provide an educational environment that maximizes achievement.

Although Down syndrome is genetic in the sense that it results from an imbalance in the genetic material—an extra chromosome—it is not hereditary in the sense that it does not run in families. The incidence of Down syndrome shows a striking increase with maternal age, increasing dramatically (to one in fifty births) in women giving birth beyond age thirty-five.

A normal human has twenty-two pairs of autosomes and one pair of sex chromosomes—XX if a female, XY if a male. Cases involving an extra chromosome or a missing chromosome, particularly if the missing chromosome is one of the autosomes, usually lead to spontaneous abortion. The few that survive have severe malformations, including those of the brain, and are likely to have severe mental retardation. Malformations as a result of abnormalities involving the sex chromosomes are usually less severe. Females with an extra X chromosome (XXX) tend to have lower IQs than their siblings. Males with an extra X chromosome (XXY), a condition called Klinefelter syndrome, usually are not mentally retarded but may develop psychosocial problems. Males with an extra Y chromosome (XXY) may have speech, language, and reading problems.

**SINGLE-GENE DISORDERS.** Fragile X syndrome is the second most common genetic cause of mental retardation. It is the most common inherited form of mental retardation. As is true of other disorders due to sex-linked recessive genes, more males are affected than are females. The frequency of fragile X males is about 1 in 1,000; for females, it is about 1 in 2,500. It is estimated that up to 8 percent of the males in institutions for mental retardation have a fragile X chromosome. Grant R. Sutherland and John C. Mulley in 1996 provided a useful review of the characteristics of fragile X syndrome.

Features include a prominent forehead and jaws; prominent, long, and mildly dysmorphic ears; hyperextensible finger joints; enlarged testes (macroorchidism); and mitral value prolapse. About 80 percent of fragile X males have mental retardation. Most of them have moderate retardation, but some are only mildly retarded. They tend to have better verbal than spatial abilities. They show speech abnormalities such as echolalia (compulsively repeating the speech of others). In general, they tend to be hyperactive. Only about one-half of girls with the fragile X chromosome are affected, and limited studies of females estimate that perhaps up to 7 percent of female mental retardation is due to fragile X syndrome. The specific gene involved in fragile X syndrome has been identified: The syndrome is caused by an expanded triplet repeat, a form of mutation in which deoxyribonucleic acid (DNA) nucleotides are repeated a number of times.

Phenylketonuria (PKU) is one of the inborn errors of metabolism that results in mental retardation if left untreated. PKU is a disorder of amino acid metabolism in which individuals cannot metabolize normally the amino acid phenylalanine because they are deficient in the liver enzyme phenylalanine hydroxylase. As a result, phenylalanine and other metabolites accumulate in the blood. At birth, children are normal, but clinical features gradually appear during the first twelve months. Some affected persons have a "mousy" odor about them because of the excretion of phenylacetic acid. They tend to have light skin and hair, seizures, mental retardation, and other neurologic symptoms. PKU occurs in about one in fourteen thousand births and once accounted for about 1 percent of severely retarded individuals in institutions. Some interesting variations in the incidence of PKU are seen among different populations. In Turkey, a very high incidence is seen, 1 in 2,600 births, whereas in Japan the rate is only 1 in 143,000 births. The disorder is inherited as autosomal recessive, and most of the affected children are born to parents who are not affected.

PKU represents the prototype of genetic disorders for which newborn screening can be done: babies with high blood levels of phenylalanine can be identified, and treatment can begin immediately. Dietary management of phenylalanine levels does not correct the underlying gene defect, but it keeps the levels sufficiently low that adverse effects on the brain and nervous system do not occur, and mental retardation is avoided. It is thought necessary to maintain the special diet through the adolescent years. It also is necessary for women with PKU who become pregnant to resume a diet low in phenylalanine to prevent high intrauterine levels from affecting the developing fetus, even though the latter may not be genetically "programmed" to inherit PKU. Untreated patients with PKU have mean IQs around 50, whereas treated patients will have IQs close to normal.

## ENVIRONMENTAL CAUSES

Numerous cases of mental retardation are a result of damage to a fetus during pregnancy. Other problems may arise during birth or after birth. Physical or chemical agents that cause an increase in congenital defects are known as teratogens. Because teratogens affect embryos and fetuses directly, the effects are not likely to produce heritable changes. A woman who uses or is exposed to various teratogens during pregnancy runs the risk of producing a child with a developmental malformation. Potential teratogens include alcohol, drugs, viral infections, radiation, diabetes mellitus, malnutrition, and environmental toxins.

Since its initial clinical delineation in 1973, fetal alcohol syndrome has been noted as a major cause of mental retardation in countries where alcohol is consumed regularly. Estimates indicate that it may be responsible for as many as one to three cases of mental retardation out of every thousand births. Fortunately, fetal alcohol syndrome is easily preventable through abstinence from alcohol during pregnancy. Children affected with fetal alcohol syndrome have a characteristic facial appearance, with a small skull, upturned nose, thin upper lip, underdeveloped upper jaw, epicanthal folds, and a long philtrum (the vertical groove on the median line of the upper lip). There is growth retardation, which has its onset prenatally and continues during the postnatal period with some catch-up growth taking place thereafter. Head and brain size remain well below normal. Children show developmental delays, attention deficits, hyperactivity, and mental deficiency. Although the average IQ of children with fetal alcohol syndrome is low, 60 to 65, there is considerable variation, with some children having normal or near-normal intelligence but experiencing learning disorders. Severe physical defects found in many of these children include cardiac and skeletal defects.

Although it is evident that the risk of fetal alcohol syndrome is related to the amount and timing of the alcohol consumed by the pregnant woman, an exact close relationship has been difficult to establish. Even with moderate consumption (one to two ounces of absolute alcohol), the serious effects of fetal alcohol syndrome have been observed in approximately 10 percent of births. Many physicians now recommend that women practice total abstinence from alcohol during the entire pregnancy.

## PREVENTION AND TREATMENT

Although it is not possible to treat some underlying causes of mental retardation, many of the genetic and teratogenic cases can be prevented through genetic counseling, prenatal diagnosis, and education to alert people of the risk to developing fetuses of teratogens such as alcohol. It also is essential to have an accurate diagnosis of the cause and nature of the problems associated with individual cases of mental retardation in order for parents to be able to undertake the best possible intervention program for their children.

Newborn screening programs can detect certain disorders that will lead to mental retardation, including PKU, congenital hypothyroidism, galactosemia, maple syrup urine disease, and other inherited metabolic disorders. Prenatal testing (such as amniocentesis and chorionic villi sampling) can be used to detect chromosomal disorders, including Down syndrome and several hundred single-gene disorders that may lead to severe physical or mental disorders in children. Neural tube defects can be detected prenatally by testing the amniotic fluid for elevated levels of alpha-fetoprotein. Most of the cases of prenatal testing are done for individuals in which there is a reason to suspect that the fetus is at an increased risk for a particular genetic disease or birth defect. These risks include increased maternal age, birth of a previous child with a disorder, and a family history of a disorder. Genetic counseling also is used to aid a couple in understanding genetic risks before a pregnancy has commenced, however, most mentally retarded children are born to parents with no history of mental retardation.

## SOURCES FOR FURTHER STUDY

Baroff, George S., and J. Gregory Olley. *Mental Retardation: Nature, Cause, and Management.* 3d ed. Philadelphia: Brunner-Routledge, 1999. This textbook presents information on the biological and psychological causes of mental retardation and its management.

Beirne-Smith, Mary, James R. Patton, and Richard F. Ittenback. *Mental Retardation.* 6th ed. Upper Saddle River, N.J.: Prentice Hall, 2002. A comprehensive book that deals with historical, biological, psychological and sociological aspects of mental retardation.

Burack, Jacob A., Robert M. Hodapp, and Edward Zigler, eds. *Handbook of Mental Retardation and Development.* New York: Cambridge University Press, 1997. Provides comprehensive information emphasizing the developmental aspects of mental retardation.

Durkin, M. S., et al. "Prenatal and Postnatal Risk Factors for Mental Retardation Among Children in Bangladesh." *American Journal of Epidemiology* 152, no. 11 (2000): 1024-1033. This study examines the roles of different factors in causing mental retardation in rural and urban children.

Igumnov, S., and V. Drozdovitch. "The Intellectual Development, Mental, and Behavioural Disorders in Children from Belarus Exposed in Utero Following the Chernobyl Accident." *European Psychiatry* 15, no. 4 (2000): 244-253. The authors report borderline intellectual functioning and emotional disorders in children exposed in utero to fallout from Chernobyl, along with factors thought to contribute (such as relocation).

McKusick, Victor A. *Mendelian Inheritance in Man.* 12th ed. Baltimore: John Hopkins University Press, 1999. A comprehensive catalog of human genes and genetic disorders including mitochondrial genes.

Rimoin, David L., J. Michael Connor, and Reed E. Pyeritz. *Emery and Rimoin's Principles and Practice of Medical Genetics.* 3d ed. New York: Churchill Livingstone, 1997. This voluminous book includes several chapters dealing with mental and behavioral disorders.

*Donald J. Nash*

SEE ALSO: Developmental Disabilities; Intelligence; Thought: Study and Measurement.

# Mood Disorders

Type of psychology: Psychopathology
Field of study: Depression

*The diagnosis of a mood disorder requires the presence or absence of a mood episode such as a major depressive episode, manic episode, mixed episode, or hypomanic episode. Mood disorders include major depressive disorder, dysthymic disorder, bipolar I disorder, bipolar II disorder, and cyclothymic disorder. The mood disorders can be specified with seasonal pattern, rapid-cycling, or postpartum onset.*

Key concepts
- bipolar I disorder
- cyclothymic disorder
- depressive episode
- dysthymic disorder
- hypomanic episode
- major depressive disorder
- manic episode
- postpartum onset
- rapid-cycling
- seasonal pattern

Descriptions of mood disorders can be found in ancient texts such as the Bible and the writings of Hippocrates (c. 460-c. 377 B.C.E.). In about 30 C.E., Aulus Cornelius Celsus, a medical writer, described melancholia as a depression caused by black bile.

Mood disorders are characterized predominantly by a disturbance in mood. The American Psychiatric Association's *Diagnostic and Statistical Manual of Mental Disorders: DSM-IV-TR* (rev. 4th ed., 2000) describes mood episodes that characterize the mood disorders: major depressive episode, manic episode, mixed episode, and hypomanic episode.

In a major depressive episode, a person experiences depressed mood for a period of at least two weeks. For the diagnosis of a depressive episode, the person must experience at least four of the following symptoms: changes in appetite or weight, sleep, and psychomotor activity; decreased energy; feelings of worthlessness or guilt; difficulty concentrating; recurrent thoughts of death or suicide. There is significant impairment in occupational or social functioning.

In a manic episode, a person experiences an abnormally elevated or irritable mood for at least one week. In addition, the person must experience at least three of the following symptoms: inflated self-esteem, decreased need for sleep, pressured (loud, rapid) speech, racing thoughts, excessive planning of or participation in multiple activities, distractibility, psychomotor agitation (such as pacing), or excessive participation in activities that may have negative consequences (such as overspending). There is severe impairment in social or occupational functioning, or there are psychotic features.

A hypomanic episode is characterized by a period of at least four days of abnormally elevated or irritable mood. The affected person must experience at least three of the following symptoms: inflated self-esteem, decreased need for sleep, pressured speech, flight of ideas, increased involvement in goal-directed activities, psychomotor agitation, or excessive participation in activities that may lead to negative consequences. The hypomanic episode is differentiated from the manic episode by less severe impairment in social or occupational functioning and a lack of psychotic features.

A person experiencing a mixed episode displays symptoms of both manic and major depressive episodes nearly every day for a period of one week.

Major depressive disorder is characterized by one or more major depressive episodes. Dysthymic disorder involves at least two years of depressed mood with symptoms that do not meet the criteria for a major depressive episode. Bipolar I disorder includes one or more manic or mixed episodes with major depressive episodes. Bipolar II disorder is characterized by one or more major depressive episodes with at least one hypomanic episode. Cyclothymic disorder is represented by at least two years of hypomanic episodes and depressive symptoms that do not meet the criteria for a major depressive episode.

## MAJOR DEPRESSIVE DISORDER

Major depressive disorder involves disturbances in mood, concentration, sleep, activity, appetite, and social behavior. It is much more than temporarily feeling sad. It is estimated that one out of every five women and one in fifteen men will suffer from major depression in his or her lifetime. An estimated eighteen million Americans are affected. In 1990, $30.4 billion was lost as a result of the illness.

A major depressive episode may develop gradually or appear quite suddenly, without any relation to environmental factors. The symptoms of major depressive disorder will vary among individuals, but there are some common symptoms. People with major depressive disorder may have difficulty falling asleep, sleep restlessly or excessively, and wake up without feeling rested. They may experience a decrease or increase in a desire to eat. They may crave certain foods, such as carbohydrates. They may be unable to pay attention to things. Even minor decisions may seem impossible to make. A loss of energy is manifested in slower mental processing, an inability to perform normal daily routines, and slowed reaction time. Sufferers may experience anhedonia, an inability to experience pleasure. They lose interest in activities they used to enjoy. They ruminate about failures and feel guilty and helpless. People with major depressive disorder tend to seek negative feedback about themselves from others. They see no hope for improvement and may be thinking of death and suicide. In adolescents, depression may be manifested in anger, aggressiveness, delinquency, drug abuse, poor performance in school, or running away. Depression is a primary risk factor in the third leading cause of death among young people, suicide.

There is probably no single cause of major depressive disorder, although it is primarily a disorder of the brain. A chemical dysfunction and genetics are thought to be parts of the cause. Neural circuits, which regulate mood, thinking, sleep, appetite, and behavior, do not function normally. Neurotransmitters are out of balance. One neurotransmitter implicated in depression is serotonin. It is thought that in major depressive disorder there is a reduced amount of serotonin available in the neural circuits (specifically, in the synapses). This results in reduced or lacking nerve impulse. In many patients with the disorder, the hormonal system that regulates the body's response to stress is overactive. Stress, alcohol or drug abuse, medication, or outlook on life may trigger depressive episodes.

Cognitive theories of depression state that a negative cognitive style, such as pessimism, represents a diathesis (a predisposition) which, in the presence of stress, triggers negative cognitions such as hopelessness. Negative cognitions increase the person's vulnerability to depression. Some common precipitants of depression in vulnerable people include marital conflict, academic or work-related difficulty, chronic medical problems, and physical or sexual abuse.

In most cases, medication or psychotherapy is the treatment of choice. Treatment depends on the severity and pattern of the symptoms. With treatment, 80 percent of people with major depressive disorder return to normal functioning.

Antidepressant drugs influence the functioning of certain neurotransmitters (serotonin, which regulates mood, and norepinephrine, which regulates the body's energy). Tricyclic antidepressants act simultaneously to increase both these neurotransmitters. This type of antidepressant often produces intolerable side effects such as sleepiness, nervousness, dizziness, dry mouth, or constipation. Monoamine oxidase inhibitors (MAOIs) increase levels of these same neurotransmitters plus dopamine, which regulates attention and pleasure. MAOIs can cause dizziness and interact negatively with some foods. Selective serotonin reuptake inhibitors (SSRIs) have fewer side effects but can cause nausea, insomnia or sleepiness, agitation, or sexual dysfunction. SSRIs have also been linked to violent behavior and suicide in children and adults, although this association is contested. Aminoketones increase norepinephrine and dopamine, with agitation, insomnia, and anxiety being common side effects. Selective norepinephrine reuptake inhibitors (SNRIs) increase levels of norepinephrine and can cause dry mouth, constipation, increased sweating, and insomnia. The selective serotonin reuptake inhibitors and blockers (SSRIBs) increase serotonin and elicit the fewest side effects (nausea, dizziness, sleepiness). Herbal remedies, such as St. John's wort, may act like SSRIs; there is some evidence that St. John's wort contributes to infertility. Some drugs blunt the action of a neurotransmitter known as substance P. Other drugs reduce the level and effects of a stress-sensitive brain chemical known as corticotropin-releasing factor (CRF). The hypothalamus, the part of the brain that manages hormone release, increases production of CRF when a threat is detected. The body responds with reduced appetite, decreased sex drive, and heightened alertness. Persistent overactivation of this hormone may lead to depression. The effects of antidepressants are due to slow-onset adaptive changes in neurons. They may take several weeks to have a noticeable effect.

Psychotherapy works by changing the way the brain functions. Cognitive-behavioral therapy helps patients change the negative styles of thinking and behaving associated with depression. Therapies teach patients new skills to cope better with life, increase self-esteem, cope with stress, and better deal with interpersonal relationships. There is evidence that severe depression responds most favorably with a combination of medication and psychotherapy.

Electroconvulsive therapy (ECT) is an effective treatment for major depressive disorder. The treatment was first developed in 1934. Between 80 percent and 90 percent of people with the disorder show great improvement with ECT, which produces a seizure in the brain by applying electrical stimulation to the brain through electrodes placed on the scalp. ECT reduces the level of CRF. The treatment is usually repeated to obtain a therapeutic response. Common, yet short-lived, side effects include memory loss and other cognitive deficits.

## DYSTHYMIC DISORDER

Dysthymic disorder was first introduced as a category of mood disorder in 1980. Dysthymia means "ill humor." It is characterized as a mild, chronic depression lasting at least two years and affects 3 to 5 percent of all Americans. The majority of people with dysthymia also develop major depressive disorder, a state called double depression. The disorder is more prevalent in women than in men.

Essentially, dysthymic disorder is a low-grade, chronic depression. Diagnosis of dysthymic disorder requires the impairment of physical and social functioning. Treatment may include cognitive and behavioral therapy as well as pharmacotherapy, especially SSRIs.

## BIPOLAR DISORDER

In 1686, Theophile Bonet, a French pathologist, described a mental illness he called *maniaco-melancholicus*. In 1854, Jules Falret, a French physician, described *folie circulaire*, distinguished by alternating moods of depression and mania. In 1899, Emil Kraepelin, a German psychologist, described manic-depressive psychosis. Bipolar disorder has a lifetime prevalence of 1.2 percent. It affects more than 2.3 million adult Americans each year. It is equally common in men and women.

There is a genetic link to bipolar disorder. About 50 percent of all bipolar disorder patients have at least one parent with a mood disorder. An increased level of calcium ions is found in the blood of patients with bipolar disorder. There is also a lowered blood flow in the brain as well as slower overall metabolism. Some research suggests that bipolar disorder may be caused by disturbed circadian rhythms and related to disturbances in melatonin secretion.

The DSM-IV-TR divides bipolar disorder into bipolar I disorder, bipolar II disorder, and cyclothymic disorder. Bipolar I disorder is characterized by the occurrence of one or more manic episodes or mixed episodes and one or more major depressive episodes. Bipolar II disorder is characterized by the occurrence of one or more major depressive episodes accompanied by at least one hypomanic episode. Cyclothymic disorder is a chronic, fluctuating mood disturbance involving periods of hypomanic episodes and periods of major depressive episodes.

Treatment options include psychotherapy and medication. Mood stabilizers, such as lithium and divalproex sodium, are the most commonly used medications. Lithium is a naturally occurring substance that increases serotonin levels in the brain. Side effects can include dry mouth, high overdose toxicity, nausea, and tremor. Divalproex sodium increases GABA (gamma-amino butyric acid) in the brain. Neurotransmitters trigger either "go" signals that allow messages to be passed on to other cells in the brain or "stop" signals that prevent messages from being forwarded. GABA is the most common message-altering neurotransmitter in the brain. Possible side effects of divalproex sodium include constipation, headache, nausea, liver damage, and tremor. Olanzapine increases levels of dopamine and serotonin. Side effects include drowsiness, dry mouth, low blood pressure, rapid heartbeat, and tremor. Anticonvulsants are also widely prescribed. Carbamazepine, for example, increases GABA and serotonin. Possible side effects include blurred vision, dizziness, dry mouth, stomach upset, or sedation. In the case of severe mania, patients may take a tranquilizer or a neuroleptic (antipsychotic drug) in addition to the mood stabilizer. During the depressive episode, the person may take an antidepressant. ECT may also be helpful during severe depressive episodes.

## SPECIFIERS FOR MOOD DISORDERS

Specifiers allow for a more specific diagnosis, which assists in treatment and prognosis. A postpartum onset specifier can be applied to a diagnosis of major depressive disorder or bipolar I or II disorder if the onset is within four weeks after childbirth. Symptoms include fluctuations in mood and intense (sometimes delusional) preoccupation with infant well-being. Severe ruminations or delusional thoughts about the infant are correlated with increased risk of harm to the infant. The mother may be uninterested in the infant, afraid of being alone with the infant, or may even try to kill the child while experiencing auditory hallucinations instructing her to do so or delusions that the child is possessed. Postpartum mood episodes severely impair functioning, which differentiates them from the "baby blues" that affects about 70 percent of women within ten days after birth.

Seasonal pattern specifier can be applied to bipolar I or II disorder or major depressive disorder. Occurrence of major depressive episodes is correlated with seasonal changes. In the most common variety, depressive episodes occur in the fall or winter and remit in the spring. The less common type is characterized by depressive episodes in the summer. Symptoms include lack of energy, oversleeping, overeating, weight gain, and carbohydrate craving. Light therapy, which uses bright visible-spectrum light, may bring relief to patients with a seasonal pattern to their mood disorder.

The rapid cycler specifier can be applied to bipolar I or II disorder. Cycling is the process of going from depression to mania, or hypomania, and back or vice versa. Cycles can be as short as a few days or as long as months or years. Rapid cycling involves the occurrence of four or more mood episodes during the previous twelve months. In extreme cases, rapid cyclers can change from depression to mania and back or vice versa in as short as a few days without a normal mood period between episodes. Seventy to ninety percent of rapid cyclers are both premenopausal and postmenopausal women. Rapid cycling is associated with a poorer prognosis.

## SOURCES FOR FURTHER STUDY

Copeland, Mary Ellen. *The Depression Workbook: A Guide for Living with Depression and Manic Depression.* Oakland, Calif.: New Harbinger, 1992. This workbook for coping with depression is based on a study of 120 people with depression and manic depression. The author includes sections on possible causes of mood disorders and offers advice about building a support system, finding a health care professional, building self-esteem, and preventing suicide.

Court, Bryan L., and Gerald E. Nelson. *Bipolar Puzzle Solution: A Mental Health Client's Perspective.* Philadelphia: Taylor & Francis, 1996. The authors provide answers to questions asked by support group members about living with manic-depressive illness.

Cronkite, Kathy. *On the Edge of Darkness.* New York: Dell, 1994. A collection of celebrity accounts of their personal experiences with depression. The reader is invited into their experiences of what depression feels like, how it is treated, and the consequences to the individual and family.

Dowling, Colette. *"You Mean I Don't Have to Feel This Way?" New Help for Depression, Anxiety, and Addiction.* New York: Macmillan, 1991. Presents the biological basis of disorders including bulimia, depression, and panic disorder. Includes a section on getting help through psychotherapy and medication.

Gold, Mark S. *The Good News About Depression: Breakthrough Medical Treatments That Can Work for You.* New York: Bantam Books, 1995. The author, a biopsychiatrist, guides the reader through treatments available to people with depression. He describes conditions that mimic the symptoms of depression.

Healy, David. *The Creation of Psychopharmacology.* Cambridge, Mass.: Harvard University Press, 2002. Details the discovery and development of psychiatric medications (including antidepressants), the extremely profitable partnership between psychiatrists and the large pharmaceutical companies, and the frightening consequences for today's culture and society.

Ingersoll, Barbara D., and Sam Goldstein. *Lonely, Sad, and Angry.* New York: Doubleday, 1995. Provides information about depressive disorders in children and adolescents. Includes guidelines on how to react to a crisis, what to expect in the future, and how to get family help. There is also a section on recognizing depression in the classroom.

Moreines, Robert N., and Patricia L. McGuire. *Light Up Your Blues: Understanding and Overcoming Seasonal Affective Disorders.* Washington, D.C.: The PIA Press, 1989. The authors, both biopsychiatrists, describe the symptoms, causes, and effects of seasonal affective disorder. They also describe phototherapy.

Nelson, John E., and Andrea Nelson, eds. *Sacred Sorrows: Embracing and Transforming Depression.* New York: Jeremy P. Tarcher/Putnam, 1996. This is an anthology of personal experiences, biological research, psychological research, and spiritual traditions written by psychiatrists, psychologists, social workers, novelists, philosophers, and teachers. The book provides a firsthand experience of depression and a look at theories about why people become depressed. Some of the essays discuss treatments including medication, physical exercise, psychotherapy, and raising planetary awareness.

Radke-Yarrow, Marian. *Children of Depressed Mothers.* New York: Cambridge University Press, 1998. Presents a developmental perspective on the children of depressed mothers. The book reports the results of a longitudinal study of children and their families.

Thompson, Tracy. *The Beast: A Journey Through Depression.* New York: Penguin, 1996. A journalist tells the story of how she came to terms with her depression. Good firsthand discussion of symptoms such as short-term memory deficits, anxiety, anhedonia, and changes in sleep patterns, sensation, and perception. Her account includes a frank discussion of feelings of isolation and thoughts of suicide.

*Elizabeth M. McGhee Nelson*

SEE ALSO: Bipolar Disorder; Clinical Depression; Depression; Drug Therapies.

# Moral Development

Type of psychology: Developmental psychology
Fields of study: Infancy and childhood; social perception and cognition

*Moral development is the process of internalizing society's rules and principles of right and wrong. In order to maintain a stable social order, the achievement of morality is necessary. Acquiring morals is a sequential process linked to a person's stage of moral reasoning and cognitive understanding.*

Key concepts

- cognitive development
- empathy
- moral development
- moral rules
- morality
- social order

Morality is a set of standards that a person has about the rightness and wrongness of various kinds of behavior. Moral development is the way in which these sets of standards change over a period of time and experiences. Without moral rules—obligatory social regulations based on the principles of justice and welfare for others—society would be chaotic and without order. Most societies, for example, agree that certain behaviors (such as murder and theft) are wrong, and most people follow those moral principles. Not everyone has the same way of reasoning about the morality of a situation, however, as seen in the following two scenarios from the work of psychologist Jean Piaget.

A little boy named John is in his room. He is called to dinner, and he goes into the dining room. Behind the door on a chair is a tray with fifteen cups on it. John does not know this; when he goes in, the door knocks against the tray, and all fifteen cups are broken. There is another boy, named Henry. One day when his mother is out, he tries to get some jam from the cupboard. He climbs onto a chair but cannot reach it; he knocks over a cup. The cup falls down and breaks.

When asked which of the above two boys is more naughty, most adults would immediately reply that Henry is more guilty. Conversely, a child between six and ten years of age usually will say that John is more guilty. The differences between the two scenes consist of both the amount of damage done and the intentions of the two children. It is obvious that children and adults do not view the situations in the same way.

## Influence of Freud and Piaget
Human morality has been an issue in philosophy since the days of Aristotle; the topic was first studied by psychologists in the early twentieth century. At

this time, both Sigmund Freud and Piaget addressed the issue of children's moral development.

Freud proposed that children around four years of age assimilate the morals and standards of their same-sex parent, resulting in the onset of the child's superego, which is the storehouse for one's conscience. Thus, children have a rudimentary sense of right and wrong based on the morals of their parental figure. Since Freud's concept was based on his theory of psychosexual development, it was discredited by his European colleagues for most of his lifetime. Thus, his theory of moral acquisition has not generally been the basis of research on the development of morality.

Piaget began observing children when he was giving intelligence tests in the laboratory of Alfred Binet. He observed that children do not reason in the same way that adults do. Thus, by questioning Swiss schoolchildren about their rules in a game of marbles, Piaget adapted his theory of cognitive development to moral development. Lawrence Kohlberg elaborated on Piaget's theory by studying children's, as well as adults', reasoning concerning moral dilemmas. Kohlberg is still generally considered the leading theorist of moral development.

## STAGES OF MORAL DEVELOPMENT

According to Piaget and Kohlberg, moral judgments are related to the stage of cognitive development from which a person is operating when making these judgments. According to Piaget's theory, the development of morality includes several stages. People cannot progress to higher stages of moral development until they have also progressed through higher stages of cognitive understanding. Cognition refers to the mental processes of thinking, reasoning, knowing, remembering, understanding, and problem solving. During the premoral stage (birth through five years of age), children have little awareness of morals. As they grow, children learn about cooperative activity and equality among peers. This cognitive knowledge leads to a new respect for rights and wrongs. At this stage (age six to ten), children cannot judge that Henry is more guilty than John, because they are not capable of understanding the differences in the children's intentions. The only understanding is of the degree of damage done. Therefore, the number of cups broken is the basis for the judgment of the wrongness of the act, regardless of the actor's good or bad intentions.

Finally, as children develop, they learn that rules can be challenged, and they are able to consider other factors, such as a person's intentions and motivation. Once this shift in perception occurs, children's moral development will progress to a higher stage.

## ROLE OF REASONING

Kohlberg expanded Piaget's theory by investigating how people reasoned the rightness or wrongness of an act and not how people actually behaved. For example, Kohlberg proposed the following moral dilemma. A man named Heinz had a wife who was dying from a disease that could be cured with a drug manufactured by a local pharmacist. The drug was expensive to make, but the druggist was charging ten times the amount it cost. Heinz could not afford the drug and pleaded with the man to discount the drug or let him pay a little at a time. The druggist refused, so Heinz broke into the pharmacy and stole the drug for his wife. Should Heinz have stolen the drug?

By listening to people's reasoning concerning Heinz's actions, Kohlberg proposed that there are three levels (of two stages each) of moral reasoning. The first level is called the preconventional level; in this stage, a person's feelings of right and wrong are based on an external set of rules that have been handed down by an authority figure such as a parent, teacher, or religious figure. These rules are obeyed in order to avoid punishment or to gain rewards. In other words, people at this stage of moral reasoning would not steal the drug—not because they believed that stealing was wrong but rather because they had been told not to and would fear being caught and punished for their action.

The second level of moral reasoning is the conventional level, at which judgments of right and wrong are based on other people's expectations. For example, at this level there are two substages. One is known as the "good boy/nice girl" orientation, in which morality is based on winning approval and avoiding disapproval by one's immediate group. In other words, people may or may not steal the drug based on what they believe their peers would think of them. The second substage is called the "law and order" orientation, under which moral behavior is thought of in terms of obedience to the authority figure and the established social order. Social order refers to the way in which a society or culture functions, based on the rules, regulation, and standards that are held and taught by each member of the society. The "laws" are usually obeyed without question, regardless of the circumstances, and are seen as the mechanism for the maintenance of social order. A person operating from this stage would say that Heinz should not steal the drug because it was against the law—and if he did steal the drug, he should go to jail for his crime.

The third level of moral reasoning is called the postconventional orientation. At this stage, the person is more concerned with a personal commitment to higher principles than with behavior dictated by society's rules. Disobeying the law would be in some instances far less immoral than obeying a law that is believed to be wrong, and being punished for the legal disobedience would be easier than the guilt and self-condemnation of disobeying the personal ethical principles held by that person. For example, many civil rights workers and Vietnam War conscientious objectors were jailed, beaten, and outcast from mainstream society, but those consequences were far less damaging to them than transgressing their own convictions would have been.

According to Kohlberg, the preconventional stage is characteristic of young children, while the conventional stage is more indicative of the general population. It has been estimated that only about 20 percent of the adult population reach the postconventional stage. Thus, the course of moral development is not the same for everyone. Even some adults operate at the preconventional level of moral reasoning. Education, parental affection, observation and imitation, and explanations of the consequences of behavior are factors in determining the course of moral development in a child.

## ROLE-PLAYING

Moral development is a progression from one stage to a different, higher stage of reasoning. One cannot proceed to a higher stage of morality without the accompanying cognitive understanding. Thus, if a child thinks that John, who broke fifteen cups, is more guilty than Henry, who broke one cup, then merely telling the child that Henry's intentions were not as good as John's, and therefore John is not as guilty, is not going to change the child's perceptions. The child's understanding of the situation must be actively changed. One way of doing this is through role-playing. The child who thinks that John is more guilty can be told to act out the two scenes, playing each of the two boys. By asking the child questions about his or her feelings while going through each of the scenes, one can help the child gain empathy (the capacity for experiencing the feelings and thoughts of other people) for each of the characters and a better understanding of intentions and actions. Once the child has the cognitive understanding of intentions, he or she is then able to reason at a higher level of moral development.

In other words, in trying to elevate someone's moral reasoning, the first goal is to elevate his or her cognitive understanding of the situation. This can also be done by citing similar examples within the person's own experience and chaining them to the event at hand. For example, if last week the child had accidentally broken something, asking the child how he or she remembers feeling when that event happened will remind the child of the emotions experienced at the time of the event. The child must then associate the remembered emotions with the situation at hand. This can be accomplished by asking questions, such as "Do you think that John might have felt the same way as you did when you broke the vase?" or "How do you think John felt when the cups fell down? Have you ever felt the same?" If one merely tells the child that John felt bad, the child may or may not comprehend the connection, but if one asks the child to reason through the situation by having empathy for John, then the child is more likely to progress to the next stage of moral reasoning.

This type of empathetic role-playing can be very important in trying to change deviant behavior. If a child is stealing, then having the child imagine or play a role in a situation where he or she is the one being stolen from is the quickest way for the child to change his or her judgments of the rightness or wrongness of the situation. Punishment may deter the behavior, but it does not result in a change in cognitive understanding or moral reasoning.

~~In addition to changing moral reasoning powers, this type of role-playing is also more likely to aid the child from an understimulated home environment. The child whose social environment includes many incidents of undesirable behaviors or who lacks examples of positive behaviors must be stimulated in ways that appeal to current cognitive understanding but that show ways of thinking that differ from current examples in his or her~~ life.

## STUDY OF SOCIAL COGNITIONS

Other areas of psychological research are concerned with the topic of children's ~~"social cognitions," which subsumes the topic of morals and considers other issues such as empathy, attribution, and motivations~~. One area that ~~has come to light is the issue of the effect of the emotions on cognitions~~ and their contribution to moral judgments. For example, it has been shown that people in a good mood are more likely to help someone else than those in a bad mood. Expanding on this premise, other research has demonstrated that even the way people perceive an object or situation is closely linked to their psychological or emotional states at the time. Even concrete perceptions can be changed by a person's state of being. One example is that people who are poor actually judge the size of a quarter to be larger than do people who are rich.

As cognitive theories begin to consider the interactive components that emotions have in cognitions, new methods of study and new theoretical predictions will change the way cognitive psychologists study such areas as problem solving, decision making, reasoning, and memory. Each of these areas is independently related to the study of moral development and should affect the way psychologists think about how people acquire and think about morality within society.

~~In addition, as society increases in sophistication and technology~~, new issues will emerge that will strain old theories. Issues that are particular to new generations will result in new ways of thinking about morality that were not faced by past generations. The direction that moral development goes is ultimately highly dependent on the problems of the current society.

## SOURCES FOR FURTHER STUDY

Duska, Ronald F., and Mariellen Whelan. *Moral Development: A Guide to Piaget and Kohlberg.* New York: Paulist Press, 1975. Presents Jean Piaget's theory and its implications for Lawrence Kohlberg's expansion into his own theory of moral development. All of the moral stories used by Piaget and Kohlberg in their research are replicated in this book. Also includes research findings and ways in which to apply these theories to everyday situations in teaching children. This book can be read easily by the high school or college student.

Gilligan, Carol, Janie Victoria Ward, and Jill McLean Taylor, eds. *Mapping the Moral Domain*. Cambridge, Mass.: Harvard University Press, 1990. A collection of essays presenting the contribution of women's studies to Kohlbergian theories of moral development.

Nucci, Larry P. *Education in the Moral Domain*. New York: Cambridge University Press, 2001. Brings together theoretical and practical approaches to creating a classroom environment that nurtures moral development in children.

Reed, Donald R. C. *Following Kohlberg: Liberalism and the Practice of Democratic Community*. South Bend, Ind.: University of Notre Dame Press, 1998. Offers a comprehensive overview of Kohlberg's research, from an empirical and psychological perspective as well as a more abstract philosophy.

Rich, John Martin, and Joseph L. DeVitis. *Theories of Moral Development*. 2d ed. Springfield, Ill.: Charles C Thomas, 1996. Presents a range of psychologists' theories on moral development, including Sigmund Freud, Alfred Adler, Carl Jung, and David Sears. In addition, it places moral development within the framework of higher education and relates it to a life-span perspective. Certain sections of the book would be difficult for a novice student to follow; however, in terms of a summary review of theoretical positions, the book is a handy reference.

*Donna Frick-Horbury*

SEE ALSO: Adolescence: Cognitive Skills; Cognitive Development: Jean Piaget; Crowd Behavior; Development; Helping; Women's Psychology: Carol Gilligan.

# MOTIVATION

TYPE OF PSYCHOLOGY: Biological bases of behavior; emotion; learning;
    memory; motivation; social psychology
FIELDS OF STUDY: Attitudes and behavior; aversive conditioning;
    behavioral and cognitive models; cognitive learning; methodological
    issues; motivation theory; Pavlovian conditioning; personality theory;
    social motives

*Central to the study of psychology is motivation, which is fundamentally concerned
with emotion, personality, learning, memory, and gaining an understanding of how
behavior is most effectively activated, organized, and directed toward the achievement
of goals.*

KEY CONCEPTS
- activation theory
- behavioral approach
- cognitive approach
- hedonistic theory
- humanistic approach
- hydraulic model
- incentive theory
- Pavlovian conditioning
- psychodynamic approach
- teacher expectations

Research in motivation is pivotal to such fields as educational psychology, social psychology, behavioral psychology, and most other subareas of psychology. Motivation is centrally concerned with the goals people set for themselves and with the means they take to achieve these goals. It is also
concerned with how people react to and process information, activities directly related to learning. Motivation to process information is influenced
by two major factors: the relevance of the topic to the person processing the
information, which affects the willingness to think hard about the topic; and
the need for cognition, or the willingness to think hard about varied topics,
whether they are directly relevant or not. The relevance of a topic is central
to people's motivation to learn about it.

For example, if the community in which a person lives experiences a severe
budgetary crisis that will necessitate a substantial increase in property taxes,
every resident in that community, home owners and renters alike, is going to
be affected directly or indirectly by the increase. Because this increase is relevant to all the residents, they will, predictably, be much concerned with the
topic and will likely think hard about its salient details. If, on the other hand,
a community in a distant state faces such a crisis, residents in other communities, reading or hearing about the situation, will not have the motivation to
do much hard thinking about it because it does not affect them directly.

The second category of motivation rests in the need of some individuals for cognition. Their inherent curiosity will motivate them to think deeply about various topics that do not concern them directly but that they feel a need to understand more fully. Such people are deliberative, self-motivated thinkers possessed of an innate curiosity about the world that surrounds them. They generally function at a higher intellectual level than people who engage in hard thinking primarily about topics that affect them directly. One of the aims of education at all levels is to stimulate people to think about a broad variety of topics, which they will do because they have an inherent curiosity that they long to satisfy.

## EARLY CONCERNS WITH MOTIVATION

During the late nineteenth century, Austrian psychoanalyst Sigmund Freud (1856-1939) developed theories about motivation that are usually categorized as the psychodynamic approach. He contended that people have psychic energy that is essentially sexual or aggressive in its origins. Such energy seeks results that please, satisfy, or delight. This pleasure principle, as it was called, had to function within the bounds of certain restraints, identified as the reality principle, never violating the demands of people's conscience or of the restraints or inhibitions that their self-images imposed. In Freudian terms, the superego served to maintain the balance between the pleasure principle and the reality principle. In *Beyond the Pleasure Principle* (1922), Freud reached the conclusion that all motivation could be reduced to two opposing sources of energy, the life instinct and the death instinct.

Heinz Hartmann (1894-1970) went a step beyond Freud's psychodynamic theory, emphasizing the need for people to achieve their goals in ways that do not produce inner conflict, that are free of actions that might compromise or devastate the ego. More idealistic was Robert White, who denied Freud's contention that motivation is sexual or aggressive in nature. White contended that the motivation to achieve competence is basic in people. Everyone, according to White, wishes to be competent and, given proper guidance, will strive to achieve competence, although individual goals and individual determinations of the areas in which they wish to be competent vary greatly from person to person.

Such social psychologists as Erik Erikson (1902-1994), Carl Jung (1875-1961), and Karen Horney (1885-1952) turned their attention away from the biological and sexual nature of motivation, focusing instead upon its social aspects. They, like Freud, Hartmann, and White before them, sought to understand the unconscious means by which psychic energy is distributed as it ferrets out sources of gratification.

## THE BEHAVIORISTS

The behavioral approach to motivation is centrally concerned with rewards and punishments. People cultivate behaviors for which they are rewarded. They avoid behaviors that experience has shown them will result in pain or punishment. B. F. Skinner (1904-1990) was probably the most influential behaviorist. Many educators accepted his theories and applied them to social as well as teaching situations.

Clark Hull (1884-1952), working experimentally with rats, determined that animals deprived of such basic requirements as food or punished by painful means such as electric shock, develop intense reactions to these stimuli. John Dollard (1900-1980) and Neal Miller (1909-2002) extended Hull's work to human subjects. They discovered that the response elicited by these means depends on the intensity of the stimulus, not on its origin. The stimuli employed also evoke previously experienced stimulus-response reactions, so that if subjects are hurt or punished following a volitional act, they will in future avoid such an act. In other words, if the negative stimuli are rapidly reduced, the responses that immediately preceded the reduction are reinforced. These researchers concluded that physiological needs such as hunger are innate, whereas secondary drives and the reaction to all drives, through conditioning, are learned.

Ivan Pavlov (1849-1936) demonstrated the strength of conditioned responses in his renowned experiments with dogs. He arranged for a bell to sound immediately before the dogs in his experiment were fed. The dogs came to associate the sound of a bell with being fed, a pleasurable and satisfying experience. Eventually, when Pavlov rang the bell but failed to follow its ringing with feeding, the dogs salivated merely on hearing the sound, because they anticipated the feeding to which they had become conditioned. Over time, the motivation to satisfy their hunger came to be as much related to hearing the bell as it was to their actually being fed. Pavlovian conditioning is directly related to motivation, in this case the motivation to satisfy hunger.

## KONRAD LORENZ'S HYDRAULIC MODEL

Freud argued that if instinctive urges are bottled up, they will eventually make the individual ill. They demand release and will find it in one way or another as the unconscious mind works to direct the distribution of the individual's psychic energy.

Konrad Lorenz (1903-1989) carried this notion a step beyond what Freud had postulated, contending that inherent drives that are not released by external means will explode spontaneously through some inherent releasing mechanism. This theory, termed Lorenz's hydraulic model, explains psychic collapses in some people, particularly in those who are markedly repressed.

Erich Fromm (1900-1980) carried Freud's notions about the repression of innate drives one step beyond what Lorenz espoused. Fromm added a moral dimension to what Freud and Lorenz asserted, by postulating that humans develop character as a means of managing and controlling their innate physiological and psychological needs. He brought the matter of free will into his consideration of how to deal in a positive way with innate drives.

## THE HEDONISTIC THEORY OF MOTIVATION

Hedonism emphasizes pleasure over everything else. The hedonistic theory of motivation stems from Freud's recognition of the pleasure principle, which stipulates that motivation is stimulated by pleasure and inhibited by pain.

Laboratory experiments with rats demonstrated unequivocally that, given a choice, rats work harder to get food that tastes good to them than to get food that is nutritious. Indeed, laboratory animals will take in empty calories to the point of emaciation as long as the food that contains such calories tastes good. It is thought that hedonistic motivation is directly related to pleasure centers in the brain, so that organisms work both consciously and unconsciously toward stimulating and satisfying these pleasure centers.

## THE INCENTIVE THEORY OF MOTIVATION

Alfred Adler (1870-1937), the Austrian psychologist who founded the school of individual psychology, rejected Freud's emphases on sex and aggression as fundamental aspects of motivation. Breaking from Freud, who had been among his earliest professional associates, Adler contended that childhood feelings of helplessness led to later feelings of inferiority. His means of treating the inferiority complex, as this condition came to be known, was to engage his patients in positive social interaction. To do this, he developed an incentive theory of motivation, as articulated in his two major works, *Praxis und Theorie der Individual psychologie* (1920; *The Practice and Theory of Individual Psychology,* 1924) and *Menschenkenntnis* (1927; *Understanding Human Nature,* 1927).

Adler's theory focused on helping people to realize the satisfaction involved in achieving superiority and competence in areas in which they had some aptitude. The motivation to do so is strictly personal and individual. Adler's entire system was based on the satisfactions to be derived from achieving a modicum of superiority. The incentive approach views competence as a basic motivation activated by people's wish to avoid failure. This is a reward/punishment approach, although it is quite different from that of the behaviorists and is, in essence, humanistic. The reward is competence; the punishment is failure. Both factors stimulate subjects' motivation.

## THE ACTIVATION THEORY OF MOTIVATION

Drive reductionists believed that if all of an organism's needs are fulfilled, that organism will lapse into a lethargic state. They conclude that increasing needs will cause the organism to have an increased drive to fulfill those needs. Their view is that the inevitable course that individual organisms select is that of least resistance.

Donald O. Hebb, however, takes a more sanguine view of motivation, particularly in humans. In his activation theory, he contends that a middle ground between lethargy at one extreme and incapacitating anxiety at the other produces the most desirable level of motivation. This theory accounts for states of desired arousal such as that found in such pursuits as competitive sports.

The drive reductionists ascribe to the reward/punishment views of most of the behaviorists, who essentially consider organisms to be entities in need of direction, possibly of manipulation. The drive inductionists, on the other hand, have faith in the innate need of organisms to be self-directive and to work individually toward gaining competence. Essentially they accept the Greek ideal of the golden mean as a guiding principle, which has also been influential in the thinking of such humanistic psychologists.

### THE HUMANISTIC APPROACH TO MOTIVATION

Abraham Maslow (1908-1970) devised a useful though controversial hierarchy of needs required to satisfy human potential. These needs proceed from low-level physiological needs such as hunger, thirst, sex, and comfort, through such other needs as safety, love, and esteem, finally reaching the highest level, self-actualization. According to Maslow, human beings progress sequentially through this hierarchy as they develop. Each category of needs proceeds from the preceding category, and no category is omitted as the human develops, although the final and highest category, self-actualization, which includes curiosity, creative living, and fulfilling work, is not necessarily attained or attainable by all humans.

The humanists stipulate that people's primary motives are those that lead toward self-actualization, those that capitalize on the unique potential of each individual. In educational terms, this means that for education to be effective, it must emphasize exploration and discovery over memorization and the rote learning of a set body of material. It must also be highly individualized, although this does not imply a one-on-one relationship between students and their teachers. Rather than acting as fonts of knowledge, teachers become facilitators of learning, directing their students individually to achieve the actualization of the personal goals that best suit them.

Carl Rogers (1902-1987) traced much psychopathology to conflicts between people's inherent understanding of what they require to move toward self-actualization and society's expectations, which may run counter to individual needs. In other words, as many people develop and pass through the educational system, they may be encouraged or required to adopt goals that are opposed to those that are most realistic for them. Humanistic views of human development run counter to the views of most of the psychodynamic and behaviorist psychologists concerned with learning theory and motivation as it relates to such theory.

### COGNITIVE APPROACHES TO MOTIVATION

Research of Kurt Lewin (1890-1947) in the subjective tension systems that work toward resolution of problems in humans, along with his research done in collaboration with Edward C. Tolman (1886-1959) that emphasizes expectancies and the subjective value of the results of actions, has led to a cognitive approach to motivation. Related to this research is that of Leon Festinger (1919-1989), whose theory of cognitive dissonance stipulates that if a person's beliefs are not in harmony with one another, the person will experience a discomfort that he or she will attempt to eliminate by altering his or her beliefs.

People ultimately realize that certain specific behaviors will lead to anticipated results. Behavior, therefore, has a purpose, but the number of goals related to specific behaviors is virtually infinite. People learn to behave in ways that make it most likely to achieve expected results.

Robert Rosenthal and Lenore Jacobson demonstrated that teacher expectations have a great deal to do with the success of the students with whom they work. Their experiment, detailed fully in *Pygmalion in the Classroom* (1968), relates how they selected preadolescent and adolescent students randomly and then told the teachers of those students that they had devised a way of determining which students were likely to show spurts of unusual mental growth in the coming year. Each teacher was given the names of two or three students who were identified as being on the brink of rapid intellectual development. The researchers tested the students at the end of the school year and found that those who had been designated as poised on the brink of unusual mental development tested above the norm, even though they had been selected randomly from all the students in the classes involved. In this experiment, teacher motivation to help certain students succeed appears to have been central to those students' achieving goals beyond those of other students in the class.

**SOURCES FOR FURTHER STUDY**

Boekaerts, Monique, Paul R. Pintrich, and Moshe Zeidner. *Handbook of Self-Regulation.* San Diego, Calif.: Academic Press, 2000. Chapters 5 and 15 deal specifically with motivation, offering unique perspectives that are both physiological and social. The approach of this volume is essentially humanistic.

Ferguson, Eva Dreikurs. *Motivation: A Biosocial and Cognitive Integration of Motivation and Emotion.* New York: Oxford University Press, 2000. This book requires some background in the field of motivation. It is carefully researched and accurately presented. Its focus is more on the physiological aspects of motivation than on the social.

Glover, John A., Royce R. Ronning, and Cecil R. Reynolds, eds. *Handbook of Creativity.* New York: Plenum Press, 1989. Of special interest to those seeking information about motivation will be chapter 7, "Cognitive Processes in Creativity," and those parts of chapter 5, "The Nature-Nurture Problem in Creativity," that deal with cognitive and motivational processes.

Greenwood, Gordon E., and H. Thompson Fillmer. *Educational Psychology: Cases for Teacher Decision-Making.* Columbus, Ohio: Merrill, 1999. Of particular value in this book of case studies is part 5, which deals with motivation and classroom management. In this section, chapter 25, "Motivation or Control?," is particularly relevant to readers interested in motivation. The approach in this book is eminently practical. The writing is easily accessible to beginners in the field.

Kendrick, Douglas T., Steven L. Neuberg, and Robert B. Cialdini. *Social Psychology: Unraveling the Mystery*. Boston: Allyn & Bacon, 1999. This is one of the best-written, most accessible books in introductory psychology. It is replete with examples to illustrate what is being said. The prose style is enticing, and the intellectual content is exceptional. The chapter titled "The Motivational Systems: Motives and Goals" is particularly relevant to those studying motivation. Strongly recommended for those unfamiliar with the field.

Lawler, Edward E., III. *Rewarding Excellence: Pay Strategies for the New Economy*. San Francisco: Jossey-Bass, 2000. Approached from the standpoint of a professor of management, this book discusses various motivational protocols employed by industry. Some of them are easily transferable to broader contexts. The tactics suggested are largely behavioral. They deal extensively with reward/punishment scenarios.

Lesko, Wayne A., ed. *Readings in Social Psychology: General, Classic, and Contemporary Selections*. Boston: Allyn & Bacon, 2000. This entire collection is worth reading. Nearly every selection in it relates in some way to motivation.

Rosenthal, Robert, and Lenore Jacobson. *Pygmalion in the Classroom*. 1968. Reprint. New York: Irvington, 1992. This report of an experiment that deals with teacher expectations and their relation to student achievement is compelling and provocative.

Wagner, Hugh. *The Psychobiology of Human Motivation*. New York: Routledge, 1999. Demonstrates how humans can adapt to complex social environments by controlling and channeling their basic physiological drives. Wagner points out the fallacy of attempting to explain human motivation in terms of models based on animal physiology. He also questions Abraham Maslow's hierarchy of needs. Wagner's skepticism is at once challenging, thought-provoking, and refreshing.

Wong, Roderick. *Motivation: A Biobehavioural Approach*. New York: Cambridge University Press, 2000. Wong's focus is sharply on behaviorism and on the physiological aspects of motivation, although chapter 9, "Social Motivation: Attachment and Altruism," moves into the area of social psychology. This in not a book for beginners, although its ideas are well presented, often with cogent examples.

*R. Baird Shuman*

SEE ALSO: Behaviorism; Conditioning; Drives; Pavlovian Conditioning; S-R Theory: Neal E. Miller and John Dollard.

# Multiple Personality

Type of psychology: Psychopathology
Fields of study: Coping; models of abnormality; personality disorders

*Multiple personality is the name of abnormal behavior in which a person behaves as if under the control of distinct and separate parts of the personality at different times. It is caused by severe childhood abuse and responds to long-term psychotherapy that addresses the past abuse and the resulting symptoms of dissociation.*

Key concepts
- alternate personality
- dissociation
- dissociative identity disorder
- integration
- repression

Multiple personality has had considerable research and clinical attention focused on it since the early 1980's, and this interest has increased significantly from that point forward. However, multiple personality was known and studied even prior to the work of Sigmund Freud (1856-1939), the Austrian psychiatrist and founder of psychoanalysis. Well-known French psychologists Pierre Janet (1859-1947) and Alfred Binet (1857-1911), among others, had written about it in the late nineteenth century, prior to Freud's writings. With the rise of psychoanalysis in the early twentieth century, the study of multiple personality and dissociation waned dramatically for many years. Two famous multiple personality cases in the United States were popularized by books and then films: *The Three Faces of Eve* in 1957 and *Sybil* in 1973.

In 1980, multiple personality disorder (MPD) was officially sanctioned as a legitimate psychiatric disorder by its inclusion in the *Diagnostic and Statistical Manual of Mental Disorders* (3d ed., 1980, DSM-III) published by the American Psychiatric Association. The official diagnostic label was changed in the fourth edition, DSM-IV (1994), to dissociative identity disorder (DID), though it is still commonly known as multiple personality.

## Cause

Research has shown that multiple personality is most probably caused by severe childhood abuse, usually both physical and sexual. Psychotherapists who specialize in treating disorders caused by trauma hypothesize that the human mind or personality divides to cope with the terror of the trauma. It is as if one part of the mind handles the abuse to protect another part of the mind from the pain. This splitting of consciousness is a psychological defense called dissociation. Instead of memories, bodily sensations, emotions, and thoughts all being associated with an experience (which is the normal process of human experience), these aspects lose their association and seem

~~to separate. A common example would be that a person who was sexually abused as a child loses the memory of those events and may have no recall of them until later in adulthood.~~ In this case, the whole experience is dissociated. For example, in multiple personality, a so-called alternate personality ("alter" for short) named Ann experienced the abuse, while alter Jane, who deals with normal, everyday living, was not abused. Thus, Jane has no memories of abuse. ~~A variation is that only certain aspects of the experience are dissociated, so that, for instance, the abused person has the memory that the sexual abuse happened but has no emotions regarding the pain and trauma~~ of it. ~~Freud coined the term "repression" to describe the process by which emotions that are too threatening to be admitted into consciousness are pushed into the unconscious.~~

## DIAGNOSIS

Several well-researched psychological tests and structured interviews aid in diagnosing a client. For a formal diagnosis of DID, the *Diagnostic and Statistical Manual of Mental Disorders: DSM-IV-TR* (rev. 4th ed., 2000) states that the following four criteria must be present: two or more distinct identities or personality states (each with its own relatively enduring pattern of perceiving, relating to, and thinking about the environment and self); at least two

*Chris Costner Sizemore, the subject of the book and film* The Three Faces of Eve *about multiple personality disorder.* (AP/Wide World Photos)

of these identities or personality states recurrently take control of the person's behavior; there is an inability to recall important personal information that is too extensive to be explained by ordinary forgetfulness; and the disturbance is not due to the direct physiological effects of a substance (such as blackouts due to alcohol, drugs, or seizures).

The central paradox of multiple personality is that it is both real and not real at the same time. It is not real in that the mind or personality does not literally split. There is only one brain and one body. It is a creation of a person's imagination. At the same time, however, the person with DID experiences very real separations and is not faking them. The perceived separate parts must be dealt with as if they were separate, while teaching them the reality that they must live in the same body and jointly suffer the consequences of the actions of any one part.

Multiple personality goes unrecognized too often as a result of several reasons. First, it has only received considerable attention since the early 1980's. Second, it was wrongly thought to be extremely rare, so psychotherapists were previously taught that they would probably never see a case of it. Third, the trauma that causes DID produces so many symptoms, such as depression, anxiety, hearing voices, and mood changes, that it is wrongly diagnosed as schizophrenia, bipolar disorder, or something else. Fourth, there is skepticism about its validity as a true diagnosis.

Alters can be categorized in various ways. Some are victims who took most of the abuse. Some are persecutors who identified with the abuser and try to control other alters internally. Some are functioning alters who handle work or school. Alters may believe they are the opposite sex of the body and can see themselves as almost any age. Some may know a great deal about other alters. Others may only know of themselves and have no knowledge that others even exist.

Because at least some alters are usually dissociated from other alters, the person with DID will typically experience time loss when one alter has had control of the body and a different alter, who does not know what has happened previously, takes control. Dissociation is experienced in degrees. When it is present to a lesser degree, DID patients hear voices inside their heads. They are hearing alters talking. This may scare them when they first experience it, or it may be so normal for them that they mistake these voices for their own thoughts.

## TREATMENT

Clinical experience and research have shown that this disorder is treatable to full remission, and therefore the prognosis is more hopeful than with some other psychiatric disorders. The negative side of treatment is that it takes a long time, usually five to seven years and in some cases longer. The guidelines for treatment established by the International Society for the Study of Dissociation call for psychotherapy two to three times a week for several years.

The initial goal of psychotherapy is stabilization, to stop any destructive behaviors such as suicide or other forms of self-harm. The intermediate goal is to become aware of the alters, counsel their individual needs, and then bring about cooperation and communication between alters to make daily functioning more effective. The long-range goal is to bring about the integration of all split personalities into one unified personality. Integration is the combining of all aspects of the self, even the ones that may seem destructive or feel great pain. The goal is not to get rid of certain alters, as every part is an aspect of the self and needs to be integrated into the self.

Part of treatment consists of recounting and processing the memories of abuse. Ignoring past abuse is not helpful. However, this memory work needs to be done slowly and carefully, going at a pace that does not overwhelm the client. One goal is to keep the client functioning as normally as possible in daily life. Mistakes have been made by therapists who go too fast, too far, and who focus on talking about memories without addressing other needs, such as helping clients stabilize, encouraging cooperation and communication of alters, gradually integrating alters, teaching toleration of uncomfortable emotions, and instilling new coping mechanisms other than dissociating. The therapist should not suggest to the client that he or she was abused but should let the client discover this on his or her own.

Hypnosis may be used as part of the treatment but it is not required. Experienced trauma therapists talk easily with the various alters and usually learn to recognize the different parts with little trouble. The switch between alters most often, but not always, is subtle and not dramatic. Psychiatric medications are often used as an adjunct to talking therapy, to help with the symptoms accompanying DID such as depression and anxiety. As DID is a disorder caused by personal experience, it is not cured by medications.

What does not work is ignoring or denying the presence of alters, focusing only on the present and ignoring the past, trying to get rid of so-called bad alters, and exorcising alters who are psychological entities. Obviously, a person with DID will succeed best in counseling with a psychotherapist who is experienced and has specialized training in the treatment of trauma disorders.

## IMPACT

People who suffer from multiple personality are adults who live with a coping mechanism that worked well to survive the horrors of abuse in childhood but is not working as well in a normal adult environment. All patients with DID suffer to some extent, which usually drives them to find relief. Some of these forms of relief are healthy, such as psychotherapy, and some may be unhealthy, such as addictions used to drown the painful feelings.

Some people with multiple personality appear to function normally and may not themselves know that they have more than one personality. They may be able to function at a very high level at a job, for instance, while those close to them sense things are not normal. They may function normally for years and then have a crisis that seems to develop very rapidly. Other people with DID have trouble functioning normally and have a long history of psychological problems. These people may be unable to work to support themselves and need multiple hospitalizations. It is common for someone with DID to function at an extremely high level in one area or at one time and, conversely, to function at a very low level in another area or at another time. This leaves those around them very puzzled and confused.

### CONTROVERSY

Unfortunately, there is controversy regarding multiple personality. Some critics inside and outside the mental health profession claim that it is not a legitimate psychiatric disorder, perhaps because the idea of having multiple personality and repressed memories does not make sense to them. They may believe that this disorder is created by people seeking attention through being dramatic, caused by incompetent therapists suggesting this diagnosis to their clients, or used by people wanting an excuse for irresponsible or even criminal behavior. Some of these critics also attack the concept of recovered memories of child sexual abuse. They believe this profound loss of memory is not real and that these recovered memories are actually false memories that serve the same purposes mentioned above.

The result is that the trauma field has tended to become polarized into true believers and extreme skeptics. A balanced position has sometimes been lost. Trauma experts with a balanced view will admit that some memories are inaccurate, that some clients labeled as having DID have indeed been misdiagnosed for the reasons the critics offer, and that some therapists do a poor job. However, these experts argue that the research base and clinical evidence supporting the existence of a distinct diagnosis called DID is strong and that the repression of memories of childhood abuse is real.

### SOURCES FOR FURTHER STUDY

Cohen, L., J. Berzhoff, and M. Elin, eds. *Dissociative Identity Disorder: Theoretical and Treatment Controversies.* Northvale, N.J.: Jason Aronson, 1995. This book gives the differing views regarding the controversies around DID. Each chapter offers both sides of the position on the topic at hand. It is somewhat technical.

Hocking, Sandra J. *Living with Your Selves: A Survival Manual for People with Multiple Personalities.* Rockville, Md.: Launch Press, 1992. This is a self-help book written by and for someone who has multiple personality. It contains helpful and accurate information.

Putnam, Frank. *Diagnosis and Treatment of Multiple Personality Disorder.* New York: Guilford Press, 1989. A textbook meant for professionals, written by an expert at the National Institute of Mental Health.

Ross, Colin A. *Dissociative Identity Disorder: Diagnosis, Clinical Features, and Treatment of Multiple Personality.* New York: John Wiley & Sons, 1997. Perhaps the leading textbook on DID. Everything you wanted to know and more by an international psychiatric expert. It is written for the professional, though it is very readable. It also contains the author's psychological test, called the DDIS, to help diagnose DID.

_____. *The Osiris Complex: Case Studies in Multiple Personality Disorder.* Toronto: University of Toronto Press, 1994. An interesting and readable book for both lay and professional audiences, giving specific cases with details that illustrate features of DID.

*Dennis Bull*

SEE ALSO: Personality Disorders.

# NERVOUS SYSTEM

TYPE OF PSYCHOLOGY: Biological bases of behavior; language; learning;
memory; sensation and perception
FIELDS OF STUDY: Auditory, chemical, cutaneous, and body senses;
biological treatments; endocrine system; nervous system; organic
disorders; schizophrenias; thought; vision

*The nervous system represents the interconnections of cells that recognize and coordinate the senses of the body. The nervous system is divided into two major components: the central nervous system, which includes the brain and spinal cord, and the peripheral nervous system, which communicates impulses to and from the regions of the body.*

KEY CONCEPTS

- central nervous system
- endocrine system
- endorphins and enkephalins
- limbic system
- neuron
- neurotransmitters
- peripheral nervous system

The functions of the human nervous system are in many ways analogous to that of a computer. The brain receives information in the form of stimuli from the senses open to the outside world. Within the brain are specific regions, analogous to programs, that interpret the stimuli and allow for a response. More specifically, such responses take the form of physiological or behavioral changes. Some of these stimuli result from activation of tissues or organs within the endocrine system, a network of glands which secrete hormones directly into the bloodstream for regulation of target organs.

The functional unit of the nervous system is the neuron, a cell which receives or sends information in the form of electrical impulses. The major component of the neuron is the cell body, the portion which contains the nucleus and most of the internal organelles. Two major forms of neurons are found within the nervous system: sensory neurons, which transmit the impulse toward the central nervous system (brain and spinal cord), and motor neurons, which receive impulses from the brain or spinal cord and transmit the impulse to muscles or other tissues.

Depending upon the type of neuron, a variety of processes may emanate from the cell body. Axons transmit the impulse away from the cell body and toward the target cell or tissue. Dendrites receive the impulse from other neurons or other sources of stimuli. The actual nerve consists of bundles of thousands of axons wrapped within a form of connective tissue.

The surface of a resting, or unstimulated, neuron has a measurable electrical potential across the membrane. When the nerve is stimulated, whether mechanically such as by pressure or electrically as in the sense of sight, an influx of electrically charged ions such as sodium occurs; the result is referred to as an action potential. The electrical discharge flows along the axon until it reaches the end of the neuron. Eventually the resting potential is restored, and the neuron may again undergo stimulation.

At its tip, the axon divides into numerous terminal branches, each with a structure called a synaptic bulb on the end. Within the bulb are vessels containing chemicals called neurotransmitters, molecules which transmit the electrical signal from one neuron to another, or to target tissues such as those in the endocrine system.

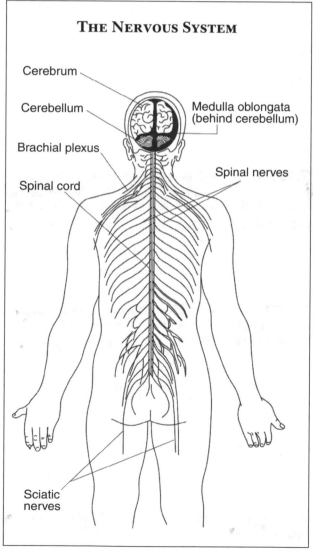

THE NERVOUS SYSTEM

Cerebrum

Cerebellum

Medulla oblongata
(behind cerebellum)

Brachial plexus

Spinal cord

Spinal nerves

Sciatic
nerves

(Hans & Cassidy, Inc.)

There exist within the nervous system a large number of different forms of neurons, many of which respond to different types of neurotransmitters. Alterations in production of these chemicals, or in the ability of nerves to respond to their stimuli, form the physiological basis for a variety of psychological problems.

## CENTRAL NERVOUS SYSTEM

The central nervous system is composed of two principal structures: the brain and the spinal cord. The brain is one of the largest organs in the human body, weighing on average about three pounds and consisting of one trillion neurons by early adulthood.

The brain is subdivided into four major functional areas. The cerebrum, the largest portion of the brain, regulates sensory and motor functions. The convolutions characteristic of the human brain represent the physical appearance of the cerebrum. The brain stem connects the brain with the spinal cord, carrying out both sensory and motor functions. The diencephalon consists of the thalamus, the relay center for sensory functions entering the cerebrum, and the hypothalamus, which controls much of the peripheral nervous system activity and regulates endocrine processes. The fourth portion of the brain is the cerebellum, the rear of the brain where voluntary muscle activity is controlled.

## PERIPHERAL NERVOUS SYSTEM

The peripheral nervous system consists of the sensory receptors such as those that recognize touch or heat in the skin or visual stimuli in the retina of the eye, and the nerves which communicate the stimuli to the brain. The peripheral nervous system is often subdivided into two parts, according to function: the somatic portion, which recognizes stimuli in the external environment such as on the skin, and the autonomic portion, which recognizes changes in the internal environment, such as hormone or mineral concentrations in the bloodstream.

The somatic portion of the peripheral nervous system in humans consists of twelve pairs of nerves which originate in the brain and which transmit sensory input from the body. For example, nerve endings in the retina of the eye transmit images to the brain; sensory fibers in the face transmit impulses affecting the skin or teeth. An additional thirty-one pairs of nerves emerge from the spinal cord, subdivide into branches, and innervate various regions of the body.

The autonomic nervous system maintains homeostasis, or constancy, within the body. For example, receptors measure heart rate, body temperature, and the activity of hormones within the bloodstream and tissues. Any abnormality or change results in a signal sent to the brain.

The most notable of the functions of the autonomic nervous system occur in the sympathetic and parasympathetic systems. The sympathetic arm of the system is primarily associated with the stimulation tissues and organs.

For example, during times of stress, hormones are released that increase the heart rate, constrict blood vessels, and stimulate the sweat glands, a phenomenon often referred to as "fight or flight." By contrast, the parasympathetic system counteracts these effects, decreasing the heart rate, dilating blood vessels, and decreasing the rate of sweating.

## ROLE OF NEUROTRANSMITTERS

Neurons communicate with one another through the release of neurotransmitters, chemical substances that transmit nerve impulses between nerve cells. Numerous types of neurotransmitters have been identified. Some of these transmitters act to excite neurons, while others inhibit neuronal activity. The particular type of transmitter is synthesized within the cell body of the neuron, travels along the axon, and is released into the space between neurons, known as the synapse.

Among the most prominent neurotransmitters involved in the excitation of neurons is acetylcholine. The same transmitter bridges the junctions between nerves and skeletal muscles as well as glandular tissues in the body. In the brain, acetylcholine bridges the synapses between neurons throughout the central nervous system. The amino acids glutamic acid and aspartic acid are also known to be involved in excitation of some neurons within the brain. The neurotransmitter serotonin is released mainly within the brain stem, where it appears to regulate activities such as sleep, moods, and body temperature.

Certain neurotransmitters serve in the inhibition of neuronal activity. The most common of these is gamma-aminobutyric acid (GABA), found primarily in the diencephalon region of the brain. Here GABA acts to reduce the activity within the region. Antianxiety drugs such as valium or librium appear to work by enhancing the activity of GABA, resulting in the relaxation of skeletal muscles. Antidepression compounds such as Prozac and Zoloft appear to function through blockage of serotonin uptake by neurons.

## ENDORPHINS AND THE PLACEBO EFFECT

Persons who receive treatments with agents that possess no pharmacological activity for various illnesses or conditions have often been known to show improvement. Such a reaction is called the placebo effect. Whether the placebo effect is real has long been controversial. A 1955 study published in the prestigious *Journal of the American Medical Association* was the first significant report that the effect was real. More recent work has suggested the placebo effect may be sometimes more myth than reality. Nevertheless, there is evidence that such an effect may indeed occur and may be associated with forms of neurotransmitters called endorphins (endogenous morphines) and enkephalins. Endorphins and enkephalins represent a class of neurotransmitter-like chemicals called neuropeptides, small molecules which consist of between two and forty amino acids.

Enkephalins, discovered in 1975, block pain impulses within the central nervous system in ways similar to the drug morphine. The second class of molecules, subsequently called endorphins, was discovered soon afterward. They appear to act through suppression of pain impulses through suppression of a chemical called substance P. Substance P is released by neurons in the brain, the result of pain impulses from receptors in the peripheral nervous system. By inhibiting the release of substance P, these neuropeptides suppress sensory pain mechanisms. In support of a physiological basis for the placebo effect, patients treated with the endorphin antagonist naloxon produced no discernable response to placebo treatment.

Endorphins have been shown to play a role in a wide variety of body functions, including memory and learning and the control of sexual impulses. Abnormal activity of endorphins has been shown to play a role in organic psychiatric dysfunctions such as schizophrenia and depression. Deficits in endorphin levels have been observed to correlate with aggressiveness; endorphin replacement therapy results in the diminishment of such behavior. Abnormal levels of endorphins in the blood have also been found in individuals suffering from behavioral disorders such as anorexia or obesity.

## LIMBIC SYSTEM AND EMOTIONS

The limbic system is the label that applies to regions of the diencephalon such as the thalamus and hypothalamus that are associated with behaviors such as emotions, learning, and sexual behavior. Stimulation of various areas within the limbic system during surgery has resulted in the patient feeling a variety of conflicting emotions, such as happiness and pleasure or fear and depression, depending upon the area being tested.

Some of these emotions or behaviors are associated with survival. For example, stimulation of certain areas results in feelings of rage or sexual excitement. Such patterns of behavior, accompanied by increased heart rate and blood pressure, have suggested that the limbic system plays a role in the "fight or flight" phenomenon.

Neurotransmitters such as serotonin and dopamine are believed to play roles in these behaviors. The effects of recreational drugs on behaviors and emotions may in part be due to the similarity of action between these drugs and neurotransmitters. For example, the high associated with amphetamine use or abuse may result from stimulation of these neurotransmitters. Cocaine blocks the movement of dopamine, resulting in the continual activation of neurons which use dopamine as a neurotransmitter. The addiction associated with cocaine results from alterations in the affected neurons, resulting in an increase in need for stimulation by these pathways.

The disorder schizophrenia may also be the result of impaired transmission of dopamine. The symptoms of schizophrenia—hallucinations or delusions—may be decreased through the use of drugs which inhibit dopamine release. Likewise, drugs which stimulate dopamine activity increase the severity of symptoms.

**SOURCES FOR FURTHER STUDY**

Becker, J., S. Breedlove, and D. Crews. *Behavioral Endocrinology.* Cambridge, Mass.: MIT Press, 2000. Emphasis is on the role of the endocrine system and neurotransmitters on physiology of the nervous system, as well as effect on behaviors.

"The Brain." *Scientific American* 241 (September, 1979). The issue was devoted entirely to the nervous system. Though new information has subsequently become available, the issue remains an excellent general source for the subject. Excellent photographs and diagrams are included in the articles.

Kolb, Bryan, and Ian Whishaw. *An Introduction to Brain and Behavior.* New York: Worth, 2001. Textbook on the subject. In addition to thorough coverage of brain structure and function, the authors describe the role of neurophysiology and behavior.

Sherwood, Lauralee. *Human Physiology: From Cells to Systems.* Pacific Grove, Calif.: Brooks/Cole, 2001. Drawing on recent experimentation, the author provides extensive background material for those chapters which explain the function of the nervous system. The text includes extensive details, but tables and diagrams clarify the material and provide numerous examples.

*Richard Adler*

SEE ALSO: Brain Structure; Endocrine System; Hormones and Behavior; Neuropsychology; Sensation and Perception; Senses.

# NEUROPSYCHOLOGY

TYPE OF PSYCHOLOGY: Biological bases of behavior
FIELDS OF STUDY: Behavioral and cognitive models; cognitive processes; nervous system; organic disorders

*Neuropsychology is the study of the relationship between the brain and behavior. It has provided insights into the workings of the normal brain as well as innovations for diagnosing and assisting individuals with an injury to or disease of the brain.*

KEY CONCEPTS
- assessment
- cognition
- lesion
- norm
- rehabilitation

Neuropsychology is the study of the relationships between the brain and behavior. More fully, it is the study of both human and animal cerebral organization as it relates to behavior. Considerable attention is directed toward investigating the workings of both healthy and damaged neural systems; specifically, there is interest in obtaining a more complete understanding of disorders of language, perception, and motor action. The field of neuropsychology can be divided into a number of specialty areas. The discussion which follows will concentrate on experimental neuropsychology and clinical neuropsychology. While this distinction is not absolute, it serves to classify the types of work in which neuropsychologists are involved.

## BRAIN LESIONS

Clinical neuropsychology refers to the study of individuals who have lesions of the brain. These lesions are often produced by tumors, cerebral vascular accidents (strokes), or trauma (for example, an automobile crash). The clinical neuropsychologist is heavily involved in the assessment of cognitive deficits brought on by these brain lesions. By evaluating the patient's performance on a variety of paper-and-pencil tests, the neuropsychologist can make valuable diagnostic inferences. The clinician can begin to develop hypotheses concerning the location, extent, and severity of the lesion.

Similarly, an attempt is made to discern the functional significance of the brain lesion on the patient. Damage to the same part of the brain may affect two individuals very differently. Because of this fact, it is vital that the clinical neuropsychologist assess the effect of the lesion on the patient's daily functioning at work, at home, and in social contexts as well as the relatively artificial environment of the testing room. Furthermore, it is important that evaluation consider the patient's current strengths in addition to weaknesses or impairments. Intact abilities can assist the patient in coping and compensating for the loss of some other function.

## BRAIN BATTERIES

A comprehensive neuropsychological test battery should assess the integrity of the entire brain. To assure the thoroughness of the evaluation, the neuropsychologist generally administers a large number of diverse tests to the patient. The tests typically demand different mental or cognitive abilities, which are subserved by different regions of the brain. These different cognitive abilities are commonly referred to as cognitive domains and include functions such as attention, memory, perception, movement, language, and problem solving. A number of comprehensive test batteries have been created to assess the various cognitive domains. The Halstead-Reitan and Luria-Nebraska are two such batteries that have been used to diagnose the location and severity of brain damage in neurological patients.

These batteries consist of a variety of subtests that are believed to tap into different cognitive abilities. For example, the Halstead-Reitan contains subtests that have proved to be helpful in localizing brain damage. This is done by first administering the Halstead-Reitan to a large number of patients with previously diagnosed brain damage. The researcher then looks at those patients with damage to a particular region of the brain (for example, right frontal) and observes which subtests gave them difficulty. By repeating this process on each patient group (left frontal, right posterior, and so on), the researcher can establish norms.

When a patient with suspected damage is tested with the battery, his or her scores can be compared to those in each patient group. Thus, if he or she performs similarly to the right-frontal norms, damage may be diagnosed to this region. While this is an oversimplification, it provides a general model of how test batteries are used in neuropsychology to evaluate patients with suspected brain damage.

## EXPERIMENTAL NEUROPSYCHOLOGY

Experimental neuropsychology focuses on answering theoretical questions rather than solving clinical or practical ones. Because of the invasive nature of these questions, experimental neuropsychologists often use animals rather than humans in their research. Typically, animals are used in the initial stages of a line of research. After the research procedure has been proved to be safe and effective, however, it is then confirmed on a human sample. Experimental neuropsychologists have shed light on a number of cognitive functions and the parts of the brain involved in those functions.

The methods that experimental neuropsychologists use to study cognitive abilities in humans can be quite creative. The tachistoscope is a device that projects a visual image to either the right or the left half of the visual field very quickly, so that the right or left hemisphere of the brain has preferential access to the visual image. Thus, the importance of the left or right hemisphere of the brain in a given task can be identified.

While the daily routines of clinical and experimental neuropsychologists are quite different, their work can be considerably intertwined. For example, the insights of experimental neuropsychologists often improve clinicians' ability to assess and treat individuals with neurological impairment. Similarly, clinicians' descriptions of interesting patients can often open the road for further theoretical investigation by experimental neuropsychologists.

## PRACTICE AND THEORY

The fields of clinical and experimental neuropsychology have been useful in solving a number of practical problems as well as more theoretical ones. For example, clinical neuropsychological procedures have been applied in the assessment and treatment of individuals suspected of having Alzheimer's disease. This disease is difficult to confirm unless a sample of brain is removed and inspected microscopically, a procedure that is quite invasive and is rarely attempted until after the patient's death. Neuropsychological test procedures have contributed dramatically to the accurate diagnosis of Alzheimer's disease without the use of invasive measures such as surgery.

Typically, a series of memory, language, perceptual, and problem-solving tasks are given to the individual when the disease is first suspected. The patient is then tested serially at six-month intervals, and the overall pattern of test scores across time is evaluated. If the patient tends to display a decremental pattern of performance across two or more cognitive domains (for example, memory and language), a diagnosis of dementia is supported.

Along with the measurement of various cognitive functions, neuropsychology also seems particularly equipped to investigate other aspects of the disease. While a patient's performance on a test battery is helpful, other features must be examined in diagnosing the disorder. For example, depression, hallucinations, delusions, and verbal or physical outbursts are often common with the disease. Conversely, the appearance of certain other signs or symptoms make a diagnosis of Alzheimer's disease unlikely. Because of this diverse collection of psychological and behavioral symptoms, clinical neuropsychology may be the best manager of services for these patients.

A second application of neuropsychological techniques concerns the recent surge in rehabilitation efforts with the brain-injured. Many individuals who have sustained an injury to or have a disease of the brain have great difficulty returning to their premorbid jobs or avocations. Neuropsychological rehabilitation attempts to assist these patients with ongoing cognitive difficulties as they reenter the work and home settings. Very often, people who have brain injuries do not have problems with all cognitive domains but rather with a select few (for example, attention or language). Because of this selective impairment, clinical neuropsychologists can focus their efforts on improving an individual's attentional abilities or use of language.

A specific example of neuropsychological rehabilitation can be seen in the case of an individual who has been involved in a motor vehicle accident. These patients tend to sustain primary damage to the frontal aspects of the brain because they withstand the initial impact. Damage to the frontal re-

gions normally produces individuals who are very unaware of their surroundings. Furthermore, they typically lack appropriate social skills as well
as planning and organizational abilities. These abilities can be improved,
however, if the patient works with a neuropsychologist who knows what to
expect, based on the exact area of damage.

Generally, rehabilitation involves intensive exposure to the problematic
cognitive task. In the case of a patient with damage to the frontal area of the
brain, this might entail placement in a group situation in which the patient
practices social skills. Specific activities might include working on conversation skills, role-playing a job interview or asking for a date, or working on a
group project. Individual sessions with the patient might be better suited for
the treatment of the organizational and planning deficits experienced by
frontal patients. Here, the neuropsychologist might teach the patient to use
a diary to plan the week's activities and learn to solve problems to get things
done.

While neuropsychologists often assist patients in acquiring compensation strategies to work around their particular difficulties, there are other ra-
tionales for rehabilitative efforts. Many researchers and psychologists believe that practicing the impaired function assists the repairing brain in
doing that task. There appears to be a six- to twelve-month period immediately after a brain injury when the brain is developing pathways around the
damaged tissue. Many believe that during this critical period, it is important
to engage the patient in activities that were most compromised by the injury.
Thus, if the injury took a major toll on memory abilities, the patient should
be exposed to exercises and activities that demand he or she remember
things.

In general, neuropsychology has tremendous applied value for persons
who have sustained a neurological insult such as a stroke or brain injury.
Furthermore, it is useful in the initial assessment and accurate diagnosis of a
given neurological disorder, as well as in the continued care and treatment
of individuals with known brain pathology.

## BRAIN STUDY

Neuropsychology rapidly emerged as a separate branch of the neurosci-
ences in the 1970's and 1980's. During that time, there was an explosion of
training programs for neuropsychologists and scientific research concerning the relationships between the brain and behavior. While the field has
only recently evolved, however, the discipline's underpinnings can be traced
back thousands of years. Egyptian writings dating to 2500 B.C.E. describe
trauma to the brain and the behavior of the patient sustaining this damage.

A second early milestone occurred with the anatomical studies and illustrations of the 1800's. In 1861, Paul Broca demonstrated that a lesion of the
left frontal lobe of the brain caused a disruption of the production of
speech. Soon after this revelation, researchers became quite consumed with
localizing all cognitive functions to some discrete part of the brain.

Those who believed that each function could be neatly contained in a small region of the brain came to be known as localizationists. Those who believed that all areas of the brain were equally involved in all cognitive abilities were labeled equipotentialists. A third group known as interactionists suggests that more basic cognitive functions are relatively localized but interact to allow for more complex cognitive processes. This perspective was derived from the late nineteenth century research of Hughlings Jackson in his clinical work as a neurologist. In many ways, Jackson's ideas were quite advanced for his time and the available research methodology.

The twentieth century witnessed a steady accumulation of knowledge concerning the relationships between the brain and behavior. These developments occurred primarily because of the need to assist soldiers who had sustained wartime brain injuries. In the process of treating these individuals, much was learned about the role of various brain regions in carrying out various behaviors. The systematic study of brain-injured persons by Aleksandr Luria contributed tremendously to the process of assessing and localizing brain dysfunction.

This new awareness provided psychology with a better understanding of how the physical brain can produce very atypical behaviors. Before this time, it was believed that behavioral disturbance was universally caused by disruption of the nonphysical "mind." The new knowledge has given clinical psychologists much more sophisticated answers about how best to treat patients with behavioral difficulties. It has also served to remove some of the stigma attached to mental illness or dysfunction. The lay public seems more willing to tolerate atypical behavior from an individual with physical damage to the brain than from a patient labeled as being mentally ill.

The future of neuropsychology appears to be full of promise. It is expected that investigators will continue to conduct research that sheds light on the workings of the healthy brain as well as assisting those with neurological damage. Furthermore, it appears that neuropsychology will continue to advance the larger field of psychology by providing physiological explanations for behaviors and disorders that now have only hypothetical ones.

## SOURCES FOR FURTHER STUDY

Beaumont, J. Graham. *Introduction to Neuropsychology*. New York: Guilford Press, 1983. An accessible reference for the student who is new to the field. Particularly helpful in describing the methods used to investigate experimental neuropsychological phenomena.

Ellis, Andrew W., and Andrew W. Young. *Human Cognitive Neuropsychology*. Rev. ed. Hillsdale, N.J.: Lawrence Erlbaum, 1996. Presents ideas and research from the mid-1980's on the integrated workings of the brain. Particularly helpful in establishing a theoretical framework that assists the student in integrating the often divergent research findings in a more holistic manner.

Kolb, Bryan, and Ian Q. Whishaw. *Fundamentals of Human Neuropsychology*.

4th ed. New York: W. H. Freeman, 1996. A comprehensive textbook that fully covers the fields of clinical and experimental neuropsychology. Lengthy but clear and well written. Best suited to the student who has read an introductory work on the topic.

Ledoux, Joseph. *Synaptic Self: How Our Brains Become Who We Are.* New York: Viking Press, 2002. Written for a lay audience, explains the neuroscience of personality and the brain. Focuses on the working of the synapses in the brain's communication system.

Luria, Aleksandr Romanovich. *The Working Brain: An Introduction to Neuropsychology.* New York: Basic Books, 1973. Considered by many to be the seminal work in the field. Presents many of Luria's most dramatic insights about normal and damaged brains. Although the title suggests this is an introduction, the ideas presented in this source are often highly complex.

Sacks, Oliver. *The Man Who Mistook His Wife for a Hat.* New York: Harper-Perennial Library, 1990. Sacks is a gifted writer as well as successful neurologist, and he displays the best of both these talents in this work. Reads more like a novel than a textbook. Based on actual neurological cases seen by Sacks.

*Jeffery B. Allen*

SEE ALSO: Alzheimer's Disease; Brain Structure; Cognitive Psychology; Dementia; Nervous System; Parkinson's Disease.

# Obsessive-Compulsive Disorder

TYPE OF PSYCHOLOGY: Psychopathology
FIELD OF STUDY: Anxiety disorders

*Obsessions and compulsions are the cardinal features of a chronic anxiety disorder known as obsessive-compulsive disorder. The identification of repetitive, anxiety-provoking thoughts known as obsessions and of associated compulsive, ritualistic behaviors is critical in the diagnosis and assessment of this debilitating condition.*

KEY CONCEPTS
- anxiety
- checking ritual
- cleaning ritual
- compulsions
- fear of contamination
- obsessions
- response prevention

Obsessive thinking and urges to engage in ritualistic compulsive behaviors are common phenomena that most individuals experience to some extent throughout their lives. It is not uncommon, for example, for a person to reexperience in his or her mind involuntary, anxiety-provoking images of circumstances surrounding a traumatic accident or embarrassing moment. Similarly, behaviors such as returning home to make sure the iron is turned off or refusing to eat from a spoon that falls on a clean floor represent mild compelling rituals in which many persons engage from time to time. It is when these patterns of obsessive thinking and behaving become either too frequent or too intense that they may escalate into a distressing clinical condition known as obsessive-compulsive disorder.

According to the American Psychiatric Association's *Diagnostic and Statistical Manual of Mental Disorders: DSM-IV-TR* (rev. 4th ed., 2000), the primary feature of this disorder is the presence of distressing obsessions or severe compulsive behaviors that interfere significantly with a person's daily functioning. Although diagnosis requires only the presence of either obsessions or compulsions, they typically are both present in obsessive-compulsive disorder. In most cases, persons with this diagnosis spend more time, on a daily basis, experiencing obsessive thinking and engaging in ritualistic behaviors than other constructive activities, including those pertaining to occupational, social, and family responsibilities. Therefore, it is not uncommon for obsessive-compulsive patients also to experience severe vocational impairment and distraught interpersonal relationships.

## Obsessions

The word "obsession" comes from the Latin word *obsidere* ("to besiege") and can be defined as a recurrent thought, impulse, idea, or image that is intrusive, disturbing, and senseless. Among the most common types are themes of violence (for example, images of killing a loved one), contamination (for example, thoughts of catching a disease from a doorknob), and personal injury or harm (for example, impulses to leap from a bridge). Obsessional doubting is also characteristic of most patients with obsessive-compulsive disorder, which leads to indecisiveness in even the most simple matters such as selecting a shirt to wear or deciding what to order at a restaurant. The basic content of obsessive thinking distinguishes it from simple worrying. Worrying involves thinking about an event or occurrence that may realistically result in discomfort, embarrassment, or harm and has a probability of occurring; obsessive thinking is typically recognized by the patient as being senseless and not likely to occur. An example of a worry is thinking about an event that possesses a strong likelihood of occurring, such as failing a test when one has not studied. Repeatedly imagining that one might leap from the third-floor classroom during the exam, a highly unlikely event, is considered an obsession. Furthermore, because the obsessive-compulsive patient is aware that these intrusive thoughts are senseless and continuously attempts to rid the thought from his or her mind, obsessive thinking is not delusional or psychotic in nature. Although both delusional and obsessive patients may experience a similar thought (for example, that they have ingested tainted food), the obsessive patient recognizes that the thought is unlikely and is a product of his or her mind and struggles to get rid of the thought. The delusional patient adheres to the belief with little to no struggle to test its validity.

## COMPULSIONS

Most obsessive-compulsive patients also exhibit a series of repetitive, intentional, stereotyped behaviors known as compulsions, which serve to reduce the anxiety experienced from severe obsessive thinking. The most common forms include counting (for example, tapping a pencil three times before laying it down), cleaning (for example, hand washing after shaking another person's hand), checking (for example, checking pilot lights several times a day), and ordering (for example, arranging pencils from longest to shortest before doing homework). Compulsions are different from simple habits in that attempts to resist urges to engage in them result in a substantial increase in anxiety, eventually forcing the patient to engage in the compelling behavior to reduce the tension. Urges to engage in simple habits, on the other hand, can often be resisted with minimal discomfort. Furthermore, most habits result in deriving some degree of pleasure from the activity (for example, shopping, gambling, drinking), while engaging in compulsive behaviors is rarely enjoyable for the patient. Compulsions must also be distinguished from superstitious behaviors, such as an athlete's warm-up ritual or wearing the same "lucky" shoes for each sporting event. In contrast to superstitious people, who employ their rituals to enhance confidence, obsessive-compulsive patients are never certain their rituals will result in anxiety reduction. This typically forces these patients continually to expand their repertoire of ritualistic behaviors, searching for new and better ways to eliminate the anxiety produced by obsessive thinking.

It is estimated that approximately 2 percent of the adult population in the United States—a larger percentage than was once believed—has at some time experienced obsessive-compulsive symptoms severe enough to warrant diagnosis. Typically, obsessive-compulsive symptoms begin in adolescence or early adulthood, although most patients report symptoms of anxiety and nervousness as children. Regarding early developmental histories, many obsessive-compulsive patients report being raised in very strict, puritanical homes. The disorder occurs equally in males and females, although cleaning rituals occur more frequently among women. While the course of the disorder is chronic, the intensity of symptoms fluctuates throughout life and occasionally has been reported to remit spontaneously. Because of the unusual nature of the symptoms, obsessive-compulsive patients often keep their rituals hidden and become introverted and withdrawn; as a result, the clinical picture becomes complicated by a coexisting depressive disorder. It is typically the depression which forces the patient to seek psychological help.

## ETIOLOGY AND TREATMENTS

Because of the distressing yet fascinating nature of the symptoms, several theoretical positions have attempted to explain how obsessive-compulsive disorder develops. From an applied perspective, each theoretical position has evolved into a treatment or intervention strategy for eliminating the problems caused by obsessions and compulsions. According to psychoanalytic theory, as outlined by Sigmund Freud in 1909, obsessive-compulsive rituals are the product of overly harsh toilet training which leaves the patient with considerable unconscious hostility, primarily directed toward an authoritarian caregiver. In a sense, as uncomfortable and disconcerting as the obsessions and compulsive behaviors are, they are preferable to experiencing the intense emotions left from these childhood incidents. Obsessions and compulsions permit the patient to avoid experiencing these emotions. Furthermore, obsessive-compulsive symptoms force the patient to become preoccupied with anxiety-reduction strategies which prevent them from dealing with other hidden impulses, such as sexual urges and desires. Based upon the psychoanalytic formulation, treatment involves identifying the original unconscious thoughts, ideas, or impulses and allowing the patient to experience them consciously. In his classic case report of an obsessive patient, Freud analyzed a patient known as the "rat man," who was plagued by recurrent, horrifying images of a bucket of hungry rats strapped to the buttocks of his girlfriend and his father. Although periodic case reports of psychoanalytic treatments for obsessive-compulsive disorder exist, there is very little controlled empirical work suggesting the effectiveness of this treatment approach.

Behavioral theorists, differing from the psychoanalytic tradition, have

## DSM-IV-TR CRITERIA FOR OBSESSIVE-COMPULSIVE DISORDER (DSM CODE 300.3)

Either obsessions or compulsions

Obsessions defined by all of the following:

- recurrent and persistent thoughts, impulses, or images experienced, at some time during disturbance, as intrusive and inappropriate and cause marked anxiety or distress
- thoughts, impulses, or images not simply excessive worries about real-life problems
- attempts made to ignore or suppress thoughts, impulses, or images, or to neutralize them with some other thought or action
- recognition that thoughts, impulses, or images are product of his or her own mind (not imposed from without, as in thought insertion)

Compulsions defined by both of the following:

- repetitive behaviors (hand washing, ordering, checking) or mental acts (praying, counting, repeating words silently) that individual feels driven to perform in response to an obsession or according to rules that must be applied rigidly
- behaviors or mental acts aimed at preventing or reducing distress or preventing some dreaded event or situation; behaviors or mental acts either are not connected in a realistic way with what they are designed to neutralize or prevent or are clearly excessive

At some point, individual recognizes obsessions or compulsions as excessive or unreasonable; this does not apply to children

Obsessions or compulsions cause marked distress, are time-consuming, or interfere significantly with normal routine, occupational or academic functioning, or usual social activities or relationships

If another Axis I disorder is present, content of obsessions or compulsions not restricted to it

Disturbance not due to direct physiological effects of a substance or general medical condition

Specify if with Poor Insight (most of the time during current episode, obsessions and compulsions not recognized as excessive or unreasonable)

proposed that obsessive-compulsive disorder represents a learned habit that is maintained by the reinforcing properties of the anxiety reduction that occurs following ritualistic behaviors. It is well established that behaviors that are reinforced occur more frequently in the future. In the case of compulsive behaviors, the ritual is always followed by a significant reduction in anxiety, therefore reinforcing the compulsive behavior as well as the preceding obsessive activity. Based upon the behavioral perspective, an intervention strategy called response prevention, or flooding, was developed to facilitate the interruption of this habitually reinforcing cycle. Response prevention involves exposing the patient to the feared stimulus (for example, a doorknob) or obsession (for example, an image of leaping from a bridge) in order to create anxiety. Rather than allowing the patient to engage in the subsequent compulsive activity, however, the therapist prevents the response (for example, the patient is not permitted to wash his or her hands). The patient endures a period of intense anxiety but eventually experiences habituation of the anxiety response. Although treatments of this nature are anxiety provoking for the patient, well-controlled investigations have reported significant reductions in obsessive thinking and ritualistic behavior following intervention. Some estimates of success rates with response prevention are as high as 80 percent, and treatment gains are maintained for several years.

Theories emphasizing the cognitive aspects of the obsessive-compulsive disorder have focused on information-processing impairments of the patient. Specifically, obsessive-compulsive patients tend to perceive harm (for example, contamination) when in fact it may not be present and to perceive a loss of control over their environment. While most individuals perceive a given situation as safe until proved harmful, the obsessive-compulsive patient perceives situations as harmful until proved safe. These perceptions of harm and lack of control lead to increased anxiety; the belief that the patient controls his or her life or the perception of safety leads to decreased anxiety. Accordingly, compulsive rituals represent a patient's efforts to gain control over his or her environment. Cognitive interventions aim to increase the patient's perception of control over the environment and to evaluate realistically environmental threats of harm. While cognitive approaches may serve as a useful adjunct to behavioral treatments such as response prevention, evidence for their effectiveness when used in treating obsessions and compulsions is lacking.

Finally, biological models of obsessive-compulsive disorder have also been examined. There is some indication that brain electrical activity during information processing, particularly in the frontal lobes, is somewhat slower for obsessive-compulsive patients in comparison to other people. For example, metabolic activity of the frontal brain regions measured using positron emission tomography (PET) scans differentiates obsessive-compulsive patients both from normal people and depressive patients. Further, a deficiency in certain neurotransmitters (for example, serotonin, and norepinephrine) has been implicated in the etiology of the disorder. Several interventions based upon the biological model have been employed as well. Pharmacotherapy, using antidepressant medications that primarily act to facilitate neurotransmitter functioning (for example, clomipramine), has been shown to be effective in treating from 20 percent to 50 percent of obsessive-compulsive patients. More drastic interventions such as frontal lobotomies have been reported in the most intractable cases, with very limited success.

Among the interventions employed to rid patients of troublesome obsessions and compulsions, response prevention holds the most promise. Because of the intensity of this treatment approach, however, the cost may be substantial, and many patients may not immediately respond. A number of predictors of poor treatment response to behavioral interventions (characteristic of those most refractory to treatment) have been identified. These include a coexisting depression, poor compliance with exposure/response-prevention instructions, the presence of fears that the patient views as realistic, and eccentric superstition. In these cases, alternative forms of treatment are typically considered (for example, pharmacotherapy).

## PREVALENCE AND RESEARCH

Obsessions and compulsions represent human phenomena that have been a topic of interest for several centuries; for example, William Shakespeare's characterization of the hand-washing Lady Macbeth has entertained audiences for hundreds of years. Prior to the first therapeutic analysis of obsessive-compulsive disorder, then called a neurosis—Freud's description of the "rat man"—obsessive thoughts were commonly attributed to demoniac influence and treated with exorcism. Freud's major contribution was delivering the phenomenon from the spiritual into the psychological realm. Although initial case reports employing psychoanalysis were promising, subsequent developments using behavioral and pharmacological formulations have more rapidly advanced the understanding of the phenomenology and treatment of this unusual condition. In addition, with the public revelation that certain prominent individuals, such as the aircraft designer and film producer Howard Hughes, suffered from this condition, the prevalence estimates of this disorder have steadily increased. Although a number of patients have sought help for this debilitating disorder since the time it was first clinically described, it has been confirmed that this problem is far more prevalent than initially thought. The increase is probably related not to an actual increase in incidence but to individuals becoming more willing to seek help for the problem. Because of the increasing number of individuals requesting help for problems relating to obsessions and compulsions, it is becoming more and more important to foster the maturation of appropriate treatment strategies to deal with this disorder.

Further, it has become increasingly important to understand the manifestation of obsessions and compulsions from a biological, psychological, and socio-occupational level. Ongoing investigations are examining the biological makeup of the nervous systems peculiar to this disorder. Research examining the specific information-processing styles and cognitive vulnerabilities of obsessive-compulsive patients is also being conducted. Both response-prevention and biochemical-intervention strategies (for example, clomipramine) are deserving of continued research, primarily in the examining characteristics of obsessive-compulsive patients that predict treatment efficacy with either form of intervention. Finally, early markers for this condition, including childhood environments, early learning experiences, and biological predispositions, require further investigation so that prevention efforts can be provided for individuals who may be at risk for developing obsessive-compulsive disorder. With these advances, psychologists will be in a better position to reduce the chronic nature of obsessive-compulsive disorder and to prevent these distressing symptoms in forthcoming generations.

## SOURCES FOR FURTHER STUDY

American Psychiatric Association. *Diagnostic and Statistical Manual of Disorders: DSM-IV-TR.* Rev. 4th ed. Washington, D.C.: Author, 2000. The DSM-IV-TR provides specific criteria for making psychiatric diagnoses of obsessive-compulsive disorder and other anxiety disorders. Brief summaries of research findings regarding each condition are also provided.

Emmelkamp, Paul M. G. *Phobic and Obsessive Compulsive Disorders: Theory, Research, and Practice.* New York: Plenum Press, 1982. A somewhat dated but classic work outlining the importance of behavioral strategies in overcoming obsessive-compulsive, as well as phobic, conditions.

Jenike, Michael A., Lee Baer, and William E. Minichiello. *Obsessive-Compulsive Disorders: Theory and Management.* 3d ed. St. Louis: Mosby, 1998. A comprehensive overview of the topic that does not burden the reader with intricate details of analysis. Readable by the layperson. Covers the topic thoroughly.

Mavissakalian, Matig, Samuel M. Turner, and Larry Michelson. *Obsessive-Compulsive Disorders: Psychological and Pharmacological Treatment.* New York: Plenum Press, 1985. An exceptionally well written text based upon a symposium held at the University of Pittsburgh. Issues pertaining to etiology, assessment, diagnosis, and treatment are covered in detail.

Rachman, S. J. "Obsessional-Compulsive Disorders." In *International Handbook of Behavior Modification and Therapy,* edited by Alan S. Bellack, Michel Hersen, and Alan E. Kazdin. 2d ed. New York: Plenum Press, 1990. Rachman's work using behavioral strategies with obsessive-compulsive patients is unparalleled. No bibliography would be complete without a contribution from Rachman, one of the most respected authorities in the field.

Steketee, Gail, and Andrew Ellis. *Treatment of Obsessive-Compulsive Disorder.* New York: Guilford Press, 1996. A comprehensive resource for mental health professionals. Covers behavioral and cognitive approaches, biological models, and pharmacological therapies.

Turner, S. M., and L. Michelson. "Obsessive-Compulsive Disorders." In *Behavioral Theories and Treatment of Anxiety,* edited by Samuel M. Turner. New York: Plenum Press, 1984. Summarizes information regarding diagnostic issues, assessment strategies, and treatment interventions for obsessive-compulsive disorder. Provides an excellent review of intervention efforts employing response prevention and clomipramine.

*Kevin T. Larkin and Virginia L. Goetsch*

SEE ALSO: Anxiety Disorders; Cognitive Therapy; Drug Therapies.

# PARKINSON'S DISEASE

TYPE OF PSYCHOLOGY: Psychopathology
FIELDS OF STUDY: Nervous system; organic disorders

*Parkinson's disease is a chronic, progressive, neurodegenerative disorder of the nervous system. Patients are typically in their sixties when they experiences the onset of the disease. Characteristic symptoms include tremor, rigidity, and slowness of movement. Although the exact causes are not known, both genetic and environmental factors are implicated.*

KEY CONCEPTS
- akinesia
- bradykinesia
- dementia
- depression
- dopamine
- levodopa
- rigidity
- substantia nigra
- transplantation of dopamine neurons
- tremor

Parkinson's disease is one of the most common neurological disorders, affecting one person in every thousand. James Parkinson, in 1817, aptly described some of the classic symptoms in his book *An Essay on the Shaking Palsy*. Parkinson reported the patients as having a chronic and progressive disorder of the nervous system that had a late-age onset, with the first mild symptoms not appearing until middle age. He also noted a tremor or shaking which typically appeared in the hand or one side and later spread to the other side. The disease progressed for a variable number of years, eventually leading to disability and death. A significant contribution was his ability to recognize the disorder as a disease distinct from previously described diseases.

Although Parkinson's disease is thought of as a disease with its onset in middle age, there is a considerable variation in the age of onset, and there are other forms of the disease in addition to the classical form. The average age of onset is somewhere in the sixties. About 15 percent of patients develop symptoms between the ages of twenty-one and forty years of age. An extremely rare form of the disease, juvenile Parkinsonism, begins before the age of twenty-one. In addition to the severe neuromuscular symptoms, dementia may occur in some patients. In addition to tremors, other major symptoms are muscle stiffness or rigidity and bradykinesia, or slow movement, and even a difficulty in starting movement. Akinesia, an impairment of voluntary activity of a muscle, also occurs. A number of other symptoms may appear as a consequence of the major symptoms, such as difficulties with speech, bowel and bladder problems, and a vacant, masklike facial expression. There are striking variations among patients in the number and severity of the symptoms and the timing of the progression.

## CLINICAL FEATURES

The disease that subsequently became known as Parkinson's disease was called "shaking palsy" by Parkinson. The shaking refers to the tremor which, although it is thought by many people to be invariably associated with Parkinson's disease, may be completely absent, or present to a minor degree, in some patients. Four symptoms which are present in many patients are a progressive tremor, bradykinesia and even akinesia, muscular rigidity, and loss of postural reflexes. There still is no specific test that can be used to diagnose Parkinson's disease. No biochemical, electrophysiologic, or radiologic test has been found to be completely reliable. As a result, misdiagnosis and underdiagnosis have been common with the disease. The situation is complicated further as a number of other diseases and conditions share some of the same symptoms, including Wilson's disease, familial Alzheimer's disease, Huntington's disease, and encephalitis, as well as responses to certain drugs. Symptoms of Parkinson's disease may also develop consequent to trauma to the brain.

A slight tremor in the hands may indicate the first symptoms of Parkinson's disease, and the tremor may or may not also be found in the legs, jaws, and neck. An interesting symptom that may appear in later stages of the disease is seborrhea, or acne. Intellectual functioning usually remains normal, but approximately 20 percent of the patients experience dementia and have a progressive loss of intellectual abilities and impairment of memory. It is not yet clear how the dementia of Parkinson's disease is related to the dementia associated with Alzheimer's disease. Depression also may occur in patients, with approximately one-third of them having depression at any one time. The depression may be directly related to the disease, or it may be a reaction to some of the medication.

It has been convenient to divide the progression of symptoms of Parkinson's disease into five stages, according to the severity of the symptoms and the degree of disability associated with them. Stage 1 is marked by mild symptoms. In this stage, the symptom that brings the patient to a physician is likely to be a mild tremor, usually limited to one hand or arm. The tremor usually is reduced or disappears during activity, but it may increase during periods of emotional stress. During this early stage of the disease, mild akinesia of the affected side and mild rigidity may be evident. Overall, many of these changes are subtle enough that the patient is not aware of them or does not complain of them. Usually, symptoms are confined to one side, but as the disease progresses, it becomes bilateral in most patients in one or two years. In Stage 2, there is bilateral involvement. Postural changes lead to the patient having a stooped posture and a shuffling walk, with little extension of the legs. All body movements become slower and slower (bradykinesia). The difficulty and slowness of movements may cause patients to curtail many of their normal activities and, in many cases, may lead to depression. Stage 3 is characterized by an increase in the postural changes and movements, leading to retropulsion, a tendency to walk backward, and to propulsion, a tendency when walking forward to walk faster and faster with shorter and shorter steps. As the disease progresses, movements occur more and more slowly, and there are fewer total movements. By Stage 4, symptoms have become so severe as to lead to significant disability, and the patient usually needs constant supervision. The course of the disease leads to Stage 5, a period of complete disability in which the patient is confined to a chair or bed. Interestingly, the tremor which is so characteristic of the initial onset of Parkinson's disease tends to lessen considerably during the later stages of the disorder. In addition to the dementia associated with aging, patients with Parkinson's disease show an increased risk of dementia, occurring six to seven times more frequently compared to age-matched controls.

## CAUSES

The most striking pathological change noted in Parkinson's disease is a loss of nerve cells in a region of the brain known as the substantia nigra, a layer of deeply pigmented gray matter located in the midbrain. The region contains nerve cells that produce dopamine, a neurotransmitter associated with the control of movement. The levels of dopamine are normally in balance with another neurotransmitter, acetylcholine. In Parkinson's disease, the loss of dopamine-producing cells causes a decrease in the levels of dopamine, with a consequent imbalance with acetylcholine. This leads to the symptoms of Parkinson's disease.

The factors that lead to an upset of the dopaminergic system in the disease are complex. The disease is found throughout the world and occurs in nearly equal frequency in men and women, with slightly more men being affected than women. Parkinson's disease is found in all ethnic groups, although there are some striking ethnic differences. The disease is relatively high among whites and relatively low among African blacks and Asians. Ethnic differences may reflect genetic and environmental differences. American blacks have a higher incidence than African blacks, indicating a likely role of local environmental factors.

The role of genetics in Parkinson's disease has been difficult to establish. A family history of Parkinson's disease appears to be a strong indicator of an increased risk of the disease. As part of its comprehensive genetic profiling of its entire population, Iceland has gathered an immense amount of data on genetic diseases, including Parkinson's disease. In the study of late-onset Parkinson's disease, the risk ratio increased with degree of relatedness, with a 2.7 greater probability of developing the disease for nephews and nieces of patients, 3.2 for children of patients, and 6.7 for brothers and sisters of patients. Much research remains to be done to determine whether single genes are playing a major causative role or whether the disorder is multifactorial, involving genetic and environmental factors.

## TREATMENT

Once it became known that dopamine was depleted in patients with Parkinson's disease, a rationale opened for a potential treatment. Levodopa was the first drug to be used to treat Parkinson's disease successfully and is still the most effective treatment available. Dopamine can pass from the blood into the brain, and levodopa increases the synthesis of dopamine. The drug does not cure the disease, but it is used in the attempt to control the symptoms. Although the effectiveness of levodopa may diminish somewhat after several years, most patients continue to benefit from its use. It is necessary to monitor patients closely to maintain proper dose levels as well as to register the appearance of new symptoms, side effects, and other complications.

A number of other drugs, alone or in combination, are being used or being tested. Drugs that enhance the action of dopamine are dopaminergic medications. Such drugs may increase dopamine release or may inhibit the breakdown of dopamine. Other drugs are known as anticholinergic medications, and these inhibit the action of acetylcholine.

Surgery has also been used to treat symptoms of Parkinson's disease, but results have been somewhat mixed. Surgical techniques include thalamotomy, a procedure producing a lesions in the thalamus gland for relief of severe unilateral tremor, and pallidotomy, the removal of part of the globus palledus region of the brain, which is used to treat severe rigidity and akinesia. More recently, transplantation of dopamine neurons from human embryos directly into the brain of a patient with Parkinson's disease has been used. More trials are required, but results seem to indicate some improvement in symptoms, including bradykinesia and rigidity. The use of human tissue has raised many ethical issues because the tissue is taken from aborted human fetuses. Attempts to use tissues from cultured cells are in progress. None of the current treatments involving medication or surgery have produced a complete reversal of the symptoms of Parkinson's disease.

## SOURCES FOR FURTHER STUDY

Cram, David L. *Understanding Parkinson's Disease: A Self-Help Guide*. Omaha, Nebr.: Addicus Books, 1999. A physician, Cram provides a well-written account of the symptoms and progression of the disease from his personal perspective and also discusses present and future treatments.

Jahanshahi, Marian, and C. David Marsden. *Parkinson's Disease: A Self-Help Guide*. New York: Demos Medical Publishing, 2000. This book is an excellent self-help guide. In addition to chapters on the basic medical facts about Parkinson's disease, there are chapters dealing with living and coping with the disease from the personal and family point of view.

Kondracke, Morton. *Saving Milly: Love, Politics, and Parkinson's Disease*. New York: Public Affairs, 2001. The author provides a moving memoir of his life with his wife, Milly, and the development and impact of Parkinson's disease.

Lanad, Anthony E., and Andres M. Lozano. "Parkinson's Disease: The First of Two Parts." *The New England Journal of Medicine* 339, no. 15 (1998): 1044-1052. Comprehensive review of Parkinson's disease includes information on diagnosis and clinical features, pathology, epidemiology, genetics, and a list of ninety-three references.

_____. "Parkinson's Disease: The Second of Two Parts." *The New England Journal of Medicine* 339, no. 16 (1998): 1130-1143. The second part of a two-part review on Parkinson's disease. The article covers the pathophysiology and various types of treatment and includes a list of 199 references.

Weiner, William J., Lisa M. Shulman, and Anthony E. Land. *Parkinson's Disease: A Complete Guide for Patients and Families.* Baltimore: Johns Hopkins University Press, 2001. This book does an excellent job of giving current information on the features and management of Parkinson's disease and also of providing valuable information on how families and patients can deal with the practical and emotional aspects.

*Donald J. Nash*

See also: Alzheimer's Disease; Brain Structure; Neuropsychology; Stress.

# Pavlovian Conditioning

DATE: 1890's forward
TYPE OF PSYCHOLOGY: Learning
FIELD OF STUDY: Pavlovian conditioning

*Pavlovian conditioning is a basic process of learning that relates especially to reflexes and emotional behavior. Interest in this form of learning has been long-standing and continues to the present day. Pavlovian principles apply to a wide range of organisms, situations, and events.*

KEY CONCEPTS
- conditioned emotional reaction (CER)
- conditioned response (CR)
- conditioned stimulus (CS)
- discrimination
- extinction
- flooding
- second-signal system
- spontaneous recovery
- stimulus generalization
- systematic desensitization
- unconditioned response (UR)
- unconditioned stimulus (US)

Pavlovian conditioning, also known as respondent conditioning and classical conditioning (as distinguished from instrumental or operant conditioning), is an elementary learning process and has been of major interest to psychologists ever since the Russian physiologist Ivan Petrovich Pavlov (1849-1936) discovered that a dog could learn to salivate to a neutral stimulus after the stimulus was paired repeatedly with food.

Pavlov's early career focused on the study of heart circulation and digestion in animals (usually dogs), for which he received the Nobel Prize in Physiology or Medicine in 1904. By that time Pavlov had already turned his attention to experiments on conditioned reflexes, from which flowed a new psychological nomenclature.

### CONDITIONING

The core of Pavlovian conditioning is the pairing (association) of stimuli to elicit responses. Food (meat powder) placed in a dog's mouth naturally produces salivation. Pavlov called the food an unconditioned stimulus (US) and salivation, elicited by the food, the unconditioned response (UR). When a neutral stimulus—for example, a tone that does not naturally elicit salivation—is repeatedly followed by presentation of food, the tone alone eventually evokes salivation. Pavlov labeled the tone a conditioned stimulus (CS) and the response (salivation) elicited by it the conditioned response (CR).

Pavlov's formulation can be summarized as follows:

*Before conditioning:*
   Food (US) elicits Salivation (UR)

*Conditioning procedure:*
   Neutral Stimulus (Tone) plus Food (US) elicits Salivation (UR)

*After conditioning:*
   Tone (CS) elicits Salivation (CR)

Pavlov believed that conditioned responses were identical to unconditioned responses. That is usually not the case. For example, conditioned responses may be less pronounced (weaker) or a bit more lethargic than unconditioned responses.

Several phenomena turn up in studies of Pavlovian conditioning. Extinction, generalization, and discrimination are among the most important. Extinction refers to the procedure as well the elimination of a CR. If the CS is repeatedly presented without the US, extinction occurs: The dog stops salivating to the tone. During the course of extinction, the CR may return from time to time until it is finally extinguished. Pavlov called the occasional return of the CR "spontaneous recovery."

*Ivan Pavlov.*
(The Nobel Foundation)

Stimulus generalization refers to responding not only to a particular CS but also to different but similar stimuli. Further, the magnitude (amount of salivation) of a generalized response tends to decline as stimuli become less and less like the CS. For example, a dog trained to salivate to a 5,000-cycle-per-second (cps) tone is likely to salivate also to 5,300 cps and 4,700 cps tones without specific training to do so (stimulus generalization). Responses tend to weaken in an orderly way as tones become more and more unlike the CS. As the tones move away from the CS in both directions, say, to 4,400 cps from 4,100 cps, and 5,600 cps to 5,900 cps, the flow of salivation becomes less and less.

Stimulus generalization in effect extends the number of stimuli that elicit a conditioned response. Discrimination procedures restrict that number by conditioning a subject not to generalize across stimuli. The procedure involves two processes: acquisition and extinction. The CS is paired repeatedly with the US (acquisition) while the US is withheld as generalized stimuli are presented repeatedly (extinction). If the dog now salivates to the CS and not to the generalized stimuli, the dog has learned to discriminate or to act discriminatingly. Pavlov reported that some dogs displayed a general breakdown in behavior patterns (experimental neurosis) when called upon to make discriminations that were too difficult.

Pavlov's work on what he called the second-signal system implies that conditioning principles are relevant to human as well as to animal learning. Once, say, a tone is established as a CS in first-order conditioning, the tone can be paired with a neutral stimulus to establish a second-order CS. Thus, in the absence of food, a light might precede the tone (CS) several times until the light itself begins to function as a CS. Second-order conditioning appears to follow many of the same rules as first-order conditioning.

Pavlov's work has clearly provided one way to study the learning process in great detail. It has also provided the kind of data and theory that have affected research in other areas of learning, such as instrumental conditioning and, subsequently, cognitive science and neuroscience.

## RANGE OF PAVLOVIAN CONDITIONING

Pavlovian phenomena have been demonstrated with different kinds of organisms and a wide variety of stimuli and responses far beyond those studied by Pavlov. Stimuli that precede such unconditioned stimuli as sudden loud noises (leading to rapid heart rate), a puff of air delivered to the eye (evoking blinking), or a large temperature increase (eliciting sweating) may become conditioned stimuli, capable of eliciting conditioned responses on their own. The idea of second-order (higher-order) conditioning is profoundly important because it suggests how rewards such as money or words of praise are established apart from primary (biologically necessary) rewards, such as food and water. It also may, in part, explain the power of films, plays, novels, and advertisements to evoke strong emotion in the absence of direct experience with primary (unconditioned) stimuli. Studies concerned with conditioned emotional reactions (CER), especially fear and anxiety in people—a subject much more complex than simple reflexes—have been of special interest to researchers and therapists for many years.

## ADDITIONAL RESEARCH FINDINGS

Studies of conditioning essentially look at how various unconditioned and conditioned stimuli influence responses under different arrangements of time and space. Following are a few general findings.

Pavlovian conditioning tends to be readily established when stimuli or responses or both are strong rather than weak. For example, in response to a near-drowning experience, some people promptly learn to fear such conditioned stimuli as the sights of water, boats, palm trees, bathing suits, and so on. In such cases, relevant stimuli and responses (panic) are presumably quite strong.

Conditioned stimuli are most likely to elicit conditioned responses when unconditioned and conditioned stimuli are paired consistently. If a mother always hums when she rocks her infant daughter to sleep, humming is likely to become a potent and reliable CS which soothes and comforts her daughter. This outcome is less likely if mother hums only occasionally.

When several stimuli precede a US, the one most often paired with the US will likely emerge as the strongest CS. If, for example, both parents threaten to punish their young son, but only father always carries out the threats, father's threats are more likely than mother's to evoke apprehension in the child.

For some responses, such as eye blinking, conditioned stimuli tend to be strongest when they precede the US by about one-half second. The optimal interval for other responses varies from seconds to fractions of seconds: A neighbor's dog barks immediately before little Sophie falls from her swing, bumping her nose very hard. She cries. If the dog's bark subsequently makes Sophie feel uneasy, the bark is functioning as a CS. This outcome becomes less and less likely as the bark and fall increasingly separate in time.

Conditioned responses are usually not established if a US and CS occur together (simultaneous conditioning)—the potency of the UC overshadows the potential CS—or when a neutral stimulus follows the US (backward conditioning).

## SOME PRACTICAL APPLICATIONS

In a widely cited study reported in 1920, American researchers John B. Watson and Rosalie Rayner conditioned a phobic reaction in an eleven-month-old infant named Albert. The researchers discovered that Albert feared loud noises but seemed unafraid of a number of other things, including small animals.

Watson and Rayner subsequently placed a white rat in Albert's crib. When Albert reached for it, the researchers struck a piece of resonate metal with a hammer, making a "loud sound." After a few such presentations, presenting the rat alone elicited crying and various avoidance reactions. Albert also showed signs of fear to similar things, such as a rabbit, a furry object, and fluffy clumps of cotton (stimulus generalization). Thus, Watson and Rayner provided early experimental evidence that Pavlovian principles are involved in the acquisition of human emotional reactions.

While this study induced a phobic reaction in the subject, systematic desensitization is a procedure designed to eliminate phobias and anxieties. The procedure was largely developed and named by South African-born therapist Joseph Wolpe. Noting that it is very difficult to have pleasant and anxious feelings simultaneously, Wolpe fashioned a systematic technique to teach clients to engage in behavior (relaxation) that competes with anxiety.

Therapy typically begins with an interview designed to identify specific sources of the client's fears. The therapist helps the client assemble a list of items that elicit fear. Items associated with the least amount of fear are positioned at the bottom of the list; most feared items are placed near the top. For example, if a client has a strong fear of dogs, the therapist and client would develop a list of scenes that make the client fearful. Situations may vary from hearing the word "dog" to seeing pictures of dogs, being in the vicinity of a dog, hearing a dog bark, being close to dogs, and patting a dog.

The client is next taught to relax by tensing and releasing various groups of muscles—shoulders, face, arms, neck, and so on. This phase of treatment ends when the client has learned to relax fully on his or her own in a matter of minutes.

The client and therapist now move on to the next phase of therapy. While remaining fully relaxed, the client is asked to imagine being in the first situation at the bottom of the list. The image is held for several seconds. The client then relaxes for about twenty seconds before imagining the same situation again for several seconds. When the client is able to imagine an item and remain fully relaxed, the therapist presents a slightly more fearful situation to imagine. This procedure continues until an image causes distress, at which time the session ends. The next session begins with relaxation, followed by the client slowly moving up the list. As before, the client stops at the point of distress. Therapy is successful when the client can imagine all the items on the list while remaining fully relaxed. The technique is less helpful when clients have difficulty identifying fearful situations or calling up vivid images.

In the hands of a skillful therapist, systematic desensitization is an effective technique for reducing a wide variety of fears. Its Pavlovian features involve pairing imagined fearful scenes with relaxation. When relaxation successfully competes with fear, it becomes a new CR to the imagined scenes. As relaxation becomes sufficiently strong as a CR, anxiety is replaced by calmness in the face of earlier aversive stimuli.

Extinction offers a more direct route to the reduction of fear than systematic desensitization. The technique called flooding makes use of extinction. Flooding exposes the client to fear-arousing stimuli for a prolonged period of time. Suppose a child is afraid of snakes. Although likely to increase the fear initially, flooding would require the child to confront the snake directly and continuously—to be "flooded" by various stimuli associated with the snake—until the conditioned stimuli lose their power to elicit fear. Some therapists think that the application of this technique is best left to professionals.

## SOME EVERYDAY EXAMPLES

Pavlovian principles may be plausibly applied to daily life, as the following examples illustrate.

Couples sometimes refer to a certain tune as "our song." A plausible interpretation is that Pavlovian conditioning has been at work. The favored tune may have been popular and repeated often at the time of the couple's courtship and marriage. The tune has since become a CS that evokes a variety of pleasant feelings associated with initial love.

A baby-sitter notes that giving a young child a blue blanket in the absence of his mother markedly reduces his irritability. Most likely, the blanket has been sufficiently associated with the soothing actions of his mother (US) and now functions as a calming stimulus (CS).

An adolescent steadfastly avoids the location where he was seriously injured in an automobile crash. He says that just thinking about the highway makes him nervous. The location doubtless contains a number of conditioned aversive stimuli that now trigger unpleasant feelings (CR) and avoidance.

After a bitter divorce, a woman finds that the sight of household items (CS) associated with her former husband is terribly upsetting (CR). She reduces her resentment by getting rid of the offending items.

A wife often places flower arrangements in her husband's den. The flowers (CS) now bring him a measure of comfort (CR) when she is away on trips.

## RESPONDENT CONDITIONING AND REINFORCEMENT

Pavlovian behaviors are principally elicited by antecedent events (just as low temperatures elicit shivering), while many behaviors are strengthened (in reinforcement) or weakened (in punishment) by what follows behavior. In Pavlovian conditioning, two stimuli are presented, one following another, regardless of what a subject does. What follows behavior is usually not important in this form of conditioning. In studying the role of reinforcement on behavior (instrumental or operant conditioning), the consequences that follow a person's actions often determine what the person is likely to do under similar circumstances in the future. What follows is important in this type of conditioning.

The topic of reinforcement is introduced here because Pavlovian conditioning and reinforcement are intricately related in that any Pavlovian conditioning is likely to contain elements of instrumental conditioning and vice versa. For example, if someone has a near-drowning experience and now avoids bodies of water, it is plausible to say that conditioned stimuli associated with the experience evoke unsettling feelings. The person reduces the unpleasant feelings by avoiding bodies of water. In this example, negative feelings are conditioned according to Pavlovian principles. The avoidance reaction is maintained by (negative) reinforcement and involves instrumental learning. Virtually all the previous examples can be analyzed similarly.

## SOURCES FOR FURTHER STUDY

Baldwin, John D., and Janice I. Baldwin. *Behavior Principles in Everyday Life.* 4th ed. Upper Saddle River, N.J.: Prentice-Hall, 2001. Written by two sociologists, this book provides an overview of psychological principles of behavior, including many details about Pavlovian conditioning. The authors provide hundreds of plausible and interesting examples of how behavior principles show up in everyday life.

Hergenhahn, B. R., and Matthew Olson. *Introduction to Theories of Learning.* 6th ed. Upper Saddle River, N.J.: Prentice-Hall, 2001. This book describes the work of fifteen major figures in the area of learning. There are chapters about associative theorists such as Ivan Pavlov and functionalist theorists such as B. F. Skinner. A useful elementary survey of learning research and theory, spanning one hundred years of development.

Rescorla, Robert A. "Pavlovian Conditioning: It's Not What You Think It Is." *American Psychologist* 43, no. 3 (May, 1988): 151-160. A critical analysis of Pavlovian conditioning by a leading researcher in the field. The author questions orthodox descriptions of conditioning because they imply that organisms form associations blindly. His view is that organisms actually seek out information using logic and perception to form sophisticated representations of the environment. Rescorla provides a sophisticated examination of the intricacies of conditioning, concentrating on the various outcomes of conditioning and on the circumstances that create them, while citing some of his own work in support of his position.

Watson, John B., and Rosalie Rayner. "Conditioned Emotional Reactions." *Journal of Experimental Psychology* 3 (1920): 1-14. Although this research has been questioned on methodological and ethical grounds—for example, concerns have been raised about the deliberate creation of a phobic reaction in a young child—it is nonetheless a historically important experiment that provided information about how human emotions are learned.

Wolpe, Joseph. *The Practice of Behavior Therapy.* 4th ed. New York: Pergamon, 1990. A significant book by the behavior therapist largely responsible for the development of systematic desensitization. Wolpe discusses behavior therapy as it applies to simple and complex cases of fear and anxiety. He is highly critical of the view that therapy consists of little more than information processing and cognitive correction.

*Frank J. Sparzo*

SEE ALSO: Behaviorism; Conditioning; Habituation and Sensitization; Learned Helplessness; Learning; Phobias; Reflexes.

# Personal Constructs

## George A. Kelly

Type of psychology: Personality
Field of study: Behavioral and cognitive models

*Personal construct theory examines the way each person thinks about the world; it attempts to provide avenues for understanding and making use of one's subjective experiences. It demonstrates how cognitions change when one incorrectly predicts the future on the basis of those cognitions.*

Key concepts
- construct
- constructive alternativism
- dichotomy
- fixed role therapy
- fundamental postulate
- role
- Role Construct Repertory Test

Personal construct theory maintains that all people are motivated to reduce uncertainty in their lives. In this manner, each person is like a scientist who is attempting to solve complex problems. Instead of dealing with complex equations in chemistry and physics, however, one is attempting to unravel the complexities of one's own life and the relationships that one has developed. Just as scientists are constantly making changes in their theories and research claims based on the availability of new evidence, people change the way they look at their subjective worlds on the basis of new evidence. That evidence appears in the form of new interactions with significant others in people's lives, such as spouses, children, parents, and bosses. When new evidence is made available, a person will alter his or her thought patterns in order to reduce uncertainty in the future. This view forms the basis of George A. Kelly's principle of constructive alternativism—the view that people are entitled to their own views of the world and that they will make use of those views in order to reduce uncertainty in the future.

Kelly became involved in personal constructs theory late in his career. Ironically, his early experiences as a psychologist did not even involve the study of personality. It was only in 1955, twelve years prior to his death, that he published *The Psychology of Personal Constructs: A Theory of Personality*. In this work, he defined and discussed the concept of a construct. For Kelly, a construct is a thought that a person has for the purpose of attempting to interpret events; these interpretations may prove to be accurate or inaccurate. In those situations in which a construct leads to an incorrect prediction of an event, the person is likely to change the construct. All of Kelly's constructs are dichotomous in nature; that is, they are made of pairs of polar opposites that cannot be simultaneously correct when referring to the same person. For example, one cannot view one's boss as both intelligent and unintelligent at the same time. Similarly, one's boyfriend or girlfriend cannot be seen as cruel and kind at the same moment.

## FUNDAMENTAL POSTULATE AND COROLLARIES

Kelly claimed that constructs operate according to a fundamental postulate. This postulate maintains that each person directs thoughts and cognitions in a way that permits the most accurate prediction of future events. If a woman has a personal construct which states that her boyfriend is a thoughtful person, and he sends her flowers while she is in bed with the flu, her construct would be regarded as an accurate one. If, however, that same boyfriend used her illness as an opportunity to date other women and ignored her illness in the process, it would be necessary to adjust her construction system because it does not accurately predict her boyfriend's behavior. This process of changing one's construction system in order to predict future events more accurately is an ongoing one, designed to decrease uncertainty in the future.

While the fundamental postulate is critical to Kelly's attempts to predict and explain behavior, it is not sufficient to cover all aspects of a person's behavior and the choices that are made which cause that behavior. In order to address this additional detail, Kelly provided a series of eleven corollaries to his fundamental postulate. These corollaries are supporting statements that provide a detailed analysis of thoughts and behaviors which cannot be directly derived from the fundamental postulate.

The construction corollary maintains that people continue to learn as they are presented with similar events in life. For example, if a man's mother has given him a birthday present for the last thirty years, his prediction that he will receive another present from her on his next birthday makes sense. Similarly, if one has watched a particular television program at 11:30 P.M. on weeknights for the past several years, one's prediction that it will again be on television at the same time next Monday night is a reasonable one.

Another important corollary to Kelly's fundamental postulate is the dichotomy corollary. This states that all constructs consist of pairs of opposites. That is, a college course may be either interesting or uninteresting, but it cannot be both at the same time. One important aspect of the dichotomy corollary is that each construct must include three members or items, with two of the members having the same characteristic and the third member having the opposite characteristic. For example, breathing and not breathing would not be a legitimate construct in evaluating three friends. Because all of them breathe, the proposed construct would not tell how the three individuals are different as well as alike. Therefore, it would not reduce uncertainty in the future.

A third corollary to Kelly's system which is particularly important is the range corollary. This maintains that a construct is only relevant in dealing with a finite number of events. The events for which a construct is deemed applicable is called its range of convenience. Terms such as "happy" and "sad" would not be within the range of convenience in depicting the characteristics of a tree or a book, while they might be critical in evaluating one's relatives.

Varying degrees of applicability can be found within a series of constructs. For example, the construct "kind versus cruel" would be more relevant in evaluating a relative or girlfriend than it would be in considering the qualities of an elevator operator one occasionally encounters. Kelly's fundamental postulate and supporting corollaries provide considerable information. The theory also provides some interesting applications in terms of personality assessment and therapeutic intervention.

## USE WITH CAREER GOALS

Kelly's personal construct theory has been used to explain, predict, and attempt to modify behavior in a wide range of circumstances. One interesting application involves the use of personal constructs in formulating career goals. A high school student, for example, may establish a goal of becoming a successful surgeon in the future. The nature of her constructs can then be examined to determine whether her constructs (as they relate to her own characteristics) are likely to lead to a medical career. She currently views herself as unintelligent rather than intelligent, dedicated to immediate gratification rather than delayed gratification, and lazy rather than hardworking. If she is eventually to become a successful physician, she must reject those constructs and develop a new construction system which is consistent with her career goals. The application of Kelly's theory to career choice is important. While one does not expect first-grade children to examine their own characteristics realistically in considering career options, much more is required of high school and college students. It is not sufficient to state that one wants to pursue a given career. The nature of one's constructs must be evaluated to determine if they are consistent with one's career goals. In those circumstances in which inconsistencies exist, either the constructs or the career goals must change.

## ROLE CONSTRUCT REPERTORY TEST

One of the most interesting applications of Kelly's personal construct theory involves the development of an assessment device, the Role Construct Repertory Test. This test defines a role as a set of behaviors that are performed by a person in response to the construction systems and behaviors of others. The test itself determines the nature of a person's system of constructs as it is related to the significant others in that person's life. The test can be used as a means of evaluating progress during psychotherapy or as a vehicle for detecting changes in interpersonal relationships.

The test involves the creation of a grid in which the person's significant others are listed. Examples would be self, mother, spouse, boss, friend, and successful person. The client then considers these individuals in groups of three provided by the therapist. The client comes up with a word that typifies two of these individuals, and a second word that is the opposite of the first word but typifies the third person. This procedure is followed for a group of twenty sorts, or sets of comparisons. This enables the therapist to determine the behaviors and thoughts of the client concerning the significant others in her life.

One of the determinations that can be made involves the flexibility of the client in dealing with others. That is, in listing those individuals on the grid who possess certain positive characteristics, the therapist would examine whether the same individuals on the grid are given credit for all the positive characteristics listed, while a second group is always viewed negatively. This would indicate a lack of flexibility in the client and might offer an area for needed change in the future.

## FIXED ROLE THERAPY

As an application of Kelly's theory, the Role Construct Repertory Test is an initial step in the therapeutic process. An interesting follow-up provided by Kelly is fixed role therapy. This technique begins by asking the client to develop an in-depth description of himself or herself, written in the third person. This is called a self-characterization sketch. The third-person style is used to produce greater objectivity than would be achieved with first-person narratives. This gives the therapist a clear look at the client from the client's own perspective. The therapist then establishes a role for the client which is directly opposite many of the characteristics in the self-characterization sketch. The client is asked to act out that new role for a period of time. The role would include positive characteristics not found in the self-characterization sketch. The ultimate goal of the technique is to have the client maintain many of those new positive characteristics on a long-term basis.

In evaluating applications of Kelly's work, the emphasis must be placed on the importance of knowing one's own construction system and, when appropriate, taking steps to change that system. While this may be handled through formal techniques such as fixed role therapy, many therapists make use of Kelly's emphasis upon cognitive change without strictly employing his terminology. To this extent, the influence of Kelly's work should increase in the future.

## KELLY'S CAREER

Kelly did not begin his career with the intention of developing personal construct theory. In fact, his initial training was not even in the field of personality psychology. Kelly's original specialty in graduate school was physiological psychology, and his dissertation was concerned with the areas of speech and reading disabilities. Having received his degree around the time of the Great Depression, however, Kelly came to the conclusion that the principles

and concepts contained within his areas of specialization offered little so-
lace to those who were emotionally and financially devastated in the after-
math of the Depression. He turned to clinical psychology, with an initial emphasis on the psychoanalytic approach. He noted that concepts such as the
id and the libido seemed of no use in dealing with victims of the Depression.
Kelly's initial academic position was at Fort Hays State College in Kansas.
While at Fort Hays, he developed a series of traveling psychological clinics
designed to treat the emotional and behavioral problems of students. This
experience was crucial in the eventual formulation of personal construct
theory. Kelly tried numerous forms of treatment with the students and determined that the optimal technique varied across cases. This led him to
conclude that any clinical technique that is successful should be retained,
while techniques that result in repeated treatment failure should be discarded. This flexibility, reflected in his later theoretical claims regarding
constructive alternativism and his fundamental postulate, has made Kelly
unique among personality theorists. His willingness to respect subjective reality as determined by each human being is reflective of his unwillingness to
commit himself totally to any one theoretical perspective. Although Kelly
was influenced by many theorists, he clearly traveled his own path in the development of his psychology of personal constructs.

## SOURCES FOR FURTHER STUDY

Bannister, Donald, and Fay Fransella. *Inquiring Man: The Theory of Personal
Constructs.* 3d ed. New York: Routledge, 1986. Provides an excellent introduction to George A. Kelly's theory. In addition, a wide range of applications are provided within the overall field of clinical psychology as well as
social psychology. The authors are dedicated advocates of Kelly's perspective.

Bannister, Donald, and J. M. M. Mair, eds. *The Evaluation of Personal Constructs.* New York: Academic Press, 1968. This excellent work provides insights into the types of theoretical and research efforts that have been un-
dertaken as a result of George A. Kelly's contributions. Particularly
relevant because it was published shortly after Kelly's death and therefore
provides an interesting analysis of his influence at that time.

Kelly, George Alexander. *Clinical Psychology and Personality: The Selected Papers
of George Kelly.* Edited by Brendan Maher. New York: John Wiley & Sons,
1969. This offering is unique in that it contains many of Kelly's last papers. Includes papers that account for the origins of the theory and depicts Kelly's analysis of his work shortly before his death. The presentation is accurate, and it faithfully depicts the essence of Kelly's work.

_____. *The Psychology of Personal Constructs: A Theory of Personality.* New
York: W. W. Norton, 1955. This two-volume series, still in print after almost half a century, provides the essence of Kelly's theory. Covers the theoretical basis for the theory by presenting an analysis of personal constructs, constructive alternativism, and the fundamental postulate as well

as the Role Construct Repertory Test and fixed role therapy. Kelly's views of the appropriate place of assessment in the therapeutic process are particularly interesting.

Neimeyer, Robert A. *The Development of Personal Construct Psychology.* Lincoln: University of Nebraska Press, 1985. Looks at the origins, development, and impact of George A. Kelly's theory. Includes many relevant insights into his early work, while including applications of the theory in areas such as personality, clinical psychology, and social psychology.

*Lawrence A. Fehr*

SEE ALSO: Abnormality: Psychological Models; Cognitive Psychology; Cognitive Social Learning: Walter Mischel; Cognitive Therapy.

# PERSONALITY DISORDERS

TYPE OF PSYCHOLOGY: Psychopathology
FIELDS OF STUDY: Personality assessment; personality disorders

*The personality disorders are a cluster of psychological disorders characterized by inflexible and long-standing patterns of relating to others and the environment that create significant impairment in functioning.*

KEY CONCEPTS
- antisocial personality disorder
- avoidant personality disorder
- borderline personality disorder
- dependent personality disorder
- histrionic personality disorder
- narcissistic personality disorder
- paranoid personality disorder
- personality
- obsessive-compulsive disorder
- schizoid personality disorder
- schizotypal personality disorder

Personality is a term used to describe long-standing patterns of thinking, behaving, and feeling. A group of traits which are consistently displayed are considered to be part of a person's personality. A person's mood, for example, is considered to be a more fleeting expression of one's overall personality. Personality comprises traits, attitudes, behaviors, and coping styles which develop throughout childhood and adolescence. Developmental theorist Erik Erikson (1902-1981) proposed that personality unfolds over the entire life cycle according to a predetermined plan. Personality can be thought of as a relatively consistent style of relating to others and the environment, developing as a result of genetic and environmental influences. Psychologists have developed several theories to explain personality development. Austrian psychoanalyst Sigmund Freud (1856-1939) believed that personality development originates in early childhood. Freud proposed that personality emerges as a result of unconscious conflicts between unacceptable aggressive and hedonistic instincts and societal mores. According to Freud, unresolved unconscious conflicts from childhood later influence personality development. In contrast to Freud's psychoanalytic theories about personality, other researchers focused on specific traits as the building blocks of personality development. Many classification systems have been developed in an attempt to organize and categorize personality traits and styles. The Big Five system proposes that five basic trait dimensions underlie personality structure: extroversion versus introversion, agreeableness versus disagreeableness, conscientiousness versus impulsiveness, emotional stability versus neuroticism, and openness to experience versus rigidity. Personality disorders may reflect extreme variants of these basic personality dimensions.

The personality disorders are a group of psychological disorders characterized by inflexible and maladaptive patterns of relating to others that result in impairments in day-to-day functioning. The personality disorders are reflected by personality traits which are significantly extreme or exaggerated, making it difficult to establish functional relationships with others. According to the *Diagnostic and Statistical Manual of Mental Disorders: DSM-IV-TR* (rev. 4th ed., 2000), the personality disorders are defined by an enduring pattern of inner experience and behavior which is consistently dysfunctional and creates impairment in functioning. Symptoms of personality disorders are usually evident by early adulthood, coinciding with the developmental period when personality patterns have become established in most people. The DSM-IV-TR identifies ten major personality disorders: paranoid personality disorder, schizoid personality disorder, schizotypal personality disorder, borderline personality disorder, antisocial personality disorder, narcissistic personality disorder, histrionic personality disorder, avoidant personality disorder, dependent personality disorder, and obsessive-compulsive personality disorder. The personality disorders are broken down into three groups, or clusters, based upon similar symptomatology.

## CLUSTER A

The personality disorders in Cluster A consist of paranoid personality disorder, schizoid personality disorder, and schizotypal personality disorder. The behavior of people with a cluster A personality disorder is described as odd or eccentric.

Paranoid personality disorder is characterized by a pervasive distrust of others, chronic suspicion about others' motives, and paranoid thinking. Others often avoid individuals with paranoid personality disorder, which reinforces the individual's mistrust of others. The suspicion is chronic and creates a difficulty in establishing and maintaining interpersonal relationships. Paranoid personality disorder is more prevalent in males than females.

Schizoid personality disorder is characterized by a pervasive and long-lasting indifference toward others. The term "schizoid" was initially chosen to refer to the preliminary symptoms, or latent symptoms of schizophrenia. A person with this disorder has little or no interest in interacting with others and is viewed as a loner. People with schizoid personality disorder have little interest in intimacy and tend to display a limited range of emotions. These individuals often are dull and lack a sense of humor. They are perceived by others as being aloof or apathetic and may appear disheveled or unkempt.

Schizotypal personality disorder is characterized by peculiar patterns of behaving and thinking. A person with this disorder may express superstitious beliefs or may engage in fantasy-based thinking. Although their thought processes might be unusual, their beliefs are not considered to be of delusional proportions. Because the symptoms of cluster A personality

---

## DSM-IV-TR GENERAL CRITERIA FOR A PERSONALITY DISORDER

Enduring pattern of inner experience and behavior deviating markedly from expectations of individual's culture

Manifested in two or more of the following areas:
- cognition (ways of perceiving and interpreting self, other people, and events)
- affectivity (range, intensity, lability, and appropriateness of emotional response)
- interpersonal functioning
- impulse control

Enduring pattern inflexible and pervasive across a broad range of personal and social situations

Enduring pattern leads to clinically significant distress or impairment in social, occupational, or other important areas of functioning

Pattern stable and of long duration, and its onset can be traced back at least to adolescence or early adulthood

Enduring pattern not better accounted for as manifestation or consequence of another mental disorder

Enduring pattern not due to direct physiological effects of a substance or general medical condition

DSM-IV-TR personality disorders:
- Cluster A: Paranoid; Schizoid; Schizotypal
- Cluster B: Antisocial; Borderline; Histrionic; Narcissistic
- Cluster C: Avoidant; Dependent; Obsessive-Compulsive

---

disorders resemble symptoms of schizophrenia, researchers believe these disorders may be genetically related to schizophrenia.

### CLUSTER B

The personality disorders of cluster B are borderline personality disorder, antisocial personality disorder, narcissistic personality disorder, and histrionic personality disorder. The cluster B personality disorders are described as dramatic, erratic, and emotional. The behavior of people with such a disorder creates significant impairment in establishing and maintaining interpersonal relationships. Borderline personality disorder (BPD) is the most prevalent personality disorder. It is diagnosed twice as often among women as men and is characterized by a long-standing and inflexible pattern of emotional instability and unstable personal relationships. Individuals with BPD have an intense fear of abandonment and tend to form intense and unstable relationships with others. They tend to fluctuate between having positive and negative feelings about significant people in their lives. This behavior is referred to as splitting and may contribute to the emotional instability displayed by these people. People with BPD often engage in self-destructive behavior, such as self-mutilation, suicidal acts, or drug abuse. Those with BPD report chronic feelings of emptiness.

Antisocial personality disorder is exemplified by an enduring pattern of behavior that disregards and violates the rights of others. The term "antisocial" refers to behaviors that are antisociety. Antisocial personality disorder is preceded by conduct disorder in the adolescent stages of development. People with antisocial personality disorder often appear initially to be charming and intelligent yet are also manipulative and grandiose. They lack a moral code which would disallow unacceptable or hurtful behaviors. Therefore, an individual with antisocial personality disorder is likely to engage in criminal acts, manipulative behavior, and the exploitation of others.

Freud coined the term "narcissistic personality disorder" in reference to the Greek myth of Narcissus, who fell in love with his own reflection in a pool of water, preventing him from forming relationships with others. The essential feature of narcissistic personality disorder is an exaggerated sense of self-importance. This disorder is characterized by a need to be the center of attention and a preoccupation with fantasies of one's success or power. A person with narcissistic personality disorder has difficulty understanding the feelings of others and constantly is demanding of attention. These grandiose behaviors typically mask feelings of insecurity.

Symptoms of histrionic personality disorder include excessive emotionality and attention-seeking behavior. A person with histrionic personality disorder is overly dramatic and emotional and inappropriately seductive in order to gain the attention of others. Histrionic personality disorder is more prevalent among females than males.

## CLUSTER C

Cluster C disorders include avoidant personality disorder, dependent personality disorder, and obsessive-compulsive personality disorder. The behavior of people with a cluster C personality disorder is described as anxious or fearful.

People with avoidant personality disorder display a pervasive pattern of social discomfort and a fear of being disliked by others. Because of these feelings, a person with this disorder avoids social interactions with others. People with avoidant personality disorder are extremely shy and have great difficulty establishing interpersonal relationships. They want to be liked by others, but their social discomfort and insecurities prevent them from engaging in interpersonal relationships.

Dependent personality disorder is characterized by a chronic pattern of dependent and needy behavior, with an intense fear of being alone. People with this disorder attempt to please other people in order to avoid potential abandonment. They may say certain things just to be liked by others. They have difficulty making their own decisions and are submissive with others. Individuals with this disorder have difficulty separating from others.

Obsessive-compulsive personality disorder is characterized by an inflexible and enduring need for control and order. People who suffer from obsessive-compulsive personality disorder are so preoccupied with order and organization that they may lose sight of the main objective of an activity. People with this disorder are usually excessively work-oriented and have little patience for leisure time. They are intolerant of indecisiveness or emotionality in others and favor intellect over affect. People with this disorder are perceived as difficult to get along with and unwilling to be a team player. Obsessive-compulsive personality disorder is different from obsessive-compulsive disorder (OCD), which is categorized as an anxiety disorder and involves obsessive thoughts and compulsive behaviors.

## DIAGNOSIS

A number of issues have created debate related to the difficulty in and reliability of the diagnosis of personality disorders. The distinction between "normal" personality characteristics and a personality disorder is not necessarily clear in the clinical definition of a personality disorder. The DSM-IV-TR notes that when personality traits are inflexible and create distress or impairment in functioning, they constitute a personality disorder. Some argue that there is considerable room for debate about the point at which a trait is considered to create impairment.

The personality disorders have been the subject of criticism by researchers because of the difficulty in diagnosing them reliably. Individuals with a personality disorder often display symptoms of other personality disorders. For example, researchers have debated about the distinction between schizoid personality disorder and avoidant personality disorder, as both disorders are characterized by an extreme in social isolation. Individuals with personality disorders are more likely than the general population to suffer from other psychological disorders, such as depression, bulimia, or substance abuse. This overlap of symptoms may lead to difficulty with diagnostic reliability. The personality disorders occur so frequently with other types of psychological disorders that it is challenging to sort through symptoms to determine what is evidence of each disorder. It is difficult to estimate the prevalence of personality disorders in the United States, as individuals with these disorders do not recognize that they are dysfunctional and are therefore less likely to seek treatment.

Researchers have explored the problem of gender bias in the diagnosis of personality disorders. It is believed that some of the symptoms of certain personality disorders are more characteristic of one gender than the other. For example, the aggression and hostility associated with antisocial personality disorder may be traits associated more frequently with the average male population, thus affecting the diagnosis among men compared to women.

This supposed gender bias is theorized to be related to the greater prevalence of borderline personality disorder and histrionic personality disorder among women compared to men. Perhaps some of the diagnostic symptoms of this disorder, such as emotionality or fears of abandonment, have been behaviors more often associated with the female population than the male population.

## CAUSES

Various theories have been developed to explain the etiology of personality disorders. The biological perspective examines the roles of genetics and brain functioning in the development of personality disorders. Evidence suggests that the cluster A disorders (paranoid, schizoid, and schizotypal personality disorders) are more prevalent among first-degree relatives of individuals suffering from schizophrenia, suggesting a possible genetic commonality among those disorders.

The underlying symptoms of borderline personality disorder (impulsivity and emotionality) are inherited. Much research confirms that borderline patients are more likely to report a childhood family history that included sexual abuse, domestic violence, and the early loss (either through death or abandonment) of a parental figure. It is believed that this history may be related to the later development of borderline personality disorder. According to Erikson, a sense of basic trust during childhood is an essential component of normal personality development. Erikson stated that a basic sense of trust or mistrust in the self and the world develops in the first year of life. The experience of being abandoned by a parent, then, would foster a sense of mistrust in the world and would affect personality development. In the 1950's, University of Wisconsin psychologist Harry Harlow (1905-1981) explored the effects of attachment on later personality development. Harlow concluded that rhesus monkeys who were separated from their mothers shortly after birth displayed abnormal behaviors later in life, such as unusual fear or aggression, difficulty engaging in mating behaviors, and difficulty with parenting their offspring. Maternally deprived animals, therefore, were more likely to display dysfunction, as is seen in individuals with disorders associated with maternal deprivation, such as borderline and antisocial personality disorders.

Genetic factors may be influential in the development of antisocial personality disorder, as children of biological parents who engage in criminal behavior are more likely to engage in criminal behavior themselves. Learning theorists propose that antisocial behaviors may be learned by mimicking parents with similar behaviors. Individuals with antisocial personality disorder have displayed an abnormally low arousal level, which might enable them to ignore physiological cues that indicate danger or punishment. Research has also suggested that the unusually low level of arousal may cause the antisocial individual to engage in behaviors which increase physiological arousal, or create a "rush."

## TREATMENT

Treatment of a personality disorder is difficult because of certain key issues related to these disorders. People with personality disorders tend to lack insight about their dysfunctional ways of interacting with others. Because they do not see themselves as having a problem, they are unlikely to pursue treatment. When a person with a personality disorder does seek treatment, it is usually for some secondary issue, such as alcoholism or depression. People suffering from personality disorders tend to end therapy prematurely, a result of their perception that their behavior is not the source of problems. One of the central features of the personality disorders is an impaired ability to maintain relationships with others; therefore, developing a relationship with a therapist is difficult. When the opportunity for treatment does arise, treatment approaches differ depending on the unique characteristics of each of the personality disorders.

The treatment of borderline personality disorder has received much research attention. American psychologist Marsha M. Linehan is credited with the development of dialectical behavior therapy (DBT), a treatment approach for borderline personality disorder which integrates cognitive, behavioral, and Zen principles to help the patient to develop essential coping skills. One of the basic tenets of DBT is that individuals with borderline personality disorder may react abnormally to a normal stimulus (such as an interaction with another person) because of negative or traumatic past experiences (such as sexual abuse). Such individuals may quickly display an increase in emotion and may take a longer period of time to reduce their emotional arousal. Treatment focuses on decreasing self-destructive behaviors and helping individual to regulate their emotions.

People with antisocial personality disorder who participate in treatment usually are made to do so by the legal system. Efficacy of treatment interventions for the person with antisocial personality disorder is often measured in terms of the number of crimes committed by the person after treatment, rather than by any significant change in personality characteristics. Treating any substance abuse issues is an integral component of treatment of antisocial personality disorder. Some believe that prevention is the most important part of managing antisocial behavior.

Researchers have found that low levels of antipsychotic medications are effective in alleviating some symptoms of schizotypal personality disorder. Several studies suggest that antipsychotic medications such as haloperidol may decrease symptoms of depression and impulsivity in the schizotypal individual. People with narcissistic personality disorder are more apt than those with other personality disorders to seek out treatment, using the therapist's office as yet another stage to be the center of attention.

## SOURCES FOR FURTHER STUDY

Claridge, Gordon. *Origins of Mental Illness.* 2d ed. Cambridge, Mass.: Malor Books, 1996. The author explores the basic dimensions of personality,

personality theories, and basic research and treatment of mental disorders.

Erikson, Erik H. *Identity: Youth and Crisis*. New York: W. W. Norton, 1968. A compilation of Erikson's notable essays about adolescent identity crisis. Articles explore theories of personality development and intrapersonal conflict.

Linehan, Marsha M. *Cognitive-Behavioral Treatment of Borderline Personality Disorder*. New York: Guilford Press, 1993. The author provides an overview of the symptoms of borderline personality disorder followed by an extensive description of an exploration of the foundations of dialectical behavioral therapy. Specific treatment strategies are clearly described, and the book contains several helpful charts and checklists.

Livesley, W. John, Marsha L. Schroeder, Douglas Jackson, and Kerry L. Jang. "Categorical Distinctions in the Study of Personality Disorder—Implications for Classification." *Journal of Abnormal Psychology* 103, no. 1 (1994): 6-17. This article focuses on the foundation of the classification of personality disorders and challenges some of the empirical evidence regarding the effectiveness of classification.

Maxmen, Jerrold S., and Nicholas G. Ward. *Essential Psychopathology and Its Treatment*. New York: W. W. Norton, 1995. The authors provide a comprehensive overview of the various forms of psychopathology and treatment approaches.

Nathan, Peter E., Jack M. Gorman, and Neil J. Salkind. *Treating Mental Disorders: A Guide to What Works*. New York: Oxford University Press, 1999. Outlines current standards of care for mental illnesses in a question-and-answer format. Offers guides for further information.

Paris, Joel. "A Diathesis-Stress Model of Personality Disorders." *Psychiatric Annals* 29, no. 12 (1999): 692-697. The author explores the possible relationship between life stressors and the development of personality disorders.

Widiger, Thomas A., and Paul T. Costa. "Personality and Personality Disorders." *Journal of Abnormal Psychology* 103, no. 1 (1994): 78-91. The authors review the belief that personality disorders are representative of extreme variants of normal personality traits. Using the five-factor model, the authors explore the correlation between personality and personality disorders.

*Janine T. Ogden*

SEE ALSO: Obsessive-Compulsive Disorder; Schizophrenia: Background, Types, and Symptoms.

# PERSONALITY
## PSYCHOPHYSIOLOGICAL MEASURES

TYPE OF PSYCHOLOGY: Personality
FIELD OF STUDY: Personality assessment

*Psychophysiological studies comparing individuals with different personality traits have sought to determine the physical characteristics of particular behavioral characteristics. Such research can provide information that helps clarify the importance of various personality types with regard to risk of psychological and physical disorders.*

KEY CONCEPTS
- anxiety sensitivity
- locus of control
- personality
- psychophysiology
- Type A behavior pattern

A broad definition of personality typically includes the dimensions of stability, determinism, and uniqueness. That is, personality changes little over time, is determined by internal processes and external factors, and reflects an individual's distinctive qualities. Personality also can be thought of as unique, relatively stable patterns of behavior, multiply determined over the course of an individual's life. There are many theories for understanding the development of these patterns of behavior.

Twin studies have provided evidence that biological factors help to shape personality; such studies support Hans Eysenck's theory that personality is inherited. The psychodynamic perspective holds that personality is determined primarily by early childhood experiences. Some of the most influential contributions to this perspective came from Sigmund Freud. He argued that unconscious forces govern behavior and that childhood experiences strongly shape adult personality via coping strategies people use to deal with sexual urges. B. F. Skinner, founder of modern behavioral psychology, assumed that personality (or behavior) is determined solely by environmental factors. More specifically, he believed that consequences of behavior are instrumental in the development of unique, relatively stable patterns of behavior in individuals. According to Albert Bandura's social learning perspective, models have a great impact on personality development. That is, patterns of behavior in individuals are influenced by the observation of others. Finally, the humanistic perspective of Carl Rogers suggests that personality is largely determined by the individual's unique perception of reality in comparison to his or her self-concept.

## PERSONALITY ASSESSMENT
Assessment of personality can be accomplished from three domains: subjec-

tive experience, behavior, and physiology. Traditional means for assessing personality have included objective and projective paper-and-pencil or interview measurements that tap the domain of subjective experience. Behavioral assessment techniques such as direct observation of behavior, self-monitoring (having the individual record occurrences of his or her own behavior), self-report questionnaires, role-play scenarios, and behavioral avoidance tests (systematic, controlled determination of how close an individual can approach a feared object or situation) tap the domains of subjective experience and objective behavior. These techniques have been used in clinical settings to aid in the diagnosis and treatment of deviant or abnormal behavior patterns.

Although psychophysiological measurement of personality has not gained popular use in clinical settings, it complements the techniques mentioned above and contributes to understanding the nature and development of psychological and physical disorders. Just as patterns of responding on traditional personality tests can indicate the possibility of aberrant behavior, so too can tests of physiological patterns. Typical measures taken during this type of assessment include heart rate, blood pressure, muscle tension (measured via electromyography), brain-wave activity (measured via electroencephalography), skin temperature, and palmar sweat gland or electrodermal activity. These measures of physiological activity are sensitive to "emotional" responses to various stimuli and have been instrumental in clarifying the nature of certain psychological and physical conditions. One of the fundamental assumptions of psychophysiology is that the responses of the body can help reveal the mechanisms underlying human behavior and personality.

Physiological responsivity can be assessed in a number of different ways. Two primary methodologies are used in the study of the relations between personality and physiology. The first method simply looks at resting or baseline differences of various physiological measures across individuals who either possess or do not possess the personality characteristic of interest. The second method also assesses individuals with or without the characteristic of interest but does this under specific stimulus or situational conditions rather than during rest. This is often referred to as measuring reactivity to the stimulus or situational condition. Resting physiological measures are referred to as tonic activity (activity evident in the absence of any known stimulus event). It is postulated that tonic activity is relatively enduring and stable within the individual while at rest, although it can be influenced by external factors. It is both of interest in its own right and important in determining the magnitude of response to a stimulus. On the other hand, phasic activity is a discrete response to a specific stimulus. This type of activity is suspected to be influenced to a much greater extent by external factors and tends to be less stable than tonic activity. Both types of activity, tonic and phasic, are important in the study of personality and physiology.

Standard laboratory procedures are typically employed to investigate tonic activity and phasic responses to environmental stimuli. For example, a typical assessment incorporating both methodologies might include the following phases: a five-minute baseline to collect resting physiological measures, a five-minute presentation of a task or other stimulus suspected to differentiate individuals in each group based on their physiological response or change from baseline, and a five-minute recovery to assess the nature and rate of physiological recovery from the task or stimulus condition. Investigations focusing on the last phase attempt to understand variations in recovery as a response pattern in certain individuals. For example, highly anxious individuals tend to take much longer to recover physiologically from stimulus presentations that influence heart rate and electrodermal activity than individuals who report low levels of anxiety.

Studies of physiological habituation—the decline or disappearance of response to a discrete stimulus—also have been used to investigate personality differences. Physiological responses to a standard tone, for example, eventually disappear with repeated presentations of the tone. The rate at which they disappear varies across individuals; the disappearance generally takes longer in individuals who tend to be anxious. Thus, individuals who tend to have anxious traits may be more physiologically responsive, recover from the response less rapidly, and habituate to repeated stimulation more slowly than those who tend to be less anxious. Such physiological differences may be an important characteristic that determines anxious behavior or results from subjective feelings of anxiousness.

## RELATIONSHIP TO PHYSIOLOGY AND HEALTH

Research has demonstrated that there is considerable variability across individuals in their physiological response patterns, both at rest and in response to various situational stimuli or laboratory manipulations. Evidence indicates that part of this variability across individuals may, in some cases, be attributable to certain personality traits or characteristic patterns of behavior. Furthermore, research suggests that these personality traits may also be related to the development of psychological or physical disorders. Although the causal links are not well understood, a growing body of research points to relations among personality, physiological measures, and psychopathology/health.

Examples of these relationships are evident in the field of psychopathology, or the study of abnormal behavior. Hans Eysenck proposed that the general characteristics of introversion and extroversion lead individuals to interact very differently with their environment. Some psychophysiological studies support this notion and suggest that the behaviors characteristic of these traits may be driven by physiological differences. Anxiety sensitivity and locus of control are two personality traits that some suggest are related to the development of anxiety disorders and depression, respectively. To varying degrees, anxiety disorders and depression have been investigated in the psychophysiology laboratory and have been found to differentiate individuals with high and low levels of the personality trait, based on their physiological responses.

Introversion describes the tendency to minimize interaction with the environment; extroversion is characterized by the opposite behaviors, or the tendency to interact more with the environment. Eysenck proposed that such traits reflect physiological differences that are genetically determined and reflected in the individual's physiology. Introverted individuals are thought to be chronically physiologically hyperaroused and thus to seek to minimize their arousal by minimizing external stimulation. Extroverted individuals are believed to be chronically physiologically underaroused and to seek a more optimal level of arousal through increased environmental stimulation. It should be easy to confirm or disprove such a theory with psychophysiological studies of resting physiological activity in introverts and extroverts. Electroencephalograph (EEG) studies have produced contradictory evidence about the validity of Eysenck's theory, however; problems in EEG methodology, experimental design, and measurement of the traits themselves have led to considerable confusion about whether the traits actually do have a physiological basis.

## ANXIETY SENSITIVITY

Anxiety sensitivity describes the tendency for individuals to fear sensations they associate with anxiety because of beliefs that anxiety may result in harmful consequences. Research in the development and assessment of this construct was pioneered by Steven Reiss and his associates in the late 1980's. They developed a sixteen-item questionnaire, the Anxiety Sensitivity Index (ASI), to measure anxiety sensitivity and found it to be both reliable and valid. Anxiety sensitivity has been most closely related to panic disorder, an anxiety disorder characterized by frequent, incapacitating episodes of extreme fear or discomfort. In fact, as a group, individuals with panic disorder score higher on the ASI than individuals with any other anxiety disorder. Furthermore, some researchers have demonstrated that individuals scoring high on the ASI are five times more likely to develop an anxiety disorder after a three-year follow-up.

Research investigating responses to arithmetic, caffeine, and hyperventilation challenges in the laboratory has demonstrated that individual differences in anxiety sensitivity levels are probably more closely related to the subjective experience of anxiousness than to actual physiological changes. Individuals high and low on anxiety sensitivity, however, have exhibited differential heart-rate reactivity to a mental arithmetic stressor. That is, individuals high on anxiety sensitivity show a greater acceleration in heart rate than individuals low on anxiety sensitivity when engaging in an arithmetic challenge. Individuals scoring high on the ASI also more accurately perceive actual changes in their physiology when compared with their low-scoring counterparts. Such heightened reactivity and sensitivity to physiological change may partially explain how anxiety sensitivity influences the development of anxiety disorders. Individuals high in anxiety sensitivity may be more reactive to environmental threat; therefore, their increased sensitivity may have a physiological basis. They also may be more likely to detect changes in their physiology, which they are then more likely to attribute to threat or danger.

On a more general note, cardiovascular and electrodermal measures can differentiate between anxiety patients and other people at rest. The differences become greater under conditions of stimulation. Delayed habituation rates in anxiety patients are also part of the pattern of physiological overarousal typically seen in individuals with heightened anxiety. Indeed, heightened physiological arousal is one of the hallmark characteristics of anxiety.

## LOCUS OF CONTROL

Locus of control, made popular by Julian Rotter in the 1960's, refers to individuals' perceptions of whether they have control over what happens to them across situations. This personality construct has been related to the development of depression. Specifically, it is believed that individuals who attribute failures to internal factors (self-blame) and successes to external factors (to other people or to luck) are more susceptible to developing feelings of helplessness, often followed by despair and depression. Locus of control also is hypothesized to have implications in the management of chronic health-related problems.

In oversimplified categorizations, individuals are labeled to have an "internal" or "external" locus of control. "External" individuals, who believe they have little control over what happens to them, are said to be more reactive to threat, more emotionally labile, more hostile, and lower in self-esteem and self-control. Psychophysiological assessment studies have revealed heart-rate acceleration and longer electrodermal habituation for "externals" in response to the presentation of tones under passive conditions. When faced with no-control conditions in stress situations such as inescapable shock, "internals" show elevated physiological arousal, while findings for "externals" are mixed. Thus, the locus of control has varying effects on physiology, depending on the circumstances. Such effects may play a role in psychological disorders such as depression and anxiety. Heightened physiological reactivity may also inhibit recovery from acute illness or affect the course of chronic health problems such as hypertension.

In addition to the relevance of personality to physiological reactivity and psychopathology, research has demonstrated that certain personality types may be risk factors or serve protective functions with regard to physical health. Type A behavior pattern and hardiness are two examples. Type A behavior pattern is characterized by competitiveness, time urgency, and hostility. It has been identified as a potential risk factor for the development of coronary heart disease. Psychophysiological studies have suggested that, under certain laboratory conditions, males who exhibit the Type A pattern are more cardiovascularly responsive. This reactivity is the proposed mechanism by which Type A behavior affects the heart. More recent research has suggested that not all components of the Type A pattern are significantly associated with heightened cardiovascular reactivity. Hostility seems to be the most critical factor in determining heightened reactivity. Males who respond to stress with hostility tend to show greater heart-rate and blood-pressure increases than individuals low in hostility. Some research suggests that hostility is also a risk factor for heart disease in women.

In contrast to hostility, hardiness is proposed to buffer the effects of stress on physiology. Hardy individuals respond to stressors as challenges and believe that they have control over the impact of stressors. They also feel commitment to their life, including work and family. Psychophysiological studies have supported the buffering effect of hardiness. Individuals who are more hardy tend to be less physiologically responsive to stressors and to recover from stressors more rapidly. Again, the construct of hardiness seems to be more relevant for males, partially because males have been studied more often.

These studies show that various personality types can be distinguished to varying degrees by psychophysiological measurement. The implications of such findings include possible physiological contributions to the development of various psychological problems as well as personality contributions to the development or course of physical disease.

### EVOLUTION OF RESEARCH

Although the sophisticated techniques and instruments that have enabled psychologists to study physiological events were not developed until the twentieth century, the notion that physiology and psychology (body and mind) are linked dates back as far as ancient Greece. Hippocrates, for example, described four bodily humors or fluids thought to influence various psychological states such as melancholy and mania. Although the link between mind and body has received varying degrees of emphasis in scientific thinking across the centuries, it regained prominence in the mid-1900's with the development of the field of psychosomatic medicine, along with the widespread influence of Sigmund Freud's theories of personality.

Psychosomatic medicine embraced the notion that personality and physiology are intertwined. Psychosomatic theorists believed that certain diseases, such as diabetes, asthma, and hypertension, were associated with particular personality characteristics. They suggested that personality influenced the development of specific diseases. Although much of this theorizing has been disproved, these theorists did return the focus to investigating the interactive nature of a person's psychological and physiological makeup.

Psychophysiologists acknowledge the influence of personality characteristics on physiology and vice versa, and they are working to characterize these relationships. Future work will better measure particular personality constructs and will clarify the interaction of gender with personality and physiology. ~~Psychophysiologists also must be concerned with the external validity of the data they obtain in the laboratory. It~~ has not been satisfactorily demonstrated that physiological responses measured in a given individual in the laboratory are at all related to that individual's response in the natural environment. ~~Thus, in order to establish fully the~~ usefulness of laboratory findings, psychophysiologists must also study individuals in their natural environments. ~~Recent technological advances will~~ enable ongoing physiological measurement, which should achieve this goal and further establish the relations among personality, physiology, and behavior.

## SOURCES FOR FURTHER STUDY

Cacioppo, John T., Louis G. Tassinary, and Gary G. Berntson, eds. *Handbook of Psychophysiology.* 2d ed. New York: Cambridge University Press, 2000. A general guidebook, aimed at advanced students and professionals.

Eysenck, Hans J. *The Biological Basis of Personality.* Springfield, Ill.: Charles C Thomas, 1967. This older book provides a thorough, in-depth discussion of Eysenck's theories of the relations between neuroticism, introversion, and extroversion with physiology.

Stern, Robert Morris, William J. Ray, and Karen S. Quigley. *Psychophysiological Recording.* 2d ed. New York: Oxford University Press, 2001. The authors provide an excellent, readable introduction to basic principles of psychophysiology. Part 2, the main body of the text, covers physiology of and recording procedures for the brain, muscles, eyes, respiratory system, gastrointestinal system, cardiovascular system, and skin. Illustrations depicting typical recordings and a glossary of psychophysiological terms are helpful additions.

Surwillo, Walter W. *Psychophysiology for Clinical Psychologists.* Norwood, N.J.: Ablex, 1990. This text provides basic knowledge of psychophysiology and highlights some areas of application. Surwillo also incorporates helpful diagrams and relevant references for research in the area.

Weiten, Wayne, Margaret A. Lloyd, and R. L. Lashley. "Theories of Personality." In *Psychology Applied to Modern Life: Adjustment at the Turn of the Century.* 6th ed. Belmont, Calif.: Wadsworth, 1999. This text, written for undergraduate students, contains a very readable chapter on personality and theories of personality development. Other chapters highlight the dynamics of adjustment, interpersonal factors, developmental transitions, and the impact that personality and styles of coping can have on psychological and physical health.

*Virginia L. Goetsch and Lois Veltum*

SEE ALSO: Emotions; Nervous System; Neuropsychology.

# PERSONALITY THEORY

TYPE OF PSYCHOLOGY: Personality
FIELD OF STUDY: Personality theory

*Personality theories seek to describe and explain the characteristics of thought, feeling, and behavior that differ among individuals and the coherence of these characteristics within a single individual. Personality theories describe approaches to human nature and provide the foundation for psychological therapies.*

KEY CONCEPTS
- attribution theory
- humanistic theory
- personality trait
- psychoanalytic theory
- social learning theory

Psychologists who study personality are interested in explaining both the coherence of an individual's behavior, attitudes, and emotions, and how that individual may change over time. To paraphrase Clyde Kluckhohn, personality theorists seek to describe and explain how each individual is unique, how groups of people meaningfully differ from one another, and how all people share some attributes. In developing answers to these questions, theorists use widely varying definitions of personality that may differ from the way the term "personality" is used in everyday language. Indeed, if there is a single overriding basic issue in personality theory, it is: What is personality?

## PERSONALITY AND ESSENCE

Theorists agree that people have an internal "essence" that determines who they are and that guides their behavior, but the nature of that essence differs from theory to theory. Psychoanalytic theory such as Sigmund Freud's see the essence of personality as arising from conflict among internal psychic processes. For Freud, the conflict is viewed as occurring among the urges for instinctual gratification (called the id), the urges for perfection (the superego), and the demands of reality (the ego).

Humanistic theories such as those of Carl Rogers and Abraham Maslow also see people as often engaged in conflict. For these theorists, however, the conflicts are between an internal self, which is striving for positive expression, and the constraints of a restrictive external social world. In general, the humanists have a much more optimistic outlook on human nature than do psychoanalytic theorists.

Still other theorists are more neutral with respect to human nature. George A. Kelly's cognitive personality theory, for example, views people as scientists, developing and testing hypotheses to understand themselves better and to predict events in their world. Social learning theorists such as Walter Mischel, Albert Bandura, and Julian Rotter see people as developing expectations and behavioral tendencies based on their histories of rewards and punishments and their observations of others.

To some extent, the question of "essence" is also the question of motivation. Psychoanalytic theorists view people as trying to achieve a balance between instinctual urges and the demands of reality. In contrast, humanistic theorists view people as motivated toward personal growth rather than homeostatic balance. Social learning theorists view people as motivated to avoid punishments and obtain rewards.

Related to the question of the "essence" of personality is the notion of whether part, or all, of the personality can be hidden from the individual. Psychoanalytic theorists believe that the driving forces of the personality are in the unconscious and thus are not directly accessible to the person except under exceptional circumstances such as those which arise in therapy. Humanists are much more optimistic about the possibility of people coming to know their inner selves. According to Rogers, parts of the self which were once hidden can, when the individual receives acceptance from others, become expressed and incorporated into self-awareness. Social learning theories do not place much weight on hidden personality dynamics. From the social learning perspective, people are viewed as unable to verbalize easily some of their expectations, but no special unconscious processes are hypothesized.

## PERSONALITY CHANGE

Theories also differ in the degree to which a person's personality is seen as changing over time. Most personality theories address the development of personality in childhood and the possibility for change in adulthood. Psychoanalytic theorists believe that the most basic personality characteristics are established by the age of five or six, although there are some minor further developments in adolescence. While the person may change in adulthood in the course of psychotherapy and become better able to cope with the conflicts and traumas experienced during the early years, major personality transformations are not expected. Again, humanists are more optimistic than psychoanalytic theorists about personality change, although humanists, too, see the childhood years as important. For example, Rogers suggests that during childhood the parents may communicate their approval of some of the child's feelings and their disapproval of others, leaving the child with a distorted self-concept. Yet, from the humanistic point of view, the person's true inner self will constantly strive for expression. Thus, positive personality change is always seen as possible. Social learning theorists also see personality as changeable. Behaviors learned in childhood may later be changed by direct training, by altering the environment, or by revising one's expectations.

A final issue is the relationship between personality and behavior. For social learning theorists, behaviors and related expectations are personality. A person's behaviors are taken as a sample of a full behavioral repertoire which forms who the person is. Both psychoanalytic and humanistic theorists view behavior as a symptom or sign of underlying, internal personality dynamics rather than a sample of the personality itself. According to this viewpoint, a person's behaviors reflect personality only when interpreted in the light of the underlying traits they reveal. Diverse behaviors may thus be related to a single internal characteristic.

## PERSONALITY MEASURES

The study of personality is a scientific discipline, with roots in empirical research; a philosophical discipline, seeking to understand the nature of people; and the foundation for the applied discipline of psychological therapy. While these three aspects of personality often support and enrich one another, there are also tensions as the field accommodates specialists in each of these three areas.

The approach which focuses on personality as a scientific discipline has produced an array of methods to measure personality characteristics. They range from projective tests, such as having people tell stories inspired by ambiguous pictures, to more standardized paper-and-pencil personality tests in which people respond on bipolar numerical or multiple-choice scales to questions about their attitudes or behaviors. Methodologically, personality testing is quite sophisticated; however, people's scores on personality tests often are rather poor predictors of behavior. The poor record of behavioral prediction based on personality traits, coupled with evidence that suggests that behavior does not have the cross-situational consistency that one might expect, has led Walter Mischel and many other personality specialists to question the utility of most traditional personality theories. Social learning approaches, which emphasize the power of the situation in determining a person's behavior, tend to fare better in these analyses.

## PREDICTING BEHAVIOR

Research has found circumstances under which people's behavior can be predicted from knowledge of their underlying personality characteristics. If one classifies personality characteristics and behaviors at a very general level, combining observations and predicting to a group of behaviors, prediction improves. For example, predictions would be more accurate if several measures of a person's conscientiousness were combined, and then used to predict an overall level of conscientious behavior in a variety of situations, than if one measured conscientiousness with a single scale and then attempted to predict behavior in one specific situation. Prediction on the basis of personality traits also improves when the situations in which one seeks to predict behaviors allow for individual variation, as opposed to being highly constrained by social norms. Five basic personality traits often emerge in investigations: extroversion, agreeableness, conscientiousness, emotional stability, and culture (high scores on culture reflect characteristics such as intelligence and refinement). Some researchers view these trait terms as accurately describing consistent personality differences among people, while others view them as reflecting the "eye of the beholder" more than the core of personality.

Ultimately, people's personality traits and situations interact to produce behavior. Situations may often determine behavior, but people choose to place themselves in specific situations that elicit their traits. A child with a predisposition to aggression may provoke others and thus set the stage for the expression of aggression; one who is highly sociable may seek out others in cooperative situations. The relation between personality and behavior is very complex, and it is difficult to describe fully using standard research methods.

Research is highly unlikely to answer philosophical questions concerning human nature; however, considering people from the different points of view offered by various theories can be an enriching experience in itself. For example, a Freudian perspective on former United States president Lyndon Johnson might see his leadership during the Vietnam War as guided by aggressive instincts or even sublimated sexual instincts. On the other hand, a humanist might look at Johnson's presidency and find his decisions to be guided by the need for self-fulfillment, perhaps citing his vision of himself as the leader of the "Great Society" as an example of self-actualization. Social learning theorists would view Johnson's actions as president as determined by the rewards, punishments, and observational learning of his personal learning history, including growing up relatively poor in Texas and accruing power and respect during his years in the U.S. Senate, as well as by the reinforcements and punishments Johnson perceived to be available in the situations in which he found himself during his presidency. In the final analysis, none of these interpretations could be shown to be blatantly false or absolutely true. Historians, biographers, and others might find each to be an enriching viewpoint from which to consider this complex individual.

## THERAPY

Multiple points of view also characterize the therapies derived from theories of personality. Most therapists take an eclectic approach, sampling from the ideas of various theories to tailor their treatment to a specific client. Each therapist, however, also may have her or his own biases, based on a particular theoretical orientation. For example, a client who often feels anxious and seeks help from a psychoanalytic therapist may find that the therapist encourages the client to explore memories of childhood experiences to discover the unconscious roots of the anxiety. Slips of the tongue, dreams, and difficulty remembering or accepting therapeutic interpretations would be viewed as important clues to unconscious processes. The same client seeking treatment from a humanistic therapist would have a different experience. There, the emphasis would be on current experiences, with the therapist providing a warm and supportive atmosphere for the client to explore feelings. A behavioral therapist, from the social learning orientation, would help the client pinpoint situations in which anxiety occurs and teach the client alternative responses to those situations. Again, no one form of therapy is superior for all clients. Successes or failures in therapy depend on the combination of client, therapist, and mode of treatment.

## THEORIES AND EXPERIMENTATION

While people have long speculated on the causes and types of individual differences in personality, the theory of Sigmund Freud was the first and most influential psychological personality theory. All subsequent theories have directly or indirectly addressed the central concerns of motivation, development, and personality organization first proposed by Freud. Psychoanalytic theorists such as Carl Jung and Alfred Adler, while trained by Freud, disagreed with Freud's emphasis on sexual instincts and developed their own theories, emphasizing different motivations. Similarly, Karen Horney, Erich Fromm, and others developed theories placing greater emphasis on the ego and its interaction with society than did Freud's.

Psychoanalytic theory has had somewhat less of an influence in the United States than it did in Europe. Personality psychology in the United States is relatively more research-oriented, practical, and optimistic. In the United States, Gordon Allport developed one of the first trait approaches to personality. The humanistic theories of Carl Rogers and Abraham Maslow, social learning theories of Albert Bandura and Julian Rotter, and cognitive theory of George A. Kelly flourished in the 1950's and 1960's and continue to have their advocates. Modern personality psychologists, however, are much more likely to confine themselves to personality measurement and research than to propose broad theories of personality.

Many have questioned personality's status as a scientific subdiscipline of psychology. In 1968, Walter Mischel's *Personality and Assessment*, arguing that the consistency and behavior-prediction assumptions inherent in all personality theories are unsupported by the evidence, was published. At the same time, attribution theories in social psychology were suggesting that personality traits are largely in the "eye of the beholder" rather than in the person being observed. For example, Edward Jones and Richard Nisbett argued that people are more inclined to see others as possessing personality traits than they are to attribute traits to themselves. The continued existence of personality as a subdiscipline of scientific psychology was debated.

The result has been a refined approach to measurement and personality analysis. Current research on personality does not boldly assert the influence of internal personality characteristics on behavior. There are no new theories purporting to explain all of personality or the nature of all people. Rather, attention is paid to careful assessment of personality and to the complex interactions of persons and situations. For example, research on loneliness has found that people who describe themselves as lonely often lack social skills and avoid interactions with others, thus perpetuating their feelings of loneliness. All personality characteristics, including loneliness, are most meaningfully seen as the product of a complex interrelationship between the person and the environment.

## SOURCES FOR FURTHER STUDY

Hall, Calvin Springer, Gardner Lindzey, and John Campbell. *Theories of Personality.* 4th ed. New York: John Wiley & Sons, 1998. A classic textbook describing personality theories. Personality research is mentioned but not discussed in detail. Includes particularly readable, thorough, and accurate descriptions of psychoanalytic theories. Chapter 1 introduces the topic of personality theories and describes many dimensions upon which theories can be contrasted.

Hampden-Turner, Charles. *Maps of the Mind.* New York: Collier Books, 1982. Presents brief descriptions and pictorial representations (termed "maps") of basic psychological and philosophical concepts. The organization and presentation are a bit idiosyncratic; the summaries are very good and the diagrams helpful in synthesizing complex information. Descriptions and maps relevant to the theories of Sigmund Freud, Carl Jung, Erich Fromm, Rollo May, Hans Eysenck, Carl Rogers, Harry Stack Sullivan, and Erik Erikson are particularly relevant to basic issues in personality theory.

Mischel, Walter. *Introduction to Personality.* 6th ed. Fort Worth, Tex.: Harcourt Brace Jovanovich, 1999. A college-level personality textbook with an emphasis on modern issues and research. Each major orientation to personality—psychodynamic, trait, phenomenological (humanistic), and behavioral—is presented with thorough discussions of measurement and research. The reader may find that this text alone is incomplete in its description of personality theories per se, but it makes an excellent companion reading to Hall, Lindzey, and Campbell's *Theories of Personality* (above). Mischel's approach to social learning theory is presented.

_____. *Personality and Assessment.* 1968. Reprint. Hillsdale, N.J.: Analytic Press, 1996. The text that inspired debate about the utility of traditional personality theories. Readable but detailed; primarily of historical importance.

Pervin, Lawrence A., and Oliver John, eds. *Handbook of Personality: Theory and Research.* 2d ed. New York: Guilford Press, 2001. A compilation of personality theory and research for the sophisticated reader. Chapters by Walter Mischel ("Personality Dispositions Revisited and Revised: A View After Three Decades"), David Magnusson ("Personality Development from an Interactional Perspective"), and Bernard Weiner ("Attribution in Personality Psychology") may be of particular interest.

Storr, Anthony. *Churchill's Black Dog, Kafka's Mice, and Other Phenomena of the Human Mind.* New York: Grove Press, 1988. This fascinating book demonstrates how personality theories can be used to interpret lives. Storr describes the creative process in general and the lives of Winston Churchill, Franz Kafka, and others from his psychological point of view, primarily psychoanalytic in orientation. The perspectives of Sigmund Freud, Carl Jung, and Erik Erikson are featured.

*Susan E. Beers*

SEE ALSO: Analytical Psychology: Carl Jung; Cognitive Social Learning: Walter Mischel; Humanistic Trait Models: Gordon Allport; Psychoanalytic Psychology; Psychoanalytic Psychology and Personality: Sigmund Freud; Social Learning: Albert Bandura.

# PERSONOLOGY
## HENRY A. MURRAY

TYPE OF PSYCHOLOGY: Personality
FIELDS OF STUDY: Humanistic-phenomenological models; personality
theory

*Murray's study of personality, or personology, as he preferred to call it, highlights the uniqueness of the individual and the interaction between individual needs and environmental constraints. His theory precipitated the in-depth study of human needs and provided an instrument for assessing human personality.*

KEY CONCEPTS
- alpha press
- beta press
- need
- need for achievement
- press
- thematic apperception test (TAT)

Henry A. Murray was born into a wealthy family in New York City in 1893. His early life was unremarkable, and unlike numerous other personality theorists, he experienced no major traumas that obviously influenced his theory. He was not trained in psychology (in fact, he greatly disliked psychology classes); rather, he studied biology and later received his Ph.D. in biochemistry from the University of Cambridge. His interest in psychology and personality processes was ignited during a three-week stay with Carl Jung, the eminent Swiss psychoanalyst. This meeting led to a change in career aspirations, whereupon Murray was brought to Harvard University to engage in personality research and establish the Harvard Psychological Clinic. Murray's biomedical training is reflected in his belief that personality processes are dependent on brain functioning. He did not believe that personality actually existed; he believed that descriptions of personality were shorthand methods of describing various aspects of individuals and their behaviors. He thought that personality helped explain and predict an individual's actions, drives, needs, goals, and plans. He stated that his system of personality, "personology," was a tentative theory, as psychologists did not yet know enough to capture completely the essence of each individual.

As opposed to personality theorists who developed their ideas in the clinic, working with emotionally disturbed individuals, Murray believed that the best way to investigate personality was to study normal individuals in their natural environments. While at Harvard, he undertook an intensive study of fifty-one male undergraduates during a six-month period. The undergraduates were examined by a council of twenty-eight specialists of various training and expertise so that the personalities of the students might be fully understood.

From these studies, Murray developed his ideas about human needs. He believed that these needs helped individuals focus their attention on certain events and guided their behaviors to meet those needs. There are primary needs that originate from internal bodily processes (for example, air, water, food, and sex) and secondary needs that are concerned with mental and emotional satisfaction (for example, achievement, dominance, understanding, and affiliation). He proposed a hierarchy of needs, a concept later elaborated on by Abraham Maslow, in which the most basic needs, such as that for food, must be met before others can be addressed. Murray originally proposed a list of twenty basic human needs, although this list was later revised and expanded by his students and followers.

## "PRESS" CONCEPT

Although Murray's elaboration and description of human needs was one of his major contributions to psychology, his focus on the situational context for behavior foreshadowed psychology's future emphasis on environmental events. He proposed the concept of "press," or forces provided by situations or events in the environment. These forces may help or hinder individuals in reaching their goals. For example, a student may have a need for achievement that would result in her attending college and receiving a degree. Environmental conditions such as poverty, however, may hinder her progress or pressure her away from these goals and necessitate that she take a job to support her family. In this situation, Murray also distinguished between "alpha press," or actual pressure resulting from environmental situations, and "beta press," or subjective pressure that results from individual interpretation of the events. In the example of going to college given above, alpha press might be the college board scores or the money necessary to go to certain colleges. These are real, and they involve little interpretation. Beta press might be the interpretation that if the student does not get into a certain college, she will be viewed as an embarrassment and a failure. This type of pressure comes from an internal evaluation of environmental events.

## USE OF THE TAT

A final major contribution of Murray's personology theory comes from the device he used to determine individual needs and more generally measure personality. Along with Christiana Morgan, Murray developed the Thematic Apperception Test (TAT), which continues to be a widely used instrument for assessing human personality. The TAT consists of thirty ambiguous black-and-white pictures for which an individual is instructed to make up a story. The test subject is asked to tell what led up to the event in the picture, what is happening in the picture, including how the characters are thinking and feeling, and what will happen to the characters in the future. Murray's idea was that test subjects will project their needs into the picture, much as individuals who are on a diet will notice food in most situations that they encounter. It is similar to the children's game of identifying the shapes of clouds. Children may identify clouds with children's themes of dragons, monsters, or dinosaurs. Adolescents may view these same clouds as other boys and girls, cars, or sports figures. Murray hypothesized that certain themes would emerge from individuals' responses to the figures and that themes and expectations for the future would become evident. Mental health professionals continue to use the TAT for this purpose.

## ACHIEVEMENT NEED

Henry A. Murray's theoretical focus was to catalog all possible human needs. This led to a wide range of understanding; however, it was left to later researchers to add depth to the understanding of needs. One of the best researched of the secondary needs is the need for achievement. This need of individuals to overcome obstacles and accomplish what often are very difficult tasks has been investigated in detail by David McClelland and his colleague John Atkinson. They developed a system for scoring individuals' responses to TAT cards to abstract achievement-oriented themes. They observed that individuals who had a high need for achievement completed more tasks under competitive conditions, were more productive in their jobs, and tended to get better grades. They used this information and measuring system to develop a training program for industry that has been shown to increase employees' need for achievement and job productivity. Their system was found to be working even two years after the program was begun. Interesting questions remain, however; for example, at what level does the need for achievement become unproductive? At some point it will lead to unrealistic expectations, unnecessary stress, and related health problems.

One of the fascinating things about the McClelland and Atkinson method of assessing an individual's need for achievement is that it is not restricted to measuring responses from TAT cards. Their scoring system can be used with any written material; therefore, it can be adapted to a vast amount of literary, historical, and biographical information. McClelland conjectured that he could predict the economic growth and decline of a country from the number of achievement themes evident in its children's stories. He looked at the economic conditions of twenty-three nations from 1929 to 1950 and scored their children's stories from the prior decade (1920-1929). While it is apparent that children's stories are not the only factor related to economic well-being, McClelland did discover that those countries with a higher number of achievement themes in the children's stories experienced the most economic growth.

## GENDER DIFFERENCES IN ACHIEVEMENT

Another example of the importance of Murray's pioneering work on the need for achievement comes from research on how this need is demonstrated differently by men and women. It had been evident for many years that the expression of achievement was more acceptable for men than for women. It has only been in recent years that the issues surrounding the achievement of women have been investigated. It is clear that these issues, in general, have been experienced much differently by women from the way they have been experienced by men. The paths for understanding and expressing ideas of achievement for men and women clearly differ very early in life. A series of studies supports the idea that women with a high need for achievement come from relatively stressful and difficult home lives, whereas men with a similar level of achievement strivings come from supportive, nonstressful homes. Additionally, girls tend to evidence their needs for achievement because of a desire for adult approval, while boys do not demonstrate this motivation.

One of the more interesting, as well as distressing, findings regarding sex differences in the need for achievement comes from the research of Matina Horner. She found that women experience considerable conflict and distress when faced with their need to achieve, whereas men do not experience a similar state. She proposed that the "smart girl" faced the prospect of considerable loss of social status and peer rejection as a result of her strivings to achieve. This may result in the behavior of acting "dumb" in order to prosper socially. Horner elaborated on Sigmund Freud's original idea that women actually may fear success because of its social consequences.

In a famous study by Horner, she had men and women write a story after being given an opening line. The women were to write a story about a woman who found herself at the top of her medical school class after the first semester. The men had the same story, except that it was a man who was at the top of the class. Far more women wrote stories of the unappealing and sometimes tragic consequences for the smart woman in class. They wrote about possible rejections and losses of friends and indicated that she would have a poorer chance of getting married. Many of the women came up with situations related to removing the student from the conflict situation, such as dropping out of medical school or settling for becoming a nurse. Finally, some of the students even indicated that she might receive bodily harm as a result of her stellar performance.

The conflicting messages of society regarding achievement for women are clearly shown by this study. It is apparent that women face considerable struggles in their attempts to compete and achieve equally with men. The factors that will alleviate this internal distress and aid women in the full expression of their abilities await further investigation. It was Murray's pioneering study of human needs that laid the groundwork for these types of investigation, which have the potential to inspire long-overdue social changes.

## THEORETICAL CONTRIBUTIONS

Murray's theory of personology was a unique contribution to the early years of personality theorizing. His system differed from those before it (for example, Freud's psychoanalytic theory) in that it was not developed in a clinic as a result of working with clients. Murray studied normal individuals in great detail and gained knowledge from experts in a number of disciplines. This gave personality theory a certain degree of academic respectability it had not had previously acquired. Murray was also a highly influential teacher, with many students who made significant contributions to psychology.

Murray's description of "needs" was a major contribution to the psychological study of motivation. His research spurred many investigations of individual human needs. Additionally, his complementary emphasis on environmental events (that is, "press") was later to become a major shift in American psychology. The behavioral school of psychology, with its leaders John B. Watson and B. F. Skinner, was to become the dominant force for many years. Their focus on the manipulation of environmental events (for example, rewards and punishments) was to have a major influence on education, therapy, and childrearing. The subjective interpretation of environmental events (that is, "beta press") also was a precursor to a major shift in theory. The cognitive school of psychology now focuses on these mental rearrangements of events and makes predictions based on individuals' expectations and fears. Murray's emphasis on the fact that the idiosyncratic perception of an event is not always the same as what actually happened is the foundation for this approach.

Finally, Murray's development of the TAT (with Christiana Morgan) was an early and influential contribution to the area of personality assessment. It and similar tests, such as the Rorschach inkblot test and the incomplete sentences blank, are frequently used for gathering personality information in the clinic. Even the weaknesses of the TAT (for example, different investigators may score it very differently) led to the development of more objective personality tests with standardized questions and scoring. Murray's influence, both in the classroom and in the clinic, was substantial.

## SOURCES FOR FURTHER STUDY

Anderson, James W. "Henry A. Murray's Early Career: A Psychobiographical Exploration." *Journal of Personality* 56, no. 1 (1988): 139-171. An interesting presentation of the factors that led Henry Murray to become a psychologist and of how his experiences interacted with his theory. An excellent example of how one's life cannot be extricated from one's beliefs about human nature.

Boring, Edwin G., and Gardner Lindzey, eds. *A History of Psychology in Autobiography.* Vol. 5. New York: Appleton-Century-Crofts, 1967. In an autobiographical essay in volume 5 of this survey, Henry Murray presents a detailed view of his concepts and the influence of his work.

Hall, Calvin Springer, Gardner Lindzey, and John Campbell. *Theories of Personality.* 4th ed. New York: John Wiley & Sons, 1998. A definitive reference for information on most personality theorists. A thorough book that gives a detailed explanation of most of Murray's concepts. Not recommended for the casual reader.

Schultz, Duane P. *Theories of Personality.* 5th ed. Belmont, Calif.: Brooks/Cole, 1994. A review of the major aspects of Henry Murray's theory in an easy-to-read format. Provides substantial biographical information about Murray and how this influenced his theory.

Smith, M. B., and J. W. Anderson. "Henry A. Murray (1893-1988)." *American Psychologist* 44 (1989): 1153-1154. This obituary is a personal account of Murray's career and his impact on his students as well as on psychology. Covers not only the facts of Murray's work but also his perceptions of his work.

*Brett L. Beck*

SEE ALSO: Aggression; Psychoanalytic Psychology.

# PHOBIAS

TYPE OF PSYCHOLOGY: Psychopathology
FIELD OF STUDY: Anxiety disorders

*Phobias are exaggerated, unjustified fears of everyday objects or situations, such as fear of certain types of animals or fears of doing things in front of other people. Though many people experience irrational fears or phobias, few seek treatment; as a result, they suffer emotional pain and may find their lives limited by their phobias.*

KEY CONCEPTS
- conditioned response (CR)
- conditioned stimulus (CS)
- instrumental conditioning
- Pavlovian conditioning
- unconditioned response (UR)
- unconditioned stimulus (US)

Phobias are a type of anxiety disorder characterized by a persistent, exaggerated, irrational fear of certain objects or situations and by efforts to avoid the object or situation. In many cases, the distress and the avoidance efforts significantly interfere with an individual's daily life. Phobias are common in the general population; approximately one person in ten suffers from mild phobias, and severe, disabling phobias are found in one person in five hundred.

The three major types of phobias are agoraphobia (a fear of situations in which escape is perceived to be difficult or assistance unavailable), social phobias, and specific (or "simple") phobias. In social phobias, being observed by others may elicit anxiety and the desire to avoid such situations. The person fears doing something which will lead to embarrassment or humiliation, such as being unable to speak or showing nervousness through trembling hands or other signs. Persons with specific phobias avoid a certain type of object or situation or suffer extreme anxiety when in the presence of these objects or situations. Some examples of common specific phobias are acrophobia, fear of heights; arachnophobia, fear of spiders; claustrophobia, fear of being in small, enclosed spaces; pathophobia, fear of diseases and germs; and xenophobia, fear of strangers.

In the presence of the feared object or situation, the severely phobic person's experience and reaction differ dramatically from the average person's. Physiologically, changes in the body cause an increase in heart rate and blood pressure, tensing of muscles, and feelings of fear. In many cases, a panic state develops, characterized by muscular trembling and shaking, rapid, shallow breathing, and feelings of unbearable anxiety and dizziness. Behaviorally, the person will stop or redirect whatever activity in which he or she is engaged, then try to escape from or avoid the phobic object or situation. Cognitively, a phobic person at a distance from the object or situation can recognize it as posing little actual danger; but upon approaching it, fear rises, and the estimation of risk increases.

## THEORETICAL EXPLANATIONS

The many theories which attempt to explain how phobias develop can be grouped under three general headings: those which stress unconscious emotional conflicts, those which explain phobias based on the principles of learning, and those which consider biological factors. For Sigmund Freud, phobias represented the external manifestation of unconscious internal emotional conflicts which had their origin in early childhood. These conflicts typically involved the inhibition of primitive sexual feelings.

Learning-theory explanations of phobias are based on Pavlovian conditioning, instrumental conditioning, and social learning theory. According to a Pavlovian conditioning model, phobias result when a neutral stimulus—a dog, for example—is paired with an unconditioned stimulus (US), for example, a painful bite to the leg. After this event, the sight of the dog has become a conditioned stimulus (CS) which elicits a conditioned response (CR), fear; thus, a dog phobia has been learned. Instrumental conditioning (the modification of behavior as a result of its consequences) has been combined with Pavlovian conditioning in the two-factor model of phobias. After the establishment of the phobia by Pavlovian conditioning, as above, a person will attempt to escape from or avoid the phobic object or situation whenever it is encountered. When this is successful, the fear subsides. The reduction in fear is a desirable consequence which increases the likelihood of escape/avoidance behavior in the future (that is, the escape/avoidance behavior is reinforced). The two-factor model thus accounts for both the development and maintenance of phobias. Social learning theory suggests that human learning is based primarily on the observation and imitation of others; thus, fears and phobias would be acquired by observing others who show fearful behavior toward certain objects or situations. This learning occurs primarily during childhood, when children learn many behaviors and attitudes by modeling those of others.

Two theories suggest that inherited biological factors contribute to the development of phobias. The preparedness theory suggests that those stimuli which are most easily conditioned are objects or situations which may have posed a particular threat to humans' early ancestors, such as spiders, heights, small spaces, thunder, and strangers. Thus, people are genetically prepared to acquire fear of them quickly. Similarly, people vary in susceptibility to phobias, and this is also thought to be based at least partly on an inherited predisposition. A phobia-prone person may be physiologically highly arousable; thus, many more events would reach a threshold of fear necessary for conditioning.

Stressful life situations, including extreme conflict or frustration, may also predispose a person to develop a phobia or exacerbate an existing phobia. Further, a sense of powerlessness or lack of control over one's situation

## DSM-IV-TR CRITERIA FOR PHOBIAS

### SPECIFIC PHOBIA (DSM CODE 300.29)

Marked and persistent fear that is excessive or unreasonable and cued by presence or anticipation of specific object or situation (flying, heights, animals, receiving an injection, seeing blood)

Exposure to phobic stimulus almost invariably provokes immediate anxiety response, which may take the form of situationally bound or situationally predisposed panic attack; in children, anxiety may be expressed by crying, tantrums, freezing, or clinging

Person recognizes fear as excessive or unreasonable; in children, this feature may be absent

Phobic situation(s) avoided or endured with intense anxiety or distress

Avoidance, anxious anticipation, or distress in feared situation(s) interferes significantly with normal routines, occupational (or academic) functioning, or social activities or relationships, or marked distress about phobia present

In individuals under age eighteen, duration of at least six months

Anxiety, panic attacks, or phobic avoidance associated with specific object or situation not better accounted for by another mental disorder, such as Obsessive-Compulsive Disorder, Post-traumatic Stress Disorder, Separation Anxiety Disorder, Social Phobia, Panic Disorder with Agoraphobia, or Agoraphobia Without History of Panic Disorder

Specify:

- Animal Type
- Natural Environment Type (such as heights, storms, water)
- Blood-Injection-Injury Type
- Situational Type (such as airplanes, elevators, enclosed places)
- Other Type (such as phobic avoidance of situations that may lead to choking, vomiting, or contracting an illness; in children, avoidance of loud sounds or costumed characters)

may increase susceptibility; this may partly explain why phobias are more common in women than in men, as these feelings are reported more often by women than by men. Once initiated, phobias tend to persist and even worsen over time, and the fear may spread to other, similar objects or situations. Even phobias which have been successfully treated may recur if the person is exposed to the original US, or even to another US which produces extreme anxiety. Thus, many factors—unconscious, learned, and biological—may be involved in the onset and maintenance of phobias. As every person is unique in terms of biology and life experience, each phobia is also unique and represents a particular interaction of the factors above and possibly other, unknown factors.

**SOCIAL PHOBIA (DSM CODE 300.23)**

Marked and persistent fear of one or more social or performance situations involving exposure to unfamiliar people or to possible scrutiny by others; individual fears that he or she will act in a way (or show anxiety symptoms) that will be humiliating or embarrassing

In children, evidence requires the capacity for age-appropriate social relationships with familiar people and anxiety must occur in peer settings, not just in interactions with adults

Exposure to feared social situation almost invariably provokes anxiety, which may take the form of situationally bound or situationally predisposed panic attack; in children, anxiety may be expressed by crying, tantrums, freezing, or shrinking from social situations with unfamiliar people

Person recognizes fear as excessive or unreasonable; in children, this feature may be absent

Feared social or performance situations avoided or endured with intense anxiety or distress

Avoidance, anxious anticipation, or distress in feared social or performance situation(s) interferes significantly with normal routines, occupational (academic) functioning, or social activities or relationships, or marked distress about phobia present

In individuals under age eighteen, duration of at least six months

Fear or avoidance not due to direct physiological effects of a substance or general medical condition

Not better accounted for by another mental disorder such as Panic Disorder with or Without Agoraphobia, Separation Anxiety Disorder, Body Dysmorphic Disorder, a Pervasive Developmental Disorder, or Schizoid Personality Disorder

If general medical condition or another mental disorder present, fear unrelated to it

Specify if Generalized (fears include most social situations)

## CASE STUDIES AND THERAPY TECHNIQUES

The following two case studies of phobias illustrate their onset, development, and the various treatment approaches typically used. These studies are fictionalized composites of the experiences of actual clients.

Ellen P. entered an anxiety disorders clinic requesting large amounts of tranquilizers. She revealed that she wanted them to enable her to fly on airplanes; if she could not fly, she would probably lose her job as a sales representative. Ellen described an eight-year history of a fear of flying, during which she had simply avoided all airplane flights and had driven or taken a train to distant sales appointments. She would sometimes drive through the night, keep her appointments during the day, then again drive through the night back to the home office. As these trips occurred more often, she became increasingly exhausted, and her work performance began to decline noticeably.

A review of major childhood and adolescent experiences revealed only that Ellen was a chronic worrier. She also reported flying comfortably on many occasions prior to the onset of her phobia but remembered her last flight in vivid detail. She was flying to meet her husband for a honeymoon cruise, but the plane was far behind schedule because of poor weather. She began to worry that she would miss the boat and that her honeymoon, and possibly her marriage, would be ruined. The plane then encountered some minor turbulence, and brief images of a crash raced through Ellen's mind. She rapidly became increasingly anxious, tense, and uncomfortable. She grasped her seat cushion; her heart seemed to be pounding in her throat; she felt dizzy and was beginning to perspire. Hoping no one would notice her distress, she closed her eyes, pretending to sleep for the remainder of the flight. After returning from the cruise, she convinced her husband to cancel their plane reservations and thus began her eight years of avoiding flying.

Ellen's psychologist began exposure therapy for her phobia. First she was trained to relax deeply. Then she was gradually exposed to her feared stimuli, progressing from visiting an airport to sitting on a taxiing plane to weekly flights of increasing length in a small plane. After ten weeks of therapy and practice at home and the airport, Ellen was able to fly on a commercial airliner. Two years after the conclusion of therapy, Ellen met her psychologist by chance and informed her that she now had her own pilot's license.

In the second case, Steve R. was a high school junior who was referred by his father because of his refusal to attend school. Steve was described as a loner who avoided other people and suffered fears of storms, cats, and now, apparently, school. He was of above-average intelligence and was pressured by his father to excel academically and attend a prestigious college. Steve's mother was described as being shy, like Steve. Steve was her only child, and she doted on him, claiming she knew what it felt like to be in his situation.

When interviewed, Steve sat rigidly in his chair, spoke in clipped sentences, and offered answers only to direct questions. Questioning revealed that Steve's refusal to attend school was based on a fear of ridicule by his classmates. He would not eat or do any written work in front of them for fear he was being watched and would do something clumsy, thus embarrassing himself. He never volunteered answers to teachers' questions, but in one class, the teacher had begun to call on Steve regularly for the correct answer whenever other students had missed the question. Steve would sit in a near-panic state, fearing he would be called on. After two weeks of this, he refused to return to school.

Steve was diagnosed as having a severe social phobia. His therapy included a contract with his teachers in which it was agreed that he would not be called upon in class until therapy had made it possible for him to answer with only moderate anxiety. In return, he was expected to attend all his classes. To help make this transition, a psychiatrist prescribed an antianxiety drug to help reduce the panic symptoms. A psychologist began relaxation training for use in exposure therapy, which would include Steve volunteering answers in class and seeking social interactions with his peers. Steve finished high school, though he left the state university at the end of his first semester because of a worsening of his phobias. His therapy was resumed, and he graduated from a local community college, though his phobias continued to recur during stressful periods in his life.

These cases illustrate many of the concepts related to the study of phobias. In both cases, it is possible that a high emotional reactivity predisposed the person to a phobia. In Ellen's case, the onset of the phobia was sudden and appeared to be the result of Pavlovian conditioning, whereas in Steve's case, the phobia likely developed over time and involved social learning: modeling of his mother's behavior. Steve's phobia may also have been inadvertently reinforced by his mother's attention; thus, instrumental conditioning may have been involved as well. Ellen's phobia could be seen to involve a sense of lack of control, combined with a possibly inherited predisposition to fear enclosed spaces. Steve's phobia illustrated both a spreading of the phobia and recurrence of the phobia under stress.

## HISTORICAL VARIATIONS IN PERSPECTIVES

As comprehensive psychological theories of human behavior began to emerge in the early 1900's, each was faced with the challenge of explaining the distinct symptoms, but apparently irrational nature, of phobias. For example, in 1909, Sigmund Freud published his account of the case of "Little Hans," a young boy with a horse phobia. Freud hypothesized that Hans had an unconscious fear of his father which was transferred to a more appropriate object: the horse. Freud's treatment of phobias involved analyzing the unconscious conflicts (through psychoanalysis) and giving patients insight into the "true" nature of their fears.

An alternative explanation of phobias based on the principles of Pavlovian conditioning was proposed by John B. Watson and Rosalie Rayner in 1920. They conditioned a fear of a white rat in an infant nicknamed "Little Albert" by pairing presentation of the rat with a frightening noise (an unconditioned stimulus). After a few such trials, simply presenting the rat (now a conditioned stimulus) produced fear and crying (the conditioned response).

## EXPERIMENTAL MODELS

As B. F. Skinner's laboratory discoveries of the principles of instrumental conditioning began to be applied to humans in the 1940's and 1950's, experimental models of phobias in animals were developed. In the 1950's, Joseph Wolpe created phobia-like responses in cats by shocking them in experimental cages. He was later able to decrease their fear by feeding them in the cages where they had previously been shocked. Based on this counterconditioning model, Wolpe developed the therapy procedure of systematic desensitization, which paired mental images of the feared stimulus with bodily relaxation.

Social learning theory as advanced by Albert Bandura in the 1960's was also applied to phobias. Bandura conducted experiments showing that someone might develop a phobia by observing another person behaving fearfully. It was later demonstrated that some phobias could be treated by having the patient observe and imitate a nonfearful model. Cognitive approaches to phobias were also developed in the 1970's and 1980's by therapists such as Albert Ellis and Aaron T. Beck. These theories focus on the role of disturbing thoughts in creating bodily arousal and associated fear. Therapy then consists of altering these thought patterns.

### APPLICATIONS TO PSYCHOLOGY

Phobias can thus be seen as providing a testing ground for the major theories of psychology. Whether the theorist adopts a psychodynamic, learning/behavioral, or cognitive perspective, some account of the development and treatment of phobias must be made. No one theory has been shown to be completely adequate, so research continues in each area. The study of phobias also illustrates the importance to psychology of animal research in helping psychologists to understand and treat human problems. For example, Susan Mineka has used monkeys to demonstrate the relative importance of social learning versus biology in the development of phobias. Future research will also likely consider the interactions among the various models of phobias and the conditions that might predict which models would be most effective in explaining and treating specific cases of phobias. As the models mature and are integrated into a comprehensive theory of phobias, this knowledge can then be applied to the prevention of phobias.

### SOURCES FOR FURTHER STUDY

Beck, Aaron T., and Gary Emery. *Anxiety Disorders and Phobias: A Cognitive Perspective.* Reprint. New York: Basic Books, 1990. Though cognitive explanations and treatments for phobias are stressed, this book considers other perspectives as well, and it could serve as an introduction to the topic for the interested high school or college student.

Bourne, Edmund. *The Anxiety and Phobia Workbook.* 3d ed. Oakland, Calif.: New Harbinger, 2000. An excellent self-help book for those who suffer from an anxiety disorder. Also an accessible introduction to the causes and treatments of phobias for high school and college students. Contains self-diagnostic and therapy exercises as well as other resources for the phobia sufferer.

Gold, Mark S. *The Good News About Panic, Anxiety, and Phobias.* New York: Random House, 1989. For a general audience. Outlines many biological factors which may be associated with phobias. Presents a one-sided approach, heavily promoting a biopsychiatric view of phobias and their treatment.

Marks, Issac Meyer. *Fears, Phobias, and Rituals.* New York: Oxford University Press, 1987. With more than five hundred pages and a bibliography with more than two thousand references, this text provides comprehensive coverage of all aspects of phobias. Written for the professional and researcher but accessible to college students who are interested in pursuing some aspect of phobias in detail.

Mineka, Susan. "Animal Models of Anxiety-Based Disorders: Their Usefulness and Limitations." In *Anxiety and the Anxiety Disorders,* edited by A. Hussain Tuma and Jack Maser. Hillsdale, N.J.: Lawrence Erlbaum, 1985. The phobia portion of this chapter reviews the major experiments done with animals which demonstrate the many similarities between human phobias and experimental phobias in animals. Clearly illustrates the relevance of animal research to human behavior. Difficult yet indispensable for a thorough understanding of phobias.

Wilson, R. Reid. *Breaking the Panic Cycle: Self-Help for People with Phobias.* Rockville, Md.: Anxiety Disorders Association of America, 1987. A publication of a nonprofit organization which is dedicated to disseminating information and providing help to phobia sufferers. The ADAA also publishes the *National Treatment Directory,* which lists treatment programs throughout the country.

*David S. McDougal*

SEE ALSO: Anxiety Disorders; Conditioning; Learning; Nervous System; Pavlovian Conditioning; Reflexes.

# PSYCHOANALYSIS

DATE: The 1880's forward

TYPE OF PSYCHOLOGY: Developmental psychology; psychological methodologies; psychotherapy

FIELDS OF STUDY: Classic analytic themes and issues; general constructs and issues; humanistic-phenomenological models; humanistic therapies; models of abnormality; motivation theory; personality theory; psychodynamic and neoanalytic models; psychodynamic therapies; thought

*Psychoanalysis is a form of intensive psychotherapy to treat emotional suffering, based on the concept that people are often unaware of what determines their emotions and behavior. By talking freely, while in an intensive relationship with the psychoanalyst, a person is able to overcome worries that may have limited his or her choices in life. Psychoanalysis is also a comprehensive theory of the mind and a method for understanding everyday behavior.*

KEY CONCEPTS

- anxiety
- certification
- countertransference
- depression
- free association
- inhibitions
- psychoanalyst
- psychoanalytic institutes
- psychoanalytic psychotherapy
- psychotherapy
- symptoms
- transference
- unconscious

Psychoanalysis began as a method for treating emotional suffering. Sigmund Freud (1856-1939), the founder of psychoanalysis, made many discoveries by studying patients with symptoms such as excessive anxiety (fear that is not realistic) or paralysis for which no physical cause could be found. He became the first psychoanalyst (often called analyst) when he developed the method of free association, in which he encouraged his patients to say whatever came to mind about their symptoms and their lives. He found that by talking in this way, his patients discovered feelings and thoughts they had not known they had. When they became aware of these unconscious thoughts and feelings, their symptoms lessened or disappeared.

Psychoanalysis as a form of psychotherapy continues to be an effective method for treating certain forms of emotional suffering, such as anxieties and inhibitions (inner constraints) that interfere with success in school, work, or relationships. It is based on the understanding that each individual is unique, that the past shapes the present, and that factors outside people's awareness influence their thoughts, feelings, and actions. As a comprehensive treatment, it has the potential to change many areas of a person's functioning. Although modern psychoanalysis is different in many ways from what was practiced in Freud's era, talking and listening remain important. Psychoanalytic psychotherapy is a modified form of psychoanalysis, usually with less frequent meetings and more modest goals.

From the beginning, psychoanalysis was more than just a treatment. It was, and continues to be, a method for investigating the mind and a theory to explain both everyday adult behavior and child development. Many of Freud's insights, which seemed so revolutionary at the beginning of the twentieth century, are now widely accepted by various schools of psychological thought and form the basis for several theories of psychological motivation, most theories of child development, and all forms of psychodynamic psychotherapy. Some of Freud's ideas, such as his theories about women, turned out to be wrong and were revised by other psychoanalysts during the 1970's and 1980's. Other ideas, such as those about the nature of dreams, although rejected by some scientists during the 1980's and 1990's, were revisited by other scientists by the beginning of the twenty-first century. Psychoanalytic ideas and concepts are used in communities to solve problems such as bullying in schools and can be applied in many other fields of study.

In the early years of psychoanalysis, Freud trained most psychoanalysts. Later, different schools of psychoanalytic thought branched out from this original source. Groups of psychoanalysts joined together in organizations, and each organization developed its own standards for training psychoanalysts. There were no nationally accepted standards for psychoanalytic training in the United States until the beginning of the twenty-first century, when several of these groups joined together to establish an Accreditation Council of Psychoanalytic Education. This council agreed to core standards for psychoanalytic institutes (schools that train psychoanalysts). Psychoanalytic psychotherapy, while practiced by trained psychoanalysts, is also practiced by psychotherapists, who are not trained as psychoanalysts.

## PSYCHOANALYTIC TREATMENT

Psychoanalysis is a method for helping people with symptoms that result from emotional conflict. Common symptoms in the modern era include anxiety (fear that is not realistic), depression (excessive sadness that is not due to a current loss), frequent unhealthy choices in relationships, and trouble getting along well with peers or family members. For example, some people may feel continuously insecure and worried about doing well in school or work despite getting good grades or reviews. Other people may be attracted to sexual and emotional partners who treat them poorly. Others may experience loneliness and isolation because of fears about close relationships. Others may sabotage their success by always changing direction before reaching their goals. Children may have tantrums beyond the age when these are normal or be afraid of going to sleep every night or feel unhappy with their maleness or femaleness.

The same symptom can have several different causes, an etiology Freud termed overdetermination. For example, depression may be caused by inner emotional constraints that prevent success, by biological vulnerability, or by upsetting events (such as the death of a loved one), or it may result from a combination of these. Therefore, most psychoanalysts believe in meeting with a person several times before deciding upon the best treatment. Psychoanalysis is not for everyone who has a symptom. Sometimes psychoanalysis is not needed because the problems can be easily helped using other, less intensive forms of therapy. Sometimes biological problems or early childhood experiences leave a person too vulnerable to undertake the hard work of psychoanalysis. When psychoanalysis is not necessary, or not the best treatment for a particular person, a psychoanalyst may recommend psychoanalytic psychotherapy, a treatment that is based on the same principles as psychoanalysis but with less ambitious goals and, usually, less frequent sessions.

Psychoanalysis can treat specific emotional disorders, as described in the *Diagnostic and Statistical Manual of Mental Disorders: DSM-IV-TR* (rev. 4th ed., 2000) and can also help with multiple sets of problematic symptoms, behaviors, and personality traits (such as being too perfectionistic or rigid). Because psychoanalysis affects the whole person rather than just treating symptoms, it has the potential to promote personal growth and development. For adults, this can mean better relationships or marriages, jobs that feel more satisfying, or the ability to enjoy free time when this was difficult before. Children may do better in school after fears about competition and success diminish, or they may have more friends and get along better with parents after they begin to feel better about themselves.

Because psychoanalysis is a very individual treatment, the best way to determine whether it would be beneficial for an individual is through consulting an experienced psychoanalyst. In general, people who benefit from psychoanalysis have some emotional sturdiness. They tend to be capable of understanding themselves and learning how to help themselves. Usually, they have had important accomplishments in one or more areas of their life before seeking psychoanalytic treatment. Often, they have tried other forms of treatment that may have been helpful but have not been sufficient to deal with all their difficulties. Sometimes they are people who work with others (therapists, rabbis, teachers) whose emotions have been interfering with their ability to do their jobs as well as possible. Psychoanalysts understand such problems in the context of each individual's strengths, vulnerabilities, and life situation.

## METHOD OF TREATMENT IN PSYCHOANALYSIS

A person who goes to a psychoanalyst for consultation usually meets with the analyst at least three times face-to-face before the analyst recommends psychoanalysis. Sometimes the patient and analyst meet for several weeks, months, or years in psychoanalytic psychotherapy; they decide upon psychoanalysis if they identify problems that are unlikely to be solved by less intensive treatment.

Once they begin psychoanalysis, the analyst and patient usually meet four or five times per week for fifty-minute sessions, as this creates the intensive personal relationship that plays an important role in the therapeutic process. The frequent sessions do not mean that the patient is very sick; they are necessary to help the patient reach deeper levels of awareness. (People with the severest forms of mental illness, such as schizophrenia, are not usually treated with psychoanalysis.) Often the adult patient lies on a couch, as this may make it easier to speak freely. The couch is not essential, and some patients feel more comfortable sitting up.

By working together to diminish obstacles to free expression in the treatment sessions, the analyst and patient come to understand the patient's worries and learn how the patient's mind works. The patient learns about thoughts and feelings he or she has kept out of awareness or isolated from one another. Through the intensity that comes from frequent meetings with the analyst, the patient often experiences the analyst as if the analyst were a parent or other important person from the past. This is called transference. Eventually, the patient has a chance to see these feelings from a more mature point of view. Although the patient may experience intense emotions within the analytic sessions, the anxieties and behaviors that brought him or her to treatment gradually diminish and feel more under control. The patient feels freer and less restricted by worries and patterns that belong to the past.

For example, a patient may be very fearful of angry feelings and avoid telling the analyst about them, expecting punishment or rejection. As a result, the patient may turn the anger on himself or herself in a form of self-sabotage. Often this is the way the patient dealt with angry feelings toward significant people while growing up. Over time, as the patient and analyst understand this behavior, the patient feels freer to express angry feelings directly and eventually feels less need to sabotage or self-punish.

Gradually, in the course of the intensive analytic relationship, the patient learns more about his or her maladaptive ways of dealing with distressing thoughts and feelings that have developed during childhood. By understanding them in adulthood or (for a child) at a later age, the patient gains a different perspective and is able to react in a more adaptive way. Rigid personality traits that had been used to keep the childhood feelings at a distance are no longer necessary, and the patient is able to react to people and situations in a more flexible way.

During the course of the treatment, the analyst will often have strong feelings toward the patient, called countertransference. Well-trained analysts are required to undergo psychoanalysis themselves before treating patients. In their own analysis, they learn how to cope with their countertransference feelings in ways that will not hurt the patient. For example, they learn not to take the patient's expressions of anger personally but to help the patient express the emotion more fully and understand where it originates.

Children and adolescents can be treated with psychoanalysis or psychoanalytic psychotherapy by using methods suitable for their ages. Most children play with toys, draw, or explore the room, in addition to talking, during their sessions with the analyst, and these activities provide ways to explore inner thoughts and feelings. The analyst meets with the parents before the treatment starts and continues to do so regularly during the course of the child's therapy or analysis. Adolescents usually sit face-to-face or draw or write about their feelings and worries. Occasionally, older adolescents want to lie on the couch. Adolescents often prefer that the analyst not meet with the parents on a regular basis. Instead, the analyst and adolescent usually develop some way to keep the parents informed about what they might need to know about the treatment.

## PSYCHOANALYTIC PSYCHOTHERAPY

Psychoanalytic psychotherapy is more varied than psychoanalysis. It may be very intensive, or it may be focused on a specific problem, such as a recent loss or trouble deciding about a job. In psychoanalytic psychotherapy, the patient and therapist usually sit face-to-face and approach the patient's problems, whatever they are, in a more interactive way. Most often, patient and therapist meet twice per week in fifty-minute sessions. Once per week is also common but not considered to be as helpful. More frequent meetings (three to five times per week) may be necessary if the patient is in crisis or has chronic problems that are not treatable with psychoanalysis.

Although psychoanalysts are well trained to practice psychoanalytic psychotherapy, this treatment is also practiced by psychotherapists who are not psychoanalysts. Some of these therapists have taken courses at psychoanalytic institutes.

## MEDICATION AND CONFIDENTIALITY ISSUES

In the early days of psychoanalysis, analysts believed that treatment with medication would interfere with psychoanalysis. Most modern psychoanalysts believe that, although medicine can sometimes interfere, there are times when it can be used in a helpful way in combination with psychoanalytic psychotherapy or even with psychoanalysis.

"Confidentiality" is the term used to describe the privacy necessary for individuals to be able to speak freely about all their thoughts and feelings. Responsible psychoanalysts and psychotherapists agree to keep private everything about their patients, including the fact that the patient has come for treatment, unless the patient gives permission to release some specific information. One exception is when patients are at risk for hurting themselves or someone else. In *Jaffe v. Redmond*, an important case decided by the U.S. Supreme Court in 1995, the Supreme Court confirmed that confidentiality is necessary for the patient to speak freely in psychotherapy.

## TRAINING AND QUALIFICATIONS FOR PSYCHOANALYSTS

The International Psychoanalytic Association (IPA), formed during Freud's lifetime, is a worldwide organization of psychoanalysts that remained in place throughout the twentieth century. The American Psychoanalytic Association (APsA) was founded in 1911 and grew to three thousand members during the course of the twentieth century. All its members also belonged to the IPA. Many schools for psychoanalysts, or psychoanalytic institutes, were accredited (examined and found to meet a set of standards) by APsA over the years. APsA also developed an examination called certification to test graduate psychoanalysts.

Because the first psychoanalysts in the United States believed that psychoanalysis would be more highly valued if connected with the medical profession, the APsA initially only accepted psychiatrists (who are medical doctors) as members. Exceptions were made for professionals who applied to train as researchers. This contrasted with the practice in Europe, where many nonmedical psychoanalysts became members of the IPA. Nonmedical professionals, such as psychologists and social workers, who wanted to become psychoanalysts in the United States often trained in psychoanalytic institutes not recognized by the APsA. Some were recognized by the IPA and later banded together under the name of the International Psychoanalytic Societies (IPS). Other institutes developed outside both organizations, sometimes creating their own standards for training. By the last quarter of the twentieth century, nonmedical mental health professionals (such as psychologists and social workers) were accepted as members of APsA and grew in numbers, becoming a large proportion of the membership.

Because the title "psychoanalyst" was not protected by federal or state law in the twentieth century, anyone, even untrained persons, could call themselves a psychoanalyst in the United States. Many institutes developed in large cities, such as New York and Los Angeles, that were not connected with APsA or IPS and admitted trainees with varying backgrounds and qualifications. Some of these defined psychoanalysis in their own way, so that arguments developed about the dividing line between psychoanalysis and psychoanalytic psychotherapy. The American Psychological Association eventually developed its own examination to qualify a psychologist as a psychoanalyst.

## TRAINING IN THE TWENTY-FIRST CENTURY

Because, by the beginning of the twenty-first century, no laws were yet in place in the United States to define who could practice psychoanalysis, it remained difficult for the public to tell who was qualified. In the late 1990's, several national organizations of the core mental health disciplines came together in a coalition called the Consortium for Psychoanalysis. By the turn of the century, they had agreed upon baseline standards that would be used to develop a national organization to accredit psychoanalytic institutes. These organizations were the American Psychoanalytic Association, the division of psychoanalysis of the American Psychological Association, the National Membership Committee on Psychoanalysis in Clinical Social Work, and the American Academy of Psychoanalysis.

Trained psychoanalysts in the twenty-first century who meet these standards already have a mental health degree, except in unusual cases, before becoming psychoanalysts. Once accepted for training at a psychoanalytic institute, these mental health professionals study many more years to become qualified psychoanalysts. They take courses and treat patients while supervised by experienced psychoanalysts. In addition, they are required to undergo psychoanalysis themselves in order to gain enough self-knowledge to keep their own problems from interfering with the treatment of patients.

## PSYCHOANALYSIS AS A THEORY

All psychoanalytic theories are based on the idea that people are motivated by thoughts and feelings outside their awareness, that the past influences the present, and that each individual is unique. Because so much change and growth has occurred since Freud's era, psychoanalysis is no longer a single theory but encompasses many different theories. All psychoanalytic theories are theories of motivation (what makes people do what they do), theories of development (how people get to be the way they are), and theories of change (how psychoanalytic treatment works). Psychoanalytic theories are usually also theories of personality development (who people are) and personality disturbance.

Most theories emphasize the complexity of each person's symptoms and behavior and take into account many different influences. For example, the psychoanalytic theory called ego psychology describes development as a complex interaction of biology (inborn factors) and experience over time. Early childhood experiences are especially important because they influence the way a person's ability to cope with the world (ego functioning) develops. Each person adapts to the environment in a unique way that gradually becomes more consistent by the time the person grows to adulthood.

Psychoanalytic theories are comprehensive theories of mental functioning and disorder. For this reason, they originally formed the basis for the diagnosis and classification of mental disorders in the United States. The American Psychiatric Association published its *Diagnostic and Statistical Manual of Mental Disorders* (DSM) in 1952 and the second edition (DSM-II) in 1968. Many changes and developments took place in psychoanalytic theory during the second half of the twentieth century. The greatest changes took place in theories about psychotic illness, female psychology, homosexuality, and the nature of the patient/analyst relationship. By the turn of the twenty-first century, it was unusual to find, in real life, the silent analysts who were still sometimes depicted in films and cartoons.

Because of their complexity, psychoanalytic theories are more difficult to study and test than other theories. For example, Freud believed that dreams have meaning and are based on the fulfillment of unconscious wishes. Neuroscientists dismissed this theory for many years because it could not be demonstrated. Behavioral psychologists, who based their theories on observable behavior, did not consider thoughts and feelings outside a person's awareness to be important. Because of the emphasis on experimental testing and the increasing public expectation for quick cures during the last quarter of the twentieth century, psychoanalytic theories became less popular. The DSM-III, the third edition of the diagnostic manual for mental disorders which came out in 1980, was based on categories of symptoms and behaviors, without any reference to underlying theory. The categories of mental disturbance in DSM-III (and in later editions) were described in a way that would be easy to test in controlled experiments. People, and particularly insurance companies, became more interested in medicines and short-term treatments for symptoms and were less willing to pay for treatments like psychoanalysis that address the whole person.

Toward the end of the twentieth century and the beginning of the twenty-first, cognitive scientists (scientists who study the way people think) and neuroscientists (scientists who study the way the brain works) began to make discoveries that proved psychoanalytic theory to be correct in some important areas. For example, cognitive scientists proved that much of mental functioning goes on outside a person's awareness. Mark Solms, a neuroscientist, proved that dreams are formed in the part of the brain that deals with motivation and emotional meaning. Psychoanalysts began a dialogue with neuroscientists and cognitive scientists. Although some psychoanalysts thought psychoanalysis could not be studied experimentally in the same way as shorter-term therapies, others began to publicize studies demonstrating the effectiveness of psychoanalysis and psychoanalytic psychotherapy. Others began to develop further ways to study psychoanalytic theory and treatment.

## PSYCHOANALYTIC THEORY APPLICATIONS

Psychoanalytic ideas have been applied in many fields of study. For example, psychoanalytic theories about loss and mourning have been used to help inner-city children cope with their reactions to losses in mourning groups. Psychoanalytic ideas about power and helplessness have been used in schools to decrease violence by changing the atmosphere in which bullies can thrive. Psychoanalytic ideas led to the concept of social and emotional learning whereby educators have demonstrated that intelligence is not just based on the ability to think but includes emotions and social abilities. Psychoanalytic ideas have been used in the study of literature to understand characters such as Hamlet or Othello. They have been used in the study of culture to understand terrorists and the societies that support them. Psychoanalysts apply psychoanalytic theories in the help they offer to day-care centers, businesses, diplomats, police officers, firefighters, rabbis, priests, and others.

## Sources for Further Study

Brenner, Charles. *An Elementary Textbook of Psychoanalysis.* Rev. ed. Garden City, N.Y.: Doubleday, 1974. This book introduces interested readers to the fundamentals of psychoanalysis, explaining core psychoanalytic concepts in clear language. Although originally written in 1955 (so it does not deal with some modern developments), it remains a good resource for understanding the basics from the point of view of ego psychology.

Gabbard Glenn. *Psychodynamic Psychiatry in Clinical Practice.* 3d ed. Washington, D.C.: American Psychiatric Press, 2000. A textbook that approaches the *Diagnostic and Statistical Manual of Mental Disorders* (rev. 4th ed., 2000) from a psychoanalytic point of view. It includes an introductory section describing psychodynamic principles and sections describing Axis I and Axis II disorders from a psychodynamic perspective.

Gay, Peter. *Freud: A Life for Our Times.* New York: W. W. Norton, 1988. This is a biography of Sigmund Freud, written by his physician. It describes the history of psychoanalysis during Freud's lifetime.

Vaughan, Susan. *The Talking Cure: The Science Behind Psychotherapy.* New York: Henry Holt, 1998. This book is written for people who may want to visit a psychoanalyst or who want to learn about models of mind and brain that integrate psychoanalytic theories with other scientific theories. It includes several descriptions of what happens when patients visit psychoanalysts.

Wallerstein, R. S. *The Talking Cures: The Psychoanalyses and the Psychotherapies.* New Haven, Conn.: Yale University Press, 1995. This book provides a comprehensive history of psychoanalytic thought, including a detailed view of trends and developments in psychoanalysis from the 1940's onward. It describes conflicting and compatible psychoanalytic theories and the debate about the dividing line between psychoanalysis and psychotherapy.

*Judith M. Chertoff*

See also: Analytic Psychology: Jacques Lacan; Analytical Psychology: Carl Jung; Analytical Psychotherapy; Ego Psychology: Erik Erikson; Individual Psychology: Alfred Adler; Personality Theory; Psychoanalytic Psychology; Psychoanalytic Psychology and Personality: Sigmund Freud; Social Psychological Models: Erich Fromm; Social Psychological Models: Karen Horney; Women's Psychology: Sigmund Freud.

# PSYCHOANALYTIC PSYCHOLOGY

TYPE OF PSYCHOLOGY: Origin and definition of psychology
FIELDS OF STUDY: Psychodynamic and neoanalytic models; psychodynamic
  therapies

*Psychoanalytic and neoanalytic schools of thought provide explanations of human
and neurotic behavior. Each of these models contributes to the understanding of personality development and psychological conflict by presenting unique theoretical
conceptualizations, assessment techniques, research methodologies, and psychotherapeutic strategies for personality change.*

KEY CONCEPTS
- analytic psychology
- dynamic cultural schools of psychoanalysis
- individual psychology
- neoanalytic psychology
- psychoanalytic psychology
- psychosocial theory

One grand theory in psychology that dramatically revolutionized the way in
which personality and its formation were viewed is psychoanalysis. Orthodox psychoanalysis and later versions of this model offer several unique perspectives of personality development, assessment, and change.

The genius of Sigmund Freud (1856-1939), the founder of psychoanalysis, is revealed in the magnitude of his achievements and the monumental
scope of his works. Over the course of his lifetime, Freud developed a theory
of personality and psychopathology (disorders of psychological functioning
that include major as well as minor mental disorders and behavior disorders), a method for probing the realm of the unconscious mind, and a therapy for dealing with personality disorders. He posited that an individual is
motivated by unconscious forces that are instinctual in nature. The two major instinctual forces are the life instincts, or eros, and the death instinct, or
thanatos. Their source is biological tension whose aim is tension reduction
through a variety of objects. Freud viewed personality as a closed system
composed of three structures: the id, ego, and superego. The irrational id
consists of the biological drives and libido, or psychic energy. It operates according to the pleasure principle, which seeks the immediate gratification
of needs. The rational ego serves as the executive component of personality
and the mediator between the demands of the id, superego, and environment. Governed by the reality principle, it seeks to postpone the gratification of needs. The superego, or moral arm of personality, consists of the
conscience (internalized values) and ego ideal (that which the person aspires to be).

According to Freud, the origins of personality are embedded in the first
seven years of life. Personality develops through a sequence of psychosexual

stages which each focus upon an area of the body (erogenous zone) that gives pleasure to the individual; they are the oral, anal, phallic, latency, and genital stages. The frustration or overindulgence of needs contributes to a fixation, or arrest in development at a particular stage.

Freud also developed a therapy for treating individuals experiencing personality disturbances. Psychoanalysis has shown how physical disorders have psychological roots, how unbearable anxiety generates conflict, and how problems in adulthood result from early childhood experiences. In therapy, Freud surmounted his challenge to reveal the hidden nature of the unconscious by exposing the resistances and transferences of his patients. His method for probing a patient's unconscious thoughts, motives, and feelings was based upon the use of many clinical techniques. Free association, dream interpretation, analyses of slips of the tongue, misplaced objects, and humor enabled him to discover the contents of an individual's unconscious mind and open the doors to a new and grand psychology of personality.

## RESPONSES TO FREUDIAN THEORY

The theory of psychosocial development of Erik Erikson (1902-1994) occupies a position between orthodox psychoanalysis and neoanalytic schools of thought. His theory builds upon the basic concepts and tenets of Freudian psychology by illustrating the influential role of social and cultural forces in personality development. Erikson's observations of infants and investigations of the parent-child relationship in various societies contributed to his development of the model of the eight stages of human development. He proposes that personality unfolds over the entire life cycle according to a predetermined plan. As an individual moves through this series of stages, he or she encounters periods of vulnerability that require him or her to resolve crises of a social nature and develop new abilities and patterns of behavior. Erikson's eight psychosocial stages not only parallel Freud's psychosexual ones but, more important, have contributed immensely to recent thought in developmental psychology.

Several other schools of thought arose in opposition to Freudian orthodoxy. Among the proponents of these new psychoanalytic models were Carl Jung (1875-1961), Alfred Adler (1870-1937), Karen Horney (1885-1952), and Harry Stack Sullivan (1892-1949). These theorists advocated revised versions of Freud's psychoanalytic model and became known as the neoanalysts.

## JUNG'S APPROACH

Carl Jung's analytical psychology stresses the complex interaction of opposing forces within the total personality (psyche) and the manner in which these inner conflicts influence development. Personality is driven by general life process energy, called libido. It operates according to the principle of opposites, for example, a contrast between conscious and unconscious. An individual's behavior is seen as a means to some end, whose goal is to create a balance between these polar opposites through a process of self-realization. Personality is composed of several regions, including the ego (a unifying force at the center of consciousness), the personal unconscious (experiences blocked from consciousness), and the collective unconscious (inherited predispositions of ancestral experiences). The major focus of Jung's theory is the collective unconscious, with its archetypes (primordial thoughts and images), persona (public self), anima/animus (feminine and masculine components), shadow (repulsive side of the personality), and self (an archetype reflecting a person's striving for personality integration). Jung further proposed two psychological attitudes that the personality could use in relating to the world: introversion and extroversion. He also identified four functions of thought: sensing, thinking, feeling, and intuiting. Eight different personality types emerge when one combines these attitudes and functions. Like Freud, Jung proposed developmental stages: childhood, young adulthood, and middle age. Through the process of individuation, a person seeks to create an inner harmony that results in self-realization. In conjunction with dream analysis, Jung used painting therapy and a word-association test to disclose underlying conflicts in patients. Therapy helped patients to reconcile the conflicting sides of their personalities and experience self-realization.

## ADLER'S APPROACH

The individual psychology of Alfred Adler illustrates the significance of social variables in personality development and the uniqueness of the individual. Adler proposed that an individual seeks to compensate for inborn feelings of inferiority by striving for superiority. It is lifestyle that helps a person achieve future goals, ideals, and superiority. Adler extended this theme of perfection to society by using the concept of social interest to depict the human tendency to create a productive society. He maintained that early childhood experiences play a crucial role in the development of a person's unique lifestyle. An individual lacking in social interest develops a mistaken lifestyle (for example, an inferiority complex). Physical inferiority, as well as spoiling or pampering and neglecting children, contributes to the development of faulty lifestyles. Adler examined dreams, birth order, and first memories to trace the origins of lifestyle and goals. These data were used in psychotherapy to help the patient create a new lifestyle oriented toward social interest.

## HORNEY'S APPROACH

Karen Horney's social and cultural psychoanalysis considers the influence of social and cultural forces upon the development and maintenance of neurosis. Her theory focuses upon disturbed human relationships, especially between parents and children. She discussed several negative factors, such as parental indifference, erratic behavior, and unkept promises, which contributed to basic anxiety in children. This basic anxiety led to certain defenses or neurotic needs. Horney proposed ten neurotic needs that are used to reestablish safety. She further summarized these needs into three categories that depicted the individual's adjustment to others: moving toward people (compliant person), moving against people (aggressive person), and moving away from people (detached person). Horney believed that neurosis occurs when an individual lives according to his or her ideal rather than real self. She also wrote a number of articles on feminine psychology that stressed the importance of cultural rather than biological factors in personality formation. Like Freud, she used the techniques of transference, dream analysis, and free association in her psychotherapy; however, the goal of therapy was to help an individual overcome his or her idealized neurotic self and become more real as he or she experienced self-realization.

## SULLIVAN'S APPROACH

Harry Stack Sullivan's interpersonal theory examines personality from the perspective of the interpersonal relationships that have influenced it, especially the mother-infant relationship. Sullivan believed that this relationship contributed to an individual's development of a "good me," "bad me," or "not me" personification of self. He also proposed six stages of development: infancy, childhood, juvenile epoch, preadolescence, early adolescence, and late adolescence. These stages illustrate an individual's experiences and need for intimacy with significant others. Overall, his theory emphasizes the importance of interpersonal relations, the appraisals of others toward an individual, and the need to achieve interpersonal security and avoid anxiety.

## USE OF CASE STUDIES

Psychoanalytic psychology and its later versions have been used to explain normal and abnormal personality development. Regardless of their perspectives, psychologists in all these schools have relied upon the case study methodology to communicate their theoretical insights and discoveries.

The theoretical roots of orthodox psychoanalysis may be traced to the famous case of "Anna O.," a patient under the care of Josef Breuer, Freud's friend and colleague. Fascinated with the hysterical symptoms of this young girl and with Breuer's success in using catharsis (the talking cure) with her, Freud asked Breuer to collaborate on a work titled *Studien über Hysterie* (1895; *Studies in Hysteria*, 1950) and discuss his findings. It was the world's first book on psychoanalysis, containing information on the unconscious, defenses, sexual cause of neurosis, resistance, and transference. Freud's own self-analysis and analyses of family members and other patients further contributed to the changing nature of his theory. Among his great case histories are "Dora" (hysteria), "Little Hans" (phobia), the "Rat Man" (obsessional neurosis), the "Schreiber" case (paranoia), and the "Wolf Man" (infantile neurosis). His method of treatment, psychoanalysis, is also well documented in later cases, such as the treatment for multiple personality described in the book *Sybil* (1974).

*Josef Breuer, Sigmund Freud's close associate.* (Library of Congress)

In his classic work *Childhood and Society* (1950), Erikson discussed the applicability of the clinical method of psychoanalysis and the case-history technique to normal development in children. His case analyses of the Sioux and Yurok Indians and his observations of children led to the creation of a psychosocial theory of development that emphasized the significant role played by one's culture. Moreover, Erikson's psychohistorical accounts, *Young Man Luther: A Study in Psychoanalysis and History* (1958) and *Gandhi's Truth on the Origins of Militant Nonviolence* (1969), illustrated the applications of clinical analyses to historical and biographical research so prominent today.

The founders of other psychoanalytic schools of thought have similarly shown that their theories can best be understood in the context of the therapeutic situations and in the writings of case histories. Harold Greenwald's *Great Cases in Psychoanalysis* (1959) is an excellent source of original case histories written by Freud, Jung, Adler, Horney, and Sullivan. Jung's case of "The Anxious Young Woman and the Retired Business Man" clarifies the differences and similarities between his theory and Freud's psychoanalytic model. In "The Drive for Superiority," Adler uses material from several cases to illustrate the themes of lifestyle, feelings of inferiority, and striving for superiority. Horney's case of "The Ever Tired Editor" portrays her use of the character analysis method; that is, she concentrates upon the way in which a patient characteristically functions. Sullivan's case of "The Inefficient Wife" sheds some light on the manner in which professional advice may be given to another (student) practitioner. In retrospect, all these prominent theorists have exposed their independent schools of thought through case histories. Even today, this method continues to be used to explain human behavior and to enhance understanding of personality functioning.

### EVOLUTION OF STUDY

Historically, the evolution of psychoanalytic psychology originated with Freud's clinical observations of the work conducted by the famous French neurologist Jean-Martin Charcot and his collaborations on the treatment of hysteria neurosis with Breuer. The publication of *Studies in Hysteria* marked the birth of psychoanalysis because it illustrated a theory of hysteria, a therapy of catharsis, and an analysis of unconscious motivation. Between 1900 and 1920, Freud made innumerable contributions to the field. His major clinical discoveries were contained in the publications *Die Traumdeutung* (1900; *The Interpretation of Dreams*, 1913) and *Drei Abhandlungen zur Sexualtheorie* (1905; *Three Contributions to the Sexual Theory*, 1910; also translated as *Three Essays on the Theory of Sexuality*, 1949) as well as in various papers on therapy, case histories, and applications to everyday life. During this time, Freud began his international correspondence with people such as Jung. He also invited a select group of individuals to his home for evening discussions; these meetings were known as the psychological Wednesday society. Eventually, these meetings led to the establishment of the Vienna Psychoanalytical Society, with Adler as its president, and the First International Psychoanalytical Congress, with Jung as its president. In 1909, Freud, Jung, and others were invited by President G. Stanley Hall of Clark University to come to the United States to deliver a series of introductory lectures on psychoanalysis. This momentous occasion acknowledged Freud's achievements and gave him international recognition. In subsequent years, Freud reformulated his theory and demonstrated how psychoanalysis could be applied to larger social issues.

Trained in psychoanalysis by Anna Freud, Erikson followed in Sigmund Freud's footsteps by supporting and extending his psychosexual theory of development with eight stages of psychosocial identity. Among the members of the original psychoanalytic group, Adler was the first to defect from the Freudian school, in 1911. Protesting Freud's theory of the Oedipus complex, Adler founded what he called individual psychology. Two years later, in 1913, Jung parted company with Freud to establish analytical psychology; he objected to Freud's belief that all human behavior stems from sex. With Horney's publications *New Ways in Psychoanalysis* (1939) and *Our Inner Conflicts: A Constructive Theory of Neurosis* (1945), it became quite clear that her ideas only remotely resembled Freud's. Objecting to a number of Freud's major tenets, she attributed the development of neurosis and the psychology of being feminine to social, cultural, and interpersonal influences. Similarly, Sullivan extended psychoanalytic psychology to interpersonal phenomena, arguing that the foundations of human nature and development are not biological but rather cultural and social.

## ACCOMPLISHMENTS AND INFLUENCE

The accomplishments of Freud and his followers are truly remarkable. The creative genius of each theorist spans a lifetime of effort and work. The magnitude of their achievements is shown in their efforts to provide new perspectives on personality development and psychopathology, theories of motivation, psychotherapeutic methods of treatment, and methods for describing the nature of human behavior. Clearly, these independent schools of thought have had a profound influence not only upon the field of psychology but also upon art, religion, anthropology, sociology, and literature. Undoubtedly, they will continue to serve as the foundations of personality theory and provide the basis for new and challenging theories of tomorrow—theories that seek to discover the true nature of what it means to be human.

## SOURCES FOR FURTHER STUDY

Adler, Alfred. *Social Interest: A Challenge to Mankind.* Translated by John Linton and Edward Vaughan. New York: Capricorn Books, 1964. An excellent summary of Adler's theories of human nature and social education, incorporating his ideas on lifestyle, inferiority and superiority complexes, neurosis, childhood memories, and social feelings. Also contains a chapter on the consultant and patient relationship and a questionnaire for understanding and treating difficult children.

Erikson, Erik Homburger. *Identity, Youth, and Crisis.* New York: W. W. Norton, 1968. An impressive summation of Erikson's theories of human nature and development and the importance of societal forces. Erikson discusses his clinical observations, the life cycle and the formation of identity, and case histories to illustrate identity confusion and other relevant issues. This book carries forward concepts expressed in *Childhood and Society* (1963).

Freud, Sigmund. *A General Introduction to Psychoanalysis.* New York: W. W. Norton, 1977. An easy-to-read account of Freud's complete theory of psychoanalysis. Freud presents twenty-eight lectures to reveal major aspects of his theory, essential details in his method of psychoanalysis, and the results of his work. He also examines the psychology of errors, dream analysis technique, and general theory of neurosis.

Greenwald, Harold, ed. *Great Cases in Psychoanalysis.* Reprint. New York: Aronson, 1973. An outstanding source of case histories written by the theorists themselves. Greenwald uses these case histories to portray the historical context of the psychoanalytic movement. These original case studies provide insight into therapeutic methods used by the great analysts as well as their assessments. Included are Sigmund Freud, Alfred Adler, Carl Jung, Karen Horney, and Harry Stack Sullivan.

Horney, Karen. *The Neurotic Personality of Our Time.* New York: W. W. Norton, 1937. This classic work contains Horney's portrayal of the neurotic personality and the relevance of cultural forces in the etiology of psychological disturbances. This post-Freudian document examines Horney's theoretical conceptualizations, including basic anxiety, neurotic trends, methods of adjustment, and the role played by culture.

Mitchell, Stephen A. *Freud and Beyond: A History of Modern Psychoanalytic Thought.* New York: Basic Books, 1996. A short overview of psychoanalysis, with chapters devoted to Sigmund Freud, Harry Stack Sullivan, Melanie Klein, and other important thinkers.

Sullivan, Harry Stack. *The Interpersonal Theory of Psychiatry.* New York: W. W. Norton, 1953. A classic work on human development from an interpersonal perspective. Sullivan provides a comprehensive overview of his theory by describing his key concepts and developmental stages. He further illustrates the application of his theory by focusing upon inappropriate interpersonal relationships.

*Joan Bartczak Cannon*

SEE ALSO: Analytical Psychology: Carl Jung; Dreams; Ego Psychology: Erik Erikson; Individual Psychology: Alfred Adler; Psychoanalysis; Psychoanalytic Psychology and Personality: Sigmund Freud; Social Psychological Models: Erich Fromm; Social Psychological Models: Karen Horney; Women's Psychology: Karen Horney; Women's Psychology: Sigmund Freud.

# Psychoanalytic Psychology and Personality
## Sigmund Freud

Type of psychology: Personality
Fields of study: Classic analytic themes and issues; personality theory; psychodynamic and neoanalytic models

*Freud's theory of personality, emphasizing unconscious motivation, sexual instincts, and psychological conflict, is one of the most profound and unique contributions in psychology. Freud described both the normal and abnormal personality, and he proposed a therapy for the treatment of mental problems.*

Key concepts
- anal stage
- ego
- genital stage
- id
- instincts
- latency
- Oedipal conflict
- oral stage
- phallic stage
- superego

Sigmund Freud (1856-1939) saw people as engaged in a personal struggle between their instinctual urges and the requirements of society. According to Freud, this conflict often takes place outside one's awareness, in the unconscious, and affects all aspects of people's lives. The instinctual energy which fuels the mind has its source in the unconscious. It is highly mobile and once engaged must achieve expression, however disguised the expression might be.

Freud said that most of the mind is below the level of awareness—in the unconscious—just as most of the mass of an iceberg is below the surface of the water. The id, the most primitive structure in the mind, is in the unconscious. The id is composed of the instincts (psychological representations of biological needs and the source of all psychological energy), including the sexual and other life instincts and the aggressive and other death instincts. For Freud, the sexual instincts were particularly important. They take a long time to develop, and society has a large investment in their regulation.

The instincts press for gratification, but the id itself cannot satisfy them, because it has no contact with reality. Therefore, the ego, which contacts the id in the unconscious but also is partly conscious, develops. The ego can perceive reality and direct behavior to satisfy the id's urges. To the extent that the ego can satisfy the id's instincts, it gains strength, which it can then use to energize its own processes, perceiving and thinking. It is important that the ego can also use its energy to restrict or delay the expression of the id. The ego uses psychological defense mechanisms to protect the individual from awareness of threatening events and to regulate the expression of the instincts. For example, a strong ego can use the defense mechanism of sublimation to direct some sexual energy into productive work rather than sexual activity itself.

In the course of a child's development, the superego develops from the ego. The ego attaches energy to the significant people in the child's world—the caregivers—and their values are then adopted as the child's own ideal and conscience. This process becomes particularly significant during the phallic stage, between the ages of four and six. At that time, the child becomes sexually attracted to the opposite-sex parent. In giving up that passion, the child adopts the characteristics of the same-sex parent; this process shapes the child's superego. The superego is mostly unconscious, and it strives for perfection. Throughout life, the id will strive for instinctual gratification, and the superego will strive for perfection. It is the task of the ego to mediate between the two, when necessary, and to chart a realistic life course.

### IMPORTANCE OF CHILDHOOD YEARS

Freud considered the childhood years particularly significant, not only because during these years the ego and superego develop from energy cap-

*Sigmund Freud, shown here with his daughter, psychiatrist Anna Freud.* (Library of Congress)

tured from the id but also because during this time the sexual instincts manifest themselves in a variety of forms. The sexual instincts become focused on particular erogenous zones of the child's body in a set order. This produces a series of psychosexual stages, each characterized by instinctual urges, societal response, conflict, and resolution. During the course of this process, lasting personality traits and defenses develop. At first, the sexual energy is focused on the mouth. In this, the oral stage, conflicts may surround feeding. At approximately age two, the anal stage begins. The sexual instincts focus on the anus, and conflicts may occur around toilet training. The phallic stage, in which the child is attracted to the opposite-sex parent, follows. According to Freud, for boys this Oedipal conflict can be severe, as they fear castration from their father in retribution for their attraction to their mother. For girls, the conflict is somewhat less severe; in Freudian psychology, this less severe conflict means that in adulthood women will have less mature personalities than men. At approximately age six, the sexual instincts go into abeyance, and the child enters a period of latency. In adolescence, the sexual instincts again come to the fore, in the genital stage, and the adolescent has the task of integrating the impulses from all the erogenous zones into mature genital sexuality.

Psychological problems occur when the psychosexual stages have left the instinctual urges strongly overgratified or undergratified, when the instincts are overly strong, when the superego is overly tyrannical, or when the ego has dealt with childhood traumas by severe repression of its experiences into the unconscious. Undergratification or overgratification of the instincts during childhood can result in fixations, incomplete resolutions of childhood conflicts. For example, a person who is severely toilet trained can develop an "anal character," becoming either excessively neat, miserly, or otherwise "holding things inside." If the id urges are too strong, they may overwhelm the ego, resulting in psychosis. An overly strong superego can lead to excessive guilt. If the ego represses childhood trauma, relegating it to the unconscious, that trauma will persist, outside awareness, in affecting a person's thoughts and behaviors.

Freud believed that no one could escape the conflicts inherent in the mind but that one could gain greater familiarity with one's unconscious and learn to direct instinctual energies in socially appropriate ways. This was the task of psychoanalysis, a form of therapy in which a client's unconscious conflicts are explored to allow the individual to develop better ways of coping.

## IMPACT ON WESTERN SOCIETY

Freud's theory has had a dramatic impact on Western society, strongly influencing the ways people view themselves and their interactions with others. Terms such as "Freudian slip," "Oedipus complex," and "unconscious" are part of everyday language. Emotions may be seen as "buried deep," and emotional expression may be called therapeutic. Assumptions about the unconscious influence both popular and professional conceptions of mental life.

The assumption that the expression of emotion is healthy and the repression of emotion is unhealthy may be traced to Freud. To some extent, this idea has received support from research which suggests that unresolved anger may contribute to physical health problems. Unfortunately, the release of anger in verbal or physical aggression may cause those aggressive behaviors to increase rather than decrease. The vicarious experience of aggression via watching television or films may also teach aggression rather than reduce the urge to act aggressively.

## ROLE OF DREAMS

Freud believed that dreams were one vehicle of unconscious expression. He viewed dreams as expressing the fulfillment of a wish, generally of a sexual nature. During sleep, the ego relaxes its restrictions on the id; instinctual wishes from the id, or repressed material from the unconscious, may be manifested in a dream. The bizarre sense of time and the confusing combinations of people and odd incidents in dreams reflect that the unconscious is without a sense of time, logic, or morality.

In dreams, the ego transforms material from the id to make it less threatening. Once one awakens, the ego disguises the true meaning of the dream further. Important points will be repressed and forgotten, and distortions will occur as the dream is remembered or told. For this reason, it is virtually impossible, according to Freud, to interpret one's own dreams accurately. A psychoanalyst interprets dreams by asking a patient to free associate—to say whatever comes to mind—about the dream content. In this fashion, the censoring of the ego may be relaxed, and the true meaning will be revealed to the therapist.

Revealing unconscious material is at the center of Freudian psychotherapy. Since Freud, many have viewed psychological problems as the result of childhood conflicts or traumas. Once the source is revealed, the patient is expected to improve. The nature of treatment is considerably more complicated than this might suggest, because the patient's ego may actively defend against acknowledging painful unconscious material. One of the few cases that Freud reported in detail was that of "Dora." Dora was referred to Freud because of a persistent cough that was assumed to be of psychological origin. According to Freud, such physical symptoms often are the result of childhood sexual conflict. Dora's cough and other psychosomatic complaints were found to be rooted in her sexual attraction to her father and to other men who were seen as resembling him—including a family friend, and even Freud himself. Her attraction was accompanied by jealousy of her mother and the family friend's wife. The situation was complicated, because Dora's father was having an affair with the family friend's wife, to whom Dora was also attracted, and the family friend had expressed his attraction for Dora.

All this and more is revealed in two dreams of Dora's that Freud analyzes in detail. The first is a dream of being awakened by her father, dressing quickly, and escaping a house that is on fire. The dream does its work by equating her father with the family friend, who once really was beside her bed as she awoke from a nap. This caused her to decide to "dress quickly" in the mornings, lest the friend come upon her unclothed. Her unconscious attraction for the friend, however, is belied by the symbol of fire, which might be likened to consuming passion. In her second dream, Dora dreamed that her father was dead and that a man said "Two and a half hours more." The dream symbolizes both Dora's turning away from her father as an object of her sexual interest and her intention (not evident to Freud at the time) of leaving therapy after two more sessions.

If Dora had not stopped therapy prematurely, Freud would have continued to bring his interpretation of her unconscious conflicts to the fore. In particular, he would have used her transference of childhood emotions to Freud himself as a vehicle for making the material revealed by her dreams, free associations, and behaviors evident to consciousness. The use of such transference is a key element of psychoanalysis. While this would not have completely resolved Dora's strong instinctual urges, it would have allowed her to come to terms with them in more mature ways, perhaps by choosing an appropriate marriage partner. Indeed, Freud reveals at the end of his report of this case that Dora married a young man she mentioned near the end of her time in therapy.

## IMPACT AND CRITICISMS

Freud was a unique, seminal thinker. His theory was controversial from its inception. At the same time, however, it is such a powerful theory that, while many have criticized it, no subsequent personality theorist has been able to ignore the ideas Freud advanced. Psychoanalytic theory has also provided an interpretive framework for literary critics, historians, philosophers, and others.

Freud's theory was a product of his personal history, his training in science and medicine, and the Viennese culture in which he lived. Freud's early training was as a neurologist. As he turned from neurology to psychology, he continued to apply the skills of careful observation to this new discipline and to assume that the human mind followed natural laws that could be discovered. Viennese society at the time of Freud was one of restrictive social attitudes, particularly for women, and of covert practices that fell far short of public ideals. Thus it was relatively easy to see the psychological problems of the middle-class Viennese women who often were Freud's patients as being attributable to sexual conflicts.

Although Freud himself was dedicated to developing a science of mental life, his methods are open to criticism on scientific grounds. His theory is based upon his experiences as a therapist and his own self-analysis. His conclusions may therefore be restricted to the particular people or time his work encompassed. He did not seek to corroborate what his patients told him by checking with others outside the therapy room. Freud was not interested in the external "truth" of a report as much as its inner psychological meaning. He did not make details of his cases available to scrutiny, perhaps because of confidentiality. Although he wrote extensively about his theory, only five case histories were published. In all, these difficulties make the assessment of Freudian theory in terms of traditional scientific criteria problematic.

Freud's theory has had strong adherents as well as critics. Although theorists such as Alfred Adler and Carl Jung eventually broke with Freud, arguing against the primacy of the sexual instincts, his influence can be seen in their theories. Similarly, the important work of Erik Erikson describing human development through the life span has its roots in psychoanalytic theory. Many modern psychoanalytic theorists place a greater emphasis on the ego than did Freud, seeing it as commanding its own source of energy, independent of and equal to the id. Much literature and social criticism also possess a Freudian flavor.

## Sources for Further Study

Freud, Sigmund. *General Psychological Theory: Papers on Metapsychology.* New York: Macmillan, 1997. A collection of Freud's papers about the practice of psychoanalysis.

_____. *An Outline of Psychoanalysis.* Translated by Helena Ragg-Kirkby . New York: Penguin Books, 2003. A brief introduction to Freudian theory. Beginning students of Freud may find the tone too didactic and the treatment too abbreviated; however, it is valuable when read in conjunction with a good summary of Freud from a secondary source.

Gay, Peter. *Freud: A Life for Our Time.* 1988. Reprint. New York: W. W. Norton, 1998. Well-written biography of Freud places his work in historical and psychological context. Accessible to the reader who may only have a passing familiarity with Freudian theory.

_____, ed. *The Freud Reader.* Reprint. New York: W. W. Norton, 1995. A well-edited volume of selections of Freud's work. *The Interpretation of Dreams, Fragment of an Analysis of a Case of Hysteria ("Dora"),* and *Three Essays on the Theory of Sexuality* are particularly important in defining the basics of Freud's theory.

Hall, Calvin Springer, Gardner Lindzey, and John Campbell. "Freud's Classical Psychoanalytical Theory." In *Theories of Personality.* 4th ed. New York: John Wiley & Sons, 1998. This chapter is the classic textbook summary of Freud's theory. Readable, thorough, and accurate. Also presents a brief discussion of psychoanalytic research methods and criticisms of the theory.

Jones, Ernest. *The Life and Work of Sigmund Freud.* Edited and abridged by Lionel Trilling and Steven Marcus.3 vols. New York: Basic Books, 1981. Jones was a confidant of Freud and his official biographer. Interesting as an insider's account of Freud's life.

Kardiner, Abram. *My Analysis with Freud.* New York: W. W. Norton, 1977. Kardiner is a well-known analyst. This brief volume is a personal account of his own analysis, with Freud as the therapist. A fascinating insider's account of Freudian analysis and the forces that shaped the psychoanalytic movement.

*Susan E. Beers*

SEE ALSO: Abnormality: Psychological Models; Dreams; Psychoanalysis; Psychoanalytic Psychology; Psychotherapy: Goals and Techniques; Women's Psychology: Karen Horney; Women's Psychology: Sigmund Freud.

# PSYCHOLOGY

## DEFINITION

TYPE OF PSYCHOLOGY: Origin and definition of psychology
FIELDS OF STUDY: Classic analytic themes and issues; methodological issues

*The term "psychology" first appeared in written form during the early sixteenth century and meant the systematic study of the soul and mind. The meaning of the concept changed gradually during the following three centuries, until psychology emerged in the 1880's as a separate field of study. Defined as the scientific study of mind and consciousness, the discipline was by the 1920's redefined as the scientific study of behavior and mental processes, creating some significant problems. In spite of definitional ambiguities, modern psychology is a vigorous and broad field of study.*

KEY CONCEPTS
- act psychology
- behaviorism
- functionalism
- psychological domain
- structuralism

The term "psyche," while personified by the ancient Greeks as a goddess, essentially means "breath," which was equated with soul or mind. The suffix "ology" means "science" or "study of." Psychology, as originally defined, then, means the scientific study of soul or mind. The term "scientific," as used here, means systematic; scientific fields of study did not emerge until the seventeenth century.

Apparently, the concept of psychology was not formulated until the early to middle sixteenth century, appearing first in 1530 as part of the title of a series of academic lectures given by Philipp Melanchthon, a German scholar. The first book with the Latin word *psychologia* (psychological) as part of the title was published in 1594. When used by philosophers and theologians during the following three centuries, the term had a gradually changing meaning, with the focus being much more on the study of mind and consciousness than on the soul.

Psychology, as a separate field of study, came into being in Germany in 1879 and, during the 1880's, in many other European countries and the United States. The field was defined as the scientific or systematic study of mind and consciousness and was largely modeled after physics and chemistry. Wilhelm Wundt (1832-1920), the acknowledged founder of the new discipline, believed that psychologists should be concerned primarily with investigating the structure of mind and consciousness using rigorous introspective techniques. Psychology was, according to Wundt, to focus on identifying the properties of simple mental elements and the laws by which these elements combined to form the more complex structures of mind and consciousness, for example, percepts and ideas. This approach, and a derivative of it developed in the United States by Edward Titchener, became known as structuralism. Animal research, the study of infants and children, the study of people with psychological problems, and concern with individual differences were not seen as central to psychology.

Some of Wundt's European contemporaries, however, such as Franz Brentano and Oswald Külpe, argued that psychology should focus on processes associated with mind and consciousness, such as perceiving, thinking, and intending, rather than attempting to divide the mental domain into simple elements. Brentano's approach became known as act psychology, in contrast to Wundt's mental-content psychology, and the two perspectives generated some interesting controversies. They did agree, though, that psychology should be concerned primarily with the study of mind and consciousness in normal adult human beings; animals, children, and people with mental and emotional problems were not of particular interest to them as subjects of research.

Also emphasizing conceptions of mind and consciousness as process rather than content were prominent early American psychologists such as William James, John Dewey, James Rowland Angell, and Harvey Carr. In contrast to Brentano and Külpe, however, these psychologists were primarily interested in the functions served by the processes. It was generally assumed that each of these capabilities evolved to help humans survive and that it was the job of psychologists to determine how seeing, hearing, feeling, thinking, willing, planning, and so forth contributed to individuals' survival. Because not everyone adapts equally well to the challenges of life, this approach to psychology, which became known as functionalism, as emphasized the study of individuals differences in intelligence, personality, social skills, and so forth, as well as applied psychology and animal research. Psychology, however, was still defined as the systematic study of mind and consciousness. Functionalism has its foundations in Charles Darwin's theory of evolution and in late nineteenth century British psychology and applied statistics.

With the introduction of animal research into psychology and continuing controversies over the meanings of the concepts of mind, consciousness, and terms referring to the varying aspects of private experience, some psychologists increasingly believed that a scientific psychology could only be created if research centered on behavior (responses) and environmental features (stimuli), both of which are observable. Therefore, when American psychologist John B. Watson proclaimed, in 1913, that psychology should abandon attempts to study mind and consciousness introspectively and redefine itself as the scientific study of behavior, many of his peers were ready to follow his call; behaviorism had its formal beginning.

The behavioral orientation had its greatest influence on American psychology from about the 1920's until the early 1970's, undergoing a number of transformations. During that time, most textbooks defined psychology as the scientific study of behavior, or of behavior and mental and affective processes. Even as the limits of behavioral psychology, in its various forms, became apparent by the late 1960's, definitions of psychology changed very little. According to most modern psychologists in the United States and in many other countries, psychology is primarily the study of behavior, and only secondarily—and sometimes grudgingly—the study of such difficult-to-define mental and affective states and processes as thoughts, percepts, images, and feelings. Nevertheless, even the concepts of mind and consciousness, the original concerns of psychology, have somewhat reluctantly been readmitted to the field as necessary research concerns.

## DEFINITIONAL PROBLEMS

There are a number of serious problems associated with defining psychology as the scientific study of behavior and mental and affective states. Not only is the definition imprecise, but it also has apparently made it very difficult to generate an integrated body of psychological knowledge. While impressive research on the behavior of animals and humans has been conducted, and some progress has been made in understanding mental and affective processes and states, the knowledge generated is fragmented and therefore of limited value.

One could argue, in fact, that psychology is not the study of behavior at all but is rather the study of the information each person or animal has available that makes behavior—that is, directed and controlled actions—possible. While this information has traditionally been referred to as mind and consciousness, there might be some virtue in calling it "the psychological domain" in order to avoid long-standing arguments. Behavior is a methodological concept because it refers to something researchers must study in order to make inferences about the psychological domain. On the other hand, researchers can also investigate the products of human actions, such as the languages people develop, the buildings they construct, and the art and music they share, to the same end. Some psychologists perform research on the physiological processes associated with seeing, hearing, feeling, and thinking. Definitions of psychology should include the terms "culture" and "physiological and biochemical correlates" as well as the concept of behavior.

A better approach might be to define psychology as the systematic study of the psychological domain, this domain being the personal information that makes it possible for individual human beings and other life-forms to move with direction and control. To go beyond this definition is to describe how psychologists do research rather than what the field is about.

Another problem associated with standard definitions of psychology is the assumption that there is general agreement concerning the meaning of the concept of behavior. As has been pointed out by many analysts, that is not the case. The term has been used to refer to sensory responses, cognitive and affective processes, muscle movements, glandular secretions, activity taking place in various parts of the nervous system, and the outcomes or consequences of particular complex actions. Behavior, in other words, is an ambiguous concept. In a strict sense, the only actions or changes relevant to the psychological level of analysis are those that are self-initiated and unique to the total-life-form level of organization in nature, because it is these changes that depend on the psychological domain. Changes in the individual cells or subsystems of life-forms, on the other hand, do not constitute behavior in the psychological sense.

## THE DEVELOPMENT OF A FIELD

Even though a clear and generally agreed-upon definition of psychology has not emerged, psychology today is a vigorous and broad scholarly field and profession, extending from biological subdisciplines and animal research laboratories to the study of humans in social, political, economic, industrial, educational, clinical, and religious contexts. It is not surprising, therefore, that psychologists have made contributions in a wide variety of areas. Among the most notable are those having to do with cognitive and emotional development, child rearing, formulating new ways to view and treat psychological problems, devising ways to deal with the crises of life associated with each stage of human experience from infancy to old age, consumer research and marketing, group dynamics, and the development of tests and educational procedures.

Psychology is one of the most popular majors in American colleges, and the discipline has experienced dramatic growth since the 1940's. There were about 4,000 psychologists in the United States during the 1940's; by the early 1990's, there were approximately 100,000. Since the mid-1970's, the number of women majoring in psychology has held steady, while the number of men has decreased significantly; as a consequence, by the late 1980's, more women than men were earning Ph.D.'s in psychology.

One of the most challenging new areas of study is health psychology, which emerged during the 1980's in response to the health care crisis, brought about by increasing costs associated with an aging population, expensive high-technology medical techniques, the acquired immunodeficiency syndrome (AIDS) epidemic, economic restructuring and stagnation, and a variety of other factors. Pressures have also been emerging for people to reexamine their values and roles and, in a sense, their personal and national identities. These pressures derive from such powerful forces and dynamics as the women's and multicultural movements, the emergence of nontraditional social and child-rearing arrangements, and the change from a production to a service society. A mass identity crisis may, in fact, provide the psychologists of the twenty-first century with their major challenge.

## SOURCES FOR FURTHER STUDY

Carr, Harvey A. *Psychology: A Study of Mental Activity.* New York: Longmans, Green, 1925. Presents a clear picture of the functionalist view of psychology. Carr was one of the American psychologists who formalized functionalism.

Gilgen, Albert R. *American Psychology Since World War II: A Profile of the Discipline.* Westport, Conn.: Greenwood, 1982. Presents an overview of the major developments and trends in American psychology during World War II, which ended in 1945, and from the postwar period through the 1970's.

_____. "The Psychological Level of Organization in Nature and Interdependencies Among Major Psychological Concepts." In *Annals of Theoretical Psychology.* Vol. 5, edited by Arthur W. Staats and Leendert P. Mos. New York: Plenum Press, 1987. Presents a detailed rationale for defining psychology as the systematic study of the information available to each person that allows each individual to move with direction and control.

Lapointe, Franois H. "Who Originated the Term 'Psychology'?" *Journal of the History of the Behavioral Sciences* 8, no. 3 (1972): 328-335. A thorough analysis of the origination of the term "psychology." An essential reference for anyone interested in the history of the concept.

Murray, David J. *A History of Western Psychology.* 2d ed. Englewood Cliffs, N.J.: Prentice-Hall, 1988. Includes clear discussions of the origins of the term "psychology" and the meaning of the concept for the act psychologists, the structuralists, the functionalists, and the behaviorists.

Porter, Roy. *Madness: A Brief History.* New York: Oxford University Press, 2002. A history of Western ideas about mental illness by one of the most respected historians of medicine. Changing ideas about "madness" help trace the evolution of the definition of psychology.

Titchener, Edward Bradford. *A Primer of Psychology.* 1899. Reprint. New York: Macmillan, 1925. Presents a clear and detailed analysis of psychology from the structuralist perspective and in the process identifies many of the challenges involved in attempting to decipher the structure of mind and consciousness.

*Albert R. Gilgen*

SEE ALSO: Behaviorism; Cognitive Psychology; Psychoanalytic Psychology; Psychology: Fields of Specialization; Structuralism and Functionalism.

# PSYCHOLOGY
## FIELDS OF SPECIALIZATION

TYPE OF PSYCHOLOGY: Origin and definition of psychology
FIELDS OF STUDY: Behavioral therapies; cognitive development;
  experimental methodologies; general constructs and issues;
  psychodynamic and neoanalytic models

*Psychology is both a theoretical and an applied science. Psychologists use observational and experimental methods to reach a greater understanding of the human mind and human behavior. They then use this knowledge in a variety of settings to help people in their daily lives.*

KEY CONCEPTS
- behaviorism
- cognitive psychology
- Gestalt psychology
- social psychology
- structuralism

Because the fields of specialization within psychology are so numerous, one must first examine the science as an entity unto itself. This involves defining psychology, exploring the reasons for its existence, reviewing its history, and surveying the diverse specialists who assist various populations. Although the semantics of defining psychology differ from text to text, the actual explanation remains constant: It is the science of human behavior as it relates to the functions of the mind. More specifically, it provides evidence for why people experience a gamut of emotions, think rationally or irrationally, and act either predictably or unpredictably.

The discipline's very existence reflects humankind's need to plumb the depths of its interior to search for the self, to process conflict, to solve problems, and to think critically as well as act pragmatically. Its challenge is to assist people in understanding themselves. Humans have a natural curiosity; it moves them to try to determine their relationship to the world in which they live. With this comes the inclination to observe and compare other people: their ideas, behavior patterns, and abilities. These analyses and comparisons, which people cannot help but make, involve the self as well as others. People may be either overly harsh or selectively blind when examining themselves; both these situations can be handicaps, and both can be helped by psychology.

At times, one's anxiety level may peak uncontrollably. Through the science of the mind, one seeks to temper one's agitation by becoming familiar with and acknowledging vague fears and uncomfortable feelings. Thus, the person learns about the source of his or her tension. From this, experts learn how behavior originates. They assist an individual in learning to cope with change; the person discovers how to make adequate adjustments in daily living. The fast pace that humans in industrialized society keep requires them now, more than ever before, to have a working knowledge of people—their thought processes and behavior patterns. From all of this, experts are able to arrive at reasonable predictions and logical conclusions about humankind's future behavior.

### HISTORY AND SYSTEMS OF PSYCHOLOGY

Psychology did not become accepted as a formal discipline until the late nineteenth century. Prior to that time, even back to antiquity, questions were directed to philosophers. Though they were versed in reasoning, logic, and scholarship, only a few of these thinkers could deal with the complexities of the human mind. Their answers were profound and lengthy, but these scholars frequently left their audiences bewildered and without the solutions they sought. Some of these logicians used the Socratic method of reasoning; they often frustrated those who questioned them and expected realistic replies. Inquires were redirected to the questioner, whose burden it was to arrive at his or her own solutions.

Gustav Fechner, a nineteenth century philosopher and physicist, postulated that the scientific method should be applied to the study of mental processes. It was his contention that experimentation and mathematical procedures should be used to study the human mind. From the middle of the nineteenth century onward, many disciplines contributed to what was to become the science of psychology. Wilhelm Wundt and Edward Titchener were the leaders of the structuralist school, which identified the elements and principles of consciousness.

Other early giants of the field included William James and John Dewey. They inaugurated the study of functionalism, which taught that psychological knowledge should be applied to practical knowledge in fields such as education, business law, and daily living. A champion of behaviorism, John B. Watson, advocated that the study of psychology should concentrate on observable behavior; he urged that objective methods be adopted. The Gestalt movement was originated by Max Wertheimer. In concert with Kurt Koffka and Wolfgang Köhler, he embraced the premise that the whole may be different from its parts studied in isolation.

Psychoanalysis was developed by Sigmund Freud. He studied the unconscious using techniques of free association, hypnosis, and body language. The neobehaviorist model, in contrast, defended the behaviorist position that complicated phenomena such as mental and emotional activities cannot be observed. Love, stress, empathy, trust, and personality cannot be observed in and of themselves. Their effects, however, are readily apparent.

Carl Rogers and Abraham Maslow pioneered the area known as humanism in the 1950's and 1960's. Areas of interest to humanistic psychologists are self-actualization, creativity and transcendence, the search for meaning, and social change. The humanists' goals are to expand and to enrich human lives through service to others and an increased understanding of the complexity of people, as individuals, in groups, organizations, and communities.

In the mid-twentieth century, with the development of cognitive psychology, mental processes such as attention, memory, and reasoning became the focus of direct study. This approach to understanding human thought analyzes cognitive processes into a sequence of ordered stages; each stage reflects an important step in the processing of information. In the 1980's and 1990's, the fields of cognitive science and cognitive neuroscience emerged. Psychologists began working with computer scientists, linguists, neurobiologists, and others to develop detailed models of brain and mind relationships.

## Major Fields in Psychology

Psychology is both a theoretical and an applied science with over a dozen major fields. In 2004, the American Psychological Association listed fifty-five divisions, representing psychologists working in settings as diverse as community mental health clinics and large corporations and with interests ranging from the adult development and aging to the study of peace, conflict, and violence. Academic and research psychologists use observational and experimental methods to reach a greater understanding of the human mind and human behavior. Psychologists in the clinical specialties then use this knowledge to help people in their daily lives.

For example, children who are abused or neglected, or who suffer as a result of being members of dysfunctional families, require the services of child psychologists, who evaluate, diagnose, and treat youngsters. This usually occurs in a clinical setting. Thus, child psychologist are considered clinical practitioners. More than one-half of the Ph.D.'s awarded in 1999 were in either clinical or counseling psychology.

Many psychologists also work in the area of education. Educational psychologists develop and analyze materials and strategies for effective educational curricula. School psychologists design instructive programs, consult with teachers, and assist students with problems.

Genetic psychologists study the activities of the human organism in relation to the hereditary and evolutionary factors involved; functions and origin play a central role. Physiological psychologists examine the biological bases of behavior. They are often interested in the biochemical reactions underlying memory and learning. Engineering psychologists design and evaluate equipment, training devices, and systems. The goal is to facilitate relationships between people and their environment. Industrial/organizational (I/O) psychologists research and develop programs that promote on-the-job efficiency, effectiveness, challenge, and positive disposition. They study ability and personality factors, special training and experience, and work and environment variables as well as organizational changes.

Personality psychologists study the many ways in which people differ from one another; they are instrumental in analyzing how those differences

---

## DEGREE FIELDS OF PSYCHOLOGY PH.D.'S

Arranged in descending order by number of degrees awarded in 1999:
- Clinical
- Counseling
- Developmental
- All other subfields (such as community psychology, sport psychology)
- Experimental/Physiological
- General
- Social and Personality
- Industrial/Organizational'
- Cognitive
- School
- Educational

---

may be assessed and what their impact is. Criminal psychologists study the complexities of a perpetrator's thought process. They are keenly interested in a criminal's habits, idiosyncrasies, and possible motives. Developmental psychologists study changes in people as they age and mature. Their work may be protracted over the span of an individual's life; their theories may be advanced several years after they were first conceived.

Social psychologists study how people influence one another. They may be interested, for example, in the concept of leaders and followers. Environmental psychologists monitor the physical and social effects of the environment on behavior. They are interested in how elements such as heat, noise, health, and activity affect the human condition. Their contributions are in the areas of urban planning, architecture, and transportation.

Consumer psychologists determine factors that influence consumer decisions, exploring such issues as the effect of advertising on purchasing decisions, brand loyalty, and the rejection or acceptance of new products. Experimental psychologists design and conduct basic and applied research in a variety of areas, including learning, sensation, attention and memory, language, motivation, and the physiological and neural bases of behavior. Comparative psychologists study the behavior, cognition, perception, and social relationships of diverse animal species. Their research can be descriptive as well as experimental and is conducted in the field or with animals in captivity.

### TESTS AND MEASURES OF INDIVIDUAL DIFFERENCES

The scope of psychology's fields of specialization is great. The professionals who work in these areas strive to help humans know, understand, and help themselves. To accomplish this, psychologists use numerous tests to help them ascertain specific information about an individual, a group of people, or a particular population. Ability tests measure multiple aptitudes, creativity, achievement, and intelligence levels. Psychologists may perform occupational and clinical assessments. Also included in the area of assessment are personality tests, which encompass self-report inventories, measures of interests, attitudes and values, projective techniques, and performance and situational evaluations.

An example of a multiple-aptitude test is the Differential Aptitude Test (DAT), first published in 1947, then revised in 1963, 1973, and 1991. Its primary purpose is to counsel students in grades eight through twelve in educational and vocational matters. Creativity tests have received much attention from researchers and practitioners alike. The Aptitudes Research Project (ARP) was developed by the University of Southern California. It is a structure-of-intellect (SI) model, which encompasses all intellectual functions. Although its initial platform was reasoning, creativity, and problem solving, its base was expanded to divergent production. Until the ARP, research resources in this area were very limited.

Achievement tests, which differ from aptitude tests, measure the effects of specific instruction or training. Some of the most respected tests are the California Achievement Tests, the Iowa Tests of Basic Skills, the Metropolitan Achievement Test, and the Stanford Achievement Test. Their significance lies in reporting what the individual can do at the time of test administration. Aptitude instruments, on the other hand, make recommendations about future skills. Intelligence tests speak their own language; it is unfortunate, though, that so much importance is placed upon the results they yield. One should always remember that the scores identified in the Stanford-Binet test and in the various Wechsler intelligence scales are only part of a big picture about any given human being and should be evaluated accordingly.

Personality tests measure the emotional, motivational, interpersonal, and attitudinal characteristics of an individual. The Kuder Interest Inventories list occupations according to a person's interest area. The Rorschach Inkblot Projective Technique investigates the personality as a whole. The Thematic Apperception Test (TAT) researches personality and attitude. The Myers-Briggs Type Indicator is a widely used measure of personality dispositions and interests based on Carl Jung's theory of types.

## PSYCHOLOGY AND SOCIETY

Psychology as a formal discipline is still relatively new; of its many specializations, some have found their way to maturity, while others are still in their early stages. The development of diverse fields has been justified by the changing nature of social and psychological problems as well as by changing perceptions as to how best to approach those problems. For example, because more people live closer together than ever before, they must interact with one another to a greater degree; finding ways to deal with issues such as aggression, racism, and prejudice therefore becomes crucial. Several divisions of the American Psychological Association reflect the diverse groups that interest psychologists: the Society of Pediatric Psychology, the Society for the Psychological Study of Ethnic Minority Issues, and the Society for the Psychological Study of Lesbian, Gay, and Bisexual Issues.

Economic conditions require most parents to work—whether they are single parents or parents in a two-parent family—thus depriving children of time with their parents. This has created a need for day-care centers; the care and nurturing of young people is being transferred, to a significant degree, to external agents. Moreover, older children may be expected to assume adult responsibilities before they are ready. All these issues point to an increasing need for family counseling. Educational institutions demand achievement from students; this can daunt students who have emotional or family problems that interfere with their ability to learn. The availability of school counselors or psychologists can make a difference in whether such children succeed or fail. Businesses and organizations use psychologists and psychological testing to avoid hiring employees who would be ineffective or incompatible with the organization's approach and to maximize employee productivity on the job.

The specialized fields of psychology have played both a facilitative and a reflective role. Therapists and counselors, for example, have enabled individuals to look at what they have previously accomplished, to assess the present, and to come to terms with themselves and the realities of the future. The future of psychology itself will hold further developments both in the refining of specializations that already exist and in the development of new ones as inevitable societal changes require them.

## SOURCES FOR FURTHER STUDY

Butler, Gillian, and Freda McManus. *Psychology: A Very Short Introduction.* New York: Oxford University Press, 2000. Provides an understanding of some of psychology's leading ideas and their practical relevance. The authors answer some of the most frequently asked questions about psychology: What is psychology? How do humans use what is in the mind? How does psychology work? How do people influence one another? What can a psychologist do to help?

Colman, Andrew M. *What Is Psychology?* 2d ed. New York: Routledge, 1999. Extensively revised and updated, this introduction to psychology as a discipline assumes no prior knowledge of the subject. Examples are used throughout to illustrate fundamental ideas, with a self-assessment quiz focusing readers on a number of intriguing psychological problems. The book explains the differences between psychology, psychiatry, and psychoanalysis and offers an exploration of the professions and careers associated with psychology.

Koch, Sigmund, and David E. Leary, eds. *A Century of Psychology as Science.* Washington, D.C.: APA Books, 1992. This reissued edition, originally published in 1985, comprehensively accesses the accomplishments, status, and prospects of psychology at the end of its first century as a science, while offering a new postscript. The forty-three contributors are among psychology's foremost authorities. Among the fields addressed are sensory processes and perception, learning, motivation, emotion, cognition, development, personality, and social psychology.

Rieber, Robert W., and Kurt Salzinger, eds. *Psychology: Theoretical-Historical Perspectives.* 2d ed. Washington, D.C.: APA Books, 1998. The approach to theory and history adapted by the contributors is to focus on some of the central figures in the development of the discipline. Within this approach, the authors offer analyses of three major theoretical currents in psychology: psychoanalysis, behaviorism, and the Geneva school. Other chapters focus on psychophysics (the oldest incarnation of experimental psychology) and on Gestalt, cognitive, and evolutionary psychology. Provides the reader with a broad overview of the development of a continually evolving field.

Simonton, Dean Keith. *Great Psychologists and Their Times: Scientific Insights into Psychology's History.* Washington, D.C.: APA Books, 2002. Integrates relevant research on the psychology of eminent psychologists, from the pioneering work of Francis Galton to work published in the twenty-first century. Of particular interest are chapters exploring what aspects of the sociocultural context are most conducive to the emergence of illustrious psychologists and how these sociocultural conditions—including political events, economic disturbances, or cultural values—affect not only the magnitude of achievement but also the nature of that achievement.

*Denise S. St. Cyr; updated by Allyson Washburn*

SEE ALSO: Behaviorism; Cognitive Psychology; Development; Industrial and Organizational Psychology; Neuropsychology; Psychoanalytic Psychology; Psychology: Definition.

# PSYCHOPATHOLOGY

TYPE OF PSYCHOLOGY: Psychopathology
FIELDS OF STUDY: Behavioral therapies; general constructs and issues;
   models of abnormality; organic disorders; personality disorders

*As a field of study, psychopathology has as its focus the description and causes of abnormal behavior and of psychological and emotional problems. Models or approaches to psychopathology differ with respect to the assumed causes of psychological problems. Many clinicians integrate different models to understand the basis of a client's problems and combine different treatment approaches to maximize effectiveness.*

KEY CONCEPTS
- behavior therapy
- biological approach
- biopsychosocial approach
- cognitive approach
- cognitive therapy
- culture and psychopathology
- learning approach
- mental illness
- somatic therapy

Psychopathology refers to psychological dysfunctions that either create distress for the person or interfere with day-to-day functioning in relationships or at the workplace. "Psychological disorders," "abnormal behavior," "mental illness," and "behavior and emotional disorders" are terms often used in place of psychopathology.

As a topic of interest, psychopathology does not have an identifiable, historical beginning. From the writings of ancient Egyptians, Hebrews, and Greeks it is clear, however, that ancient societies believed that abnormal behavior had its roots in supernatural phenomena, such as the vengeance of God and evil spirits. Although modern scientists have opposed that view, in the twenty-first century many people who hold fundamentalist religious beliefs or live in isolated societies still maintain that abnormal behavior can be caused by demoniac possession.

The Greek physician Hippocrates (460-377 B.C.E.) rejected demoniac possession and believed that psychological disorders had many natural causes, including heredity, head trauma, brain disease, and even family stress. Hippocrates was wrong when it came to specific details, but it is remarkable how accurate he was in identifying broad categories of factors that do influence the development of psychopathology. The Roman physician Galen (c. 129-198 C.E.) adopted the ideas of Hippocrates and expanded upon them. His school of thought held that diseases, including psychological disorders, were due to an imbalance among four bodily fluids, which he called humors: blood, black bile, yellow bile, and phlegm. For example, too much black bile, called melancholer, was believed to cause depression. Galen's beliefs have been discredited, but many of the terms he used have lived on. For instance, a specific subtype of depression is named after Galen's melancholer: Major Depression with Melancholic Features.

A major figure in the history of psychopathology is the German psychiatrist Emil Kraepelin (1856-1926). He claimed that mental illnesses, like physical illnesses, could be classified into distinct disorders, each having its own biological causes. Each disorder could be recognized by a cluster of symptoms, called a syndrome. The way in which he classified mental disorders continues to exert a strong influence on approaches to categorizing mental illnesses. The official classification system in the United States is published by the American Psychiatric Association in the *Diagnostic and Statistical Manual of Mental Disorders: DSM-IV-TR* (rev. 4th ed., 2000). Many features of this manual can be traced directly to the writings of Kraepelin in the early years of the twentieth century.

## EXAMPLES OF PSYCHOPATHOLOGY

There is a very broad range of psychological disorders. The DSM-IV-TR lists more than two hundred psychological disorders that differ in symptoms and the degree to which they affect a person's ability to function.

It is normal for someone to feel anxious on occasion. Generalized anxiety disorder is diagnosed when a person engages in excessive worry about all sorts of things and feels anxious and tense much of the time. Most people who have this disorder function quite well. They can do well at work, have good relationships, and be good parents. It is the fact that they suffer so much from their anxiety that leads to a diagnosis. In contrast, schizophrenia can be completely debilitating. Many people with schizophrenia cannot hold a job, are hospitalized frequently, have difficulty in relationships, and are incapable of good parenting. Common symptoms of schizophrenia include delusions (a system of false beliefs, such as believing there is a vast conspiracy among extraterrestrial beings to control the government); hallucinations (seeing things that are not there or hearing voices that other people cannot hear); incoherence (talking in a way that no one can understand); or emotions that are expressed out of context (laughing when telling a sad story). The symptoms of schizophrenia make it difficult or impossible for the person to function normally.

Many disorders are marked by both subjective distress and impaired functioning. One such disorder is obsessive-compulsive disorder (OCD). An obsession is a recurrent, usually unpleasant thought, image, or impulse that intrudes into a person's awareness. Some examples are believing that one is contaminated by germs, picturing oneself stabbing one's children, or thinking that every bump hit in the road while driving could have been a person struck by the car. Obsessions cause a great deal of distress. Obsessions typically lead to the development of compulsions. A compulsion is a repetitive act that is used by the person to stop the obsession and decrease the anxiety caused by the obsession. People who believe they have been contaminated may wash themselves for hours on end; those who believe that they have hit another person while driving may not be able to resist the urge to stop and look for someone injured. Behavioral compulsions can sometimes occupy so much time that the person cannot meet the demands of everyday life.

## CAUSES OF PSYCHOPATHOLOGY

The most important goal of researchers in the field of psychopathology is to discover the causes (etiology) of each disorder. If the causes for disorders were known, then psychologists could design effective treatments and, it would be hoped, be able to prevent the development of many disorders. Unfortunately, theories of psychological disorders are in their infancy, and there are many more questions than there are answers. There is no general agreement among psychologists as to where to look for answers to the question of etiology. Consequently, some researchers stress the importance of biological causes, other researchers focus on psychological processes in the development of disorders, while still others emphasize the crucial role of learning experiences in the development of behavior disorders. All these approaches are important, and each supplies a piece of the puzzle of psychopathology, but all approaches have their limitations.

THE LEARNING APPROACH. Psychologists who work within this model of psychopathology believe that abnormal behavior is learned through past experiences. The same principles that are used to explain the development of normal behavior are used to explain the development of abnormal behavior. For example, a child can learn to be a conscientious student by observing role models who are conscientious in their work. Another child may learn to break the rules of society by watching a parent break the same rules. In each case, observational learning is at work, but the outcome is very different. In another example of a learning principle, a person who is hungry and hears someone preparing food in the kitchen may begin to salivate because the sounds of food preparation have, in the past, preceded eating food and food makes the person salivate. Those sounds from the kitchen are stimuli that have become conditioned so that the person learns to have the same reaction to the sounds as to food (salivation). This learning process is called classical conditioning. In a different example, experiencing pain and having one's life threatened causes fear. A person who is attacked and bitten by a dog might well develop a fear response to all dogs that is severe enough to lead to a diagnosis of a phobia. Just as the sounds in the kitchen elicit salivation, the sight of a dog elicits an emotional response. The same underlying principle of classical conditioning can account for the development of normal behavior as well as a disorder. There are many other principles of learning besides observational learning and classical conditioning. Together, psychologists use them to account for forms of psychopathology more complex than are exemplified here. Nonetheless, there are many disorders in which a learning approach to etiology seems farfetched. For example, no one believes that mental retardation, childhood autism, or schizophrenia can be explained by learning principles alone.

**THE PSYCHOLOGICAL APPROACH.** This model, sometimes called the cognitive approach, holds that many forms of psychopathology are best understood by studying the mind. Some psychologists within this tradition believe that the most important aspect of the mind is the unconscious. The Austrian psychoanalyst Sigmund Freud (1856-1939) believed that many forms of psychopathology are due to intense conflicts of which the person is unaware but which, nevertheless, produce symptoms of disorders.

Many psychological disorders are associated with obvious problems in thinking. Schizophrenics, people with attention-deficit hyperactivity disorder (ADHD), and those who suffer from depression all show difficulties in concentration. Memory problems are central in people who develop amnesia in response to psychological trauma. People who are paranoid show abnormalities in the way they interpret the behavior of others. Indeed, it is difficult to find examples of psychopathology in which thinking is not disordered in some way, be it mild or severe. Within the cognitive approach, depression is one of the disorders that receives the most attention. People who are depressed often show problems in emotion (feeling sad), behavior (withdrawing from people), and thinking. The cognitive formulation assumes that thinking is central, specifically the way depressed people think about the world, themselves, and the future. Dysfunctional thinking is believed to give rise to the other aspects of depression. Most of the research in the field of psychopathology derives from the cognitive perspective. One of the major challenges to this approach is determining whether thinking patterns cause disorders or whether they are aspects of disorders that, themselves, are caused by nonpsychological factors. For example, depressed people have a pessimistic view of their futures. Does pessimism figure into the cause of the depression, or might depression be caused by biological factors and pessimism is just one of the symptoms of depression?

**THE BIOLOGICAL APPROACH.** The biological (biogenic) approach assumes that many forms of psychopathology are caused by abnormalities of the body, usually the brain. These abnormalities can be inherited or can occur for other reasons. What these "other reasons" are is unclear, but they may include birth complications, environmental toxins, or illness of the mother during pregnancy.

Schizophrenia is one disorder that receives much attention among those researchers who follow the biogenic approach. A great deal of research has been conducted on the importance of neurotransmitters. Nerve cells in the brain are not connected; there is a small space between them. A nerve impulse travels this space by the release of chemicals in one nerve cell, called neurotransmitters, which carry the impulse to the receptors of the next cell. There are a large number of neurotransmitters, and new ones are discovered periodically. Early research on the relationship between neurotransmitters and psychopathology tended to view the problem as "too much" or "too little" of the amount of neurotransmitters. It is now known that the situation is much more complicated. In schizophrenia, the neurotransmitter dopamine has received most of the attention, with many studies suggesting that excessive amounts of dopamine cause some of the symptoms of schizophrenia. In fact, drugs that reduce the availability of dopamine to the cells are successful in alleviating some symptoms of the disorder. However, not all people with schizophrenia are helped by these drugs, and some people are helped by drugs that one would not prescribe if the sole cause of schizophrenia is too much dopamine. Researchers are finding that the way in which dopamine and another neurotransmitter, serotonin, work together may lead to a better biological theory of schizophrenia than the excessive dopamine hypothesis.

The biological approach is a highly technical field, and it relies heavily on advances in technologies for studying the brain. Powerful new tools for studying the brain are invented at a rapid pace. For example, researchers are now able to use neuroimaging techniques to watch how the brain responds and changes from second to second.

Heredity appears to be important in understanding who develops what kind of psychological disorder, but it is often unknown exactly what is inherited that causes the disorder. The fact that schizophrenia runs in families does not reveal what is being passed on from generation to generation. The fact that inheritance works at the level of gene transmission places hereditary research squarely within the biological approach.

One method for addressing the question of whether a disorder can be inherited is by studying twins. Some twins are identical; each twin has the same genes as the other. Other twins share only half of their genes; these are fraternal twins. If one identical twin has schizophrenia and the disorder is entirely inherited, the other twin should also develop schizophrenia. Among identical twins, if one twin is schizophrenic, the other twin has a 48 percent chance of having the same disorder, not a 100 percent chance. For fraternal twins, if one is schizophrenic, there is a 17 percent chance that the other twin will have the disorder. If neither twin has schizophrenia, and no one else in the immediate family has the disorder, there is only a 1 percent chance of developing this form of psychopathology.

Two important points can be made. First, genes matter in the transmission of schizophrenia. Second, the disorder is not entirely due to heredity. Researchers who focus on heredity have found that some other disorders seem to have a genetic component, but no mental illness has been found to be entirely due to heredity. Clearly, there are other factors operating, and the biological approach must be integrated with other approaches to gain a full picture of the etiology of psychopathology.

**THE BIOPSYCHOSOCIAL APPROACH.** As its name suggests, the biopsychosocial approach seeks to understand psychopathology by examining the interactive influences of biology, cognitive processes, and learning. This is the most popular model of psychopathology and, in its most basic form, is also referred to as the diathesis-stress model. A diathesis is a predisposing factor, and the diathesis may be biological or psychological. When discussing biological diatheses, most theories assume that the diathesis is present at birth. A problem with the regulation of neurotransmitters, which may lead to schizophrenia or depression, is one example. An example of a psychological diathesis is when a person's style of thinking predisposes him or her to a disorder. For instance, pessimism—minimizing good things that happen, maximizing negative events, and attributing failures to personal defects—may predispose a person to depression. The stress aspect of the diathesis-stress model refers to the negative life experiences of the person. An early, chaotic family environment, child abuse, and being raised or living in a high-crime neighborhood are examples of stressful environments. From this perspective, a person will develop a disorder who has a predisposition for the disorder, in combination with certain life experiences that trigger the disorder.

Because the biological, learning, and psychological approaches have all contributed to the understanding of psychopathology, it is no surprise that most psychologists want to combine the best of each approach—hence, the biopsychosocial model. Given the present state of knowledge, each model represents more of an assumption about how psychopathology develops rather than a single theory with widespread scientific support. For virtually every psychological disorder, psychologists debate the causes of the disorder.

## Culture and Psychopathology

The importance of understanding the cultural context of psychopathology cannot be overstated. To be sure, some disorders that span populations—depression, mental retardation, and schizophrenia are examples—but a population both defines what should be considered abnormal behavior and determines how psychopathology is expressed. "Cultural relativism" refers to the fact that abnormality is relative to its cultural context; the same behavior or set of beliefs can be viewed as abnormal in one population and perfectly familiar and normal in another population. When viewed from an American perspective, the remedies, rituals, and beliefs of a witch doctor may seem to reflect some disorder within the witch doctor rather than a valued and culturally sanctioned means of treatment within that culture. No doubt members of a given tribal population in South America may regard the behavior of North American adolescents on prom night as grossly abnormal.

Some disorders only exist in certain cultures. A disorder known as *pibloktoq* occurs in Eskimo communities. The symptoms include tearing off one's clothes, shouting obscenities, breaking furniture, and performing other irrational and dangerous acts. The afflicted individual often follows this brief period of excited behavior by having a seizure, falling into a coma for twelve hours, and, upon awakening, having no memory of his or her behavior.

Some disorders may be very similar across two populations but contain a cultural twist. For instance, in the United States, the essential feature of social anxiety disorder is a fear of performance situations that could lead to embarrassment and disapproval. In Japan and Korea, the main concern of people with social anxiety disorder is the fear that one's blushing, eye contact, or body odor will be offensive to others.

There are numerous examples of culturally based psychopathologies; the DSM-IV-TR lists twenty-five of them in an appendix. Moreover, throughout the manual, a brief statement accompanies the description of most disorders on the roles of ethnic and cultural factors that are relevant for the given disorder, which can help the clinician arrive at an accurate diagnosis.

## TREATMENT

The major forms of treatment for psychological disorders can be grouped according to the most popular models of psychopathology. Thus, there exists behavior therapy (learning approach), cognitive therapy and psychoanalysis (psychological approach), and somatic treatment, such as the use of medications (biological approach). Consistent with the biopsychosocial model, many therapists practice cognitive behavior therapy while their clients are taking medication for their disorders. These treatments, as well as the models from which they derive, represent common and popular viewpoints, but the list is not exhaustive (for instance, family systems is a model of disorders, and the treatment is family therapy). The link between models of psychopathology and treatment is not as strong as it appears. Therapists tend to adopt the treatment belief of "whatever works," despite the fact that all therapists would prefer to know why the person is suffering from a disorder and why a specific treatment is helpful. In addition, even if the therapist is sure that the problem is a consequence of learning, he or she might have the client take medication for symptom relief during therapy. In other words, psychologists who are aligned with a specific model of psychopathology will still employ an array of treatment techniques, some of which are more closely associated with other models.

**BEHAVIOR THERAPY.** Based on learning theory, behavior therapy attempts to provide new learning experiences for the client. Those with problems that are fear-based, such as phobias, may benefit from gradual exposure to the feared situation. If social anxiety is determined to be caused by a deficit in social skills, a behavior therapist can help the person learn new ways of relating to others. If the disorder is one of excess, as in substance abuse, the behavior therapist will provide training in self-control strategies. The parents of children who show conduct disorders will be taught behavior modification techniques that they could use in the home. Behavior therapy focuses on the client's present and future. Little time is spent discussing childhood experiences, except as they clearly and directly bear on the client's presenting problem. The therapist adopts a problem-solving approach, and sessions are focused on a learning-theory-based conceptualization of the client's problems and discussions of strategies for change. Homework assignments are common, which leads behavior therapists to believe that therapy takes place between sessions.

**COGNITIVE THERAPY.** The basic tenet of cognitive therapy is that psychological problems stem from the way people view and think about the events that happen to them. Consequently, therapy focuses on helping patients change their viewpoints. For example, with a patient who becomes depressed after the breakup of a relationship, the cognitive therapist will assess the meaning that the breakup has for the person. Perhaps he or she holds irrational beliefs such as, "If my partner does not want me, no one will," or "I am a complete failure for losing this relationship." The assumption is that the patient's extreme, negative thinking is contributing to the depression. The therapist will challenge these beliefs and help the patient substitute a more rational perspective; for example, "Just because one person left me does not mean that the next person will," and "Even if this relationship ended, it does not mean that I am a failure in everything I do."

Cognitive therapy has some similarity to behavior therapy. There is a focus on the present, history-taking is selective and related to the presenting problem, and homework assignments are routine. Indeed, because the two approaches have many things in common, many therapists use both forms of treatment and refer to themselves as cognitive-behavioral therapists.

**SOMATIC THERAPY.** Somatic therapy is the domain of physicians (psychiatrists) because this form of treatment requires medical training. By far the most common example of somatic therapy is the use of psychotropic medications, medicine that will relieve psychological symptoms. Less common examples are electroconvulsive shock treatment, in which the client is tranquilized and administered a brief electric current to the brain to induce a convulsion, and brain surgery, such as leucotomy and lobotomy (rarely practiced).

The use of medications for psychological disorders has become enormously popular since 1970. Three main reasons are that the biological approach to understanding psychopathology is becoming more prominent; new drugs are being released each year that have fewer side effects; and a great deal of research is being conducted to show that an ever-increasing number of disorders are helped by medication. The use of medication for psychological disorders is not viewed as a cure. Sometimes drugs are used to help a person through a difficult period. At other times they are an important adjunct to psychotherapy. Only in the most severe forms of psychopathology would a person be medicated for the rest of his or her life.

## WHICH THERAPY IS BEST?

Researchers approach the question of which therapy is best in the context of specific disorders. No one therapy is recommended for every disorder. For instance, behavior therapy has proven to be highly successful with phobias, cognitive therapy shows good results with depression, and a trial of medication is usual for schizophrenia and bipolar disorder.

No matter what the presumed cause is of a specific disorder, a common practice is to provide medication for symptom relief, along with some form of psychotherapy to improve the person's condition over the long run.

## SOURCES FOR FURTHER STUDY

American Psychiatric Association. *Diagnostic and Statistical Manual of Mental Disorders: DSM-IV-TR.* Rev. 4th ed. Washington, D.C.: Author, 2000. The manual is the official listing of psychological disorders and their diagnostic criteria. Some of the technical words are not defined, theories are not discussed, and treatment is ignored. Nonetheless, the reader can gain a great deal of knowledge about the different forms of psychopathology and how therapists arrive at diagnoses.

Barlow, David H., and Vincent M. Durand. *Abnormal Psychology.* 3d ed. Belmont, Calif.: Wadsworth/Thomson, 2002. This undergraduate textbook is written for an audience with little or no background in psychology. The book covers a broad range of psychological disorders and is an excellent beginning text to learn about the biopsychosocial model of psychopathology. Hundreds of references are provided.

Kanfer, Frederick, H., and Arnold P. Goldstein, eds. *Helping People Change: A Textbook of Methods.* New York: Pergamon General Psychology, 1991. This is a classic in the field of clinical psychology. It covers many cognitive-behavioral techniques that are used for an array of psychological disorders. The target audience is undergraduate and graduate students in psychology and practitioners who want to learn about this treatment modality. Each chapter is easy to understand and assumes only a basic knowledge of therapy and psychopathology.

Millon, Theodore, Paul H. Blaney, and Roger D. Davis, eds. *Oxford Textbook of Psychopathology.* New York: Oxford University Press, 1999. An advanced textbook for readers who have, at least, a college background in psychology and basic knowledge of the field of psychopathology. Twenty-seven chapters, authored by experts, span almost seven hundred pages. Theory and assessment of disorders is emphasized.

*Laurence Grimm and Lindsey L. Henninger*

SEE ALSO: Abnormality: Psychological Models; Cognitive Behavior Therapy; Cognitive Therapy; Drug Therapies; Psychotherapy: Goals and Techniques.

# PSYCHOSOMATIC DISORDERS

TYPE OF PSYCHOLOGY: Psychopathology
FIELDS OF STUDY: Cognitive processes; organic disorders; stress and illness

*Psychosomatic disorders are physical disorders produced by psychological factors such as stress, mental states, or personality characteristics. A variety of psychological or psychotherapeutic interventions have been developed to alter the individual's ability to cope with stressful situations and to change the personality or behavior of the individual.*

KEY CONCEPTS
- behavior modification
- biogenic
- biopsychosocial
- cognitive
- locus of control
- psychogenic
- psychological factors affecting physical condition
- psychosomatic disorders
- self-efficacy
- Type A behavior pattern

The term "psychosomatic" was introduced by physician Flanders Dunbar in the early 1940's, shortly after Hans Selye presented the concept of "stress." Psychosomatic disorders are physical disorders which are caused by, or exacerbated by, psychological factors. These psychological factors fall into three major groups: stress resulting from encounters with the environment, personality characteristics, and psychological states. Psychosomatic disorders are different from two other conditions with which they are often confused. Psychosomatic disorders are real—that is, they are actual physical illnesses that have underlying psychological causes or that are made worse by psychological factors. In somatoform disorders (such as hypochondriasis), by contrast, there is no physiological cause; another condition, malingering, is the faking of an illness.

Psychosomatic disorders can affect any of the organ systems of the body. Certainly, not all physical disorders or illnesses are psychosomatic disorders; in many cases, an illness or physical disorder is caused entirely by biogenic factors. In many other cases, however, there is no question about the importance of psychogenic factors. The American College of Family Physicians has estimated that 90 percent of the workload of doctors is the result of psychogenic factors.

Many familiar and common psychosomatic disorders that can affect the body's various organ systems. Included among them are skin disorders, such as acne, hives, and rashes; musculoskeletal disorders, such as backaches, rheumatoid arthritis, and tension headaches; respiratory disorders, such as asthma and hiccups; and cardiovascular disorders, such as hypertension, heart attacks, strokes, and migraine headaches. Other disorders have also been related to psychological factors, including anemia, weakening of the immune system, ulcers, and constipation. Genitourinary disorders such as menstrual problems, vaginismus, male erectile disorder, and premature ejaculation are included among psychosomatic disorders, as are certain endocrine and neurological problems.

The relationship between the mind and the body has long been the subject of debate. Early societies saw a clear link between the two. Early Greek and Roman physicians believed that body fluids determined personality types and that people with certain personality types were prone to certain types of diseases. Beginning during the Renaissance, the dominant line of thought held that there was little or no connection between the mind and the body. Illness was seen as the result of organic, cellular pathology. Destruction of body tissue and invasion by "germs," rather than personality type, were seen as the causes of illness.

Sigmund Freud's work with patients suffering from conversion hysteria began to demonstrate both the importance of psychological factors in the production of physical symptoms of illness and the value of psychological therapy in changing the functioning of the body. Research conducted in the 1930's and 1940's suggested that personality factors play a role in the production of a variety of specific illnesses, including ulcers, hypertension, and asthma.

## THE ROLE OF STRESS

Even though Freud demonstrated the role of psychological factors in illness, the medical field has still focused upon the biological roots of illness and has still largely rejected or ignored the role of emotions and personality. Nevertheless, the ascending line of thought can be described as a biopsychosocial view of illness, which begins with the basic assumption that health and illness result from an interplay of biological, psychological, and social factors. This view provides a conceptual framework for incorporating human elements into the scientific paradigm. A man who suffers a heart attack at age thirty-five is not conceptualized simply as a person who is experiencing the effects of cellular damage caused by purely biological processes that are best treated by surgery or the administration of drugs. The victim, instead, is viewed as a person who also has engaged in practices that adversely affected his health. In addition to drugs and surgery, therefore, treatment for this man might include changing his views on the relative value of work and family as well as emphasizing the importance of daily exercise and diet. If he smokes, he will be encouraged to quit smoking. He might receive training in stress management and relaxation techniques.

Few people today would argue with the proposition that stress is a fact of life. Most have far more experience with stressors—those events that humans find stressful—than they would willingly choose for themselves. Stress is one of the major causes of psychosomatic disorders. Stressors are often assumed to be external events, probably because stressful external events are so easily identified and recognized. Many stressors, however, come from within oneself. For example, an individual alone often sets strict standards for himself or herself and, in failing to meet those standards, often makes harsher personal judgments than anyone else would make. Especially since the late 1970's and early 1980's, cognitive psychologists have focused attention on the internal thinking processes, thoughts, values, beliefs, and expectations that lead people to put unnecessary pressure on themselves that results in the subjective sense of stress.

Another contribution made by cognitive psychologists was the realization that a situation can be a stressor only if the individual interprets it as stressful. Any event that people perceive as something with which they can cope will be perceived as less stressful than an event that taxes or exceeds their resources, regardless of the objective seriousness of the two events. In other words, it is the cognitive appraisal of the event, coupled with one's cognitive appraisal of one's ability to deal with the event, rather than the objective reality of the event, that determines the degree to which one subjectively experiences stress.

## PERSONALITY TYPES

Continuing the tradition of the early Greek and Roman physicians, modern personality theorists have often noted that certain personality characteristics seem to be associated with a propensity to develop illness, or even specific illnesses. Other personality characteristics appear to reduce vulnerability to illness. One of the best-known examples of a case in which personality characteristics affect health is that of the Type A behavior pattern (or Type A personality). The person identified as a Type A personality typically displays a pattern of behaviors which includes easily aroused hostility, excessive competitiveness, and a pronounced sense of time urgency. Research suggests that hostility is the most damaging of these behaviors. Type A personalities typically display hyperreactivity to stressful situations, with a corresponding slow return to the baseline of arousal. The hostile Type A personality is particularly prone to coronary heart disease. By contrast, the less driven Type B personality does not display the hostility, competitiveness, and time urgency of the Type A personality and is about half as likely to develop coronary heart disease.

Studies conducted in the 1970's and 1980's led to the suggestion that there is a Type C, or cancer-prone, personality. Although the role of personality characteristics is heavily debated in terms of the development of cancer, various characteristics related to stress have been found to suppress the immune system, thereby making an individual more vulnerable to some cancers. Personality characteristics have therefore also been found to be somewhat influential in the course of the disease. It is well known that many natural and artificial substances produce cancer, but many researchers have also noted that people with certain personality characteristics are more likely to develop cancer, are more likely to develop fast-growing cancers, and are less likely to survive their cancers, whatever the cause. These personality characteristics include repression of strong negative emotions, acquiescence in the face of stressful life situations, inhibition, depression, and hopelessness. Encounters with uncontrollable stressful events appear to be particularly related to the development or course of cancer. In addition, some research suggests that not having strong social support systems may contribute to the development or affect the outcome of cancer.

Research has begun to focus on the possible interaction among risk factors for cancer. For example, depressed smokers are many more times likely to develop smoking-related cancers than are either nondepressed smokers or depressed nonsmokers. One theory suggests that the smoking provides exposure to the carcinogenic substance that initiates the cancer, and depression promotes its development.

It has been suggested that hardiness is a broad, positive personality variable that affects one's propensity for developing stress-related illness. Hardiness is made up of three more specific characteristics: commitment (becoming involved in things that are going on around oneself), challenge (accepting the need for change and seeing new opportunities for growth in what others see as problems), and control (believing that one's actions determine what happens in life and that one can have an effect on the environment). It has been hypothesized that people who possess these characteristics are less likely to develop stress-related disorders because they view stressful situations more favorably than do other people. Commitment and control seem to be more influential in promoting health. Locus of control is a related concept which has received much attention.

## CONTROL AND HELPLESSNESS

Locus of control refers to the location where one believes control over life events originates. An external locus of control is outside oneself; an internal locus of control is within oneself. The individual who perceives that life events are the result of luck, or are determined by others, is assuming an external locus of control. The belief that one's efforts and actions control one's own destiny reflects an internal locus of control. Internalizers are thought to be more likely to assume responsibility for initiating necessary lifestyle changes, to employ direct coping mechanisms when confronted with stressful situations, and to be more optimistic about the possibility of successfully instituting changes that are needed. This last characteristic is sometimes called self-efficacy. Self-efficacy refers to the belief that one is able to do what is needed and attain the intended effect.

The concept of learned helplessness, on the other hand, produces feelings of complete lack of control and a fatalistic acceptance of events. Martin E. P. Seligman began to investigate this phenomenon in 1964. He found that when people are faced with a situation which they can do nothing to prevent or escape, they learn the attitude of helplessness. Seligman and colleagues later investigated the question of why some people do not adopt this attitude. They concluded that people who adopt a pessimistic explanatory style become helpless when adversity is encountered, but that an optimistic explanatory style prevents the development of learned helplessness.

Seligman has described the chain of events by which the pessimistic explanatory style may lead to illness. Beginning with unfortunate experiences such as a serious loss, defeat, or failure, the person with a pessimistic explanatory style becomes depressed. The depression leads to depletion of a neurotransmitter substance called catecholamine, and the body increases the secretion of endorphins—the body's naturally produced form of morphine. When receptors in the immune system detect the increased presence of the endorphins, the immune system begins to turn itself down. Any disease agents that are encountered while the immune system is weakened have a much greater likelihood of overwhelming the remaining defenses of the immune system. This process is very similar to the situation faced by the individual who contracts the human immunodeficiency virus (HIV) and develops acquired immunodeficiency syndrome (AIDS). When the immune system of the person with AIDS is unable to function effectively, opportunistic infections against which the body could normally defend itself are able to overtake it. It is those opportunistic infections that kill, rather than the HIV itself.

### INTERVENTIONS

Because the hyperreactivity of the Type A behavior pattern is thought to be at least partially genetically based, there are probably some limits on what can be done to reduce the incidence of coronary heart disease resulting from physiological hyperreactivity. There is, however, much that can be done in other areas. Persons who are prone to such disorders can be taught to exercise properly, eliminate unhealthy dietary practices, and reduce or quit smoking. Of particular interest to psychologists is the opportunity to help these individuals by teaching effective coping strategies, stress management, values training, behavior modification to control Type A behaviors, and cognitive control of depression and other negative emotions.

Studies by psychologists have demonstrated a wide range of interventions that can be helpful in reducing the danger of cardiovascular disease in Type A personalities. Exercise produces positive effects on physiological functioning, appears to improve general psychological functioning, and reduces Type A behaviors. Cognitive behavioral stress management techniques have been shown to reduce behavioral reactivity. Values training focusing on changing the person's perceptions of the importance of occupational success and competitiveness has enabled the individual to concentrate on more beneficial behaviors. Behavior modification techniques have been used to alter the kinds of behavior that appear to be most dangerous for the Type A person, substituting other behavioral responses in place of explosive speech and hostility. Cognitive control of emotions produces more rapid physiological recovery after stress.

Efforts by psychologists to help the Type C personality might focus on assertiveness training and altering the person's belief that it is not appropriate to display strong negative emotions, such as anger or frustration. Teaching the Type C person to fight back against stressful life situations, rather than acquiescing to them, might also be of benefit. Imagery therapy appears to be beneficial to some cancer patients, perhaps for that reason, but also because it promotes the development of learned optimism in place of learned pessimism. Promoting the development of effective social support systems is another means for psychologists to have a positive impact in the fight against cancer.

### PSYCHOSOMATICS AND THE FUTURE

It is important that a distinction be made between psychosomatic disorders and three other conditions listed in the *Diagnostic and Statistical Manual of Mental Disorders: DSM-IV-TR* (rev. 4th ed., 2000), which is the official classification system for mental disorders published by the American Psychiatric Association. Psychosomatic disorders, which are covered by the category Psychological Factors Affecting Physical Conditions, are not themselves considered mental disorders. While the psychological factors that cause the physical illness are unhealthy or abnormal from a psychiatric or psychological perspective, the psychosomatic disorder is a real, physical illness or condition controlled by real, physical processes.

Somatoform disorders, on the other hand, are mental disorders which manifest themselves through real or imagined physical symptoms for which no physical cause exists. These symptoms are not intentionally produced by the client. Conversion disorder is one of the somatoform disorders that laypeople often confuse with psychosomatic disorders. Unlike the case with psychosomatic disorders, there is no organic or physiological pathology that would account for the presence of the physical symptoms displayed by the person suffering from a conversion disorder. Hypochondriasis is the second somatoform disorder that is often confusing for laypeople. The person suffering from hypochondriasis fears or believes that he or she has the symptoms of a serious disease, but the imagined "symptoms" are actually normal sensations or body reactions which are misinterpreted as symptoms of disease.

Malingering is the third condition which is sometimes confused with psychosomatic disorders. The person who is malingering is faking illness and is reporting symptoms that either do not exist at all or are grossly exaggerated. The malingering is motivated by external goals or incentives.

By eliminating many of the diseases that used to be epidemic, especially those which killed people early in life, medical science has increased the average life expectancy of Americans by about thirty years since the beginning of the twentieth century. Eliminating the psychological factors that cause psychosomatic disorders holds promise for another increase in average life expectancy in the next few decades. Heart disease, cancer, and strokes are the top three killer diseases in the United States, and each has a powerful psychosomatic component. The reduction in human suffering and the economic benefits that can be gained by controlling nonfatal psychosomatic disorders are equally promising.

Cognitive and health psychologists have, particularly since the 1970's, tried to determine the degree to which cognitive psychotherapy interventions can boost immune system functioning in cancer patients. They have also used behavioral and cognitive therapy approaches to alter the attitudes and behaviors of people who are prone to heart disease and strokes, with considerable success. In the near future, they can be expected to focus their efforts on two major fronts. The first will involve further attempts to identify the psychological factors which might increase people's propensity to develop psychosomatic disorders. The second will involve continuing efforts to develop and refine the therapeutic interventions intended to reduce the damage done by psychosomatic disorders, and possibly to prevent them entirely.

### SOURCES FOR FURTHER STUDY

Chopra, Deepak. *Creating Health.* Reprint. Boston: Houghton Mifflin, 1991. Chopra is a proponent of meditation, an approach that not all American psychologists feel comfortable advocating. Nevertheless, this book is written by a practicing physician for the layperson. He covers a wide variety of psychosomatic disorders, suggests a variety of healthy habits, and presents the viewpoint that "health is our natural state."

Pert, Candace B. *Molecules of Emotion.* New York: Simon & Schuster, 1997. This is a highly accessible book written in an engaging style with wit and humor. Pert discusses her research on the scientific bases of mind-body medicine and the difficulties in integrating these concepts into Western medicine. The book contains appendices with a list of resources and practitioners, an extensive glossary, and recommended readings.

Seligman, Martin E. P. *Learned Optimism.* New York: Alfred A. Knopf, 1991. Chapter 2 provides an especially interesting account of how two young graduate students can upset one of the most basic assumptions of a well-entrenched viewpoint and promote the development of a new way of looking at things. Chapter 10 describes how explanatory styles might affect health and the mechanism by which this is thought to occur. A readable book which examines an interesting concept.

Simonton, O. Carl, Stephanie Matthews-Simonton, and James L. Creighton. *Getting Well Again.* New York: Bantam Books, 1980. Cancer researchers and therapists examine the mind-body connection, effects of beliefs, causes of cancer, effects of stress and personality, and effects of expectations on the development and progress of cancer. They describe a holistic approach to treatment, emphasizing relaxation and visual imagery, that is reported to produce cancer survival rates that are twice the national norm.

Taylor, Shelley E. *Health Psychology*. 5th ed. Boston: McGraw-Hill, 2003. A moderately high-level college textbook that comprehensively covers the general field of health psychology. As could be expected, many research studies are presented, and not all of them corroborate one another. The general reader should have no particular difficulty handling this material; the writing is reader-friendly.

Wedding, Danny, ed. *Behavior and Medicine*. 3d ed. Seattle: Hogrefe & Huber, 2001. This large volume covers an extensive area of behavior and medicine, which include stress and various behaviors which may affect physiological health. The articles cover such behavioral issues as substance abuse, stress management, pain, placebos, AIDS, cardiovascular risk, and adherence to medical regimens. Other behavioral issues are covered which relate to love and work, as well as developmental issues from infancy to death, dying and grief. The book is readable and includes illustrations, bibliographies, summaries, and study questions at the end of each article.

*John W. Nichols; updated by Martha Oehmke Loustaunau*

SEE ALSO: Cognitive Behavior Therapy; Cognitive Therapy; Emotions; Endocrine System; Learned Helplessness; Stress-Related Diseases.

# PSYCHOSURGERY

DATE: The 1930's forward
TYPE OF PSYCHOLOGY: Psychological methodologies
FIELDS OF STUDY: Anxiety disorders; biological treatments; depression;
  endocrine system; schizophrenias

*Psychosurgery is brain surgery in which brain parts are disconnected or removed to do away with psychiatric problems such as aggression, anxiety, and psychoses. It was used most from 1935 to 1965, until psychoactive drugs began to replace it. Psychosurgery is not used to relieve psychiatric symptoms resulting from structural brain disease such as brain tumors.*

KEY CONCEPTS
* electroconvulsive therapy
* psychopharmaceuticals
* psychosurgery techniques
* somatic theory of insanity

In the early twentieth century, the treatment of mental disease was limited to psychotherapy for neurotics and long-term care of psychotics in asylums. In the 1930's, these methods were supplemented by physical approaches using electroconvulsive therapy (ECT) and brain operations. Psychosurgical operations were in vogue from the mid-1930's to the middle to late 1960's. They became, and still are, hugely controversial, although their use had drastically declined by the last quarter of the twentieth century. Controversy arose because, for its first twenty-five years of existence, crude psychosurgery was too often carried out on inappropriate patients.

ECT developed after the 1935 discovery that schizophrenia could be treated by convulsions induced through camphor injection. Soon, convulsion production was accomplished by passage of electric current through the brain, as described in 1938 by Italian physicians Ugo Cerletti and Lucio Bini. ECT was most successful in alleviating depression and is still used for that purpose. In contrast, classic psychosurgery by bilateral prefrontal leucotomy (lobotomy) is no longer performed because of its deleterious effects on the physical and mental health of many subjects. These effects included epilepsy and unwanted personality changes such as apathy, passivity, and low emotional responses. It should be remembered, however, that psychosurgery was first planned to quiet chronically tense, delusional, agitated, or violent psychotic patients.

## HISTORY AND CONTEXT OF PSYCHOSURGERY

Psychosurgery is believed to have originated with the observation by early medical practitioners that severe head injuries could produce extreme changes in behavior patterns. In addition, physicians of the thirteenth to sixteenth centuries reported that sword and knife wounds that penetrated the skull could change normal behavior patterns. From the mid-1930's to the mid-1960's, reputable physicians performed psychosurgery on both indigent patients in public institutions and on the wealthy at expensive private hospitals and universities.

Psychosurgery was imperfect and could cause adverse reactions, but it was performed because of the arguments advanced by powerful physician proponents of the method; the imperfect state of knowledge of the brain at the time; the enthusiasm of the popular press, which lauded the method; and many problems at overcrowded mental hospitals. The last reason is thought to have been the most compelling, as asylums for the incurably mentally ill were hellish places. Patients were beaten and choked by attendants, incarcerated in dark, dank, padded cells, and subjected to many other indignities. At the same time, little could be done to cure them.

### EGAS MONIZ INVENTS LEUCOTOMY

The two main figures in psychosurgery were António Egas Moniz, the Portuguese neurologist who invented lobotomy, and the well-known American neuropathologist and neuropsychiatrist Walter Freeman, who roamed the world convincing others to carry out the operations. The imperfect state of knowledge of the brain in relation to insanity was expressed in two theories of mental illness. A somatic (organic) theory of insanity proposed it to be of biological origin. In contrast, a functional theory supposed life experiences to cause the problems.

The somatic theory was shaped most by Emil Kraepelin, the foremost authority on psychiatry in the first half of the twentieth century. Kraepelin distinguished twenty types of mental disorder, including dementia praecox (schizophrenia) and manic-depressive (bipolar) disorder. Kraepelin and his colleagues viewed these diseases as genetically determined, and practitioners of psychiatry developed complex physical diagnostic schema that identified people with various types of psychoses. In contrast, Sigmund Freud was the main proponent of the functional theory. Attempts to help mental patients included ECT as well as surgical removal of tonsils, sex organs, and parts of the digestive system. All these methods had widely varied success rates that were often subjective. Further differences depended on which surgeon used them. By the 1930's, the most widely effective curative procedures were several types of ECT and lobotomy (psychosurgery).

The first lobotomy was carried out on November 12, 1935, at a hospital in Lisbon, Portugal. There, Pedro A. Lima, Egas Moniz's neurosurgeon collaborator, drilled two holes into the skull of a mental patient and injected ethyl alcohol directly into the frontal lobes of her brain to destroy nerve cells. After similar operations on several patients, the tissue-killing procedure was altered to use an instrument called a leucotome. After its insertion into the brain, the knifelike instrument, designed by Egas Moniz, was rotated like an apple corer to destroy chosen lobe areas.

*António Egas Moniz,*
*inventor of the lobotomy.*
(The Nobel Foundation)

Egas Moniz—already a famous neurologist—named the procedure prefrontal leucotomy. He won a Nobel Prize in Physiology or Medicine in 1949 for his invention of the procedure. Within a year of his first leucotomy, psychosurgery (another term invented by Egas Moniz) spread through Europe. Justification for its wide use was the absence of any other effective somatic treatment and the emerging concept that the cerebral frontal lobes were the site of intellectual activity and mental problems. The selection of leucotomy target sites was based on two considerations using the position in the frontal lobes where nerve fibers—not nerve cells—were most concentrated and avoiding damage to large blood vessels. Thus, Egas Moniz targeted the frontal lobe's centrum ovale, which contains few blood vessels.

After eight operations—50 percent performed on schizophrenics—Egas Moniz and Lima stated that their cure rates were good. Several other psychiatric physicians disagreed strongly. After twenty operations, it became fairly clear that psychosurgery worked best on patients suffering from anxiety and depression, while schizophrenics did not benefit very much. The main effect of the surgery was to calm patients and make them docile. Retrospectively, it is believed that Egas Moniz's evidence for serious improvement in many cases was very sketchy. However, many psychiatric and neurological practitioners were impressed, and the stage was set for wide dissemination of psychosurgery.

## LOBOTOMY PROCEDURES

The second great proponent of leucotomy—the physician who renamed it lobotomy and greatly modified the methodology used—was Freeman, professor of neuropathology at George Washington University Medical School in Washington, D.C. In 1936, he tested the procedure on preserved brains from the medical school morgue and repeated Egas Moniz's efforts. After six lobotomies, Freeman and his associate James W. Watts became optimistic that the method was useful to treat patients exhibiting apprehension, anxiety, insomnia, and nervous tension, while pointing out that it would be impossible to determine whether the procedure had effected the recovery or cure of mental problems until a five-year period had passed.

As Freeman and Watts continued to operate, they noticed problems, including relapses to the original abnormal state, a need for repeated surgery, a lack of ability on the part of patients to resume jobs requiring the use of reason, and death due to postsurgical hemorrhage. This led them to develop a more precise technique, using the landmarks on the skull to identify where to drill entry holes, cannulation to assure that lobe penetration depth was not dangerous to patients, and use of a knifelike spatula to make lobotomy cuts. The extent of surgery also varied, depending upon whether the patient involved was suffering from an affective disorder or from schizophrenia. Their method, the "routine Freeman-Watts lobotomy procedure," became popular throughout the world.

Another method used for prefrontal lobotomy was designed by J. G. Lyerly in 1937. He opened the brain so that psychosurgeons could see exactly what was being done to the frontal lobes. This technique also became popular and was used throughout the United States. Near the same time, in Japan, Mizuho Nakata of Nigata Medical College began to remove from the brain parts of one or both frontal lobes. However, the Freeman-Watts method was most popular as the result of a "do-it-yourself manual" for psychosurgery that Freeman and Watts published in 1942. The book theorized that the brain pathways between cerebral frontal lobes and the thalamus regulate intensity of emotions in ideas, and acceptance of this theory led to better scientific justification of psychosurgery.

Another lobotomy procedure that was fairly widespread was Freeman's transorbital method, designed not only to correct shortcomings in his routine method but also in attempt to aid many more schizophrenics. The simple, rapid, but frightening procedure drove an ice-pick-like transorbital leukotome through the eye socket, above the eyeball, and into the frontal lobe. Subjects were rendered unconscious with ECT, and the procedure was done before they woke up. Use of this method gained many converts and, gruesome as it sounds, the method caused less brain damage than other psychosurgery procedures. It was widely used at state hospitals for the insane and was lauded by the press as making previously hopeless cases normal immediately.

Subsequently developed tereotaxic surgical techniques, such as stereotactic cingulatory, enabled psychosurgeons to create much smaller lesions by means of probes inserted into accurately located brain regions, followed by nerve destruction through the use of radioactive implants or by cryogenics. Currently, psychosurgery is claimed to be an effective treatment for patients with intractable depression, anxiety, or obsessional problems and a method that improves the behavior of very aggressive patients. Opponents say that these therapeutic effects can be attained by means of antipsychotic and antidepressant drugs. The consensus is that psychosurgery can play a small part in psychiatric treatment when long-term use of other treatments is unsuccessful and patients are tormented by mental problems.

## MODE OF ACTION OF PSYCHOSURGERY

Collectively, the brain's limbic system is composed of the hippocampus, amygdala, hippocampal and cingulate gyri, limen insulae, and posterior orbital regions of cerebral frontal lobes. This system, its components linked by nerve pathways, controls emotional expression, seizure activity, and memory storage and recall. Moreover, cerebral lobe limbic system connections from the dorsal convexity of a frontal lobe comprise two pathways running to the cingulate gyrus and hippocampus and the hypothalamus and midbrain. The frontal lobe orbital surface also projects to the septal area of the hypothalamus. The limbic brain architecture therefore yields two neurotransport circuits in a frontolimbic-hypothalamic-midbrain axis. These are a medial frontal, cingulate, hippocampus circuit (MFCHC) and an orbital frontal, temporal, amygdala circuit (OFTAC), which control hypothalamic autonomic and endocrine action. The MFCHC and OFTAC connect in the septa, preoptic area, midbrain, and hypothalamus.

The original Egas Moniz lobotomy divided the frontolimbic structures, and its bad effects were due to the disabling impairment of frontal lobe function. Psychosurgery on the anterior cingulate gyrus and on the thalamofrontal bundle (bimedial leucotomy) divided different parts of the same main circuit. Orbital undercutting severs red nerve tracts running from the posterior orbital cortex to the limbic system. Although psychosurgery is currently an uncommon procedure, when it is performed, the methods used are lower medial quadrant leucotomy, making lesions just before the fourth ventricle; stereotactic-subcaudate-tractotomy, making lesions with rear halves in the subcaudate area; removal of the anterior two inches of the cingulate gyrus; and stereotactic limbic leucotomy, lesioning the lower medial frontal lobe quadrant. These operations cause varied endocrine and autonomic disconnections and are thus chosen to suit the mental condition being treated.

## DIAGNOSIS AND TREATMENT

Diagnosis of a need for psychosurgery is based on observation of symptoms supporting abnormal psychological behavior. Examples are extremes of aggression, anxiety, obsession, or compulsiveness as well as psychoses other than schizophrenia. The exclusion of schizophrenics, except for those having marked anxiety and tension, is based on data supporting poor responses by schizophrenics to lobotomy and other leucotomies. Surveys have shown that good surgical outcomes were only obtained in 18 percent of schizophrenics who underwent lobotomy, as compared with 50 percent of depressives.

Psychosurgery's unfavorable record between 1935 and 1965, and its postoperative irreversibility, speak to the need for careful study before suggesting such brain surgery. In addition, many members of the medical community believe that the choice of psychosurgery should be based on the long-term nature of symptoms untreatable by other means, as well as a severe risk of suicide. Before psychosurgery is attempted, other methods must be exhausted, such as repeated ECT, prolonged psychoanalysis, and aggressive pharmaceutical treatments with antipsychotic drugs. Some sources suggest, as criteria for choosing psychosurgery, the persistence of symptoms for more than ten years of treatment under conditions where all possible nonsurgical methodology has been exhausted after its aggressive use. Others believe it inhumane to require a decade of illness before allowing the possibility of a cure.

Symptom severity is another hugely important criterion for psychosurgery. Examples of this are the complete inability to work at a job or carry out household chores, as well as long-term and severe endogenous depression. It is also suggested that patients who have strong psychological support from their families and stable environments are the best candidates. Careful assessment of patient symptoms, handicaps, and problems should always be carried out. Formal rating scales, personality assessment via school and work records, and information coming from close relatives or friends are also viewed as crucial.

The use of psychosurgery is limited to a very small number of patients not helped by existing chemotherapeutic or psychoanalytical methodology. It is fortunate that a wide variety of new techniques have made psychosurgery capable of destroying smaller and smaller targets. As knowledge of the brain and its functioning increases, it appears possible that modern psychosurgery may yet prove to be useful where other methods fail.

## SOURCES FOR FURTHER STUDY

Feigenbaum, Ernes. *Stereotactic Cingulotomy as a Means of Psychosurgery.* Rockville, Md.: U.S. Department of Health and Human Services, Public Health Service, 1985. A useful description of one of the newer psychosurgical methods.

Fulton, John F. *Frontal Lobotomy and Affective Behavior: A Neuropsychological*

*Analysis.* New York: W. W. Norton, 1951. A prominent member of the American medical profession contemporary with António Egas Moniz and Pedro A. Lima discusses human and animal lobotomy. Fulton is strongly for lobotomy and lauds its achievements and prospects. The book has good references and illustrations.

Lader, Malcolm H., and Reginald Herrington. *Biological Treatments in Psychiatry.* 2d ed. New York: Oxford University Press, 1996. Covers the human brain, mental illness and principles of its treatment, neuropharmacology, psychosurgery, and ECT. Contains a good bibliography.

Rodgers, Joann Ellison. *Psychosurgery: Damaging the Brain to Save the Mind.* New York: HarperCollins, 1992. Covers psychosurgery in healing the chronically mentally ill. Describes methods which destroy only a few brain cells and their efficacy compared to drugs. Examines moral and medical pros and cons.

Turner, Eric A. *Surgery of the Mind.* Birmingham, England: Carmen Press, 1982. Answers questions regarding the ethics of carrying out psychosurgery, its consequences, and its justifications. Topics include the brain, its function and operation, selection and management of lobotomy patients, various types of psychosurgery, and follow-up of five hundred psychosurgeries.

Valenstein, Elliot S. *Great and Desperate Cures: The Rise and Decline of Psychosurgery and Other Radical Treatments for Mental Illness.* New York: Basic Books, 1986. Well-thought-out history of psychosurgery. Includes theories of mentation leading to psychosurgery, methodology of its great proponents, and reasons for its replacement and limited use. Illustrated.

_____, ed. *The Psychosurgery Debate: Scientific, Legal, and Ethical Perspectives.* New York: W. F. Freeman, 1980. Includes an overview of the history, rationale for, and extent of psychosurgery; patient selection; evaluation of methods used; description of legal and ethical issues; and an extensive bibliography.

*Sanford S. Singer*

SEE ALSO: Anxiety Disorders; Bipolar Disorder; Brain Structure; Depression; Madness: Historical Concepts; Schizophrenia: Background, Types, and Symptoms; Schizophrenia: Theoretical Explanations.

# PSYCHOTHERAPY
## GOALS AND TECHNIQUES

TYPE OF PSYCHOLOGY: Psychotherapy
FIELD OF STUDY: Evaluating psychotherapy

*The goals to be reached in psychotherapy and the techniques employed to accomplish them vary according to the needs of the patient and the theoretical orientation of the therapist.*

KEY CONCEPTS
- behavioral therapy
- corrective emotional experience
- desensitization
- eclectic therapy
- humanistic therapy
- interpretation
- psychodynamic therapy
- resistance
- shaping
- therapeutic alliance

Psychotherapy involves an interpersonal relationship in which clients present themselves to a psychotherapist in order to gain some relief from distress in their lives. It should be noted that although people who seek psychological help are referred to as "clients" by a wide range of psychotherapists, this term is used interchangeably with the term "patients," which is traditionally used more often by psychodynamically and medically trained practitioners. In all forms of psychotherapy, patients must tell the psychotherapist about their distress and reveal intimate information in order for the psychotherapist to be helpful. The psychotherapist must aid patients in the difficult task of admitting difficulties and revealing themselves, because a patient's desire to be liked and to be seen as competent can stand in the way of this work. The patient also wants to find relief from distress at the least possible cost in terms of the effort and personal changes to be made, and, therefore, patients often prevent themselves from making the very changes in which they are interested. This is termed resistance, and much of the work of the psychotherapist involves dealing with such resistance.

The goals of the patient are determined by the type of life problems that are being experienced. Traditionally, psychotherapists make a diagnosis of the psychiatric disorder from which the patient suffers, with certain symptoms to be removed in order for the patient to gain relief. The vast majority of patients suffer from some form of anxiety or depression, or from certain failures in personality development which produce deviant behaviors and rigid patterns of relating to others called personality disorders. Relatively few patients suffer from severe disorders, called psychoses, which are characterized by some degree of loss of contact with reality. Depending on the particular symptoms involved in the patient's disorder, psychotherapeutic goals will be set, although the patient may not be aware of the necessity of these changes at first. In addition, the diagnosis allows the psychotherapist to anticipate the kinds of goals that would be difficult for the patient to attain. Psychotherapists also consider the length of time they will likely work with the patient. Therefore, psychotherapeutic goals depend on the patient's wishes, the type of psychiatric disorder from which the patient suffers, and the limitations of time under which the psychotherapy proceeds.

Another factor that plays a major role in determining psychotherapeutic goals is the psychotherapist's theoretical model for treatment. This model is based on a personality theory that explains people's motivations, how people develop psychologically, and how people differ from one another. It suggests what occurred in life to create the person's problems and what must be achieved to correct these problems. Associated with each theory is a group of techniques that can be applied to accomplish the goals considered to be crucial within the theory used. There are three main models of personality and treatment: psychodynamic therapies, behavioral therapies, and humanistic therapies. Psychodynamic therapists seek to make patients aware of motives, of which they were previously unconscious or unaware, for their actions. By becoming aware of their motives, patients can better control the balance between desires for pleasure and the need to obey one's conscience. Behavioral therapists attempt to increase the frequency of certain behaviors and decrease the frequency of others by reducing anxiety associated with certain behavior, teaching new behavior, and rewarding and punishing certain behaviors. Humanistic therapists try to free patients to use their innate abilities by developing relationships with patients in which patients can be assured of acceptance, making the patients more accepting of themselves and more confident in making decisions and expressing themselves.

Most psychotherapists use a combination of theories, and therefore of goals and techniques, in their practice. These "eclectic" therapists base their decisions about goals and techniques upon the combined theory they have evolved or upon a choice among other theories given what applies best to a patient or diagnosis. It also appears that this eclectic approach has become popular because virtually all psychotherapy cases demand attention to certain common goals associated with the various stages of treatment, and different types of therapy are well suited to certain goals and related techniques at particular stages.

## THERAPEUTIC RELATIONSHIPS

When patients first come to a psychotherapist, they have in mind some things about their lives that need to be changed. The psychotherapist recognizes that before this can be accomplished, a trusting relationship must be established with patients. This has been termed the "therapeutic alliance" or a "collaborative relationship." Establishing this relationship becomes the first goal of therapy. Patients must learn that the therapist understands them and can be trusted with the secrets of their lives. They must also learn about the limits of the therapeutic relationship: that the psychotherapist is to be paid for the service, that the relationship will focus on the patients' concerns and life experiences rather than the psychotherapist's, that the psychotherapist is available to patients during the scheduled sessions and emergencies only, and that this relationship will end when the psychotherapeutic goals are met.

The therapist looks early for certain recurring patterns in what the patient thinks, feels, and does. These patterns may occur in the therapy sessions, and the patient reports about the way these patterns have occurred in the past and how they continue. These patterns become the focal theme for the therapy and are seen as a basic reason for the patient's troubles.

For example, a patient may complain that he has never had the confidence to think for himself. He reports that his parents always told him what to do, without explanation. In his marriage, he finds himself unable to feel comfortable with making any decisions, and he always looks to his spouse for the final say. This pattern of dependence may not be as clear to the patient as to the psychotherapist, who looks specifically for similarities across past and present relationships. Furthermore, the patient will probably approach the psychotherapist in a similar fashion. For example, the patient might ask for the psychotherapist's advice, stating that he does not know what to do. When the psychotherapist points out the pattern in the patient's behavior, or suggests that it may have developed from the way his parents interacted with him, the psychotherapist is using the technique of interpretation. This technique originated in the psychodynamic models of psychotherapy.

When patients are confronted with having such patterns or focal themes, they may protest that they are not doing this, that they find it difficult to do anything different, or that they cannot imagine that there may be a different way of living. These tendencies to protest and to find change to be difficult are called "resistance." Much of the work of psychotherapy involves overcoming this resistance and achieving the understanding of self called insight.

One of the techniques the psychotherapist uses to deal with resistance is the continued development of the therapeutic relationship in order to demonstrate that the psychotherapist understands and accepts the patient's point of view and that these interpretations of patterns of living are done in the interest of the achievement of therapeutic goals by the patient. Humanistic psychotherapists have emphasized this aspect of psychotherapeutic technique. The psychotherapist also responds differently to the patient from the way others have in the past, so that when the patient demonstrates the focal theme in the psychotherapy session, this different outcome to the pattern encourages a new approach to the difficulty. This is called the corrective emotional experience, a psychotherapeutic technique that originated in psychodynamic psychotherapy and is emphasized in humanistic therapies as well.

For example, when the patient asks the psychotherapist for advice, the psychotherapist might respond that they could work together on a solution, building on valuable information and ideas that both may have. In this way, the psychotherapist has avoided keeping the patient dependent in the relationship with the psychotherapist, as the patient has been in relationships with parents, a spouse, or others. This is experienced by the patient emotionally, in that it may produce an increase in self-confidence or trust rather than resentment, because the psychotherapist did not dominate. With the repetition of these responses by the psychotherapist, the patient's ways of relating are corrected. Such a repetition is often called working through, another term originating in psychodynamic models of therapy.

Psychotherapists have recognized that many patients have difficulty with changing their patterns of living because of anxiety or lack of skill and experience in behaving differently. Behavioral therapy techniques are especially useful in such cases. In cases of anxiety, the patient can be taught to relax through relaxation training exercises. The patient gradually imagines performing new, difficult behaviors while relaxing. Eventually, the patient learns to stay relaxed while performing these behaviors with the psychotherapist and other people. This process is called desensitization, and it was originally developed to treat persons with extreme fears of particular objects or situations, termed phobias. New behavior is sometimes taught through modeling techniques in which examples of the behavior are first demonstrated by others. Behavioral psychotherapists have also shown the importance of rewarding small approximations to the new behavior that is the goal. This shaping technique might be used with the dependent patient by praising confident, assertive, or independent behavior reported by the patient or shown in the psychotherapy session, no matter how minor it may be initially.

## ALLEVIATING DISTRESS

The goals and techniques of psychotherapy were first discussed by the psychodynamic theorists who originated the modern practice of psychotherapy. Sigmund Freud and Josef Breuer are generally credited with describing the first modern case treated with psychotherapy, and Freud went on to develop the basis for psychodynamic psychotherapy in his writings between 1895 and his death in 1939. Freud sat behind his patients while they lay upon a couch, so that they could concentrate on saying anything that came to mind in order to reveal themselves to the psychotherapist. This also prevented the patients from seeing the psychotherapist's reaction, in case they expected the psychotherapist to react to them as their parents had reacted. This transference relationship provided Freud with information about the patient's relationship with parents, which Freud considered to be the root of the problems that his patients had. Later psychodynamic psychotherapists sat facing their patients and conversing with them in a more conventional fashion, but they still attended to the transference.

Carl Rogers is usually described as the first humanistic psychotherapist, and he published descriptions of his techniques in 1942 and 1951. Rogers concentrated on establishing a warm, accepting, honest relationship with his patients. He established this relationship by attempting to understand the patient from the patient's point of view. By communicating this "accurate empathy," patients would feel accepted and therefore would accept themselves and be more confident in living according to their wishes without fear.

Behavioral psychotherapists began to play a major role in this field after Joseph Wolpe developed systematic desensitization in the 1950's. In the 1960's and 1970's, Albert Bandura applied his findings on how children learn to be aggressive through observation to the development of modeling techniques for reducing fears and teaching new behaviors. Bandura focused on how people attend to, remember, and decide to perform behavior they observe in others. These thought processes, or "cognitions," came to be addressed in cognitive psychotherapy by Aaron T. Beck and others in the 1970's and 1980's. Cognitive behavioral therapy became a popular hybrid that included emphasis on how thinking and behavior influence each other.

In surveys of practicing psychotherapists beginning in the late 1970's, Sol Garfield showed that the majority of therapists practice some hybrid therapy or eclectic approach. As it became apparent that no one model produced the desired effects in a variety of patients, psychotherapists used techniques from various approaches. An example is Arnold Lazarus's multimodal behavior therapy, introduced in 1971. It appears that such trends will continue and that, in addition to combining existing psychotherapeutic techniques, new eclectic models will produce additional ways of understanding psychotherapy as well as different techniques for practice.

## SOURCES FOR FURTHER STUDY

Garfield, Sol L. *Psychotherapy: An Eclectic Approach.* New York: John Wiley & Sons, 1980. Focuses on the patient, the therapist, and their interaction within an eclectic framework. Written for the beginning student of psychotherapy and relatively free of jargon.

Goldfried, Marvin R., and Gerald C. Davison. *Clinical Behavior Therapy.* New York: Holt, Rinehart and Winston, 1976. An elementary, concise description of basic behavioral techniques. Includes clear examples of how these techniques are implemented.

Goldman, George D., and Donald S. Milman, eds. *Psychoanalytic Psychotherapy.* Reading, Mass.: Addison-Wesley, 1978. A very clear, concise treatment of complicated psychodynamic techniques. Explains difficult concepts in language accessible to the layperson.

Phares, E. Jerry. *Clinical Psychology: Concepts, Methods, and Profession.* 3d ed.

Pacific Grove, Calif.: Brooks/Cole, 1988. An overview of clinical psychology that includes excellent chapters summarizing psychodynamic, behavioral, humanistic, and other models of psychotherapy. Written as a college-level text.

Rogers, Carl Ransom. *Client-Centered Therapy.* Boston: Houghton Mifflin, 1965. A classic description of the author's humanistic psychotherapy that is still useful as a strong statement of the value of the therapeutic relationship. Written for a professional audience, though quite readable.

Teyber, Edward. *Interpersonal Process in Psychotherapy: A Guide to Clinical Training.* 3d ed. Pacific Grove, Calif.: Brooks/Cole, 1997. An extremely clear and readable guide to modern eclectic therapy. Full of practical examples and written as a training manual for beginning psychotherapy students.

Wolpe, Joseph. *The Practice of Behavior Therapy.* 4th ed. Elmsford, N.Y.: Pergamon, 1990. Written by the originator of behavioral psychotherapy. Introduces basic principles, examples of behavioral interventions, and many references to research. Initial chapters are elementary, but later ones tend to be complicated.

*Richard G. Tedeschi*

SEE ALSO: Cognitive Therapy; Drug Therapies; Psychoanalysis; Psychoanalytic Psychology.

# RACE AND INTELLIGENCE

TYPE OF PSYCHOLOGY: Biological bases of behavior; intelligence and intelligence testing
FIELDS OF STUDY: Biological influences on learning; general issues in intelligence; intelligence assessment

*The relationship between race and intelligence has long been the subject of heated debate among social scientists. At issue is whether intelligence is an inherited trait or is primarily attributable to environmental influences.*

KEY CONCEPTS
• intelligence quotient (IQ) tests
• nature versus nurture
• twin studies

In 1969, educational psychologist Arthur Jensen published an article in the *Harvard Educational Review* titled "How Much Can We Boost I.Q. and Scholastic Achievement?" He attempted to explain multiple findings that whites, on the average, outperform blacks by about 15 points on intelligence quotient (IQ) tests. His major conclusion was that racial differences in intelligence are primarily attributable to heredity and that whites, as a racial group, are born with abilities superior to those of blacks.

Jensen, as well as William Shockley, presents the hereditarian hypothesis of intelligence. It argues that some people are born smarter than others and that this fact cannot be changed with training, education, or any alteration in the environment. Because they believe that African Americans as a group are not as smart as Caucasians, they suggest that special programs, such as Head Start, which are designed to help disadvantaged children improve in school achievement, are doomed to fail.

In contrast to the hereditarians, Urie Bronfenbrenner and Ashley Montagu can be described as environmentalists. They believe that although intelligence has some genetic component, as do all human characteristics, the expression of intelligent behavior is defined, determined, and developed within a specific cultural context. Therefore, what people choose to call intelligence is primarily caused by the interaction of genetics with environmental influences. Environmentalists believe that a person can improve in his or her intellectual functioning with sufficient changes in environment.

Richard Herrnstein and Charles Murray's *The Bell Curve* (1994) reopened the issue of heredity versus environment in the attainment of intelligence. The authors argue that Caucasians are inherently superior to African Americans in IQ levels, presenting a mass of statistical evidence to support their position. Critics of *The Bell Curve* attack it on a number of fronts. There is a failure to separate hereditary from genetic variables. The definition of race proves a difficult one. The IQ tests themselves come into the same culture bias category. The statistical tests hide more than they reveal. There is difficulty replicating Hernnstein and Murray's results. The defects mount up rather quickly.

Much of the hereditarian argument is based on two types of studies: those comparing IQ test performances of twins and those of adopted children. Because identical twins have the same genetic endowment, it is thought that any differences observed between them should be attributable to the effects of the environment. Hereditarians also suggest that one should observe more similarities in the IQs of parents and their biological children (because they share genes) than between parents and adopted children (who are biologically unrelated and therefore share no genes).

Statistical formulas are applied to comparisons between family members' IQs to determine the relative contributions of heredity and environment. Using this method, Sir Cyril Burt in 1958 reported a heritability estimate of .93. This means that 93 percent of the variability in intelligence could be explained genetically. People have also interpreted this to mean that 93 percent of the intelligence level is inherited. Jensen has more recently reported heritability estimates of .80 and .67, depending on what formula is used. Hereditarians have also pointed out that when they compare African Americans and Caucasians from similar environments (the same educational level, income level, or occupation), the reported IQ differences remain. This, they argue, supports their view that heredity is more important than environment in determining intelligence. The same arguments have been made for the work of Hernnstein and Murray.

For environmentalists, it is not so much the reported IQ differences between different racial groups that are in question. Of more concern are the basic assumptions made by the hereditarians and the reasons they give for the reported differences. Not surprisingly, environmentalists challenge the hereditarian arguments on several levels. First, they point out that there is no evidence of the existence of an "intelligence" gene or set of genes. They say that scientists have been unsuccessful in distinguishing the genetic from the environmental contributions to intelligence.

Environmentalists also refute the assumption that IQ tests adequately measure intelligence. Although IQ has been noted to be a good predictor of success in school, it turns out to have little relationship to economic success in life. S. E. Luria reports an analysis that shows that the son of a Caucasian businessman with an IQ of 90 has a greater chance of success than an African American boy with an IQ of 120. This example calls into question what actually is being assessed. It is not at all clear that "intelligence" is being measured—especially as there is no generally accepted definition of intelligence among social scientists.

The definition of race is also problematic. Although most people may identify several racial groups (such as African, or black; Caucasian, or white; and so on), Montagu and many other social scientists agree that race is a pseudoscientific concept, used as a social or political category to assign social status and to subordinate nonwhite populations. Because of intermin-

*Intelligence, as measured by tests, involves both genetics and environmental factors such as good schools.*
(CLEO Photography)

gling among different cultural groups, it is also difficult to identify strict biological boundaries for race, which in turn makes genetic interpretations of racial comparisons of IQ differences much less meaningful.

In addition to questioning what IQ tests measure, many psychologists have criticized IQ tests as being biased against individuals who are culturally different from the mainstream group (Caucasians) and who have not assimilated the white, middle-class norms upon which the tests were based. Tests developed in one culture may not adequately measure the abilities and aptitude of people from another culture, especially if the two cultures emphasize different skills, ways of solving problems, and ways of understanding the world.

Environmentalists have also criticized the research and statistical techniques used by the hereditarians. It is now widely acknowledged that the data reported by Burt, upon which Jensen heavily relied, were false. In many different studies, he came up with the same figures (to the third decimal point) for the similarities between IQ scores for twins. This is statistically impossible. He also did not take into account how other variables, such as age and gender, might have produced higher IQ values in the twins he studied. Rather, he assumed that they shared genes for intelligence.

It is also charged that the concept of heritability is misunderstood by the hereditarians. This is a statistic that applies to groups, not to individuals. If one states that the heritability estimate of a group of IQ scores is .80, that does not mean that 80 percent of each IQ score is attributable to genetics, but that 80 percent of the difference in the group of scores can be attributed to genetic variation. Therefore, according to the enviromentalists, it is incorrect for hereditarians to establish heritability within one group (such as Caucasian children) and then apply that figure to a different racial group (such as African American children).

## CONSEQUENCES OF VARIOUS POSITIONS

Several examples may help clarify the relationships between heredity, environment, and characteristics such as IQ. The first example involves a highly heritable characteristic, height. In this example, a farmer has two fields, one rich in nutrients (field A) and the other barren (field B). The farmer takes seeds from a bag that has considerable genetic variety, plants them in the two fields, and cares for the two fields of crops equally well. After several weeks, the plants are measured. The farmer finds that within field A, some plants are taller than others in the same field. Because all these plants had the same growing environment, the variation could be attributed to the genetic differences in the seeds planted. The same would be the case with the plants in field B.

The farmer also finds differences between the two fields. The plants in field A are taller than the plants in field B, because of the richer soil in which they grew. The difference in the average heights of the plants is attributable to the quality of the growing environment, even though the genetic variation (heritability) within field A may be the same as that within field B. This same principle applies to IQ scores of different human groups.

Taking the example further, the farmer might call a chemist to test the soil. If the chemist was able to determine all the essential missing nutrients, the farmer could add them to the soil in field B for the next season. The second batch of plants would grow larger, with the average height being similar to the average height of plants in field A. Similarly, if one is comparing African Americans and Caucasians—or any racial groups—on a characteristic such as IQ test scores, it is important to understand that unless the groups have equivalent growing environments (social, political, economic, educational, and so on), differences between them cannot be easily traced to heredity.

As another example, one might take a set of identical twins who were born in Chicago, separate them at birth, and place one of the twins in the !Kung desert community in Africa. The life experiences of the twin in Africa would differ significantly from those of his Chicago counterpart because of the differences in diet, climate, and other relevant factors required for existence and survival in the two environments. The twin in Africa would have a different language and number system; drawing and writing would not likely be an important part of daily life. Therefore, if one were to use existing IQ tests, one would have to translate them from English to the !Kung language so that they could be understood. The translation might not truly capture the meaning of all the questions and tasks, which might interfere with the !Kung twin's understanding of what was being asked of him. More problems would arise when the !Kung twin is asked to interpret drawings or to copy figures, because he would not be very familiar with these activities.

It is likely that the !Kung twin would perform poorly on the translated IQ test, because it does not reflect what is emphasized and valued in his society. Rather, it is based on the schooling in society in which the Chicago twin lives. This does not mean that the !Kung twin is less intelligent than his Chicago twin. Similarly, the Chicago twin would do poorly on a test developed from the experience of !Kung culture, because the !Kung test would emphasize skills such as building shelter, finding water, and other activities that are not important for survival in Chicago. In this case, the !Kung test would not adequately measure the ability of the Chicago twin.

Studies done by psychologist Sandra Scarr show that evidence for a genetic basis for racial differences in IQ is far from clear. She looked at the IQ scores of African American children who were born into working-class families but were adopted and raised by white middle-class families. The IQ scores of these children were close to the national average and were almost 10 to 20 points higher than would have been expected had they remained in their birth homes.

Change in children's environments seems to be a critical factor in enhancing their ability to perform on the IQ tests, as seen in the research done by Scarr. Bronfenbrenner found similar results. He examined a dozen studies that looked at early intervention in children's lives; he found that whenever it was possible to change the environment positively, children's scores on IQ tests increased.

### HISTORICAL DEVELOPMENT OF RACIAL CONTEXT

The notion of inherited differences is an ancient one; however, the concept of racial classifications is more recent. According to psychologist Wade Nobles, the Western idea of race emerged during the sixteenth century as Europeans began to colonize other parts of the world. As they came into contact with people who looked different from them, many Europeans developed the notion that some races were superior to others. This belief often was given as a justification for slavery and other oppressive activities.

Charles Darwin's theory of evolution was critical in promoting the belief that human differences were a result of heredity and genetics. His notion of "the survival of the fittest" led psychologists to research racial differences in intelligence in order to understand the successes and failures of different human groups. Francis Galton, Darwin's cousin, was instrumental in furthering the hereditarian perspective in psychology. In his book *Hereditary Genius: An Inquiry into Its Laws and Consequences* (1869), he attempted to illustrate that genius and prominence follow family lines. He also began the eugenics movement, which supported the use of selective mating and forced sterilization to improve racial stock. *The Bell Curve* is simply a more recent argument along the same lines. Nothing really new is added to the argument. There is a bit more sociobiological jargon and a mass of statistics, but they do not hold up to careful scrutiny.

Following Galton's lead, many psychologists embraced the notions of inherited racial differences in intelligence. The pioneering work of anthropologist Franz Boas, in attacking the popular conception of race, fostered research to attack the myths attached to that concept, including the myth of inherent superiority or inferiority. G. Stanley Hall, the founder of the American Psychological Association, believed that African people were at a lower evolutionary stage than Caucasians. By the beginning of the 1900's, psychological testing was being widely used to support the view that intelligence was hereditary and was little influenced by the environment. More recently, Burt, Herrnstein, and Jensen have argued in favor of an overriding genetic factor in intelligence.

There were also early efforts to challenge the hereditarian perspective in psychology. During the 1920's and 1930's, Herman Canady and Howard Long, two of the first African Americans to receive graduate degrees in psychology, produced evidence showing the importance of environmental influences on IQ test performance. They were concerned about increasingly prevalent "scientific" justifications for the inequality and injustice experienced by African Americans, American Indians, and other groups. Fighting racism was a major reason Leon Kamin became involved in the debate about race and intelligence. He gathered the original information that had been reported by scientists and reexamined it; Kamin was responsible for discovering that Burt had reported false information. He also noted that many hereditarians misused and misinterpreted their statistics.

Hereditarians maintain that racial differences in IQ test scores are primarily caused by genetics and that these scores do reflect differences in intelligence; environmentalists say no. It has not been proved definitively that IQ tests measure intelligence; however, the evidence does suggest that performance on IQ tests is determined by the interaction between genetic and environmental influences. The quality of the environment will determine how well people will reach their potential. In a society where the history of certain groups includes oppression, discrimination, and exclusion from opportunity, it is difficult to explain differences in achievement as being primarily inherited. Instead, it would seem to be a more important goal to eliminate injustices and to change the conditions of life so that all people could do well.

## SOURCES FOR FURTHER STUDY

Devlin, Bernie, et al., eds. *Intelligence, Genes, and Success: Scientists Respond to "The Bell Curve."* New York: Springer, 1997. A number of psychologists and social scientists respond to the claims of Richard Hernnstein and Charles Murray.

Fancher, Raymond E. *The Intelligence Men: Makers of the IQ Controversy.* New York: W. W. Norton, 1985. Examines the historical contexts of the IQ controversy. The life experiences of the major hereditarians and environmentalists and how these experiences influenced their perspectives are emphasized. This book is easy to read and does an excellent job of making complex statistics understandable.

Goldsby, Richard. *Race and Races.* 2d ed. New York: Macmillan, 1977. Provides straightforward and accurate information about issues of race, racial differences, and racism. There is a balanced discussion of both the hereditarian and environmentalist perspectives of the IQ controversy. Enjoyable and easy to read for high school and college students alike.

Gould, Stephen Jay. *The Mismeasure of Man.* Revised and expanded ed. New York: Norton, 1997. Gould replies to the work of Richard Hernnstein and Charles Murray, questioning both their motives and their methods.

Guthrie, Robert V. *Even the Rat Was White.* 2d ed. Boston: Allyn and Bacon, 2004. Provides an excellent historical view of how psychology has dealt with race as an issue. The first section of the book focuses on methods of study, early psychological testing, and the development of racism in the profession of psychology.

Hernnstein, Richard, and Charles Murray. *The Bell Curve.* New York: Free Press, 1994. This book argues that differences in black and white IQ scores are genetically based.

Jensen, Arthur R. *Bias in Mental Testing.* New York: Free Press, 1980. An attempt to deal comprehensively with the issues of IQ testing and bias. Jensen challenges the criticisms against IQ tests and offers research to support his view that group differences in IQ test scores are not attributable to bias.

Kamin, Leon J. *The Science and Politics of IQ.* New York: Halstead Press, 1974. Discusses the political nature of the role psychologists have played in support of IQ testing. The role of psychologists in the eugenics movement and in education is discussed. Includes strong critiques of the work done by Cyril Burt and Arthur Jensen.

Montagu, Ashley, ed. *Race and IQ.* New York: Oxford University Press, 1975. Written to challenge the interpretations offered by the hereditarians. Most of the articles included were previously published in professional journals or popular magazines. Some of the chapters contain very technical material; however, the authors generally do an effective job translating this into more understandable language.

*Derise E. Tolliver; updated by Frank A. Salamone*

SEE ALSO: Intelligence; Intelligence Tests.

# Radical Behaviorism

## B. F. Skinner

Type of psychology: Personality
Fields of study: Behavioral and cognitive models; instrumental
   conditioning

*Radical behaviorism describes the views of Skinner, an influential figure in American psychology since the 1930's. Skinner argued that most behavior is controlled by its consequences; he invented an apparatus for observing the effects of consequences, advocated a technology of behavior control, and believed that everyday views about the causes of behavior were an obstacle to its true understanding.*

Key concepts
- contingency of reinforcement
- discriminative stimulus
- experimental analysis of behavior
- mentalism
- operant
- private events
- rule-governed behavior
- shaping

According to B. F. Skinner (1904-1990), the behavior of an organism is a product of current and past environmental consequences and genetic endowment. Because little can be done, at least by psychology, about genetic endowment, Skinner focused on those things that could be changed or controlled: the immediate consequences of behavior. By consequences, Skinner meant the results or effects that a particular behavior (a class of responses, or "operant") produces. There are many ways to open a door, for example, but because each one allows a person to walk to the next room, one would speak of a "door-opening" operant. The consequences not only define the class of responses but also determine how often members of the class are likely to occur in the future. This was termed the Law of Effect by early twentieth century American psychologist Edward L. Thorndike, whose work Skinner refined.

Skinner analyzed behavior by examining the antecedents and consequences which control any specific class of responses in the individual organism. From this view, he elaborated a psychology that encompassed all aspects of animal and human behavior, including language. By the late 1970's, historians of psychology ranked Skinner's work as the second most significant development in psychology since World War II; the general growth of the field was ranked first. Three journals arose to publish work in the Skinnerian tradition: *Journal of the Experimental Analysis of Behavior, Journal of Applied Behavior Analysis*, and *Behaviorism*. Moreover, an international organization, the Association for Behavior Analysis, was formed, with its own journal.

## CONTROLLING VARIABLES

Skinner theorized that behavior has several kinds of consequences, or effects. Events that follow behavior and produce an increase in the rate or frequency of the behavior are termed reinforcers. In ordinary language, they might be called rewards, but Skinner avoided this expression because he defined reinforcing events in terms of the effects they produced (their rate of occurrence) rather than the alleged feelings they induced (for example, pleasure). To attribute the increase in rate of response produced by reinforcement to feelings of pleasure would be regarded by Skinner as an instance of mentalism—the attribution of behavior to a feeling rather than an event occurring in the environment. Other consequences which follow a behavior produce a decrease in the rate of behavior. These are termed punishers. Skinner strongly objected to the use of punishment as a means to control behavior because it elicited aggression and produced dysfunctional emotional responses such as striking back and, in a small child, crying. Consequences (reinforcers and punishers) may be presented following a behavior (twenty dollars for building a doghouse, for example, or an electric

*B. F. Skinner.*
(Alfred A. Knopf)

shock for touching an exposed wire) or taken away (a fine for speeding, the end of a headache by taking aspirin). Consequences may be natural (tomatoes to eat after a season of careful planting and watering) or contrived (receiving a dollar for earning an A on a test).

Reinforcing and punishing consequences are one example of controlling variables. Events that precede behaviors are also controlling variables and determine under what circumstances certain behaviors are likely to appear. Events occurring before a response occurs are called discriminative stimuli because they come to discriminate in favor of a particular piece of behavior. They set the occasion for the behavior and make it more likely to occur. For example, persons trying to control their eating are advised to keep away from the kitchen except at meal times. Being in the kitchen makes it more likely that the person will eat something, not simply because that is where the food is kept but also because being in the kitchen is one of the events which has preceded previous eating and therefore makes eating more likely to occur. This is true even when the person does not intend to eat but goes to the kitchen for other reasons. Being in the kitchen raises the probability of eating. It is a discriminative stimulus (any stimulus in the presence of which a response is reinforced) for eating, as are the table, the refrigerator, or a candy bar on the counter. Any event or stimulus which occurs immediately before a response is reinforced becomes reinforced with the response and makes the response more likely to occur again if the discriminative stimulus occurs again. The discriminative stimulus comes to gain some control over the behavior.

## DISCRIMINATIVE AND REINFORCING STIMULI

Discriminative stimuli and reinforcing stimuli are the controlling variables Skinner used to analyze behavior. These events constitute a chain of behavior called a contingency of reinforcement. It is a contingency because reinforcement does not occur unless the response is made in the presence of the discriminative stimuli. Contingencies of reinforcement are encountered every day. For example, a soda drink is purchased from a machine. The machine is brightly colored to act as a discriminative stimulus for dropping coins in a slot, which in turn yields a can or bottle of soft drink. The machine comes to control a small portion of a person's behavior. If the machine malfunctions, a person may push the selector button several times repeatedly, perhaps even putting in more coins, and still later, strike the machine. By carefully scheduling how many times an organism must respond before reinforcement occurs, the rate of response can be controlled as is done in slot or video machines or gambling devices in general. Responses are made several hundred or thousand times for very little reinforcement—a near win or a small payoff. Schedules of reinforcement are another important set of controlling variables which Skinner explored.

Contingencies are relationships among controlling variables. Some of the relationships become abstracted and formulized, that is, put in the form of rules. When behavior is under the control of a rule, it is termed rule-governed behavior, as opposed to contingency-shaped behavior. As a person first learns any skill, much of his or her behavior is rule governed, either through written instructions or by the person's repeating the rule to himself or herself. For example, a novice golfer might review the rules for a good swing, even repeating them aloud. Eventually, though, swing becomes automatic; it seems to become "natural." The verbal discriminative stimuli have shifted to the very subtle and covert stimuli associated with swing without the golfer's thinking about it, and the natural consequences of a successful swing take over.

## OPERANT CHAMBER EXPERIMENTS

The operant chamber is a small experimental space or cage that Skinner invented to observe the effects that consequences have on behavior. A food-deprived organism (Skinner first used rats and later switched to pigeons) is placed in the chamber containing a lever that, when depressed, releases a small piece of food into a cup from which the organism eats. The first bar-press response is produced through the process of shaping, or reinforcing approximations to bar pressing (for example, being near the bar, having a paw above the bar, resting a paw on the bar, nearly depressing the bar) until bar pressing is regularly occurring. Once the operant of bar pressing is established, an experimental analysis of the variables which influence it can be done. The schedule of reinforcement can be changed, for example, from one reinforcer for each response to five responses required for each reinforcer. Changes in the rate of response can be observed on a device Skinner invented, a cumulative record, which automatically displays the rate at which the operant is occurring. A discriminative stimulus can be introduced in the form of a small light mounted on the wall of the chamber. If bar presses are reinforced only when the light is turned on, the light will come to have some control over the operant. Turning the light on and off will literally turn bar pressing on and off in a food-deprived rat.

Skinner controlled his own behavior in the same fashion that he had learned to control the behavior of laboratory organisms. He arranged a "writing environment," a desk used only for that purpose; wrote at a set time each day; and would keep careful records of time spent writing. Other examples of self-management may be found in Skinner's novel of his research, *Walden Two* (1948). In this fictionalized account, children learn self-control through a set of exercises that teach ways to tolerate increasing delays of reinforcement.

## BEHAVIORAL ANALYSIS OF LANGUAGE

Skinner also performed a behavior analysis of language (*Verbal Behavior*, 1957). For example, a behavioral analysis of the word "want," "believe," or "love," an operational definition in Skinner's sense, would be all those circumstances and situations which control the use of the word, that is, the discriminative stimuli for the verbal response. Skinner tried to show in *Verbal Behavior* that speaking and writing could be explained with the same principle he had used to explain animal behavior. Many of Skinner's works, and much of his private notebooks, are taken up with the recording of how words are used. His purpose was to de-mentalize them, to show that what controls their use is some aspect of the environment or some behavioral practice on the part of the verbal community, rather than some internal or mental event. The earliest uses of the word "to know," for example, referred to action, something the individual could do, rather than something he or she possessed or had stored inside the mind.

## UNDERSTANDING SKINNER'S CONTRIBUTIONS

So much has been written about Skinner, some of it misleading or false, that it is important to clarify what he did not do. He did not raise either of his daughters in a "Skinner box." His youngest daughter was raised during her infancy with the aid of an "aircrib," a special enclosed crib Skinner built that allowed control of air temperature and humidity, and in which the infant could sleep and play without the burden of clothes. "Aircribs" were later available commercially. Skinner did not limit his analysis of behavior only to publicly observable events, as did the methodological behaviorists. Part of what made Skinner's behaviorism radical was his insistence that a science of behavior should be able to account for those private events—events to which only the individual has access, such as the pain of a toothache—to which only the individual has access. He described how the community teaches its members to describe covert events such as toothaches and headaches. He did not regard such events as anything other than behavior. That is, he did not give them a special status by calling them "mental events."

Skinner did not argue that reinforcement explains everything. He allowed, especially in his later works, that genetic endowment plays a role in the determination of behavior, as do rules and antecedent events. He did not reject physiological explanations of behavior when actual physiology was involved. He did object to the use of physiological terms in psychological accounts, unless the physiological mechanisms were known. For Skinner, physiology was one subject matter and behavior was another. Finally, he did not ignore complex behavior. Many of his works, particularly *Verbal Behavior* and *The Technology of Teaching* (1968), offered behaviorist analyses of what in other psychologies would be termed cognitive phenomena, such as talking, reading, thinking, problem solving, and remembering.

Skinner made many contributions to twentieth century psychology. Among them was his invention of the operant chamber and its associated methodology. Operant equipment and procedures are employed by animal and human experimental psychologists in laboratories around the world. Most of these psychologists do not adhere to Skinner's radical behaviorism or to all the features of his science of behavior. They have, however, found the techniques that he developed to be productive in exploring a wide variety of problems, ranging from the fields of psychopharmacology to learning in children and adults to experimental economics. Skinner and his followers developed a technology of behavior that included techniques for working with the developmentally disabled, children in elementary classrooms, and persons with rehabilitation or health care problems. They also considered approaches to public safety, employee motivation and production, and any other field which involved the management of behavior. Although the technology developments never reached the vision described in *Walden Two*, the efforts are ongoing.

Skinner may have exhausted the Law of Effect. The idea which states that consequences influence behavior can be found in many forms in the literature of psychology and philosophy, especially since the middle of the nineteenth century, but it is only in the work of B. F. Skinner that one sees how much of human and animal behavior can be brought within its purview. Because Skinner took behavior as his subject matter, he greatly expanded what could be regarded as being of interest to psychologists. Behavior was everywhere, in the classroom, at the office, in the factory. Nearly any aspect of human activity could become the legitimate object of study by a Skinnerian psychologist, a point well illustrated in Skinner's description of a utopian community which takes an experimental attitude toward its cultural practices and designs a culture based on a science of behavior (*Walden Two*). Finally, Skinner conceptualized an epistemology, a way of understanding what it means for humans to know something, that may be a lasting contribution to twentieth century philosophy.

### RELATIONSHIP WITH DARWINISM AND PRAGMATISM

In placing the radical behaviorism of B. F. Skinner in historical context, two nineteenth century doctrines are often invoked. One view, shared by Skinner, is that operant psychology represents an extension of the principle of natural selection which Charles Darwin described at the level of the species. Natural selection explained the origin of species; contingencies of reinforcement and punishment explain the origin of classes of responses. The environment selects in both cases. In operant psychology, the role of the environment is to reinforce differentially and thereby select from among a pool of responses which the organism is making. The final effect is some one particular operant which has survival or adaptive value for the individual organism. Skinner has suggested that cultural evolution occurs in a similar fashion.

It is also observed that Skinner's psychology resembles nineteenth century pragmatism. The pragmatists held that beliefs are formed by their outcome, or practical effect. To explain why someone does something by reference to a belief would be regarded as mentalism by Skinner; he would substitute behavior for beliefs. Yet he comes to the same doctrine: one in which environmental consequences act in a Darwinian fashion. Finally, Skinner's philosophy shows the influence of the nineteenth century positivism of physicist Ernst Mach. Skinner desired a description of behavior and its causes, while avoiding mental states or other cognitive or personality entities that intervene between behavior and the environment.

## SOURCES FOR FURTHER STUDY

Kazdin, Alan E. *Behavior Modification in Applied Settings.* 6th ed. Belmont, Calif.: Wadsworth/Thomson Learning, 2001. An introduction to behavior modification that can be understood by the high school or college student. Operant techniques are clearly described, with the emphasis on how they are applied in a wide range of settings. Excellent discussion of recent developments in the field.

Modgil, Sohan, and Celia Modgil, eds. *B. F. Skinner: Consensus and Controversy.* New York: Falmer Press, 1987. A collection of essays by psychologists and philosophers. Each topic has a pro and contrary opinion, with replies and rebuttals. Although written at a professional level, this is an excellent volume for a global view of Skinner's ideas and for the clearest understanding of what is "radical" about Skinner's behaviorism.

O'Donoghue, William, and Kyle Ferguson. *The Psychology of B. F. Skinner.* Thousand Oaks, Calif.: Sage Publications, 2001. An attempt to clarify Skinner's psychology through discussion of his life, contributions to psychology, and philosophy of science.

Skinner, B. F. *About Behaviorism.* New York: Vintage Books, 1976. In this work Skinner argues for his radical behaviorism by contrasting it with methodological behaviorism and by illustrating how it treats topics such as perception, memory, verbal behavior, private events, and thinking.

_____. *Particulars of My Life.* New York: New York University Press, 1984.

_____. *The Shaping of a Behaviorist.* New York: New York University Press, 1984.

_____. *A Matter of Consequences.* New York: Alfred A. Knopf, 1983. Skinner published his autobiography in three separate volumes, listed as the three previous titles. The first describes his life from birth, through his college years, to his entering Harvard University for graduate study in psychology. *The Shaping of a Behaviorist* presents his years at Harvard and his rise to national prominence. *A Matter of Consequences* begins with his return to Harvard as a professor in the late 1940's.

_____. *Science and Human Behavior.* Reprint. New York: Classics of Psychiatry & behavioral Sciences Library, 1992. A fine introduction to Skinner's thought. The principles of operant psychology are described, with numerous examples of the applicability to an individual's life and the major institutions of society. The chapter on private events illustrates one important way in which Skinner's radical behaviorism differs from methodological behaviorism.

_____. *Walden Two.* Reprint. New York: Macmillan, 1990. A description of a fictional community based upon experimental practices and behavioral principles. The book was the source of inspiration for several communes and illustrates how all aspects of culture can be submitted to a behavioral analysis. Contains a lengthy criticism of democracy as a form of government.

Vargas, Julie S. "B. F. Skinner, Father, Grandfather, Behavior Modifier." In *About Human Nature: Journeys in Psychological Thought,* edited by Terry J. Knapp and Charles T. Rasmussen. Dubuque, Iowa: Kendall/Hunt, 1987. An intimate description of Skinner by his eldest daughter, who is herself a psychologist. Skinner's home, study, and the activities occurring over a Thanksgiving weekend are described.

*Terry J. Knapp*

SEE ALSO: Behaviorism; Cognitive Behavior Therapy; Conditioning; Learning.

# REFLEXES

TYPE OF PSYCHOLOGY: Biological bases of behavior
FIELD OF STUDY: Nervous system

*A reflex is one of the most basic types of behavior that can be elicited; over the years, psychologists and physiologists have studied the behavioral and biological processes associated with reflex production in the hope of understanding principles and processes involved in generating both simple behaviors and a variety of more complex behaviors such as learning, memory, and voluntary movement.*

KEY CONCEPTS
- classical (Pavlovian) conditioning
- infantile reflexes
- monosynaptic reflex
- polysynaptic reflex
- spinal reflex

The reflex is undoubtedly the simplest form of behavior that has been studied widely by psychologists and neuroscientists. Reflexes involve two separate yet highly related events: the occurrence of an eliciting stimulus and the production of a specific response. Most organisms are capable of displaying a variety of complex behaviors; however, because these behaviors are complex, it has been very difficult, if not impossible, to understand biological or psychological processes involved in generating or modifying the variety of behaviors that most organisms can display. In attempts to study these complex behaviors, a number of researchers have adopted a strategy of studying simpler behaviors, such as reflexes, that are thought to make up, contribute to, or serve as a model of the more complex behavior.

## SPINAL REFLEX

A number of reflexes can be generated in the mammalian spinal cord even after it has been surgically isolated from the brain. The stretch reflex is an example of a spinal reflex. When a muscle is stretched, such as when a tendon is tapped or when an attempt is made to reach for an object, sensory "detectors" or receptors within the muscle are activated to signal the muscle stretch. These receptors are at the end of very long nerve fibers that travel from the muscle receptor to the spinal cord, where they activate spinal motor neurons. The motor neurons control the same muscle on which the stretch receptor that initiated the stretch signal is located. When activated, the spinal motor neurons signal the muscle, causing it to contract. In this manner, when a muscle stretch is detected, the stretch reflex ensures that a contraction is generated in the muscle to counteract and balance the stretch. This type of reflex is referred to as a "monosynaptic reflex" because it involves only one synapse: the synapse between the sensory receptor neuron and the motor neuron (where a synapse is the junction between two neurons).

Another example of a spinal reflex is the flexion or withdrawal reflex. Anyone who has accidentally touched a hot stove has encountered this reflex. Touching a hot stove or applying any aversive stimulus to the skin activates pain receptors in the skin. These receptors are at the end of long sensory fibers that project to neurons in the spinal cord. The spinal neurons that receive input from the sensory fibers are not motor neurons, as in the stretch reflex, but rather very small neurons called spinal interneurons. The interneurons make synaptic contact on other interneurons as well as on motor neurons that innervate flexor muscles. When activated, the flexor muscles typically cause limb withdrawal. The flexor reflex ensures that a relatively rapid withdrawal of one's hand from a hot stove will occur if the stove is accidentally touched. The flexor reflex is an example of a "polysynaptic reflex" because there are two or more synapses involved in the reflex (the presence of at least one synapse between a sensory neuron and an interneuron and a second synapse between the interneuron and a motor neuron).

One functional difference between monosynaptic and polysynaptic reflexes is the amount of information processing that can take place in the two reflex systems. The monosynaptic reflex is somewhat limited, because information flow involves only the synapse between the sensory and motor neurons. This type of reflex is ideal for quick adjustments that must be made in muscle tension. Conversely, polysynaptic reflexes typically involve a number of levels of interneurons. Hence, convergence and divergence of information can occur as information flows from sensory to motor elements. In essence, the polysynaptic system, in addition to having afferent and efferent components, has a "processor" of sorts between the sensory and motor elements. In intact organisms, the integration that takes place within the processor allows information to be shared by other regions of the nervous system. For example, some of the interneurons send information upward to the brain. When a hot stove is touched, the brain is informed. This sensory experience is likely to be evaluated and stored by the brain, therefore making it less likely that the hot stove will be touched a second time.

## MUSCULATURE REFLEXES

Reflexes are not limited to the spinal cord. Responses involving the musculature of the face and neck can also be reflexive in nature. For example, a puff of air that strikes the cornea of the human eye elicits a brisk, short-latency eyelid closure. Like the polysynaptic spinal reflexes, this eyeblink reflex appears to involve three elements: a sensory nerve, called the trigeminal nerve, that carries information from receptors in the cornea of the eye to the trigeminal nucleus (a cranial nerve nucleus); interneurons that connect the trigeminal nucleus with several other brain-stem neurons; and a motor nerve that originates from brain-stem motor neurons and contracts the muscles surrounding the eye to produce the eyeblink. This reflex is defensive in nature because it ensures that the eyeball is protected from further stimulation if a stimulus strikes the cornea.

## USE OF AUTONOMIC NERVOUS SYSTEM

Not all reflexes involve activation of skeletal muscles. For example, control of the urinary bladder involves a spinal reflex that activates smooth muscles. Also, temperature regulation is partially the product of a reflexive response to changes in external or internal environments. Many of these types of reflexes engage the autonomic nervous system, a division of the nervous system that is involved in regulating and maintaining the function of internal organs.

Not all reflexes involve simple, local, short-latency responses. The maintenance of posture when standing upright is a generally automatic, reflexive system that one does not think about. This system includes neurons in the spinal cord and brain stem. The body's equilibrium system (the vestibular or balance system) involves receptors in the middle ear, brain-stem structures, and spinal motor neurons, while locomotion requires the patterned activation of several reflex systems. Finally, a number of behavioral situations require a rapid response that integrates the motor system with one of the special senses (such as quickly applying the car brakes when a road hazard is seen). These are generally referred to as reaction-time situations and require considerable nervous system processing, including the involvement of the cerebral cortex, when engaged. Nevertheless, these responses are considered reflexive in nature because they involve an eliciting stimulus and a well-defined, consistent response.

## ROLE IN LEARNING AND MEMORY

Reflexes have been widely studied by psychologists and biologists interested in learning and memory. Russian physiologists Ivan Sechenov and Ivan Pavlov have generally been credited with the first attempts to study systematically how reflexes could be used to examine relationships between behavior and physiology. Pavlov in particular had a huge influence on the study of behavior. Most students are familiar with the story of Pavlov and his successful demonstration of conditioned salivation in dogs produced by pairing a bell with meat powder. Over the years, the Pavlovian conditioning procedure (also known as classical conditioning) has often been used to study the behavioral principles and neural substrates of learning. The conditioning of a variety of reflexes has been observed, including skeletal muscle responses such as forelimb flexion, hindlimb flexion, and eyelid closure as well as autonomic responses such as respiration, heart rate, and sweat gland activity.

One of the most widely studied classical conditioning procedures is classical eyelid conditioning. This reflex conditioning procedure has been studied in a variety of species, including rabbits, rats, cats, dogs, and humans. Mostly because of the research efforts of Isadore Gormezano and his colleagues, which began in the early 1960's, much is known about behavioral aspects of classical eyelid conditioning in rabbits. In this paradigm, a mild electric shock or air puff is presented to elicit reliably a reflexive blink from the rabbit. The blink is typically measured by means of devices that are attached to the nictitating membrane, a third eyelid that is present in a variety of species, including the rabbit. During training sessions, a neutral stimulus such as a tone or light is delivered 0.3 to 1.0 second prior to the air puff. After about one hundred of these tone and air-puff pairings, the rabbit learns to blink when the tone or light is presented (the rabbit begins to interpret the tone as a signal of the impending air-puff presentation).

This preparation has yielded a wealth of data concerning the parameters of behavioral training that produce the fastest or slowest learning rates (such as stimuli intensities, time between stimuli, and number of trials per day). Furthermore, this simple reflexive learning situation has been used to study how the brain codes simple forms of learning and memory. A number of researchers (most notably Richard F. Thompson) have studied the activity of a variety of brain structures during learning and performance of the classically conditioned eyelid response. These studies have shown that discrete brain regions such as the cerebellum and hippocampus alter their activity to generate or modify the conditioned response. In brief, these researchers have used the conditioning of a very simple reflex to advance the understanding of how the brain might code more complex learning and memory processes.

## INNATE REFLEXES

The study of reflexes has not been limited to learning and memory. Developmental psychologists have studied a variety of innate reflexes that are generated by newborn infants. Sucking is a very prominent reflex that is readily observed in newborns. Also related to feeding is the rooting reflex, which can be elicited when the cheek of an infant is stroked softly. The skin stimu-

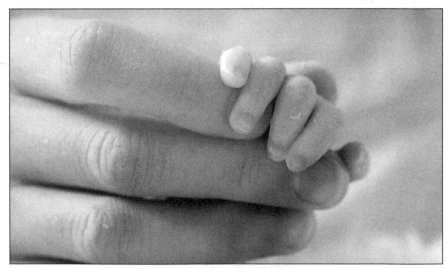

*Newborns possess a grasping reflex that allows them to hold tightly to objects.* (PhotoDisc)

lation causes the infant to open his or her mouth and turn toward the point of stimulation. This reflex has obvious applications in helping the infant locate food. The infant's ability to hold on to objects is, in part, attributable to the presence of the grasp reflex. When an object touches the palm of a newborn's hand, the newborn's fist will close immediately around the object, thus allowing the infant to hold the object for a short period of time. The infantile reflexes disappear within a few months after birth and are replaced by voluntary responses. Most developmental researchers believe that the infantile reflexes are temporary substitutes for the voluntary responses. Apparently, the voluntary responses are not present during the first few months of life because various parts of the infant's nervous system, including the cerebral cortex, have not matured sufficiently to support the behavior. Therefore, the disappearance of the infantile reflexes serves as an important marker of neural and behavioral development.

## CONTRIBUTIONS TO PSYCHOLOGY

The study of reflexes has played a prominent role in shaping the field of psychology. During the late nineteenth century and early twentieth century, Sir Charles Sherrington, a British physiologist, conducted an extensive series of studies concerned with spinal reflexes. He showed that a number of skin stimulations, such as pinching or brushing, produced simple responses even when a spinal transection separated the spinal cord from the rest of the nervous system. From these experiments, he argued that the basic unit of movement was the reflex, which he defined as a highly stereotyped, unlearned response to external stimuli. This work created a flurry of activity among physiologists and psychologists, who tried to trace reflexes throughout the nervous system and assemble them into more complex behaviors.

Early in the twentieth century, many psychologists and physiologists, including Sherrington and Pavlov, adopted the reflex as the basic unit of behavior to study, in part because of the relative simplicity of the behavior and in part because of the ease with which the behavior could be reliably elicited by applying external stimuli. Based on his research, Sherrington believed that complex behaviors were produced by chaining together simple reflexes in some temporal order. This basic idea provided the framework for much of the physiological and behavioral work completed early in the twentieth century. Sechenov and Pavlov also believed that the concept of the reflex could explain more complex behaviors. Pavlov, for example, showed that not all reflexes were innate; rather, new reflexes could be established by associating a "neutral" stimulus (a stimulus that did not initially produce a reflex) with a stimulus that reliably elicited a reflex. As a result of this demonstration, Pavlov proposed an elaborate theory of reflex learning that involved forming associations between stimuli in the cerebral cortex.

In the latter half of the twentieth century, many psychologists interested in studying overt behavior and physiologists interested in studying nervous system function adopted the study of reflexes as a means of simplifying behavior or nervous system activity. Psychologists such as Gormezano, Robert Rescorla, and Allan Wagner, who have studied classical conditioning phenomena, hope to develop a comprehensive understanding of the learning process that occurs when simple paradigms such as classical conditioning are used. Behavioral neuroscientists and neurobiologists (such as Thompson and Eric Kandel) who study nervous system function have used reflexes as the basic unit of behavior in hope of catching a glimpse of nervous system function when a fairly simple behavioral response is being generated and modified by learning experiences. In both cases, a major reason for using the reflex as the unit of behavior is to simplify the experimental situation. Indeed, researchers are not likely to understand complex behavioral processes without first understanding how simpler behaviors and nervous system functions are generated, modified, and maintained. The study of reflexes, from both a behavioral and biological standpoint, has provided and should continue to provide a valuable approach for understanding human behavior as well as understanding how the nervous system generates activity to produce the behavior.

## SOURCES FOR FURTHER STUDY

Carlson, Neil R. *Foundations of Physiological Psychology.* 5th ed. Boston: Allyn & Bacon, 2002. An up-to-date textbook on the neuroscience of behavior.

Domjan, Michael, and Barbara Burkhard. *The Principles of Learning and Behavior.* 5th ed. Belmont, Calif.: Thomson/Wadsworth, 2003. This text is widely used by students interested in learning and behavior. The sections on the history of the reflex and its use in the learning research field is particularly applicable to the present discussion.

Fancher, Raymond E. *Pioneers of Psychology.* 3d ed. New York: W. W. Norton, 1996. This book provides biographies of several prominent psychologists who have had an impact on the field. Included is a chapter detailing the experiments and theories of Ivan Pavlov. Valuable for understanding how the study of the reflex fits into the history of psychology.

Gleitman, Henry, Alan J. Fridlund, and Daniel Weisberg. *Psychology.* 6th ed. New York: W. W. Norton, 2004. This text provides broad coverage of the field of psychology. The chapters on development, learning, and memory should provide the reader with additional information concerning reflexes and other simple behaviors.

*Joseph E. Steinmetz*

SEE ALSO: Brain Structure; Nervous System; Pavlovian Conditioning.

# S-R Theory
## Neal E. Miller and John Dollard

Type of psychology: Personality
Fields of study: Behavioral and cognitive models; models of
abnormality; personality theory

*Miller and Dollard developed a personality theory that was based on Clark Hull's stimulus-response learning theory. They used this theory and a number of psychoanalytic concepts to explain how neurosis developed. They also showed how psychotherapy could be conceptualized as a learning process by using an S-R model of higher mental processes.*

Key concepts
- conflict
- cue
- cue-producing response
- drive
- habit
- imitation
- reinforcement
- response
- response hierarchy
- secondary drive

Much, if not most, human behavior is learned. How human beings learn is one of the central and most controversial topics in psychology. Neal E. Miller and John Dollard used principles of learning developed by Clark Hull, who studied how animals learn, and applied them to explain complex human behavior.

According to Miller and Dollard, human behavior occurs in response to cues. A red traffic light, for example, is a cue to stop, whereas a green light is a cue to go. A cue is simply any stimulus that is recognized as different from other stimuli. A cue may bring about a variety of responses, but some responses are more likely to occur than others. The response to a cue most likely to occur is called the dominant response. Responses to a cue are arranged in a response hierarchy, from the dominant response to the response least likely to occur. A person's response hierarchy can change. The hierarchy that a person has originally is called the initial hierarchy. If the initial hierarchy is inborn, it is known as the innate hierarchy. When a hierarchy changes, the result is known as the response hierarchy.

## RESPONSE HIERARCHY AND LEARNING
Change in a response hierarchy occurs as a result of learning. There are four fundamental considerations in the explanation of how learning occurs: drive, cue, response, and reinforcement.

A drive is an intense stimulus, such as hunger, that motivates a response. The cue is the stimulus that elicits the response. If the dominant response in the hierarchy results in a reduction in the drive, then reinforcement will occur. Reinforcement means that the association, or connection, between the cue (stimulus) and response is strengthened; the next time the cue occurs, therefore, that response will be even more likely to occur. Reinforcement occurs when a person realizes that the response has led to a reward, although such awareness is not always necessary; reinforcement can also occur automatically. In other words, Miller and Dollard's theory states that for persons to learn, they must want something (drive), must do something (response) in the presence of a distinct stimulus (cue), and must get some reward for their actions (reinforcement).

If the dominant response does not result in a reward, the chance that the dominant response will occur again is gradually lessened. This process is called extinction. Eventually, the next response in the hierarchy will occur; in other words, the person will try something else. If that response results in reward, it will be reinforced and may become the dominant response in the hierarchy. In this way, according to Miller and Dollard, humans learn and change their behavior. According to this theory, connections between stimulus and response are learned; these are called habits. Theories that view learning in this way are called stimulus-response, or S-R, theories. The total collection of a person's habits make up his or her personality.

## ROLE OF DRIVES

Drives, as previously noted, motivate and reinforce responses. Some drives, such as hunger, thirst, sex, and pain, are inborn and are known as primary drives. These drives are naturally aroused by certain physiological conditions; through learning, however, they may also be aroused by cues to which they are not innately connected. For example, one may feel hungry when one sees a favorite restaurant, even though one has recently eaten. Drives aroused in this way (that is, by previously neutral cues) are called secondary, or learned, drives.

The natural reaction to an aversive stimulus is pain. Pain is a primary drive; it motivates a person to act, and any response which reduces pain will be reinforced. Neutral cues associated with pain may also produce a response related to pain called fear (or anxiety). Fear motivates a person to act; a response which reduces fear will be reinforced. Fear is therefore a drive; it is a drive which is especially important for understanding neurotic behavior, according to Miller and Dollard. For example, a fear of a harmless cue such as an elevator (an elevator phobia) will motivate a person to avoid elevators, and such avoidance will be reinforced by reduction of fear.

## CUE RESPONSES

A response to one cue may also occur to cues which are physically similar to that cue; in other words, what one learns to do in one situation will occur in other, similar situations. This phenomenon is called stimulus generalization.

Many responses are instrumental responses; that is, they act on and change some aspect of the environment. Other responses are known as cue-producing responses; the cues from these responses serve to bring about other responses. Words are especially important cue-producing responses; someone says a word and another person responds, or one thinks a word and this is a cue for another word. Thinking can be considered as chains of cue-producing responses—that is, as a sequence of associated words; in this way Miller and Dollard sought to describe the higher mental processes such as thinking, reasoning, and planning.

## SOCIAL ROLE OF LEARNING

In their book *Social Learning and Imitation* (1941), Miller and Dollard pointed out that to understand human behavior one must know not only the process of learning (as described above) but also the social conditions under which learning occurs. Human learning is social—that is, it occurs in a social context, which can range from the societal level to the interpersonal level. The process of imitation is one example of how what an individual learns to do depends on the social context.

Imitation involves matching, or copying, the behavior of another person. If the matching behavior is rewarded, it will be reinforced, and the individual will therefore continue to imitate. The cue that elicits the imitating response is the person being imitated (the model), so that the imitative behavior, in Miller and Dollard's analysis, is dependent on the presence of the model. In this way, Miller and Dollard used S-R theory to explain how individuals learn what to do from others and thereby learn how to conform to society.

## PSYCHOANALYTIC APPROACH TO NEUROSIS

In their best-known work, *Personality and Psychotherapy: An Analysis in Terms of Learning, Thinking, and Culture* (1950), Dollard and Miller applied S-R theory to explain how neurosis is learned and how it can be treated using learning principles. They pointed out three central characteristics of neurosis that require explanation: misery, stupidity, and symptoms. The misery that neurotics experience is a result of conflict. Conflict exists when incompatible responses are elicited in an individual. An approach-approach conflict exists when a person has to choose between two desirable goals; once a choice is made, the conflict is easily resolved. An avoidance-avoidance conflict exists when an individual must choose between two undesirable goals. An approach-avoidance conflict exists when an individual is motivated both to approach and to avoid the same goal. The last two types of conflicts may be difficult to resolve and under certain conditions may result in a neurosis.

Dollard and Miller tried to explain some aspects of psychoanalytic theory in S-R terms; like Sigmund Freud, the founder of psychoanalysis, they emphasized the role of four critical childhood training situations in producing conflicts that can result in neurosis. These are the feeding situation, cleanliness training, sex training, and anger-anxiety conflicts. Unfortunate training experiences during these stages of childhood may result in emotional problems. Childhood conflicts arising from such problems may be repressed and may therefore operate unconsciously.

The "stupidity" of the neurotic is related to the fact that conflicts which produce misery are repressed and unconscious. Dollard and Miller explained the psychoanalytic concept of repression in terms of S-R theory in the following manner. Thinking about an experience involves the use of cue-producing responses (that is, the use of words) in thinking. If no words are available to label an experience, then a person is unable to think about it—that is, the experience is unconscious. Some experiences are unconscious because they were never labeled. Early childhood experiences before the development of speech and experiences for which the culture and language do not provide adequate labels are examples of experiences which are unconscious because they are unlabeled. Labeled painful experiences may also become unconscious if a person stops thinking about them. Consciously deciding to stop thinking about an unpleasant topic is called suppression. Repression is similar to suppression except that it is automatic—that is, it occurs without one consciously planning to stop thinking. For Dollard and Miller, therefore, repression is the automatic response of stopping thinking about very painful thoughts; it is reinforced by drive reduction and eventually becomes a very strong habit.

The third characteristic of neuroses requiring explanation are symptoms. Phobias, compulsions, hysteria, and alcoholism are examples of symptoms. Symptoms arise when an individual is in a state of conflict-produced misery. This misery is a result of the intense fear, and other intense drives (for example, sexual drives), involved in conflict. Because the conflict is unconscious, the individual cannot learn that the fear is unrealistic. Some symptoms of neurosis are physiological; these are direct effects of the fear and other drives which produce the conflict. Other symptoms, such as avoidance in a phobia, are learned behaviors that reduce the fear or drives of the conflict. These symptoms are reinforced, therefore, by drive reduction.

## THERAPEUTIC TECHNIQUES

Dollard and Miller's explanation of psychotherapy is largely a presentation of key features of psychoanalysis described in S-R terms. Therapy is viewed as a situation in which new learning can occur. Because neurotic conflict is unconscious, new learning is required to remove repression so that conflict can be resolved. One technique for doing this, taken directly from psychoanalysis, is free association; here, neurotic patients are instructed to say whatever comes to their consciousness. Because this can be a painful experience, patients may resist doing this, but, because the therapist rewards patients for free associating, they eventually continue. While free associating, patients become aware of emotions related to their unconscious conflicts and so develop a better understanding of themselves.

Another technique borrowed from psychoanalysis involves a phenomenon known as transference. Patients experience and express feelings about the therapist. Such feelings really represent, in S-R terms, emotional reactions to parents, teachers, and other important persons in the patient's past, which, through stimulus generalization, have been transferred to the therapist. The therapist helps the patient to recognize and label these feelings and to see that they are generalized from significant persons in the patient's past. The patient in this way learns how she or he really feels. The patient learns much about herself or himself that was previously unconscious and learns how to think more adaptively about everyday life. The patient's symptoms are thereby alleviated.

## EXTENDING THE BEHAVIORIST APPROACH

The S-R theory used by Miller and Dollard had its intellectual roots in the thinking of the seventeenth century, when human beings were thought of as being complicated machines which were set in motion by external stimuli. At the beginning of the twentieth century, the stimulus-response model was adopted by John B. Watson, the founder of behaviorism. Watson used the S-R model to explain observable behavior, but he avoided applying it to mental processes because he believed that mental processes could not be studied scientifically.

Miller and Dollard extended the behaviorism of Watson to the explanation of mental events through their concept of the cue-producing response and its role in the higher mental processes. This was an S-R explanation: Mental processes were seen as arising from associations between words that represent external objects; the words are cues producing responses. Miller and Dollard's approach, therefore, represented a significant departure from the behaviorism of Watson. Miller and Dollard tried to explain mental events in their book *Personality and Psychotherapy*, in which they attempted to explain many psychoanalytic concepts in S-R terms. Because psychoanalysis is largely a theory of the mind, it would have been impossible for them not to have attempted to describe mental processes.

## CONTRIBUTIONS TO MENTAL PROCESSES RESEARCH

The approach to explaining mental processes used by Miller and Dollard, though it represented a theoretical advance in the 1950's, was gradually replaced by other explanations, beginning in the 1960's. The drive-reduction theory of learning that Miller and Dollard advocated came under criticism, and the S-R view that humans passively react to external stimuli was criticized by many psychologists. As a result, new theories of learning emphasizing cognitive (mental) concepts were developed.

New ways of thinking about mental processes were also suggested by fields outside psychology; one of these was computer science. The computer and its programs were seen as analogous to human mental processes, which, like computer programs, involve the input, storage, and retrieval of information. The computer and its programs, therefore, suggested new ways of thinking about the human mind. Miller and Dollard's S-R theory has largely been replaced by concepts of modern cognitive science.

Miller and Dollard's theory still exercises an important influence on modern thinking in psychology. Their analysis of psychoanalysis in terms of learning theory made the important point that neuroses could be unlearned using the principles of learning. Behaviorally oriented treatments of emotional disorders owe a debt to the intellectual legacy of Miller and Dollard.

### SOURCES FOR FURTHER STUDY

Dollard, John, et al. *Frustration and Aggression.* 1939. Reprint. Westport, Conn.: Greenwood Press, 1980. An early application of S-R theory to complex human behavior. The presentation of the hypothesis that aggression is inevitably caused by frustration is seen here.

Dollard, John, and Neal E. Miller. *Personality and Psychotherapy: An Analysis in Terms of Learning, Thinking, and Culture.* New York: McGraw-Hill, 1950. The best-known of the works of Miller and Dollard. Presents a theory of personality and an S-R presentation of psychoanalytic theory and psychoanalytic therapy.

Hall, Calvin Springer, Gardner Lindzey, and John Campbell. *Theories of Personality.* 4th ed. New York: John Wiley & Sons, 1998. This book has a chapter on S-R theory and presents a detailed overview of the theory of Miller and Dollard.

Miller, Neal E. "Studies of Fear as an Acquirable Drive: I. Fear as a Motivator and Fear-Reduction as Reinforcement in the Learning of New Responses." *Journal of Experimental Psychology* 38 (1948): 89-101. A classic paper that served as the experimental basis for postulating that fear is a secondary drive.

Miller, Neal E., and John Dollard. *Social Learning and Imitation.* 1949. Reprint. Westport, Conn.: Greenwood Press, 1979. Presents an application of S-R theory to social motivation with a special emphasis on imitation.

*Sanford Golin*

SEE ALSO: Behaviorism; Conditioning; Drives; Learning; Social Learning: Albert Bandura.

# SCHIZOPHRENIA
## BACKGROUND, TYPES, AND SYMPTOMS

TYPE OF PSYCHOLOGY: Psychopathology
FIELD OF STUDY: Schizophrenias

*Schizophrenia is a severe mental illness that interferes with a person's ability to think and communicate. Researchers have studied the illness for decades, but the specific genetic mechanisms and how they interact with environmental factors in contributing to the illness remain unknown.*

KEY CONCEPTS
- affect
- antipsychotic medication
- delusions
- genetic factors
- hallucinations
- insight
- neuroleptics
- psychosis
- tardive dyskinesia

Schizophrenia affects approximately one out of every hundred individuals. It is considered to be one of the most severe mental illnesses because its symptoms can have a devastating impact on the lives of patients and their families. The patient's thought processes, communication abilities, and emotional expressions are disturbed. As a result, many patients with schizophrenia are dependent on others for assistance with daily life activities.

Schizophrenia is often confused, by the layperson, with multiple personality disorder. The latter is an illness which is defined as two or more distinct personalities existing within the person. The personalities tend to be intact, and each is associated with its own style of perceiving the world and relating to others. Schizophrenia, in contrast, does not involve the existence of two or more personalities; rather, it is the presence of psychotic symptoms and characteristic deficits in social interaction that define schizophrenia.

The diagnostic criteria for schizophrenia have changed over the years; however, certain key symptoms, including disturbances in thought, perception, and emotional experiences, have remained as defining features. The most widely used criteria for diagnosing schizophrenia are those listed in the *Diagnostic and Statistical Manual of Mental Disorders: DSM-IV-TR* (rev. 4th ed., 2000). This manual is published by the American Psychiatric Association and is periodically revised to incorporate changes in diagnostic criteria.

The DSM-IV-TR contains the following symptoms for diagnosing schizophrenia: delusions, hallucinations, disorganized thought, speech, or behavior, and flattened (less responsive) affect; symptoms must have been present for at least six months, and the individual must show marked impairment in a major area of functioning such as work or interpersonal relations. Further, the presence of other disorders, such as drug reactions or organic brain disorders associated with aging, must be ruled out. Thus, the diagnosis of schizophrenia typically involves a thorough physical and mental assessment. While no single individual symptom is necessary for a person to receive a diagnosis of schizophrenia, according to the DSM-IV-TR, the persistent and debilitating presence of bizarre hallucinations, which can include a hallucinated voice commenting on the individual or hallucinated conversations between two voices, is a strong indication of schizophrenia. The presence of delusions or hallucinations and loss of contact with reality is referred to as psychosis and is often present in schizophrenia, but psychotic symptoms can be seen in other mental disorders (for example, bipolar disorder or substance-induced psychotic disorder), so the term "psychosis" is not synonymous with the diagnosis of schizophrenia.

While not emphasized by the DSM-IV-TR, international and cross-cultural study of the symptoms of schizophrenia has noted that the most frequently observed symptom in schizophrenia is patients' lack of insight. That is, despite sometimes overwhelming evidence of gross abnormalities in perception and behavior, patients with schizophrenia are likely to deny that those problems are symptomatic of a disorder.

Each of these symptoms can take a variety of forms. Delusions are defined as false beliefs based on incorrect inferences about external reality. Delusions are classified based on the nature of their content. For example, grandiose delusions involve false beliefs about one's importance, power, or knowledge. The patient might express the belief that he or she is the most intelligent person in the world but that these special intellectual powers have gone unrecognized. As another example, persecutory delusions involve beliefs of being persecuted or conspired against by others. The patient might claim, for example, that there is a government plot to poison him or her.

Hallucinations are sensory experiences that occur in the absence of real stimuli. In the case of auditory hallucinations, the patient may hear voices calling or conversing when there is no one in physical proximity. Visual hallucinations may involve seeing people who are deceased or seeing inanimate objects move on their own accord. Olfactory (smell) and tactile (touch) hallucinations are also possible.

The term "affect" is used to refer to observable behaviors that are the expression of an emotion. Affect is predominantly displayed in facial expressions. "Flat" affect describes a severe reduction in the intensity of emotional expressions, both positive and negative. Patients with flat affect may show no observable sign of emotion, even when experiencing a very joyful or sad event.

Among the symptoms of schizophrenia, abnormalities in the expression of thoughts are a central feature. When speech is incoherent, it is difficult for the listener to comprehend because it is illogical or incomplete. As an

## DSM-IV-TR CRITERIA FOR SCHIZOPHRENIA

Characterized by two or more of the following, each present for significant portion of time during one-month period (less if treated successfully):

- delusions
- hallucinations
- disorganized speech (such as frequent derailment or incoherence)
- grossly disorganized or catatonic behavior
- negative symptoms (affective flattening, alogia, or avolition)

Only one criterion symptom required if delusions are bizarre or hallucinations consist of a voice keeping running commentary on person's behavior or thoughts, or two or more voices conversing with each other

For a significant portion of time since onset, one or more major areas of functioning (work, interpersonal relations, self-care) markedly below level achieved prior to onset; when onset in childhood or adolescence, failure to achieve expected level of interpersonal, academic, or occupational achievement

Continuous signs of disturbance persist for at least six months, including at least one month of active-phase symptoms (less if treated successfully) and possibly including periods of prodromal or residual symptoms; during prodromal or residual periods, signs of disturbance may be manifested by only negative symptoms or two or more symptoms present in attenuated form (such as odd beliefs, unusual perceptual experiences)

Schizoaffective Disorder and Mood Disorder with Psychotic Features ruled out because either no Major Depressive, Manic, or Mixed Episodes have occurred concurrently with active-phase symptoms or mood episodes have occurred during active-phase symptoms, but their total duration brief relative to duration of active and residual periods

Disturbance not due to direct physiological effects of a substance or a general medical condition

If history of Autistic Disorder or another Pervasive Developmental Disorder present, additional diagnosis of Schizophrenia made only if prominent delusions or hallucinations are also present for at least one month (less if treated successfully)

Classification of longitudinal course (applied only after at least one year has elapsed since initial onset of active-phase symptoms):

- Episodic with Interepisode Residual Symptoms: Episodes defined by reemergence of prominent psychotic symptoms; also specify if with Prominent Negative Symptoms
- Episodic with No Interepisode Residual Symptoms
- Continuous: Prominent psychotic symptoms present throughout period of observation; also specify if with Prominent Negative Symptoms
- Single Episode in Partial Remission; also specify if with Prominent Negative Symptoms
- Single Episode in Full Remission
- Other or Unspecified Pattern

example, in response to the question "Where do you live?" one patient replied, "Yes, live! I haven't had much time in this or that. It is an area. In the same area. Mrs. Smith! If the time comes for a temporary space now or whatever." The term "loose associations" is applied to speech in which ideas shift from one subject to another subject that is unrelated. If the loosening of associations is severe, speech may be incoherent. As an illustration of loose associations, a patient described the meaning of "A rolling stone gathers no moss" by saying, "Inside your head there's a brain and it's round like a stone and when it spins around it can't make connections the way moss has little filaments."

With regard to speech, a variety of other abnormalities are sometimes shown by patients. They may use neologisms, which are new words invented by the patient to convey a special meaning. Some show clang associations, which involve the use of rhyming words in conversation: "Live and let live, that's my motto. You live and give and live-give." Abnormalities in the intonation and pace of speech are also common.

In addition to these symptoms, some patients manifest bizarre behaviors, such as odd, repetitive movements or unusual postures. Odd or inappropriate styles of dressing, such as wearing winter coats in the summer, may also occur in some patients. More deteriorated patients frequently show poor hygiene. In order to meet the diagnostic criteria for schizophrenia, the individual must show signs of disturbance for at least six months.

### TYPES AND TREATMENT OF SCHIZOPHRENIA

Because no one symptom is sufficient for a diagnosis of schizophrenia, patients vary in the numbers and intensity of their symptoms. Four subtypes of schizophrenia are recognized; the differentiation among them is based upon the symptom profile, and the criteria are clearly described in DSM-IV-TR.

Catatonic schizophrenia is predominantly characterized by abnormal motor behavior. The patient may be in a "catatonic stupor," which means that he or she shows a marked reduction in movement and is sometimes mute. Other catatonic schizophrenic patients adopt a rigid posture (catatonic rigidity), which they will maintain despite efforts to move them. In disorganized schizophrenia, the primary symptoms are incoherence, catatonic behavior, and flat or inappropriate affect. In paranoid schizophrenia, the predominant symptom is a preoccupation with a systematized delusion. The label undifferentiated schizophrenia is applied to cases that do not meet the specific criteria for catatonic, disorganized, or paranoid schizophrenia but do show prominent delusions, hallucinations, incoherence, or disorganized behavior. Residual schizophrenia is a diagnosis used to refer to the presence of flattened affect or limited speech and less severe delusions or hallucinations in individuals with a prior history of schizophrenia.

In his writings, Eugen Bleuler often used the phrase "the group of schizophrenias," because he believed the disorder could be caused by a variety of factors. In other words, he believed that schizophrenia may not be a single disease entity. Today, some researchers and clinicians who work in the field take the same position. They believe that the differences among patients in symptom patterns and the course of the illness are attributable to differences in etiology. Despite the assumption that there may be different subtypes of schizophrenia, however, each with its own etiology, there is no definitive evidence to support this. In fact, the five subtypes listed in DSM-IV-TR show similar courses and receive the same medications and psychotherapeutic treatments. Thus the distinctions among them are purely descriptive at this point.

Because schizophrenic symptoms have such a devastating impact on the individual's ability to function, family members often respond to the onset of symptoms by seeking immediate treatment. Clinicians, in turn, often respond by recommending hospitalization so that tests can be conducted and an appropriate treatment can be determined. Consequently, almost all patients who are diagnosed with schizophrenia are hospitalized at least once in their lives. The majority experience several hospitalizations.

Research on the long-term outcome of schizophrenia indicates that the illness is highly variable in its course. A minority of patients have only one episode of illness, then go into remission and experience no further symptoms. Unfortunately, however, the majority of patients have recurring episodes that require periodic rehospitalizations. The most severely ill never experience remission but instead show a chronic course of symptomatology. For these reasons, schizophrenia is viewed as having the poorest prognosis of all the major mental illnesses.

Prior to the 1950's, patients with schizophrenia were hospitalized for extended periods of time and frequently became "institutionalized." There were only a few available somatic treatments, and those proved to be of little efficacy. Included among them were insulin coma therapy (the administration of large doses of insulin in order to induce coma), electroconvulsive therapy (ECT; the application of electrical current to the temples in order to induce a seizure), and prefrontal lobotomy (a surgical procedure in which the tracts connecting the frontal lobes to other areas of the brain are severed).

In the 1950's, a class of drugs referred to as antipsychotic medications were discovered to be effective in treating schizophrenia. Antipsychotic drugs significantly reduce some of the symptoms of schizophrenia in many patients. The introduction of antipsychotic medications (also called neuroleptics) in combination with changes in public policy led to a dramatic decline in the number of patients in public mental hospitals. Antipsychotic medications have freed many patients from confinement in hospitals and have enhanced their chances for functioning in the community. Not all patients benefit from typical antipsychotic medications, and the discovery of new classes of medications has offered hope to patients and families. Despite the benefits of antipsychotic medications, they can also produce serious side effects, particularly tardive dyskinesia, a movement disorder associated in some patients with chronic use of typical antipsychotic medications.

The public policy that has contributed to the decline in the number of hospitalized patients with schizophrenia is the nationwide policy of deinstitutionalization. This policy, which has been adopted and promoted by most state governments in the years since 1970, emphasizes short-term hospitalizations, and it has involved the release of some patients who had been in institutions for many years. Unfortunately, the support services that were needed to facilitate the transition from hospital to community living were never put in place. Consequently, the number of homeless schizophrenic patients has increased dramatically. Some of these are patients whose family members have died or have simply lost touch with them. Other patients have withdrawn from contact with their families, despite efforts by concerned relatives to provide assistance. The plight of the homeless mentally ill is of great concern to mental health professionals.

## HISTORY AND FUTURE DIRECTIONS

Writing in the late 1800's, the eminent physician Emil Kraepelin was among the first to document the symptoms and course of schizophrenia, referring to it as "dementia praecox" (dementia of early life). Subsequently, Eugen Bleuler applied the term "schizophrenia," meaning splitting of the mind, to the disorder. Both Kraepelin and Bleuler assumed that organic factors are involved in schizophrenia. Later research confirmed this assumption; brain scans reveal that a significant proportion of schizophrenic patients do have organic abnormalities. The precise nature and cause of these abnormalities remain unknown.

In the majority of cases, the onset of schizophrenic symptoms occurs in late adolescence or early adulthood. The major risk period is between twenty and twenty-five years of age, but the period of risk extends well into adult life. For some patients, there are no readily apparent abnormalities prior to the development of illness. For others, however, the onset of schizophrenia is preceded by impairments in social, academic, or occupational functioning. Some are described by their families as having had adjustment problems in childhood. Childhood schizophrenia is relatively rare. It is estimated to occur in about one out of every ten thousand children. When schizophrenia is diagnosed in childhood, the same diagnostic criteria and treatments are applied.

Schizophrenia shows no clear pattern in terms of its distribution in the population. It occurs in both males and females, although it tends to have a slightly earlier onset in males than in females. The illness strikes individuals of all social, economic, and ethnic backgrounds. Some patients manifest high levels of intelligence and are excellent students prior to becoming ill; others show poor academic performance and signs of learning disability. While the specific pathophysiology associated with schizophrenia remains obscure, the preponderance of evidence demonstrates a significant role for genetic factors in the risk for developing schizophrenia.

Schizophrenia is an illness that has been recognized by medicine for more than one hundred years. During this time, only modest progress has been made in research on its etiology. Some significant advances have been achieved in treatment, however, and the prognosis for schizophrenia is better now than ever before. Moreover, there is reason to believe that the availability of new technologies for studying the central nervous system will speed the pace of further discovery.

**SOURCES FOR FURTHER STUDY**

Bleuler, Eugen. *Dementia Praecox: Or, The Group of Schizophrenias.* Translated by Joseph Zinkin. New York: International Universities Press, 1957. Original German first published in 1911. A classic book in the field, this provides excellent descriptions of the symptoms and very interesting discussions of possible causal factors.

Gottesman, Irving I. *Schizophrenia Genesis: The Origins of Madness.* New York: W. H. Freeman, 1991. An accessible overview for both general and professional readers; includes numerous first-person accounts of the experience of schizophrenia from the perspective of patients and family members.

Herz, Marvin I., Samuel J. Keith, and John P. Docherty. *Psychosocial Treatment of Schizophrenia.* New York: Elsevier, 1990. This book, volume 4 in the Handbook of Schizophrenia series, examines psychosocial causes of schizophrenia and psychosocial treatment approaches. Discusses early intervention, behavior therapy and supportive living arrangements. Results of long-term outcome studies are also reviewed.

Hirsch, Steven R., and Daniel R. Weinberger. *Schizophrenia.* Oxford: Blackwell Science, 1995. A comprehensive review by two masters in the field.

Kraepelin, Emil. *Clinical Psychiatry.* Translated by A. Ross Diefendorf. Delmar, N.Y.: Scholars' Facsimiles & Reprints, 1981. A facsimile reprint of the seventh (1907) edition of Kraepelin's classic text. Reveals the origins of the study of schizophrenia and other mental disorders.

Maj, Mario, and Norman Sartorius. *Schizophrenia.* New York: John Wiley & Sons, 1999. This book is an integration of the worldwide research literature on schizophrenia.

Neale, John M., and Thomas F. Oltmanns. *Schizophrenia.* New York: John Wiley & Sons, 1980. This book provides a comprehensive overview of the illness and examines many of the research methods for exploring its causes.

Walker, Elaine F., ed. *Schizophrenia: A Life-Span Developmental Perspective.* San Diego, Calif.: Academic Press, 1991. The entire life-course of schizophrenic patients is addressed in this book, from early childhood precursors to geriatric outcome.

*Elaine F. Walker; updated by Loring J. Ingraham*

SEE ALSO: Abnormality: Psychological Models; Diagnosis; Drug Therapies; Madness: Historical Concepts; Psychosurgery; Schizophrenia: Theoretical Explanations.

# SCHIZOPHRENIA
## THEORETICAL EXPLANATIONS

TYPE OF PSYCHOLOGY: Psychopathology
FIELDS OF STUDY: Models of abnormality; schizophrenias

*Schizophrenia is one of the most severe and potentially devastating of all psychological disorders. Over the years, a variety of theoretical explanations, sometimes poorly supported by direct experimental evidence, have been proposed. Current empirical research supports the operation of genetic factors in schizophrenia and suggests that such factors may act in concert with environmental factors during early development to elevate the risk for subsequent illness.*

KEY CONCEPTS
- environment
- genetic factors
- interaction
- neurodevelopment
- neurotransmitter
- organic
- schizophrenia spectrum
- schizotypal

Schizophrenia, an illness that strikes one percent of adults, involves changes in all aspects of psychological functioning. Thinking disorders, perceptual distortions and hallucinations, delusions, and emotional changes are the most prominent of such changes. Although some people recover completely, in many others the illness is chronic and deteriorative. For many years, because the causes of schizophrenia were poorly understood, a wide range of theories were proposed to account for the development of schizophrenia. These early theories about schizophrenia can be classified into four types: psychodynamic, family interaction, learning/attention, and organic. Current theories of schizophrenia focus primarily on genetic factors and their interaction with environmental conditions, particularly the environment experienced before birth and during early development.

### PSYCHODYNAMIC THEORIES
Psychodynamic theories originated with Sigmund Freud, who believed that schizophrenia results when a child fails to develop an attachment to his or her parent of the opposite sex. This causes a powerful conflict (called an Oedipal conflict in males) in which unconscious homosexual desires threaten to overwhelm the conscious self. To prevent these desires from generating thoughts and feelings that cause painful guilt or behaviors that would be punished, the ego defends itself by regressing to a state in which awareness of the self as a distinct entity is lost. Thus, the person's behavior becomes so-

cially inappropriate; the person mistakes fantasies for reality and experiences hallucinations and delusions.

Harry Stack Sullivan, a follower of Freud, believed that failure of maternal attachment creates excessive anxiety and sets the pattern for all future relationships. Unable to cope in a world seen as socially dangerous, the individual retreats into fantasy. Having done so, the individual cannot grow socially or develop a sense of trust in or belonging with others. By late adolescence or early adulthood, the person's situation has become so hopeless that all pretense of normality collapses, and he or she withdraws totally into a world of fantasy and delusion.

### FAMILY AND LEARNING THEORIES

Family interaction theories dwell even more intensely on parent-child, especially mother-child, relationships. Theodore Lidz and coworkers, after conducting studies on families with a schizophrenic member, concluded that one or both parents of a future schizophrenic are likely to be nearly, if not overtly, psychotic. They proposed that the psychotogenic influence of these parents on a psychologically vulnerable child is most likely the cause of schizophrenia.

Gregory Bateson and colleagues proposed a family interaction theory called the double-bind theory. Bateson suggested that schizophrenia results when parents expose a child to a family atmosphere in which they never effectively communicate their expectations, and therefore the child is unable to discover which behaviors will win approval. Scolded for disobeying, for example, the child changes his or her behavior only to be scolded for being "too obedient." Subjected to such no-win situations constantly, the child cannot develop an attachment to the family, and this failure generalizes to all subsequent relationships.

Learning theories propose that failure of operant conditioning causes the bizarre behavior of schizophrenia. In one version, conditioning fails because mechanisms in the brain that support operant learning, such as reinforcement and attention, are faulty, thus preventing the learning of appropriate, adaptive behaviors.

For example, a person who is unable to focus attention on relevant stimuli would be unable to learn the stimulus associations and discriminations necessary for successful day-to-day behavior. Such an individual's behavior would eventually become chaotic. This learning/attention theory proposes a defect in perceptual filtering, a function of the brain's reticular formation. This system filters out the innumerable stimuli that impinge upon one's senses every moment but are unimportant. In schizophrenia, the theory proposes, this filtering system fails, and the individual is overwhelmed by a welter of trivial stimuli. Unable to cope with this confusing overstimulation, the person withdraws, becomes preoccupied with sorting out his or her thoughts, and becomes unable to distinguish internally generated stimuli from external ones.

## ORGANIC THEORIES

Organic theories of schizophrenia are influenced by the knowledge that conditions known to have organic causes (that is, causes stemming from biological abnormalities) often produce psychological symptoms that mimic the psychotic symptoms of schizophrenia. Among these are viral encephalitis, vitamin-deficiency diseases, temporal-lobe epilepsy, and neurodegenerative disease such as Huntington's disease and Wilson's disease. In contradistinction to historical theories of schizophrenia that have little empirical support, considerable research supports the operation of genetic factors in schizophrenia. Such factors are most often assumed to influence the development of the brain and its resilience to a variety of physiological and psychological stressors. In the diathesis-stress model, such a genetic defect is necessary for the development of chronic schizophrenia but is not sufficient to produce it; stressful life events must also be present. The genetic abnormality then leaves the person unable to cope with life stresses, the result being psychosis. Research demonstrating the operation of genetic factors in schizophrenia in no way implies the absence of environmental factors which operate to influence the course of the disorder.

Many brain abnormalities have been proposed as causes of schizophrenia. One suggestion is that schizophrenia results from generalized brain pathology. For example, some researchers suggest that widespread brain deterioration caused by either environmental poisoning or infection by a virus causes schizophrenia.

Alternatively, some biochemical abnormality may be at fault. The endogenous psychotogen theory proposes that abnormal production of a chemical substance either inside or outside the brain produces psychotic symptoms by affecting the brain in a druglike fashion. Substances similar to the hallucinogenic drugs lysergic acid diethylamide (LSD) and mescaline are popular candidates for the endogenous psychotogen. The dopamine theory, however, proposes that schizophrenia results when a chemical neurotransmitter system in the brain called the dopamine system becomes abnormally overactive or when dopamine receptors in the brain become abnormally sensitive to normal amounts of dopamine. In addition to dopamine, other neurotransmitters have been proposed as important in the development and maintenance of schizophrenia.

## NEUROLOGICAL AND GENETIC STUDIES

Theories of schizophrenia are instrumental in generating experiments that provide definite knowledge of the condition. Experimental support for psychodynamic theories of the development and progression of schizophrenia has not been forthcoming. Therefore, most empirical researchers regard psychodynamic theories of schizophrenia as having little scientific merit. Family interaction theories also have not been supported by subsequent experiments. Although studies have found disturbed family relationships, the evidence suggests that these are most likely the result of, not the cause of, having a schizophrenic individual in the family. Family interaction has, however, been shown to be influential in modifying the course of illness and the risk of relapse. Studies consistently fail to find that parent-child interactions are psychotogenic, and the once-popular notion of the schizophrenogenic parent has been discarded. Only learning/attention and organic theories are strongly supported by experimental evidence. The evidence for attentional or learning deficits resulting from a fault in the reticular formation is strong, and it stems from electrophysiological and behavioral studies.

The electroencephalogram (EEG) is often found to be abnormal in schizophrenic patients, showing excessive activation that indicates overarousal. Furthermore, studies of evoked potentials, electrical events recorded from the cortex of the brain in response to specific sensory stimuli, often find abnormalities. Significantly, these occur late in the evoked potential, indicating abnormality in the brain's interpretation of sensory stimuli rather than in initial reception and conduction.

Behavioral studies show that schizophrenic patients often overreact to low-intensity stimuli, which corresponds to their complaints that lights are too bright or sounds are too loud. In addition, patients are often unusually distractible—unable to focus attention on the most relevant stimuli. Orienting responses to novel stimuli are deficient in about half of schizophrenic patients. Patient self-reports also indicate that, subjectively, the individual feels overwhelmed by sensory stimulation.

Thus, considerable evidence suggests that, at least in many patients, there is an abnormality in the sensory/perceptual functioning in the brain, perhaps in the perceptual filtering mechanism of the reticular formation.

Franz J. Kallmann's twin studies of the 1940's provided convincing evidence of a genetic factor in schizophrenia. He found that genetically identical monozygotic twins are much more likely to be concordant for schizophrenia (that is, both twins are much more likely to be psychotic) than are dizygotic twins, who are not genetically identical. Studies using genealogical techniques also showed that schizophrenia runs in families.

The criticism of these studies was that twins not only are genetically similar but also are exposed to the same family environment, and therefore genetic and environmental factors were confounded. Seymour Kety and colleagues, working with adoption records in Scandinavia, effectively answered this criticism by showing that adoptees with schizophrenia are more likely to have biological relatives with schizophrenia or related illnesses than the biological relatives of unaffected adoptees. These studies showed that schizophrenia is more closely associated with genetic relatedness than with family environment. In addition, these studies showed that the genetic liability is not a liability to psychopathology in general (that is, relatives of individuals with schizophrenia are not at elevated risk for all forms of mental disorder) but that there is a range of severity of illness observed in the relatives of individuals with schizophrenia. The range of less severe schizophrenia-like conditions observed is called the schizophrenia spectrum of illness; schizotypal personality is the most frequently studied form. Schizotypal personality disorder occurs more frequently than schizophrenia itself among the relatives of individuals with schizophrenia.

Presumably, this genetic predisposition works by producing some organic change. Studies using advanced brain-imaging techniques indicate that, in many patients, there is nonlocalized brain degeneration, which is revealed by the increased size of the ventricles, fluid-filled spaces within the brain. What causes this degeneration is unknown, but some researchers suggest that it is caused by a virus and that a genetic factor increases susceptibility to infection and the subsequent damaging effects of a viral disease. Although direct evidence of a virus has been found in a minority of patients, the viral theory is still considered speculative and unproved. There is no evidence that schizophrenia is contagious.

## BIOCHEMICAL STUDIES

Experimental evidence of biochemical abnormalities in the brain's dopamine neurotransmitter systems is, however, impressive. Antipsychotic drugs are effective in relieving the symptoms of schizophrenia, especially positive symptoms such as hallucinations and delusions. These drugs block dopamine receptors in the brain. Furthermore, the more powerfully the drugs bind to and block dopamine receptors, the smaller the effective dose that is necessary to produce a therapeutic result.

Further evidence comes from a condition called amphetamine psychosis, which occurs in people who abuse amphetamine and similar stimulants such as cocaine. Amphetamine psychosis so closely mimics some forms of schizophrenia that misdiagnoses have been common. Furthermore, amphetamine psychosis is not an artifact of disturbed personality; experiments show that normal control subjects will develop the condition if they are given high doses of amphetamines every few hours for several days. Amphetamine psychosis, which is believed to result from the overactivation of dopamine systems in the brain, is treated with antipsychotic drugs such as chlorpromazine.

Direct evidence of abnormality in the dopamine systems comes from studies using advanced techniques such as positron emission tomography (PET) scanning. These studies show that the brains of schizophrenic patients, even those who have never been treated with antipsychotic medications, may have abnormally large numbers of dopamine receptors in an area called the limbic system, which is responsible for emotional regulation.

Dopamine-blocking drugs, however, help only a subset of patients. Studies show that those most likely to benefit from medication are patients who display primarily positive symptoms. Patients who show negative symptoms—such as withdrawal, thought blocking, and catatonia—are less likely to be helped by medication.

## HISTORY OF THE CONCEPT OF SCHIZOPHRENIA

The disorders that are now called schizophrenia were first characterized in the nineteenth century. Emil Kraepelin first grouped these disorders, referring to them by the collective name dementia praecox, in 1893.

Many early neurologists and psychiatrists thought these dementias were organic conditions. This view changed, however, after Swiss psychiatrist Eugen Bleuler published his classic work on the disorder in 1911. Bleuler proposed that the primary characteristic of the condition was a splitting of intellect from emotions. He introduced the term "schizophrenia" (literally, "split mind"). Bleuler, influenced by the psychodynamic theories of Freud, believed that the bizarre content of schizophrenic thoughts and perceptions represented a breaking away from an external reality that was too painful or frightening. His ideas became especially influential in the United States.

Attempts to treat schizophrenia with traditional psychotherapies were, however, unsuccessful. Success rates rarely surpassed the rate of spontaneous recovery, the rate at which patients recover without treatment. Because medical interventions such as lobotomy, insulin shock therapy, and electroconvulsive therapy were also ineffective, psychiatric hospitals were filled with patients for whom little could be done.

The discovery of antipsychotic drugs and changing public policy about institutionalization in the 1950's changed things dramatically. Hospital populations declined. The surprising effectiveness of these medications, in concert with the discovery of amphetamine psychosis in the 1930's and the genetic studies of the 1940's, renewed the belief that schizophrenia is an organic condition.

Two problems impeded further understanding. First, techniques available for investigating the brain were primitive compared with modern techniques. Therefore, reports of organic changes in schizophrenia, although common, were difficult to confirm. Second, because the routinely administered medications powerfully influenced brain functioning, it became a problem to distinguish organic changes that were important in causing the disorder from those that were merely secondary to the action of antipsychotic drugs in the brain.

*Eugen Bleuler.*

Indeed, it became "common wisdom" among many psychologists that organic factors identified by researchers were not primary to the disorder but were, rather, side effects of medication. Soft neurological signs such as eye-movement dysfunctions, abnormal orienting responses, and unusual movements were considered drug related, even though Kraepelin and others had described them decades before the drugs were discovered. The drugs came to be called "major tranquilizers," implying that medication allowed patients to function more effectively by relieving the overwhelming anxiety that accompanied the disorder but that the drugs did not influence the schizophrenic process itself.

The fact that antipsychotic drugs have little usefulness as antianxiety agents in nonschizophrenics did not shake this opinion. Neither did the discovery of more powerful antianxiety agents such as Librium (chlordiazepoxide) and Valium (diazepam), even after they were shown to be almost useless in treating schizophrenia.

The next dramatic change in understanding schizophrenia came in the 1960's with the discovery of monoamine neurotransmitters, including dopamine, and the discovery that these chemical systems in the brain are strongly affected in opposite ways by psychotogenic drugs, such as cocaine and amphetamine, and antipsychotic drugs, such as chlorpromazine. Carefully conducted twin and adoption studies confirmed the role of genetic factors in schizophrenia and encouraged the search for the mechanism by which genes influenced the risk for developing schizophrenia. In the following decades, evidence that prenatal and perinatal factors are instrumental in the development of schizophrenia has led to the emerging consensus that schizophrenia should be considered from a neurodevelopmental perspective.

### SOURCES FOR FURTHER STUDY

Bowers, Malcolm B. *Retreat from Sanity: The Structure of Emerging Psychosis.* New York: Human Sciences Press, 1974. A fascinating description, often in the words of patients, of the experiences many people have in the very early stages of psychosis. Especially interesting are descriptions of "peak" and "psychedelic" experiences resulting from sensory alterations during the onset of the disorder.

Gottesman, Irving I. *Schizophrenia Genesis: The Origins of Madness.* New York: W. H. Freeman, 1991. An excellent, well-written book that is easily accessible to the general reader. Highly recommended.

Gottesman, Irving I., James Shields, and Daniel R. Hanson. *Schizophrenia: The Epigenetic Puzzle.* Cambridge, England: Cambridge University Press, 1982. More technical than *Schizophrenia Genesis* but still accessible to anyone with a solid background in genetics of the type obtained in a good general biology course. Concentrates on genetic studies and gives complete references to original technical articles.

Hirsch, Steven R., and Daniel R. Weinberger. *Schizophrenia.* Malden, Mass.:

Blackwell Science, 1995. A comprehensive review by two masters in the field.

Kraepelin, Emil. *Clinical Psychiatry*. Translated by A. Ross Diefendorf. Delmar, N.Y.: Scholars' Facsimiles & Reprints, 1981. A facsimile reprint of the seventh (1907) edition of Kraepelin's classic text. Reveals the origins of the study of schizophrenia and other mental disorders.

Maj, Mario, and Norman Sartorius. *Schizophrenia*. New York: John Wiley & Sons, 1999. This book is an integration of the worldwide research literature on schizophrenia.

Myslobodsky, Michael S., and Ina Weiner. *Contemporary Issues in Modeling Psychopathology*. Boston: Kluwer Academic, 2000. Presents several theories of schizophrenic psychopathology and empirical approaches to and evidence from tests of those theories.

Raine, Adrian, Todd Lencz, and Sarnoff A. Mednick. *Schizotypal Personality*. New York: Cambridge University Press, 1995. An overview of the less severe schizophrenia-like disorder seen in some relatives of patients with schizophrenia. Discusses links (and differences) between schizotypal personality and schizophrenia.

Snyder, Solomon H. *Madness and the Brain*. New York: McGraw-Hill, 1974. Written in a lively, breezy style, this short volume deals with biomedical factors in many psychological disorders, including schizophrenia. Especially interesting is Snyder's discussion of drug effects, neurotransmitters, and schizophrenia.

Torrey, Edwin Fuller. *Surviving Schizophrenia: A Family Manual*. Rev. ed. New York: Perennial Library, 1988. One of the best books available for the general reader on schizophrenia. Intended primarily for family members of schizophrenics, this book is appropriate for anyone who is interested in the disorder, including mental health care workers. Torrey writes wonderfully and pulls no punches when dealing with outmoded theories and poorly done experiments. Many libraries have only the first edition; the revised edition is recommended.

*William B. King; updated by Loring J. Ingraham*

SEE ALSO: Abnormality: Psychological Models; Diagnosis; Drug Therapies; Madness: Historical Concepts; Psychosurgery; Schizophrenia: Background, Types, and Symptoms.

# SELF

TYPE OF PSYCHOLOGY: Personality; developmental psychology; social psychology; consciousness
FIELDS OF STUDY: Attitudes and behavior; general constructs and issues; personality theory; social perception and cognition

*The self is a term that is widely used and variously defined. It has been examined by personality theorists as a central structure. Social cognitive psychology has explored the individual and interpersonal processes that influence such dimensions as self-systems, self-concept, self-consciousness, and self-efficacy. Recent research has challenged psychology to rethink its concept of the self.*

KEY CONCEPTS
- being-in-the-world
- identity
- identity crisis
- narrative
- self-awareness
- self-concept
- self-efficacy
- self-in-relation
- self-system
- subjectivity

The concept of the self was invoked in Western thought long before the advent of the discipline of psychology. During the Renaissance and Enlightenment, scholars often depicted humans as having a soul, spirit, or metaphysical essence. The famous argument by French Renaissance philosopher René Descartes (1596-1650), "I think, therefore I am," placed its fundamental confidence in the assumption that the "I"—an active, unique identity—could be directly experienced through introspection and therefore trusted to exist. Descartes's dualistic formulation of the mind-body relation set the stage for a number of assumptions about the self: that the self is an active, unitary, core structure of the person which belongs to and is consciously accessible to the individual.

During the Enlightenment, empiricist and associationist philosophers retained the mind-body distinction but emphasized the material, objectively observable behaviors of the body, with more stress on observable information, as seen in the rephrasing of Descartes by Scottish philosopher David Hume (1711-1776): "I sense, therefore I am." William James (1842-1930), philosopher and founder of American scientific psychology, recognized that the personal experience of one's own stream of consciousness—the sense of "I" or subjectivity—is fleeting and fluid and less measurable than the objective "me" with its body, relationships, and belongings. However, he considered the self to be made up of both subjective and objective components, a perspective reflected in the various theories of the self present in modern psychology.

Many psychologists believe that there is an internal self *in potentia* that takes shape and grows as long as an adequate environment is provided. Others emphasize a social component, suggesting that the self develops directly out of interpersonal interactions.

## PSYCHOANALYTIC AND PSYCHODYNAMIC THEORIES

Sigmund Freud (1856-1939), Austrian founder of psychoanalysis at the turn of the twentieth century, had little use in his tripartite theory of the psyche for the idea of self as one's central identity. He conceptualized the ego as an important but secondary structure that mediates between the instincts of the id and the strictures of the superego. However, other psychodynamic theorists of the first half of the twentieth century returned to the idea of a center of personality. Carl Jung (1875-1961), a Swiss psychiatrist, thought of the self as an important archetype—an energized symbol in the collective unconscious—that organizes and balances the contradictory influences of other archetypes and, in fact, transcends opposing forces within the psyche. The archetype itself is an inborn potential, while its actual development is informed by personal experiences. Karen Horney (1885-1952), a German psychiatrist, believed that each individual is born with a real self, containing healthy intrinsic potentials and capabilities. However, because of basic anxiety and a belief that one is unlovable, some individuals become alienated from their real selves and pursue an unrealistic idealized self. Margaret Mahler (1897-1985), a Hungarian-born pediatrician and psychoanalyst, described the separation-individuation process of the first three years of life, by which a child achieves individual personhood through psychologically separating from other people.

In contrast, Harry Stack Sullivan (1892-1949), an American psychiatrist, believed that personality and self can never be fully disconnected from interpersonal relations. His concept of the self-system is thus a set of enduring patterns of relating to others that avoids anxiety by striving for others' approval (the "good-me"), avoiding their disapproval (the "bad-me"), and dissociating from whatever causes their revulsion (the "not-me"). Heinz Kohut (1931-1981), Austrian founder of self psychology, also stressed that healthy selfhood is only attained through satisfying, empathically attuned interactions between infants and caregivers. Caregivers initially provide the self with a sense of goodness and strength and are therefore termed self-objects. The healthy self then develops its own ambitions, ideals, and skills, while deprivation from self-objects results in an injured self.

## DEVELOPMENTAL THEORIES

While these psychodynamic theorists focused on the emotional and relational dimensions of early development, others, such as German-born Erik

Erikson (1902-1994), also emphasized cognitive and identity development over the entire life span. Erikson's theory, in which the ego confronts a series of psychosocial crises, recognized such childhood stages as autonomy versus shame and doubt, initiative versus guilt, and industry versus inferiority as important to ego development. However, it was his conceptualization of the identity crisis during adolescence that has been highly influential on modern research on self-concept and self-esteem. By searching out and eventually choosing life strategies, values, and goals, the adolescent establishes a sense of inner assuredness and self-definition, which serve to promote healthy intimacy, productivity, and integration later in life. James Marcia, an American developmental psychologist, demonstrated in the 1960's, 1970's, and 1980's that adolescents who actively explore the question "Who am I?" and achieve their own sense of identity are more likely to have positive outcomes, including high self-esteem, self-direction, and mature relationships. Erikson, Marcia, and other developmental scholars recognize that the task of establishing identity can be facilitated or hampered by the values and traditions presented in families and social structures.

## HUMANISTIC AND EXISTENTIAL/PHENOMENOLOGICAL PERSPECTIVES
Since the 1920's, humanistic and existential traditions have focused on the human being as a whole, and division into parts or structures is resisted insofar as it leads to dehumanizing the person. Thus, the self as such is often renamed or deemphasized in these theories. Gordon Allport (1897-1967), an American psychologist, used the concept of "proprium" to describe the unique, holistic organization of personality and awareness that develops over the life span, culminating in ownership of one's own consciousness in adulthood. American psychologist Carl Rogers (1902-1987) also deemphasized the role of self, which he thought was merely one differentiated aspect of one's phenomenological, conscious experience. Rogers's self-image was a complex representation of the total organism as perceived through self-reflection. Abraham Maslow (1908-1970), another American psychologist, proposed that one of the most advanced human needs was the pull to be true to one's own nature. While he called this pull "self-actualization," he did not theorize the self to be a central structure but a unique range of capacities, talents, and activities. American existentialist psychologist Rollo May (1909-1994) suggested that instead of thinking of a person as having a central, internal self that is separated from the world, a person should be considered to be a being-in-the-world (*Dasein* in German), who is in all ways related to the physical and especially the social environment.

## THE SELF AS A REGULATOR OF INDIVIDUAL PROCESSES
Beginning in the 1950's and accelerating through the turn of the twenty-first century, much research on personality has moved away from extensive personality theories toward empirically testable hypotheses. Models of the self focus on describing and observing the mental mechanisms by which in-

dividuals moderate and control their internal processes and their interactions with the world within specific social traditions and expectations.

Albert Bandura, the American founder of social cognitive psychology, conceptualizes the person as part of an interactive triad consisting of individual, behavior, and environment. Like radical behaviorism, social cognitive theory assumes that all human behavior is ultimately caused by the external environment. However, Bandura also describes individuals as having cognitions with which they regulate their own behavior, through the establishment of guiding performance standards. His idea of the self-system consists of internal motivations, emotions, plans, and beliefs which are organized into three processes: self-observation, judgmental processes, and self-reaction. In self-observation, the individual consciously monitors his or her own behavior and describes it. Through judgmental processes, values are placed on the observations, according to personal standards internalized from past experience and comparisons to others. The self-reaction is the self-system's way of punishing, rewarding, changing, or continuing with renewed motivation the behavior that has been self-observed.

Bandura's concept of self-observation has been further refined in research on self-awareness, self-consciousness, and self-monitoring. American social psychologists such as Robert Wicklund, Arnold Buss, Mark Davis, and Stephen Franzoi have defined self-awareness as a state of focusing attention on oneself, while self-consciousness is defined as a traitlike tendency to spend time in the state of such self-awareness. Most such research distinguishes between private self-awareness or self-consciousness, in which a person attends to internal aspects of self, such as thoughts and emotions, and public self-awareness or self-consciousness, in which a person attends to external aspects of self that can be observed by others, such as appearance, physical movements, and spoken words. Private self-awareness and self-consciousness have been associated with intense emotional responses, clear self-knowledge, and actions that are consistent with one's own attitudes and values. Self-monitoring is related primarily to public self-consciousness and is described by American psychologist Mark Snyder as the tendency to engage in attempts to control how one is perceived in social interactions. Snyder's research suggests that high self-monitors use current situations to guide their reactions more than do low self-monitors, which can lead to the relationships of high self-monitors being dependent on situations or activities.

Social cognitive theory has also directed research on self-efficacy, the belief that one will be capable of using one's own behavior, knowledge, and skills to master a situation or overcome an obstacle. For example, Bandura showed in 1986 that people in recovery from a heart attack were more likely to follow an exercise regimen when they learned to see themselves as having physical efficacy. Perceived self-efficacy was demonstrated throughout the 1980's and 1990's as contributing to a wide range of behaviors, from weight loss to maternal competence to managerial decision making.

A final theme coming to prominence since the 1970's relates to identity and self-concept. Self-concept has been defined by American psychologist Roy Baumeister as one's personal beliefs about oneself, including one's attributes and traits and one's self-esteem, which is based on self-evaluations. American developmental psychologists such as Jerome Kagan, Michael Lewis, and Jeanne Brooks-Gunn found that by their second year, children become capable of recognizing and cognitively representing as their own their actions, intentions, states, and competencies. With further development, people appear to form not one unitary self-concept, but a collection of self-schemas or ideas about themselves in relation to specific domains such as school or work. American psychologist Hazel Markus has also found time to be a relevant dimension of self-concept, in that persons develop possible selves: detailed concepts of who they hope and fear to become in the future.

Identity is defined as who a person is, including not only the personal ideas in the self-concept but also the public perceptions of a person in his or her social context (for instance, birth name or roles in cultural institutions). Identity consists of two major features: continuity or sameness of the person over time and differentiation of the person as unique compared to others and groups of others. As mentioned with regard to Erikson's theory and Marcia's research, adolescence has been demonstrated to be a primary stage for exploring the values, beliefs, and group memberships that constitute identity. However, identity continues to evolve during adulthood with changes in roles (such as student versus parent) and activities (work versus retirement).

### NEUROPSYCHOLOGICAL PERSPECTIVES

From a neuropsychological perspective, brain functions underlie all dimensions and activities of the self. Yet an important question is how the functioning of biophysical structures such as the brain and nervous system can give rise to the self, which can be consciously experienced, either directly or through its activity. This question relies on the same mind-body problem that first arose with Descartes. One solution to this mental-physical divide proposed by such neuroscientists as Australian Sir John Eccles and Hungarian-born Michael Polanyi is the concept of emergent systems, or marginal control of lower systems by the organizational rules of higher systems. As the nervous system evolved into a complex set of structures, neural circuitry gained a concomitant complexity of organized functioning such that a new property, consciousness, emerged. This emergent property has capabilities and activities (such as the experience of mental images) that are a result of the organization of neural patterns but are not reducible to its component neural parts, much as water molecules have different qualities from those of hydrogen and oxygen atoms alone. Yet consciousness and thus experience of the self are necessarily embodied in and constrained by these patterned brain and biological processes.

Thus, the sense of self as having continuity relies on the capacity of several structures of the brain (such as the hippocampus and specialized areas of the association cortex) for forming, storing, and retrieving personal memories as well as representations of background bodily and emotional states. A specific self-concept, as explored in social cognitive research, can only be developed through the organizational capacity of the prefrontal cortex to self-observe and construct cognitive schemas. The prefrontal cortex is also involved in carrying out many actions attributed to the self, such as the planned action of self-efficacy, and the techniques of presenting the self in a particular light, as in self-monitoring. Research such as that by Antonio Damasio, an American neurologist, indicates that when normal functioning of specific neural circuits is disturbed, deficits also occur in these experiences of self as knower and owner of mental and physical states. For example, with anasagnosia, damage to the right somatosensory cortices impairs a person's ability to be aware of damage to the body or associated problems in the functioning of the self. The body itself may become completely disowned by the person, and the unified sense of "me" is fractured.

## CULTURE AND GENDER DIFFERENCES IN THE EXPERIENCE OF SELF

Empirical and theoretical scholarship since the 1970's has presented alternatives to the universality of the self across culture and gender, and has challenged the utility of the construct as heretofore defined. Humans' experiences of self have been found to vary substantially across cultures and gender, especially regarding the importance of independence and separation versus interdependence and relationship. For example, American psychologist Hazel Markus, Japanese psychologist Shinobu Kitayama, and their colleagues found in their 1991 and 1997 studies that the concept of an individualized self as uniquely differentiated from others is descriptive of Americans' psychological experience. In contrast, Japanese personal experience is often more consistent with collective, relational roles, a conclusion that has been replicated with other collectivist cultures.

Feminist psychologists working at the Stone Center in Massachusetts have drawn on the developmental psychological work of Americans Nancy Chodorow and Carol Gilligan, observing that many women find the notion of a discrete and individualized self places too much emphasis on separation between people. This research group proposed the concept of self-in-relation to capture the extent to which one's core sense of being is defined by one's relationships with and commitments to other individuals. Likewise, as American developmental psychologist Mary Field Belenky and her colleagues interviewed women about their learning processes, they found that the sense of self as an individual, separate knower and speaker is only one stage of development. The individualist stage is often followed by respect for the ways one's subjectivity is informed by empathy and intimacy with others. These empirical observations suggest that theories of the self should attend more carefully to the interplay of individual and interpersonal or social experience.

## POSTMODERN, DIALOGICAL, AND NARRATIVE THEORIES

The advancement since the 1970's of postmodernism has led many psychologists to recognize that persons construct their own realities through social rules, roles, and structures. Kenneth Gergen, an American social psychologist, proposes that the self gains its unity and identity from the consistency of the social roles a person plays. He points out that the more a person's roles multiply and conflict, as is common in fast-paced technological societies, the less cohesive and the more obsolete the concept of self becomes.

New Zealand-born cognitive psychologist Rom Harré and American psychologists Edward Sampson and Frank Richardson have each advanced alternative theories in which the concept of self is still viable but which emphasize the necessity of recognizing the multiplicity of perspectives within a self. Drawing on the sociological traditions of symbolic interactionism, especially the "looking-glass self" of American sociologists George Herbert Mead and Charles Cooley, these theorists see the self as constructed only through intimate involvement in interpersonal interaction and especially language, which allow one to reflect on oneself and create the social bonds that define one as a self. The unique and specific manner with which one articulates oneself appears to reflect one's culture and social audience but also one's beliefs and commitments about identity.

American developmental psychologist Dan McAdams has led research on the narratives people tell to describe and explain their lives to themselves and others, concluding that the linguistic construction of the self is a continuous and central task of the entire life span. Jerome Bruner, an American cognitive psychologist, suggests that through narrative, the various dimensions of self—public and private, structure and activity—become interrelated in meaningful stories and serve to promote both the growth of the individual and the survival of human culture.

## SOURCES FOR FURTHER STUDY

Bandura, Albert. "The Self-System in Reciprocal Determinism." *American Psychologist* 33 (1978): 344-358. Lays out major concepts of social cognitive theory with respect to the role of the self-system. Theory and research are well elaborated and accessible to nonprofessionals.

Damasio, Antonio R. *Descartes' Error: Emotion, Reason, and the Human Brain.* New York: Avon Books, 1994. Provides a review of neural circuitry and an overview of modern neurological research on personality and the self, especially regarding the role of the body and emotions in reasonable, planned action. The content is complex but is presented in an engaging and straightforward style.

Derlega, Valerian J., Barbara A. Winstead, and Warren H. Jones. *Personality: Contemporary Theory and Research.* Chicago: Nelson-Hall, 1999. Provides clear overviews of modern research in self-concept, identity, self-awareness, and self-consciousness.

Gergen, Kenneth J. *The Saturated Self.* New York: Basic Books, 1991. This influential text is written for nonprofessionals to describe how modern society has undermined traditional concepts of the self. The author's nontechnical, entertaining style makes this a good introduction to post-modernism and its new theories of self.

Hall, Calvin S., Gardner Lindzey, and John B. Campbell. *Theories of Personality*. 4th ed. New York: John Wiley & Sons, 1998. A popular text used in undergraduate and graduate courses, explaining the major theories' tenets about the self and personality.

Kitayama, Shinobu, Hazel Rose Markus, Hisaya Matsumoto, and Vinai Norasakkunkit. "Individual and Collective Processes in the Construction of the Self: Self-Enhancement in the United States and Self-Criticism in Japan." *Journal of Personality and Social Psychology* 72, no. 6 (1997): 1245-1267. Explores the role of culture in people's experiences of and formulations of self and describes cross-cultural differences in the maintenance of the self.

Lewis, Michael, and Jeanne Brooks-Gunn. *Social Cognition and the Acquisition of Self*. New York: Plenum Press, 1979. Describes the authors' classic series of studies on development of self-recognition and other aspects of self-concept and places the empirical work in the context of self theories and philosophy of science.

Snodgrass, Joan Gay, and Robert L. Thompson, eds. *The Self Across Psychology*. New York: New York Academy of Sciences, 1997. This text is written at a fairly high level of professional conceptualization, yet provides a diverse representation of empirical and theoretical approaches to studying the self.

Stevens, Richard. *Understanding the Self*. Thousand Oaks, Calif.: Sage Publications, 1996. An undergraduate text integrating various perspectives on the self into other topics of psychology, such as phenomenology and biopsychology.

*Mary L. Wandrei*

SEE ALSO: Analytic Psychology: Jacques Lacan; Analytical Psychology: Carl Jung; Cognitive Psychology; Consciousness; Crowd Behavior; Ego Psychology: Erik Erikson; Gender-Identity Formation; Identity Crises; Multiple Personality; Personality Theory; Psychoanalytic Psychology and Personality: Sigmund Freud; Self-Esteem; Social Psychological Models: Erich Fromm; Social Psychological Models: Karen Horney; Thought: Study and Measurement.

# SELF-ESTEEM

TYPE OF PSYCHOLOGY: Social psychology
FIELDS OF STUDY: Childhood and adolescent disorders; cognitive
    development; social perception and cognition

*Self-esteem research examines how individuals come to feel as they do about themselves. Psychologists seek to understand how self-esteem develops and what can be done to change negative views of the self once they have been established.*

KEY CONCEPTS
- attributions
- identity negotiation
- inheritable traits
- self-concept
- self-efficacy
- self-esteem

"Self-esteem" is a term with which almost everyone is familiar, yet it is not necessarily easily understood. Psychologist William James gave the first clear definition in 1892 when he said that self-esteem equals success divided by pretensions. In other words, feelings of self-worth come from the successes an individual achieves tempered by what the person had expected to achieve. If the person expected to do extremely well on an exam (his or her pretensions are quite high) and scores an A, then his or her self-esteem should be high. If, however, the person expected to do well and then scores a D, his or her self-esteem should be low.

This important but simplistic view of self-esteem started a movement toward a better understanding of the complex series of factors that come together to create the positive or negative feelings individuals have about who they are. Once a person has developed a self-concept (a global idea of all the things that define who and what a person is), that person is likely to exhibit behaviors that are consistent with that self-concept. If a young woman believes that she is a good tennis player, then she is likely to put herself in situations in which that factor is important. Once she behaves (in this case, plays her game of tennis), she is likely to receive feedback from others as to how she did. This feedback determines how she will feel about her tennis-playing ability. Over time, these specific instances of positive or negative feedback about tennis-playing ability will come together to create the more global feelings of positivity or negativity a person has about the self in general.

Even though an individual may believe that she is good at tennis, her ability may not live up to those expectations, and she may receive feedback telling her so (for example, losing in the early rounds of a tournament). In this case, the individual may come to feel somewhat negative about her tennis ability. If this continues to happen, she will adjust her view of her ability and come to believe that she is not a good tennis player after all. To the extent that the person truly wanted to be good, this realization can cause her to feel quite negative about all aspects of her self. When this happens, the person is said to have developed low self-esteem.

## ROLE OF ATTRIBUTIONS

The reality of how self-esteem develops, however, is more complicated than this example demonstrates. People do not always accept the feedback that others offer, and they may believe that their failure means nothing more than having an off day. In order to understand the impact that success and failure will have on self-esteem, it is important to understand the kinds of attributions people make for their successes and failures. When a person succeeds or fails, there are three levels of attributions that can be made for explaining the occurrence. First, the individual must decide if the event occurred because of something internal (something inside caused it to happen) or something external (something in the environment caused it to happen). Second, it must be decided whether the event occurred because of a stable factor (because it happened this time, it will happen again) or a temporary circumstance (it probably will not happen again). Finally, it must be decided whether the event occurred because of something specific (this failure resulted because of poor tennis ability) or something global (failure resulted at this undertaking because of lack of ability to do anything).

It is easy to see that the kinds of attributions individuals make for their successes and failures will have a profound impact on how a particular event influences their self-esteem. If a decision is made that a failure at tennis occurred because of something internal (lack of ability), stable (the ability will never be present), and global (lack of any ability), then a failure is going to damage self-esteem severely. Self-esteem is created through the blending of expectations for success, actual levels of success, and the kinds of attributions made for why success or failure occurred.

## CYCLIC PERPETUATION

Once positive or negative self-esteem has developed, it will perpetuate itself in a cycle. If a person believes that he is a failure, he may put himself into situations in which he is destined to fail. If he does not think he can succeed, he may not put forth the amount of effort that success would require. Similarly, if a person believes that he is a success, he will not let one little failure cause him to change his entire opinion of himself. Self-esteem, once it is created, is very difficult to change. If a person dislikes who she is, yet someone else tries to tell her that she is wonderful, she probably will not believe that person. More likely, she will wonder what this person could possibly want from her that he or she is willing to lie and be so nice to get it. On the other hand, if the person feels positive about herself, a single instance of failure will be written off as bad luck, poor effort, or a simple fluke. A negative self-esteem cycle, once it gets started, is very difficult to change, and learning how to break this cycle is the single greatest challenge to self-esteem therapists.

## UNDERSTANDING NEGATIVE SELF-ESTEEM

Understanding self-esteem has considerable practical importance in daily life. If it is believed that all successes come from external sources (luck or someone's pity), then good things coming from others can be seen as an attempt to degrade the individual or offer a bribe. People feeling this way relate to others in a judgmental way and cause them to turn away. When others turn away, the person takes it as a signal that he or she was correct about his or her unworthiness, and the negative self-esteem level is perpetuated.

If this negative self-esteem cycle is to be broken, it is important to convince the person of the critical point made by George Herbert Mead. According to Mead, self-esteem is a product of people's interpretation of the feedback that they receive from others. A person with low self-esteem often misinterprets that feedback. If someone with low self-esteem is told, "You look really nice today," he or she is likely to misinterpret that to mean, "You usually look terrible; what did you do different today?"

Ralph Turner has said that the self is not fixed and that the person with low self-esteem must be convinced that he or she is not at the mercy of a self: He or she can be, and is, the creator of a self. It helps to put the person into a situation in which he or she can succeed with no possibility for the wrong attributions to be made. If a person cannot read, this failure will generalize to other situations and is likely to be considered a stable and global deficiency. If this person is taught to read, however, even a person with low self-esteem would find it difficult to argue that the success was situational. In this way, the person begins to see that he or she can take control and that failures need not be catastrophic for the other self-conceptions he or she might hold.

A person with negative self-esteem is extremely difficult to help. It takes more than the providing of positive feedback to assist such a person. Imagine a series of circles, one inside the other, each one getting smaller. Take that smallest, innermost circle and assign it a negative value. This represents an overall negative self-esteem. Then assign negative values to all the outer circles as well. These represent how the person feels about his or her specific attributes.

If positive messages are directed toward a person with negative values assigned to all these layers of self-esteem, they will not easily penetrate the negative layers; they will be much more likely to bounce off. Negative messages, on the other hand, will easily enter the circles and will strengthen the negativity. Penetration of all the negative layers can, however, sometimes be achieved by a long-term direction of positive and loving messages toward the person with low self-esteem. In effect, the innermost circle, that of global self-esteem, will eventually be exposed. Self-esteem can then be improved if enough positive, loving messages can be directed at the level of the person's global self-esteem. This is a difficult process, partly because as soon as the person's negative self-image comes into serious question, confusion about his or her identity results; living in self-hate, although often painful, is still more secure than suddenly living in doubt.

Once the negative signs have been replaced with positive ones, the new self-esteem level will be as impervious to change as the negative one was. Now, when the person enters a situation, he or she will have more realistic expectations as to what he or she can and cannot do. The person has been taught to make realistic attributions about success and failure. Most important, the individual has been taught that one need not succeed at everything to be a worthy person. William James suggested in 1892 that striving does as much to alleviate self-esteem problems as actual success. Once the individual is convinced that setting a goal and striving, rather than not trying at all, is all it takes to feel good about himself or herself, the person is truly on the way to having high self-esteem.

## IMPORTANCE OF CHILDHOOD AND ADOLESCENCE

An interest in self-esteem developed along with interest in psychological questions in general. Early psychologists such as Sigmund Freud, Carl Jung, William James, and others all realized that an important part of what makes individuals think and act the way they do is determined by the early experiences that create their sense of self and self-esteem. A very important aspect

*Feedback from parents plays a crucial role in the development of a child's self-esteem.* (CLEO Photography)

of psychological inquiry has been asking how and why people perceive and interpret the same event so differently. Self-esteem and self-concept play a big role in these interpretations. Knowing an individual's self-esteem level helps one to predict how others will be perceived, what kind of other individuals will be chosen for interaction, and the kinds of attitudes and beliefs the person may hold.

An understanding of childhood development and adolescence would be impossible without an understanding of the forces that combine to create a person's sense of self-esteem. Adolescence has often been described as a time of "storm and stress" because the teenager is trying to negotiate an identity (create a sense of self and self-esteem that he or she would like to have). Teenagers' wishes and desires, however, are not the only things they must consider. They are receiving pressure from parents, peers, and society as a whole to be a certain kind of person and do certain kinds of things. Only when self-esteem development is fully understood will it be known how to alleviate some of the trials and tribulations of adolescence and ensure that teenagers develop a healthy and productive view of their worth.

## ROLE IN CONTEMPORARY SOCIETY

The role of self-esteem will probably be even greater as psychological inquiry moves ahead. Modern society continues to tell people that if they want to succeed, they have to achieve more. Yet economic downturns and increasing competition to enter colleges and careers make it difficult for young people to live up to those expectations and feel good about who they are. The large role that psychologists with experience in self-esteem enhancement training will play in the future cannot be overemphasized. In order for adults to lead healthy, productive, and satisfied lives, they must feel good about who they are and where they are going. This requires an intimate understanding of the factors that combine to create people's expectations for success and the likelihood that they will be able to achieve that level of success. Self-esteem development must be kept in mind in helping young people create for themselves a realistic set of expectations for success and an ability to make realistic attributions for why their successes and failures occur.

## SOURCES FOR FURTHER STUDY

Butler, Gillian. *Overcoming Social Anxiety and Shyness: A Self-Help Guide Using Cognitive-Behavioral Techniques.* New York: New York University Press, 2001. A practical guide to changing negative thought patterns in order to increase self-esteem.

Coopersmith, Stanley. *The Antecedents of Self-Esteem.* Palo Alto, Calif.: Consulting Psychologists Press, 1981. A well written and informative look at the background factors that influence the development of self-esteem. Includes statistics and figures but is fairly nontechnical, and the comprehensiveness of the book is well worth the effort.

Jones, Warren H., Jonathan M. Cheek, and Stephen R. Briggs. *Shyness: Perspectives on Research and Treatment.* New York: Plenum Press, 1986. Presents a thorough view of the development of shyness and the impact it has on social relationships. Many individuals with low self-esteem suffer from shyness, and it is difficult to understand one without the other. The writing is technical; appropriate for a college audience.

Kernis, Michael. *Efficacy, Angency, and Self-Esteem.* New York: Plenum Press, 1995. A collection of papers that challenge existing notions of self-esteem in modern therapy or offer suggestions for new areas of research.

Rosenberg, Morris. *Society and the Adolescent Self-Image.* Reprint. Collingdale, Pa.: DIANE, 1999. Although written in the mid-1960's, this is still one of the best books available on self-esteem. Rosenberg's influence remains strong, and the self-esteem scale he included in this book is still widely used to measure self-esteem. Appropriate for both college and high school students.

*Randall E. Osborne*

SEE ALSO: Affiliation and Friendship; Identity Crises; Self.

# SENSATION AND PERCEPTION

TYPE OF PSYCHOLOGY: Sensation and perception
FIELDS OF STUDY: Auditory, chemical, cutaneous, and body senses; vision

*The study of sensation and perception examines the relationship between input from the world and the manner in which people react to it. Through the process of sensation, the body receives various stimuli that are transformed into neural messages and transmitted to the brain. Perception is the meaning and interpretation given to these messages.*

KEY CONCEPTS
- absolute threshold
- acuity
- attention
- sensory deprivation
- sensory receptors

Although the distinction between sensation and perception is not always clear, psychologists attempt to distinguish between the two concepts. Sensation is generally viewed as the initial contact between organisms and their physical environment. It focuses on the interaction between various forms of sensory stimulation and how these sensations are registered by the sense organs (nose, skin, eyes, ears, and tongue). The process by which an individual then interprets and organizes this information to produce conscious experiences is known as perception.

The warmth of the sun, the distinctive sound of a jet airplane rumbling down a runway, the smell of freshly baked bread, and the taste of an ice cream sundae all have an impact on the body's sensory receptors. The signals received are transmitted to the brain via the nervous system; there, interpretation of the information is performed. The body's sensory receptors are capable of detecting very low levels of stimulation. Eugene Galanter's studies indicated that on a clear night, the human eye is capable of viewing a candle at a distance of 30 miles (48 kilometers), while the ears can detect the ticking of a watch 20 feet (6 meters) away in a quiet room. He also demonstrated that the tongue can taste a teaspoon of sugar dissolved in 2 gallons (about 7.5 liters) of water. People can feel a bee wing falling on the cheek and can smell a single drop of perfume in a three-bedroom apartment. Awareness of these faint stimuli demonstrates the absolute thresholds, defined as the minimum amount of stimulus that can be detected 50 percent of the time.

## SIGNAL RECOGNITION
A person's ability to detect a weak stimulus, often called a signal, depends not only on the strength of the signal or stimulus but also on the person's

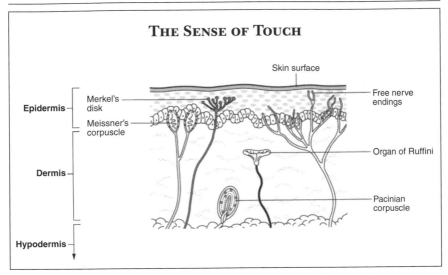

## THE SENSE OF TOUCH

*The sensation of touch is produced by special receptors in the skin that respond to temperature and pressure.* (Hans & Cassidy, Inc.)

psychological state. For example, a child remaining at home alone for the first time may be startled by an almost imperceptible noise. In a normal setting, with his or her parents at home, the same noise or signal would probably go unnoticed. Scientists who study signal detection seek to explain why people respond differently to a similar signal and why the same person's reactions vary as circumstances change. Studies have shown that people's reactions to signals depend on many factors, including the time of day and the type of signal.

Much controversy has arisen over the subject of subliminal signals—signals that one's body receives without one's conscious awareness. It has long been thought that these subliminal signals could influence a person's behaviors through persuasion. Many researchers believe that individuals do sense subliminal sensations; however, it is highly unlikely that this information will somehow change an individual's behaviors. Researchers Anthony Pratkanis and Anthony Greenwald suggest that in the area of advertising, subliminal procedures offer little or nothing of value to the marketing practitioner.

### ADAPTATION AND SELECTIVE ATTENTION

An individual's response to a stimulus may change over time. For example, when a swimmer first enters the cold ocean, the initial response may be to complain about the water's frigidity; however, after a few minutes, the water feels comfortable. This is an example of sensory adaptation—the body's ability to diminish sensitivity to stimuli that are unchanging. Sensory receptors are initially alert to the coldness of the water, but prolonged exposure reduces sensitivity. This is an important benefit to humans in that it allows an individual not to be distracted by constant stimuli that are uninformative. It would be very difficult to function daily if one's body were constantly aware of the fit of shoes and garments, the rumble of a heating system, or constant street noises.

The reception of sensory information by the senses, and the transmission of this information to the brain, is included under the term "sensation." Of equal importance is the process of perception: the way an individual selects information, organizes it, and makes an interpretation. In this manner, one achieves a grasp of one's surroundings. People cannot absorb and understand all the available sensory information received from the environment. Thus, they must selectively attend to certain information and disregard other material. Through the process of selective attention, people are able to maximize information gained from the object of focus while at the same time ignoring irrelevant material. To some degree, people are capable of controlling the focus of their attention; in many instances, however, focus can be shifted undesirably. For example, while one is watching a television show, extraneous stimuli such as a car horn blaring may change one's focus.

The fundamental focus of the study of perception is how people come to comprehend the world around them through its objects and events. People are constantly giving meaning to a host of stimuli being received from all their senses. While research suggests that people prize visual stimuli above other forms, information from all other senses must also be processed. More difficult to understand is the concept of extrasensory perception (ESP). More researchers are becoming interested in the possible existence of extrasensory perception—perceptions that are not based on information from the sensory receptors. Often included under the heading of ESP are such questionable abilities as clairvoyance and telepathy. While psychologists generally remain skeptical as to the existence of ESP, some do not deny that evidence may someday be available supporting its existence.

## FIVE LAWS OF GROUPING

Knowledge of the fields of sensation and perception assists people in understanding their environment. By understanding how and why people respond to various stimuli, scientists have been able to identify important factors which have proved useful in such fields as advertising, industry, and education.

Max Wertheimer discussed five laws of grouping that describe why certain elements seem to go together rather than remain independent. The laws include the law of similarity, which states that similar objects tend to be seen as a unit; the law of nearness, which indicates that objects near one another tend to be seen as a unit; the law of closure, which states that when a figure has a gap, the figure still tends to be seen as closed; the law of common fate, which states that when objects move in the same direction, they tend to be seen as a unit; and the law of good continuation, which states that objects organized in a straight line or a smooth curve tend to be seen as a unit. These laws are illustrated in the figure on the following page.

## USE IN ADVERTISING AND MARKETING

The laws of grouping are frequently used in the field of advertising. Advertisers attempt to associate their products with various stimuli. For example, David L. Loudon and Albert J. Della Bitta, after studying advertising dealing with menthol cigarettes, noted that the advertisers often show mentholated cigarettes in green, springlike settings to suggest freshness and taste. Similarly, summertime soft-drink advertisements include refreshing outdoor scenes depicting cool, fresh, clean running water, which is meant to be associated with the beverage. Advertisements for rugged four-wheel-drive vehicles use the laws of grouping by placing their vehicles in harsh, rugged climates. The viewer develops a perception of toughness and ruggedness.

The overall goal of advertisers is to provide consumers with appropriate sensations that will cause them to perceive the products in a manner that the advertisers desire. By structuring the stimuli that reach the senses, advertisers can build a foundation for perceptions of products, making them seem durable, sensuous, refreshing, or desirable. By using the results of numerous research studies pertaining to perception, subtle yet effective manipulation of the consumer is achieved.

## COLOR STUDIES

Another area that has been researched extensively by industry deals with color. If one were in a restaurant ordering dinner and received an orange steak with purple French fries and a blue salad, the meal would be difficult to consume. People's individual perceptions of color are extremely important. Variations from these expectations can be very difficult to overcome. Researchers have found that people's perceptions of color also influence their beliefs about products. When reactions to laundry detergents were examined, detergent in a blue box was found to be too weak, while detergent in a yellow box was thought to be too strong. Consumers believed, based on coloration, that the ideal detergent came in a blue box with yellow accentuation. Similarly, when individuals were asked to judge the capsule color of drugs, findings suggested that orange capsules were frequently seen as stimulants, white capsules as having an analgesic action, and lavender capsules as having a hallucinogenic effect.

Studies have shown that various colors have proved more satisfactory than others for industrial application. Red has been shown typically to be perceived as a sign of danger and is used to warn individuals of hazardous situations. Yellow is also a sign of warning. It is frequently used on highway signs as a warning indicator because of its high degree of visibility in adverse weather conditions. Instrument panels in both automobiles and airplanes are frequently equipped with orange- and yellow-tipped instrument indicators, because research has demonstrated that these colors are easily distinguished from the dark background of the gauges. Finally, industry has not overlooked the fact that many colors have a calming and soothing effect on people. Thus, soft pastels are often used in the workplace.

## USE IN EDUCATION

The field of education has also benefited from research in the areas of sensation and perception. Knowing how young children perceive educational materials is important in developing ways to increase their skills and motivation. Textbook publishers have found that materials need to be visually attractive to children in order to help them focus on activities. Graphics and illustrations help the young learner to understand written materials. Size of printed text is also important to accommodate the developmental level of the student. For example, primers and primary-level reading series typically have large print, to assist the student in focusing on the text. As the child's abilities to discriminate letters and numbers become more efficient with age, the print size diminishes to that of the size of characters in adult books. Similar techniques continue into high school and college; especially in introductory courses, the design of texts use extensive amounts of color, along with variation in page design. The reader's eyes are attracted by numerous stimuli to pictures, figures, definitions, and charts strategically placed on each page. This technique allows the author to highlight and accent essential points of information.

## EARLY RESEARCH

The study of sensation and perception began more than two thousand years ago with the Greek philosophers and is one of the oldest fields in psychology. There are numerous theories, hypotheses, and facts dealing with how people obtain information about their world, what type of information they obtain, and what they do with this information once it has been obtained. None of this information has been sufficient to account for human perceptual experiences and perceptual behavior, so research in the area of sensation and perception continues.

The philosopher Thomas Reed made the original distinction between sensations and perceptions. He proposed that the crucial difference between them is that perceptions always refer to external objects, whereas sensations refer to the experiences within a person that are not linked to external objects. Many psychologists of the nineteenth century proposed that sensations are elementary building blocks of perceptions. According to their ideas, perceptions arise from the addition of numerous sensations. The sum of these sensations thus creates a perception. Other psychologists believed that making a distinction between sensations and perceptions was not useful.

The first psychologists saw the importance of perception when they realized that information from the senses was necessary in order to learn, think, and memorize. Thus, research pertaining to the senses was a central research component of all the psychological laboratories established in Europe and the United States during the late nineteenth and early twentieth centuries.

## APPLICATIONS IN MODERN SOCIETY

By studying perceptions, researchers can identify potential environmental hazards that threaten the senses. Studying perception has also enabled people to develop devices that ensure optimal performance of the senses. For example, on a daily basis, one's senses rely on such manufactured objects as telephones, clocks, televisions, and computers. To be effective, these devices must be tailored to the human sensory systems.

The study of sensations and perceptions has also made it possible to build and develop prosthetic devices to aid individuals with impaired sensory function. For example, hearing aids amplify sound for hard-of-hearing individuals; however, when all sounds are amplified to the same degree, it is often difficult for people to discriminate between sounds. From the work of Richard Gregory, a British psychologist, an instrument was developed that would amplify only speech sounds, thus allowing a person to attend more adequately to conversations and tune out background noise.

Finally, understanding perception is important for comprehending and appreciating the perceptual experience called art. When knowledge of perception is combined with the process of perceiving artistic works, this understanding adds an additional dimension to one's ability to view a work of art.

## SOURCES FOR FURTHER STUDY

Goldstein, E. Bruce. *Sensation and Perception*. 6th ed. Pacific Grove, Calif.: Wadsworth-Thomson Learning, 2002. Excellent overview of the field of sensation and perception study. Chapters focus on subjects dealing with vision, hearing, and touch as well as perceived speech and the chemical senses.

Gregory, R. L. *Eye and Brain: The Psychology of Seeing*. 5th ed. New York: Oxford University Press, 1998. A broad book on vision for the general reader. Beneficial for students in the areas of psychology, biology, and physiology. Includes many illustrations that help to explain complex matters in an understandable fashion.

Matlin, M. W. *Sensation and Perception*. 4th ed. Boston: Allyn & Bacon, 1997. An introductory text covering all general areas of sensation and perception. Themes carried throughout the text are intended to provide additional structure for the material; these themes reflect the author's eclectic, theoretical orientation.

Schiff, William. *Perception: An Applied Approach*. Boston: Houghton Mifflin, 1980. Schiff's book is concerned with how people can, and do, use their senses to comprehend their world and their relation to it. Interesting chapters cover such topics as social-event perception, personal perception, and individual differences in perception.

Sekuler, Robert, and Robert R. Blake. *Perception.* 4th ed. Boston: McGraw-Hill, 2002. Sekuler and Blake attempt to explain seeing, hearing, smelling, and tasting to students of perception. Extensive use of illustrations allows the reader to understand materials more fully. A series of short illustrations is also used to depict additional concepts.

*Eugene R. Johnson*

SEE ALSO: Nervous System; Senses.

# SENSES

TYPE OF PSYCHOLOGY: Sensation and perception
FIELDS OF STUDY: Auditory, chemical, cutaneous, and body senses; vision

*Humans process information using at least five sensory modalities: sight, sound, taste, smell, and the body senses, which include touch, temperature, balance, and pain. Because people's sensation and perception of external stimuli define their world, knowledge of these processes is relevant to every aspect of daily life.*

KEY CONCEPTS
- cutaneous
- perception
- proximate
- receptor
- sensation
- ultimate studies
- *Umwelt*

Humans have five sense organs: the eyes, ears, taste buds, nasal mucosa, and skin. Each sense organ is specialized to intercept a particular kind of environmental energy and then to convert that energy into a message that the brain can interpret. Together, these two processes are called sensation.

The first step of sensation, the interception of external energy, is done by the part of the sense organ that is in direct contact with the environment. Each sense organ has a specialized shape and structure designed to intercept a particular form of energy. The second step, conversion of the captured energy into signals the brain can understand, is done by cells inside the sense organ called receptors. Receptors are structures to which physicists and engineers refer as transducers: They convert one form of energy into another. Artificial transducers are common. Hydroelectric plants, for example, intercept flowing water and convert it to electricity; then appliances convert the electricity into heat, moving parts, sound, or light displays. Receptors are biological transducers which convert environmental energy intercepted by the sense organ into neural signals. These signals are then sent to the brain, where they are interpreted through a process called perception.

The eye, the best understood of all the sense organs, consists of a lens which focuses light (a kind of electromagnetic energy) through a small hole (the pupil) onto a sheet of cells (the retina). The retina contains the eye's receptor cells: the rods, which are sensitive to all wavelengths of light in the visible spectrum, and three kinds of cones, which are sensitive to those wavelengths that the brain perceives as blue, green, and yellow.

The ear funnels air pressure waves onto the tympanic membrane (more commonly known as the eardrum), where vibrations are transmitted to the inner ear. In the inner ear, receptors called hair cells are stimulated by different frequency vibrations; they then send signals to the brain, which interprets them as different pitches and harmonics.

Taste buds are small bumps on the tongue and parts of the throat which are continuously bathed in liquid. Receptors in the taste buds intercept any chemicals which have been dissolved in the liquid. Molecules of different shapes trigger messages from different receptors. Humans have several kinds of taste receptors which send signals the brain interprets as bitter, at least two kinds of receptors which send signals interpreted as sweet, and one kind of receptor each that sends messages interpreted as salty and sour.

The nasal mucosa, the sense organ for smell, is a layer of cells lining parts of the nasal passageways and throat; it intercepts chemicals directly from inhaled air. Apparently, cells in the nasal mucosa can produce receptor cells (called olfactory receptors) throughout life. This way, people can develop the capacity to smell "new" chemicals which they could not smell before. New olfactory receptors seem to be created in response to exposure to novel chemicals, analogous to the production of antibodies when the immune system is exposed to foreign material. Because of this ability to create new olfactory receptors, it is not possible to list and categorize all the different types of smells.

The skin is the largest sense organ in the human body; its sense, touch, actually consists of several different senses, collectively referred to as the cutaneous senses. Receptors called mechanoreceptors are triggered by mechan-

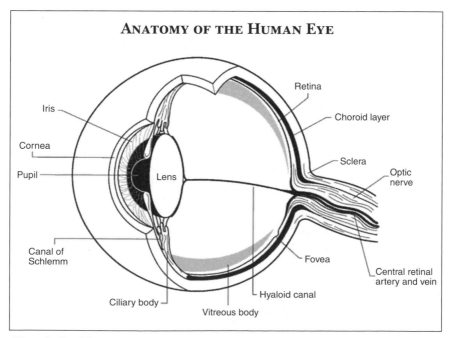

**ANATOMY OF THE HUMAN EYE**

Iris

Cornea

Pupil

Canal of Schlemm

Ciliary body

Vitreous body

Hyaloid canal

Lens

Retina

Choroid layer

Sclera

Optic nerve

Fovea

Central retinal artery and vein

(Hans & Cassidy, Inc.)

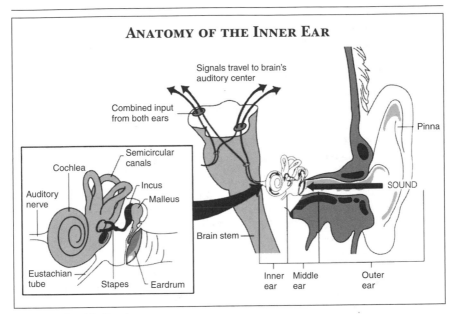

## ANATOMY OF THE INNER EAR

Signals travel to brain's auditory center

Combined input from both ears

Pinna

Semicircular canals

Cochlea

Incus

Auditory nerve

Malleus

SOUND

Brain stem

Eustachian tube

Stapes

Eardrum

Inner ear

Middle ear

Outer ear

(Hans & Cassidy, Inc.)

ical movements of the skin and send signals that the brain interprets as vibration, light or deep pressure, and stretching. Thermoreceptors intercept heat passing in or out of the body through the skin; their signals are interpreted by the brain as warmth and cold, respectively. Receptors which are triggered when skin cells are damaged are called nociceptors; their signals to the brain are interpreted as pain.

### ANIMAL SENSES

Some animals have sense organs that humans do not and can thereby sense and perceive stimuli that humans cannot. Many birds and probably a variety of marine creatures can detect variations in the earth's magnetic field; some fish and invertebrates can detect electrical fields. Other animals have sense organs similar to, but more sensitive than, those of humans; they can intercept a broader range of energy or detect it at lower levels. Insects can see ultraviolet light, while pit vipers can sense infrared. Elephants can hear infrasound, and mice can hear ultrasound. The olfactory sensitivity of most animals far surpasses that of humans. Because of differences in sensory apparatus, each animal experiences a different sensory reality; this is termed each animal's *Umwelt.*

### BIOENGINEERING USES

One application of the knowledge of sensory modalities is in the field of bioengineering. Knowing that sense organs are biological transducers allows the possibility of replacing damaged or nonfunctional sense organs with artificial transducers, the same way artificial limbs replace missing ones. To-day's most advanced artificial limbs can be connected directly to nerves that send information from the motor (movement) areas of the brain; thus, a person can direct movement of the artificial limb with neural messages via thoughts. Similarly, bioengineers are researching the use of small sensors that can be set up to send electrical signals directly to a person's sensory nerves or the sensory cortex of the brain. Researchers have already developed the first version of a hearing aid to help people who have nerve deafness in the inner ear but whose auditory processing centers in the brain are still intact.

## HUMAN-FACTORS ENGINEERING

Another field which applies the findings of experimental sensory psychologists is called human-factors engineering. People who design complicated instrument panels (for example, in jet cockpits or nuclear reactors) must have an understanding of what kinds of stimuli will elicit attention, what will be irritating, and what will fade unnoticed into the background. Using knowledge of how sound is transmitted and how the human brain perceives sound, human-factors engineers have designed police and ambulance sirens which make one type of sound while the vehicle is moving quickly (the air-raid-type wailing sound) and another while the vehicle is moving slowly, as through a crowded intersection (alternating pulses of different pitches). These two types of sounds maximize the likelihood that the siren will be noticed in the different environmental settings. Research by human-factors engineers has also prompted many communities to change the color of fire engines from red to yellow; because red is difficult to see in twilight and darkness, and bright yellow can be seen well at all times of day, yellow makes a better warning color.

Research by human-factors engineers and environmental psychologists is also used to improve commercial products and other aspects of day-to-day living, answering questions such as, How loud should the music be in a dentist's waiting office? What color packaging will attract the most buyers to a product? How much salt does a potato chip need? How much light is necessary to maximize production in a factory? Will noise in a domed stadium cause damage to fans? Research on sensation and perception is applied in almost every setting imaginable.

## INFLUENCING ANIMAL BEHAVIOR

Knowledge of sensation and perception can also be used to influence the behavior of other animals. Because people visit zoos during the daytime, nocturnal animals are often housed in areas bathed in only red light. Most nocturnal animals are colorblind, and as red light by itself is so difficult to see, the animals are tricked into perceiving that it is nighttime and become active for the viewers. Knowing that vultures have an exceptionally good sense of smell and that they are attracted to the scent of rotting meat allowed scientists to find an invisible but dangerous leak in a long, geographically isolated pipeline; after adding the aroma of rotting meat into the pipeline fuel, they simply waited to see where the vultures started circling—and knew where they would find the leak.

## LEARNING THEORY

The knowledge that sensation and perception differ across species has also influenced the biggest and perhaps most important field in all of psychology: learning theory. The so-called laws of learning were derived from observations of animals during the acquisition of associations between two previously unassociated stimuli, between a stimulus and a response, or between a behavior and a consequent change in the environment. These laws were originally thought to generalize equally with regard to all species and all stimuli. This belief, along with the prevailing *Zeitgeist* which held that learning was the basis of all behavior, led to the assumption that studies of any animal could serve as a sufficient model for discovering the principles guiding human learning and behavior. It is now known that such is not the case.

Although laws of learning do generalize nicely in the acquisition of associations between biologically neutral stimuli, each animal's sensory apparatus is designed specifically to sense those stimuli that are relevant for its lifestyle. How it perceives those stimuli will also be related to its lifestyle. Therefore, the meaning of a particular stimulus may be different for different species, so results from studies on one animal cannot be generalized to another; neither can results from studies using one stimulus or stimulus modality be generalized to another.

Finally, it is important to note that scientific inquiry itself is dependent upon human understanding of the human senses. Scientific method is based on the philosophy of empiricism, which states that knowledge must be obtained by direct experience using the physical senses (or extensions of them). In short, all scientific data are collected through the physical senses; thus, the entirety of scientific knowledge is ultimately based upon, and limited by, human understanding of, and the limitations of, the human senses.

## EVOLUTION OF STUDY

In the late nineteenth and early twentieth centuries, Wilhelm Wundt, often considered the founder of scientific psychology, aspired to study the most fundamental units (or structures) of the mind. Wundt and other European psychologists (called structuralists) focused much of their attention on the description of mental responses to external stimuli—in other words, on sensation and perception. Around the same time, educational philosopher William James developed functionalism in the United States. Functionalists avoided questions about what was happening in the mind and brain and focused on questions about why people respond the way they do to different stimuli.

Today, both the structuralist and the functionalist methodologies have been replaced, but the fundamental questions they addressed remain. Psychologists who study sensation and perception still conduct research into how sense organs and the brain work together to produce perceptions (proximate studies) and why people and other animals have their own particular *Umwelts* (ultimate studies). Results from proximate and ultimate studies typically lead to different kinds of insights about the human condition. Proximate studies lead to solutions for real-world problems, while studies of ultimate functions provide enlightenment about the evolution of human nature and humans' place in the world; they help identify what stimuli were important throughout human evolutionary history.

For example, the human ear is fine-tuned so that its greatest sensitivity is in the frequency range that matches sounds produced by the human voice. Clearly, this reflects the importance of communication—and, in turn, cooperation—throughout human evolution. More specifically, hearing sensitivity peaks nearer to the frequencies produced by female voices than male voices. This suggests that human language capacity may have evolved out of mother-infant interactions rather than from the need for communication in some other activity, such as hunting.

### STIMULI ADAPTATIONS FOR SURVIVAL

Knowing what kinds and intensities of stimuli the human sense organs can detect suggests what stimuli have been important for human survival; furthermore, the way the brain perceives those stimuli says something about their role. Most stimuli that are perceived positively are, in fact, good for people; food tastes and smells "good" because without some kind of psychological inducement to eat, people would not survive. Stimuli that are perceived negatively are those that people need to avoid; the fact that rotting foods smell "bad" is the brain's way of keeping one from eating something that might make one sick. To give an example from another sensory modality, most adults find the sound of a crying baby bothersome; in order to stop the sound, they address the needs of the infant. Cooing and laughing are rewards that reinforce good parenting.

### SOURCES FOR FURTHER STUDY

Ackerman, Diane. *A Natural History of the Senses.* Reprint. New York: Vintage, 1991. A best-selling rumination on the senses, written by a poet. A remarkable mixture of science and art.

Brown, Evan L., and Kenneth Deffenbacher. *Perception and the Senses.* New York: Oxford University Press, 1979. This text differs from most textbooks on sensation in that it integrates ethological, cross-species information with the traditional coverage of human sensory physiology and psychophysics. Although technical, the book is user-friendly. Each chapter has its own outline, glossary, and set of suggested readings.

Buddenbrock, Wolfgang von. *The Senses.* Ann Arbor: University of Michigan Press, 1958. Easy-to-read descriptions of different *Umwelts*, with many fascinating examples. Because the focus is almost entirely on ultimate explanations rather than sensory mechanisms, new technologies have not made this book outdated.

Gescheider, George. *Psychophysics: The Fundamentals*. 3d ed. Mahwah, N.J.: Lawrence Erlbaum, 1997. A thorough introduction to psychophysics, focusing on measurement techniques and the theory of signal detection.

Hall, Edward Twitchell. *The Hidden Dimension*. 1969. Reprint. Garden City, N.Y.: Anchor Books, 1990. Written by an anthropologist, this book on cross-cultural differences in use of space includes three chapters on the perception of space as influenced by each sensory modality. These provide good examples of using human factors and environmental psychology to address real-world problems, particularly problems in architecture and interpersonal communication.

Scharf, Bertram, ed. *Experimental Sensory Psychology*. Glenview, Ill.: Scott, Foresman, 1975. Includes an introduction, a chapter on psychophysics, a chapter on each sensory modality, and a postscript on the direction of modern studies. Provides excellent detailed descriptions of sensory mechanisms and psychophysical laws. Includes many diagrams, formulas, and technical terms but is still very readable.

Seligman, Martin E. P. "On the Generality of the Laws of Learning." *Psychological Review* 77, no. 5 (1970): 406-418. The article that triggered the ongoing debate over the generalizability of the results of learning studies across different species and different types of stimuli. Although written for a professional audience, the paper describes the basic assumptions of learning studies, so previous familiarity with learning theory is not necessary.

Stone, Herbert, and Joel L. Sidel. *Sensory Evaluation Practices*. 2d ed. Orlando, Fla.: Academic Press, 1997. Although written for professionals, this text can provide the layperson with insight into the world of product research. Mostly describes techniques for designing studies of the sensory evaluation of food products, but most of the principles are generalizable to other products and industries.

*Linda Mealey*

SEE ALSO: Sensation and Perception.

# Sexual Variants and Paraphilias

Type of psychology: Psychopathology
Field of study: Sexual disorders

*Sexual variations, or paraphilias, are unusual sexual activities in that they deviate from what is considered normal at a particular time in a particular society. Paraphilias include behaviors such as exhibitionism, voyeurism, and sadomasochism. It is when they become the prime means of gratification, displacing direct sexual contact with a consenting adult partner, that paraphilias are technically present.*

Key concepts
- exhibitionism
- fetishism
- frotteurism
- sexual masochism
- sexual sadism
- transvestic fetishism
- voyeurism
- zoophilia

Paraphilias are sexual behaviors that are considered a problem for the person who performs them or a problem for society because they differ from the society's norms. Psychologist John Money, who has studied sexual attitudes and behaviors extensively, claims to have identified about forty such behaviors.

## Types of Paraphilias

**EXHIBITIONISM.** Exhibitionism is commonly called indecent exposure. The term refers to behavior in which an individual, usually a male, experiences recurrent, intense sexually arousing fantasies or urges about exposing his genitals to an involuntary observer, who is usually a female. A disorder is present if the individual acts on these urges or if the thoughts cause marked distress. The key point in exhibitionistic behavior is that it involves observers who are unwilling. After exposing himself, the exhibitionist often masturbates while fantasizing about the observer's reaction. Exhibitionists tend to be most aroused by shock and typically flee if the observer responds by laughing or attempts to approach the exhibitionist. Most people who exhibit themselves are males in their twenties or thirties. They tend to be shy, unassertive people who feel inadequate and are afraid of being rejected by another person. People who make obscene telephone calls have similar characteristics to the people who engage in exhibitionism. Typically, they are sexually aroused when their victims react in a shocked manner. Many masturbate during or immediately after placing an obscene call.

**VOYEURISM.** Voyeurism is the derivation of sexual pleasure through the repetitive seeking or intrusional fantasies of situations that involve looking, or "peeping," at unsuspecting people who are naked, undressing, or engaged in sexual intercourse. Most individuals who act on these urges masturbate during the voyeuristic activity or immediately afterward in response to what they have seen. Further sexual contact with the unsuspecting stranger is rarely sought. Like exhibitionists, voyeurs are usually not physically dangerous. Most voyeurs are not attracted to nude beaches or other places where it is acceptable to look, because they are most aroused when the risk of being discovered is high. Voyeurs tend to be men in their twenties with strong feelings of inadequacy.

**SADOMASOCHISM.** Sadomasochistic behavior encompasses both sadism and masochism; it is often abbreviated "SM." The term "sadism" is derived from name of the Marquis de Sade (1740-1814), a French writer and army officer who was horribly cruel to people for his own erotic purposes. Sexual sadism involves acts in which the psychological or physical suffering of the victim, including his or her humiliation, is deemed sexually exciting. In masochism, sexual excitement is produced in a person by his or her own suffering; preferred means of achieving gratification include verbal humiliation and being bound or whipped. The dynamics of the two behaviors are similar. Sadomasochistic behaviors have the potential to be physically dangerous, but most people involved in these behaviors participate in mild or symbolic acts with a partner they can trust. Most people who engage in SM activities are motivated by a desire for dominance or submission rather than pain. Interestingly, many nonhuman animals participate in pain-inflicting behavior before coitus. Some researchers think that the activity heightens the biological components of sexual arousal, such as blood pressure and muscle tension. It has been suggested that any resistance between partners enhances sex, and SM is a more extreme version of this behavior. It is also thought that SM offers people the temporary opportunity to take on roles that are the opposite of the controlled, restrictive roles they play in everyday life. Both sadism and masochism are considered disorders when the fantasies, sexual urges, or behaviors cause significant distress or impairment in social, occupational, or other important areas.

**FETISHISM.** Fetishism is a type of behavior in which a person becomes sexually aroused by focusing on an inanimate object or part of the human body. Many people are aroused by looking at undergarments, legs, or breasts, and it is often difficult to distinguish between normal activities and fetishistic ones. It is when a person becomes focused on the objects or body parts, called fetishes, to the point of causing significant distress or impairment that a disorder is present. Fetishists are usually males. Common fetish objects include women's lingerie, high-heeled shoes, boots, stockings, leather, silk, and rubber goods. Common body parts involved in fetishism are hair, buttocks, breasts, and feet.

**PEDOPHILIA.** The term "pedophilia" is from the Greek language and means "love of children." It is characterized by a preference for sexual activity with prepubescent children and is engaged in primarily by men. The activity varies in intensity and ranges from stroking the child's hair to holding the child while secretly masturbating, manipulating the child's genitals, encouraging the child to manipulate his or her own genitals, or, sometimes, engaging in sexual intercourse. Generally, the pedophile, or sexual abuser of children, is related to, or an acquaintance of, the child, rather than a stranger. Studies of imprisoned pedophiles have found that the men typically had poor relationships with their parents, drink heavily, show poor sexual adjustment, and were themselves sexually abused as children. Pedophiles tend to be older than people convicted of other sex offenses. The average age at first conviction is thirty-five. For a diagnosis of pedophilia, the abuser should be at least sixteen years old and at least five years older than the child or children who are abused.

**TRANSVESTIC FETISHISM.** Transvestic fetishism involves dressing in clothing of the opposite sex to obtain sexual excitement. In the majority of cases, it is men who are attracted to transvestism. Several studies show that cross-dressing occurs primarily among married heterosexuals. The man usually achieves sexual satisfaction simply by putting on the clothing, but sometimes masturbation and intercourse are engaged in while the clothing is being worn. A disorder is diagnosed if the fantasies, sexual urges, or behaviors cause clinically significant distress or impairment. In some cases, gender dysphoria, persistent discomfort with gender role or identity, is also present.

**FROTTEURISM.** Frotteurism encompasses fairly common fantasies, sexual urges, or behaviors of a person, usually a male, obtaining sexual pleasure by pressing or rubbing against a fully clothed female in a crowded public place. Often it involves the clothed penis rubbing against the woman's buttocks or legs and and thus appear accidental.

**ZOOPHILIA AND NECROPHILIA.** Zoophilia involves sexual contact between humans and animals as the repeatedly preferred method of achieving sexual excitement. In this disorder, the animal is preferred despite other available sexual outlets. Necrophilia is a rare dysfunction in which a person obtains sexual gratification by looking at or having intercourse with a corpse.

## DIAGNOSIS AND THERAPY

A problem in the definition and diagnosis of sexual variations is that it is difficult to draw the line between normal and abnormal behavior. Patterns of sexual behavior differ widely across history and within different cultures and communities. It is impossible to lay down the rules of normality; however, attempts are made in order to understand behavior that differs from the majority and in order to help people who find their own atypical behavior to be problematic or to be problematic in the eyes of the law.

Unlike most therapeutic techniques in use by psychologists, many of the treatments for paraphilias are painful, and the degree of their effectiveness is questionable. Supposedly, the methods are not aimed at punishing the individual, but perhaps society's lack of tolerance toward sexual deviations can be seen in the nature of the available treatments. In general, all attempts to treat the paraphilias have been hindered by the lack of information available about them and their causes.

Traditional counseling and psychotherapy alone have not been very effective in modifying the behavior of paraphiliacs, and it is unclear why the clients are resistant to treatment. Some researchers believe that the behavior might be important for the mental stability of paraphiliacs; if they did not have the paraphilia, they would experience mental deterioration. Another idea is that, although people are punished by society for being sexually deviant, they are also rewarded for it. For the paraphilias that put the person at risk for arrest, the danger of arrest often becomes as arousing and rewarding as the sexual activity itself. Difficulties in treating paraphiliacs may also be related to the emotionally impoverished environments that many of them experienced throughout childhood and adolescence. Convicted sex offenders report more physical and sexual abuse as children than do the people convicted of nonsexual crimes. It is difficult to undo the years of learning involved.

Surgical castration for therapeutic purposes involves removal of the testicles. Surgical castration for sexual offenders in North America is very uncommon, but the procedure is sometimes used in northern European countries. The reason castration is used as a treatment for sex offenders is the inaccurate belief that testosterone, is necessary for sexual behavior. The hormone testosterone is produced by the testicles. Unfortunately, reducing the amount of testosterone in the blood system does not always change sexual behavior. Furthermore, contrary to the myth that a sex offender has an abnormally high sex drive, many sex offenders have a low sex drive or are sexually dysfunctional.

In the same vein as surgical castration, other treatments use the administration of chemicals to decrease desire in sex offenders without the removal of genitalia. Estrogens have been fairly effective in reducing the sex drive, but they sometimes make the male appear feminine by increasing breast size and simulating other female characteristics. There are also drugs that block the action of testosterone and other androgens but do not feminize the body; these drugs are called antiandrogens. Used together with counseling, antiandrogens do benefit some sex offenders, especially those who are highly motivated to overcome the problem. More research on the effects of chemicals on sexual behavior is needed; the extent of the possible side effects, for example, needs further study.

Aversion therapy is another technique that has been used to eliminate inappropriate sexual arousal. In aversion therapy, the behavior that is to be decreased or eliminated is paired with an aversive, or unpleasant, experience. Most approaches use pictures of the object or situation that is problematic. The pictures are then paired with something extremely unpleasant, such as an electric shock or a putrid smell, thereby reducing arousal to the problematic object or situation in the future. Aversion therapy has been found to be fairly effective but is under ethical questioning because of its drastic nature.

For example, chemical aversion therapy involves the administration of a nausea-inducing drug. Electrical aversion therapy involves the use of electric shock. An example of the use of electric shock would be to show a pedophile pictures of young children whom he finds sexually arousing and to give an electric shock immediately after showing the pictures, in an attempt to reverse the pedophile's tendency to be sexually aroused by children.

Other techniques have been developed to help patients learn more socially approved patterns of sexual interaction skills. In general, there has not been a rigorous testing of any of the techniques mentioned. Furthermore, most therapy is conducted while the offenders are imprisoned, providing a less than ideal setting.

### DISTURBANCES OF COURTSHIP BEHAVIOR

Beliefs regularly change with respect to what sexual activities are considered normal, so most therapists prefer to avoid terms such as "perversion," instead using "paraphilia." Basically, "paraphilia" means "love of the unusual." Aspects of paraphilias are commonly found within the scope of normal behavior; it is when they become the prime means of gratification, replacing direct sexual contact with a consenting adult partner, that paraphilias are technically said to exist. People who show atypical sexual patterns might also have emotional problems, but it is thought that most people who participate in paraphilias also participate in normal sexual behavior with adult partners, without complete reliance on paraphilic behaviors to produce sexual excitement. Many people who are arrested for paraphilic behaviors do not resort to the paraphilia because they lack a socially acceptable sex partner. Instead, they have an unusual opportunity, a desire to experiment, or perhaps an underlying psychological problem.

According to the approach of Kurt Freund and his colleagues, some paraphilias are better understood as disturbances in the sequence of courtship behaviors. Freund has described courtship as a sequence of four steps: location and appraisal of a potential partner; interaction that does not involve touch; interaction that does involve touch; and genital contact. Most people engage in behavior that is appropriate for each of these steps, but some do not. The ones who do not can be seen as having exaggerations or distortions in one or more of the steps. For example, Freund says that voyeurism is a disorder in the first step of courtship. The voyeur does not use an acceptable means to locate a potential partner. An exhibitionist and an obscene phone caller would have a problem with the second step: They have interaction with people that occurs before the stage of touch, but the talking and showing of exhibitionistic behaviors are not the normal courtship procedures. Frotteurism would be a disruption at the third step, because there is physical touching that is inappropriate. Finally, rape would be a deviation from the appropriate fourth step.

As a result of social and legal restrictions, reliable data on the frequency of paraphilic behaviors are limited. Most information about paraphilias comes from people who have been arrested or are in therapy. Because the majority of people who participate in paraphilias do not fall into these two categories, it is not possible to talk about the majority of paraphiliacs in the real world. It is known, however, that males are much more likely to engage in paraphilias than are females.

## SOURCES FOR FURTHER STUDY

Allgeier, E. R., and A. R. Allgeier. "Atypical Sexual Activity." In *Sexual Interactions*. Boston: Houghton Mifflin, 1998. A highly readable description of sexual variations. Contains photographs, charts, and tables which help make the material understandable. Provides a multitude of references. An excellent, thorough textbook.

Laws, D. Richard, and William O'Donohue, eds. *Sexual Deviance*. New York: Guilford Press, 1997. Twenty-five essays providing a complete reference on paraphilias such as exhibitionism, fetishism, masochism, voyeurism, and transvestic fetishism.

Rosen, Michael A. *Sexual Magic: The S/M Photographs*. Reprint. San Francisco: Shaynew Press, 1992. Contains essays written by people who engage in sadomasochistic activities. Includes photographs. In general, provides a personal, honest look into the lives of real people, using a case-study approach.

Stoller, Robert J. "Sexual Deviations." In *Human Sexuality in Four Perspectives*, edited by Frank A. Beach and Milton Diamond. Baltimore: Johns Hopkins University Press, 1977. Provides a review of several common atypical sexual behaviors, along with several case studies. Concise and readable. Part of an interesting, well-rounded book on sexuality in general.

Weinberg, Thomas S., and G. W. Levi Kamel, eds. *S and M: Studies in Sadomasochism*. Rev. ed. Buffalo, N.Y.: Prometheus Books, 1995. Composed of eighteen articles that provide thought-provoking information on a variety of issues relating to sadism and masochism.

*Deborah R. McDonald*

SEE ALSO: Abnormality: Psychological Models; Adolescence: Sexuality; Homosexuality.

# SLEEP

TYPE OF PSYCHOLOGY: Consciousness
FIELD OF STUDY: Sleep

*The study of sleep stages and functions involves descriptions of the electrophysiological, cognitive, motor, and behavioral components of various sleep stages as well as the potential functions served by each. The sleep-wake cycle is one of several human circadian rhythms that regulate human attention, alertness, and performance.*

KEY CONCEPTS
- circadian rhythms
- desynchronized electroencephalogram (EEG)
- hypnagogic imagery
- myoclonia
- nonrapid eye movement (NREM) sleep
- paradoxical sleep
- rapid eye movement (REM) sleep
- synchronized electroencephalogram (EEG)

Sleep, one of the most mysterious of human circadian rhythms (biological cycles that fluctuate on a daily basis), can be characterized as a naturally induced alteration in consciousness. Although the sleeper may appear to be unconscious, many complex cognitive, physiological, and behavioral processes occur during sleep. For example, parents may sleep through a nearby police siren yet easily awaken to the sound of their crying infant.

Efforts to understand sleep have focused on behavioral and electrical changes that occur each night. During every moment of a person's life, the brain, eyes, and muscles are generating electrical potentials that can be recorded by a polygraph. In polygraph use, minute electrical signals are conveyed through tiny disk electrodes attached to the scalp and face, which are recorded by the instrument as wave patterns that can be described in terms of frequency, amplitude, and synchronization. Frequency is measured by the number of cycles that occur per second (cps), amplitude by the distance between the peaks and troughs of waves, and synchronization by the regular, repetitive nature of the waves.

## MEASURING STAGES OF SLEEP

Use of the polygraph has resulted in the identification of four stages of nonrapid eye movement (NREM) sleep, as well as a special stage referred to as rapid eye movement (REM) sleep. Each stage is described in terms of electrical changes in brain-wave patterns, speed and pattern of eye movements, and muscular activity in the body. Brain-wave activity is measured by the electroencephalogram (EEG), eye movement patterns by the electrooculogram (EOG), and muscle activity by the electromyogram (EMG).

Three EEG patterns can be described for NREM sleep. First, as a sleeper progresses from stages one through four, the waves increase in amplitude or voltage from approximately 50 to 100 microvolts in stage one to about 100 to 200 microvolts in stage four. Second, the frequency of the waves decreases gradually from 4 to 8 cps in stages one and two to 1 to 4 cps in stages three and four. Last, the waves become progressively more synchronized from stages one to four, so that by stage four, the waves assume a slow, regular pattern sometimes called S sleep, for slow-wave sleep or synchronized sleep. Each of these patterns is reflected in the type of brain-wave activity present, with stages one and two consisting predominantly of theta waves and stages three and four of delta waves.

In addition to the changes in brain electrical activity, the EMG records a gradual diminution of muscular activity as the sleeper progresses through each stage of NREM sleep. By the onset of stage four, the EMG is relatively flat, revealing a deep state of muscular relaxation. In fact, virtually all physiological activity is at its lowest during stage four, including respiration, heart rate, blood pressure, digestion, and so on. In this sense, stage four is considered to be the deepest stage of sleep.

### COGNITIVE ACTIVITY CYCLES DURING SLEEP

As stated previously, the sleeper is not in an unconscious state but is in a different level of consciousness. Cognitive activity is present in all stages of NREM sleep. Hypnagogic imagery, consisting of dreamlike images sometimes indistinguishable from REM dreams, is present in stage one. Subjects are easily awakened during this sleep stage, and regressions to a waking state are quite common. Often, these regressions occur because of myoclonias, which are brief jerking movements of the muscles. Because stage one is sometimes viewed as a transitional state between sleeping and waking, it should not be too surprising that sleep talking occurs primarily in this stage. Stage one sleep lasts for approximately fifteen minutes.

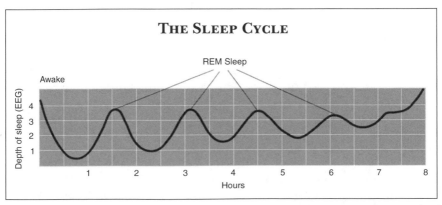

*Over an eight-hour sleep period, the depth of sleep fluctuates and is punctuated by periods of rapid-eye movement (REM). (Hans & Cassidy, Inc.)*

The sleeper is somewhat more difficult to arouse during stage two, and the cognitive activity present is more fragmentary than in stage one. If the subject recalls any mental activity, it is rather sparse. Stage two also lasts for approximately fifteen minutes.

It was once assumed that dreams only occur in REM sleep, but it is now common knowledge that dreams of a different variety occur in stages three and four. These dreams are not of the narrative or storylike variety found in REM sleep; rather, they resemble nonsequential thoughts, images, sensations, or emotions. As might be expected in the deepest sleep stage, it is quite difficult to awaken the sleeper who is in stage four. Paradoxically, a subject awakened in stage four will often claim not to be sleeping. Finally, sleepwalking, night terrors, and bed-wetting, all of which are developmental disorders, occur predominantly in stage four. Stage three lasts approximately ten minutes, while the first episode of stage four usually lasts about fifty minutes.

Suddenly, about ninety minutes after falling asleep, the subject rapidly regresses back through the stages of NREM sleep to a special stage usually called stage one-REM sleep, or sometimes simply REM sleep. Three major changes occur in the electrical activity measured in this stage. First, the EEG pattern becomes highly desynchronized, resembling a combination of waking and stage one-NREM brain-wave activity. For this reason, REM sleep is sometimes called paradoxical sleep, because it is paradoxical that elements of a waking EEG should be present in a sleeping condition. Second, the EMG recordings become almost completely flat for most skeletal muscles, resembling paralysis. Finally, there is an onset of rapid eye movements, as measured by the EOG.

Cognitive activity, in the form of narrative or storylike dreams, is rich and varied in REM sleep—hence the term "D sleep," for dreaming or desynchronized sleep. It is interesting to note that the rapid eye movements correspond closely with dream content. For example, if a person dreams of something running from left to right, the direction of rapid eye movements will also be left to right.

Throughout the remainder of the night, a cycle of approximately ninety minutes will be established from one REM episode to the next. All together, the sleeper will experience four to five REM episodes in a typical eight-hour sleep period, with each one lasting for a longer interval than the previous one. The first REM episode may last only five to ten minutes, while the final one may be thirty to forty minutes or longer in duration. In contrast, S sleep episodes decrease in length throughout the evening, and will disappear completely after two to three episodes.

## STUDY OF SLEEP DEPRIVATION

Although a description of sleep stages can be provided with relative ease, identifying a clear function for sleep is a more difficult proposition. Yet applications of sleep research are inextricably linked with the functions of sleep. For the typical layperson, the seemingly obvious function of sleep is to repair and restore the body after daily mental and physical exertion. This commonsense approach has been formalized by science as the repair and restoration theory. One of the most frequently used methods to assess this theory is to examine the mental and physical effects of sleep deprivation. If the primary function of sleep is to repair the body, then loss of sleep should disrupt cognitive, motor, and behavioral processes. Early laboratory research with animals seemed to support this position. If sleep deprivation persisted for a sufficient time, usually between three and twenty days, death ensued in laboratory animals. Unfortunately, to maintain sleep deprivation in animals, it is necessary to keep them active. Perhaps the continuous activity, rather than the sleep deprivation, killed the animals.

If it were possible to allow animals to rest and relax but not sleep, would the sleep deprivation still prove fatal? This question was addressed by anecdotal accounts of human sleep deprivation during the Korean War. As a means of extracting confessions from American soldiers, Korean military intelligence operatives commonly subjected prisoners of war to sustained bouts of sleep deprivation. In the face of overwhelming exhaustion and clear signs of personality disintegration, American soldiers were often induced to sign confessions of their alleged war crimes. However, Randy Gardner, a seventeen-year-old high school student, experienced sleep deprivation for 264 hours to get his name in the *Guinness Book of World Records* with no apparent permanent effects and no profound temporary deficits. Why would people respond in such radically different ways to sleep deprivation? One hypothesis proposes that severe adverse effects arise as a function of stress and inability to rest and relax, rather than from the loss of sleep. Furthermore, laboratory investigations with volunteer subjects suggest that those individuals who exhibit severe reactions to sleep deprivation almost always have some predisposition to abnormal behavior. Sleep researchers would not deny that sleep serves to restore the body; however, rest and relaxation may serve the same restorative functions in the absence of sleep, which would suggest that repair and restoration is not the sole or even primary function of sleep.

## ADAPTIVE THEORY OF SLEEP

To redress the shortcomings of the repair and restoration theory, an alternative theory of a need to sleep has been proposed. The adaptive or evolutionary theory postulates that the need to sleep arose in the course of biological evolution as an adaptive mechanism to conserve energy during the evening hours, when it would be inefficient to search for food and other resources. Sleep, according to this view, serves a function similar to the hibernation observed in several species of mammals. These animals reduce their metabolic processes to barely detectable levels during winter to conserve energy when food resources are scarce. To do otherwise would threaten the survival of these animals. It is important to note that the adaptive theory still considers sleep to be a real need; in essence, sleep is a remnant of the human evolutionary past when human forebears did not have the convenience of twenty-four-hour supermarkets to acquire their sustenance. Humans deprived of sleep will become just as irritable and ill-tempered as a groundhog prevented from hibernating.

Several predictions have been generated from the adaptive theory, most of which have been supported by scientific observations. First, the theory predicts that predators such as large cats and bears, which obtain most of their nutrients in one large meal per day, would sleep much more than grazing animals such as cattle and horses, who must eat frequently to survive. A second prediction of the theory is that predators such as wolves and mountain lions, which have few natural enemies, would sleep more than prey such as rabbits and guinea pigs, which are at risk if they fail to maintain constant vigilance. Finally, animals such as bats, which are well protected by the environment in which they live, would sleep for relatively long periods of time. These predictions are documented by scientific observations, which provide support for the adaptive or evolutionary theory of sleep.

**CLINICAL APPLICATIONS**

The functions of sleep are extremely important in clinical applications. If the repair and restoration theory lacks strong scientific support, attempting to recover lost sleep time may serve no functional purpose. Indeed, most subjects expect to sleep for several hours longer than normal after staying awake for twenty-four hours, presumably because they believe sleep is required for repair and restoration of the body. In practice, however, most subjects report only four to six total hours of poor-quality sleep following such deprivation. Even after 264 hours of sleep deprivation, Randy Gardner slept for only fourteen hours and forty minutes the first evening, then resumed a normal nocturnal sleep pattern of eight hours per evening.

Knowledge of sleep stages may be especially valuable in diagnosing and treating sleep disorders, because the frequency, patterns, and symptoms of these disorders may be associated with specific stages of sleep. For example, knowledge of the muscular paralysis that accompanies REM sleep has been instrumental in diagnosing the cause of male impotence. Partial or total erections are present in about 95 percent of REM periods. Therefore, men who complain of impotence yet demonstrate normal REM erections can be diagnosed as suffering from psychologically based impotence. These patients may benefit from psychotherapy or sexual counseling. In contrast, men who do not achieve REM erections are diagnosed as suffering from organically based impotence and require hormone therapy or surgical implantations.

Nocturnal enuresis, or bed-wetting, is a stage four developmental disorder present in about four million to five million children annually in the United States. The exact cause of this disorder is undetermined, although the extreme muscular relaxation during stage four sleep likely contributes to its occurrence. To prevent nocturnal enuresis, the patient must learn to associate a full bladder with waking up. Typically, a special apparatus is placed under the child, which sounds a loud buzzer when urine contacts it. Eventually, the child will learn to associate the feeling of a full bladder with waking up in the absence of the buzzer.

## EMERGENCE OF RESEARCH

Because sleep is a universal human experience, it has probably interested people since the dawn of humanity; however, scientific inquiry into sleep is a relatively recent phenomenon. Early interest in sleep arose during the late nineteenth century from a need to isolate the brain structure responsible for lethargy syndromes. Similarly, the electrophysiological study of sleep originated with a discovery in 1875 by the English physiologist Richard Caton that the brain continually produces low-voltage waves. This discovery was largely ignored until 1929, when a German psychiatrist, Hans Berger, found that he could record from large groups of neurons by attaching electrodes to the scalp and the forehead. Berger's discovery marked the beginning of modern electroencephalography. With the advent of EEG recordings, it was not long before A. L. Loomis, E. N. Harvey, and G. A. Hobart found, in 1937, that EEG recordings could be used to differentiate stages of sleep. In 1952, Nathaniel Kleitman at the University of Chicago gave Eugene Aserinsky, one of his new graduate students, the assignment of watching the eye movements of sleeping subjects. Aserinsky quickly noted the rapid, darting nature of eye movements during certain times of the night, which differed from the usual slow, rolling eye movements observed at other times. William Dement later coined the term "REM sleep"; sleep in which slow, rolling eye movements predominate later came to be known as NREM sleep (for nonrapid eye movement sleep). Finally, in 1957, Dement and Kleitman presented the current system of four NREM sleep stages and stage one-REM sleep.

## IMPORTANCE TO PSYCHOLOGY OF CONSCIOUSNESS

As a naturally induced alteration in consciousness that can be studied objectively with electrophysiological recording equipment, sleep has assumed a prominent role in the psychology of consciousness. Electrophysiological recording techniques that were originally developed in sleep research are now widely used to study other aspects of consciousness, such as hemispheric asymmetries, meditation, sensory isolation, biofeedback, dreams, and drug effects on the brain and behavior. In addition, sleep is one of the few alterations in consciousness that plays a central role in several areas of psychological inquiry. For example, physiological psychologists are concerned with the neurobiological mechanisms underlying sleep, as well as the functions of sleep. From their perspective, sleep is simply one of many human behaviors and cognitive processes whose biological basis must be ascertained. Developmental psychologists are interested in age-related changes that occur in sleep and attempt to develop applications of those findings for concerned parents of young children. Finally, physicians and clinical psychologists are often presented with patients who suffer from physical or psychological stress as a function of sleep disorders. These professionals are interested in developing effective drug and psychological therapies that can be used to treat sleep-disordered patients. Sleep is a concern in many areas of psychology.

Because sleep is universal in humans, it will continue to play a major role in consciousness studies and throughout the discipline of psychology. Future research will likely focus on applications of sleep research to industrial settings that employ shift workers. The emphasis will be on reducing fatigue and improving performance among employees by gradually adjusting them to shift work and by changing employee work schedules infrequently. In addition, research will seek ways to improve diagnostic procedures and treatments for a variety of sleep disorders, including insomnia, hypersomnia, sleep apnea, narcolepsy, and enuresis. The focus will be on developing effective drug and psychological therapies. Finally, pure research will continue to examine the functions of sleep, and to delineate more clearly the adverse effects of sleep, even those of a temporary nature.

### Sources for Further Study

Coren, Stanley. *Sleep Thieves*. New York: Free Press, 1997. A wide-ranging exploration of sleep research. Coren is one of the major researchers in the relationship between sleep deficit and major industrial accidents, such as the 1989 Exxon *Valdez* oil spill, the 1986 Chernobyl nuclear plant disaster, and the 1986 *Challenger* space shuttle explosion.

Dement, William C. *The Promise of Sleep*. New York: Dell, 2000. Dement, founder of the sleep disorders clinic at Stanford University, provides a nontechnical, personal report of current findings in sleep research, drawing a connection between sleep and general health. Offers a guide to remedying sleep deficits and alleviating insomnia.

Empson, Jacob, and Michael B. Wang. *Sleep and Dreaming*. 3d ed. New York: St. Martin's Press, 2002. An overview of scientific sleep research and popular beliefs about sleep.

Hobson, J. Allan. *Sleep*. Reprint. New York: W. H. Freeman, 1995. A broad and interdisciplinary view of sleep research, combining knowledge drawn from neurology, psychology, and animal behavior studies. The nontechnical language and lavish illustrations are two major advantages of this book. Highly recommended for high school and college students.

Jouvet, Michel. *The Paradox of Sleep*. Translated by Laurence Gary. Cambridge, Mass.: MIT Press, 1999. The scientist who discovered the relationship between REM sleep and dreaming discusses the stages of sleep, the meaning and evolutionary function of dreams, and many other topics.

*Richard P. Atkinson*

See also: Brain Structure; Consciousness; Consciousness: Altered States; Dreams.

# Social Learning

## Albert Bandura

Type of psychology: Personality
Fields of study: Behavioral and cognitive models; cognitive learning

*Bandura's social learning theory, later called social cognitive theory, provides a theoretical framework for understanding and explaining human behavior; the theory embraces an interactional model of causation and accords central roles to cognitive, vicarious, and self-regulatory processes.*

Key concepts
- determinism
- model
- observational learning
- outcome expectancies
- reciprocal determinism
- reinforcement
- self-efficacy

Social learning theory, later amplified as social cognitive theory by its founder, social psychologist Albert Bandura, provides a unified theoretical framework for analyzing the psychological processes that govern human behavior. Its goal is to explain how behavior develops, how it is maintained, and through what processes it can be modified. It seeks to accomplish this task by identifying the determinants of human action and the mechanisms through which they operate.

Bandura lays out the conceptual framework of his approach in his book *Social Learning Theory* (1977). His theory is based on a model of reciprocal determinism. This means that Bandura rejects both the humanist and existentialist position viewing people as free agents and the behaviorist position viewing behavior as controlled by the environment. Rather, external determinants of behavior (such as rewards and punishments) and internal determinants (such as thoughts, expectations, and beliefs) are considered part of a system of interlocking determinants that influence not only behavior but also the various other parts of the system. In other words, each part of the system—behavior, cognition, and environmental influences—affects each of the other parts. People are neither free agents nor passive reactors to external pressures. Instead, through self-regulatory processes, they have the ability to exercise some measure of control over their own actions. They can affect their behavior by setting goals, arranging environmental inducements, generating cognitive strategies, evaluating goal attainment, and mediating consequences for their actions. Bandura accepts that these self-regulatory functions initially are learned as the result of external rewards and punishments. Their external origin, however, does not invalidate the fact that, once internalized, they in part determine behavior.

## COGNITIVE MEDIATING FACTORS

As self-regulation results from symbolic processing of information, Bandura in his theorizing assigned an increasingly prominent role to cognition. This was reflected in his book *Social Foundations of Thought and Action: A Social Cognitive Theory* (1986), in which he no longer referred to his approach as social learning but as social cognitive theory. People, unlike lower animals, use verbal and nonverbal symbols (language and images) to process information and preserve experiences in the form of cognitive representations. This encoded information serves as a guide for future behavior. Without the ability to use symbols, people would have to solve problems by enacting various alternative solutions until, by trial and error, they learned which ones resulted in rewards or punishments. Through their cognitive abilities, however, people can think through different options, imagine possible outcomes, and guide their behavior by anticipated consequences. Symbolic capabilities provide people with a powerful tool to regulate their own behavior in the absence of external reinforcements and punishments.

According to Bandura, the central mechanism of self-regulation is self-efficacy, defined as the belief that one has the ability, with one's actions, to bring about a certain outcome. Self-efficacy beliefs function as determinants of behavior by influencing motivation, thought processes, and emotions in ways that may be self-aiding or self-hindering. Specifically, self-efficacy appraisals determine the goals people set for themselves, whether they anticipate and visualize scenarios of success or failure, whether they embark on a course of action, how much effort they expend, and how long they persist in the face of obstacles. Self-efficacy expectations are different from outcome expectations. While outcome expectancies are beliefs that a given behavior will result in a certain outcome, self-efficacy refers to the belief in one's ability to bring about this outcome. To put it simply, people may believe that something can happen, but whether they embark on a course of action depends on their perceived ability to make it happen.

## RELEVANCE TO OBSERVATION AND MODELING

Perhaps the most important contribution of social learning theory to the understanding of human behavior is the concept of vicarious, or observational, learning, also termed learning through modeling. Before the advent of social learning theory, many psychologists assigned a crucial role to the process of reinforcement in learning. They postulated that without performing responses that are followed by reinforcement or punishment, a person cannot learn. In contrast, Bandura asserted that much of social behavior is not learned from the consequences of trial and error but is acquired through symbolic modeling. People watch what other people do and what happens to them as a result of their actions. From such observations, they form ideas of how to perform new behaviors, and later this information guides their actions.

Symbolic modeling is of great significance for human learning because of its enormous efficiency in transmitting information. Whereas trial-and-error learning requires the gradual shaping of the behavior of individuals through repetition and reinforcement, in observational learning, a single model can teach complex behaviors simultaneously to any number of people. According to Bandura, some elaborate and specifically human behavior patterns, such as language, might even be impossible to learn if it were not for symbolic modeling. For example, it seems unlikely that children learn to talk as a result of their parents' reinforcing each correct utterance they emit. Rather, children probably hear and watch other members of their verbal community talk and then imitate their behavior. In a similar vein, complex behaviors such as driving a car or flying a plane are not acquired by trial and error. Instead, prospective drivers or pilots follow the verbal rules of an instructor until they master the task.

In summary, Bandura's social learning theory explains human action in terms of the interplay among behavior, cognition, and environmental influences. The theory places particular emphasis on cognitive mediating factors such as self-efficacy beliefs and outcome expectancies. Its greatest contribution to a general theory of human learning has been its emphasis on learning by observation or modeling. Observational learning has achieved the status of a third learning principle, next to classical and operant conditioning.

## STUDIES OF LEARNING AND PERFORMANCE

From its inception, social learning theory has served as a useful framework for the understanding of both normal and abnormal human behavior. A major contribution that has important implications for the modification of human behavior is the theory's distinction between learning and performance. In a now-classic series of experiments, Bandura and his associates teased apart the roles of observation and reinforcement in learning and were able to demonstrate that people learn through mere observation.

In a study on aggression, an adult model hit and kicked a life-size inflated clown doll (a "Bobo" doll), with children watching the attack in person or on a television screen. Other children watched the model perform some innocuous behavior. Later, the children were allowed to play in the room with the Bobo doll. All children who had witnessed the aggression, either in person or on television, viciously attacked the doll, while those who had observed the model's innocuous behavior did not display aggression toward the doll. Moreover, it was clearly shown that the children modeled their aggressive behaviors after the adult. Those who had observed the adult sit on the doll and hit its face, or kick the doll, or use a hammer to pound it, imitated exactly these behaviors. Thus, the study accomplished its purpose by demonstrating that observational learning occurs in the absence of direct reinforcement.

In a related experiment, Bandura showed that expected consequences, while not relevant for learning, play a role in performance. A group of children watched a film of an adult model behaving aggressively toward a Bobo doll and being punished, while another group observed the same behavior with the person being rewarded. When the children subsequently were allowed to play with the Bobo doll, those who had watched the model being punished displayed fewer aggressive behaviors toward the doll than those who had seen the model being rewarded. When the experimenter then offered a reward to the children for imitating the model, however, all children, regardless of the consequences they had observed, attacked the Bobo doll. This showed that all children had learned the aggressive behavior from the model but that observing the model being punished served as an inhibiting factor until it was removed by the promise of a reward. Again, this study showed that children learn without reinforcement, simply by observing how others behave. Whether they then engage in the behavior, however, depends on the consequences they expect will result from their actions.

### DISINHIBITORY EFFECTS

Models not only teach people novel ways of thinking and behaving but also can strengthen or weaken inhibitions. Seeing models punished may inhibit similar behavior in observers, while seeing models carry out feared or forbidden actions without negative consequences may reduce their inhibitions.

The most striking demonstrations of the disinhibitory effects of observational learning come from therapeutic interventions based on modeling principles. Baudura, in his book *Principles of Behavior Modification* (1969), shows how social learning theory can provide a conceptual framework for the modification of a wide range of maladaptive behaviors. For example, a large number of laboratory studies of subjects with a severe phobia of snakes showed that phobic individuals can overcome their fear of reptiles when fearless adult models demonstrate how to handle a snake and directly assist subjects in coping successfully with whatever they dread.

### SELF-EFFICACY MECHANISM

In later elaborations, the scope of social learning theory was amplified to include self-efficacy theory. Self-efficacy is now considered the principal mechanism of behavior change, in that all successful interventions are assumed to operate by strengthening a person's self-perceived efficacy to cope with difficulties.

How can self-efficacy be strengthened? Research indicates that it is influenced by four sources of information. The most important influence comes from performance attainments, with successes heightening and failures lowering perceived self-efficacy. Thus, having people enact and master a difficult task most powerfully increases their efficacy percepts. A second influence comes from vicarious experiences. Exposing people to models

works because seeing people similar to oneself successfully perform a difficult task raises one's own efficacy expectations. Verbal persuasion is a third
way of influencing self-efficacy. Convincing people that they have the ability
to perform a task can encourage them to try harder, which indeed may
lead to successful performance. Finally, teaching people coping strategies
to lower emotional arousal can also increase self-efficacy. If subsequently
they approach a task more calmly, the likelihood of succeeding at it may increase.

Bandura and his associates conducted a series of studies to test the idea
that vastly different modes of influence all improve coping behavior by
strengthening self-perceived efficacy. Severe snake phobics received interventions based on enactive, vicarious, cognitive, or emotive treatment (a
method of personality change that incorporates cognitive, emotional, and
behavioral strategies, designed to help resist tendencies to be irrational, sug-
gestible, and conforming) modalities. The results confirmed that the degree to which people changed their behavior toward the reptiles was closely
associated with increases in self-judged efficacy, regardless of the method
of intervention. It is now widely accepted among social learning theorists
that all effective therapies ultimately work by strengthening people's self-
perceptions of efficacy.

## THEORETICAL INFLUENCES
Social learning theory was born into a climate in which two competing and
diametrically opposed schools of thought dominated psychology. On one
hand, psychologists who advocated psychodynamic theories postulated that
human behavior is governed by motivational forces operating in the form of
largely unconscious needs, drives, and impulses. These impulse theories
tended to give circular explanations, attributing behavior to inner causes
that were inferred from the very behavior they were supposed to cause. They
also tended to provide explanations after the fact, rather than predicting
events, and had very limited empirical support.

On the other hand, there were various types of behavior theory that
shifted the focus of the causal analysis from hypothetical internal determinants of behavior to external, publicly observable causes. Behaviorists were
able to show that actions commonly attributed to inner causes could be produced, eliminated, and reinstated by manipulating the antecedent (stimulus) and consequent (reinforcing) conditions of the person's external environment. This led to the proposition that people's behavior is caused by
factors residing in the environment.

Social learning theory presents a theory of human behavior that to some
extent incorporates both viewpoints. According to Bandura, people are neither driven by inner forces nor buffeted by environmental stimuli; instead,
psychological functioning is best explained in terms of a continuous reciprocal interaction of internal and external causes. This assumption, termed reciprocal determinism, became one of the dominant viewpoints in psychology.

An initial exposition of social learning theory was presented in Bandura and Richard H. Walters's text *Social Learning and Personality Development* (1963). This formulation drew heavily on the procedures and principles of operant and classical conditioning. In his later book *Principles of Behavior Modification*, Bandura placed much greater emphasis on symbolic events and self-regulatory processes. He argued that complex human behavior could not be satisfactorily explained by the narrow set of learning principles behaviorists had derived from animal studies. He incorporated principles derived from developmental, social, and cognitive psychology into social learning theory.

## EVOLUTION OF THEORETICAL DEVELOPMENT

During the 1970's, psychology had grown increasingly cognitive. This development was reflected in Bandura's 1977 book *Social Learning Theory*, which presented self-efficacy theory as the central mechanism through which people control their own behavior. Over the following decade, the influence of cognitive psychology on Bandura's work grew stronger. In *Social Foundations of Thought and Action*, he finally disavowed his roots in learning theory and renamed his approach "social cognitive theory." This theory accorded central roles to cognitive, vicarious, self-reflective, and self-regulatory processes.

Social learning/social cognitive theory became the dominant conceptual approach within the field of behavior therapy. It has provided the conceptual framework for numerous interventions for a wide variety of psychological disorders and probably will remain popular for a long time. Bandura, its founder, was honored with the Award for Distinguished Scientific Contributions to Psychology from the American Psychological Foundation in 1980 in recognition of his work.

## SOURCES FOR FURTHER STUDY

Bandura, Albert. *Principles of Behavior Modification*. New York: Holt, Rinehart and Winston, 1969. Presents an overview of basic psychological principles governing human behavior within the conceptual framework of social learning. Reviews theoretical and empirical advances in the field of social learning, placing special emphasis on self-regulation and on symbolic and vicarious processes. Applies these principles to the conceptualization and modification of a number of common behavior disorders such as alcoholism, phobias, and sexual deviancy.

_____. *Social Foundations of Thought and Action: A Social Cognitive Theory*. Englewood Cliffs, N.J.: Prentice-Hall, 1986. Presents a comprehensive coverage of the tenets of current social cognitive theory. Besides addressing general issues of human nature and causality, provides an impressive in-depth analysis of all important aspects of human functioning, including motivational, cognitive, and self-regulatory processes.

_____. *Social Learning Theory*. Reprint. Englewood Cliffs, N.J.: Prentice-Hall, 1986. Lays out Bandura's theory and presents a concise overview of its theoretical and experimental contributions to the field of social learning. Redefines many of the traditional concepts of learning theory and emphasizes the importance of cognitive processes in human learning.

Evans, Richard I. *Albert Bandura, the Man and His Ideas: A Dialogue.* New York: Praeger, 1989. An edited version of an interview with Bandura. Easy to read, presenting Bandura's thoughts on the major aspects of his work in an accessible form. The spontaneity of the discussion between Evans and Bandura gives a glimpse of Bandura as a person.

Feist, Jess, and Gregory Feist. *Theories of Personality.* 5th ed. Boston: McGraw-Hill, 2001. Chapter 11 of this book contains an excellent summary of Bandura's work. Gives an easy-to-read overview of his philosophical position (reciprocal determinism), discusses his theory (including observational learning and self-regulatory processes), and presents a summary of relevant research conducted within the framework of social cognitive theory. An ideal starting point for those who would like to become familiar with Bandura's work.

*Edelgard Wulfert*

SEE ALSO: Aggression; Cognitive Behavior Therapy; Cognitive Social Learning: Walter Mischel; Learning; Phobias.

# Social Psychological Models
## Erich Fromm

Type of psychology: Personality
Fields of study: Humanistic-phenomenological models; psychodynamic and neoanalytic models

*Fromm studied the effects of political, economic, and religious institutions on human personality. Fromm's work provides powerful insight into the causes of human unhappiness and psychopathology as well as ideas about how individuals and social institutions could change to maximize mental health and happiness.*

Key concepts
- dynamic adaptation
- escape from freedom
- freedom from external constraints
- freedom to maximize potential
- mental health
- personality
- productive love
- productive work

The approach of Erich Fromm (1900-1980) to the study of human personality starts from an evolutionary perspective. Specifically, Fromm maintained that humans, like all other living creatures, are motivated to survive and that survival requires adaptation to their physical surroundings. Humans are, however, unique in that they substantially alter their physical surroundings through the creation and maintenance of cultural institutions. Consequently, Fromm believed, human adaptation occurs primarily in response to the demands of political, economic, and religious institutions.

Fromm made a distinction between adaptations to physical and social surroundings that have no enduring impact on personality (static adaptation—for example, an American learning to drive on the left side of the road in England) and adaptation that does have an enduring impact on personality (dynamic adaptation—for example, a child who becomes humble and submissive in response to a brutally domineering, egomaniacal parent). Fromm consequently defined personality as the manner in which individuals dynamically adapt to their physical and social surroundings in order to survive and reduce anxiety.

Human adaptation includes the reduction of anxiety for two reasons. First, because humans are born in a profoundly immature and helplessly dependent state, they are especially prone to anxiety, which, although unpleasant, is useful to the extent that it results in signs of distress (such as crying) which alert others and elicit their assistance. Second, infants eventually mature into fully self-conscious human beings who, although no longer help-less and dependent, recognize their ultimate mortality and essential isola-tion from all other living creatures.

Fromm believed that humans have five basic inorganic needs (as op-posed to organic needs associated with physical survival) resulting from the anxiety associated with human immaturity at birth and eventual self-consciousness. The need for relatedness refers to the innate desire to acquire and maintain social relationships. The need for transcendence sug-gests that human beings have an inherent drive to become creative individu-als. The need for rootedness consists of a sense of belonging to a social group. The need for identity is the need to be a unique individual. The need for a frame of orientation refers to a stable and consistent way of perceiving the world.

## FREEDOM AND INDIVIDUAL POTENTIAL

Mental health for Fromm consists of realizing one's own unique individual potential, and it requires two kinds of freedom that are primarily dependent on the structure of a society's political, economic, and religious institutions. Freedom from external constraints refers to practical concerns such as free-dom from imprisonment, hunger, and homelessness. This is how many peo-ple commonly conceive of the notion of freedom. For Fromm, freedom from external constraints is necessary, but not sufficient, for optimal mental health, which also requires the freedom to maximize one's individual poten-tial.

Freedom to maximize individual potential entails productive love and productive work. Productive love consists of interpersonal relationships based on mutual trust, respect, and cooperation. Productive work refers to daily activities that allow for creative expression and provide self-esteem. Fromm hypothesized that people become anxious and insecure if their need for transcendence is thwarted by a lack of productive work and love. Many people, he believed, respond to anxiety and insecurity by an "escape from freedom": the unconscious adoption of personality traits that reduce anxiety and insecurity at the expense of individual identity.

## PERSONALITY TYPES AND FREEDOM ESCAPE

Fromm described five personality types representing an escape from free-dom. The authoritarian person reduces anxiety and insecurity by fusing himself or herself with another person or a religious, political, or economic institution. Fromm distinguished between sadistic and masochistic authori-tarians: The sadistic type needs to dominate (and often hurt and humiliate) others, while the masochistic type needs to submit to the authority of others. The sadist and the masochist are similar in that they share a pathetic depen-dence on each other. Fromm used the people in Nazi Germany (masoch-ists) under Adolf Hitler (a sadist) to illustrate the authoritarian personality type.

Destructive individuals reduce anxiety and insecurity by destroying other persons or things. Fromm suggested that ideally people derive satisfaction and security through constructive endeavors, but noted that some people lack the skill and motivation to create and therefore engage in destructive behavior as an impoverished substitute for constructive activities.

Withdrawn individuals reduce anxiety and insecurity by willingly or unwillingly refusing to participate in a socially prescribed conception of reality; instead, they withdraw into their own idiosyncratic versions of reality. In one social conception, for example, many devout Christians believe that God created the earth in six days, that Christ was born approximately two thousand years ago, and that he has not yet returned to Earth. The withdrawn individual might singularly believe that the earth was hatched from the egg of a giant bird a few years ago and that Christ had been seen eating a hamburger yesterday. Psychiatrists and clinicians today would generally characterize the withdrawn individual as psychotic or schizophrenic.

Self-inflated people reduce anxiety and insecurity by unconsciously adopting glorified images of themselves as superhuman individuals who are vastly superior to others. They are arrogant, strive to succeed at the expense of others, are unable to accept constructive criticism, and avoid experiences that might disconfirm their false conceptions of themselves.

Finally, Fromm characterized American society in the 1940's as peopled by automaton conformists, who reduce anxiety and insecurity by unconsciously adopting the thoughts and feelings demanded of them by their culture. They are then no longer anxious and insecure, because they are like everyone else around them. According to Fromm, automaton conformists are taught to distrust and repress their own thoughts and feelings during childhood through impoverished and demoralizing educational and socializing experiences. The result is the acquisition of pseudothoughts and pseudofeelings, which people believe to be their own but which are actually socially infused. For example, Fromm contended that most Americans vote the same way that their parents do, although very few would claim that parental preference was the cause of their political preferences. Rather, most American voters would claim that their decisions are the result of a thorough and rational consideration of genuine issues (a pseudothought) instead of a mindless conformity to parental influence (a genuine thought—or, in this case, a nonthought).

## IMPACT OF HISTORICAL CONSTRAINTS

In *Escape from Freedom* (1941), Fromm applied his theory of personality to a historical account of personality types by a consideration of how political, economic, and religious changes in Western Europe from the Middle Ages to the twentieth century affected "freedom from" and "freedom to." Fromm argued that the feudal political system of the Middle Ages engendered very little freedom from external constraints. Specifically, there was limited physical mobility; the average person died in the same place that he or she was born, and many people were indentured servants who could not leave their feudal lord even if they had somewhere to go. Additionally, there was no choice of occupation: One's job was generally inherited from one's father.

Despite the lack of freedom from external constraints, however, economic and religious institutions provided circumstances that fostered freedom to maximize individual potential through productive work and productive love. Economically, individual craftsmanship was the primary means by which goods were produced. Although this was time-consuming and inefficient by modern standards, craftsmen were responsible for the design and production of entire products. A shoemaker would choose the design and materials, make the shoes, and sell the shoes. A finished pair of shoes thus represented a tangible manifestation of the creative energies of the producer, thus providing productive work.

Additionally, the crafts were regulated by the guild system, which controlled access to apprenticeships and materials and set wages and prices in order to guarantee maximum employment and a fair profit to the craftsmen. The guilds encouraged relatively cooperative behavior between craftsmen and consequently engendered productive love. Productive love was also sustained by the moral precepts of the then-dominant Catholic church, which stressed the essential goodness of humankind, the idea that human beings had free will to choose their behavior on Earth and hence influence their ultimate fate after death, the need to be responsible for the welfare of others, and the sinfulness of extracting excessive profits from commerce and accumulating money beyond that which is necessary to exist comfortably.

The dissolution of the feudal system and the consequent transition to parliamentary democracy and capitalism provided the average individual with a historically unprecedented amount of freedom from external constraints. Physical mobility increased dramatically as the descendants of serfs were able to migrate freely to cities to seek employment of their choosing; however, according to Fromm, increased freedom from external constraints was acquired at the expense of the circumstances necessary for freedom to maximize individual potential through productive work and productive love.

## IMPACT OF CAPITALISM

Capitalism shifted the focus of commerce from small towns to large cities and stimulated the development of fast and efficient means of production, but assembly-line production methods divested the worker of opportunities for creative expression. The assembly-line worker has no control over the design of a product, does not engage in the entire production of the product, and has nothing to do with the sale and distribution of the product. Workers in a modern automobile factory might put on hub caps or install radios for eight hours each day as cars roll by on the assembly line. They have no control over the process of production and no opportunity for creative expression, given the monotonous and repetitive activities to which their job confines them.

In addition to the loss of opportunities to engage in productive work, the inherent competitiveness of capitalism undermined the relatively cooperative interpersonal relationships engendered by the guild system, transforming the stable small-town economic order into a frenzied free-for-all in which people compete with their neighbors for the resources necessary to survive, hence dramatically reducing opportunities for people to acquire and maintain productive love. Additionally, these economic changes were supported by the newly dominant Protestant churches (represented by the teachings of John Calvin and Martin Luther), which stressed the inherent evilness of humankind, the lack of free will, and the notion of predestination—the idea that God has already decided prior to one's birth if one is to be consigned to heaven or hell after death. Despite the absence of free will and the idea that an individual's fate was predetermined, Protestant theologians claimed that people could get a sense of God's intentions by their material success on Earth, thus encouraging people to work very hard to accumulate as much as possible (the so-called Protestant work ethic) as an indication that God's countenance is shining upon them.

### CALL TO EMBRACE POSITIVE FREEDOM

In summary, Fromm argued that the average person in Western industrial democracies has freedom from external constraints but lacks opportunities to maximize individual potential through productive love and productive work; the result is pervasive feelings of anxiety and insecurity. Most people respond to this anxiety and insecurity by unconsciously adopting personality traits that reduce anxiety and insecurity, but at the expense of their individuality, which Fromm referred to as an escape from freedom. For Fromm, psychopathology is the general result of the loss of individuality associated with an escape from freedom. The specific manifestation of psychopathology depends on the innate characteristics of the individual in conjunction with the demands of the person's social environment.

Fromm argued that while escaping from freedom is a typical response to anxiety and insecurity, it is not an inevitable one. Instead, he urged people to embrace positive freedom through the pursuit of productive love and work, which he claimed would require both individual and social change. Individually, Fromm advocated a life of spontaneous exuberance made possible by love and being loved. He described the play of children and the behavior of artists as illustrations of this kind of lifestyle. Socially, Fromm believed strongly that the fundamental tenets of democracy should be retained but that capitalism in its present form must be modified to ensure every person's right to live, to distribute resources more equitably, and to provide opportunities to engage in productive work.

## THEORETICAL INFLUENCES

Fromm's ideas reflect the scientific traditions of his time as well as his extensive training in history and philosophy, in addition to his psychological background. Fromm is considered a neo-Freudian (along with Karen Horney, Harry Stack Sullivan, and others) because of his acceptance of some of Freud's basic ideas (specifically, the role of unconsciously motivated behaviors in human affairs and the notion that anxiety-producing inclinations are repressed or prevented from entering conscious awareness) while rejecting Freud's reliance on the role of biological instincts (sex and aggression) for understanding human behavior. Instead, the neo-Freudians were explicitly concerned with the influence of the social environment on personality development.

Additionally, Fromm was very much influenced by Charles Darwin's theory of evolution, by existential philosophy, and by the economic and social psychological ideas of Karl Marx. Fromm's use of adaptation in the service of survival to define personality is derived from basic evolutionary theory. His analysis of the sources of human anxiety, especially the awareness of death and perception of isolation and aloneness, is extracted from existential philosophy. The notion that human happiness requires productive love and work and that capitalism is antithetical to mental health was originally proposed by Marx. Fromm's work has never received the attention that it deserves in America because of his open affinity for some of Marx's ideas and his insistence that economic change is utterly necessary to ameliorate the unhappiness and mental illness that pervade American society. Nevertheless, his ideas are vitally important from both a theoretical and practical perspective.

## SOURCES FOR FURTHER STUDY

Becker, Ernest. *The Birth and Death of Meaning.* 2d ed. Reprint. New York: Free Press, 1985. Becker presents a general description of Fromm's ideas embedded in a broad interdisciplinary consideration of human social psychological behavior.

Fromm, Erich. *Anatomy of Human Destructiveness.* 1973. Reprint. New York: Henry Holt, 1992. An in-depth examination of the destructive personality type.

_____. *The Art of Loving.* 1956. Reprint. New York: HarperCollins, 2000. A detailed analysis of how to love and be loved. Distinguishes between genuine love and morbid dependency.

_____. *Escape from Freedom.* 1941. Reprint. New York: Henry Holt, 1995. Fromm's early seminal work, in which his basic theory about the relationship between political, economic, and religious institutions and personality development was originally articulated. All of Fromm's later books are extensions of ideas expressed here.

_____. *Marx's Concept of Man.* 1962. Reprint. New York: Frederick Ungar, 1982. An introduction to Marx's ideas, including a translation of Marx's economic and philosophical manuscripts of 1844.

_____. *The Revolution of Hope: Toward a Humanized Technology*. New York: Harper & Row, 1968. A detailed discussion of how capital-based economies can be transformed to provide opportunities for productive work without sacrificing productive efficiency, technological advances, or democratic political ideals.

*Sheldon Solomon*

SEE ALSO: Psychoanalytic Psychology and Personality: Sigmund Freud; Self; Self-Esteem; Social Psychological Models: Karen Horney.

# SOCIAL PSYCHOLOGICAL MODELS
## KAREN HORNEY

TYPE OF PSYCHOLOGY: Personality
FIELDS OF STUDY: Personality theory; psychodynamic and neoanalytic
  models; psychodynamic therapies

*Horney's social psychoanalytic theory focuses on how human relationships and cultural conditions influence personality formation. The theory describes how basic anxiety, resulting from childhood experiences, contributes to the development of three neurotic, compulsive, rigid personality styles: moving toward others, moving away from others, and moving against others. Normal personality is characterized by flexibility and balance among interpersonal styles.*

KEY CONCEPTS
- basic anxiety
- externalization
- idealized self
- neurosis
- neurotic trends
- search for glory
- self-realization
- tyranny of the should

Karen Horney (1885-1952) spent the major part of her career explaining how personality patterns, especially neurotic patterns, are formed, how they operate, and how they can be changed in order to increase individual potential. In contrast to Sigmund Freud's view that people are guided by instincts and the pleasure principle, Horney proposed that people act out desires to achieve safety and satisfaction in social relationships. She was optimistic about the possibility for human growth and believed that, under conditions of acceptance and care, people move toward self-realization, or the development of their full potential. She wrote almost exclusively, however, about personality problems and methods for solving them.

### ROLE OF CULTURE
Horney believed that it is impossible to understand individuals or the mechanisms of neurosis (inflexible behaviors and reactions, or discrepancies between one's potential and one's achievements) apart from the cultural context in which they exist. Neurosis varies across cultures, as well as within the same culture, and it is influenced by socioeconomic class, gender, and historical period. For example, in *The Neurotic Personality of Our Time* (1937), Horney noted that a person who refuses to accept a salary increase in a Western culture might be seen as neurotic, whereas in a Pueblo Indian culture, this person might be seen as entirely normal.

The neurotic person experiences culturally determined problems in an exaggerated form. In Western culture, competitiveness shapes many neurotic problems because it decreases opportunities for cooperation, fosters a climate of mistrust and hostility, undermines self-esteem, increases isolation, and encourages people to be more concerned with how they appear to others than with fulfilling personal possibilities. It fosters the overvaluing of external success, encourages people to develop grandiose images of superiority, and leads to intensified needs for approval and affection as well as to the distortion of love. Moreover, the ideal of external success is contradicted by the ideal of humility, which leads to further internal conflict and, in many cases, neurosis.

### ROLE OF THE FAMILY

Cultural patterns are replicated and transmitted primarily in family environments. Ideally, a family provides the warmth and nurturance that prepares children to face the world with confidence. When parents have struggled unsuccessfully with the culture, however, they create the conditions that

*Karen Horney.* (Courtesy of Marianne Horney Eckardt, M.D.)

lead to inadequate parenting. In its most extreme form, the competitiveness of the larger culture leads to child abuse, but it can also lead to parents' preoccupation with their own needs, an inability to love and nurture effectively, or a tendency to treat children as extensions of themselves. Rivalry, overprotectiveness, irritability, partiality, and erratic behavior are other manifestations of parental problems.

Within a negative environment, children experience fear and anger, but they also feel weak and helpless beside more powerful adults. They recognize that expressing hostility directly might be dangerous and result in parental reprisals or loss of love. As a result, children repress legitimate anger, banishing it to the unconscious. By using the defense mechanism of reaction formation, they develop emotions toward parents that are the opposite of anger, and they experience feared parents as objects of admiration. Children unconsciously turn their inner fears and anger against themselves and lose touch with their real selves. As a result, they develop basic anxiety, or the feeling of being alone and defenseless in a world that seems hostile.

## DEFENSE AND COPING STRATEGIES

In order to cope with basic anxiety, individuals use additional defensive strategies or neurotic trends to cope with the world. These involve three primary patterns of behavior: moving away from others, moving toward others, and moving against others. In addition, neurotic individuals develop an idealized self, an unrealistic, flattering distortion of the self-image that encourages people to set unattainable standards, shrink from reality, and compulsively search for glory (compulsive and insatiable efforts to fulfill the demands of the idealized self) rather than accept themselves as they are.

Horney wrote about these in rich detail in *Our Inner Conflicts: A Constructive Theory of Neurosis* (1945), a highly readable book. The person who moves toward others believes: "If I love you or give in, you will not hurt me." The person who moves against others believes: "If I have power, you will not hurt me." The person who moves away from others thinks: "If I am independent or withdraw from you, you will not hurt me."

The person who moves toward others has chosen a dependent or compliant pattern of coping. The person experiences strong needs for approval, belonging, and affection and strives to live up to the expectations of others through behavior that is overconsiderate and submissive. This person sees love as the only worthwhile goal in life and represses all competitive, hostile, angry aspects of the self. The moving-against type, who has adopted an aggressive, tough, exploitive style, believes that others are hostile, that life is a struggle, and that the only way to survive is to win and to control others. This person sees herself or himself as strong and determined, and represses all feelings of affection for fear of losing power over others. Finally, the moving-away type, who has adopted a style of detachment and isolation, sees himself or herself as self-sufficient, private, and superior to others. This person represses all emotion and avoids any desire or activity that would result in dependency on others.

The interpersonal patterns that Horney discussed are no longer known as neurotic styles but as personality disorders. Many of the behaviors that she described can be seen in descriptions of diagnostic categories that appear in the American Psychiatric Association's *Diagnostic and Statistical Manual of Mental Disorders: DSM-IV-TR* (rev. 4th ed., 2000), such as dependent personality disorder, narcissistic personality disorder, and obsessive-compulsive personality disorder. Like Horney's original criteria, these categories describe inflexible and maladaptive patterns of behavior and thinking that are displayed in various environments and result in emotional distress or impaired functioning.

## USE OF PSYCHOANALYSIS

In her practice of psychoanalysis, Horney used free association and dream analysis to bring unconscious material to light. In contrast to Freud's more passive involvement with patients, she believed that the psychoanalyst should play an active role not only in interpreting behavior but also in inquiring about current behaviors that maintain unproductive patterns, suggesting alternatives, and helping persons mobilize energy to change.

Horney also made psychoanalysis more accessible to the general population. She suggested that by examining oneself according to the principles outlined in her book *Self-Analysis* (1942), one could increase self-understanding and gain freedom from internal issues that limit one's potential. Her suggestions indicate that a person should choose a problem that one could clearly identify, engage in informal free association about the issue, reflect upon and tentatively interpret the experience, and make specific, simple choices about altering problematic behavior patterns. Complex, long-standing issues, however, should be dealt with in formal psychoanalysis.

## INFLUENCES

Horney was one of the first individuals to criticize Freud's psychology of women. In contrast to Freudian instinct theory, she proposed a version of psychoanalysis that emphasized the role that social relationships and culture play in human development. She questioned the usefulness of Freud's division of the personality into the regions of the id, ego, and superego, and she viewed the ego as a more constructive, forward-moving force within the person.

Horney's work was enriched by her contact with psychoanalysts Harry Stack Sullivan, Clara Thompson, and Erich Fromm, who also emphasized the role of interpersonal relationships and sociocultural factors and were members at Horney's American Institute of Psychoanalysis when it was first established. Horney's work also resembled Alfred Adler's personality theory. Her concepts of the search for glory and idealized self are similar to Adler's concepts of superiority striving and the superiority complex. Furthermore, Adler's ruling type resembles the moving-against personality, his getting type is similar to the moving-toward personality, and his avoiding type is closely related to the moving-away personality.

## CONTRIBUTIONS TO THE FIELD

Horney anticipated many later developments within cognitive, humanistic, and feminist personality theory and psychotherapy. Abraham Maslow, who was inspired by Horney, built his concept of self-actualization on Horney's optimistic belief that individuals can move toward self-realization. Carl Rogers's assumptions that problems are based on distortions of real experience and discrepancies between the ideal and real selves are related to Horney's beliefs that unhealthy behavior results from denial of the real self as well as from conflict between the idealized and real selves. In the field of cognitive psychotherapy, Albert Ellis's descriptions of the mechanisms of neurosis resemble Horney's statements. He borrowed the phrase "tyranny of the should" from Horney and placed strong emphasis on how "shoulds" influence irrational, distorted thinking patterns. Finally, Horney's notion that problems are shaped by cultural patterns is echoed in the work of feminist psychotherapists, who believe that individual problems are often the consequence of external, social problems.

## SOURCES FOR FURTHER STUDY

Horney, Karen. *Neurosis and Human Growth: The Struggle Toward Self-Realization.* 1950. Reprint. New York: W. W. Norton, 1991. Presents Horney's theory in its final form. Describes the ways in which various neurotic processes operate, including the tyranny of the should, neurotic claims, self-alienation, and self-contempt. Discusses faulty, neurotic solutions that are developed as a way to relieve internal tensions through domination, dependency, resignation, or self-effacement.

_____. *The Neurotic Personality of Our Time.* 1937. Reprint. New York: W. W. Norton, 1994. Outlines the manner in which culture influences personality difficulties and describes typical behavior problems that result from the exaggeration of cultural difficulties in one's life.

_____. *New Ways in Psychoanalysis.* 1939. Reprint. New York: W. W. Norton, 2000. Describes major areas of agreement and disagreement with Sigmund Freud as well as important elements of Horney's theory; highly controversial when first published.

_____. *Our Inner Conflicts: A Constructive Theory of Neurosis.* 1945. Reprint. New York: W. W. Norton, 1993. Identifies and describes, through rich detail and examples, the three neurotic trends of moving toward others, moving away from others, and moving against others. Highly readable and a good introduction to Horney's main ideas.

_____. *Self-Analysis.* 1942. Reprint. New York: W. W. Norton, 1994. Provides guidance for readers who may wish to engage in informal free association, self-discovery, and personal problem solving.

Quinn, Susan. *A Mind of Her Own: The Life of Karen Horney.* Reading, Mass.: Addison-Wesley, 1988. Readable, honest, fascinating biography of Horney's life; provides insights into personal factors that influenced Horney's theoretical and clinical work.

Westkott, Marcia. *The Feminist Legacy of Karen Horney.* New Haven, Conn.: Yale University Press, 1986. This book integrates Karen Horney's early papers on the psychology of women with the more complete personality theory that emerged over time.

*Carolyn Zerbe Enns*

SEE ALSO: Individual Psychology: Alfred Adler; Psychoanalysis; Psychoanalytic Psychology and Personality: Sigmund Freud; Social Psychological Models: Erich Fromm; Women's Psychology: Karen Horney; Women's Psychology: Sigmund Freud.

# SPEECH DISORDERS

TYPE OF PSYCHOLOGY: Language
FIELDS OF STUDY: Behavioral therapies; infancy and childhood; organic
    disorders

*Speech disorders may have an organic or learned origin, and they often affect a person's ability to communicate efficiently. As a result of a speech disorder, a person may exhibit a number of effects on behavior, such as the avoidance of talking with others and low self-esteem.*

KEY CONCEPTS
- communication
- self-esteem
- social interaction
- speech
- vocal folds

The ability to communicate is one of the most basic human characteristics. Communication is essential to learning, working, and, perhaps most important, social interaction. Normal communication involves hearing sounds, interpreting and organizing sounds, and making meaningful sounds. The ear takes in sounds, changes them into electrical impulses, and relays these impulses to the brain. The brain interprets the impulses, assigns meaning, and prepares a response. This response is then coded into the precisely coordinated changes in muscles, breath, vocal folds, tongue, jaw, lips, and so on that produce understandable speech.

Between 5 percent and 10 percent of Americans experience speech or language difficulties, often referred to as speech disorders. For these individuals, a breakdown occurs in one of the processes of normal communication described above. People with speech disorders may exhibit one or more of the following problems: They may be difficult to understand, use and produce words incorrectly, consistently use incorrect grammar, be unable to hear appropriately or to understand others, consistently speak too loudly, demonstrate a hesitating speech pattern, or simply be unable to speak. Speech disorders can be categorized as one of three disorder types: disorders of articulation, of fluency, or of voice. Articulation disorders are difficulties in the formation and stringing together of sounds to produce words. Fluency disorders, commonly referred to as stuttering, are interruptions in the flow or rhythm of speech. Finally, voice disorders are characterized by deviations in a person's voice quality, pitch, or loudness.

## TYPES OF SPEECH DISORDERS
Articulation disorders are the most common types of speech errors in children. Articulation errors may take the form of substitutions, omissions, or distortions of sounds. An example of a substitution would be the substitu-

tion of the *w* sound for the *r* sound, as in "wabbit" for "rabbit." Substitutions are the most common form of articulation errors. An example of an omission would be if the *d* sound was left out of the word "bed," as in "be_." Finally, sounds can also be distorted, as in "shleep" for "sleep."

Stuttering is defined as an interruption in the flow or rhythm of speech. Stuttering can be characterized by hesitations, interjections, repetitions, or prolongations of a sound, syllable, word, or phrase. "I wa-wa-want that" is an example of a part-word repetition, while "I, I, I want that" is an example of a whole-word repetition. When a word or group of words such as "uh," "you know," "well," or "oh" is inserted into an utterance, it is termed an interjection. "I want uh, uh, you know, uh, that" is an example of a sentence containing interjections. There may also be secondary behaviors associated with

## DSM-IV-TR CRITERIA FOR SPEECH DISORDERS

### PHONOLOGICAL DISORDER (DSM CODE 315.39)

Failure to use developmentally expected speech sounds appropriate for age and dialect

Examples include errors in sound production, use, representation, or organization (substitutions of one sound for another, omissions of sounds such as final consonants)

Speech sound production difficulties interfere with academic or occupational achievement or with social communication

If mental retardation, speech-motor or sensory deficit, or environmental deprivation is present, speech difficulties exceed those usually associated with these problems

### STUTTERING (DSM CODE 307.0)

Disturbance in the normal fluency and time patterning of speech inappropriate for age

Characterized by frequent occurrences of one or more of the following:

- sound and syllable repetitions
- sound prolongations
- interjections
- broken words (such as pauses within a word)
- audible or silent blocking (filled or unfilled pauses in speech)
- circumlocutions (word substitutions to avoid problematic words)
- words produced with an excess of physical tension
- monosyllabic whole-word repetitions

Fluency disturbance interferes with academic or occupational achievement or with social communication

If speech-motor or sensory deficit is present, speech difficulties exceed those usually associated with these problems stuttering. In order for an individual to extricate himself or herself from a stuttering incident, secondary behaviors may be used. A stutterer may blink the eyes, turn the head, tap his or her leg, look away, or perform some other interruptive behavior to stop the stuttering. In therapy, secondary behaviors are very difficult to extinguish.

While articulation disorders and stuttering are often seen in children, voice disorders are common among adults. Voice disorders are categorized into disorders of pitch, intensity, nasality, and quality. A person with a voice disorder of pitch may have a vocal pitch which is too high. A person may speak too softly and thus exhibit a voice disorder of intensity. Still others may sound as though they talk through their nose (hypernasality) or always have a cold (hyponasality). The most common voice disorder is a disorder of quality. Examples of disorders of vocal quality include a voice that sounds hoarse, breathy, harsh, or rough. This type of voice disorder may be caused by vocal abuse, or an overusage of the voice, and might be found among singers, actors, or other individuals who abuse or overuse their voices. If the vocal abuse continues, vocal nodules (like calluses) may appear on the vocal folds. Vocal nodules may be surgically removed, and a person may be put on an extended period of vocal rest.

Speech disorders may be caused by a variety of factors. They may result from physical problems, health problems, or other problems. Physical problems such as cleft lip and palate, misaligned teeth, difficulty in controlling movements of the tongue, injury to the head, neck, or spinal cord, poor hearing, mental retardation, and cerebral palsy can contribute to poor articulation. The exact causes of stuttering are not known; however, a variety of factors are thought to be involved, including learning problems, emotional difficulties, biological defects, and neurological problems. Problems with voice quality can be caused by too much strain on the vocal folds (for example, yelling too much or clearing the throat too often), hearing loss, inflammation or growths on the vocal folds (vocal nodules), or emotional problems.

### SPEECH AND COMMUNICATION

Speaking, hearing, and understanding are essential to human communication. A disorder in one or more of these abilities can interfere with a person's capacity to communicate. Impaired communication can influence all aspects of life, creating many problems for an individual. Behavioral effects resulting from the speech disorder can be found in both children and adults. Children with speech disorders can experience difficulties in learning and find it hard to establish relationships with others. Speech disorders in adults can adversely affect social interactions and often create emotional problems, which may interfere with a person's ability to earn a living. Disorders such as those described above can interfere with a person's relationships, independence, well-being, and ability to learn. People who have trouble communicating thoughts and ideas may have trouble relating to others, possibly resulting in depression and isolation. Furthermore, job opportunities are often limited for people who cannot communicate effectively. Thus, they may have trouble leading independent, satisfying lives. Emotional problems may develop in people who exhibit speech disorders as a result of embarrassment, rejection, or poor self-image. Finally, learning is difficult and frustrating for people with speech disorders. As a consequence, their performance and progress at school and on the job can suffer.

When trying to communicate with others, individuals with speech disorders may experience other negative behavioral effects as a result of the disorder. These effects include frustration, anxiety, guilt, and hostility. The emotional experience of speech-disordered persons is often a result of their experiences in trying to communicate with others. Both the listener and the speech-disordered person react to the disordered person's attempts to communicate. In addition, the listener's reactions may influence the disordered individual. These reactions may include embarrassment, guilt, frustration, and anger and may cause the disordered individual to experience a sense of helplessness that can subsequently lower the person's sense of self-worth. Many speech-disordered people respond to their problem by being overly aggressive, by denying its existence, by projecting reactions in listeners, or by feeling anxious or timid.

### TREATMENT AND PREVENTION
Treatment of speech disorders attempts to eliminate or minimize the disorder and related problems. Many professionals may be involved in providing therapy, special equipment, or surgery. In therapy, specialists teach clients more effective ways of communicating. They may also help families learn to communicate with the disordered individual. Therapy may also include dealing with the negative behavioral effects of having a speech disorder, such as frustration, anxiety, and a feeling of low self-worth. In some cases, surgery can correct structural problems that may be causing speech disorders, such as cleft palate or misaligned teeth. For children with articulation disorders, therapy begins with awareness training of the misarticulations and the correct sound productions. After awareness is established, the new sound's productions are taught. For individuals who exhibit voice disorders, therapy is designed to find the cause of the disorder, eliminate or correct the cause, and retrain the individuals to use their voices correctly. Therapy for stutterers, however, is an entirely different matter. There are many methods for treating stuttering. Some are called "cures," while others help individuals live with their stuttering. Still other types of stuttering therapy help the stutterer overcome his or her fear of communicating or help him or her develop a more normal breathing pattern.

Though there are many ways to treat speech disorders, disorder prevention is even more important. Certain things can be done to help prevent many speech disorders. All the methods focus on preventing speech disorders in childhood. Children should be encouraged to talk, but they should not be pushed into speaking. Pushing a child may cause that child to associate anxiety or frustration with communicating. Infants do not simply start talking; they need to experiment with their voice, lips, and tongue. This experimentation is often called babbling, and it should not be discouraged. Later on, one can slowly introduce words and help with correct pronunciation. When talking with young children, one should talk slowly and naturally, avoiding "baby talk." Children will have difficulty distinguishing between the baby-talk word (for example, "baba") and the real word ("bottle"). Having children point to and name things in picture books and in real-world surroundings allows them to put labels (words) on the objects in their environment. Increases in the number of labels a child has learned can subsequently increase the number of topics about which the child can communicate. It is most important to listen to what the child is trying to say rather than to how the child is saying it. Such prevention strategies will encourage positive behavioral effects regarding the act of communicating. These positive effects include feelings of self-efficiency, independence, and a positive self-image.

### SPEECH-LANGUAGE PATHOLOGY

Early identification of a speech disorder improves the chances for successful treatment, and early treatment can help prevent a speech disorder from developing into a lifelong handicap. Professionals who identify, evaluate, and treat communication disorders in individuals have preparations in the field of speech-language pathology. A speech-language pathologist is a professional who has been educated in the study of human communication, its development, and its disorders. By evaluating the speech and language skills of children and adults, the speech-language pathologist determines if communication problems exist and decides on the most appropriate way of treating these problems.

Speech-language pathology services are provided in many public and private schools, community clinics, hospitals, rehabilitation centers, private practices, health departments, colleges and universities, and state and federal governmental agencies. There are more than fourteen hundred clinical facilities and hundreds of full-time private practitioners providing speech services to people throughout the United States. Service facilities exist in many cities in every state. A speech-language pathologist will have a master's or doctoral degree and should hold a Certificate of Clinical Competence (CCC) from the American Speech-Language-Hearing Association or a license from his or her state.

Responsibilities of a speech-language pathologist include evaluation and diagnosis, therapy, and referral to other specialists involved with speech disorders. By gathering background information and by direct observation and testing, the speech-language pathologist can determine the extent of the disorder as well as a probable cause. The speech-language pathologist chooses an appropriate treatment to correct or lessen the communication problem and attempts to help the patient and family understand the problem. When other treatment is needed to correct the problem, the patient is referred to another specialist. Audiologists, special educators, psychologists, social workers, neurologists, pediatricians, otolaryngologists (also known as ear, nose, and throat specialists), and other medical and dental specialists may be involved in the diagnosis and treatment of a speech disorder. For example, psychologists may be best suited to treat the emotional or behavioral aspects of having a speech disorder (that is, anxiety, frustration, anger, denial, and so on). Otolaryngologists are often involved in the diagnosis of voice disorders. Audiologists determine whether an individual's hearing is affecting or causing a speech disorder.

Speech disorders can affect anyone at any time. The chances are good that everyone at one time has either had or known someone with a speech disorder. Because communication is so overwhelmingly a part of life, disordered speech is not something to take lightly. With good prevention, early identification, and early treatment, lifelong difficulties with communication can be prevented.

### Sources for Further Study

Curlee, Richard F. "Counseling in Speech, Language, and Hearing." *Seminars in Speech and Language* 9, no. 3 (1988). In his introductory article to this issue, Curlee presents a clear and interesting overview of counseling strategies for the speech-language pathologist. Counseling of parents and spouses of persons with speech disorders is detailed.

Riekehof, Lottie L. *The Joy of Signing.* 2d ed. Springfield, Mo.: Gospel Publishing House, 1987. A comprehensive book of sign language. Includes origins of the signs, usage of the signs, and sign variations.

Shames, George H., and Norma B. Anderson, eds. *Human Communication Disorders.* Boston: Allyn & Bacon, 2001. This general text covers a wide range of communication disorders. Includes a section on speech-language pathology as a profession. Also includes sections on cleft palate, aphasia, and cerebral palsy.

The Speech Foundation of America. *Counseling Stutterers.* Memphis, Tenn.: Author, 1989. The Speech Foundation of America is a nonprofit, charitable organization dedicated to the prevention and treatment of stuttering. It provides a variety of low-cost publications about stuttering and stuttering therapy. This publication is written to give clinicians a better understanding of the counseling aspect of therapy and to suggest ways in which it can be used most effectively.

_____. *Therapy for Stutterers.* Memphis, Tenn.: Author, 1989. A general guide to help those who work or plan to work in therapy with adult and older-adolescent stutterers.

*Jennifer A. Sanders Wann and Daniel L. Wann*

See also: Language.

# Stress

TYPE OF PSYCHOLOGY: Stress
FIELDS OF STUDY: Coping; critical issues in stress; stress and illness

*The stress response consists of physiological arousal, subjective feelings of discomfort, and the behavioral changes people experience when they confront situations that they appraise as dangerous or threatening. Because extreme situational or chronic stress causes emotional distress and may impair physical functioning, it is important to learn effective stress coping strategies.*

KEY CONCEPTS
- cognitive appraisal
- emotion-focused coping
- learned helplessness
- problem-focused coping
- stressor

In the past, the term "stress" designated both a stimulus (a force or pressure) and a response (adversity, affliction). More recently, it has usually been used to denote a set of changes that people undergo in situations that they appraise as threatening to their well-being. These changes involve physiological arousal, subjective feelings of discomfort, and overt behaviors. The terms "anxiety" and "fear" are also used to indicate what people experience when they appraise circumstances as straining their ability to cope with them.

The external circumstances that induce stress responses are called stressors. Stressors have a number of important temporal components. Exposure to them may be relatively brief, with a clear starting and stopping point (acute stressors), or may persist for extended periods without clear demarcation (chronic stressors). Stressors impinge on people at different points in their life cycles, sometimes occurring "off time" (at times that are incompatible with personal and societal expectations of their occurrence) or at a "bad time" (along with other stressors). Finally, stress may be induced by the anticipation of harmful circumstances that one thinks one is likely to confront, by an ongoing stressor, or by the harmful effects of stressors already encountered. All these factors affect people's interpretations of stressful events, how they deal with them, and how effective they are at coping with them.

Although there are some situations to which almost everyone responds with high levels of stress, there are individual differences in how people respond to situations. Thus, though most people cringe at the thought of having to parachute from an airplane, a substantial minority find this an exciting, challenging adventure. Most people avoid contact with snakes, yet others keep them as pets. For most people, automobiles, birds, and people with deep voices are largely neutral objects, yet for others they provoke a stress reaction that may verge on panic.

The key concept is cognitive appraisal. Situations become stressors for an individual only if they are construed as threatening or dangerous by that individual. As demonstrated in a study of parachuters by psychologists Walter D. Fenz and Seymour Epstein, stress appraisals can change markedly over the course of exposure to a stressor, and patterns of stress arousal differ as a function of experience with the stressor. Fenz and Epstein found that fear levels of veteran jumpers (as evaluated by a self-report measure) were highest the morning before the jump, declined continuously up to the moment of the jump, and then increased slightly until after landing. Fear levels for novice jumpers, in contrast, increased up to a point shortly before the jump and then decreased continuously. For both groups, the peak of stress occurred during the anticipatory period rather than at the point of the greatest objective danger, the act of jumping.

## MEASURING STRESS

Stress reactions are measured in three broad ways: by means of self-report, through behavioral observations, and on the basis of physiological arousal. The self-report technique is the technique most commonly used by behavioral scientists to evaluate subjective stress levels. The State Anxiety Scale of the State-Trait Anxiety Inventory, developed by psychologist Charles Spielberger, is one of the most widely used self-report measures of stress. Examples of items on this scale are "I am tense," "I am worried," and "I feel pleasant." Subjects are instructed to respond to the items in terms of how they currently feel.

Self-report state anxiety scales may be administered and scored easily and quickly. Further, they may be administered repeatedly and still provide valid measures of momentary changes in stress levels. They have been criticized by some, however, because they are face valid (that is, their intent is clear); therefore, people who are motivated to disguise their stress levels can readily do so.

Overt behavioral measures of stress include both direct and indirect observational measures. Direct measures focus on behaviors associated with stress-related physiological arousal such as heavy breathing, tremors, and perspiration; self-manipulations such as nail biting, eyeblinks, and postural orientation; and body movement such as pacing.

Speech disturbances, both verbal (for example, repetitions, omissions, incomplete sentences, and slips of the tongue) and nonverbal (for example, pauses and hand movements), have been analyzed intensively, but no single measure or pattern has emerged as a reliable indicant of stress. Another way in which people commonly express fear reactions is by means of facial expressions. This area has been studied by psychologists Paul Ekman and Wallace V. Friesen, who concluded that the facial features that take on the most distinctive appearance during fear are the eyebrows (raised and drawn together), the eyes (open, lower lid tensed), and the lips (stretched back).

Indirect observational measures involve evaluating the degree to which people avoid feared objects. For example, in one test used by clinical psychologists to assess fear level, an individual is instructed to approach a feared stimulus (such as a snake) and engage in increasingly intimate interactions with it (for example, looking at a caged snake from a distance, approaching it, touching it, holding it). The rationale is that the higher the level of fear elicited, the earlier in the sequence the person will try to avoid the feared stimulus. Other examples include asking claustrophobics (people who are fearful of being in an enclosed space) to remain in a closed chamber as long as they can and asking acrophobics (people who fear heights) to climb a ladder and assessing their progress.

Physiological arousal is an integral component of the stress response. The most frequently monitored response systems are cardiovascular responses, electrodermal responses, and muscular tension. These measures are important in their own right as independent indicants of stress level, and in particular as possible indices of stress-related diseases.

## ULCERS AND LEARNED HELPLESSNESS

The concept of stress has been used to help explain the etiology of certain diseases. Diseases that are thought to be caused in part by exposure to stress or poor ability to cope with stress are called psychophysiological or psychosomatic disorders. Among the diseases that seem to have strong psychological components are ulcers and coronary heart disease. The role of stress in ulcers was highlighted in a study by Joseph V. Brady known as the "executive monkey" study. In this study, pairs of monkeys were yoked together in a restraining apparatus. The monkeys received identical treatment except that one member of each pair could anticipate whether both of them would be shocked (it was given a warning signal) and could control whether the shock was actually administered (if it pressed a lever, the shock was avoided). Thus, one monkey in each pair (the "executive monkey") had to make decisions constantly and was responsible for the welfare of both itself and its partner. Twelve pairs of monkeys were tested, and in every case the executive monkey died of peptic ulcers within weeks, while the passive member of each pair remained healthy. This experiment was criticized because of flaws in its experimental design, but it nevertheless brought much attention to the important role that chronic stress can play in the activation of physiological processes (in this case, the secretion of hydrochloric acid in the stomach in the absence of food) that can be damaging or even life threatening.

Although being in the position of a business executive who has to make decisions constantly can be very stressful, research indicates that it may be even more damaging to be exposed to stress over long periods and not have the opportunity to change or control the source of stress. People and animals who are in aversive situations over which they have little or no control for prolonged periods are said to experience learned helplessness. This concept was introduced by psychologist Martin E. P. Seligman and his colleagues. In controlled research with rats and dogs, he and his colleagues demonstrated that exposure to prolonged stress that cannot be controlled produces emotional, motivational, and cognitive deficits. The animals show signs of depression and withdrawal, they show little ability or desire to master their environment, and their problem-solving ability suffers.

Learned helplessness has also been observed in humans. Seligman refers to Bruno Bettelheim's descriptions of some of the inmates of the Nazi concentration camps during World War II, who, when faced with the incredible brutality and hopelessness of their situation, gave up and died without any apparent physical cause. Many institutionalized patients (for example, nursing home residents and the chronically ill) also live in environments that are stressful because they have little control over them. Seligman suggests that the stress levels of such patients can be lowered and their health improved if they are given as much control as possible over their everyday activities (such as choosing what they want for breakfast, the color of their curtains, and whether to sleep late or wake up early).

## STRESS AND CONTROL

Research findings have supported Seligman's suggestions. For example, psychologists Ellen Langer and Judith Rodin told a group of elderly nursing home residents that they could decide what they wanted their rooms to look like, when they wanted to go see motion pictures, and with whom they wanted to interact. A second, comparable group of elderly residents, who were randomly assigned to live on another floor, were told that the staff would care for them and try to keep them happy. It was found that the residents in the first group became more active and reported feeling happier than those in the second group. They also became more alert and involved in different kinds of activities, such as attending movies and socializing. Further, during the eighteen-month period following the intervention, 15 percent of the subjects in the first group died, whereas 30 percent of the subjects in the second group died.

Altering people's perception of control and predictability can also help them adjust to transitory stressful situations. Studies by psychologists Stephen Auerbach, Suzanne Miller, and others have shown that for people who prefer to deal with stress in active ways (rather than by avoiding the source of stress), adjustment to stressful surgical procedures and diagnostic examinations can be improved if they are provided with detailed information about the impending procedure. It is likely that the information enhances their sense of predictability and control in an otherwise minimally controllable situation. Others, who prefer to control their stress by "blunting" the stressor, show better adjustment when they are not given detailed information.

## REACTION TO STRESS

Physiologist Walter B. Cannon was among the first scientists to describe how people respond to stressful circumstances. When faced with a threat, one's body mobilizes for "fight or flight." One's heart rate increases, one begins to perspire, one's muscles tense, and one undergoes other physiological changes to prepare for action either to confront the stressor or to flee the situation.

Physician Hans Selye examined the fight-or-flight response in more detail by studying physiological changes in rats exposed to stress. He identified three stages of reaction to stress, which he collectively termed the general adaptation syndrome (GAS). This includes an initial alarm reaction, followed by a stage of resistance, and finally by a stage of exhaustion, which results from long-term unabated exposure to stress and produces irreversible physiological damage. Selye also brought attention to the idea that not only clearly aversive events (for example, the death of a spouse or a jail sentence) but also events that appear positive (for example, a promotion at work or meeting new friends) may be stressful because they involve changes to which people must adapt. Thus, these ostensibly positive events (which he called eustress) will produce the nonspecific physiological stress response just as obviously negative events (which he called distress) will.

How an individual cognitively appraises an event is the most important determinant of whether that event will be perceived as stressful by that person. Psychologist Richard Lazarus has delineated three important cognitive mechanisms (primary appraisals, secondary appraisals, and coping strategies) that determine perceptions of stressfulness and how people alter appraisals. Primary appraisal refers to an assessment of whether a situation is neutral, challenging, or potentially harmful. When a situation is judged to be harmful or threatening, a secondary appraisal is made of the coping options or maneuvers that the individual has at his or her disposal. Actual coping strategies that may be used are problem focused (those that involve altering the circumstances that are eliciting the stress response) or emotion focused (those that involve directly lowering physiological arousal or the cognitive determinants of the stress response). Psychologists have used concepts such as these to develop stress management procedures that help people control stress in their everyday lives.

## SOURCES FOR FURTHER STUDY

Goldberger, Leo, and Shlomo Breznitz, eds. *The Handbook of Stress: Theoretical and Clinical Aspects.* 2d ed. New York: Free Press, 1993. A wide-ranging collection of essays on the diagnosis and treatment of stress. A good starting point for investigating the field.

Greenberg, Jerrold S. *Comprehensive Stress Management.* 7th ed. New York: McGraw-Hill, 2001. An easy-to-read text giving an overview of psychological and physiological stress responses and stress-management techniques. Separate sections on applications to occupational stress, the college student, the family, and the elderly.

Janis, Irving Lester. *Psychological Stress.* 1958. Reprint. New York: Academic Press, 1974. Describes some of Janis's early investigations evaluating relationships between stress and behavior. The focus is on his pioneering study evaluating the relationship between preoperative stress levels in surgical patients and their ability to adapt to the rigors of the postoperative convalescent period.

Monat, Alan, and Richard S. Lazarus, eds. *Stress and Coping.* 2d ed. New York: Columbia University Press, 1985. This anthology consists of twenty-six brief readings under the headings of effects of stress, stress and the environment, coping with the stresses of living, coping with death and dying, and stress management.

Rabin, Bruce S. *Stress, Immune Function, and Health: The Connection.* New York: Wiley-Liss, 1999. A psychoneuroimmunological approach to the physiological effects of stress.

Sapolsky, Robert. *Why Zebras Don't Get Ulcers: An Updated Guide to Stress, Stress-Related Diseases, and Coping.* New York: W. H. Freeman, 1998. An entertaining comparison of the physiology of stress in humans and other mammals, written by a neuroscientist. Argues that the human nervous system evolved to cope with short-term stressors, and that stress-related diseases, such as heart disease and diabetes, are the result of living in an environment that produces long-term stress instead.

Silver, R. L., and C. Wortman. "Coping with Undesirable Life Events." In *Human Helplessness,* edited by Judy Garber and Martin E. P. Seligman. New York: Academic Press, 1980. Silver and Wortman examine the behavioral consequences of encountering and adjusting to cataclysmic stressful events such as a disabling accident, a serious illness, or the death of a loved one.

*Stephen M. Auerbach*

SEE ALSO: Stress: Physiological Responses; Stress-Related Diseases.

# STRESS
## BEHAVIORAL AND PSYCHOLOGICAL RESPONSES

TYPE OF PSYCHOLOGY: Stress
FIELDS OF STUDY: Coping; critical issues in stress; stress and illness

*Stress is an adaptive reaction to circumstances that are perceived as threatening. It motivates people and can enhance performance. Learning to cope with adversity is an important aspect of normal psychological development, but exposure to chronic stress can have severe negative consequences if effective coping mechanisms are not learned.*

KEY CONCEPTS
- circumplex model
- coping strategies
- daily hassles
- phobias
- state anxiety
- trait anxiety

The term "stress" is used to designate how human beings respond when they confront circumstances that they appraise as dangerous or threatening and that tax their coping capability. Stressful events (stressors) elicit a wide range of responses in humans. They not only bring about immediate physiological changes but also affect one's emotional state, the use of one's intellectual abilities and one's efficiency at solving problems, and one's social behavior. When experiencing stress, people take steps to do something about the stressors eliciting the stress and to manage the emotional upset they are producing. These maneuvers are called coping responses. Coping is a key concept in the study of the stress process. Stress-management intervention techniques are designed to teach people the appropriate ways to cope with the stressors that they encounter in their everyday lives.

### ANXIETY AND PHOBIAS

The emotional state most directly affected by stress is anxiety. In fact, the term "state anxiety" is often used interchangeably with the terms "fear" and "stress" to denote a transitory emotional reaction to a dangerous situation. Stress, fear, and state anxiety are distinguished from trait anxiety, which is conceptualized as a relatively stable personality disposition or trait. According to psychologist Charles Spielberger, people high in trait or "chronic" anxiety interpret more situations as dangerous or threatening than do people who are low in trait anxiety, and they respond to them with more intense stress (state anxiety) reactions. Instruments that measure trait anxiety ask people to characterize how they usually feel, and thus they measure how people characteristically respond to situations. Measures of trait anxiety (such as the trait anxiety scale of the State-Trait Anxiety Inventory) are especially useful in predicting whether people will experience high levels of stress in situations involving threats to self-esteem or threat of failure at evaluative tasks.

The recently developed two-dimensional circumplex model (see the figure "Circumplex Model") has been adopted as a model for illustrating how emotion relates to stress. The activation-deactivation dimension of the circumplex relates to how much the emotion invokes a sense of alertness, energy, and mobilization, in contrast to the deactivation end of the continuum that connotes drowsiness and lethargy. The second dimension of the circumplex relates to the degree of pleasantness/unpleasantness associated with the emotion. For example, perceived stress and anxiety relate to unpleasant activation. In contrast, serenity is associated with deactivation and positive affect. Richard Lazarus has argued that the relational meaning of a stressful event determines the particular emotion associated with the event. For example, the relational meaning of anger is "a demeaning offense against me and mine." The relational meaning of anxiety is "facing an uncertain or existential threat." The relational meaning of fright is "facing an immediate, concrete, and overwhelming physical danger." Coping alters the emotion by either changing reality (problem-focused coping) or changing the interpretation of the event (emotion-focused coping).

Common phobias or fears of specific situations, however, especially when the perceived threat has a strong physical component, are not related to individual differences in general trait anxiety level. Measures of general trait anxiety are therefore not good predictors of people's stress levels when they are confronted by snakes, an impending surgical operation, or the threat of electric shock. Such fears can be reliably predicted only by scales designed to evaluate proneness to experience fear in these particular situations.

Seemingly minor events that are a constant source of irritation can be very stressful, as can more focalized events that require major and sometimes sudden readjustments. Psychologists Richard Lazarus and Susan Folkman have dubbed these minor events "daily hassles." The media focus attention on disasters such as plane crashes, earthquakes, and epidemics that suddenly disrupt the lives of many people, or on particularly gruesome crimes or other occurrences that are likely to attract attention. For most people, however, much of the stress of daily life results from having to deal with ongoing problems pertaining to jobs, interpersonal relationships, and everyday living circumstances.

Often, people have no actual experience of harm or unpleasantness regarding things that they come to fear. For example, many people are at least somewhat uneasy about flying on airplanes or about the prospect of having a nuclear power plant located near them, though few people have personally experienced harm caused by these things. Although people tend to pride themselves on how logical they are, they are often not very rational in appraising how dangerous or risky different events actually are. For example, there is great public concern about the safety of nuclear reactors, though they have, in fact, caused few deaths.

## POSITIVE STRESS

People tend to think of stress as being uniformly negative—something to be avoided or at least minimized as much as possible. Psychologists Carolyn Aldwin and Daniel Stokols point out, however, that studies using both animals and humans have indicated that exposure to stress also has beneficial effects. Being handled by humans is stressful for rats, but rats handled as infants are less fearful, are more exploratory, are faster learners, and have more robust immune systems later in life. In humans, physical stature as adults is greater in cultures that expose children to stress (for example, circumcision, scarification, sleeping apart from parents) than in those that are careful to prevent stress exposure—even when nutrition, climate, and other relevant variables are taken into account. Although failure experiences in dealing with stressful circumstances can inhibit future ability to function under stress, success experiences enable learning of important coping and problem-solving skills that are then used to deal effectively with future stressful encounters. Such success experiences also promote a positive self-concept and induce a generalized sense of self-efficacy that, in turn, enhances persistence in coping with future stressors.

Psychologists Stephen Auerbach and Sandra Gramling note that stress is a normal, adaptive reaction to threat. It signals danger and motivates people to take defensive action. Over time, individuals learn which coping strategies are successful for them in particular situations. This is part of the normal process of mental growth and maturation.

Stress can, however, cause psychological problems if the demands posed by stressors overwhelm a person's coping capabilities. If a sense of being overwhelmed and unable to control events persists over a period of time, one's stress signaling system ceases to work in an adaptive way. One misreads and overinterprets the actual degree of threat posed by situations, makes poor decisions as to what coping strategies to use, and realizes that one is coping inefficiently. A cycle of increasing distress and ineffective coping may result. Some people who have experienced high-level stress for extended periods or who are attempting to deal with the aftereffects of traumatic stressors may become extremely socially withdrawn and show other signs of severe emotional dysfunction.

In severe cases where these symptoms persist for over a month, a psychological condition known as post-traumatic stress disorder (PTSD) may develop. Common symptoms of PTSD include reliving the traumatic event, avoiding anything that reminds the person of the event, insomnia, nightmares, wariness, poor concentration, chronic irritability resulting in angry or aggressive outbursts, and a numbing of emotions. The symptom of numbing of emotions has been referred to as alexithymia, a condition in which the person lacks the ability to define and express their emotions to themselves and others. James Pennebaker believes that although alexithymics cannot express their emotions, these emotions are still present in an unconscious cycle of rumination; this suppression and rumination of negative thoughts is associated with increased psychological and physiological arousal. That is, it takes a lot of work to inhibit one's emotions.

Although anxiety is the most common emotion associated with stress, chronic stress may induce chronic negative emotions such as hostility and depression. Chronic hostility and depression have been shown to have damaging effects on social relationships and physical health. The known physical costs of chronic stress include poor immune functioning, not engaging in health-promoting activities (such as exercise and following the advice of a physician), and a shortened life expectancy.

When people are faced with a stressful circumstance that overwhelms their coping mechanisms, they may react with depression and a sense of defeat and hopelessness. According to Martin Seligman, learned helplessness is the result of a person coming to believe that events are uncontrollable or hopeless, and it often results in depression.

### ASSESSING AND MEASURING STRESS

The fact that stress has both positive and negative effects can be exemplified in many ways. Interpersonally, stress brings out the "worst" and the "best" in people. A greater incidence of negative social behaviors, including less altruism and cooperation and more aggression, has generally been observed in stressful circumstances. Psychologist Kent Bailey points out that, in addition to any learning influences, this may result from the fact that stress signals real or imagined threats to survival and is therefore a potent elicitor of regressive, self-serving survival behaviors. The highly publicized murder of Kitty Genovese in Queens, New York, in 1964, which was witnessed by thirty-eight people (from the safety of their apartments) who ignored her pleas for help, exemplifies this tendency. So does the behavior during World War II of many Europeans who were aware of the oppression of Jews and other minorities by the Nazis but who turned their heads. Everyone has heard, however, of selfless acts of individual heroism being performed by seemingly ordinary people who in emergency situations rose to the occasion and risked their own lives to save others. After the terrorist attacks on the World Trade Center on September 11, 2001, firefighters continued to help victims and fight fires after more than two hundred of their fellow firefighters had been killed in the buildings' collapse. In addition, in stressful circumstances in which cooperation and altruism have survival value for all concerned, as in the wake of a natural disaster, helping-oriented activities and resource sharing are among the most common short-term reactions.

Stress may enhance as well as hinder performance. For example, the classic view of the relationship between stress and performance is represented in the Yerkes-Dodson inverted-U model, which posits that both low and high levels of arousal decrease performance, whereas intermediate levels en-

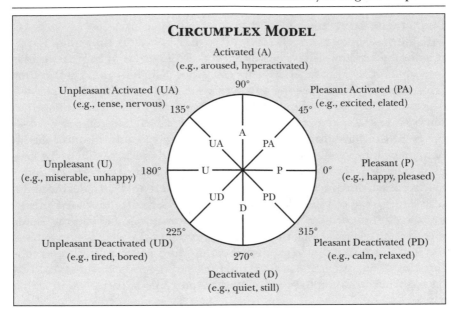

## CIRCUMPLEX MODEL

Activated (A)
(e.g., aroused, hyperactivated)

Unpleasant Activated (UA)
(e.g., tense, nervous)

Pleasant Activated (PA)
(e.g., excited, elated)

Unpleasant (U)
(e.g., miserable, unhappy)

Pleasant (P)
(e.g., happy, pleased)

Unpleasant Deactivated (UD)
(e.g., tired, bored)

Pleasant Deactivated (PD)
(e.g., calm, relaxed)

Deactivated (D)
(e.g., quiet, still)

hance performance. Although this model has not been unequivocally validated, it seems to be at least partially correct, and its correctness may depend upon the circumstances. On one hand, psychologists Gary Evans and Sheldon Cohen concluded that, in learning and performance tasks, high levels of stress result in reduced levels of working-memory capacity and clearly interfere with performance of tasks that require rapid detection, sustained attention, or attention to multiple sources of input. On the other hand, psychologist Charles Spielberger found that in less complex tasks, as learning progresses, high stress levels may facilitate performance.

Psychologist Irving Janis examined the relationship between preoperative stress in surgical patients and how well they coped with the rigors of the postoperative convalescent period. He found that patients with moderate preoperative fear levels adjusted better after surgery than those with low or high preoperative fear. He reasoned that patients with moderate fear levels realistically appraised the situation, determined how they would deal with the stressful aspects of the recovery period, and thus were better able to tolerate those stressors. Patients low in preoperative fear engaged in unrealistic denial and thus were unprepared for the demands of the postoperative period, whereas those high in preoperative fear became overanxious and carried their inappropriately high stress levels over into the recovery period, in which that stress continued to inhibit them from realistically dealing with the demands of the situation. Janis further found that giving people information about what to expect before the surgery reduced their levels of fear and stress and allowed them to recover from surgery more quickly.

## BENEFITS OF CONTROL

Janis's investigation was particularly influential because it drew attention to the question of how psychologists can work with people to help them cope with impending stressful events, especially those (such as surgery) that they are committed to confronting and over which they have little control.

Research by Judith Rodin and others has shown that interventions designed to increase the predictability of and perceived control over a stressful event can have dramatic effects on stress and health. In one control-enhancing intervention study, nursing home residents were told by the hospital administrator to take responsibility for themselves, were asked to decide what activities in which to participate, and were told what decisions for which they were responsible. Patients who received the control-enhancing intervention reported being happier in the nursing home, and the death rate was half of that among nursing home residents who were told that it was the staff's responsibility to care for them. Rodin's research has been replicated by other researchers. More intensive stress reduction interventions have even been shown to increase survival rates among patients with breast cancer.

Findings by psychologists Thomas Strentz and Stephen Auerbach indicate that in such situations it may be more useful to teach people emotion-focused coping strategies (those designed to minimize stress and physiological arousal directly) than problem-focused strategies (those designed to change the stressful situation itself). In a study with volunteers who were abducted and held hostage for four days in a stressful simulation, they found that hostages who were taught to use emotion-focused coping techniques (such as deep breathing, muscular relaxation, and directed fantasy) adjusted better and experienced lower stress levels than those who were taught problem-focused techniques (such as nonverbal communication, how to interact with captors, and how to gather intelligence).

Finally, in a series of studies, Pennebaker and others have found that writing for just twenty minutes a day for three or four consecutive days about the most stressful experience one has ever experienced has widespread beneficial effects that may last for several months. In a series of studies, he found that his writing task improved immune functioning, reduced illness and perceived stress, and even improved students' grade point averages. He believes that his writing task may help people to release their inhibited emotions about past stressful events. This release of emotions decreases physiological arousal and psychological anxiety associated with repressing negative past events.

## ADAPTIVE AND MALADAPTIVE FUNCTIONS

Stress has many important adaptive functions. The experience of stress and learning how to cope with adversity is an essential aspect of normal growth and development. Coping strategies learned in particular situations must be generalized appropriately to new situations. Exposure to chronic stress that cannot be coped with effectively can have severe negative consequences. Work by pioneering stress researchers such as Hans Selye brought attention to the physiological changes produced by exposure to chronic stress, which contribute to diseases such as peptic ulcers, high blood pressure, and cardiovascular disorders. Subsequent research by psychiatrists Thomas Holmes and Richard Rahe and their colleagues indicated that exposure to a relatively large number of stressful life events is associated with the onset of other diseases, such as cancer and psychiatric disorders, which are less directly a function of arousal in specific physiological systems.

Studies by these researchers have led psychologists to try to understand how best to teach people to manage and cope with stress. Learning to cope with stress is a complex matter because, as Lazarus has emphasized, the stressfulness of given events is determined by how they are cognitively appraised, and this can vary considerably among individuals. Further, the source of stress may be in the past, the present, or the future. The prospect of an impending threatening encounter (such as a school exam) may evoke high-level stress, but people also experience stress when reflecting on past unpleasant or humiliating experiences or when dealing with an immediate, ongoing danger. Sometimes people deal with past, present, and future stressors simultaneously.

It is important to distinguish among present, past, and future stressors, because psychological and behavioral responses to them differ, and different kinds of coping strategies are effective in dealing with them. For example, for stressors that may never occur but are so aversive that people want to avoid them if at all possible (for example, cancer or injury in an automobile crash), people engage in preventive coping behavior (they stop smoking or they wear seat belts) even though they are not currently experiencing a high level of anxiety. In this kind of situation, an individual's anxiety level sometimes needs to be heightened in order to motivate coping behavior.

When known stressors are about to affect one (for example, a surgical operation the next morning), it is important for one to moderate one's anxiety level so that one can function effectively when actually confronting the stressor. The situation is much different when one is trying to deal with a significant stressor (such as sexual assault, death of a loved one, or a war experience) that has already occurred but continues to cause emotional distress. Important aspects of coping with such stressors include conceptualizing one's response to the situation as normal and rational rather than "crazy" or inadequate, and reinstating the belief that one is in control of one's life and environment rather than subject to the whims of circumstance.

## SOURCES FOR FURTHER STUDY

Auerbach, Stephen M. "Assumptions of Crisis Theory and Temporal Model of Crisis Intervention." In *Crisis Intervention with Children and Families*, edited by Stephen M. Auerbach and Arnold L. Stolberg. Washington, D.C.: Hemisphere, 1986. This chapter examines some basic issues pertaining to psychological responses to extremely stressful events, including the role of the passage of time, individual differences, and previous success in dealing with stressful events. Crisis intervention and other stress-management programs are also reviewed.

_____. "Temporal Factors in Stress and Coping: Intervention Implications." In *Personal Coping: Theory, Research, and Application,* edited by B. N. Carpenter. Westport, Conn.: Praeger, 1992. Focuses on how behavioral and psychological stress responses differ depending on whether the stressor is anticipated, is currently ongoing, or has already occurred. The types of coping strategies that are likely to be most effective for each kind of stressor are described, and many examples are given.

Davis, Martha, Elizabeth Eshelman, and Matthew McKay. *The Relaxation and Stress Reduction Workbook.* 5th ed. Oakland, Calif.: New Harbinger, 2000. An overview of techniques used to reduce stress. Sections include body awareness, progressive relaxation, visualization, biofeedback, coping skills training, job stress management, and assertiveness training.

Janis, Irving Lester. *Stress and Frustration.* New York: Harcourt Brace Jovanovich, 1971. Describes some of Janis's early investigations evaluating relationships between stress and behavior. The focus is on his pioneering study evaluating the relationship between preoperative stress levels in surgical patients and their ability to adapt to the rigors of the postoperative convalescent period.

Lazarus, Richard S. "From Psychological Stress to the Emotions: A History of Changing Outlooks." *Annual Review of Psychology* 44 (1993): 1-21. Discusses the history of the study and treatment of stress. Discusses his recent research that has involved the cognitive-mediational approach to the appraisal and coping processes that cause stress.

Miller, Todd, et al. "A Meta-analytic Review of Research on Hostility and Physical Health." *Psychological Bulletin* 119, no. 2 (1996): 322-348. Reviews more than sixty studies on hostility and health to show that cynical people have shorter life spans. In addition, those who display signs of anger are at increased risk for heart disease.

Pennebaker, James W. *Opening Up: The Healing Power of Expressing Emotions.* Rev. ed. New York: Guilford Press, 1997. Presents evidence that personal self-disclosure not only benefits emotional health but also boosts physical health. Explains how writing about problems can improve one's physical and psychological health.

Rodin, Judith, and Christine Timko. "Control, Aging and Health." In *Aging, Health, and Behavior,* edited by Marcia Ory, Ronald Abeles, and Paula Lipman. Newbury Park, Calif.: Sage, 1992. Reviews research on the relationship among stress and health.

Russell, James A., and Lisa F. Barrett. "Core Affect, Prototypical Emotional Episodes, and Other Things Called Emotion: Dissecting the Elephant." *Journal of Personality and Social Psychology* 76 (1999): 805-819. This article discusses the validation of the circumplex model of emotion.

Silver, R. L., and C. Wortman. "Coping with Undesirable Life Events." In *Human Helplessness*, edited by Judy Garber and Martin E. P. Seligman. New York: Academic Press, 1980. The authors examine the behavioral consequences of encountering and adjusting to cataclysmic stressful events such as a disabling accident, a serious illness, or the death of a loved one. They review different theoretical formulations of reactions to stressful events and examine whether people's actual emotional and behavioral reactions are consistent with theories. They emphasize social support, the ability to find meaning in the outcome of the event, and experience with other stressors as important factors that determine how well people adjust.

*Stephen M. Auerbach; updated by Todd Miller*

SEE ALSO: Stress-Related Diseases.

# STRESS
## PHYSIOLOGICAL RESPONSES

TYPE OF PSYCHOLOGY: Stress
FIELDS OF STUDY: Biology of stress; critical issues in stress; stress and illness

*The human body contains a number of regulatory mechanisms that allow it to adapt to changing conditions. Stressful events produce characteristic physiological changes that are meant to enhance the likelihood of survival. Because these changes sometimes present a threat to health rather than serving a protective function, researchers seek to determine relationships among stressors, their physiological effects, and subsequent health.*

KEY CONCEPTS
- fight-or-flight response
- general adaptation syndrome
- homeostasis
- parasympathetic nervous system
- stress response
- stressor
- sympathetic nervous system

Although the term "stress" is commonly used (if not overused) to refer to various responses to events that individuals find taxing, the concept involves much more. For centuries, scientific thinkers and philosophers have been interested in learning about the interactions among the environment (stressful events), the emotions, and the body. Much is now known about this interaction, although there is still more left to discover. In the late twentieth century, particularly, much has been learned about how stressful events affect the activity of the body (or physiology). For example, it has been established that these physiological responses to stressors sometimes increase one's vulnerability to a number of diseases. In order to understand the body's response to stressful events (or stressors), the general sequence of events and the specific responses of various organ systems must be considered.

Almost all bodily responses are mediated, at least partially, by the central nervous system: the brain and spinal cord. The brain takes in and analyzes information from the external environment as well as from the internal environment (the rest of the body), and it regulates the body's activities to optimize adaptation or survival. When the brain detects a threat, a sequence of events occurs to prepare the body to fight or to flee the threat. Walter B. Cannon, in the early twentieth century, was the first to describe this "fight-or-flight" response It is characterized by generalized physiological activation. Heart rate, blood pressure, and respiration increase to enhance the amount of oxygen available to the tissues. The distribution of blood flow changes to optimize efficiency of the tissues most needed to fight or flee: Blood flow to the muscles, brain, and skin increases, while it decreases in the stomach and other organs less important for immediate survival. Increased sweating and muscle tension help regulate the body's temperature and enhance movement if action is needed. Levels of blood glucose and insulin increase to provide added energy sources, and immune function is depressed. Brain activity increases, resulting in enhanced sensitivity to incoming information and faster reactions to this information.

Taken together, these physiological changes serve to protect the organism and to prepare it to take action to survive threat. They occur quite rapidly and are controlled by the brain through a series of neurological and hormonal events. When the brain detects a threat (or stressor), it sends its activating message to the rest of the body through two primary channels, the sympathetic nervous system (SNS) and the pituitary-adrenal axis. The SNS is a branch of the nervous system that has multiple, diffuse neural connections to the rest of the body. It relays activating messages to the heart, liver, muscles, and other organs that produce the physiological changes already described. The sympathetic nervous system also stimulates the adrenal gland to secrete two hormones, epinephrine and norepinephrine (formerly called adrenaline and noradrenaline), into the bloodstream. Epinephrine and norepinephrine further activate the heart, blood vessels, lungs, sweat glands, and other tissues.

Also, the brain sends an activating message through its hypothalamus to the pituitary gland, at the base of the brain. This message causes the pituitary to release hormones into the bloodstream that circulate to the peripheral tissues and activate them. The primary "stress" hormone that the pituitary gland releases is adrenocorticotropic hormone (ACTH), which in turn acts upon the adrenal gland to cause the release of the hormone cortisol. The actions of cortisol on other organs cause increases in blood glucose and insulin, among many other reactions.

In addition to isolating primary stress mechanisms, research has demonstrated that the body secretes naturally occurring opiates—endorphins and enkephalins—in response to stress. Receptors for these opiates are found throughout the body and brain. Although their function is not entirely clear, some research suggests that they serve to buffer the effects of stressful events by counteracting the effects of the SNS and stress hormones.

## GENERAL ADAPTATION SYNDROME

One can see that the human body contains a very sophisticated series of mechanisms that have evolved to enhance survival. When stressors and the subsequent physiological changes that are adaptive in the short run are chronic, however, they may produce long-term health risks. This idea was first discussed in detail in the mid-twentieth century by physiologist Hans Selye, who coined the term "general adaptation syndrome" to describe the body's physiological responses to stressors and the mechanisms by which these responses might result in disease.

Selye's general adaptation syndrome involves three stages of physiological response: alarm, resistance, and exhaustion. During the alarm stage, the organism detects a stressor and responds with SNS and hormonal activation. The second stage, resistance, is characterized by the body's efforts to neutralize the effects of the stressor. Such attempts are meant to return the body to a state of homeostasis, or balance. (The concept of homeostasis, or the tendency of the body to seek to achieve an optimal, adaptive level of activity, was developed earlier by Walter Cannon.) Finally, if the resistance stage is prolonged, exhaustion occurs, which can result in illness. Selye referred to such illnesses as diseases of adaptation. In this category of diseases, he included hypertension, cardiovascular disease, kidney disease, peptic ulcer, hyperthyroidism, and asthma.

Selye's general adaptation syndrome has received considerable attention as a useful framework within which to study the effects of stressors on health, but there are several problems with his theory. First, it assumes that all stressors produce characteristic, widespread physiological changes that differ only in intensity and duration. There is compelling evidence, however, that different types of stressors can produce very different patterns of neural and hormonal responses. For example, some stressors produce increases in heart rate, while others can actually cause heart rate deceleration. Thus, Selye's assumption of a nonspecific stress response must be questioned.

Also, Selye's theory does not take into account individual differences in the pattern of response to threat. Research during the later twentieth century demonstrated that there is considerable variability across individuals in their physiological responses to identical stressors. Such differences may result from genetic or environmental influences. For example, some studies have demonstrated that normotensive offspring of hypertensive parents are more cardiovascularly responsive to brief stressors than individuals with normotensive parents. Although one might conclude that the genes responsible for hypertension have been passed on from the hypertensive parents, these children might also have different socialization or learning histories that contribute to their exaggerated cardiovascular reactivity to stressors. Whatever the mechanism, this research highlights the point that individuals vary in the degree to which they respond to stress and in the degree to which any one organ system responds.

## STRESS AND ILLNESS

Coinciding with the scientific community's growing acknowledgment that stressful events have direct physiological effects, much interest has developed in understanding the relations between these events and the development or maintenance of specific diseases. Probably the greatest amount of research has focused on the link between stress and heart disease, the primary cause of death in the United States. Much empirical work also has focused on gastrointestinal disorders, diabetes, and pain (for example, headache and arthritis). Researchers are beginning to understand the links between stress and immune function. Such work has implications for the study of infectious disease (such as flu and mononucleosis), cancer, and acquired immunodeficiency syndrome (AIDS).

Several types of research paradigms have been employed to study the effects of stressors on health and illness. Longitudinal studies have identified a number of environmental stressors that contribute to the development or exacerbation of disease. For example, one study of more than four thousand residents of Alameda County, California, spanning two decades, showed that a number of environmental stressors such as social isolation were significant predictors of mortality from all causes. Other longitudinal investigations have linked stressful contexts such as loud noise, crowding, and low socioeconomic status with the onset or exacerbation of disease.

A major drawback of such longitudinal research is that no clear conclusions can be made about the exact mechanism or mechanisms by which the stressor had its impact on health. Although it is possible, in the Alameda County study, that the relationship between social isolation and disease was mediated by the SNS/hormonal mechanisms already discussed, individuals who are isolated also may be less likely to engage in behaviors such as eating healthy diets, exercising, and maintaining preventive health care. Thus, other research paradigms have been used to try to clarify the causal mechanisms by which stressors may influence particular diseases. For example, laboratory stress procedures are used by many scientists to investigate the influence of brief, standardized stressors on physiology. This type of research has the advantage of being more easily controlled. That is, the researcher can manipulate one or a small number of variables (for example, noise) in the laboratory and measure the physiological effects. These effects are then thought to mimic the physiological effects of such a variable in the natural environment.

This research primarily is conducted to ask basic questions about the relations between stressors, physiology, and subsequent health. The findings also have implications, however, for prevention and intervention. If a particular stressor is identified that increases risk of a particular disease, prevention efforts could be developed to target the populations exposed to this stressor. Prevention strategies might involve modifying the stressor, teaching people ways to manage more effectively their responses to it, or both.

During the last two or three decades of teh twentieth century, applied researchers attempted to develop intervention strategies aimed at controlling the body's physiological responses to stress. This work has suggested that a number of stress management strategies can actually attenuate physiological responsivity. Most strategies teach the individual some form of relaxation (such as deep muscle relaxation, biofeedback, hypnosis, or meditation), and most of this work has focused on populations already diagnosed with a stress-related disease, such as hypertension, diabetes, or ulcer. The tech-

*In biofeedback therapy, patients monitor their own physiological responses, such as blood pressure or heart rate.* (Hans & Cassidy, Inc.)

niques are thought to produce their effects by two possible mechanisms: lowering basal physiological activation (or changing the level at which homeostasis is achieved) or providing a strategy for more effectively responding to acute stressors to attenuate their physiological effects. Research has not proceeded far enough to make any statements about the relative importance of these mechanisms. Indeed, it is not clear whether either mechanism is active in many of the successful intervention studies. While research does indicate that relaxation strategies often improve symptoms of stress-related illnesses, the causal mechanisms of such techniques remain to be clarified.

## THE MIND-BODY CONNECTION

The notion that the mind and body are connected has been considered since the time of ancient Greece. Hippocrates described four bodily humors (fluids) that he associated with differing behavioral and psychological characteristics. Thus, the road was paved for scientific thinkers to consider the interrelations among environment, psychological state, and physiological state (that is, health and illness). Such considerations developed most rapidly in the twentieth century, when advancements in scientific methodology permitted a more rigorous examination of the relationships among these variables.

In the early twentieth century, as noted already, Cannon was the first to document and discuss the "fight or flight response" to threatening events. He also reasoned that the response was adaptive, unless prolonged or repeated. In the 1940's, two physicians published observations consistent with Cannon's of an ulcer patient who had a gastric fistula, enabling the doctors to observe directly the contents of the stomach. They reported that stomach acids and bleeding increased when the patient was anxious or angry, thus documenting the relations between stress, emotion, and physiology. Shortly after this work was published, Selye began reporting his experiments on the effects of cold and fatigue on the physiology of rats. These physical stressors produced enlarged adrenal glands, small thymus and lymph glands (involved in immune system functioning), and increased ulcer formation.

Psychiatrists took this information, along with the writings of Sigmund Freud, to mean that certain disease states might be associated with particular personality types. Efforts to demonstrate the relationship between specific personality types and physical disease endpoints culminated in the development of a field known as psychosomatic medicine. Research, however, does not support the basic tenet of this field, that a given disease is linked with specific personality traits. Thus, psychosomatic medicine has not received much support from the scientific community. The work of clinicians and researchers in psychosomatic medicine paved the way for late twentieth century conceptualizations of the relations between stress and physiology. Most important, biopsychosocial models that view the individual's health status in the context of the interaction between his or her biological vulnerability, psychological characteristics, and socio-occupational environment have been developed for a number of physical diseases.

Future research into individual differences in stress responses will further clarify the mechanisms by which stress exerts its effects on physiology. Once these mechanisms are identified, intervention strategies for use with patients or for prevention programs for at-risk individuals can be identified and implemented. Clarification of the role of the endogenous opiates in the stress response, for example, represents an important dimension in developing new strategies to enhance individual coping with stressors. Further investigation of the influence of stressors on immune function should open new doors for prevention and intervention, as well.

Much remains to be learned about why individuals differ in their responses to stress. Research in this area will seek to determine the influence of genes, environment, and behavior on the individual, elucidating the important differences between stress-tolerant and stress-intolerant individuals. Such work will provide a better understanding of the basic mechanisms by which stressors have their effects and should lead to exciting new prevention and intervention strategies that will enhance health and improve the quality of life.

## SOURCES FOR FURTHER STUDY

Craig, Kenneth D., and Stephen M. Weiss, eds. *Health Enhancement, Disease Prevention, and Early Intervention: Biobehavioral Perspectives.* New York: Springer, 1990. Includes, among other chapters of interest, an excellent chapter by Neal Miller (the "father of biofeedback") on how the brain affects the health of the body.

Feist, Jess, and Linda Brannon. *Health Psychology: An Introduction to Behavior and Health.* 5th ed. Belmont, Calif.: Thomson/Wadsworth, 2004. Written for undergraduate students. A very readable overview of the field of health psychology. Provides the reader with chapters on stress and health, and various stress-related diseases.

Fuller, M. G., and V. L. Goetsch. "Stress and Stress Management." In *Behavior and Medicine*, edited by Danny Wedding. 3d ed. Seattle: Hogrefe & Huber, 2001. Provides an overview of the field, focusing particularly on the physiological response to stress.

Jacobson, Edmund. *You Must Relax*. New York: McGraw-Hill, 1934. A rare classic which may be available in the special collections section of the library. Jacobson is considered the father of modern relaxation training. This book is worth seeking for the pictures of Jacobson's patients after undergoing his relaxation procedure as well as for Jacobson's thoughtful insights.

Ornstein, Robert, and D. S. Sobel. "The Brain as a Health Maintenance Organization." In *The Healing Brain: A Scientific Reader*, edited by Robert Ornstein and Charles Swencionis. New York: Guilford Press, 1990. Discusses the body's responses to stressors from an evolutionary perspective.

Selye, Hans. *The Stress of Life*. 2d ed. New York: McGraw-Hill, 1978. First published in 1956. A thoroughly readable account of Selye's work and thinking about stress and health. Available at most bookstores, a must for those interested in learning more about stress.

*Virginia L. Goetsch and Kevin T. Larkin*

SEE ALSO: Emotions; Endocrine System; Nervous System; Psychosomatic Disorders; Stress: Behavioral and Psychological Responses; Stress-Related Diseases.

# STRESS-RELATED DISEASES

TYPE OF PSYCHOLOGY: Stress
FIELD OF STUDY: Stress and illness

*As a person undergoes stress, physical responses occur that have been associated with a host of physical diseases. Understanding the stress-disease relationship, including how to control and lower stress levels, is important in maintaining a healthy life.*

KEY CONCEPTS
- biofeedback
- endorphin
- general adaptation syndrome
- locus of control
- psychoneuroimmunology
- relaxation response
- stressor
- Type A personality
- Type B personality

The term "stress," as it is used in the field of psychology, may be defined as the physical or psychological disturbance an individual experiences as a result of what he or she perceives to be an adverse or challenging circumstance. Four observations concerning this definition of stress should be made. First, stress is what the individual experiences, not the circumstance causing the stress (the stressor). Second, individuals differ in what they perceive to be stressful. What may be very stressful for one may not be at all stressful for another. Hans Selye, the researcher who did more than anyone else to make the medical community and the general public aware of the concept and consequences of stress, once noted that, for him, spending the day on the beach doing nothing would be extremely stressful. This difference in people's perceptions is behind the familiar concept that events do not cause stress. Instead, stress comes from one's perception or interpretation of events.

Third, stress occurs in response to circumstances that are seen as negative, but stress may also arise from challenging circumstances, even positive ones. The well-known Social Readjustment Rating Scale developed by Thomas Holmes and Richard Rahe includes both positive and negative life events. A negative event, such as the death of a spouse, is clearly stressful; however, marriage, generally viewed as a positive life event, can also be stressful. Fourth, stressors can lead to stress-related disturbances that are psychological, physiological, or both. The psychological response is rather unpredictable. A given stressor may result in one individual responding with anger, another with depression, and another with a new determination to succeed.

## GENERAL ADAPTATION SYNDROME

The physiological response is more predictable. Beginning in the 1930's, Selye began studying the human response to stressors. Eventually he identified what he termed the general adaptation syndrome (GAS) to describe the typical pattern of physical responses. Selye divided the GAS into three stages: alarm, resistance, and exhaustion.

The first stage begins when an individual becomes frightened, anxious, or even merely concerned. The body immediately undergoes numerous physical changes to cope with the stressor. Metabolism speeds up. Heart and respiration rates increase. The hormones epinephrine, norepinephrine, and cortisol are secreted. Sugar is released from the liver. The muscles tense. Blood shifts from the internal organs to the skeletal musculature. These and a host of other changes are aimed at helping the body cope, but the price paid for this heightened state of arousal typically includes symptoms such as headache, upset stomach, sleeplessness, fatigue, diarrhea, and loss of appetite. The body's increase in alertness and energy is accompanied by a lowered state of resistance to illness.

Obviously, people cannot remain in the alarm stage for long. If the stressor is not removed, the body enters the resistance stage—a stage which may last from minutes to days or longer. During this stage, the body seeks to adapt to the stressor. The physical changes that occurred during the alarm stage subside. Resistance to illness is actually increased to above-normal levels. Because the body is still experiencing stress, however, remaining in this stage for a long period will eventually lead to physical and psychological exhaustion—the exhaustion stage.

Selye has noted that over the course of life, most people go through the first two stages many, many times. Such is necessary to adapt to the demands and challenges of life. The real danger is found in not eliminating the stressor. During the exhaustion stage, the body is very vulnerable to disease and in extreme cases may suffer collapse or death. Although newer research has found subtle differences in the stress response, depending on the stressor involved, the basic findings of Selye have continued to be supported. In addition to the direct physiological effects of stress on the body, indirect effects may also lead to illness. For example, stress may cause or exacerbate behavioral risk factors such as smoking, alcohol use, and overeating.

## HEART DISEASE AND IMMUNE EFFECTS

Specific illnesses can also be caused or exacerbated by stress. For many years Americans have been aware of the relationship between stress and heart disease. The biochemical changes associated with stress lead to higher blood pressure, an increased heart rate, and a release of fat into the bloodstream. If the fat is completely consumed by the muscles through physical activity (for example, defending oneself from an attacker), no serious health consequences follow. If, however, a person experiences stress without engaging in physical activity (a more common scenario in Western culture), the fat is simply deposited on the walls of the blood vessels. As these fatty deposits accumulate, life is threatened.

The work of two cardiologists, Meyer Friedman and Ray Rosenman, is of particular importance to a discussion of heart disease and stress. Friedman and Rosenman demonstrated, based originally on personal observation and subsequently on clinical research, that there is a personality type that is particularly prone to heart disease. The personality type that is at the greatest risk was found to be one which is highly stressed—impatient, hostile, hard-driving, and competitive. They termed this a Type A personality. The low-risk person, the Type B personality, is more patient, easygoing, and relaxed.

Numerous studies have examined health based on the Type A-Type B concept. Virtually all have supported Friedman and Rosenman's conclusions. One major report, however, did not; subsequent analysis of that report and other research generally has indicated that the aspects of the Type A personality which are threatening to one's health are primarily the hostility, cynicism, and impatience, not the desire to achieve.

A newer area of research that is even more fundamental to understanding how stress is related to disease involves the immune system. As the physiological changes associated with stress occur, the immune system is suppressed. The immune system has two primary functions: to identify and destroy hazardous foreign materials called antigens (these include bacteria, viruses, parasites, and fungi) and to identify and destroy the body's own cells

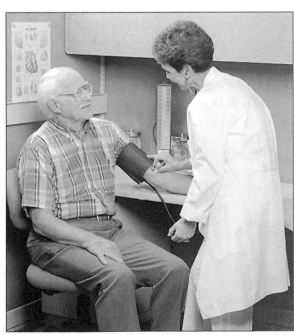

*Physiological changes produced by exposure to chronic stress can contribute to conditions such as high blood pressure, peptic ulcers, and cardiovascular disease.*
(Digital Stock)

that have undergone changes associated with malignancy. Thus, if the immune system is suppressed, the body is less able to detect and defend against a host of diseases. An example of this effect again involves research with laboratory rats. One such investigation involved placing tumor cells in the bodies of rats. Some of the rats were then exposed to an abundance of stress. Those that were given this treatment were less resistant to the cancer. Their tumors were larger, and they developed sooner than those found in the "low-stress" rats.

The recent growth of the field of psychoneuroimmunology focuses specifically on the chemical bases of communication between mind and body. Research in this area provides evidence that the body's immune system can be influenced by psychological factors which produce stress. One study, for example, showed that during students' examination periods, the levels of students' antibodies that fight infections were lowest. Thus they were most vulnerable to illness at that most stressful time. Health centers confirm that students tend to report more illness during examination times.

As research continues, the number of specific diseases that can be linked to stress grows. Stress-related diseases and disorders for which recent research is available include acne, asthma, cancers (many types), colds, coronary thrombosis, diabetes mellitus, gastric ulcers, herpes simplex (types 1 and 2), human immunodeficiency virus (HIV) infection, hyperlipidemia, hypertension, infertility, irritable bowel syndrome, migraine headache, mononucleosis syndrome, rheumatoid arthritis, streptococcal infection, stroke, systemic lupus erythematosus, and tuberculosis.

Research has shown that stress may also play a role in depression, sleep disturbances, ovulation, and brain atrophy associated with Alzheimer's disease. Stress as a cause of stomach ulcers has been essentially negated, with the discovery that these ulcers are generally caused by the bacterium *Helicobacter pylori*, which can be treated with antibiotics. However, stress may still play a role in decreasing the mucous lining of the stomach, which makes it more vulnerable to ulcer formation. Some experts feel that there is no illness that is not in some way influenced by stress.

It should be emphasized that few, if any, of these physical problems are caused solely by stress. Many other factors influence risk, including genetic composition, gender, race, environmental conditions, nutritional state, and so forth. Nevertheless, stress is frequently an important factor in determining initial resistance as well as the subsequent course of a given disease.

## STRESS REDUCTION AND COPING

Why is it that some individuals who appear to live with many stressors generally avoid physical and psychological illness? This question is important because the answer can provide insight as to what the average person can and should do to lower stress levels. Dispositional factors (optimistic versus pessimistic, easygoing versus hard-driving, friendly versus hostile) are probably most important in determining one's stress level. The Type A-Type B research noted above is an example of research demonstrating the influence of dispositional factors.

Research with twins has found that temperament is largely inborn; however, any individual can choose to be more optimistic, generous, and patient. Norman Cousins is often cited as an example of a person who decided to change his outlook and mental state in order to preserve his life. He had read Selye's *The Stress of Life* (1956), which describes how negative emotions can cause physical stress and subsequent disease. Cousins, who had a rare and painful illness from which he was told he would likely never recover, decided that if negative emotions could harm one's health, then positive emotions could possibly return one's health.

As Cousins describes his experience in *Anatomy of an Illness as Perceived by the Patient* (1979), he left his hospital room for a more pleasant environment, began taking massive doses of vitamin C instead of massive doses of drugs, and decided to stop worrying. To the surprise of his medical team, his recovery began at once. Though this now-classic example is merely anecdotal, the research on disposition and stress would support the assumption that Cousins's decision to change his mental state and stop worrying—not his avoidance of traditional medical care—was a truly important influence.

A related area of research has investigated how psychological hardiness helps people resist stress. Studies by Suzanne Kobasa and her colleagues examined business executives who all had an obvious abundance of stressors in their lives. In comparing those hardy individuals who handled the stressors well with the nonhardy individuals, the researchers found that the two groups differed in three important but basic ways.

The first was commitment. Stress-resistant executives typically possessed a clear sense of values. They had clear goals and a commitment to those goals. Less hardy executives were more likely to feel alienation. The second was challenge. The hardy executives welcomed challenges and viewed change rather than stability as the norm in life. Their less healthy counterparts viewed change with alarm. The third factor was control. The hardy executives felt more in control of their lives. This aspect of Kobasa's research overlaps with research conducted since the 1960's involving a concept known as the "locus of control." People with an internal locus of control are those individuals who believe they are influential rather than powerless in controlling the direction of their lives. This area of research has also found that such a belief lowers stress.

Many years ago it was estimated that more than a thousand studies had been completed that examined the relationship between physical fitness and mental health. What has emerged from this heavily researched area is a clear conclusion: Exercise can lower stress levels. Though regular, sustained aerobic exercise is generally advocated, research has found that even something as simple as a daily ten-minute walk can have measurable beneficial effects. During exercise, there is a release of chemical substances, including neurotransmitters called endorphins. Endorphins act to decrease pain and produce feelings of well-being, somewhat like an opiate. Exposure to stress has been shown to increase the level of endorphins in the body. For example, studies were conducted with runners, one group using naloxone, a substance which blocks effects of opiates, and the other group a placebo which had no effect on the body. After strenuous runs, those taking the placebo reported feelings of euphoria, sometimes known as "runners' high." Those taking naloxone reported no such feelings. Other chemicals are released during exercise as well and include dopamine, which is thought to act as an antidepressant. Thus there is abundant evidence of the stress-reducing benefits of exercise.

Another approach to reducing stress involves learning to evoke a physical "relaxation response," a term coined by Harvard Medical School cardiologist Herbert Benson. Benson became intrigued by the ability of some people who practice meditation to lower their blood pressure, heart rate, and oxygen consumption voluntarily. He discovered that the process is not at all mystical and can be easily taught. The process involves getting comfortable, closing the eyes, breathing deeply, relaxing muscles, and relaxing one's mind by focusing on a simple word or phrase.

Others are helped by using an electronic device which closely monitors subtle physiological changes. By observing these changes (typically on a monitor), a person can, for example, learn to slow down a heart rate. This is known as biofeedback training. Many other techniques and suggestions arising from research as well as common sense can lower stress. A strong social support system has been found to be very important; disciplining oneself not to violate one's own value system is essential. Even having a pet that needs love and attention has been found to lower stress.

## RESEARCH AND THE FUTURE

A general recognition that a relationship exists between mind and body is at least as old as the biblical Old Testament writings. In the book of Proverbs, for example, one reads, "A cheerful heart is good medicine,/ but a crushed spirit dries up the bones" (Proverbs 17:22). Hippocrates (460-377 B.C.E.), generally considered the "father of medicine," sought to understand how the body could heal itself and what factors could slow or prevent this process. He clearly perceived a relationship between physical health and what is now termed "stress," though his understanding was shallow.

Several physiologists of the nineteenth century made contributions; however, it was not until the twentieth century that the classic studies of American physiologist Walter B. Cannon proved the link scientifically. Cannon and his student Phillip Bard began their analysis of stress and physiological arousal to disprove the idea espoused by others, that emotion follows physiological arousal.

Cannon found a variety of stressors that led to the release of the hormones adrenaline and noradrenaline (or, properly now, epinephrine and norepinephrine). Heat, cold, oxygen deprivation, and fright all led to hormonal changes as well as a number of additional physiological adaptations. Cannon was excited about this discovery and impressed with the body's remarkable ability to react to stressors. All these changes were aimed at preparing the body for what Cannon termed the "fight-or-flight" response. It was Selye's task to build on Cannon's work. His description of the reaction subsequently termed the general adaptation syndrome first appeared in a scientific journal in 1936. As knowledge of the stress concept began to spread, interest by the public as well as the research community increased.

Literally tens of thousands of stress research studies conducted throughout the world were completed during the last half of the twentieth century. Of particular importance was the discovery by three American scientists that the brain produces morphinelike antistress substances. The discovery of these substances, named endorphins, won a 1977 Nobel Prize for the scientists involved and opened a whole new area of research.

Research has shown that the brain itself produces neuropeptides, or brain message transmitters, which may also be produced by macrophages—white blood cells that attack viruses and bacteria. Because some forms of stress-reduction, such as relaxation, also seem to result in production of neuropeptides, if the brain could be caused to produce more of these substances, the immune system could be strengthened. The hope remains that someday an endorphin-type drug could be used to counter some of the unhealthy effects of stress, ensuring better health and longer lives. Better health and longer lives are available even today, however, for all people who are willing to make lifestyle changes based on current knowledge.

**BIBLIOGRAPHY**

Benson, Herbert, and Eileen Stuart. *The Wellness Book*. New York: Simon & Schuster, 1992. Written by a physician and author of *The Relaxation Response*, a nurse, and associates of the Mind/Body Medical Institute of the New England Deaconess Hospital and Harvard Medical School, this is a self-help book on stress-related illness, very informative about mind-body interactions and the role of stress in illness.

Brown, Barbara B. *Between Health and Illness*. Boston: Houghton Mifflin, 1984. One of many books available for the nonprofessional who simply wants an overview of stress and its consequences. This easy-to-read book is full of accurate information and practical suggestions.

Greenberg, Jerrold S. *Comprehensive Stress Management*. 6th ed. New York: WCB/McGraw-Hill, 1999. This is an excellent source which includes numerous self-tests, explains the scientific foundations of stress, and offers methods and techniques used to reduce stress in a variety of life situations. Written in an introductory yet comprehensive textbook format, this book is informative and easy to read.

Leonard, Brian, and Klara Miller, eds. *Stress, the Immune System, and Psychiatry*. New York: John Wiley & Sons, 1995. This book contains difficult reading, with detailed studies from the field of psychoneuroimmunology. The focus is on the immune system as related to various aspects of stress, including discussions of depressive illness, schizophrenia, multiple sclerosis, and food allergies.

*Managing Stress: From Morning to Evening.* Alexandria, Va.: Time-Life Books, 1987. A good introduction to understanding and managing stress. Written in clear, simple language and widely available, it provides an overview of the sources of stress, the physiological changes associated with stress, the effects of stress on the immune system, a way to assess one's own stress level, and suggestions for numerous approaches to managing stress. Full of illustrations and photographs. A weakness is that the book fails to address adequately the importance of dispositional factors, focusing too heavily on some stress-reduction techniques that few are likely to use.

Pelletier, Kenneth R. *Mind as Healer, Mind as Slayer.* New York: Dell Books, 1977. This well-known work examines how stress contributes to heart disease, cancer, arthritis, migraine, and respiratory disease. Sources of stress, evaluation of personal stress levels, profiles of unhealthy personality traits, and means of preventing stress-related diseases are addressed.

Selye, Hans. *The Stress of Life.* Rev. ed. New York: McGraw-Hill, 1976. Originally published in 1956, this is the most influential book ever written about stress. It focuses on the relationship between a stressful life and subsequent illness, but it is very technical. Those wanting a less difficult introduction to Selye's writings and work should read his *Stress Without Distress.*

Wedding, Danny, ed. *Behavior and Medicine.* 3d ed. Seattle: Hogrefe & Huber, 2001. This is a large volume which covers an extensive area of behavior and medicine, with a strong focus on stress, although it covers much additional territory. In addition to stress-related issues, including substance abuse, stress management, pain, placebos, AIDS, cardiovascular risk, and adherence to medical regimens, sections include assessment of patients, foundations of behavioral science, love and work, and developmental issues from infancy to death, dying and grief. The style is quite readable and combines illustrations, relevant poetry, bibliographies, summaries, and study questions at the end of each article.

*Timothy S. Rampey; updated by Martha Oehmke Loustaunau*

SEE ALSO: Endocrine System; Nervous System; Stress: Behavioral and Psychological Responses; Stress: Physiological Responses.

# STRUCTURALISM AND FUNCTIONALISM

DATE: 1879-1913
TYPE OF PSYCHOLOGY: Origin and definition of psychology
FIELDS OF STUDY: General constructs and issues; thought

*Structualism and functionalism represent early schools of thought in psychology. While the structuralists were devoted to discovering the elements of consciousness, the functionalists believed that psychology should focus on understanding how consciousness is useful or functional.*

KEY CONCEPTS
- applied psychology
- evolution
- imageless thought
- introspection
- stimulus error
- stream of consciousness
- voluntarism

Structuralism and functionalism were two of the earliest schools of thought in psychology. To understand these early perspectives, it is important to consider the sociohistorical context in which they developed. Psychology as an independent scientific discipline was founded in 1879 by German scholar Wilhelm Wundt (1832-1920) at the University of Leipzig. Wundt was a medically trained physiologist appointed to the department of philosophy at Leipzig. In 1879, he established the first-ever laboratory devoted solely to the experimental study of psychological issues. The German *Zeitgeist* was conducive to this development. For example, the education reform movement encouraged the development of university research and promoted academic freedom. Furthermore, German scholars at the time accepted a broader definition of science compared to their counterparts in many other European countries.

Wundt defined psychology as the scientific study of conscious experience and organized it into two broad areas: experimental psychology (the study of sensation and perception, reaction time, attention, and feelings) and *Völkerpsychologie* (cultural psychology, which included the study of language, myth, and custom). Wundt made an important distinction between immediate and mediate experiences. Mediate experiences involve an interpretation of sensory input ("I see an apple"), whereas an immediate experience consists of pure and unbiased sensory experiences ("I see a roundish, red object"). Wundt emphasized the process of organizing and synthesizing the elemental components of consciousness (the immediate experiences) into higher-level thoughts. Because this process of apperception was considered to be an act of will or volition, he often referred to his system as voluntarism.

One of Wundt's students, Edward Bradford Titchener (1867-1927), an Englishman who earned his Ph.D. under Wundt in 1892, ascended to prominence by establishing the structural school of thought in psychology as a professor at Cornell University. Functionalism soon arose as a school of thought that opposed structuralism.

Titchener, it should be noted, considered structuralism to be a refined extension of, and largely compatible with, Wundt's work. Because Titchener was the main translator of Wundt's work into English and was widely considered to be a loyal and accurate representative of Wundt's system, the term "structuralism" at the time was used as a label for both Titchener's and Wundt's work. This interpretative error, which is still propagated in some textbooks, was not fully realized until the mid-1970's, when scholars started to examine Wundt's original work in detail. There are some important differences between Titchener's structuralism and Wundt's system of voluntarism. First, Titchener rejected the idea of a branch of cultural psychology. Second, structural psychology neglected the study of apperception and focused almost exclusively on the identification of the elements of consciousness. Finally, in a structuralist framework, the elements of consciousness themselves were of utmost importance; mediate and immediate experiences were considered the same event, viewed from different vantage points. There was no need for a volitional process.

## STRUCTURALISM

For Titchener, psychology was the study of consciousness. Whereas physics was said to be concerned with assessing environmental events from an objective, external standard, psychology was concerned with examining how humans experience such events subjectively. For example, an hour spent listening to a boring speech and an hour spent playing an enjoyable game last exactly the same length of time—3,600 seconds—but, psychologically, the second event goes by more quickly.

In structuralism, consciousness is defined as the sum total of experiences at any given moment, and the mind is defined as the sum of experiences over the course of a lifetime. In order to understand consciousness and thus the mind, psychology, according to structuralism, must be concerned with three primary questions: First, what are the most basic elements of consciousness? Just as chemists break down physical substances into their elemental components, psychologists should identify the basic components of consciousness. Second, how are the elements associated with one another? That is, in what ways do they combine to produce complex experiences? Third, according to Titchener, what underlying physiological conditions are associated with the elements? Most of Titchener's work was devoted to the first goal of identifying the basic elements of consciousness. The primary methodology used toward this end was systematic experimental introspection.

## INTROSPECTION

A primary goal for structuralism was to identify the basic elements of consciousness. Titchener reasoned that any science requires an observation of its subject matter, and psychology was no different. As detailed in Titchener's classic work *Experimental Psychology: A Manual of Laboratory Practice* (4 vols., 1901-1905), introspection involved the systematic analysis and reporting of conscious experiences by highly trained researchers. Such individuals were trained to report on the most basic of sensory experiences and to avoid the stimulus error of reporting perceptual interpretations. For example, to report seeing "an apple" or having "a headache" would be a stimulus error. It would be more accurate, psychologically, to report seeing a "roundish, red object" or experiencing a "throbbing sensation of moderate intensity in the lower right part of the head." This methodology was used by Wundt, but Wundt emphasized quantitative judgments (such as size, weight, duration, or intensity), whereas in Titchener's system, descriptive reports were emphasized.

Titchener concluded that there were three basic elements of consciousness: sensations, images, and feelings. Sensations were the most fundamental and were the building blocks of all perceptions. In his *An Outline of Psychology* (1896), Titchener listed more than forty-four thousand elementary sensations, including approximately thirty-two thousand visual, twelve thousand auditory, and four taste sensations. It was held that these indivisible sensations could be combined in any number of ways to produce unique perceptions and ideas. Images are the building blocks for ideas and reflect previous sensory experiences. It is possible to have an image of an apple only because of past experiences with a particular combination of sensations. All feelings were viewed as reducible to experiencing a degree of pleasantness or unpleasantness. (In contrast, Wundt postulated two other dimensions: strain/relaxation and excitement/calmness.) A feeling, when combined with certain sensations, can give rise to a complex emotional state, such as love, joy, disgust, or fear.

Later in his career, Titchener asserted that each element of consciousness could be characterized with regard to five basic dimensions: quality, intensity, protensity (duration), attensity (clearness), and extensity (space). Quality refers to the differentiation of sensations (an apple may be red or green; the water may be hot or cold). Intensity refers to the strength or magnitude of the quality (the extent to which the apple is red or the water is cold). Protensity refers to the duration or length of a sensory experience. Attensity refers to the clarity or vividness of the experience and reflects the process of attention (sensations are clearer when they are the focus of attention). Some sensations, especially visual and tactile ones, can also be characterized in terms of extensity (that is, they take up a certain amount of space). Feelings were characterized only in terms of quality, intensity, and protensity. Titchener believed that feelings dissipated when they were the subject of focused attention and therefore could not be experienced with great clarity.

## EVALUATION

Structuralism faded away after Titchener's death in 1927. However, the basic tenets of structuralism had been under attack for years. First, there were serious problems with introspection as a scientific methodology. The results of such studies were frequently unreliable, and there was no way of objectively verifying the content of someone's consciousness. The controversy over imageless thought was important. One group of researchers, most notably a former follower of Wundt, Oswald Külpe (1862-1915), at the University of Würzburg, concluded, using introspection methodology, that some thoughts occurred in the absence of any mentalistic sensations or images. This was completely at odds with structuralism, and researchers loyal to the structuralist position were not able to replicate the findings. On the other hand, researchers sympathetic to the Würzburg school were able to replicate the findings. Obviously, a theoretical bias was driving the results. It was widely concluded that introspection was lacking the objectivity needed to sustain a scientific discipline. Other methodologies were discouraged by structuralists, in part because of the limited scope of psychology they practiced. In essence, structural psychology was limited to the study of the elements of consciousness in the healthy adult human. There was no place for the use of nonhuman animals as subjects, no child psychology, and no concern with the psychology of physical or mental illness. In addition, Titchener was against applied research, that is, conducting research to help resolve practical problems. He felt that this would detract from the objectivity of the study, and that academic researchers should be devoted to advancement of pure knowledge. Finally, structuralism was criticized for focusing almost exclusively on the elements of consciousness without taking into serious consideration the idea that consciousness is experienced as a unified whole, and that this whole is different from the sum of the elements.

Today, two major contributions of structuralism are recognized. The first is the strong emphasis that Titchener and his followers placed on rigorous laboratory research as the basis for psychology. While other methods are used by modern psychologists (such as case studies and field research), the emphasis on experimentation in practice and training remains dominant. Second, structuralism provided a well-defined school of thought and set of ideas that others could debate and oppose, with the ultimate result being the development of new and different schools of thought. The most prominent opposition to structuralism was functionalism.

## FUNCTIONALISM

Unlike structuralism, functionalism was not a formal school of psychological thought. Rather, it was a label (originally used by Titchener) applied to a general set of assumptions regarding the providence of psychology and a loosely connected set of principles regarding the psychology of consciousness. In many respects, functionalism was defined in terms of its opposition or contrast to structuralism. For example, functionalists believed that psychology should focus on the functions of mental life (in contrast to the structuralist focus on elemental components); be concerned with using psychology for practical solutions to problems (structuralists were, at best, indifferent to this concern); study not only healthy adult humans (the main focus of attention of structuralists) but also nonhuman animals, children, and nonhealthy individuals; employ a wide range of methodologies to investigate psychological issues (structuralists relied almost totally on introspection); and examine individual differences, rather than being solely concerned, like the structuralists, with the establishment of universal (nomothetic) principles.

While structuralism was imported to the United States by a British scholar (Titchener) who received his psychological training in Germany (under Wundt), functionalism had a distinctly American flair. The American *Zeitgeist* at the time emphasized pragmatism and individuality. Such qualities made American psychologists especially receptive to the revolutionary work of Charles Darwin (1809-1882) on evolution and its subsequent application (as "social Darwinism") by anthropologist Herbert Spencer (1820-1903) to education, business, government, and other social institutions. Other important developments that influenced functionalism include work by Sir Francis Galton (1822-1911) on individual differences in mental abilities and the work on animal psychology by George Romanes (1848-1894) and C. Lloyd Morgan (1852-1936).

## WILLIAM JAMES

William James (1842-1910) is considered the most important direct precursor of functional psychology in the United States and one of the most eminent psychologists ever to have lived. James earned his M.D. from Harvard University in 1869 and subsequently became keenly interested in psychology. Despite his severe bouts with depression and other ailments, he accepted a post at Harvard in 1872 to teach physiology. Shortly thereafter, in 1875, James taught the first psychology course offered in the United States, "The Relations Between Physiology and Psychology," and initiated a classroom demonstration laboratory.

James published the two-volume *The Principles of Psychology* in 1890. This work was immediately a great success and is now widely regarded as the most important text in the history of modern psychology. Given the expansiveness of *Principles*—more than thirteen hundred pages arranged in twenty-eight chapters—it is impossible to summarize fully, but it includes such topics as the scope of psychology, functions of the brain, habit, methods of psychology, memory, the consciousness of self, sensation, perception, reasoning, instinct, emotions, will, and hypnotism. In this text James presented ideas that became central to functionalism. For example, in the chapter "The Stream of Consciousness," he criticized the postulate of structural psychology that sensations constitute the simplest mental elements and must therefore be the major focus of psychological inquiry. In contrast, James argued that conscious thought is experienced as a flowing and continuous stream, not as a collection of frozen elements. In critiquing introspection, the methodology championed by the structuralists, James asserted,

> The rush of the thought is so headlong that it almost always brings us up at the conclusion before we can arrest it. . . . The attempt at introspective analysis in these cases is in fact like seizing a spinning top to catch its motion, or trying to turn up the gas quickly enough to see how darkness looks.

With this new, expansive conceptualization of consciousness, James helped pave the way for psychologists interested in broadening the scope and methods of psychology. What was to emerge was the school of functionalism, with prominent camps at the University of Chicago and Columbia University.

### THE CHICAGO SCHOOL

The Chicago school of functionalism is represented by the works of American scholars John Dewey (1859-1952), James Rowland Angell (1869-1949), and Harvey A. Carr (1873-1954). Functionalism was launched in 1896 with Dewy's *Psychological Review* article, "The Reflex Arc Concept in Psychology." Here Dewey argued against reducing reflexive behaviors to discontinuous elements of sensory stimuli, neural activity, and motor responses. In the same way that James attacked elementalism and reductionism in the analysis of consciousness, Dewey argued that it was inaccurate and artificial to do so with behavior. Influenced by Darwin's evolutionary theory of natural selection, Dewey asserted that reflexes should not be analyzed in terms of their component parts but rather in terms of how they are functional for the organism; that is, how they help an organism adapt to the environment.

Angell crystalized the functional school in his 1907 *Psychological Review* paper, "The Province of Functional Psychology." In this work, three characteristics of functionalism were identified: Functional psychology is interested in discerning and portraying the typical operations of consciousness under actual life conditions, as opposed to analyzing and describing the elementary units of consciousness. Functional psychology is concerned with discovering the basic utilities of consciousness, that is, how mental processes help organisms adapt their surroundings and survive. Finally, functional psychology recognizes and insists upon the essential significance of the mind-body relationship for any just and comprehensive appreciation of mental life itself.

Carr's 1925 textbook *Psychology: A Study of Mental Activity* presents the most polished version of functionalism. As the title suggests, Carr identified such processes as memory, perception, feelings, imagination, judgment, and will as the topics for psychology. Such psychological processes were considered functional in that they help organisms gain information about the world, retain and organize that information, and then retrieve the information to make judgments about how to react to current situations. In other words, these processes were viewed as useful to organisms as they adapt their environments.

## THE COLUMBIA SCHOOL

Another major camp of functionalism was at Columbia University and included such notable psychologists as James McKeen Cattell (1860-1944), Robert Sessions Woodworth (1869-1962), and Edward Lee Thorndike (1874-1949).

In line with the functionalist's embrace of applied psychology and the study of individual differences, Cattell laid the foundation for the psychological testing movement that would become massive in the 1920's and beyond. Under the influence of Galton, Cattell stressed the statistical analysis of large data sets and the measurement of mental abilities. He developed the order of merit methodology, in which participants rank-order a set of stimuli (for instance, the relative appeal of pictures or the relative eminence of a group of scientists) from which average ranks are calculated.

Woodworth is best known for his emphasis on motivation in what he called dynamic psychology. In this system, Woodworth acknowledged the importance of considering environmental stimuli and overt responses but emphasized the necessity of understanding the organism (perceptions, needs, or desires), representing therefore an early stimulis-organism-response (S-O-R) approach to psychology.

Thorndike represented a bridge from functionalism to behaviorism, a new school of thought that was led by John Broadus Watson (1878-1958) and emerged around 1913. Thorndike was notable for his use of nonhuman subjects, a position consistent with Darwin's emphasis on the continuity among organisms. He is also famous for his puzzle box research with cats, which led to his Law of Effect, which states that when an association is followed by a satisfying state of affairs, that association is strengthened. This early operant conditioning research was later expanded on by the famous behaviorist psychologist B. F. Skinner (1904-1990).

## EVALUATION

Functionalism paved the way for the development of applied psychology, including psychological testing, clinical psychology, school psychology, and industrial and organizational psychology. Functionalism also facilitated the use of psychological research with a wide variety of subjects beyond the healthy adult male, including infants, children, the mentally ill, and nonhuman animals. Finally, functional psychologists used a wide variety of methods beyond that of introspection, including field studies, questionnaires, mental tests, and behavioral observations. These developments were responsible, in part, for the United States becoming the world center for psychological study by 1920. The term "functional psychology" faded from usage as it became clear that, by default, being simply a psychologist in the United States meant being a functional psychologist. The shift in psychological thought instigated by functionalism set the stage for the next major evolutionary phase in American psychology, behaviorism.

### SOURCES FOR FURTHER STUDY

Behnamin, Ludy T., Jr. "The Psychology Laboratory at the Turn of the Twentieth Century." *American Psychologist* 55 (2000): 318-321. This is a nontechnical and brief introduction to laboratory research in psychology from 1879 to 1900. The author discusses the importance of the laboratory for establishing psychology as a scientific discipline separate from philosophy.

Boring, E. G. *A History of Experimental Psychology.* 2d ed. New York: Appleton-Century-Crofts, 1950. This is the classic text on the history of psychology, written by one of Edward Titchener's students. The first edition of 1925 is also widely available.

Donnelly, M. E. *Reinterpreting the Legacy of William James.* Washington, D.C.: American Psychological Association, 1992. This book explores how James's masterwork might have been revised in light of his later pluralistic, pragmatic approach to psychology and philosophy. A distinguished group of psychologists, philosophers, and historians contribute twenty-three chapters that probe this and other questions in a broad-based collection focused on the relevance of the works of James.

Hergenhahn, B. R. *An Introduction to the History of Psychology.* 4th ed. Belmont, Calif.: Wadsworth/Thomson Learning, 2001. Another excellent standard textbook on the history of psychology. Written for college students; includes in-depth chapters on structuralism and functionalism.

Leys, R., and R. B. Evans. *Defining American Psychology: The Correspondence Between Adolf Meyer and Edward Bradford Titchener.* Baltimore: Johns Hopkins University Press, 1990. Adolf Meyer was a highly influential psychiatrist who exchanged a series of letters with Titchener in 1909 and again in 1918. This book represents an interesting firsthand look at how the new science of psychology was being discussed and situated among other disciplines.

Shultz, D. P., and S. E. Shultz. *A History of Modern Psychology.* 7th ed. Fort Worth, Tex.: Harcourt College, 1999. A clear, well-organized history of modern psychology, placing schools of thought within their social contexts.

Watson, R. I., and R. B. Evans. *The Great Psychologists: A History of Psychological Thought.* 5th ed. New York: HarperCollins, 1991. Psychologists and schools of psychology from ancient Greek times to the present. Chapters 19 and 20 specifically focus on structuralism and functionalism.

*Jay W. Jackson*

SEE ALSO: Behaviorism; Madness: Historical Concepts; Psychoanalytic Psychology; Psychology: Definition.

# Substance Use Disorders

Type of psychology: Biological bases of behavior; motivation; psychopathology; stress
Fields of study: Biological treatments; coping; critical issues in stress; motivation theory; nervous system; stress and illness; substance abuse

*Substance use disorders include the formal medical diagnoses of substance abuse and substance dependence for many types of drugs of abuse, including alcohol and prescription drugs. These disorders are characterized by recurrent problems in everyday life or physical or emotional distress and impairment that are caused or exacerbated by the use of the substances of abuse.*

Key concepts
- hallucinogens
- inhalants
- opioids
- psychological dependence
- sedatives/hypnotics
- self-medication
- stimulants
- tolerance
- withdrawal

Substance use is studied in psychology from personality, social, and biological perspectives. Social and personality studies of individuals with substance use disorders have produced a variety of theories. These theories have focused on issues such as difficulties people might have with tolerating stress, being unable to delay gratification, developing social skills, being socially isolated or marginalized, being attracted to taking risks, and having difficulties regulating one's own behavior. Additionally, environmental issues, such as poverty or high levels of stress, have been linked to substance use problems. Biological theories of these disorders suggest that genetic and conditioned sensitivities to substances of abuse and their effects may predispose individuals to acquire these disorders. For instance, people who have increased needs to seek relief from pain or have an increased need to seek pleasure or euphoria might be at greater risk for developing such problems. Pain is broadly defined as any feeling of dysphoria. Because both pain and euphoria can be produced by psychosomatic or somatopsychic events, these two biological categories can subsume most of the stated nonbiological correlates of substance abuse.

There are several forms of substance use disorders including abuse and dependence. These should be contrasted to normal experimentation, normal use without problems, and limited instances of misuse that are more appropriately attributed to situational factors than an underlying psychiatric disorder.

There are several types of substances of abuse, and some of these are not typically viewed as problematic. Major categories include alcohol; sedatives/hypnotics; nicotine; marijuana; opioids, such as heroin; stimulants, including amphetamines, cocaine, crack, and caffeine; inhalants, such as glue, paint, nitrous oxide (laughing gas), and shoe polish; hallucinogens, including phencyclidine (PCP or "angel dust"), LSD ("acid"), MDMA (an amphetamine-like drug with hallucinogenic effects, also known as X or ecstasy); anabolic steroids; and even some types of prescription drugs, such as Valium.

When diagnoses are given for substance use disorders, diagnoses should be given in terms of a specific type of substance. A diagnosis of "substance abuse" would be too general because it does not specify the substance causing the problem. Having problems with one substance does not automatically mean that a person has problems with all substances. Thus, any diagnosis for a substance use disorder should be substance-specific; examples might include alcohol abuse, inhalant abuse, marijuana dependence, marijuana abuse, cocaine dependence, or stimulant abuse.

For the substance abuse category, the key features of the disorder are patterns of repeated problems in individual functioning in terms of roles at work, school, or home; legal status; use of the substance in hazardous situations, or the consequences of the use on interpersonal relationships. For the substance dependence category, the key features of the disorder are patterns of repeated problems in several areas that are distinct from those considered for abuse. Diagnosis of dependence relies on factors such as tolerance, withdrawal, new or worsened physical or emotional problems directly resulting from the use of the substance, loss of control over the use of the substance, unsuccessful efforts to cut down or quit coupled with intense desire to quit, excessive periods of time spent obtaining, using, or recovering from using the substance, and the displacement of social or occupational activities in order to use the substance.

### PAIN AND EUPHORIA

The experience of pain or the seeking of euphoria as causes of substance use disorders can be measured physically or can be perceived by the individual without obvious physical indicators. The relative importance of pain and euphoria in determining the development and maintenance of substance use disorders requires consideration of the contributions of at least five potential sources of behavioral and physical status: genetic predisposition, dysregulation during development, dysregulation from trauma at any time during the life span, the environment, and learning. Any of these can result in or interact to produce the pain or feelings of euphoria that can lead to substance use disorders.

The key commonality in pain-induced substance use disorders is that the organism experiences pain that it does not tolerate. Genetic predisposers of pain include inherited diseases and conditions that interfere with normal pain tolerance. Developmental dysregulations include physical and behavioral arrests and related differences from developmental norms. Trauma from physical injury or from environmental conditions can also result in the experience of pain, as can the learning of a pain-producing response.

Several theories of pain-induced substance use disorders can be summarized as self-medication theories. In essence, these state that individuals misuse substances in order to correct an underlying disorder that presumably produces some form of physical or emotional distress or discomfort. Self-medication theories are useful because they take into account the homeostatic (tendency toward balance) nature of the organism and because they include the potential for significant individual differences in problems with pain.

Relief from pain by itself does not account entirely for drug use that goes beyond improvement in health or reachievement of normal status and certainly cannot account entirely for drug use that becomes physically self-destructive. Thus, the use of substances to achieve positive effects such as euphoria or pleasure are also important to consider as causes of these disorders. Associative conditioning and operant conditioning effects play an important role as well. This type of substance misuse can be distinguished from the relief caused by substance use to decrease pain because the substance use does not stop when such relief is achieved but continues until the person experiences the pleasurable effects.

Euphoria-inducing substance use, or pleasure seeking, is characteristic of virtually all species tested. Some theorists have proposed that pleasure seeking is an innate drive not easily kept in check even by socially acceptable substitutes. Other theorists believe that these types of substance use disorders related to the positively reinforcing aspects of the substances may have developed as a function of biological causes such as evolutionary pressure and selection. For example, organisms that could eat rotten, fermented fruit (composed partly of alcohol) may have survived to reproduce when others did not; people who could tolerate or preferred drinking alcohol instead of contaminated water reproduced when those who drank contaminated water did not live to do so.

## SUBSTANCE USE DISORDER RESEARCH

Laboratory studies of the biological bases of substance abuse and dependence involve clinical (human) and preclinical (animal) approaches. Such research has demonstrated that there are areas of the brain that can provide powerful feelings of euphoria when stimulated, indicating that the brain is primed for the experience of pleasure. Direct electrical stimulation of some areas of the brain, including an area first referred to as the medial forebrain bundle, produced such strong addictive behaviors in animals that they ignored many basic drives including those for food, water, mating, and care of offspring.

Later research showed that the brain also contains highly addictive analgesic and euphoriant chemicals that exist as a normal part of the neural milieu. Thus, the brain is also predisposed to aid in providing relief from pain

## DSM-IV-TR Criteria for Dependence and Abuse

### Substance Dependence

Maladaptive pattern of substance use, leading to clinically significant impairment or distress

Manifested by three or more of the following, occurring at any time in the same twelve-month period

Tolerance, as defined by either:
- need for markedly increased amounts of substance to achieve intoxication or desired effect
- markedly diminished effect with continued use of same amount of substance

Withdrawal, as manifested by either:
- characteristic withdrawal syndrome for substance
- same (or closely related) substance taken to relieve or avoid withdrawal symptoms

Substance often taken in larger amounts or over longer period than intended

Persistent desire or unsuccessful efforts to cut down or control substance use

Great deal of time spent in activities necessary to obtain substance, use substance, or recover from its effects

Important social, occupational, or recreational activities given up or reduced because of substance use

Substance use continues despite knowledge of persistent or recurrent physical or psychological problem likely to have been caused or exacerbated by substance

Specify if with Physiological Dependence (evidence of tolerance or withdrawal) or Without Physiological Dependence (no evidence of tolerance or withdrawal)

Course specifiers: Early Full Remission; Early Partial Remission; Sustained Full Remission; Sustained Partial Remission; on Agonist Therapy; in a Controlled Environment

### Substance Abuse

Maladaptive pattern of substance use leading to clinically significant impairment or distress

Manifested by one or more of the following, occurring within a twelve-month period:
- recurrent substance use resulting in failure to fulfill major role obligations at work, school, or home
- recurrent substance use in situations in which it is physically hazardous
- recurrent substance-related legal problems
- continued substance use despite having persistent or recurrent social or interpersonal problems caused or exacerbated by the effects of the substance (such as arguments with spouse about consequences of intoxication, physical fights)

Criteria for Substance Dependence not met for this class of substance and has coupled such relief in some cases with feelings of euphoria. It is not surprising, therefore, that substance abuse, dependence, and other behaviors with addictive characteristics can develop so readily in so many organisms.

The effects of typical representatives of the major categories of abused substances can be predicted. Alcohol can disrupt several behavioral functions. It can slow reaction time, movement, and thought processes and can interfere with needed rapid eye movement (REM) sleep. It can also produce unpredictable emotionality, including violence. Those who abuse alcohol may go on to develop the symptoms of physiological dependence (a condition where tolerance or withdrawal are present) and may develop the full diagnosis of alcohol dependence, and it is important to note that the symptoms of alcohol withdrawal can be life-threatening. Heroin, an opioid, has analgesic (pain-killing) and euphoriant effects. It is also highly addictive, but withdrawal seldom results in death. Marijuana, sometimes classified as a sedative, sometimes as a hallucinogen, has many of the same behavioral effects as alcohol.

Stimulants vary widely in their behavioral effects. Common to all is some form of physiological and behavioral stimulation. Some, such as cocaine and the amphetamines (including crystal methamphetamine), are extremely addictive and seriously life-threatening and can produce violence. Others, such as caffeine, are relatively mild in their euphoriant effects. Withdrawal from stimulants, especially the powerful forms, can result in profound depression.

Hallucinogens are a diverse group of substances that can produce visual, auditory, tactile, olfactory, or gustatory hallucinations, but most do so in only a small percentage of the population. Some, such as PCP, can produce violent behavior, while others, such as lysergic acid diethylamide (LSD), are not known for producing negative emotional outbursts. Inhalants usually produce feelings of euphoria; they are most often used by individuals in their adolescent years who cannot afford to buy other types of drugs such as marijuana, as well as by adult individuals who have easy access to these substances in their work environments or social circles.

## BRAIN CHEMISTRY

Some of the pharmacological effects of very different drugs are quite similar. Marijuana and alcohol affect at least three of the same brain biochemical systems. Alcohol can become a form of opiate in the brain following some specific chemical transformations. These similarities raise an old and continuing question in the substance use field: Is there a fundamental addictive mechanism common to everyone that differs only in the level and nature of expression? Older theories of drug-abuse behavior approached this question by postulating the "addictive personality," a type of person who would become indiscriminately addicted as a result of his or her personal and social history. With advances in neuroscience have come theories concerning the possibility of an "addictive brain," which refers to a neurological status that requires continued adjustment provided by drugs.

An example of the workings of the addictive brain might be a low-opiate brain that does not produce normal levels of analgesia or normal levels of organismic and behavioral euphoria (joy). The chemical adjustment sought by the brain might be satisfied by use or abuse of any drug that results in stimulation of the opiate function of the brain. As discussed above, several seemingly unrelated drugs can produce a similar chemical effect. Thus, the choice of a particular substance might depend both on brain status and on personal or social experience with the effects and availability of the drug used.

The example of the opiate-seeking brain raises at least two possibilities for prevention and treatment, both of which have been discussed in substance-use literature: reregulation of the brain and substitution. So far, socially acceptable substitutes or substitute addictions offer some promise, but reregulation of the dysregulated brain is still primarily a hope of the future. An example of a socially acceptable substitute might be opiate production by excessive running, an activity that can produce some increase in opiate function. The success of such a substitution procedure, however, depends upon many variables that may be quite difficult to predict or control. The substitution might not produce the required amount of reregulation, the adjustment might not be permanent, and tolerance to the adjustment might develop. There are a host of other possible problems.

### FUTURE POSSIBILITIES

Use of psychoactive substances dates from the earliest recorded history and likely predates it. Historical records indicate that many substances with the potential for abuse were used in medicinal and ceremonial or religious contexts, as tokens in barter, for their euphoriant properties during recreation, as indicators of guilt or innocence, as penalties, and in other practices.

Substance use disorders are widespread in virtually all countries and cultures and can be extremely costly, both personally and socially. There is no doubt that most societies would like to eliminate substance use disorders, as many efforts are under way to prevent and treat their occurrence. It is obvious that economic as well as social factors contribute both to substance use disorders and to the laws regulating substance use, and possibly create some roadblocks in eliminating abuse and dependence.

In psychology, the systemic and popular study of substance use became most extensive as the field of pharmacology blossomed and access to substances of abuse increased. The creation of the National Institute of Alcohol Abuse and Alcoholism and the National Institute on Drug Abuse helped to fuel research in this area in the 1970's and later. During the 1980's and 1990's, there was an increase in exploration of the biological mechanisms underlying substance use disorders and the possibility that pharmacological interventions might be useful to prevent and treat substance use disorders. The 1990's also brought an increase in awareness among the research and clinical communities that attention to specific demographic characteristics, such as age, gender, and ethnicity, was also important for understanding the etiology, prevention, and treatment of substance use disorders. As research progresses, these factors and the impact of the environment on behavior are increasingly the focus of study, and attention to the diagnosis of abuse is increasing.

Future research on substance use disorders is likely to focus on biological determinants of the problem for the purposes of prevention and treatment, environmental circumstances related to problem development, the interaction of culture and gender as they relate to substance use disorders and treatments, and how other mental illnesses can compound problems related to substance use. Many people erroneously consider biological explanations of problematic behaviors to be an excuse for such behaviors. In fact, discoveries regarding the neural contributions to such behaviors are the basis on which rational therapies for such behaviors can be developed. Recognizing that a disorder has a basis in the brain can enable therapists to address the disorder with a better armamentarium of useful therapeutic tools. In this way, simple management of such disorders can be replaced by real solutions to the problems created by substance abuse.

## SOURCES FOR FURTHER STUDY

Gitlow, Stuart. *Substance Use Disorders: A Practical Guide*. Philadelphia: Lippincott Williams & Wilkins, 2001. Provides basic explanations for different diagnoses of substance use disorders and explains other diagnostic terms.

Hardman, Joel G., and Lee E. Limbard, eds. *Goodman and Gilman's The Pharmacological Basis of Therapeutics*. 10th ed. New York: Macmillan, 2001. A standard reference for students interested in an overview of the pharmacological aspects of selected addictive drugs. Of greater interest to those interested in pursuing the study of substance abuse from a neurological and physiological perspective.

Inaba, Daryl. *Uppers, Downers, All Arounders: Physical and Mental Effects of Psychoactive Drugs*. 4th ed. Ashland, Oreg.: CNS Productions, 2000. An easy-to-read, practical book on what substance use disorders look like to the everyday person, as well as a description of related problems and concerns.

Julien, Robert M. *A Primer of Drug Action*. Rev. ed. New York: W. H. Freeman, 2001. An introductory treatment of types and actions of many abused and therapeutic substances. A useful, quick reference guide for psychoactive effects of drugs used in traditional pharmacological therapy for disorders and abused substances. Contains good reference lists and appendices that explain some of the anatomy and chemistry required to understand biological mechanisms of substance abuse.

Weil, Andrew, and Winifred Rosen. *From Chocolate to Morphine: Everything You Need to Know About Mind-Altering Drugs*. Rev. and updated ed. Boston: Houghton Mifflin, 1998. This classic text discusses mind-altering substances, from foods that alter moods to illicit drugs of abuse.

*Rebecca M. Chesire; updated by Nancy A. Piotrowski*

SEE ALSO: Motivation.

# SUICIDE

TYPE OF PSYCHOLOGY: Psychopathology
FIELD OF STUDY: Depression

*Suicide is the intentional ending of one's own life; roughly 12 per 100,000 Americans commit suicide annually. Suicide rates are higher for males than females and increase with age; risk also increases with clinical depression, so suicide may be considered among the most severe consequences of any psychological disorder.*

KEY CONCEPTS
- altruistic suicide
- anomie
- egoistic suicide
- epidemiological research
- psychological autopsy
- suicidal gesture

Suicide is the intentional taking of one's own life. Psychologists have devoted much effort to its study, attempting to identify those at greatest risk for suicide and to intervene effectively to prevent suicide.

Sociologist Émile Durkheim introduced what has become a well-known classification of suicide types. Altruistic suicides, according to Durkheim, are those that occur in response to societal demands (for example, the soldier who sacrifices himself to save his comrades). Egoistic suicides occur when the individual is isolated from society and so does not experience sufficient societal demands to live. The third type is the anomic suicide. Anomie is a sense of disorientation or alienation which occurs following a major change in one's societal relationships (such as the loss of a job or the death of a close friend); the anomic suicide occurs following such sudden and dramatic changes.

Research supports Durkheim's ideas that suicide is associated with social isolation and recent loss. Many other variables, both demographic and psychological, have also been found to be related to suicide. Numerous studies have shown that the following demographic variables are related to suicide: sex, age, marital status, employment status, urban versus rural dwelling, and race. Paradoxically, more females than males attempt suicide, but more males than females commit suicide. The ratio in both cases is about three to one. The difference between the sex ratios for attempted and completed suicide is generally explained by the fact that males tend to employ more lethal and less reversible methods than do females (firearms and hanging, for example, are more lethal and less reversible than ingestion of drugs).

Age is also related to suicide. In general, risk for suicide increases with increasing age; however, even though suicide risk is higher in older people, much attention has been devoted to suicide among children and adolescents. This attention is attributable to two factors. First, since 1960 there has been an increase in the suicide rate among people under twenty-five years of age. Second, suicide has become one of the leading causes of death among people under twenty-one, whereas suicide is surpassed by many illnesses as a cause of death among older adults. Other demographic variables are related to suicide. Suicide risk is higher for divorced than married people. The unemployed have a higher suicide rate than those who are employed. Urban dwellers have a higher suicide rate than rural dwellers. Caucasians have a higher suicide rate than African Americans.

In addition to these demographic variables, several psychological or behavioral variables are related to suicide. Perhaps the single best predictor of suicide is threatening to commit suicide. Most suicide victims have made some type of suicide threat (although, in some cases, the threat may be veiled or indirect, such as putting one's affairs in order or giving away one's belongings). For this reason, psychologists consider seriously any threat of suicide. A related index of suicide risk is the detailedness or clarity of the threat. Individuals who describe a suicide method in detail are at greater risk than those who express an intent to die but who describe the act only vaguely. Similarly, the lethality and availability of the proposed method provide additional measures of risk. Suicide risk is higher if the individual proposes using a more lethal method and if the individual has access to the proposed method.

Another useful indicator of suicide risk is previous suicide attempts. People who have made prior attempts are at higher risk for suicide than people who have not. The lethality of the method used in the prior attempt is a related indicator. An individual who survives a more lethal method (a gunshot to the head) is considered at higher risk than one who survives a less lethal attempt (swallowing a bottle of aspirin).

Suicide risk is associated with particular behavioral or psychological variables: depression, isolation, stress, pain or illness, recent loss, and drug or alcohol abuse. These factors may help explain why certain of the demographic variables are related to suicide. For example, people who are unemployed may experience higher levels of stress, depression, and isolation than people who are employed. Similarly, divorced people may experience more stress and isolation than married people. The elderly may experience more isolation, depression, and pain or illness than younger people.

Although the demographic and psychological variables summarized above have been found to be related to suicide, the prediction of suicide remains extremely difficult. Suicide is a statistically rare event; according to basic laws of probability, it is very difficult to predict such rare occurrences. What happens in actual attempts to predict suicide is that, in order to identify the "true positives" (individuals who actually attempt suicide), one must accept a very large number of "false positives" (individuals who are labeled suicidal but who, in fact, will not attempt suicide).

## RESEARCH AND PREVENTION

Several methods have been used to study the psychology of suicide. Epidemiological research determines the distribution of demographic characteristics among suicide victims. Another method is to study survivors of suicide attempts. This enables psychologists to examine intensively their psychological characteristics. A third method is to analyze suicide notes, which may explain the individual's reasons for suicide. A final method is the psychological autopsy. This involves interviewing the victim's friends and family members and examining the victim's personal materials (such as diaries and letters) in an attempt to identify the psychological cause of the suicide.

Although all these approaches have been widely used, each has its limitations. The epidemiological method focuses on demographic characteristics and so may overlook psychological influences. Studying survivors of suicide attempts has limitations because survivors and victims of suicide attempts may differ significantly. For example, some suicide attempts are regarded as suicidal gestures, or "cries for help," the intent of which is not to die but rather to call attention to oneself to gain sympathy or assistance. Thus, what is learned from survivors may not generalize to successful suicide victims. The study of suicide notes is limited by the fact that most suicide victims do not leave notes. For example, in a study of all suicides in Los Angeles County in a single year, psychologists Edwin Shneidman and Norman Farberow found that only 35 percent of the males and 39 percent of the females left notes. Finally, the psychological autopsy is limited in that the victim's records and acquaintances may not shed light on the victim's thought processes.

In 1988, Harry Hoberman and Barry Garfinkel conducted an epidemiological study to identify variables related to suicide in children and adolescents. They examined death records in two counties in Minnesota over an eleven-year period for individuals who died at age nineteen or younger. Hoberman and Garfinkel examined in detail the death records of 225 suicide victims. They noted that 15 percent of their sample had not been identified as suicides by the medical examiner but had instead been listed as accident victims or as having died of undetermined causes. This finding suggests that official estimates of suicide deaths in the United States are actually low.

Consistent with other studies, Hoberman and Garfinkel found that suicide was related to both age and sex. Males accounted for 80 percent of the suicides, females for only 20 percent. Adolescents aged fifteen to nineteen years composed 91 percent of the sample, with children aged fourteen and under 9 percent. In addition, Hoberman and Garfinkel found that a full 50 percent of the sample showed evidence of one or more psychiatric disorders. Most common were depression and alcohol or drug abuse. Finally, Hoberman and Garfinkel found that a substantial number of the suicide victims had been described as "loners," "lonely," or "withdrawn." Thus, several of the indicators of suicide in adults also are related to suicide in children and adolescents.

## ASSESSING RISK

Psychiatrist Aaron T. Beck and his colleagues developed the Hopelessness Scale in 1974 to assess an individual's negative thoughts of self and future. In many theories of suicide, an individual's sense of hopelessness is related to risk for suicide. Beck and others have demonstrated that hopelessness in depressed patients is a useful indicator of suicide risk. For example, in 1985, Beck and his colleagues reported a study of 207 patients who were hospitalized because of suicidal thinking. Over the next five to ten years, fourteen patients committed suicide. Only one demographic variable, race, differed between the suicide and nonsuicide groups: Caucasian patients had a higher rate of suicide (10.1 percent) than African American patients (1.3 percent). Of the psychological variables assessed, only the Hopelessness Scale and a measure of pessimism differed between suicide victims and other patients. Patients who committed suicide were higher in both hopelessness and pessimism than other patients. Beck and his colleagues determined the Hopelessness Scale score which best discriminated suicides from nonsuicides. Other mental health professionals can now use this criterion to identify those clinically depressed patients who are at greatest risk for suicide.

Several approaches have been developed in efforts to prevent suicide. Shneidman and Farberow developed what may be the most well-known suicide-prevention program, the Los Angeles Suicide Prevention Center. This program, begun in 1958, helped popularize telephone suicide hotlines. Staff members are trained to interact with individuals who are experiencing extreme distress. When an individual calls the center, staff members immediately begin to assess the caller's risk for suicide, considering the caller's demographics, stress, lifestyle, and suicidal intent. Staff members attempt to calm the caller, so as to prevent an immediate suicide, and to put the person into contact with local mental health agencies so that the individual can receive more extensive follow-up care.

Psychologists William Fremouw, Maria de Perczel, and Thomas Ellis published a useful guide for those who work with suicidal clients. Among their suggestions are to talk openly and matter-of-factly about suicide, to avoid dismissing the client's feelings or motives in a judgmental or pejorative way, and to adopt a problem-solving approach to dealing with the client's situation.

Suicide-prevention programs are difficult to evaluate. Callers may not identify themselves, so it is difficult to determine whether they later commit suicide. Still, such programs are generally thought to be useful, and suicide-prevention programs similar to that of Shneidman and Farberow have been developed in many communities.

## SOCIAL AND CULTURAL CONTEXTS

Suicide is one of the most extreme and drastic behaviors faced by psychologists. Because of its severity, psychologists have devoted considerable effort to identifying individuals at risk for suicide and to developing programs that are effective in preventing suicide.

Psychological studies have shown that many popular beliefs about suicide are incorrect. For example, many people erroneously believe that people who threaten suicide never attempt suicide, that all suicide victims truly wish to die, that only the mentally ill commit suicide, that suicide runs in families, and that there are no treatments that can help someone who is suicidal. Because of these and other myths about suicide, it is especially important that psychological studies of suicide continue and that the results of this study be disseminated to the public.

Suicide risk increases in clinically depressed individuals. In depressed patients, suicide risk has been found to be associated with hopelessness: As one's sense of hopelessness increases, one's risk for suicide increases. Since the 1970's, Beck's Hopelessness Scale has been used in efforts to predict risk for suicide among depressed patients. Although the suicide rate has been relatively stable in the United States since the early twentieth century, the suicide rate of young people has increased since the 1960's.

For this reason, depression and suicide among children and adolescents have become major concerns of psychologists. Whereas childhood depression received relatively little attention from psychologists before the 1970's, psychologists have devoted considerable attention to this condition since then. Much of this attention has concerned whether biological, cognitive, and behavioral theories of the causes of depression and approaches to the treatment of depression, which were originally developed and applied to depressed adults, may generalize to children. In the 1980's, psychologists developed several innovative programs that attempt to identify youths who are depressed and experiencing hopelessness, and so may be at risk for suicide; evaluations and refinements of these programs will continue.

### SOURCES FOR FURTHER STUDY

Durkheim, Émile. *Suicide.* Reprint. Glencoe, Ill.: Free Press, 1951. In this work, originally published in 1897, Durkheim introduced his classification system of suicide types—altruistic, egoistic, and anomic suicides—and examined the relationship of suicide to isolation and recent loss.

Fremouw, William J., Maria de Perczel, and Thomas E. Ellis. *Suicide Risk: Assessment and Response Guidelines.* New York: Pergamon, 1990. This book presents useful guidelines, based on both research and clinical practice, for working with suicidal individuals.

Hawton, Keith. *Suicide and Attempted Suicide Among Children and Adolescents.* Beverly Hills, Calif.: Sage Publications, 1986. This work overviews research results concerning the causes of youth suicide and treatment programs for suicidal youngsters.

Holinger, Paul C., and J. Sandlow. "Suicide." In *Violent Deaths in the United States,* edited by Paul C. Holinger. New York: Guilford Press, 1987. This chapter presents epidemiological information on suicide in the United

States, from 1900 to 1980. It also addresses demographic variables and their relationship to suicide.

Lann, Irma S., Eve K. Moscicki, and Ronald Maris, eds. *Strategies for Studying Suicide and Suicidal Behavior.* New York: Guilford Press, 1989. This book examines the various research methods used to study suicide. Considers the relative strengths and weaknesses and offers examples of each method.

Lester, David, ed. *Current Concepts of Suicide.* Philadelphia: Charles Press, 1990. A useful overview of research results on the possible causes of suicide and on programs designed both to prevent suicide and to treat suicidal patients.

Peck, Michael L., Norman L. Farberow, and Robert E. Litman, eds. *Youth Suicide.* New York: Springer, 1985. A useful overview of the psychological influences on youth suicide and on the treatment and prevention programs that have been used with suicidal youths.

Shneidman, Edwin S., Norman L. Farberow, and Robert E. Litman. *The Psychology of Suicide.* New York: Science House, 1970. This is a collection of articles, some of which are now regarded as classics in the study of suicide.

Stengel, Erwin. *Suicide and Attempted Suicide.* Rev. ed. Harmondsworth, England: Penguin Books, 1973. This classic work summarizes the demographic and psychological variables that were known at the time to be associated with suicide.

*Michael Wierzbicki*

SEE ALSO: Bipolar Disorder; Clinical Depression; Depression; Drug Therapies.

# SUPPORT GROUPS

TYPE OF PSYCHOLOGY: Cognition; emotion; language; learning; memory;
motivation; personality; psychological methodologies; psychopathology;
psychotherapy; social psychology; stress
FIELDS OF STUDY: All

*The history of support groups in modern times begins with the formation of the Oxford
Group in 1908 and the subsequent development of Alcoholics Anonymous. For the
participants, support groups reduce feelings of isolation, offer information, instill
hope, provide feedback and social support, and teach new social skills. At the opening
of the twenty-first century, support groups exist for persons suffering from all kinds of
medical and psychological conditions to support for victims of violent crime.*

KEY CONCEPTS
- cohesion
- exchange theory
- group dynamics
- networks
- norms
- roles
- social facilitation
- social inhibition
- social learning
- sociobiology

Humans are social animals—they live in groups. These networks among
people are powerful in shaping behavior, feelings, and judgments. Groups
can lead to destructive behavior such as mob violence and aggression, but
they can also encourage loyalty, nurturing of others, and achievement, as
found in cancer-support groups. Scientific investigation of how groups affect human behavior began as early as 1898, but the main body of research
on group functioning began only in the 1940's and 1950's. The study of
groups is still a major topic of scientific enquiry.

D. R. Forsyth defined a group as "two or more individuals who influence
each other through social interaction." A group may be permanent or temporary, formal or informal, structured or unstructured. Those groups known as
support groups may share any of these characteristics.

Why do human beings seek out groups? Social learning theorists believe
that humans learn to depend on other people because most are raised
within families, where they learn to look to other people for support, validation, amusement, and advice. Exchange theorists, on the other hand, reason that groups provide both rewards (such as love and approval) and costs
(such as time and effort). Membership in a group will "profit" the individual
if the rewards are greater than the costs. Yet another set of theorists, the
sociobiologists, argue that humans form groups because this has a survival

benefit for the species. They hypothesize a genetic predisposition toward affiliation with others. It is within groups that the fittest have the greatest chance of survival.

Whatever the reason for forming groups, all groups have important characteristics that must be addressed in seeking to understand why support groups work. First of all, group size is important. Larger groups allow more anonymity, while smaller groups facilitate communication, for example. Group structure includes such elements as status differences, norms of conduct, leaders and followers, and subgroups. Individuals in groups develop social roles—those expected behaviors associated with the individual's position within the group. Roles are powerful in influencing behavior and can cause individuals to act contrary even to their private feelings or their own interests. These roles carry varying degrees of status within the group—who is influential and respected and who is less so. Groups may have subgroups, based on age, residence, roles, interests, or other factors. These subgroups may contribute to the success of the whole or may become cliquish and undermine the main group's effectiveness.

Groups also have varying degrees of cohesion. Cohesion reflects the strength of attachments within the group. Sometimes cohesion is a factor of how well group members like one another, sometimes a factor of the need to achieve an important goal, and sometimes a factor of the rewards that group membership confers. All groups have communication networks, or patterns of openness and restrictions on communication among members.

Group norms are those attitudes and behaviors that are expected of members. These norms are needed for the group's success because they make life more predictable and efficient for the members. Leadership may be formal or informal, may be task oriented or people oriented, and may change over time. Finally, all groups go through fairly predictable stages as they form, do their work, and conclude. The comprehensive term for the way a group functions is "group dynamics."

## HOW GROUPS INFLUENCE INDIVIDUALS

Researchers have found that for all animals, including human beings, the mere presence of other members of the same species may enhance performance on individual tasks. This phenomenon is known as social facilitation. With more complex tasks, however, the presence of others may decrease performance. This is known as social inhibition or impairment. It is not clear whether this occurs because the presence of others arouses the individual, leads individuals to expect rewards or punishments based on past experience, makes people self-conscious, creates challenges to self-image, or affects the individual's ability to process information. Most theorists agree that the nature of the task is important in the success of a group. For example, the group is more likely to succeed if the individual members' welfare is closely tied to the task of the group.

Groups provide modeling of behavior deemed appropriate in a given situation. The more similar the individuals doing the modeling are to the individual who wants to learn a behavior, the more powerful the models are. Groups reward members for behavior that conforms to group norms or standards and punish behaviors that do not conform. Groups provide a means of social comparison—how one's own behavior compares to others' in a similar situation. Groups are valuable sources of support during times of stress. Some specific factors that enhance the ability of groups to help individuals reduce stress are attachment, guidance, tangible assistance, and embeddedness. Attachment has to do with caring and attention among group members. Guidance may be provision of information, or it may be advice and feedback provided by the group to its members. Tangible assistance may take the form of money or of other kinds of service. Embeddedness refers to the sense the individual has of belonging to the group. Some researchers have shown that a strong support system actually increases the body's immune functioning.

### ALCOHOLICS ANONYMOUS

The best-known support group is Alcoholics Anonymous (AA), formed in Akron, Ohio, in the late 1930's. AA groups now number in the tens of thousands and are found across the globe. AA is an outgrowth of the Oxford Group, a Christian student and athlete group formed at Oxford University in England in 1908. The Oxford Group's ideals of self-examination, acknowledgment of character defects, restitution for harm done, and working with others directly influenced the steps to recovery practiced by members of AA and other so-called twelve-step groups, including Al-Anon, Narcotics Anonymous, Smokers Anonymous, and many others.

For addicts, support groups are important for a number of reasons. They provide peer support for the effort to become "clean and sober." They provide peer pressure against relapsing into substance use. They assure addicts that they are not alone—that others have suffered the destruction brought about by drinking or taking drugs. Addicts in twelve-step groups learn to interact with others on an emotional level. Importantly, members of AA and other support groups for addicts are able to confront the individual's maladaptive behaviors and provide models for more functional behavior. The norm for AA is sobriety, and sobriety is reinforced by clear directions on how to live as a sober person. Another important aspect of AA is the hope that it is able to inspire in persons who, while using, saw no hope for the future. This hope comes not only from seeing individuals who have successfully learned to live as sober persons but also from the group's emphasis on dependence on a higher power and the importance of one's spiritual life.

### OTHER SUPPORT GROUPS

Not all support groups are for addicts. Support groups exist for adoptive parents, people who were adopted when they were children, people with acquired immunodeficiency syndrome (AIDS), caregivers for patients with

Alzheimer's disease, and that is just the beginning. Why are these groups so popular? Some writers believe that Americans have turned away from the "rugged individualism" that has characterized the national psyche in the past and are searching for meaning in groups to replace the extended families found in other societies. However, this does not explain why support groups are also popular in other parts of the world. The answer probably lies in the characteristics of groups.

Support groups are generally composed of small numbers of people who are facing similar challenges in their lives. They meet, with or without a trained facilitator, to explore their reactions, problems, solutions, feelings, frustrations, successes, and needs in relation to those challenges. They build bonds of trust. Members show compassion to one another. Groups may provide material support or simply assure the individual member he or she is not alone. They help minimize stress and maximize coping. They model strategies for dealing with the given challenge. They provide information. They nurture their members. They encourage application of new learning. Through this sharing, each member grows, and through individual growth, the group matures.

Support groups have traditionally met in person, but the World Wide Web has now enabled many groups to meet online. These meetings may take the form of synchronous or asynchronous chat groups, bulletin boards, listservs, Web sites with multiple links to information sources, referrals, and collaboration with professionals. These groups, while not well studied, seem to serve the same purposes as in-person groups. In addition, they may provide an advantage: The anonymity of the Web makes it possible to observe and to learn from observing without actually participating until one is comfortable doing so.

Support groups may not be sufficient in and of themselves to solve individual problems. They are probably most effective as a part of an integrated plan for addressing the challenge in the individual's life that involves other resources as appropriate. For example, the caregiver of a person with Alzheimer's disease may also need social services support, adult day care or respite care facilities, medical assistance for control of problem behaviors, and home health services to deal successfully with the day-to-day challenges of dealing with the patient. The support group can facilitate access to these other resources in addition to serving as an important stress reducer and support system for the caregiver.

### Sources for Further Study

Carlson, Hannah. *The Courage to Lead: Start Your Own Support Group: Mental Illnesses and Addictions.* Madison, Conn.: Bick, 2001. A complete how-to manual for creating small groups for persons striving against addiction or to overcome mental illnesses.

Ferguson, Tom. *Health Online: How to Find Health Information, Support Groups, and Self-Help Communities in Cyberspace.* Reading, Mass.: Addison-Wesley,

1996. A comprehensive guide to information on diseases and illnesses. Explains how to locate online medical journals and interpret articles. Covers commercial online services, Internet bulletin boards, and National Institutes of Health databases.

Kauth, Bill. *A Circle of Men: The Original Manual for Men's Support Groups.* New York: St. Martin's Press, 1992. Covers finding the right members, running meetings, training in listening, creating rituals, and dealing with problems within the group.

Kelly, Pat. *Living with Breast Cancer: A Guide for Facilitating Self-Help Groups.* Lewiston, N.Y.: B. C. Decker, 2000. A guide to starting and running a member-managed self-help group. Provides a good list of resources.

Klein, Linda L. *The Support Group Sourcebook: What They Are, How You Can Find One, and How They Can Help You.* New York: John Wiley & Sons, 2000. A comprehensive guide to how groups work and develop and how they assist people. Good advice on how to start or find a group.

O'Rourke, Kathleen, and John C. Worzbyt. *Support Groups for Children.* Washington, D.C.: Accelerated Development, 1996. Helpful description of how to find an appropriate support group for children.

Shaffer, Carolyn R., and Kristin Anundsen. *Creating Community Anywhere: Finding Support and Connection in a Fragmented World.* New York: Penguin Putnam, 1993. Focuses on how to find or create intentional communities.

Wuthnow, Robert. *Sharing the Journey: Support Groups and America's New Quest for Community.* New York: Free Press, 1994. Examines the shift from extended family through the isolation of the nuclear family and the present movement toward intentional communities.

*Rebecca Lovell Scott*

SEE ALSO: Domestic Violence; Groups; Substance Use Disorders.

# SURVEY RESEARCH
## QUESTIONNAIRES AND INTERVIEWS

TYPE OF PSYCHOLOGY: Psychological methodologies
FIELDS OF STUDY: Descriptive methodologies; experimental
  methodologies; methodological issues

*Psychologists use survey research techniques, including questionnaires and interviews, to evaluate attitudes about social or personal issues and to find out about people's behaviors directly from those people. Questionnaires are self-administered and in written form. In interviews, the psychologist asks questions of the respondent. There are strengths and limitations of both of these data collection methods.*

KEY CONCEPTS
- attitudes
- demographics
- interview
- population
- questionnaire
- respondent
- sample

Survey research is common in both science and daily life. Almost everyone in today's society has been exposed to survey research in one form or another. Researchers ask questions about the political candidate one favors, the television programs one watches, the soft drink one prefers, whether there should be a waiting period prior to purchasing a handgun, and so on.

There are many ways to obtain data about the social world; among them are observation, field studies, and experimentation. Two key methods for obtaining data—questionnaires and interviews—are survey research methods. Most of the social research conducted or published involves these two data collection methods.

In general, when using survey methods, the researcher gets information directly from each person (or respondent) by using self-report measurement techniques to ask people about their current attitudes, behaviors, and demographics (statistical features of populations, such as age, income, race, and marital status), in addition to past experiences and future goals. In questionnaires, the questions are in written format, and the research subjects check boxes and type in (or write down) their answers. In interviews, there is one-to-one verbal communication, either face-to-face or by means of a telephone, between the interviewer and respondent. Both techniques are flexible and adaptable to the group of people being studied and the particular situation. Both can range from being highly structured to highly unstructured.

## STRENGTHS AND LIMITATIONS

Questionnaires can be completed in groups or self-administered on an individual basis. They can also be mailed to people. They are generally less expensive than conducting interviews. Questionnaires also allow greater anonymity of the respondents. One drawback is that a questionnaire's design cannot guarantee that the subjects understand exactly what the questions are asking. Also, there may be a problem of motivation with responding to questionnaires, because people may get bored or find it tedious to type in the forms on their own. The survey researcher must therefore make sure that the questionnaire is not excessively long or complex.

In contrast, with an interview there is a better chance that the interviewer and subject will have good communication and that all questions will be understood. Telephone interviews are less expensive than face-to-face interviews; still, questionnaires tend to be less costly. In an interview, the respondent is presented with questions orally, whereas in the questionnaire, regardless of type or form, the respondent is presented with a written question. Each data collection device has pros and cons. The decision to use questionnaires versus interviews depends on the purpose of the study, the type of information needed, the size of the sample (the number of people who participate in a study and are part of a population), the resources for conducting the study, and the variable(s) to be measured. Overall, the interview is probably the more flexible device of the two.

## DESIGNING BIAS-FREE QUESTIONS

When creating a questionnaire, the researcher must give special thought to writing the specific questions. Researchers must avoid questions that would lead people to answer in a biased way or ones that might be easily misinterpreted. For example, the questions "Do you favor eliminating the wasteful excesses in the federal budget?" and "Do you favor reducing the federal budget?" might well yield different answers from the same respondent.

Questions are either closed-ended or open-ended, depending on the researcher's choice. In a closed-ended question, a limited number of fixed response choices are provided to subjects. With open-ended questions, subjects are able to respond in any way they like. Thus, a researcher could ask, "Where would you like a swimming pool to be built in this town?" as opposed to "Which of the following locations is your top choice for a swimming pool to be built in this town?" The first question allows the respondent to provide any answer; the second provides a fixed number of answers from which the person must choose. Use of closed-ended questions is a more structured approach, allowing greater ease of analysis because the response choices are the same for everyone. Open-ended questions require more time to analyze and are therefore more costly. Open-ended questions, however, can provide valuable insights into what the subjects are actually thinking.

## CLINICAL INTERVIEW

A specialized type of interview is the clinical, or therapeutic, interview. The specific goal of a particular clinical interview depends on the needs and the condition of the individual being interviewed. There is a distinction between a therapeutic interview, which attempts both to obtain information and to remedy the client's problem, and a research interview, which attempts solely to obtain information about people at large. Because the clinical interview is a fairly unstructured search for relevant information, it is important to be aware of the factors that might affect its accuracy and comprehensiveness. Research on hypothesis confirmation bias suggests that it is difficult to search for unbiased and comprehensive information in an unstructured setting such as the clinical interview. In the context of the clinical interview, clinicians are likely to conduct unintentionally biased searches for information that confirms their early impressions of each client. Research on self-fulfilling prophecies suggests a second factor that may limit the applicability of interviews in general: The interviewer's expectations may affect the behavior of the person being interviewed, and respondents may change their behavior to match the interviewer's expectations.

## ROLE OF SCIENTIFIC METHOD

Knowing what to believe about research is often related to understanding the scientific method. The two basic approaches to using the scientific method, the descriptive and the experimental research approaches, differ because they seek to attain different types of knowledge. Descriptive research tries to describe particular situations; experimental research tries to determine cause-and-effect relationships. Independent variables are not manipulated in descriptive research. For that reason, it is not possible to decide whether one thing causes another. Instead, survey research uses correlational techniques, which allow the determination of whether behaviors or attitudes are related to one another and whether they predict one another. For example, how liberal a person's political views are might be related to that person's attitudes about sexuality. Such a relationship could be determined using descriptive research.

Survey research, as a widely used descriptive technique, is defined as a method of collecting standardized information by interviewing a representative sample of some population. All research involves sampling of subjects. That is, subjects must be found to participate in the research whether that research is a survey or an experiment. Sampling is particularly important when conducting survey research, because the goal is to describe what a whole population is like based on the data from a relatively small sample of that population.

## KINSEY GROUP RESEARCH

One famous survey study in the mid-1930's was conducted by Alfred Kinsey and his colleagues. Kinsey studied sexual behavior. Until that time, most of

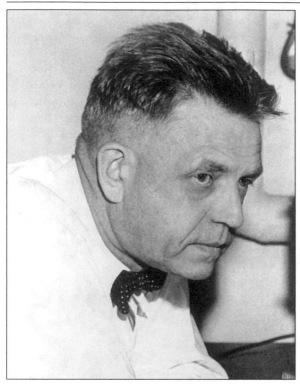

*Alfred Kinsey.*
(Library of Congress)

what was known about sexual behavior was based on what biologists knew about animal sex, what anthropologists knew about sex among indigenous peoples in non-Western, nonindustrialized societies, or what Freud learned about sexuality from his emotionally disturbed patients. Kinsey and his colleagues were the first psychological researchers to interview volunteers from mainstream American society about their sexual behaviors. The research was hindered by political investigations and threats of legal action. In spite of the harassment encountered by the scientists on the project, the Kinsey group published *Sexual Behavior in the Human Male* in 1948 and *Sexual Behavior in the Human Female* in 1953.

The findings of the Kinsey group benefited the public immensely. As a result, it is now known that the majority of people (both men and women) interviewed by the Kinsey group masturbated at various times, but that more men than women said they masturbated. Data collected by the Kinsey group on oral-genital sexual practices have allowed later researchers to discover that, since the 1930's, attitudes toward oral-genital sex have become more positive. Kinsey's research also shocked the United States with the discovery that the majority of brides at that time were not virgins.

When scientific sampling techniques are used, the survey results can be interpreted as an accurate representation of the entire population. Although Kinsey and his associates helped to pave the way for future researchers to investigate sexual behaviors and attitudes, there were some problems with the research because of its lack of generalizability. The Kinsey group's research is still the largest study of sexual behavior ever completed. They interviewed more than ten thousand people; however, they did not attempt to select a random or representative sample of the population of the United States, which meant that the responses of middle-class, well-educated Caucasians were overrepresented. There is also a problem with the accuracy of the respondents' information, because of memory errors, exaggerations, or embarrassment about telling an interviewer personal, sensitive information. Despite these limitations, the interviewing conducted by Kinsey and associates made great strides for the study of sexuality and great strides for psychology in general.

### IMPORTANCE OF SAMPLING PROCEDURES

When research is intended to reveal very precisely what a population is like, careful sampling procedures must be used. This requires defining the population and sampling people from the population in a random fashion so that no biases will be introduced. In order to learn what elderly people think about the medical services available to them, for example, a careful sample of the elderly population is needed. Obtaining the sample only from retirement communities in Arizona would bias the results because these individuals are not representative of all elderly people in the population.

Thus, when evaluating survey data, a researcher must examine how the responses were obtained and what population was investigated. Major polling organizations such as the Gallup organization typically are careful to obtain representative samples of people in the United States. Gallup polls are frequently conducted to survey the voting public's opinions about the popularity of a presidential candidate or a given policy. Many other surveys, however, such as surveys that are published in popular magazines, have limited generalizability because the results are based on people who read the particular magazine and are sufficiently motivated to complete and mail in the questionnaire. When *Redbook*, for example, asks readers to write in to say whether they have ever had an affair, the results may be interesting but would not give a very accurate estimate of the true extent of extramarital sexual activity in the United States. An example of an inaccurate sampling technique was a survey by *Literary Digest* (a now defunct magazine) sampling almost ten million people in 1936. The results showed that American presidential candidate Alfred Landon would beat Franklin D. Roosevelt by a landslide in that year's election. Although it was large, the sample was completely inaccurate.

### EARLY SURVEY METHODS

One of the earliest ways of obtaining psychological information using descriptive techniques was through clinical interviewing. The early interviews conducted by Sigmund Freud in the late 1800's were based on question-and-answer medical formats, which is not surprising, considering that Freud was originally a physician. Later, Freud relied on the less structured free-association technique. In 1902, Adolf Meyer developed a technique to assess a client's mental functioning, memory, attention, speech, and judgment. Independent of the style used, all the early clinical interviews sought to get a psychological portrait of the person, determine the source of the problem, make a diagnosis, and formulate a treatment. More detailed studies of interviews were conducted in the 1940's and 1950's to compare and contrast interviewing styles and determine how much structure was necessary. During the 1960's, much research came about as a result of ideas held by Carl Rogers, who emphasized the interpersonal elements he thought were necessary for the ideal therapeutic relationship; among them are warmth, positive regard, and genuineness on the part of the interviewer.

In the 1800's and early 1900's, interviews were used mainly by psychologists who were therapists helping people with problems such as fear, depression, and hysteria. During that same period, experimental psychologists had not yet begun to use survey research methods. Instead, they used introspection to investigate their own thought processes. For example, experimental psychologist Hermann Ebbinghaus gave himself lists of pronounceable nonsense syllables to remember; he then tested his own memory and attempted to improve it methodically. Many experimental psychologists during this period relied upon the use of animals such as dogs and laboratory rats to conduct behavioral research.

## EVOLUTION OF QUESTIONNAIRES

As mentioned above, one of the first attempts by experimental psychologists to study attitudes and behaviors by means of the interview was that of the Kinsey group in the 1930's. At about that same time, Louis Thurstone, an experimental social psychologist, formalized and popularized the first questionnaire methodology for attitude measurement. Thurstone devised a set of questionnaires, or scales, that have been widely used for decades. He is considered by many to be the father of attitude scaling. Soon thereafter, Rensis Likert made breakthroughs in questionnaire usage with the development of what are known as Likert scales. A Likert scale provides a series of statements to which subjects can indicate degrees of agreement or disagreement. Using the Likert technique, the respondent answers by selecting from predetermined categories ranging from "strongly agree" to "strongly disagree." It is fairly standard to use five categories (strongly agree, agree, uncertain, disagree, strongly disagree), but more categories can be used if necessary. An example of a question using this technique might be, "Intelligence test scores of marijuana users are higher on the average than scores of nonusers." The respondent then picks one of the five categories mentioned above in response. Likert scales have been widely used and have resulted in a vast amount of information about human attitudes and behaviors.

## Sources for Further Study

Bordens, Kenneth S., and Bruce B. Abbott. *Research Design and Methods: A Process Approach.* 5th ed. Mountain View, Calif.: Mayfield, 2001. Places the techniques of using surveys, interviews, and questionnaires for collecting data in the context of conducting research as a process from start to finish. A well-received textbook in psychology.

Converse, Jean M., and Stanley Presser. *Survey Questions: Handcrafting the Standardized Questionnaire.* Beverly Hills, Calif.: Sage Publications, 1986. Provides explicit, practical details for consideration when designing a questionnaire. Stresses the art of questionnaire creation.

Cozby, Paul C. *Methods in Behavioral Research.* 7th ed. Mountain View, Calif.: Mayfield, 2000. Examines the importance of survey research in the context of conducting experiments and doing research in psychology in general. Allows the reader to understand the research process from a broader perspective.

Judd, Charles M., Louise H. Kidder, and Eliot R. Smith. *Research Methods in Social Relations.* 6th ed. Pacific Grove, Calif.: International Thomson, 1991. A popular book whose writing style is exceptionally clear. Offers thorough information that introduces the reader to the process of doing research in psychology, including how to get an idea for a research topic, how to collect the information, how to be ethical with subjects, and how to report the results. Detailed information is provided on questionnaires and interviews.

Stewart, Charles J., and William B. Cash, Jr. *Interviewing Principles and Practices.* 9th ed. Boston: McGraw-Hill College, 2000. A hands-on introduction to interviewing which provides practical suggestions and tips along with background information.

*Deborah R. McDonald*

See also: Case-Study Methodologies.

# THIRST

TYPE OF PSYCHOLOGY: Motivation

FIELDS OF STUDY: Endocrine system; motivation theory; physical motives

*Thirst, along with hunger, is one of the basic biological drives. It motivates humans to drink, which is necessary for their survival.*

KEY CONCEPTS
- antidiuretic hormone (ADH)
- cellular dehydration thirst
- drive
- hypothalamus
- hypovolemic thirst
- motivation

The range of human motivation is quite broad in controlling behaviors. Motivation can be defined as a condition that energizes and directs behavior in a particular manner. Different aspects of motivation can be attributed to instinctive behavior patterns, the need to reduce drives, or learned experiences.

Thirst is one of many biologically based motivational factors; among other such factors are those that involve food, air, sleep, temperature regulation, and pain avoidance. Biologically based motivational factors help humans and other organisms to maintain a balanced internal environment. This is the process of homeostasis. Deviations from the norm, such as hunger, excessive water loss, and pain, will cause an organism to seek out whatever is lacking.

Biologically based motivational factors, such as thirst, have been explained by the drive-reduction hypothesis proposed by Clark Hull in 1943. The lack of some factor, such as water or food, causes the body to feel unpleasant. This motivates one to reduce this feeling of unpleasantness, thus reducing the drive. Thirst is considered what is called a primary drive. Primary drives, which are related to biologically based needs such as hunger, thirst, and sleepiness, energize and motivate one to fulfill these biological needs, thus helping the body to maintain homeostasis. Secondary drives fulfill no biological need.

One may wonder what it is that makes one thirsty and how one knows when one has had enough to drink. Seventy-five percent of a human's weight is water. The maintenance of water balance is an ongoing process. In an average day, a person will lose approximately 2.5 liters of water; 60 percent of the water loss occurs through urination, 20 percent is lost through perspiration, and the remainder is lost through defecation and exhalation from the lungs. These 2.5 liters of water must be replaced.

What is the stimulus that motivates one to drink when one is thirsty? The simplest hypothesis, which was proposed by Walter Cannon in 1934, is the dry mouth hypothesis. According to Cannon, it is a dry mouth that causes one to drink, not the need for water. This hypothesis has not held up under scrutiny. Research has shown that neither the removal of the salivary glands nor the presence of excess salivation in dogs disrupts the animals' regulation of water intake. Studies have indicated that the amount of water consumed is somehow measured and related to the organism's water deficit. This occurs even before the water has been replaced in the person's tissues and cells. Thus, dry mouth is a symptom of the need for water.

## WATER REGULATION PROCESS

When a human being's water intake is lower than its level of water loss, two bodily processes are set in motion. First, the person becomes thirsty and drinks water (provided it is available). Second, the kidneys start to retain water by reabsorbing it and concentrating the urine. Thus, the kidneys can conserve the water that is already in the body. These processes are set in motion by the central nervous system (CNS).

The CNS responds to two primary internal bodily mechanisms. One is cellular dehydration thirst, and the other is hypovolemic thirst (a change in the volume of water in the body). In order to understand these mechanisms, one must realize that the body contains two main supplies of water. One supply, the intracellular fluid, is in the cells; the other supply consists of the extracellular fluid surrounding the cells and tissues and the fluid in the circulatory system. Water moves between these two areas by means of a process called osmosis, which causes it to move from an area of higher concentration to an area of lower concentration.

A person who is deprived of water will experience cellular dehydration thirst as a result of water loss caused by perspiration and excretion through the urine. This increases the salt concentration in the extracellular fluid, thereby lowering the water concentration. Thus, the cells lose their water to the surrounding extracellular fluid. The increasing salt concentration triggers specialized osmoreceptors located in the hypothalamic region of the brain. Two events occur: First, drinking is stimulated; second, antidiuretic hormone (ADH) is secreted from the pituitary gland in the brain. The ADH helps to promote the reabsorption of water into the kidneys.

The second kind of thirst, hypovolemic thirst, occurs when there is a decrease in the volume of the extracellular fluid as a result of bleeding, diarrhea, or vomiting. This produces a decrease in the salt concentration of the extracellular fluid, which lowers the blood pressure, which in turn stimulates the kidney cells to release a chemical. Eventually, the thirst receptors in the hypothalamus are stimulated; these cause the organism to consume water. In addition, ADH is secreted in this process, which promotes the conservation of water.

The regulation of water intake in humans is thus related to a number of factors and is quite complex. Though cellular dehydration thirst and hypovolemic thirst play a role, it appears that in humans, peripheral factors such as dry mouth play an even larger role. Humans can drink rapidly, replacing a twenty-four-hour water deficit in two to three minutes. This occurs even before the cellular fluid has replaced the water, which takes approximately eight to twelve minutes.

## MOTIVATIONAL FACTOR

Thirst is a strong motivational factor. The importance of replacing lost water is underscored by the fact that a person can survive for a month without food but for only several days without water. It appears that both thirst processes help to promote drinking. Researchers have estimated that 64 to 85 percent of the drinking following water loss is caused by cellular dehydration thirst. Hypovolemic thirst accounts for 5 to 27 percent of the drinking, and the remainder is caused by peripheral factors.

The two types of thirst are independent of each other. The receptors for both thirsts are located in the hypothalamic region of the brain, but they are at different locations. Research has shown that lesions in one region will have no effect on thirst regulation in the other region.

Although the motivation to drink in humans is under conscious control by peripheral factors, unconscious control does exert a large influence. A study of cellular dehydration thirst using goats showed that the injection of a saline solution that has a salt concentration of more than 0.9 percent salt (body fluids have a salt concentration of 0.9 percent salt) into the area in which the osmoreceptors are located will produce a drinking response within sixty seconds. Similar results have been found regarding hypovolemic thirst; injecting angiotensin II (a converted protein found in the blood) into the hypothalamus causes a drinking response. This occurs even in animals that are fully hydrated. These animals will consume in direct proportion to the amount of angiotensin II injected into the hypothalamus.

Diet can have a profound effect on water balance in humans. Eating salty foods will produce cellular dehydration thirst despite adequate fluid levels, because water will flow out of the cells into the extracellular fluid. In contrast, salt-free diets will produce hypovolemic thirst by causing water to flow into the cells. Other factors also cause thirst. As stated previously, diarrhea, vomiting, and blood loss will cause hypovolemic thirst as a result of the loss of extracellular fluid. Therefore, significant blood loss will cause a person to become thirsty.

## IMPACT OF DISEASES

Diseases can also have an impact on thirst. An interesting example of such a disease is diabetes. Diabetes is a condition in which the body cannot process blood glucose (a type of sugar) properly. Improper diet or medication can cause diabetic ketoacidosis, which causes the levels of glucose and ketone bodies (derivatives from fat) in the blood to rise. This creates a major shift in the water balance of the body. Water leaves the cells and enters the blood system, causing the volume of blood to increase. This extra fluid (along with potassium and sodium) is excreted from the body in the urine, which causes the body to suffer dehydration and triggers a tremendous thirst. Because fluid is lost from both cells and extracellular fluid, this causes both types of thirst. Excessive thirst is still a symptom of diabetes, but it has become rare as a result of education and improved treatment.

## IMPACT OF EXERCISE

Thirst motivation also operates during exercise. In short-term exercise, thirst motivation does not come into play because the body usually maintains its temperature. During long-term exercise, however, water intake at intervals facilitates athletic performance by helping to maintain body temperature. The motivation to drink occurs as a result of sweating, which causes the salt concentration in the body to rise during exercise, thereby causing cellular dehydration thirst. Interestingly, voluntary thirst and peripheral factors do not motivate one to take in water during prolonged exercise in the heat until it is too late. Thus, coaches should insist that athletes drink water as they perform.

## SOURCES FOR FURTHER STUDY

Carlson, Neil. *Foundations of Physiological Psychology.* 5th ed. Boston: Allyn & Bacon, 2002. An introductory college textbook. Thirst is covered in the chapter on ingestive behavior.

Levinthal, Charles F. "Chemical Senses and the Mechanisms for Eating and Drinking." In *Introduction to Physiological Psychology.* 3d ed. Englewood Cliffs, N.J.: Prentice-Hall, 1990. A very good chapter on the thirst drive. It is quite detailed, but the clarity of the writing makes it easy to read.

Mader, Sylvia S. *Biology.* 8th ed. Boston: McGraw-Hill, 2004. An easy-to-read introductory textbook on biology that provides a good background on hormones, water regulation, and kidney function, with many fine diagrams and figures. A good basis for understanding physiological psychology.

*Lonnie J. Guralnick*

SEE ALSO: Drives; Endocrine System; Hormones and Behavior; Hunger.

# THOUGHT
## STUDY AND MEASUREMENT

TYPE OF PSYCHOLOGY: Cognition
FIELDS OF STUDY: Cognitive processes; thought

*Although the study of thought did not originate in psychology, cognitive psychology is primarily dedicated to the study and measurement of thought processes.*

KEY CONCEPTS
- cognitive psychology
- Ebbinghaus forgetting curve
- higher mental functions
- information processing model
- parallel processing
- percent savings
- personal equation
- serial processing
- subtraction technique

Cognitive psychologists study many processes basic to human nature and everyday life. Mental processes are central to who people are, what they do, and how they survive. In cognitive psychology, the study of thought necessitates its measurement. For example, much effort has been put forth in cognitive psychology to study how people understand and process information in their environment. One popular approach is to use the idea of a human information-processing system, analogous to a computer. Computers are information-processing devices that use very specific instructions to achieve tasks. A computer receives input, performs certain internal operations on the data (including memory operations), and outputs certain results. Cognitive psychologists often use the information-processing metaphor in describing human operations. People must "input" information from the environment; this process includes sensory and perceptual systems, the recognition of certain common patterns of information, and attention processes.

Once this information has entered the "system," a vast number of operations can be performed. Much of the work by cognitive psychologists has centered on the storage of information during this process—that is, on memory. While memory processes have been of interest since ancient times, it was not until the 1880's that scientists, notably Hermann Ebbinghaus, first systematically and scientifically studied memory. Scientists studying memory today talk about concepts such as short-term and long-term memory as well as about the distinction between episodic and semantic memory systems. The function of memory is essential to human thought and ultimately to the measurement of thought.

In terms of measuring what happens to incoming information, more than memory storage occurs; people manipulate these data. They make decisions based on the information available, and they have capabilities (often referred to as higher mental processes) that in many ways differentiate humans from other animals. Some of the functions commonly studied and measured include reasoning, problem solving, logic, decision making, and language development and use. The information-processing analogy is completed with the "output" of information. When a person is asked a question, the response is the output; it is based on the information stored in memory, whether those items be personal experiences, knowledge gained from books, or awareness of social customs. People do these things so effortlessly, day in and day out, that it is difficult to stop, appreciate, and comprehend how thoughts work. Psychologists have pondered these questions for many years and are only beginning to discover the answers.

## MEASURING THOUGHTS

Some of the earliest systematic studies of thought and the accompanying desire to measure it came from astronomy, not psychology or philosophy. From this beginning, Dutch physiologist Frans C. Donders set out specifically to measure a sequence of mental process—thought—in the middle of the nineteenth century. His technique was simple yet elegant in its ability to measure how much time mental processes consume; the procedure developed by Donders is typically referred to as the subtraction technique.

The subtraction technique begins with the timing and measurement of a very basic task. For example, a person might be asked to press a button after hearing a tone. Donders realized that it was fairly easy to time accurately how long subjects took to perform this task. He believed that two cognitive (thought) processes would be operating: perception of the tone and the motor response of pressing the button. Once the time of this simple task was known, Donders would make the task more difficult. If a discrimination task were added, he believed, the time taken to complete the task would increase compared to the basic perception-motor response sequence. In this discrimination task, for example, Donders might tell a person to press the button only after hearing a high-pitched sound. That person is now faced with an added demand—to make a decision about pitch. Donders believed that with this discrimination stage, the processing of the information would require more mental effort and more time; he was right. More important, Donders could now measure the amount of extra thought required for the decision by subtracting the simple-task time from the discrimination-task time. In a general sense, Donders had a method for measuring thought.

Donders also had the ability to measure and manipulate specific components of the thought process. He even added another component to the sequence of tasks, what he called choice time. For example, the task could be changed so that for a high tone the subject should press the right button and for a low tone press the left button. By subtracting the discrimination time from this new choice time, he could estimate how long the added choice contributed to the overall thought process. By means of these ingenious methods, Donders inspired generations of cognitive psychologists to study thought in terms of the time it takes to think.

### EBBINGHAUS ON LEARNING AND FORGETTING

The first recognized work done in psychology on the measurement of thought processes was Hermann Ebbinghaus's work on memory capacity and forgetting. Working independently in the 1880's in Germany, Ebbinghaus set out to study memory processes, particularly the nature of forgetting. Being the first psychologist to study the issue, he had no precedent, so Ebbinghaus invented his own procedures for measuring memory. To his credit, those procedures were so good that they are still commonly used. Before describing his measurement of memory, Ebbinghaus made two important decisions about methods for studying memory. First, he studied only one person's memory—his own. He believed he would have better control over situational and contextual variables that way.

Second, Ebbinghaus decided that he could not use everyday words in his memory studies, because they might have associations that would make them easier to study. For example, if one were memorizing a poem, the story and the writing style might help memory, and Ebbinghaus was interested in a pure measure of memory and forgetting. To achieve this, Ebbinghaus pioneered the use of nonsense syllables. He used three-letter combinations of consonant-vowel-consonant so that the items were pronounceable but meaningless. Nonsense syllables such as "geb," "fak," "jit," "zab," and "buh" were used.

Ebbinghaus used a vigorous schedule of testing and presented himself with many lists of nonsense syllables to be remembered at a later time. In fact, he spent five years memorizing various lists until he published his seminal work on the topic, *Über das Gedächtnis* (1885; *Memory: A Contribution to Experimental Psychology*, 1913). He systematically measured memory by memorizing a list, letting some time pass, and testing himself on the list. He devised a numerical measurement for memory called percent savings. Percent savings was a measure of the degree of forgetting that occurred over time. For example, it might take him ten minutes to memorize a list perfectly. He would let forty-eight hours pass, then tell himself to recall the list. Forgetting occurs during that time, and only some items would be remembered. Ebbinghaus would then look at the original list and rememorize it until he knew it perfectly; this might take seven minutes or so. He always spent less time rememorizing the list. Said another way, there was some savings from the earlier experience forty-eight hours before. This percent savings was his measure of memory. The higher the percentage of savings, the more items remembered (or the less forgotten), and Ebbinghaus could remember the list in less time.

Ebbinghaus then varied the time between original list learning and later list recall. He found that percent savings drops over time; that is, the longer one waits to remember something, the less one saves from the prior experience, so the more time he had to spend rememorizing the list. Ebbinghaus found fairly good percent savings two or nine hours later, but percent savings dropped dramatically after two or three days. Plotted on a graph, this relationship looks like a downward sloping curve, and it is called the Ebbinghaus forgetting curve. Simply stated, it means that as time passes, memories become poorer. Although this effect is not surprising today, Ebbinghaus was the first (in 1885) to demonstrate this phenomenon empirically.

## STERNBERG ON SPEED

Another example of the work in the area of cognitive psychology comes from the studies of Saul Sternberg in the 1960's at Bell Laboratories. Sternberg examined how additional information in memory influences the speed of mental operations in retrieving information stored in memory. Sternberg's task was fairly simple. He presented his subjects with a list of numbers; the list might range from one to six numbers. After the subjects saw this initial list, a single number (called a probe) was presented. People were asked to identify whether the probe number was on the initial list of numbers. The list might be 2, 3, 9, and 5, for example, and the probe might be 3.

Sternberg's primary interest was in studying how the length of the initial list affected the time it took to make the required yes-or-no decision. Two possibilities typically emerge when people consider this problem. The concept called serial processing holds that the comparison of the probe to each number in the initial list takes time, so that the more items in the initial list, the longer the memory search takes. An alternative idea, parallel processing, suggests that people instantaneously scan all the items in the memory set, and the number of items in the initial list does not make a difference. Another way of saying this is that all the items are scanned at once, in parallel fashion. Sternberg found that people search their memories using the technique of serial processing. In fact, he was able to calculate precisely the amount of additional search time needed for each added item in the memory set—38 milliseconds (a millisecond is a thousandth of a second). Although the search may seem fast, even instantaneous, the more there is to think about, the more time it takes to think.

## COGNITIVE PSYCHOLOGY

The study of thought, and particularly its measurement, is a relatively recent development. For centuries, the thinking processes of humans were believed to be somewhat mystical and certainly not available for scientific inquiry. Most philosophers were concerned more with the mind and its relationship to the body or the world than with how people think. The study of thought, although it was generally considered by the ancient Greek philosophers, did not merit serious attention until the emergence of the "personal equation" by astronomers and the realization that thought processes are indeed measurable and can be measured accurately and precisely.

The story of the first recorded measurements of thought begins with the royal astronomer to England, Nevil Maskelyne, and his assistant, David

Kinnebrook, in 1794. Astronomers of the day were mostly concerned with stellar transits (measuring the movement of stars across the sky). Using telescopes and specialized techniques, the astronomer sought to measure the time it took for a particular star to move across a portion of the telescopic field. Using a complicated procedure that involved listening to a beating clock and viewing the sky, astronomers could measure the transit time of a star fairly accurately, to within one-tenth or two-tenths of a second. These measurements were particularly important because the clocks of that period were based on stellar transits.

Maskelyne and Kinnebrook often worked together in recording the movement of the stars. While Kinnebrook had no problems during 1794, in 1795 Maskelyne began to notice that Kinnebrook's times varied from his own by as much as one-half of a second—considered a large and important difference. By early 1796, the difference between the astronomers' times had grown to eight-tenths of a second. This was an intolerable amount of error to Maskelyne, and he fired his assistant Kinnebrook.

About twenty years later, a German astronomer named Friedrich Bessel came across the records of these incidents and began to study the "error" in the differing astronomers' measurements. He believed that the different measurements were attributable in part to differences between people and that this difference was not necessarily an error. He found that even the most famous and reliable astronomers of the day differed from one another by more than two-tenths of a second.

This incident between Maskelyne and Kinnebrook, and its later study by Bessel, led to some important conclusions. First, measurements in astronomy would have to consider the specific person making the measurement. Astronomers even went to the lengths of developing what became known as the personal equation. The personal equation was a verified, quantified account of how each astronomer's thought processes worked when measuring stellar transits. In essence, the personal equation was a measurement of the thought process involved and a recognition of differences between people. Second, if astronomers differ in their particular thought processes, then many people differ in other types of thinking processes as well. Finally, and perhaps most important in the long run, this incident laid the groundwork for the idea that thought could be measured accurately and the information could be put to good use. No longer was thinking a mystical or magical process that was unacceptable for study by scientists.

It is from this historical context that the field of cognitive psychology has emerged. Cognitive psychology is chiefly concerned with the thought processes and, indeed, all the general mental processing of organisms (most often humans). The interests of a cognitive psychologist can be quite varied: learning, memory, problem solving, reasoning, logic, decision making, linguistics, cognitive development in children, and other topics. Each area of specialization continues to measure and examine how people think, using tasks and procedures as ingenious as those of Donders, Ebbinghaus, and

Sternberg. The study and measurement of thought (or, more generally, the field of cognitive psychology) will continue to play an important and vital role. Not many questions are more basic to the study of human behavior than how people think, what processes are involved, and how researchers can scientifically study and measure these processes.

## SOURCES FOR FURTHER STUDY

Anderson, John R. *Cognitive Psychology and Its Implications.* 5th ed. New York: Worth, 2000. This text is a long-standing leader in the field of cognitive psychology. Provides a wonderful overview of the fundamental issues of cognitive psychology, including attention and perception, basic principles of human memory, problem solving, the development of expertise, reasoning, intelligence, and language structure and use.

Ashcraft, Mark H. *Human Memory and Cognition.* 2d ed. Upper Saddle River, N.J.: Prentice Hall, 1994. A cognitive psychology textbook that heavily emphasizes the human information-processing metaphor. Arranged differently from Anderson's text, it too provides good coverage of all the basic areas of cognitive psychology.

Boring, Edwin G. *A History of Experimental Psychology.* 2d ed. Englewood Cliffs, N.J.: Prentice-Hall, 1957. This text is the foremost authority on the development and history of psychology in the first half of the twentieth century. Contains detailed accounts of the work of early philosophers and astronomers who contributed to the study of thought and even contains an entire chapter devoted to the personal equation. This can be a difficult text to read, but it is the authoritative overview of the early history of psychology.

Goodwin, C. James. *A History of Modern Psychology.* New York: John Wiley & Sons, 1998. A readable and understandable treatment of the history of psychology from René Descartes in the Renaissance to the present.

Lachman, Roy, Janet L. Lachman, and Earl C. Butterfield. *Cognitive Psychology and Information Processing: An Introduction.* Hillsdale, N.J.: Lawrence Erlbaum, 1979. One of the earliest texts that adequately captures the coming importance and influence of cognitive psychology. There are outstanding chapters that trace the influences of other disciplines and traditions on what is now known as cognitive psychology. Topic areas within the field are discussed as well.

Mayer, Richard E. *Thinking, Problem Solving, and Cognition.* 2d ed. New York: W. H. Freeman, 1992. A book primarily dedicated to the topic of problem solving, which is unusual. The format is interesting and creative, covering the historical perspective of problem solving, basic thinking tasks, information-processing analysis, and implications and applications. The focus on thought and its measurement is seen throughout, especially in sections discussing mental chronometry.

*R. Eric Landrum*

SEE ALSO: Cognitive Psychology; Language; Learning; Logic and Reasoning.

# WOMEN'S PSYCHOLOGY
## CAROL GILLIGAN

TYPE OF PSYCHOLOGY: Social psychology
FIELDS OF STUDY: Adolescence; classic analytic themes and issues; general
   constructs and issues; social motives

*Gilligan's theories of girls' and women's moral voice and development led many re-*
*searchers to examine the ways boys and girls, men and women develop morality, and*
*has been instrumental in drawing attention to the importance of the study of the lives*
*of girls and women.*

KEY CONCEPTS
- ethic of care
- ethic of justice
- moral orientation
- relational self
- voice

Within the fields of the moral psychology and the psychology of women, Carol Gilligan, a developmental psychologist, has raised a number of important questions about moral psychology and has generated a great deal of research on girls and their development. Her theory about the "different voice" of girls and women, described in her 1982 book, *In a Different Voice: Psychological Theory and Women's Development,* has been used to explain gender differences in such diverse fields as children's play, the speech of children, adult conversation, women in academia, leadership style, career choice, war and peace studies, the professions of law, nursing, and teaching, and theories about women's epistemologies or ways of knowing.

Originally Gilligan's work was conducted in the field of moral psychology. She followed a tradition of social scientists and moral philosophers who associated moral development with cognitive development. Gilligan argued that boys and men apply rational, abstract, or objective thought to moral questions; as a result they are likely to appeal to the principle of justice when describing their thinking about moral issues. In contrast, Gilligan asserted, girls and women are more likely than boys and men to focus on the relationships between people and the potential for human suffering and harm. When this thinking is applied to moral issues, girls and women appeal to the ethic of care. The ethic of care, she claims, reflects women's "different voice."

In the preface written to the 1993 edition of her book, Gilligan describes "voice" as the core of the self. She calls it "a powerful psychological instrument and channel, connecting inner and outer worlds . . . a litmus test of relationships and a measure of psychological health." Gilligan and colleagues in the Harvard Project on Women's Psychology and the Development of

Girls designed an interview and qualitative scoring method to study moral orientation and voice. They interviewed, held focus groups, and used sentence completion measures to examine female adolescent and adult development. They argued that girls "lose voice" in adolescence; they dissociate from their real selves, a loss that puts them at risk for depression and anxiety.

### DEVELOPMENT OF THE ETHIC OF CARE AND VOICE

Gilligan offers two explanations regarding how the ethic of care and women's different voice develop. The first draws from the psychoanalytic theory of Nancy Chodorow. According to Chodorow, from infancy both boys and girls develop a strong attachment to their mothers, which is the basis for their relational selves. However, during the Oedipal period (about age five), boys must separate from their mothers and must form an autonomous and separate identity as a male. This leads them to repress their relational selves and identify with their fathers. For girls, it is not necessary to detach themselves psychologically from their mothers in order to develop a gender role identity as a female; their attachment to their mothers is not repressed, and girls maintain a strong relational self.

*Carol Gilligan.* (Courtesy of Carol Gilligan)

Gilligan claimed to find a developmental pattern in her study of women facing a decision to have an abortion, described in her 1982 book. The first level, called "orientation to individual survival," focused on caring for oneself. The second level, called "goodness as sacrifice" focused on care of self. The third level, "the morality of nonviolence," is a morality of care for both self and others. Gilligan's levels have not been validated in any subsequent studies, raising questions about whether the ethic of care is a developmental construct.

Socialization also affects women's sense of self and is connected with the development of voice. According to Gilligan, society reinforces the male/female gender roles, rewarding boys and men for being autonomous, independent, and rational, while their relational voices are silenced. In contrast, girls' independent autonomous voices are silenced during adolescence when they experience a conflict. If they become "good women" by conforming to societal stereotypes, they risk losing their authentic (independent) self, or voice. However, if girls resist social pressures to conform to an ideal of femininity, they risk damaging their connections to others. Most girls do not resist and, as a consequence, learn to doubt their true selves.

## HISTORICAL CONTEXT FOR GILLIGAN'S THEORY

Gilligan's theory of moral development was an attempt to correct psychological theories that overlooked the experiences of women or discredited women's moral psychology. For example, Sigmund Freud (1856-1939), the "father" of psychoanalysis, had claimed that women and men differ in their moral capacity because girls' superegos are less developed than those of boys. While Freud found women's morality inferior to men's, Gilligan claimed that women's moral thinking was different from men's but of great, if not greater, moral value.

Gilligan's theory drew from the developmental work of Lawrence Kohlberg (1927-1987) but corrected what she claimed was a gender bias in Kohlberg's theory. Kohlberg's theory of moral development was based on six stages of moral thinking that develop universally in an invariant sequence as a result of maturation and experience. In 1969, Kohlberg published results comparing men's and women's moral reasoning and reported that women typically scored at stage three, "mutual interpersonal expectations, relationships, and conformity," while men typically scored at stage four, "social system and conscience maintenance." Because developmental theories such as Kohlberg's assume higher stages to be superior, this was tantamount to saying that the moral reasoning of women was less well developed than that of men. However, Kohlberg made no claim regarding gender differences in moral reasoning. It is likely that in the 1960's, when his study was conducted, his sample of working men and their wives had very different life experiences and that these differences account for his findings.

Gilligan's influential book *In a Different Voice* entered the field of the psychology of women at an important time. In the 1960's and 1970's, researchers who were studying the psychology of women had argued that empirical evidence shows that psychological differences between men and women are small, and, if they exist at all, gender differences are due to socialization and experience. If no relevant differences exist, there is no basis for assigning men and women to different spheres; gender cannot be used to exclude women from education, political life, or work.

Androgyny theorists in the 1960's and 1970's sought to discredit claims of gender differences that denigrate women or bar them from educational or career opportunities. They argued that with proper gender-role socialization, boys and girls, men and women would be equal in psychological attributes. However, by the late 1970's, feminist psychologists began pointing out that androgyny theory contained its own problems: The qualities of competitiveness, aggression, independence, and autonomy, which characterized the masculine norm, might not be the best ideal for either men or women. Some feminist psychologists, such as Jean Baker Miller, sought a new norm for human development, an ideal that celebrated the alternative, feminine virtues of care, concern for others, and the ability to maintain strong relationships with others.

In this postandrogyny period, Gilligan's theory was hailed as a corrective to psychological studies based on male samples that posited masculinity as normative. Gilligan called attention to the study of adolescent girls and claimed to map a new psychological theory that begins with the experience of girls and women and reveals women's different voice.

## RESEARCH ON MORAL REASONING, MORAL ORIENTATION, AND VOICE

Research on moral psychology shows that children are concerned with moral issues at a very early age. They care about "what's fair," and they are disturbed when someone has been hurt, suggesting that both justice and care orientations can be identified early in life. Research also shows that in Western culture, girls and women are expected to be more concerned with relationships and more in tune with their feelings than boys. However, a great deal of research since the 1970's has shown that girls and boys are not as different in moral reasoning and voice as Gilligan claims.

Studies using the Kohlbergian Moral Judgment Interview (MJI) reveal that males and females at the same age and educational levels are equally able to resolve moral dilemmas by appealing to justice principles. Similar results have been obtained with the Defining Issues Test (DIT), the most frequently used objective test of comprehension of and preference for moral issues. Meta-analysis on DIT scores reveals that education is 250 times more powerful than gender in predicting principled moral reasoning. Narrative and longitudinal studies also have shown that women are as likely as men at the same educational level to advance in the sequential order of development predicted from Kohlberg's theory. In sum, evidence does not support the assertions that, compared with females, males are more principled in their moral reasoning, more concerned with conflicts resulting from conflicting claims about rights, or more capable of using abstract principles of justice in their moral reasoning. Evidence does not support the claim that Kohlberg's theory or measure of moral reasoning is biased against girls or women.

Are women more caring or more relational than men? Are they more likely to be silenced, silence themselves, or lose their voice than men? The evidence to support or refute Gilligan's assertion that the ethic of care characterizes female morality or voice is inconclusive. In part, this is because there are so many different ways that care and voice as psychological constructs are measured; it is difficult to compare across studies that operationalize the constructs differently. Different researchers view the ethic of care as a moral theory, an interpersonal orientation, a perceptual focus, or an epistemological theory. Voice is understood variously as a theory of self, a moral perspective, or a defensive posture. Furthermore, most of Gilligan's qualitative studies of girls' development only present girls' voices, and gender differences cannot be tested.

Research on the ethic of care suggests that the majority of people, both males and females, can and do use both care and justice orientations. Some studies, particularly those conducted using Gilligan's qualitative interview, report that females tend to focus on the care orientation and males on the justice orientation, particularly in self-identified moral dilemmas. While qualitative research is very important in developing theory and understanding a construct, testing specific hypotheses (such as that there are gender differences in voice) requires quantitative studies. Most such studies fail to support Gilligan's theory of gender differences in moral orientation.

Some researchers have found that whether someone uses an ethic of care or an ethic of justice depends on the type of moral dilemma they discuss. Lawrence J. Walker and his colleagues found that when participants talked about their own moral dilemmas, females were more likely to identify interpersonal dilemmas, whereas males were more likely to choose impersonal dilemmas. If respondents focussed on people and their relationships (a friend who betrays another friend), they were more likely to see that the ethic of care had been violated. If respondents focussed on issues in which the rights of others were violated or societal rules were transgressed (breaking a law), they were more likely to be concerned about justice. Interpersonal conflicts elicited a care orientation, while issues of conflicting rights elicited a justice orientation for both men and women. However, when asked to think about an issue differently, both boys and girls were able to change and use either justice or care reasoning.

Gilligan's studies of adolescent girls' voices, using her methods of interview, focus groups, and open-ended sentence completion measures, depict a conflicted adolescence, loss of voice, and growing dissociation from what girls know. While some girls resist, most strive to retain their relationships, and thus seek to please others even if it means developing an inauthentic self.

Research conducted by Susan Harter using more standardized measures and large samples of both boys and girls indicates that adolescence is a challenging time for girls, and that they are concerned about their relationships. Girls feel silenced by others and they silence themselves, but not more so than adolescent boys. Harter's studies of loss of voice indicate there are not gender differences in voice, that girls do not have lower levels of voice than boys, and voice does not decline with age.

## GENDER DIFFERENCE RESEARCH

Given the empirical results that gender differences, when they exist, are small and usually attributable to different socialization, why do such claims persist? In part the answer lies in the methodology that is used in research on gender. Gilligan and her colleagues' work, particularly their research using qualitatively analyzed interviews, leads to the conclusion that there are large differences in the ways boys and girls view moral issues, think, react emotionally, and commit to relationships. However, studies that use standardized measures to compare men and women reveal more similarities than differences. Either conclusion has important implications.

Rachel Hare-Mustin and Jeanne Marecek claim that as knowledge in the social sciences is always incomplete, interpretation of events, including research findings, is always subject to bias. They suggest two forms of bias influence beliefs about gender differences. Alpha bias is the tendency to emphasize gender difference; beta bias is the tendency to emphasize similarity. In beta bias, underemphasizing gender differences can lead to ignoring the different resources men and women need. In contrast, alpha bias, overestimating differences, can lead one to advocate different roles for men and women. If women are more caring, ought they to be the caregivers? If men are more justice oriented, ought they to be judges? If there is no difference in moral orientation between boys and girls, ought all children to be taught to use both principles? Ought care and justice to be expected from all adults?

## GILLIGAN'S CONTRIBUTION

Gilligan raised important questions in the field of the psychology of morality and in so doing drew attention to the ethic of care. While the gender differences that she originally asserted have not been found, her work draws on the experience of girls and women in ways that value that experience. Her insistence that studying the lives of girls is as important as studying the lives of boys brought a good deal of research attention that can lead to new knowledge and new ways to promote the well-being of all boys and girls, men and women.

## SOURCES FOR FURTHER STUDY

Brown, Lyn Mikel, and Carol Gilligan. *Meeting at the Crossroads: Women's Psychology and Girls' Development.* Cambridge, Mass.: Harvard University

Press, 1992. This book describes interviews conducted at the Laurel School, a private day school for girls. The authors describe the listener's guide, a method of listening to girls' thoughts and feelings. The interviews demonstrate that relationships are central concerns for middle and high school girls.

Chodorow, Nancy. *The Reproduction of Mothering: Psychoanalysis and the Sociology of Gender.* 2d ed. Berkeley: University of California Press, 1999. Chodorow draws on psychoanalytic theory to describe how women's mothering is reproduced across culture and across time. The book requires a fairly good background in psychoanalytic theory.

Freud, Sigmund. "Some Psychical Consequences of the Anatomical Distinction Between the Sexes." In *The Standard Edition of the Complete Psychological Works of Sigmund Freud.* Vol 19. Translated and edited by James Strachey. London: The Hogarth Press, 1966-1973. Freud claimed that because of anatomical differences, girls do not have an Oedipal conflict as emotionally strong as that of boys. As a consequence, boys develop a stronger superego, the structure of the psyche responsible for morality.

Gilligan, Carol. *In a Different Voice: Psychological Theory and Women's Development.* Reprint. Cambridge, Mass.: Harvard University Press, 1993. The theory of ethic of care and girls' and women's different moral voice is described. This often-cited book launched a great deal of discussion and prompted many studies of adolescent girls. Gilligan describes her theory of gender differences in moral orientation and of women's voice as different from men's voice.

Gilligan, Carol, Nona Lyons, and Trudy Hanmer, eds. *Making Connections: The Relational Worlds of Adolescent Girls at Emma Willard School.* Cambridge, Mass.: Harvard University Press, 1990. The voices of girls and their resistance to imposed silencing of their voices are described through interviews conducted at the Emma Willard School, a private day and boarding school for girls.

Gilligan, Carol, Annie G. Rogers, and Deborah L. Tolman. *Women, Girls, and Psychotherapy: Reframing Resistance.* New York: Harrington Park Press, 1991. This collection of essays describes the social pressures that silence girls' voices and demonstrates girls' resistance to being silenced.

Gilligan, Carol, Jamie Victoria Ward, and Jill McLean Taylor, with Betty Bardige, eds. *Mapping the Moral Domain: A Contribution of Women's Thinking to Psychological Theory and Education.* Cambridge, Mass.: Harvard Graduate School of Education, 1988. These essays describe research on gender and morality and include a chapter on the origins of gender differences in moral orientation. Many of the chapters were previously published as journal articles or book chapters.

Hare-Mustin, Rachel, and Jeanne Marecek, eds. *Making a Difference: Psychology and the Construction of Gender.* New Haven, Conn.: Yale University Press, 1990. The essays describe how gender differences are socially constructed and includes Hare-Mustin and Marecek's discussion of alpha and beta bias, a distinction that is useful in interpreting findings of gender differences.

Harter, Susan. *The Construction of the Self: A Developmental Perspective.* New York: Guilford Press, 1999. Harter describes her theory and measurement of the self from a developmental perspective. This book includes an important summary and discussion of her research on gender differences in voice.

Miller, Jean Baker. *Toward a New Psychology of Women.* 2d ed. Boston: Beacon Press, 1986. Miller draws on her clinical experience with women to describe and value a relational self, as defined through connections and relationships with others. This is an essential text for understanding relational theories about women's psychology.

Walker, Lawrence J. "Sex Differences in the Development of Moral Reasoning: A Critical Review." *Child Development* 55 (1984): 677-691. Walker's first meta-analysis revealed no gender differences in moral reasoning among men and women. Subsequent studies conducted by Walker and associates have confirmed his initial findings.

*Mary Brabeck*

SEE ALSO: Moral Development; Women's Psychology: Karen Horney; Women's Psychology: Sigmund Freud.

# WOMEN'S PSYCHOLOGY
## KAREN HORNEY

TYPE OF PSYCHOLOGY: Personality
FIELDS OF STUDY: Classic analytic themes and issues; personality theory

*Horney's theories emphasize the effects of cultural influences on women's personality development. Her theories modified classical psychoanalytic views and provided new insights into women's interpersonal relationships.*

KEY CONCEPTS
- biological influences
- classical psychoanalysis
- cultural influences
- instinct
- neo-Freudians
- sexual instinct
- unconscious

Karen Horney (1885-1952) considered people to be products of their environment as well as of biology. She stressed the ways in which cultural influences affect women's personality development. These cultural influences include interpersonal relationships and society's attitudes about women.

Cultural influences are overlooked by classical psychoanalysis—a system of psychology based on Freudian doctrine and procedure that seeks the root of human behavior in the unconscious, a region of the mind that is the seat of repressed impulses and experiences of which the conscious mind is unaware. Unconscious motivation and conflict, particularly sexual conflict, according to Horney, play an important role in women's development. She viewed women as living in a male-oriented world in which they are judged by men according to male standards. Women have come to believe that these male-based standards represent their true nature. As a result, according to Horney, women live with the dilemma of having to choose between fulfilling their ambitions and meeting their needs for love by adhering to the passive role that society assigns to them. These circumstances contribute to depression and low self-esteem.

Horney described three basic patterns of behavior by which people relate to others: moving toward (or self-effacing), moving away from (or distancing), and moving against (or expanding). The moving-toward behavior involves dependency and taking care of others as well as self-effacement. Women have been conditioned since birth to relate to others in this manner, according to Horney.

### RELATIONSHIP TO FREUDIAN THEORY
Horney's theories were modifications of classical psychoanalytic beliefs. Her theories are best understood when viewed in relation to the Freudian con-

cepts that were prevalent during her lifetime. According to Sigmund Freud, who founded classical psychoanalysis during the late nineteenth century, biological influences determine human behavior. Of these biological factors, sexual instincts are the strongest motivators of human behavior. Neurosis, or mental disorder, was considered by Freud to be the result of unconscious sexual conflicts which began in early childhood.

Horney was grounded in psychoanalytic thinking and agreed with many of Freud's concepts. She disagreed radically, however, with the heavy sexual content of Freudian theory. A major point of departure was the Freudian concept of penis envy. Freud essentially viewed all psychological problems in women to be the result of the woman's inherent wish to be a man. Freud maintained that girls are not born with a natural sense of their femininity and regard themselves as inferior, castrated boys. As a result of penis envy, the female rebels against her biological inferiority. The consequences, according to Freud, are resentment, devaluation of her "negative sexual endowments," envying the opposite sex, and a constant search for compensation.

Horney considered penis envy to be contrary to biological thinking. She maintained that little girls are instinctively feminine and aware of their femaleness in early childhood. Thus, girls are not programmed to feel inferior. Women may envy men the power and freedom they have in their private and professional lives, but women do not envy men's genitals. The behaviors which Freud associated with penis envy—including greed, envy, and ambition—Horney attributed to the restrictions society places on females.

Horney also disagreed with the Freudian theory that viewed frigidity and masochism as biologically determined aspects of woman's nature. Frigidity, or the inability of a woman to experience sexual desire, is neither a normal condition for a woman nor an illness, according to Horney. She considered frigidity to be a symptom of an underlying psychological disturbance, such as chronic anxiety. Frequently, it is caused by tensions between marital partners. Powerful forces in society restrict a woman in the free expression of her sexuality. Custom and education promote female inhibitions. Men's tendency to view their wives as spiritual partners and to look for sexual excitement with prostitutes or others whom they do not respect may also cause frigidity in wives.

Masochistic tendencies, wherein a woman seeks and enjoys pain and suffering, particularly in her sexual life, result from special social circumstances, Horney maintained. Freudian theory, holding that women are biologically programmed for masochism, is associated with the Freudian concept of the female as having been rendered less powerful than the male through castration. Horney, on the other hand, believed that society encourages women to be masochistic. Women are stereotyped as weak and emotional, as enjoying dependence, and these qualities are rewarded by men. Masochistic tendencies, according to Horney, are a way of relating by which a woman tries to obtain security and satisfaction through submission and self-effacement.

Karen Horney's theories stressed the positive aspects of femininity. As her ideas developed, she became more influenced by social scientists of her period. Her theories placed increasing emphasis on interpersonal and social attitudes in determining women's feelings, relations, and roles. Her ideas about the development of women's sexuality were focused on adolescent girls, rather than on young children, as in Freudian theory. According to Horney, adolescents develop attitudes to cope with sexual conflict, and these attitudes carry over into adulthood.

## New Approach to Women and Relationships

Horney's theories opened the door for new ways of understanding women's personalities and relationships. In a 1984 study of women's reactions to separation and loss, psychotherapist Alexandra Symonds found Horney's theories to be relevant to what she encountered in her woman patients. Writing in the *American Journal of Psychoanalysis,* Symonds reported female reactions to separation and loss to be a frequent motivation for women to enter therapy. In contrast, she found that men come into therapy in these circumstances mainly because of pressure from a wife or girlfriend. According to Symonds, women are more eager than men to create relationships, and women express more feeling when the relationships end.

Symonds considered these behaviors from the viewpoint of the three basic patterns of behavior described by Horney: moving toward, moving away from, and moving against. Symonds viewed the moving-toward, self-effacing type of behavior as love oriented, or dependent; the moving-away-from, detached type as freedom oriented; and the moving-against, expansive type as power oriented. According to Symonds's views, society assigns the love-oriented, dependent pattern to women, while men are encouraged to develop power- or freedom-oriented patterns. She described a frequent combination in a couple to be a detached, expansive, power-oriented male married to a dependent, self-effacing, love-oriented female. Relationships often develop between the silent, withdrawn, noncommunicative male and the loving, dependent woman who always wants to talk about feelings.

As people develop character patterns, such as love-oriented and dependent, they suppress feelings that cause inner conflicts, such as aggressiveness, according to Symonds. By contrast, power-oriented people suppress dependent feelings. People idealize their self-values and feel contempt for what is suppressed; thus, the power-oriented person views dependency and need as contemptible weaknesses. This contempt is conveyed to those who are aware of their dependency needs. Women then add self-hate for needing others to the anxiety they feel when a relationship ends.

Extremely dependent, self-effacing women often stay in poor and even abusive relationships rather than separate, according to Symonds. They are victims of a culture that considers a woman nothing unless attached to a man. Symonds found these women to be coming from two different backgrounds: either having been held close by mother or father during childhood and adolescence, thus having no opportunity for healthy growth; or having separated prematurely from parents in childhood in an effort to become self-sufficient at an early age, often having developed a facade of self-sufficiency with deep, unresolved dependency needs.

## UNDERSTANDING FEAR OF SUCCESS

Horney's theories predicted the anxiety women feel about their own ambition and the ways in which women sabotage their competence and success. In the book *Women in Therapy* (1988), psychotherapist Harriet Goldhor Lerner discusses female work inhibition in the light of Horney's theories. Lerner views work inhibition as an unconscious attempt to preserve harmony within a relationship as well as to allay fears of being unfeminine. Women often fear success because they fear they will pay dearly for their accomplishments. Women frequently equate success, or the wish for it, with the loss of femininity and attractiveness, loss of significant relationships, loss of health, or even loss of life. Feelings of depression and anxiety are ways women either apologize for their competence and success on the one hand or ensure the lack of success on the other hand, according to Lerner. She views self-sacrifice or self-sabotage to be other common ways women react to their feelings of guilt and anxiety about becoming successful.

When faced with the choice (real or imagined) of sacrificing the self to preserve a relationship or strengthening the self at the risk of threatening a relationship, women often choose the former, according to Lerner. She applies Horney's views to the situation of a thirty-year-old married woman who entered therapy because of personal distress and marital tension over her desire to enroll in graduate school and embark on a career. Lerner found that multigenerational guilt on the part of the woman was involved, as well as fears of destroying her marriage. The woman's husband was opposed to his wife's enrolling in graduate school. In addition, the woman was the first female in her family to aspire to graduate school. In the face of these circumstances, she put aside her ambitions in order to preserve harmony in her relationships. The woman's work inhibition involved profound anxiety and guilt over striving for things previous generations of women in her family could not have. Work inhibition also may result when a woman perceives her strivings as "too masculine," a perception Lerner sees as reinforced by society. Being labeled "masculine" triggers deep guilt and anxiety in women.

## BACKGROUND AND ACCOMPLISHMENTS

Horney's theories on female psychology developed from a series of papers she wrote over a thirteen-year period in response to Freud's views on female sexuality. The last paper was published after Horney emigrated to the United States from Germany at a highly productive point in her career.

One of the first women admitted to medical school in Berlin, she had completed her psychiatric and psychoanalytic training there by 1913. By that time, Freud had passed the peak of his greatest creative years. Horney was thirty years younger than Freud and a product of the twentieth century. Her views were more in tune with the relatively open structure of twentieth century science than with the more closed science of Freud's period. Horney was influenced greatly by sociologists of her time. She and other neo-Freudians, such as Harry Stack Sullivan, Alfred Adler, and Erich Fromm, were the first psychoanalysts to emphasize cultural influences on personality development.

Horney's theories grew out of a need for a feminine psychology different from male psychology. She believed that women were being analyzed and treated according to a male-oriented psychology that considered women to be biologically inferior to men. She did not find these male theories supported by what she observed in her female patients or in her own life experience.

Horney was the first woman doctor to challenge male theory and went on to take a position in the foreground of the psychoanalytic movement. In so doing, she became a role model for women in general and professional women in particular. She was a controversial figure, and her career involved many disputes with the established psychoanalytic world. She and her followers eventually were ostracized by the establishment, and for a time her name disappeared from the psychoanalytic literature. Her biographers attribute this to a fear on the part of some Freudians of being contaminated by association with her ideas.

## MODERN-DAY IMPACT

A growing interest in her work occurred during the women's movement in the 1970's. The women's movement brought her name back into the literature as a pioneer in upgrading women's status. Her name began appearing more frequently in literature associated with women's therapy. The series of important books which she had written throughout her career remain popular and continue to be used as textbooks.

An independent thinker, Horney is considered an individual who was always ahead of her time. Her work anticipated a revival of interest in the narcissistic personality. Her theories predicted popular trends in psychology, although she often is not credited for her ideas. One of these trends is the increasing emphasis on social and cultural factors as causes of emotional illness. Systems theory is another popular trend related to Horney's concepts. Systems theory, which includes a type of psychology called family therapy, emphasizes the continuous interaction among cultural conditions, interpersonal relations, and inner emotional experience.

## SOURCES FOR FURTHER STUDY

Horney, Karen. *Feminine Psychology.* 1967. Reprint. New York: W. W. Norton, 1993. A collection of all of Horney's writings on feminine psychology.

Gives a flavor of Horney's personality and force as a psychoanalyst and educator. Includes an informative introduction by Harold Kelman, one of Horney's colleagues. Available through college libraries.

Lerner, Harriet Goldhor. *Women in Therapy.* Reprint. New York: Harper-Collins, 1989. Discusses women and their psychotherapists from a psychoanalytic perspective, with references to Horney's theories. Illustrates how Horney's theories apply to many themes and issues in women's psychology.

Paris, Bernard. *Karen Horney: A Psychoanalyst's Search for Self-Understanding.* New Haven, Conn.: Yale University Press, 1996. A biography of Horney that places her theories squarely within the context of her life history. Written by the editor of the papers unpublished during Horney's lifetime (*The Unknown Karen Horney,* 2000).

Quinn, Susan. *A Mind of Her Own: The Life of Karen Horney.* Reading, Mass.: Addison-Wesley, 1988. This biography is an excellent source of information about Horney's personal and professional life. Much of it is devoted to her female psychology. Easy to read; contains photographs, biographical essays, extensive source notes, and a complete list of Horney's work.

Rubins, Jack L. *Karen Horney: Gentle Rebel of Psychoanalysis.* New York: Dial Press, 1978. The first biography of Karen Horney. Thorough and well documented; includes detailed discussions of Horney's theories on women. Lengthy but well organized. Can be read by the college or high school student.

Symonds, Alexandra. "Separation and Loss: Significance for Women." *American Journal of Psychoanalysis* 45, no. 1 (1985): 53-58. Discusses women's feelings about separation and loss. Important illustration of how Horney's theories help explain women's role in interpersonal relationships. Available in college libraries.

*Margaret M. Frailey*

SEE ALSO: Consciousness; Dreams; Instinct Theory; Psychoanalysis; Psychoanalytic Psychology; Psychoanalytic Psychology and Personality: Sigmund Freud; Social Psychological Models: Karen Horney; Women's Psychology: Carol Gilligan; Women's Psychology: Sigmund Freud.

# WOMEN'S PSYCHOLOGY
## SIGMUND FREUD

TYPE OF PSYCHOLOGY: Personality
FIELDS OF STUDY: Classic analytic themes and issues; personality theory

*Freud, the first person to develop a comprehensive theory of personality, thought that women undergo distinct experiences in the development of their personalities. He believed that traumatic events during the phallic stage (from approximately three to five years of age) were likely to hinder normal female development, the results being a failure of same-sex identification and a diminished superego or moral capacity.*

KEY CONCEPTS
- free association
- id
- identification
- instincts
- Oedipus complex
- penis envy
- psychosexual stages of development
- superego

Two central concepts underlie Sigmund Freud's theory of personality development. The first is the notion of the unconscious; the second concept has to do with the role of infantile sexuality. Freud believed that consciousness could be viewed as a continuum of experience, with one pole being the familiar one of acute awareness of one's thoughts, feelings, and behaviors and the other pole being a state of profound unconsciousness in which one's feelings, thoughts, and wishes are completely beyond one's awareness. Midway between these poles is the preconscious, which Freud believed contained material or mental life from both the conscious and the unconscious and could, with effort, be made totally conscious. Freud believed that the bulk of mental life is represented in the unconscious, with only a small portion, "the tip of the iceberg," being conscious awareness.

Operating from the depths of the unconscious, a structure of personality known as the id operates to seek pleasure, to avoid pain at all costs, and to accomplish solely selfish aims. The id is the source of all psychic energy, including both sexual and aggressive instincts.

### PSYCHOSEXUAL STAGES OF DEVELOPMENT THEORY
Freud proposed that the sexual instincts are critical and that personality develops over time as the individual responds to these instincts. He believed that a number of component instincts arise from various regions of the body. These instincts strive for satisfaction in what he calls organ pleasure. Each of these organs is the focus of a phase or stage of development, the first

of which is the oral stage. The oral stage begins at birth and continues through the first year, as the infant seeks pleasure through the mouth, and the mouth becomes the source of all gratification. Milk from the mother's breast or a bottle is devoured, just as, later, any object that the child can reach will be manipulated and explored orally. The child takes in physical nourishment in the same way that he or she takes in, in a very rudimentary way, the behaviors, values, and beliefs of others, beginning the basis for later identification with others.

The second psychosexual stage of development is the anal stage, which Freud believed revolved around the pleasure associated with elimination. During the second year of life, the child begins taking control of urination and defecation, trying to do so within parental and societal limits.

Freud believed that both boys and girls proceed through the oral stage in essentially the same manner. For both, the mother is the primary love object. Sometime after the third year, however, Freud believed that the sexes diverge. In the third, or phallic, stage of development, both boys and girls discover the pleasurable nature of the genitals. For boys, the stage is centered on the Oedipus complex, in which they develop strong sexual feelings toward their mothers. These feelings are accompanied by others, such as anger and jealousy, as fathers are perceived as competitors for mothers' affection and attention. As sexual desires heighten, the boy begins to perceive competition and hostility from the father. The sense of peril becomes located in the physical source of the boy's feelings for his mother, the penis, and the result is a phenomenon that Freud called castration anxiety—the fear that the father will retaliate. Over time, fear of castration motivates the boy to give up the mother as a love object and turn toward the father in same-sex identification. According to Freud, this strengthening identification with the father is essential for the development of a solid superego, which, in turn, empowers the male, making possible major contributions to culture and society.

Unlike the male's experience, the onset of the phallic stage for females entails a major trauma: the realization that she does not have a penis. Often, the realization is accompanied by the notion that the mother is responsible for her own and her daughter's castrated state. Here the little girl turns away from her mother as the primary love object and turns toward her father, limiting her future chances for same-sex identification. Feelings of inferiority pervade, and she falls victim to penis envy, a chronic wish for the superior male organ. Freud believed that, as a result of this trauma, the remaining course of female development would be difficult at best and that the accomplishment of same-sex identification was questionable. The girl's life is thus spent in search of a substitute penis, which Freud thought might be a husband or a child, particularly a male child. Indeed, Freud believed that the single most rewarding relationship in a woman's life would be her relationship with her son, regarding which her feelings would be totally unambivalent.

*Sigmund Freud in London in 1938, a year before his death at age eighty-three.* (Library of Congress)

Freud believed that the foundations of personality were in place by the end of the phallic stage. He described the post-Oedipal period, beginning with the latency stage, as a period when children repress, or make unconscious, the sexual conflicts of the Oedipal period. Females during this time are said to be more passive and less aggressive than boys, but, like boys, they tend to seek out same-sex play groups.

The final psychosexual stage of development is the genital stage. Unlike the previous, more self-centered periods of stimulation and gratification, the genital stage marks a period of sexual attraction to others and a time during which social activities and career goals become important before marriage. The child is thus transformed into an adult. Freud believed that, in some cases, failure to resolve the female Oedipus complex results in neurosis, which he often observed in his practice with women patients. He believed that in other cases the lack of resolution caused a masculinity complex in which women attempt to succeed in traditionally male endeavors (he offered this explanation to his contemporary female analysts for their behavior). Freud believed that the female's failure to unite with her mother in post-Oedipal identification, and her subsequent diminished superego capacity, caused her to have a tendency toward negative personality traits and an inability to apply objective standards of justice.

## CRITICISMS

Several of Freud's contemporaries, including some women analysts, were critical of Freud's views on the psychology of women. Among his critics was Karen Horney, who rejected the idea that penis envy is central to normal female development. She acknowledged, however, that from a cultural point of view, envy of the male role might explain some of Freud's clinical observations better than the biological notion of penis envy. In addition, after many years of analyzing female patients, Horney began analyzing males; from her observations, she concluded that males often exhibit an intense envy of pregnancy, childbirth, and motherhood, as well as of the breasts and of the act of suckling.

### FREE INTERPRETATION AND DREAM ANALYSIS

Historically, psychoanalysis has represented a method of psychological observation, a set of theoretical constructs or ideas, and an approach to psychotherapy. When Freud began psychoanalysis, it was a method of observation intended to broaden the knowledge of human behavior. Believing that the unconscious is the major clue to solving problems of human behavior, Freud used two processes to understand it: free association and dream interpretation. Free association, the reporting of what comes to mind in an unedited fashion, was an important tool used to discover the contents of the unconscious. Freud believed that all thoughts are connected in some fashion and that therefore the spontaneous utterances of the patient are always meaningful clues to what has been repressed or buried in the unconscious. Freud also believed that the unconscious can be clarified by means of dream interpretation. Those thoughts and impulses that are unacceptable to the conscious mind are given symbols in dreams.

An interesting study conducted by Calvin Hall in 1964 illustrates how the interpretation of dreams has been used in research—in this case, to test Freud's observation that the superego is not as strong in females as it appears to be in males. Hall reasoned that a person with a strong internalized superego would be independent of external agents, whereas a person who has a less internalized superego would tend to disown his or her own guilt and blame external authority figures. Hall further made the assumption that dreams in which the dreamer was the victim of aggression were expressions of an externalized superego, whereas dreams in which the dreamer was the victim of misfortune (accident, circumstance) were expressions of an internalized superego. It was hypothesized that females would be more likely to dream of themselves as victims of aggression and males would be more likely to dream of themselves as victims of misfortune. Careful content analysis of more than three thousand dreams of young adults was performed. Results supported the hypotheses, although Hall cautioned that additional hypotheses should be tested and more diverse data collected to support thoroughly Freud's theory of the differences between the male and the female superego.

## TRANSFERENCE AND THE UNCONSCIOUS

Freud was also the first to understand and describe the concept of transference, the patient's positive or negative feelings that develop toward the therapist during the long, intimate process of analysis. These feelings often relate to earlier ones that the patient has had for significant others: namely, mother, father, or sibling. The analysis of transference has become extremely important to neo-Freudian analysts, particularly as it relates to the treatment of borderline and other personality disturbances.

Another aspect of Freud's legacy involves the many theoretical constructs that psychoanalysis has generated. Among these is the concept of the unconscious. Freud provided many everyday examples of the operation of the unconscious as he described slips of the tongue and other phenomena. He was convinced that such slips, now known as "Freudian slips," were not accidental at all but somehow expressed unconscious wishes, thoughts, or desires. For example, the woman who loses her wedding ring wishes she had never had it.

## MENTAL ILLNESS THERAPY

Finally, psychoanalysis also represents a method of therapy that Freud and later analysts used to treat the symptoms of mental illness. Practicing for many years, Freud refined his technique, using free association and dream interpretation to help patients gain insight into themselves by recognizing their unconscious patterns and to help them work through the unconscious conflicts that affect everyday life. Many of Freud's patients were women, and it was from these women's recollections in analysis that Freud built his theory of female development. Some of Freud's critics argue that building a theory of normal development from the observation of pathology or abnormality represents an inappropriate conceptual leap.

## SEXUAL BASIS OF NEUROSIS

During years of conducting analysis, Freud became convinced of the sexual basis of neurosis. He believed that sexual experiences occurring prior to puberty and stored in the unconscious as memories produced conflict that later caused certain neurotic conditions. These ideas, often referred to as Freud's seduction theory, were used to explain hysterical symptoms such as paralysis, blindness, inability to understand the spoken word (receptive aphasia), and sexual dysfunction as the result of sexual abuse, probably occurring before ages six to eight. It is important to note, however, that Freud later revised his thinking on infantile sexuality and concluded that it is the thought or psychic reality of the individual that counts more than the physical reality of events. In other words, a person might fantasize a seduction, store the fantasy in unconscious memory (repress it), and have that conflictual memory cause neurosis just as readily as the memory of an actual seduction. Some recent critics have suggested that Freud's reformulation represented a form of denial of his inability to recognize the prevalence of sexual abuse at that time.

## FREUD'S BACKGROUND AND IMPACT

Born in 1856 to Jewish parents, Freud lived and practiced most of his life in Vienna. He was graduated from medical school in 1881 and practiced as a clinical neurologist for several years before becoming interested in the "talking cure" that his colleague, Josef Breuer, had developed as a means of dealing with his patients' emotional symptoms. Freud's writings and lectures on the subject of hysteria and its sexual roots led him to be ostracized by most of his medical colleagues. His medical training and the influence of the work of Charles Darwin were largely responsible for his emphasis on sexual and aggressive instincts as the basis for behavior.

Freud's theory was important because it was the first of its kind and because it was controversial, generating further research into and theorizing about the female personality.

## CHALLENGES TO FREUDIAN THEORY

Over the years, many aspects of Freudian theory have been challenged. Freud's notion that penis envy is a primary motivator in the female personality was challenged by Karen Horney, who believed that, if it existed, a woman's envy was related to the male's privileged role in society. Freud's idea that the clitoral orgasm is immature and must be surrendered for the vaginal orgasm at puberty spurred work by William Masters and Virginia Johnson, who concluded, after much rigorous research, that orgasm is a reaction of the entire pelvic area.

Freud's theory has forced critics to determine what is uniquely female about personality. In *Toward a New Psychology of Women* (1976), Jean Baker Miller attempted to show how traditional theories of female behavior have failed to acknowledge the essence of the female personality. Miller suggested that affiliation is the cornerstone of the female experience and that it is in response to her relationships with others that a woman's personality grows and develops.

In her book *In a Different Voice* (1982), Carol Gilligan disputes Freud's notion that females show less of a sense of justice than males and have weak superegos. She argues that morality involves respect for the needs of self balanced with respect for the needs of others; thus, it is not that females lack the justice principle but rather that they have different expressions of justice and different internal and external demands.

Heavily influenced by Freud, many object-relations theorists continue to make contributions in the area of psychotherapy with clients whose early relationships have been disturbed or disrupted. This work will continue to constitute the basis for decisions made by courts, adoption agencies, and social-service agencies regarding the placement of children.

Freud's views on the origins of neurosis may continue to play a role in the understanding of multiple personality disorder and its roots in early sexual abuse. The concept of body memory, the physical memory that abuse has occurred, may well bridge the gap between Freud's concepts of repressed psychic memory and repressed actual memory of early sexual abuse; it may streamline the treatment of this condition. Freud's theory will no doubt continue to generate controversy, motivating both theory and research in the area of women's personality development.

## SOURCES FOR FURTHER STUDY

Freud, Sigmund. *New Introductory Lectures on Psychoanalysis*. New York: W. W. Norton, 1933. This volume contains seven lectures or papers that Freud wrote toward the end of his career. Among them is "The Psychology of Women," in which he attempts to explain some fundamental differences between the sexes. Freud describes female behavior and the Oedipus complex for males and females, and he elaborates on the role of penis envy in female development. The volume also contains lectures on dreams, on the structure of personality, and on anxiety and the instincts.

_____. *The Standard Edition of the Complete Psychological Works of Sigmund Freud*. Edited by James Strachey. London: Hogarth Press, 1966-1973. Volume 7 in this collection of Freud's works contains a detailed case history of a woman named Dora, whom Freud treated over a period of years. This case history illustrates Freud's ideas about the causes of neurosis and hysterical symptoms. The work also contains three essays on sexuality, including sexual aberrations, infantile sexuality, and puberty.

Gilligan, Carol. *In a Different Voice*. Reprint. Cambridge, Mass.: Harvard University Press, 1993. Traditional theories of development have tried to impose male thinking and values on female psychology. Gilligan discusses the importance of relationships as well as female conceptions of morality, challenging Freud's views on female superego development.

Horney, Karen. *Feminine Psychology*. Reprint. Edited by Harold Kelman. New York: W. W. Norton, 1993. A collection of some of Horney's early works in which she describes Freudian ideas on the psychology of women and offers her own observations and conclusions. Horney disputes Freud's notion of penis envy and in later essays explores such topics as distrust between the sexes, premenstrual tension, and female masochism.

Miller, Jean Baker. *Toward a New Psychology of Women*. 1976. 2d ed. Boston: Beacon Press, 1987. Miller proposes that traditional theories of female development have overlooked a critical ingredient in female behavior—affiliation—which she believes is a cornerstone of female psychology.

Miller, Jonathan, ed. *Freud: The Man, His World, His Influence*. Boston: Little, Brown, 1972. Miller has edited a series of essays that put Freud's work in historical, social, and cultural perspective. One essay, by Friedrich Heer, describes the impact of Freud's Jewish background on his life and work in Vienna. Another, by Martin Esslin, describes Vienna, the exciting and culturally rich background for Freud's work.

Rychlak, Joseph F. *Introduction to Personality and Psychotherapy*. 2d ed. Boston: Houghton Mifflin, 1981. This introductory personality text carefully reviews the work of several leading psychologists and psychotherapists, including Sigmund Freud. Rychlak describes the gradual development of Freud's structural hypothesis, and he reviews Freud's ideas about the instincts, dynamic concepts such as defense mechanisms, and the development of the Oedipus complex for males and females, noting the concerns of modern feminists who have found Freud's work offensive.

*Ruth T. Hannon*

SEE ALSO: Abnormality: Psychological Models; Consciousness; Dreams; Instinct Theory; Psychoanalysis; Psychoanalytic Psychology; Psychoanalytic Psychology and Personality: Sigmund Freud; Women's Psychology: Carol Gilligan; Women's Psychology: Karen Horney.

# GLOSSARY

*Absolute threshold:* The smallest amount of stimulus that elicits a sensation 50 percent of the time.

*Accommodation:* In Jean Piaget's theory of development, adjusting the interpretation (schema) of an object or event to include a new instance; in vision, the ability of the lens to focus light on the retina by changing its shape.

*Acetylcholine (ACh):* A cholinergic neurotransmitter important in producing muscular contraction and in some autonomic nerve transmissions.

*Achievement motivation:* The tendency for people to strive for moderately difficult goals because of the relative attractiveness of success and repulsiveness of failure.

*Acquisition:* In learning, the process by which an association is formed in classical or operant conditioning; in memory, the stage at which information is stored in memory.

*Action potential:* A rapid change in electrical charges across a neuron's cell membrane, with depolarization followed by repolarization, leading to a nerve impulse moving down an axon; associated with nerve and muscle activity.

*Actor-observer bias:* The tendency to infer that other people's behavior is caused by dispositional factors but that one's own behavior is the product of situational causes.

*Actualizing tendency:* The force toward maintaining and enhancing the organism, achieving congruence between experience and awareness, and realizing potentials.

*Adaptation:* Any heritable characteristic that presumably has developed as a result of natural selection and thus increases an animal's ability to survive and reproduce.

*Addiction:* Physical dependence on a substance; components include tolerance, psychological dependence, and physical withdrawal symptoms.

*Adolescence:* The period of life extending from the onset of puberty to early adulthood.

*Adrenal glands:* The suprarenal glands, small, caplike structures sitting each on top of one kidney; in general, they function in response to stress, but they are also important in regulating metabolic and sexual functions.

*Affect:* A class name given to feelings, emotions, or dispositions as a mode of mental functioning.

*Affective disorders:* Functional mental disorders associated with emotions or feelings (also called mood disorders); examples include depression and bipolar disorders.

*Afferent:* A sensory neuron or a dendrite carrying information toward a structure; for example, carrying sensory stimuli coming into the reticular formation.

*Affiliation motive:* The motive to seek the company of others and to be with one's own kind, based on such things as cooperation, similarity, friendship, sex, and protection.

*Aggression:* Behavior intended to harm another person or thing.

*Agoraphobia:* An intense fear of being in places or situations in which help may not be available or escape could be difficult.

*Allele:* One of the many forms of a gene; it may be dominant (needing only one copy for the trait to appear) or recessive (needing two copies).

*Altruism:* A phenomenon in human and animal behaviors in which individuals unselfishly sacrifice their own genetic fitness in order to help other individuals in a group.

*Alzheimer's disease:* A form of presenile dementia, characterized by disorientation, loss of memory, speech disturbances, and personality disorders.

*Amplitude:* The peak deviation from the rest state of the movement of a vibrating object, or the ambient state of the medium through which vibration is conducted.

*Anal stage:* According to Sigmund Freud, the second psychosexual stage of personality development, approximately from ages two to four; sexual energy is focused on the anus and on pleasures and conflicts associated with retaining and eliminating feces.

*Analgesia:* The reduction or elimination of pain.

*Analytical psychology:* A school of psychology founded by Carl Jung that views the human mind as the result of prior experiences and the preparation of future goals; it deemphasizes the role of sexuality in psychological disorders.

*Androgens:* Male sex hormones secreted by the testes; testosterone, the primary mammalian male androgen, is responsible for the development and maturation of male sexual structures and sexual behaviors.

*Androgyny:* The expression of both traditionally feminine and traditionally masculine attributes.

*Anorexia nervosa:* An eating disorder characterized by an obsessive-compulsive concern for thinness achieved by dieting, often combined with extreme exercising and sometimes part of a binge-purge cycle.

*Anterograde amnesia:* An inability to form new memories after the onset of amnesia.

*Antidepressants:* Drugs that are used in the treatment of depression, many of which affect or mimic neurotransmitters; classes of antidepressants include the tricyclics and monoamine oxidase inhibitors (MAOIs).

*Antisocial personality disorder:* A personality disorder characterized by a history of impulsive, risk-taking, and perhaps chronic criminal behavior, and by opportunistic interpersonal relations.

*Anxiety:* A chronic fearlike state that is accompanied by feelings of impending doom and that cannot be explained by an actual threatening object or event.

*Aphasia:* Partial or total loss of the use of language as a result of brain damage, characterized by an inability to use or comprehend language.

*Applied research:* Research intended to solve existing problems, as opposed to "basic research," which seeks knowledge for its own sake.

*Aptitude:* The potential to develop an ability with training or experience.

*Archetypes:* In Carl Jung's theory, universal, inherited themes—such as the motifs of the self, hero, and shadow—that exercise an influence on virtually all human beings.

*Archival data:* Information collected at an earlier time by someone other than the present researcher, often for purposes very different from those of the present research.

*Artificial intelligence:* The use of computers to simulate aspects of human thinking and, in some cases, behavior.

*Assimilation:* The interpretation of a new instance of an object or event in terms of one's preexisting schema or understanding; the fit, never perfect, is close enough.

*Attachment:* An emotional bond between infant and caregiver based on reciprocal interaction patterns.

*Attention:* The ability to focus mentally.

*Attitude:* A relatively stable evaluation of a person or thing; it can be either positive or negative, can vary in level of intensity, and has an affective, cognitive, and behavioral component.

*Attribution:* The process by which one gathers information about the self and others and interprets it to determine the cause of an event or behavior.

*Attributional biases:* Typical motivational and cognitive errors in the attribution process; tendencies that are shared among people in using information in illogical or unwarranted ways.

*Autonomic nervous system:* The division of the peripheral nervous system that regulates basic, automatically controlled life processes such as cardiovascular function, digestive function, and genital function.

*Availability heuristic:* A decision-making heuristic whereby a person estimates the probability of some occurrence or event depending on how easily examples of that event can be remembered.

*Aversion therapy:* A therapy that involves pairing something negative (such as electric shock) with an undesired behavior (such as drinking alcohol or smoking cigarettes).

*Axon:* The single fiberlike extension of a neuron that carries information away from the cell body toward the next cell in a pathway.

*Beck Depression Inventory (BDI):* A brief questionnaire used to measure the severity of depression developed by Aaron Beck.

*Behavioral therapy:* A branch of psychotherapy narrowly conceived as the application of classical and operant conditioning to the alteration of clinical problems but more broadly conceived as applied experimental psychology in a clinical context.

*Behaviorism:* A theoretical approach which states that the environment is the primary cause of behavior and that only external, observable stimuli and responses are available to objective study.

*Between-subject designs:* Experimental plans in which different participants receive each level of the independent variable.

*Biofeedback:* A psychophysiological technique in which an individual monitors a specific, supposedly involuntary, bodily function such as blood pressure or heart rate and consciously attempts to control this function through the use of learning principles.

*Bipolar disorder:* A disorder characterized by the occurrence of one or more manic episodes, usually interspersed with one or more major depressive episodes.

*Brain stem:* The lower part of the brain, between the brain and spinal cord, which activates the cortex and makes perception and consciousness possible; it includes the midbrain, pons, medulla, and cerebellum.

*Bystander effect:* The tendency for an individual to be less likely to help as the number of other people present increases.

*Cardinal trait:* According to Gordon W. Allport's theory of personality, a single outstanding characteristic that dominates a person's life; few individuals are characterized by a cardinal disposition.

*Case study:* An in-depth method of data collection in which all available background data on an individual or group are reviewed; typically used in psychotherapy.

*Catecholamines:* A neurotransmitter group derived from the amino acid tyrosine that includes dopamine, epinephrine, and norepinephrine; they are activated in stressful situations.

*Catharsis:* A reduction of psychological tension or physiological arousal by expressing (either directly or vicariously) repressed aggressive or sexual anxieties.

*Central nervous system:* The nerve cells, fibers, and other tissues associated with the brain and spinal cord.

*Central traits:* According to Gordon Allport's theory, the relatively few (five to ten) distinctive and descriptive characteristics that provide direction and focus to a person's life.

*Cerebellum:* The portion of the brain that controls voluntary muscle activity, including posture and body movement; located behind the brain stem.

*Cerebral commissures:* Fiber tracts, such as the corpus callosum and anterior commissure, that connect and allow neural communication between the cerebral hemispheres.

*Cerebral cortex:* The outer layer of the cerebrum; controls higher-level brain functions such as thinking, reasoning, motor coordination, memory, and language.

*Cerebral hemispheres:* Two anatomically similar hemispheres that make up the outer surface of the brain (the cerebral cortex); separated by the cerebral longitudinal fissure.

*Cerebrospinal fluid:* A fluid, derived from blood, that circulates in and around the ventricles of the brain and the spinal cord.

*Cerebrum:* The largest and uppermost portion of the brain; the cerebrum performs sensory and motor functions and affects memory, speech, and emotional functions.

*Chaining:* The process by which several neutral stimuli are presented in a series; they eventually assume reinforcing qualities by being ultimately paired with an innate reinforcer.

*Children's Depression Inventory (CDI):* A modified version of the Beck Depression Inventory (BDI) that was developed to measure the severity of depression in children, developed by Maria Kovacs.

*Chromosomes:* Microscopic threadlike bodies in the nuclei of cells; they carry the genes, which convey hereditary characteristics.

*Circadian rhythm:* A cyclical variation in a biological process or behavior that has a duration of about a day.

*Classical conditioning:* A form of associative learning in which a neutral stimulus, called the conditioned stimulus (CS), is repeatedly paired with a biologically significant unconditioned stimulus (US) so that the CS acquires the same power to elicit response as the US; also called Pavlovian conditioning.

*Clinical psychologist:* A person with a Ph.D. in psychology, specially trained to assess and treat mental disorders and behavior problems.

*Cognition:* Mental processes involved in the acquisition and use of knowledge, such as attention, thinking, problem solving, and perception; cognitive learning emphasizes these processes in the acquisition of new behaviors.

*Cognitive appraisal:* An assessment of the meaningfulness of an event to an individual; events that are appraised as harmful or potentially harmful elicit stress.

*Cognitive behavior therapy:* Therapy that integrates principles of learning theory with cognitive strategies to treat disorders such as depression, anxiety, and other behavioral problems (such as smoking or obesity).

*Cognitive dissonance theory:* Leon Festinger's theory that inconsistencies among one's cognitions cause tension and that individuals are motivated to reduce this tension by changing discrepant attitudes.

*Cognitive map:* A mental representation of an external area that is used to guide one's behavior.

*Cognitive processes:* The processes of thought, which include attending to an event, storing information in memory, recalling information, and making sense of information; they enable people to perceive events.

*Cognitive psychology:* An area of study that investigates mental processes; areas within cognitive psychology include attention, perception, language, learning, memory, problem solving, and logic.

*Cognitive science:* A multidisciplinary approach to the study of cognition from the perspectives of psychology, computer science, neuroscience, philosophy, and linguistics.

*Cohort:* An identifiable group of people; in developmental research, group members are commonly associated by their birth dates and shared historical experiences.

*Collective unconscious:* In Carl Jung's theory, memory traces of repeated experiences that have been passed down to all humankind as a function of evolutionary development; includes inherited tendencies to behave in certain ways and contains the archetypes.

*Color:* The brain's interpretation of electromagnetic radiation of different wavelengths within the range of visible light.

*Compensation:* In Alfred Adler's theory, a defense mechanism for overcoming feelings of inferiority by trying harder to excel; in Sigmund Freud's theory, the process of learning alternative ways to accomplish a task while making up for an inferiority—a process that could involve dreams that adjust psychologically for waking imbalances.

*Compulsions:* Ritualistic patterns of behavior that commonly follow obsessive thinking and that reduce the intensity of the anxiety-evoking thoughts.

*Concrete operational stage:* The third stage of Jean Piaget's theory, during which children acquire basic logical rules and concrete concepts; occurs between the ages of seven and eleven.

*Conditioned response (CR):* In Pavlovian conditioning, the behavior and emotional quality that occurs when a conditioned stimulus is presented; related to but not the same as the unconditioned response.

*Conditioned stimulus (CS):* A previously neutral stimulus (a sight, sound, touch, or smell) that, after Pavlovian conditioning, will elicit the conditioned response (CR).

*Conditioned taste aversion:* An avoidance of a food or drink that has been followed by illness when consumed in the past.

*Conditioning:* A type of learning in which an animal learns a concept by associating it with some object or by the administration of rewards or punishments.

*Conditions of worth:* In Carl Rogers's theory, externally based conditions for love and praise; the expectation that the child must behave in accordance with parental standards in order to receive love.

*Cone:* One type of visual receptor found in the retina of the eye; primarily for color vision and acute daytime vision.

*Confounding of variables:* The variation of other variables along with the independent variable of interest, as a result of which any effects cannot be attributed with certainty to the independent variable.

*Consciousness:* A level of awareness that includes those things of which an individual is aware at any given moment, such as current ideas, thoughts, accessed memories, and feelings.

*Consensual validation:* The verification of subjective beliefs by obtaining a consensus among other people.

*Consensus information:* Information concerning other people's responses to an object; in attribution theory, high consensus generally leads people to attribute situational rather than personal causes to a behavior.

*Conservation:* In Jean Piaget's theory, understanding that the physical properties (number, length, mass, volume) remain constant even though appearances may change; a concrete-operational skill.

*Consistency information:* Information concerning a person's response to an object over time. In attribution theory, high consistency implies that behavior is dispositional or typical of a person.

*Consolidation:* A neural process by which short-term memories become stored in long-term memory.

*Construct:* A formal concept representing the relationships between variables or processes such as motivation and behavior; may be empirical (observable) or hypothetical (inferred).

*Construct validity:* A type of validity that assesses the extent to which a test score (variable) correlates with other tests (variables) already established as valid measures of the item.

*Consumer psychology:* The subfield of psychology that studies selling, advertising, and buying; the goal of its practitioners is generally to communicate clearly and to persuade consumers to buy products.

*Context dependence:* The phenomenon in which memory functions more effectively when material is recalled in the same environment in which it was originally learned, compared with recall in a different environment.

*Contingency:* A relationship between a response and its consequence or between two stimuli; sometimes considered a dependency.

*Contingency management:* A method of behavior modification that involves providing or removing positive rewards in accordance with whether the individual being treated engages in the expected behavior.

*Continuous reinforcement:* A schedule in which each response is followed by a reinforcer.

*Control group:* A group of subjects that are like the experimental groups in all ways except that they do not experience the independent variable; used as a comparison measure.

*Controlling variable:* An extraneous factor that might influence the dependent variable, making it difficult to evaluate the effect of the independent variable; in an experiment, attempts are made to isolate or control such effects systematically.

*Convergent thinking:* Creative thinking in which possible solutions to a problem are systematically eliminated in search for the best solution; the type of ordinary thinking in which most people generally engage.

*Conversion disorder:* A psychological disorder in which a person experiences physical symptoms, such as the loss or impairment of some motor or sensory function (paralysis or blindness, for example), in the absence of an organic cause.

*Coping:* Responses directed at dealing with demands (in particular, threatening or stressful ones) upon an organism; these responses may either improve or reduce long-term functioning.

*Correlation:* The degree of relatedness or correspondence between two variables, expressed by a coefficient that can range from +1.00 to −1.00; 0.00 signifies no correspondence.

*Cortex:* The surface (or outer layer) of the brain, which receives sensory input, interprets it, and relates behavior to external stimuli; responsible for perception and conscious thought.

*Cortical brain centers:* The portions of the brain making up the cerebral cortex and controlling voluntary behavior, higher reasoning, and language skills; they develop rapidly during the first two years of life.

*Countertransference:* The phenomenon in which an analyst either shifts feelings from his or her past onto a patient or is affected by the client's emotional problems; caused by a patient's perceived similarity to individuals or experiences in the analyst's life.

*Creativity:* Cognitive abilities in areas such as fluency, flexibility, originality, elaboration, visualization, metaphorical thinking, and problem definition; the ability to originate something that is both new and appropriate.

*Criterion group:* A group used to validate a measurement instrument; in the case of interest inventories, it refers to persons in a particular occupational group.

*Critical period:* A time during which the developing organism is particularly sensitive to the influence of certain inputs or experiences necessary to foster normal development; in nonhuman animals, a specific time period during which a certain type of learning such as imprinting must occur.

*Cross-sectional design:* A design in which subgroups of a population are randomly sampled; the members of the sample are then tested or observed.

*Cue-producing response:* A response that serves as a cue for other responses; words (speech) can cue behaviors, and thoughts can cue other thoughts.

*Cutaneous senses:* Relating to the skin sense, as in responses to touch or temperature.

*Cyclothymia:* A milder version of a cyclical mood disorder in which mood swings can occur but are not as intense as in bipolar disorder.

*Daily hassles:* Seemingly minor everyday events that are a constant source of stress.

*Dark adaptation:* An increase in the sensitivity of rods and cones to light through an increase in the concentration of light-absorbing pigments.

*Data:* A collection of observations from an experiment or survey.

*Death instinct:* The unconscious desire for death and destruction in order to escape the tensions of living.

*Debriefing:* Discussing an experiment and its purpose with subjects after its completion; ethically required if the experiment involved deception.

*Decay:* The disappearance of a memory trace.

*Deduction:* A type of logic by which one draws a specific conclusion from one or more known truths or premises; often formed as an "if/then" statement.

*Defense mechanism:* According to Sigmund Freud, a psychological strategy by which an unacceptable sexual or aggressive impulse may be kept from conscious thought or expressed in a disguised fashion.

*Deindividuation:* The loss of self-awareness and evaluation apprehension that accompanies situations that foster personal and physical anonymity.

*Delusion:* A symptom of psychosis that consists of a strong irrational belief held despite considerable evidence against it; types include delusions of grandeur, reference, and persecution.

*Dementia:* Globally impaired intellectual functioning (memory reasoning) in adults as a function of brain impairment; it does not mean "craziness" but a loss or impairment of mental power.

*Dendrite:* A branching extension of a neuron through which information enters the cell; there may be one or many dendrites on a neuron.

*Dependent variable:* The outcome measure in a study; the effect of the independent variable is measured by changes in the dependent variable.

*Depolarization:* A shift in ions and electrical charges across a cell membrane, causing loss of resting membrane potential and bringing the cell closer to the action potential.

*Depression:* A psychological disorder characterized by extreme feelings of sadness, hopelessness, or personal unworthiness as well as loss of energy, withdrawal, and either lack of sleep or excessive sleep.

*Depth perception:* The ability to see three-dimensional features, such as the distance of an object from oneself and the shape of an object.

*Descriptive statistics:* Procedures that summarize and organize data sets; they include mean, median, range, correlation, and variability.

*Desensitization:* A behavioral technique of gradually removing anxiety associated with certain situations by associating a relaxed state with these situations.

*Determinism:* The theory or doctrine that acts of the will, occurrences in nature, or social or psychological phenomena are causally determined by preceding events or natural laws.

*Development:* The continuous and cumulative process of age-related changes in physical growth, thought, perception, and behavior of people and animals; a result of both biological and environmental influences.

*Developmental psychology:* The subfield of psychology that studies biological, social, and intellectual changes as they occur throughout the human life cycle.

*Deviancy:* The quality of having a condition or engaging in behavior that is atypical in a social group and is considered undesirable.

*Diagnosis:* The classification or labeling of a patient's problem within one of a set of recognized categories of abnormal behavior, determined with the aid of interviews and psychological tests.

*Diagnostic and Statistical Manual of Mental Disorders (DSM):* A handbook created by the American Psychiatric Association for diagnosing and classifying mental disorders; used by mental health professionals and insurance companies.

*Diffusion of responsibility:* The reduction of personal responsibility that is commonly experienced in group situations; diffusion of responsibility increases as the size of the crowd increases.

*Discounting:* Reducing the role of a particular cause in producing a behavior because of the presence of other plausible causes.

*Discrimination:* In perception, the ability to see that two patterns differ in some way; in intergroup relations, behavior (usually unfavorable) toward persons that is based on their group membership rather than on their individual personalities.

*Discriminative stimulus:* A stimulus that signals the availability of a consequence, given that a response occurs.

*Dispersion:* A statistical measure of variability; a measure (standard deviation, range, semi-interquartile range, or variance) that provides information about the difference among the scores.

*Displacement:* According to Sigmund Freud, a defense mechanism by which a person redirects his or her aggressive impulse onto a target that may substitute for the target that originally aroused the person's aggression.

*Display:* A visual dance or series of movements or gestures by an individual or animal to communicate such things as dominance, aggression, and courtship to other individuals.

*Display rules:* Culturally determined rules regarding the appropriate expression of emotions.

*Dispositional:* Relating to disposition or personality rather than to situation.

*Dissociative disorders:* Disorders that occur when some psychological function, such as memory, is split off from the rest of the conscious mind; not caused by brain dysfunction.

*Dissonance:* An unpleasant psychological and physiological state caused by an inconsistency between cognitions.

*Distal stimulus:* An object or other sensory element in the environment.

*Distinctiveness information:* Information concerning a person's response to an object under given conditions; in attribution theory, high distinctiveness suggests that individuals are behaving uniquely toward a given target/object.

*Diurnal enuresis:* The presence of enuretic episodes when the individual is awake.

*Divergent thinking:* Thinking that results in new and different responses that most people cannot, or do not, offer; the type of thinking most clearly involved in creativity.

*Domestic violence:* Physical, emotional, psychological, or sexual abuse perpetrated by an individual toward a member of his or her own family; typically the abuse follows a repetitive, predictable pattern.

*Dopamine:* One type of neurotransmitter, a chemical that is released from one nerve cell and stimulates receptors on another, thus transferring a message between them; associated with movement and with treatment of depression.

*Double bind:* A form of communication that often occurs when a family member sends two messages, requests, or commands that are logically inconsistent, contradictory, or impossible, resulting in a "damned if one does, damned if one doesn't" situation; a hypothesis about the development of schizophrenia.

*Double-blind method:* A procedure in which neither the experimenter nor the subjects know who is receiving treatment and who is not; this controls for subject and experimenter biases and expectations.

*Down syndrome:* A chromosomal abnormality that causes mental retardation as well as certain physical defects; caused by an extra (third) chromosome on chromosome pair 21.

*Drive:* The tendency of a person or animal to engage in behaviors brought about by some change or condition inside that organism; often generated by deprivation (hunger or thirst) or exposure to painful or other noxious stimuli.

*Drive reduction hypothesis:* The idea that a physiological need state triggers a series of behaviors aimed at reducing the unpleasant state; drive reduction is reinforcing.

*Dysfunctional family:* A family grouping that is characterized by the presence of disturbed interactions and communications; particularly an abusive, incestuous, or alcoholic family.

*Dyslexia:* Diffculties in reading, usually after damage to the left cerebral hemisphere.

*Dysphoria:* A symptom of clinical depression; extreme sadness.

*Dysthymic disorder:* A form of depression in which mild to moderate levels of depressive symptoms persist chronically.

*Early recollections:* A projective technique in which the patient attempts to remember things that happened in the distant past; these provide clues to the patient's current use of private logic.

*Eating disorders:* Afflictions resulting from dysfunctional relationships to hunger, food, and eating.

*Echoic memory:* Sensory memory for sound.

*Echolalia:* An involuntary and parrotlike repetition of words or phrases spoken by others.

*Eclectic therapy:* Therapy in which a combination of models and techniques is employed, rather than a single approach.

*Educational psychology:* The subfield of psychology that studies the effectiveness of education, usually formal education; educational psychologists seek to develop new educational techniques and to improve the learning process.

*Ego:* In psychoanalytic theory, the part of the personality responsible for perceiving reality and thinking; mediates between the demands of the pleasure-seeking id, the rule-following superego, and reality.

*Egocentric thought:* A cognitive tendency in childhood in which the child assumes that everyone shares his or her own perspective; the cognitive inability to understand the different perspective of another.

*Elaborative rehearsal:* Giving meaning to information to enable encoding it in memory.

*Electroconvulsive therapy (ECT):* A treatment for severe depression in which an electric current is passed through the brain of the patient; sometimes referred to as electric shock therapy.

*Electroencephalogram (EEG):* The graphic recording of the electrical activity of the brain (brain waves).

*Electroencephalography:* Measurement of the electrical output of the brain, which may then sometimes be brought under voluntary control by biofeedback and relaxation.

*Embryonic phase:* The period of rapid prenatal change that follows the zygote period; extends from the second to the eighth week after conception.

*Emotions:* Psychological responses that include a set of physiological changes, expressive behaviors, and a subjective experience.

*Empathy:* In therapy, the therapist's ability to focus attention on the needs and experience of the client; also refers to the therapist's ability to communicate an understanding of the client's emotional state.

*Empirical evidence:* Data or information derived objectively from the physical senses, without reliance on personal faith, intuition, or introspection.

*Empiricism:* A philosophy holding that knowledge is learned through experience and that infants begin life like blank slates, learning about their environment through experience.

*Encoding:* The transformation of incoming sensory information into a form of code that the memory system can accept and use.

*Endocrine gland:* A gland that produces one or more hormones and secretes them into the blood so that they can serve as intercellular messengers.

*Endocrine system:* A system of ductless glands in the bodies of vertebrate animals that secretes hormones which travel through the bloodstream to target tissues, whose functioning is altered by the hormones.

*Endogenous behavior:* An innate, or inborn, behavior that is established by the animal's inherited genetic code (DNA) and that is not influenced by the animal's experiences or environment.

*Endorphins:* A group of endogenous, opiate-like neuropeptides of the central nervous system that simulate analgesia and interfere with transmission of pain impulses; the brain's own morphine.

*Enkephalins:* Peptides containing five amino acids, within the endorphin group, that may act as neurotransmitters; the first of the endorphins to be discovered.

*Enmeshment:* An excessively close relationship between parent and child in which adult concerns and needs are communicated and in which over-dependence on the child is apparent.

*Entitlement:* The expectation of special or unusually favorable treatment by others; commonly seen among narcissistic personalities.

*Entropy:* In Carl Jung's analytical theory, a concept maintaining that aspects of a person's psychic energy which are not in balance will tend to seek a state of equilibrium.

*Enuresis:* The inability to control the release of urine; nocturnal enuresis is also called bed-wetting.

*Environmental psychology:* The subfield of psychology that studies the relationship between the environment and behavior, particularly the effects of the physical and social environments (such as noise or crowding) on behavior.

*Environmental stressor:* A condition in the environment, such as crowding, noise, toxic chemicals, or extreme temperatures, that produces stress (bodily or mental tension).

*Epilepsy:* A disorder of the nervous system in which the cortex produces electrical firing that causes convulsions and other forms of seizures; thought by some to be linked to the reticular formation.

*Epinephrine:* The neurotransmitter released from the adrenal gland as a result of innervation of the autonomic nervous system; formerly called adrenaline.

*Episodic memory:* A form of long-term memory involving temporal and spatial information, including personal experiences.

*Equipotentiality:* In Pavlovian conditioning, the idea that any stimulus paired with an effective unconditioned stimulus will come to elicit a conditioned response with equal facility.

*Equity theory:* A theory in attraction and work motivation that contends that individuals are motivated to remain in relationships they perceive to be fair, just, and equitable—that is, where one's outcomes are proportional to one's inputs, particularly when contrasted with others in the relationship.

*Equivalence:* A principle stating that an increase in energy or value in one aspect of the psyche is accompanied by a decrease in another area.

*Estradiol:* The primary sex hormone of mammalian females, which is responsible for the menstrual cycle and for development of secondary sex characteristics; a primary estrogen, secreted by the corpus luteum.

*Ethnocentrism:* An attitude of uncritically assuming the superiority of the in-group culture.

*Ethology:* A branch of zoology that studies animals in their natural environments; often concerned with investigating the adaptive significance and innate basis of behaviors.

*Etiology:* The factors that are thought to cause or contribute to the development of a particular disorder.

*Eustress:* Positive arousal or stress, appraised as a challenge rather than as a threat.

*Evoked potential:* A brain response that is triggered by electroencephalography using discrete sensory stimuli.

*Excitation transfer:* The theory that arousal from one source can intensify an emotional reaction to a different source (for example, that sexual arousal can increase the response to an aggressive cue).

*Existentialism:* A philosophical viewpoint emphasizing human existence and the human situation in the world that gives meaning to life through the free choice of mature values and commitment to responsible goals; the critical goal involves finding one's true self and living according to this potential.

*Exogenous substances:* Substances not normally occurring in the body, present only when administered; exogenous substances include substances such as drugs or synthetic test compounds mimicking endogenous substances.

*Expectancy confirmation bias:* Interpreting ambiguous information as being supportive of expectations; mistakenly "seeing" what is expected.

*Expectancy theory:* A cognitive motivation model which proposes that people choose to perform behaviors they believe to be the most likely to lead to positive outcomes; in work theory, workers are more motivated when they perceive congruence between their efforts, products, and rewards.

*Experimentation:* One of several data collection methods; requires systematically manipulating the levels of an independent variable under controlled conditions in order to measure its impact on a dependent variable.

*Experimenter bias:* Biases introduced into a research study as a result of the expectations of the experimenter.

*Expressive aphasia:* Difficulties in expressing language, usually after damage to Broca's area in the left frontal lobe of the cerebral cortex.

*External validity:* The extent to which the results of a research study can be generalized to different populations, settings, or conditions.

*Externalization:* A defense mechanism in which one experiences unresolved, repressed inner turmoil as occurring outside oneself; holding external factors responsible for one's problems.

*Extinction:* A process by which the probability of a response is decreased; in classical or Pavlovian conditioning, a process in which the temporal contiguity of the conditioned stimulus and the unconditioned stimulus is disrupted and the learned association is lost; in operant or instrumental conditioning, a process in which undesirable behavior is not followed by reinforcement.

*Extraneous variable:* A variable that has a detrimental affect on a research study, making it difficult to determine if the result is attributable to the variable under study or to some unknown variable not controlled for; for example, in jury decision making, the effect of defendant attractiveness.

*Extrinsic motivation:* Motivation to perform an activity only because the activity leads to a valued outcome external to the activity itself.

*Extrinsic religion:* An immature religious orientation that uses religion for self-serving purposes such as security or a sense of social or economic well-being.

*Factor analysis:* A statistical technique wherein a set of correlated variables can be regrouped in terms of the degree of commonality they share.

*Family therapy:* A type of psychotherapy that focuses on correcting the faulty interactions among family members that maintain children's psychological problems.

*Feminist analysis:* The examination of the ways in which inequality, injustice, or oppression devalues women or limits their potential, both individually and collectively.

*Fetal phase:* The third period of prenatal development, extending from the ninth week of pregnancy until birth.

*Fetishism:* A sexual behavior in which a person becomes aroused by focusing on an inanimate object or a part of the human body.

*Field research:* An approach in which evidence is gathered in a "natural" setting, such as the workplace; by contrast, laboratory research involves an artificial, contrived setting.

*Fight-or-flight response:* A sequence of physiological changes, described by Walter B. Cannon, that occurs in response to threat and prepares the organism to flee from or fight the threat; includes increases in heart rate, blood pressure, and respiration.

*Fixation:* In psychoanalytic theory, an inability to progress to the next level of psychosexual development because of overgratification or undergratification of desires at a particular stage.

*Flashback:* A type of traumatic reexperiencing in which a person becomes detached from reality and thinks, feels, and acts as if a previous traumatic experience were happening again.

*Flocking:* A defensive maneuver in many mammalian and bird species in which a scattered group of individuals implodes into a compact cluster at the approach of a predator.

*Flooding:* A type of therapy in which a phobic person imagines his or her most-feared situation until fear decreases.

*Fluid intelligence:* The form of intelligence that reflects speed of information processing, reasoning, and memory capacity rather than factual knowledge (crystallized intelligence); associated with Raymond Cattell.

*Forebrain:* A developmentally defined division of the brain that contains structures such as the cerebral hemispheres, the thalamus, and the hypothalamus.

*Forensic psychology:* The application of psychological skills in the legal profession—for example, in jury selection, sanity determination, and assessing competency to stand trial.

*Forgetting:* The loss of information from memory.

*Formal operational stage:* According to Jean Piaget, the fourth stage of cognitive development, reached at adolescence; characterized by the ability to engage in abstract thinking, hypothetical constructs, and unobserved logical possibilities.

*Free association:* The psychoanalytic method in which a patient talks spontaneously without restriction; thought to reveal repressed conflicts of the unconscious.

*Frequency:* The number of complete back-and-forth movements or pressure changes (cycles) from the rest or ambient state that occur each second; measured in units called hertz.

*Frequency distribution:* The pairing of a measurement or score with the number of people or subjects obtaining that measurement.

*Frontal lobe:* The anterior portion of each cerebral hemisphere, containing control of motor areas and most of the higher intellectual functions of the brain, including speech.

*Frustration:* A psychological state of arousal that results when a person is prevented from attaining a goal.

*Frustration-aggression hypothesis:* A concept, pioneered by John Dollard, stating that aggressive behavior is born of frustration in attempting to reach a goal.

*Fugue state:* A flight from reality in which the individual develops amnesia, leaves his or her present situation, travels to a new location, and establishes a new identity.

*Functional autonomy:* A concept, pioneered by Gordon W. Allport, that many adult motives are independent in purpose from their childhood origins.

*Functional disorders:* Signs and symptoms for which no organic or physiological basis can be found.

*Functional fixedness:* An inability to think of novel uses for objects because of a fixation on their usual functions.

*Functionalism:* An early school of American psychology that argued for the study of the human mind from the standpoint of understanding consciousness in terms of its purpose rather than its elements.

*Fundamental attribution error:* Underestimating the influence of situations and overestimating the influence of personality traits in causing behavior.

*Gamete:* A reproductive sex cell; the female cell is known as the ovum, and the male cell is known as the sperm.

*Gamma-aminobutyric acid (GABA):* The most common neurotransmitter in the brain, derived from the amino acid glutamic acid; an inhibitor that seems to affect mood and emotion.

*Gender:* Social maleness or femaleness, reflected in the behaviors and characteristics that society expects from people of one biological sex.

*Gender identity:* A child's accurate labeling of himself or herself by gender; also, a person's inner sense of femaleness or maleness.

*Gender schema:* A general knowledge framework that organizes information and guides perceptions related to males and females.

*Gene:* The basic unit of heredity; a segment of a DNA molecule that contains hereditary instructions for an individual's physical traits and abilities and for the cell's production of proteins.

*General adaptation syndrome (GAS):* The three-stage physiological response pattern of the body to stress that was proposed by Hans Selye; the three stages are the alarm reaction, resistance stage, and exhaustion stage.

*Generalization:* The process by which behavior learned in one situation transfers to new situations.

*Generativity:* In Erik Erikson's theory of personality, the seventh stage, associated with the desire to leave a legacy; the need to take care of future generations through the experiences of caring, nurturing, and educating.

*Genetics:* The biochemical basis of inherited characteristics.

*Genital stage:* In Sigmund Freud's theory, the fifth psychosexual stage, beginning at adolescence and extending throughout adulthood; the individual learns to experience sexual gratification with a partner.

*Genotype:* The genetic makeup of an individual.

*Gestalt:* A German word, for which there is no precise translation, that is generally used to refer to a form, a whole, or a configuration.

*Gestalt school of psychology:* A school of psychology which maintains that the overall configuration of a stimulus array, rather than its individual elements, forms the basis of perception.

*Gestalt therapy:* A form of psychotherapy, initiated by Fritz Perls, that emphasizes awareness of the present and employs an active therapist-client relationship.

*Giftedness:* A marked ability to learn more rapidly, perform more intricate problems, and solve problems more rapidly than is normally expected for a given age; operationally defined as an IQ score above 130 on an individually administered test.

*Goal setting:* A motivational technique used to increase productivity in which employees are given specific performance objectives and time deadlines.

*Gray matter:* Unmyelinated neurons that make up the cerebral cortex, so called because they lack the fatty covering (myelin) found on neurons of the white matter.

*Group dynamics:* The study of how groups influence individual functioning.

*Gustation:* The sense of taste.

*Gyrus:* A convolution on the surface of the brain that results from the infolding of the cortex (surface).

*Habit:* An association or connection between a cue and a response, such as stopping (the response) at a red light (the cue) while driving.

*Habituation:* A decrease in response to repeated presentations of a stimulus that is not simply caused by fatigued sensory receptors.

*Hallucinogen:* A substance that can alter perception (vision and audition, in particular); examples include LSD, PCP, peyote, psilocybin, and possibly marijuana.

*Hardiness:* A constellation of behaviors and perceptions, characterized by perceptions of control, commitment, and challenge, that are thought to buffer the effects of stress; introduced by Suzanne Kobasa.

*Hawthorne effect:* A phenomenon that occurs when a subject's behavior changes after the subject discovers that he or she is being studied.

*Hedonic:* Associated with the seeking of pleasure and the avoidance of pain.

*Helplessness:* A condition in which one has little or no control over the events in one's life; viewed by Martin Seligman as an important cause of depression.

*Heredity:* The transmission of characteristics from parent to offspring through genes in the chromosomes.

*Heuristic:* A shortcut or rule of thumb used for decision making or problem solving that often leads to, but does not guarantee, a correct response.

*Higher-order conditioning:* The linking of successive conditioned stimuli, the last of which elicits the conditioned response; higher-order associations are easily broken.

*Hindbrain:* A developmentally defined division of the brain that contains the pons, medulla, and cerebellum.

*Hippocampus:* A structure located in the temporal lobe (lateral cortical area) of the brain that has important memory functions.

*Homeostasis:* A term referring to the idea that the body tries to maintain steady states—that is, to maintain physiological characteristics within relatively narrow and optimum levels.

*Homophobia:* A fear, prejudice, or hatred toward homosexuals, usually based upon irrational stereotyping.

*Hormone:* A chemical "messenger," usually composed of protein or steroids, that is produced and secreted by an endocrine gland and released into the bloodstream; it targets specific genes in certain body tissue cells.

*Hostile aggression:* Aggressive behavior that is associated with anger and is intended to harm another.

*Humanistic psychology:* A branch of psychology that emphasizes the human tendencies toward growth and fulfillment, autonomy, choice, responsibility, and ultimate values such as truth, love, and justice; exemplified by the theories of Carl Rogers and Abraham Maslow.

*Hypnagogic hallucination:* A vivid auditory or visual hallucination that occurs at the transition from wakefulness to sleep or from sleep to wakefulness; associated with narcolepsy.

*Hypnosis:* An altered state of consciousness brought on by special induction techniques (usually progressive relaxation instructions) and characterized by varying degrees of responsiveness to suggestions.

*Hypnotic susceptibility:* A subject's measured level of responsiveness to hypnotic suggestions on standardized scales.

*Hypochondriasis:* A psychological disorder in which the person is unrealistically preoccupied with the fear of disease and worries excessively about his or her health.

*Hypothalamus:* A small region near the base of the brain that controls the pituitary gland, autonomic nervous system, and behaviors important for survival, including eating, drinking, and temperature regulation.

*Hypothesis:* An educated guess about the relationship between two or more variables, derived from inductive reasoning; often tested by an experiment.

*Iconic memory:* Brief sensory memory for vision.

*Id:* The part of the psyche that contains the instincts and is directed solely by pleasure seeking; it is the most primitive part of the psyche and was thought by Sigmund Freud to fuel the ego and superego.

*Idealized self:* Alienation from the real self that is characterized by grandiose, unrealistic conceptions of the self and unattainable standards.

*Identification:* The internalization of parental or societal values, behaviors, and attitudes; in Freudian theory, a defense and resolution of incestuous feelings toward the opposite-sex parent that is important in the development of the superego.

*Identity:* A personal configuration of occupational, sexual, and ideological commitments; according to Erik Erikson, the positive pole of the fifth stage of psychosocial development.

*Identity crisis:* According to Erik Erikson, the central developmental issue in adolescence; encompasses a struggle between an integrated core identity and role confusion.

*Idiographic study:* The study of the unique patterns of the individual through methods such as case studies, autobiographies, and tests that examine patterns of behavior within a single person.

*Illusions:* Beliefs that are unsupported by evidence or that require facts to be perceived in a particular manner.

*Imagery:* The use of visualization to imagine the physical movements involved in executing a skill.

*Imitation:* The performance of behaviors that were learned by observing the actions of others.

*Immune response:* The body's response to invasion by disease-producing organisms; proteins (antibodies) are produced that mark the unwanted cells for destruction.

*Immutable characteristics:* Physical attributes (such as gender) that are present at birth and that other people assume gives them information as to the kind of person they are seeing.

*Implosion therapy:* A therapy in which the patient imagines his or her feared situation, plus elements from psychodynamic theory that are related to the fear until fear decreases.

*Impression management:* The attempt to control the impressions of oneself that others form; synonymous with "self-presentation."

*Imprinting:* The innate behavioral attachment that a young animal forms with another individual (for example, its mother), with food, or with an object during a brief critical period shortly after birth; especially seen in ducks and chicks.

*In-group:* A social group to which a person belongs or with which a person is identified, thereby forming part of the self-concept.

*In-group bias:* The tendency to discriminate in favor of one's own group.

*Incentive:* A motivating force or system of rewards that is presented to an individual if he or she behaves or successfully performs specified tasks according to the norms of society; a goal object.

*Incompetency:* The legally established lack of sufficient knowledge and judgment to maintain a given right or responsibility.

*Incongruence:* In Carl Rogers's theory, inconsistency or distortion between one's real and ideal self; a lack of genuineness.

*Independent variable:* The factor that is manipulated by the experimenter in order to assess its causal impact on the dependent variable.

*Individual psychology:* Alfred Adler's school of personality theory and therapy; stresses the unity of the individual and his or her striving for superiority to compensate for feelings of inferiority.

*Induction:* A type of logic by which one arrives at a general premise or conclusion based on generalization from a large number of known specific cases.

*Industrial/organizational psychology:* The subfield of psychology that studies behavior in business and industry; practitioners analyze placement, training, and supervision of personnel, study organizational and communication structures, and explore ways to maximize efficiency.

*Inflection:* An addition to the stem of a word which indicates subtle modulations in meaning, such as plurality (more than one) or tense (present time or past time); in English, inflections are all suffixes.

*Information-processing model:* The approach of most modern cognitive psychologists; it interprets cognition as the flow of information through interrelated stages (input, processing, storage, and retrieval) in much the same way that information is processed by a computer.

*Innate:* A term describing any inborn characteristic or behavior that is determined and controlled largely by the genes.

*Insanity:* A legal term for having a mental disease or defect so great that criminal intent or responsibility are not possible; it renders one incompetent.

*Insight:* A sudden mental inspiration or comprehension of a problem that was previously unsolved.

*Insomnia:* Difficulty in falling asleep or in remaining asleep for sufficient periods.

*Instinct:* An innate or inherited tendency that motivates a person or animal to act in often complex sequences without reasoning, instruction, or experience; in Freudian theory, a biological source of excitation that directs the development of personality into adulthood, such as the life instinct (Eros) and death instinct (Thanatos).

*Institutional racism:* The behavior patterns followed in organizations and in society at large that produce discrimination against members of racial minorities regardless of the prejudice or lack thereof of individuals.

*Instrumental aggression:* Aggressive behavior that is a by-product of another activity; instrumental aggression occurs only incidentally, as a means to another end.

*Instrumental conditioning:* The learning of the relationship between a voluntary action and the reinforcements or punishments that follow that action; also known as operant conditioning.

*Integration:* The function of most of the neurons of the cerebral cortex; summarizing incoming sensory information and producing a consensus as to what the nervous system will do next.

*Intelligence:* The ability to perform various mental tasks, including reasoning, knowledge, comprehension, memory, applying concepts, and manipulating figures; thought to reflect one's learning potential.

*Intelligence quotient (IQ):* A measure of a person's mental ability (as reflected by intelligence test scores) in comparison with the rest of the population at a comparable age.

*Intensity:* A measure of a physical aspect of a stimulus, such as the frequency of a sound or the brightness of a color.

*Interest inventory:* A type of test designed to determine areas of interest and enjoyment, often for the purpose of matching a person with a career.

*Interference:* The loss or displacement of a memory trace because of competing information that is presented.

*Intermittent reinforcement:* Any reinforcement schedule in which some but not all responses are rewarded; particularly difficult to extinguish.

*Internal validity:* The extent to which the dependent variable is caused by the independent variable; if relevant plausible rival alternative hypotheses can be ruled out, the study has strong internal validity.

*Interneuron:* A neuron that receives information from a sensory neuron and transmits a message to a motor neuron; very common in the brain and important in integration.

*Interrater reliability:* The obtained level of agreement between two observers when scoring the same observations with the same behavioral taxonomy.

*Interval schedule:* A schedule in which reinforcer delivery is contingent upon performance of a response after a specified amount of time has elapsed.

*Intrinsic motivation:* Motivation based on the desire to achieve or perform a task for its own sake, because it produces satisfaction or enjoyment, rather than for external rewards.

*Introspection:* The self-report of one's own sensations, perceptions, experiences, and thoughts; analyses of and reports on the content of one's own conscious experiences.

*Irradiation:* Nervous excitement generated in a specific brain center by an unconditioned stimulus that spreads to surrounding areas of the cerebral cortex.

*Kinesthetic:* Related to the sensation of body position, presence, or movement, resulting mostly from the stimulation of sensory nerves in muscles, tendons, and joints.

*Korsakoff's syndrome:* Alcohol-induced brain damage that causes disorientation, impaired long-term memory, and production of false memories to fill memory gaps.

*Latency:* In Sigmund Freud's theory, the period between approximately age six and adolescence, when sexual instincts are not strongly manifested; strictly speaking, not a psychosexual stage.

*Latent content:* According to psychoanalytic theory, the hidden content of a dream, camouflaged by the manifest content.

*Lateral geniculate nucleus:* A subdivision of the thalamus in the brain, which receives the nerve impulse from the retina; it assembles visual information.

*Laterality:* Specialization by sides of almost symmetrical structures; speech is lateralized in human brains, because it is mainly controlled by the left hemispheres of almost all right-handed people.

*Law of Effect:* Thorndike's basic law of instrumental conditioning, which holds that responses followed by certain events will be either more or less likely to recur.

*Leakage:* Nonverbal behavior that reveals information that a person wishes to conceal; especially useful in deception detection.

*Learned helplessness:* The hypothesized result of experiences in which behavior performed seems to bear no relationship to the appearance or control of a stressor.

*Learning:* A modification in behavior as the result of experience that involves changes in the nervous system which are not caused by fatigue, maturation, or injury.

*Lesion:* Damage or injury to brain tissue that is caused by disease or trauma or produced experimentally using mechanical, electrical, or chemical methods.

*Levels-of-processing model:* The perspective that holds that how well something is remembered is based on how elaborately incoming information is mentally processed.

*Libido:* The energy used to direct behavior that is pleasurable either for the self or others; when it is directed toward the self, it results in self-gratification, follows the pleasure principle, and is immature.

*Limbic system:* An integrated set of cerebral structures (including the amygdala, hypothalamus, hippocampus, and septal area) that play a vital role in the regulation of emotion and motivation.

*Linguistic relativity hypothesis:* The idea that the structure of particular languages that people speak affects the way they perceive the world.

*Linguistics:* A field of inquiry that focuses on the underlying structure of language; linguists study phonology (the sound system), syntax (sentence structure), and semantics (meaning), among other topics.

*Lithium carbonate:* An alkaline compound that modulates the intensity of mood swings and is particularly effective in the dampening of symptoms of manic excitability.

*Locus of control:* Beliefs concerning the sources of power over one's life; persons who believe they can generally control the direction of their lives have an internal locus of control, whereas those who believe that their lives are influenced more by fate have an external locus of control.

*Long-term memory:* A memory system of unlimited capacity that consists of more or less permanent knowledge.

*Longitudinal study:* A research methodology that requires the testing of the same subjects repeatedly over a specified period of time.

*Loudness:* The strength of sound as heard; related to sound pressure level but also affected by frequency.

*Magnitude estimation:* A technique for measuring perceptual experience by having persons assign numbers to indicate the "magnitude" of an experience.

*Main effect:* A statistically significant difference in behavior related to different levels of a variable and not affected by any other variable.

*Major depressive episode:* A disorder of mood and functioning, meeting clearly specified criteria and present for at least two weeks, which is characterized by dysphoric mood or apathy.

*Mania:* A phase of bipolar disorder in which the mood is one of elation, euphoria, or irritability; a disorder in which manic symptoms occur, including hyperactivity, agitation, restlessness, and grandiosity, and then are followed by a return to a normal mood state.

*Manifest content:* In Freudian theory, the content of a dream just as it is experienced or recalled; masks the dream's latent content.

*Masculine protest:* The denying of inferiority feelings through rebelliousness, violence, or maintaining a tough exterior.

*Maturation:* Development attributable to one's genetic timetable rather than to experience.

*Mean:* The arithmetic average of all the data measuring one characteristic; it can be used as a descriptive or inferential statistic.

*Mechanoreceptor:* A sensory receptor that is sensitive to mechanical stimulation, such as touch, movement of a joint, or stretching of a muscle.

*Medical model:* A view in which abnormality consists of a number of diseases that originate in bodily functions, especially in the brain, and have defined symptoms, treatments, and outcomes.

*Medulla oblongata:* The bulbous portion of the brain stem that directly connects with the spinal cord; controls cardiac and respiratory activity.

*Melatonin:* A hormone produced by the pineal gland within the forebrain that is usually released into the blood during the night phase of the light-dark cycle.

*Memory:* The mental processes that are involved in storing and recalling previously experienced images, information, and events.

*Mere exposure:* A psychological phenomenon in which liking tends to increase as a person sees more of something or someone.

*Meta-analysis:* A set of quantitative (statistical) procedures used to evaluate a body of empirical literature.

*Metastasis:* The transfer of disease from one part of the body to an unrelated part, often through the bloodstream or lymphatic system.

*Midbrain:* The section of the brain just above the hindbrain; influences auditory and visual processes and arousal.

*Midlife crisis:* A sense of reevaluation, and sometimes panic, that strikes some individuals during middle age; impulsive behavior, reassessment of goals, and career changes can result.

*Mind-body problem:* A psychological question originating from philosophy and religion that concerns how to understand the relationship between a physical body or brain and a nonphysical mind or subjective experience.

*Mineralocorticoids:* The proinflammatory hormones aldosterone and deoxycorticosterone, secreted by the adrenal cortex and having a role in salt metabolism.

*Misattribution:* Attributing an event to any factor other than the true cause.

*Mnemonics:* Strategies for improving memory through placing information in an organized context.

*Monoamine oxidase inhibitors (MAOIs):* A class of antidepressant drugs.

*Monoamines:* A group of neurotransmitters derived from a single amino acid; they include serotonin and the catecholamines.

*Monosynaptic reflex:* A reflex system that consists of only one synapse, the synapse between the sensory input and motor output.

*Mood disorders:* Functional mental disorders associated with emotions or feelings (also called affective disorders); examples include depression and bipolar disorders.

*Morpheme:* The smallest part of a word that has a discernible meaning.

*Morphology:* The rules in a given language that govern how morphemes can be combined to form words.

*Motivation:* A hypothetical construct used to explain behavior and its direction, intensity, and persistence.

*Motor neurons:* The cells of the central nervous system responsible for causing muscular activity.

*Multiple personality disorder:* A rare mental disorder characterized by the development and existence or two or more relatively unique and independent personalities in the same individual.

*Nanometer:* A billionth of a meter.

*Narcolepsy:* A condition in which an individual is prone to fall suddenly into a deep sleep.

*Nativism:* A philosophy which holds that knowledge is innate and that the neonate enters the world prepared for certain kinds of environmental inputs.

*Natural selection:* The process by which those characteristics of a species that help it to survive or adapt to its environment tend to be passed along by members that live long enough to have offspring.

*Need:* A state of an organism attributable to deprivation of a biological or psychological requirement; it is related to a disturbance in the homeostatic state.

*Negative reinforcement:* The procedure whereby the probability of a response is increased by the contingent removal of an aversive stimulus.

*Neo-Freudian:* A term for psychoanalysts who place more emphasis on security and interpersonal relations as determining behavior than on the biological theories of Sigmund Freud; Neo-Freudians include Alfred Adler, Carl Jung, Karen Horney, Harry Stack Sullivan, and Erik Erikson.

*Nerve impulse:* Electrical activity transmitted through a nerve fiber.

*Nervous system:* An array of billions of neurons (conducting nerve cells) that transmits electrical information throughout the body and thereby controls practically all bodily processes.

*Neurologist:* A physician who specializes in the diagnosis and treatment of disorders of the nervous system.

*Neuron:* An individual nerve cell, the basic unit of the nervous system; receives and transmits electrical information and consists of a cell body, dendrites, and an axon.

*Neuropsychology:* The study of brain-behavior relationships, usually involving behavioral tests and correlating results with brain areas.

*Neuropsychopharmacology:* The field of study of the relationship among behavior, neuronal functioning, and drugs.

*Neurosis:* Any functional disorder of the mind or the emotions, occurring without obvious brain damage and involving anxiety, phobic responses, or other abnormal behavior symptoms.

*Neurotransmitter:* A chemical substance released from one nerve cell that communicates activity by binding to and changing the activity of another nerve cell, muscle, or gland; some stimulate, others inhibit.

*Nomothetic study:* A research approach that compares groups of people in order to identify general principles; the dominant method of personality research.

*Nonparticipant observation:* A field technique in which the researcher passively observes the behavior of the subjects, trying not to get involved in the setting.

*Nonverbal communication:* Communication through any means other than words; includes facial expression, tone of voice, and posture.

*Normal distribution:* A bell-shaped curve that often provides an accurate description of the distribution of scores obtained in research; it forms the basis of many statistical tests.

*Observational learning:* Learning that results from observing other people's behavior and its consequences.

*Observational study:* A research technique in which a scientist systematically watches for and records occurrences of the phenomena under study without actively influencing them.

*Obsessions:* Intrusive, recurrent, anxiety-provoking thoughts, ideas, images, or impulses that interfere with an individual's daily functioning.

*Obsessive-compulsive disorder:* A chronic, debilitating anxiety disorder characterized by continuous obsessive thinking and frequent compulsive behaviors.

*Occipital lobe:* The posterior portion of each cerebral hemisphere, where visual stimuli are received and integrated.

*Oedipus complex:* In Freudian theory, sexual attraction to the parent of the opposite sex, and jealousy of and fear of retribution from the parent of the same sex; first manifested in the phallic stage (in girls, sometimes called the Electra complex).

*Olfaction:* The sense of smell.

*Operant:* The basic response unit in instrumental conditioning; a response which, when emitted, operates upon its environment and is instrumental in providing some consequences.

*Operant conditioning:* Learning in which a behavior increases or decreases depending on whether the behavior is followed by reward or punishment; also known as instrumental conditioning.

*Operational definition:* A description of a measurement or manipulation in terms that are unambiguous, observable, and easily identified.

*Opiates:* A class of drugs that relieve pain; opiates include morphine, heroin, and several naturally occurring peptides.

*Oral stage:* In Freudian theory, the first stage of psychosexual development, from birth to approximately age two; sexual energy focuses on the mouth, and conflicts may arise over nursing, biting, or chewing.

*Organic disorder:* A symptomatology with a known physiological or neurological basis.

*Organizational effects:* The early and permanent effects of a hormone; for example, the sex hormones, which produce differentiation in the developing embryo of primordial gonads, internal reproductive structures, and external genitalia.

*Out-group:* Any social group to which an individual does not belong and which, as a consequence, may be viewed in a negative way.

*Overextension:* The application of a word to more objects than ordinary adult usage allows; for example, when a child refers to all small four-legged animals as "dog."

*Overjustification effect:* The tendency of external factors that are perceived to be controlling an individual's behavior to undermine the individual's intrinsic motivation to engage in that behavior.

*Papilla:* A small bundle of taste receptor cells surrounded by supportive cells and communicating with the exterior through a small pore.

*Paradoxical intervention:* A therapeutic technique in which a therapist gives a patient or family a task that appears to contradict the goals of treatment.

*Parallel distributed processing (PDP):* A neurally inspired model in which information is processed in a massively parallel and interactive network; the course of processing is determined by the connection strengths between units of the network.

*Paranoia:* A psychosis characterized by delusions, particularly delusions of persecution, and pervasive suspiciousness; paranoia rarely involves hallucinations.

*Parasympathetic nervous system:* A branch of the autonomic nervous system; responsible for maintaining or reestablishing homeostasis.

*Parietal lobe:* The side and upper-middle part of each cerebral hemisphere and the site of sensory reception from the skin, muscles, and other areas; also contains part of the general interpretive area.

*Pavlovian conditioning:* Learning in which two stimuli are presented one after the other, and the response to the first changes because of the response automatically elicited by the second; also called classical conditioning.

*Penis envy:* In Freudian theory, the strong envy that females develop of the male organ because they subconsciously believe they have been castrated; Sigmund Freud proposed that penis envy dominates the female personality.

*Perception:* The psychological process by which information that comes in through the sense organs is meaningfully interpreted by the brain.

*Perceptual constancy:* The tendency to perceive figures as constant and stable in terms of shape, color, size, or brightness.

*Peripheral nervous system:* All the nerves located outside the bones of the skull and spinal cord.

*Persona:* A major Jungian archetype representing one's public personality; the mask that one wears in order to be acceptable to society at large.

*Personality:* An individual's unique collection of behavioral responses (physical, emotional, and intellectual) that are consistent across time and situations.

*Personality disorder:* A disorder involving deep-rooted behavior patterns that are inflexible and maladaptive and that cause distress in an individual's relationships with others.

*Personality trait:* A stable disposition to behave in a given way over time and across situations.

*Phallic stage:* In Freudian theory, the third stage of psychosexual development, from approximately age four to age six, in which sexual energy focuses on the genitals.

*Phenomenology:* An approach that stresses openness to direct experience in introspective or unsophisticated ways, without using analysis, theory, expectations, or interpretation.

*Pheromone:* A hormone or other chemical that is produced and released from the tissues of one individual and targets tissues in another individual, usually with a consciously or unconsciously detectable scent.

*Phobia:* An anxiety disorder involving an intense irrational fear of a particular class of things (such as horses) or a situation (such as heights).

*Phoneme:* A minimal unit of sound that can signal a difference in meaning.

*Phonology:* The specification, for a given language, of which speech sounds may occur and how they may be combined, as well as the pitch and stress patterns that accompany words and sentences.

*Pineal gland:* A light-sensitive endocrine gland that is located toward the back of the brain and that controls reproductive cycles in many mammalian species.

*Pitch:* The highness or lowness of a sound as heard; related to frequency but also affected by loudness.

*Pituitary:* An endocrine gland located in the brain that controls several other endocrine glands and that cooperates with the hypothalamus of the nervous system in controlling physiology.

*Placebo:* A substance or treatment (such as a pill or an injection) that has no intrinsic effect but is presented as having some effect.

*Placebo effect:* The relief of pain or the causing of a desired behavioral effect as a result of a patient's belief that a substance or treatment will be effective when, in fact, the substance or treatment has no known effect; for example, a sugar pill may relieve a backache if given by a trusted doctor.

*Plasticity:* The ability of neurons and neural networks to grow into specific patterns based partially upon the organism's genetics and partially upon the organism's learned experience; in the brain, neurons can modify the structural organization in order to compensate for neural damage.

*Play therapy:* A system of individual psychotherapy in which children's play is utilized to explain and reduce symptoms of their psychological disorders.

*Pons:* A part of the brain stem that serves as the nerve connection between the cerebellum and the brain stem.

*Population:* All members of a specified group that a researcher is interested in studying.

*Positive reinforcement:* A procedure used to increase the frequency of a response by presenting a favorable consequence following the response.

*Positron emission tomography (PET):* An imaging technique that allows blood flow, energy metabolism, and chemical activity to be visualized in the living human brain.

*Post-traumatic stress disorder (PTSD):* A pathological condition caused by severe stress such as an earthquake or a divorce; it has an acute stage and a chronic stage, and symptoms involve reexperiencing the traumatic event.

*Postsynaptic potential:* A chemical stimulus that is produced in a postsynaptic cell; may excite the cell to come nearer to electrical firing, or may inhibit firing.

*Power law:* A statement of the lawful relationship between two variables that expresses one of them as the other raised to some exponent.

*Pragmatism:* A philosophical position that provided the framework of functionalism by proposing that the value of something lies in its usefulness.

*Prejudice:* Liking or disliking of persons based on their category or group membership rather than on their individual personalities; predominantly refers to unfavorable reactions.

*Preoperational stage:* In Jean Piaget's theory, a transitional stage of childhood (ages two to seven, approximately), after mental representations (symbols) are acquired but before they can be logically manipulated.

*Preparedness:* The idea that, through evolution, animals have been genetically prepared to learn certain things important to their survival.

*Primacy effect:* The tendency for things that are seen or received first to be better recalled and more influential than things that come later.

*Primary motive:* A motive that arises from innate, biological needs and that must be met for survival.

*Primary reinforcer:* A stimulus that acts as a natural, unlearned reinforcer.

*Primary sex characteristics:* The physiological features of the sex organs.

*Priming:* An increase in the availability of certain types of information in memory in response to a stimulus.

*Prisoner's dilemma:* A laboratory game used by psychologists to study the comparative strategies of cooperation and competition.

*Probability:* The proportion of times a particular event will occur; also, the study of uncertainty that is the foundation of inferential statistics.

*Progesterone:* A female sex hormone secreted by the corpus luteum of the ovary; maintains the lining of the uterus during pregnancy and the second half of the menstrual cycle.

*Programmed instruction:* A self-paced training program characterized by many small, increasingly difficult lessons separated by frequent tests.

*Progressive muscle relaxation:* A relaxation technique that systematically works through all the major muscle groups of the body by first tensing, then relaxing each group and paying attention to the changes.

*Projective task:* Any task that provides an open-ended response that may reveal aspects of one's personality; tasks or tests commonly include standard stimuli that are ambiguous in nature.

*Proposition:* A mental representation based on the underlying structure of language; a proposition is the smallest unit of knowledge that can be stated.

*Prosocial behavior:* Behavior intended to benefit another; can be motivated by either egoistic or altruistic concern.

*Prototype:* A "best example" of a concept—one that contains the most typical features of that concept.

*Proxemics:* The use of space as a special elaboration of culture; it is usually divided into the subfields of territory and personal space.

*Proximo-distal development:* Motor development that proceeds from the center of the body to its periphery.

*Psychoactive drugs:* Chemical substances that act on the brain to create psychological effects; usually classified as depressants, stimulants, narcotics (opiates), hallucinogens, or antipsychotics.

*Psychoanalytic theory:* A set of theories conceived by Sigmund Freud that see the roots of human behavior and mental disorders in unconscious motivation and in childhood and early adulthood conflict.

*Psychobiology:* The study of the interactions between biological and psychological processes.

*Psychogenic disorder:* An illness that is attributable primarily to a psychological conflict or to emotional stress.

*Psychometrics:* The theory or technique of psychological measurement; the measurement of psychological differences among people and the statistical analysis of those differences.

*Psychophysics:* The study of the relationship between physical units of a stimulus, such as amplitude, and its sensory, experienced qualities, such as loudness.

*Psychophysiology:* The study of the interaction between the psyche (mind and emotions) and the physiology (physical processes such as blood pressure and heart rate) of the organism.

*Psychosis:* A general term referring to a severe mental disorder, with or without organic damage, characterized by deterioration of normal intellectual and social function and by partial or complete withdrawal from reality; includes schizophrenia and mood disorders such as bipolar disorder.

*Psychosocial crisis:* In Erik Erikson's theory, a turning point in the process of development precipitated by the individual having to face a new set of social demands and new social relationships.

*Psychosomatic disorder:* A physical disorder that results from, or is worsened by, psychological factors; synonymous with psychophysiological disorder and includes stress-related disorders.

*Psychosurgery:* Brain surgery intended to alter an inappropriate or maladaptive behavior.

*Psychotherapy:* A general category of treatment techniques for mental disorders; most psychotherapy uses talking as a tool and centers on the client-psychotherapist relationship to develop awareness and provide support.

*Punishment:* The procedure of decreasing the probability of a behavior by the response-contingent delivery of an aversive stimulus.

*Quasi-experimental designs:* Experimental plans that do not allow subjects to be assigned randomly to treatment conditions.

*Questionnaires:* A survey tool; research subjects view questions in electronic or written format and respond in the same format.

*Random assignment:* The most common technique for establishing equivalent groups by balancing subject characteristics through the assigning of subjects to groups through some random process.

*Rapid eye movement (REM) sleep:* A special stage of sleep that involves desynchronized electrical brain activity, muscle paralysis, rapid eye movements, and narrative dream recall.

*Ratio schedule:* A reinforcement schedule in which reinforcer delivery is contingent upon the performance of a specified number of responses.

*Rational-emotive therapy:* A cognitive-based psychotherapy, pioneered by Albert Ellis, that attempts to replace or modify a client's irrational, inappropriate, or problematic thought processes, outlooks, and self-concept.

*Realistic conflict theory:* A theory from social psychology that suggests that direct competition for scarce or valued resources can lead to prejudice.

*Receptive aphasia:* Difficulties in comprehending spoken and written material, usually after damage to Wernicke's area in the left temporal lobe of the cerebral cortex.

*Receptive field:* The region and pattern in space to which a single neuron responds.

*Receptor:* A specific protein structure on a target cell to which a neurotransmitter binds, producing a stimulatory or inhibitory response.

*Recessive gene:* A gene whose corresponding trait will not be expressed unless the gene is paired with another recessive gene for that trait.

*Reciprocal determinism:* An interactional model proposing that environment, personal factors, and behavior all operate as interacting determinants of one another.

*Reductionism:* An aspect of the scientific method which seeks to understand complex and often interactive processes by reducing them to more basic components and principles.

*Reflex:* An unlearned and automatic biologically programmed response to a particular stimulus.

*Reflex arc:* The simplest behavioral response, in which an impulse is carried by a sensory neuron to the spinal cord, crosses a synapse to a motor neuron, and stimulates a response.

*Regression:* An ego defense mechanism that a person experiencing stress or conflict uses to return to an earlier stage of development.

*Regulators:* Gestures and expressions made by listeners that are informative for speakers; they convey comprehension or acceptance, or indicate when the other person may speak.

*Reinforcement:* An operation or process that increases the probability that a learned behavior will be repeated.

*Reinforcer:* A stimulus or event that, when delivered contingently upon a response, will increase the probability of the recurrence of that response.

*Relative deprivation:* The proposition that people's attitudes, aspirations, and grievances largely depend on the frame of reference within which they are conceived.

*Reliability:* The consistency of a psychological measure, which can be assessed by means of stability over repeated administrations or agreement among different observers.

*Representativeness:* A heuristic in which an estimate of the probability of an event or sample is determined by the degree to which it resembles the originating process or population.

*Repression:* In psychoanalytic theory, a defense mechanism that keeps unacceptable thoughts and impulses from becoming conscious.

*Response cost:* Negative consequences that follow the commission of an undesired behavior, decreasing the rate at which the misbehavior will recur.

*Response hierarchy:* An arrangement of alternative responses to a cue, in a hierarchy from that most likely to occur to that least likely to occur.

*Resting membrane potential:* The maintenance of difference in electrical charges between the inside and outside of a neuron's cell membrane, keeping it polarized with closed ion channels.

*Retardation:* A condition wherein a person has mental abilities that are far below average; other skills and abilities, such as adaptive behavior, may also be marginal; measured by an IQ score of less than 70.

*Reticular formation:* A core of neurons extending through the medulla, pons, and midbrain that controls arousal and sleeping/waking, as well as motor functions such as muscle tone and posture.

*Retina:* The light-sensitive area at the back of the eye, containing the photoreceptors (rods and cones) that detect light.

*Retrieval:* The process of locating information stored in memory and bringing it into awareness.

*Retrograde amnesia:* The type of amnesia that involves an inability to remember things that occurred before the onset of the amnesia.

*Rhodopsin:* The visual pigment in the cells of the rods that responds to light.

*Rod:* A photoreceptor of the retina specialized for the detection of light without discrimination of color.

*Role:* A social position that is associated with a set of behavioral expectations.

*Rule-governed behavior:* Behavior that is under the discriminative control of formalized contingencies.

*Sample:* A subset of a population; a group of elements selected from a larger, well-defined pool of elements.

*Sampling error:* The extent to which population parameters deviate from a sample statistic.

*Satiety:* A feeling of fullness and satisfaction.

*Schema:* An active organization of prior knowledge, beliefs, and experience which is used in perceiving the environment, retrieving information from memory, and directing behavior (plural, schemata).

*Schizophrenia:* Any of a group of psychotic reactions characterized by withdrawal from reality with accompanying affective, behavioral, and intellectual disturbances, including illusions and hallucinations.

*Schwann cell:* A type of insulating nerve cell that wraps around neurons located peripherally throughout the organism.

*Script:* An event schema in which a customary sequence of actions, actors, and props is specified; for example, behavior at a restaurant.

*Seasonal affective disorder (SAD):* Bipolar disorder that undergoes a seasonal fluctuation resulting from various factors, including seasonal changes in the intensity and duration of sunlight.

*Secondary reinforcement:* A learned reinforcer that has acquired reinforcing qualities by being paired with other reinforcers.

*Secondary sex characteristics:* Physical features other than genitals that differentiate women and men; for example, facial hair.

*Self:* The unified and integrated center of one's experience and awareness, which one experiences both subjectively, as an actor, and objectively, as a recipient of actions.

*Self-actualization:* A biologically and culturally determined process involving a tendency toward growth and full realization of one's potential, characterized by acceptance, autonomy, accuracy, creativity, and community; pioneered by Abraham Maslow.

*Self-concept:* The sum total of the attributes, abilities, attitudes, and values that an individual believes defines who he or she is.

*Self-efficacy:* The perception or judgment of one's ability to perform a certain action successfully or to control one's circumstances.

*Self-esteem:* The evaluative part of the self-concept; one's feeling of self-worth.

*Self-image:* The self as the individual pictures or imagines it.

*Self-perception:* A psychological process whereby individuals infer the nature of their attitudes and beliefs by observing their own behavior.

*Semantic memory:* The long-term representation of a person's factual knowledge of the world.

*Sensation:* The process by which the nervous system and sensory receptors receive and represent stimuli received from the environment.

*Sensorimotor stage:* The first of Jean Piaget's developmental stages, lasting from birth to about two years of age, during which objects become familiar and are interpreted by appropriate habitual, motor, and sensory processes.

*Sensory memory:* The persistence of a sensory impression for less than a second; it allows the information to be processed further.

*Serial processing:* A theory concerning how people scan information in memory that suggests that as the number of items in memory increases, so does the amount of time taken to determine whether an item is present in memory.

*Set point:* An organism's personal homeostatic level for a particular body weight, which results from factors such as early feeding experiences and heredity.

*Sex:* Biological maleness or femaleness, determined by genetic endowment and hormones.

*Sex typing:* The process of acquiring traits, attitudes, and behaviors seen as appropriate for members of one's gender; gender-role acquisition.

*Sexual instinct:* In Sigmund Freud's theory, the innate tendency toward pleasure seeking, particularly through achieving sexual aims and objects.

*Shaping:* The acquiring of instrumental behavior in small steps or increments through the reinforcement of successively closer approximations to the desired final behavior.

*Short-term memory:* A memory system of limited capacity that uses rehearsal processes either to retain current memories or to pass them on to long-term memory.

*Significance level:* The degree of likelihood that research results are attributable to chance.

*Skinner box:* The most commonly used apparatus for studying instrumental conditioning; manipulation of a lever (for rats, monkeys, or humans) or an illuminated disk (for pigeons) produces consequences; named for B. F. Skinner.

*Social categorization:* The classification of people and groups according to attributes that are personally meaningful.

*Social cognition:* The area of social psychology concerned with how people make sense of social events, including the actions of others.

*Social comparison:* Comparing attitudes, skills, and feelings with those of similar people in order to determine relative standing in a group or the acceptability of one's own positions.

*Social facilitation:* The enhancement of a person's most dominant response as a result of the presence of others; for some tasks, such as simple ones, performance is enhanced, while for others, such as novel tasks, performance is impaired.

*Social identity theory:* A theory maintaining that people are motivated to create and maintain a positive identity in terms of personal qualities and, especially, group memberships.

*Social learning theory:* The approach to personality that emphasizes the learning of behavior via observations and direct reward; exemplified by the theories of Albert Bandura and Walter Mischel.

*Social loafing:* The tendency to expend less effort while in the presence of others; most likely to occur on additive tasks in which one's individual effort is obscured as a result of the collective efforts of the group.

*Social phobia:* A condition characterized by fear of the possible scrutiny or criticism of others.

*Social psychology:* A subfield of psychology that studies how individuals are affected by environmental factors and particularly by other people.

*Social support:* The relationships with other people that provide emotional, informational, or tangible resources that affect one's health and psychological comfort.

*Socialization:* The process of learning and internalizing social rules and standards.

*Sociobiology:* The application of the principles of evolutionary biology to the understanding of social behavior.

*Somatization disorder:* A mental syndrome in which a person chronically has a number of vague but dramatic medical complaints that apparently have no physical cause.

*Somatoform disorders:* A group of mental disorders in which a person has physical complaints or symptoms that appear to be caused by psychological rather than physical factors; for example, hypochondriasis.

*Somnambulism:* The scientific term for sleepwalking; formerly a term for hypnosis.

*Spinal cord:* The part of the central nervous system that is enclosed within the backbone; conducts nerve impulses to and from the brain.

*Spontaneous recovery:* The recovery of extinguished behaviors over time in the absence of any specific treatment or training.

*Sports psychology:* The subfield of psychology that applies psychological principles to physical activities such as competitive sports; frequently concerned with maximizing athletic performance.

*Sprouting:* A process that occurs when remaining nerve fibers branch and form new connections to replace those that have been lost.

*Stage theory of development:* The belief that development moves through a set sequence of stages; the quality of behavior at each stage is unique but is dependent upon movement through earlier stages.

*Standard deviation:* A measure of how variable or spread out a group of scores is from the mean.

*Standardization:* The administration, scoring, and interpretation of a test in a prescribed manner so that differences in test results can be attributed to the testee.

*Statistical significance:* Differences in behavior large enough that they are probably related to the subject variables or manipulated variables by differences too large to be caused by chance alone.

*Stereotype:* A set of beliefs, often rigidly held, about the characteristics of an entire group.

*Stimulants:* Drugs that cause behavioral or physiological stimulation, including amphetamines, cocaine, and their respective derivatives; caffeine; nicotine; and some antidepressants.

*Stimulus:* An environmental circumstance to which an organism may respond; it may be as specific as a single physical event or as global as a social situation.

*Stimulus generalization:* The ability of stimuli that are similar to other stimuli to elicit a response that was previously elicited only by the first stimuli.

*Storage:* The stage of memory between encoding and retrieval; the period for which memories are held.

*Strange situation:* An experimental technique designed to measure the quality of the mother-infant attachment relationship.

*Stress:* The judgment that a problem exceeds one's available resources, resulting from a primary appraisal of the problem and a secondary appraisal of the coping resources.

*Stressor:* Anything that produces a demand on an organism.

*Striate cortex:* The region of the occipital lobe that reconstitutes visual images for recognition.

*Stroke:* A vascular injury resulting from either the rupture of a vessel or the blocking of blood flow in an artery.

*Structuralism:* An early school of psychology that sought to define the basic elements of mind and the laws governing their combination.

*Sublimation:* According to Sigmund Freud, a defense mechanism by which a person may redirect aggressive impulses by engaging in a socially sanctioned activity.

*Suffix:* A morpheme that attaches to the end of a word.

*Superego:* In Freudian theory, the part of the psyche that contains parental and societal standards of morality and that acts to prohibit expression of instinctual drives; includes the conscience and the ego-ideal.

*Syllogism:* A logical argument constructed of a major premise, a minor premise, and a conclusion, the validity of which is determined by rules of inference.

*Symbiotic relationship:* An overprotective, often enmeshed relationship between a parent and child.

*Sympathetic nervous system:* A division of the autonomic nervous system that prepares the organism for energy expenditure.

*Synapse:* The junction between two neurons over which a nerve impulse is chemically transduced.

*Synchronized electroencephalogram:* A regular, repetitive brain-wave pattern that is caused by multitudes of neurons firing at the same time and the same rate in a given brain region.

*Systematic desensitization:* An exposure therapy in which the phobic patient is gradually presented with a feared object or situation.

*Systems theory:* A concept in which the family grouping is viewed as a biosocial subsystem existing within the larger system of society; intrafamilial communications are the mechanisms of subsystem interchange.

*Tachistoscope:* An experimental apparatus for presenting visual information very briefly to the right or left visual field; sometimes called a T-scope.

*Tardive dyskinesia:* Slow, involuntary motor movements, especially of the mouth and tongue, which can become permanent and untreatable; can result from psychoactive drug treatment.

*Temporal lobe:* The lower portion on the side of each cerebral hemisphere, containing the sites of sensory interpretation, memory of visual and auditory patterns, and part of the general interpretive area.

*Test-retest reliability:* A common way of determining consistency, by administering the same test twice to the same persons.

*Testosterone:* The principal male sex hormone produced by the testes.

*Thalamus:* A portion of the diencephalon, located at the base of the forebrain, which receives sensory information from the body and relays these signals to the appropriate regions of the cerebrum.

*Thematic Apperception Test (TAT):* A personality test in which individuals demonstrate their needs by describing what is happening in a series of ambiguous pictures.

*Theory:* A model explaining the relationship between several phenomena; derived from several related hypotheses which have survived many tests.

*Therapy:* The systematic habilitation of a disorder.

*Thermoreceptor:* A sensory receptor specialized for the detection of changes in the flow of heat.

*Threshold:* The minimum stimulus intensity necessary for an individual to detect a stimulus; usually defined as that intensity detected 50 percent of the time it is presented.

*Thyroxine:* The major hormone produced and secreted by the thyroid gland; stimulates protein synthesis and the basal metabolic rate.

*Trait theory:* A way of conceptualizing personality in terms of relatively persistent and consistent behavior patterns that are manifested in a wide range of circumstances.

*Transduction:* The process of changing physical energy, such as light, into neural messages.

*Transference:* The phenomenon in which a person in psychoanalysis shifts thoughts or emotions concerning people in his or her past (most often parents) onto the analyst.

*Transvestite:* A person who, for fun or sexual arousal, often dresses and acts like a member of the opposite sex (going "in drag"); most are heterosexual males.

*Tricyclics:* A class of antidepressant drugs.

*Two-factor theory:* A behavioral theory of anxiety stating that fear is caused by Pavlovian conditioning and that avoidance of the feared object is maintained by operant conditioning.

*Type A personality:* A behavior pattern that describes individuals who are driven, competitive, high-strung, impatient, time-urgent, intense, and easily angered; some researchers have associated this pattern with increased risk of heart disease.

*Unconditional positive regard:* The attempt by a therapist to convey to a client that he or she genuinely cares for the client.

*Unconditioned response (UR):* An innate or unlearned behavior that occurs automatically following some stimulus; a reflex.

*Unconditioned stimulus (US):* A stimulus that elicits an unconditioned response; the relation between unconditioned stimuli and unconditioned responses is unlearned.

*Unconscious:* The deep-rooted aspects of the mind; Sigmund Freud claimed that the unconscious includes negative instincts and urges that are too disturbing for people to be aware of consciously.

*Unipolar depression:* A disorder characterized by the occurrence of one or more major depressive episodes but no manic episodes.

*Validity:* A statistical value that states the degree to which a test measures what it is intended to measure; the test is usually compared to external criteria.

*Vicarious learning:* Learning (for example, learning to fear something) without direct experience, either by observing or by receiving verbal information.

*Visual cortex:* The top six cell layers in the back of the brain, which are specialized for organizing and interpreting visual information.

*Visual dyslexia:* The lack of ability to translate observed written or printed language into meaningful terms.

*Voyeurism:* The derivation of sexual pleasure from looking at the naked bodies or sexual activities of others without their consent.

*Wavelength:* The distance traveled by a wave front in the time given by one cycle (the period of the wave); has an inverse relation to frequency.

*White matter:* The tissue within the central nervous system, consisting primarily of nerve fibers.

*Within-subject design:* An experimental plan in which each subject receives each level of the independent variable.

*Working through:* A psychoanalytical term that describes the process by which clients develop more adaptive behavior once they have gained insight into the causes of their psychological disorders.

*Yerkes-Dodson law:* The principle that moderate levels of arousal tend to yield optimal performance.

*Zeitgeber:* A German word meaning "time giver"; a factor that serves as a synchronizer or entraining agent, such as sunlight in the morning.

# BIOGRAPHICAL LIST OF PSYCHOLOGISTS

**ADLER, ALFRED** (1870-1937). Originally a Freudian psychologist, Adler had by 1911 broken from Sigmund Freud, resigning as president of the Vienna Psychoanalytic Society when the break became apparent. Adler was known for his work on individual personality and his theory of the creative self. He eschewed environment and heredity as the major governing factors in people's lives. He considered these factors raw materials that individuals can shape as they will.

**ALLPORT, GORDON** (1897-1967). Allport was well known for his theory of functional autonomy, which disputes Sigmund Freud's notion that adult conduct stems from instincts, desires, and needs that all people share. He resisted classifying people according to such elemental motives. For him, each personality was unique and could not be categorized according to a preconceived set of motivations.

**BANDURA, ALBERT** (1925-    ). The learning theory advanced by Bandura postulated that people learn largely through realizing what the consequences are of their behavior or of the behavior of others. He advocated observational learning. His social cognitive theory influenced learning theory in the last quarter of the twentieth century.

**BECK, AARON T.** (1921-    ). Recognized for his work in cognitive therapy, Beck sought to alter the thinking of depressed patients by encouraging them to assess their problems in alternative ways capable of solution. He also moved his patients toward understanding how their problems might be the result of their own actions or inactions. The Beck Depression Inventory, a twenty-one-item instrument based on a four-point scale, is used as a quantitative tool for ascertaining the symptoms of depression in adolescents and adults.

**BERKOWITZ, LEONARD** (1926-    ). A social psychologist, Berkowitz gained a worldwide reputation as an expert on human aggression, which he defined as an externally elicited drive to harm others. He believed that aggression could be sparked involuntarily by stimuli from the surrounding environment.

**BINET, ALFRED** (1857-1911). Binet, collaborating with Theodore Simon, devised tests for measuring intelligence, later called intelligence quotient (IQ) tests. Although he originally contended that intelligence was too complex to be reduced to mere numbers, he ultimately accepted the simplified modes of measurement, devised by William Stern and refined by Lewis Terman, that considered IQ to be equal to mental age divided by chronological age and multiplied by one hundred. Terman added the last element so that IQ could be expressed in whole numbers rather than in numbers requiring decimal points.

**BRENTANO, FRANZ CLEMENS** (1838-1917). Brentano questioned the theories of the mind espoused by many contemporary psychologists and physicians who were mainly concerned with the brain as a physical entity. Brentano denied the necessity of understanding the physiological mechanisms underlying mental events, contending that experimental psychology was more limited and limiting than many of his colleagues believed because it involves the systematic manipulation of variables, then noting their effect upon other variables. Brentano believed that any study of the mind should emphasize process over a material view of the mind's content.

**BREUER, JOSEF** (1842-1925). A noted physician and researcher, Breuer grew close to the young Sigmund Freud, fourteen years his junior. Freud said that while he was still a student preparing for his last examinations in medical school, Breuer applied the methods of psychoanalysis to one of his patients, Anna O., who suffered from hysteria and whom he treated systematically from 1880 to 1882, thereby, in Freud's eyes, inaugurating the field of psychoanalysis.

**CANNON, WALTER B.** (1871-1945). A Harvard University professor of physiology, Cannon demonstrated the effects emotions have on the human body. His work led to the mapping of the brain's hypothalamus and limbic systems. Cannon challenged the theory proposed by William James and C. G. Lange that situations caused by certain stimuli produce specific bodily reactions, such as increase heart beat or increases or decreases in blood pressure, pointing out that similar bodily reactions occur in a wide variety of emotional states. He noted that the viscera, with few sensory nerves, are unlikely to perceive changes, contending that autonomic reactions often have relatively long periods of latency.

**CATTELL, JAMES McKEEN** (1860-1944). Convinced that applied psychology underlies every aspect of human activity, Cattell was a member of the functionalist school, which demanded that psychology be a practical science. Unlike the structuralists, the functionalists were concerned with the function of the mind rather than with its contents. The approach of Cattell and other functionalists was biological rather than physiological. He was elected president of the American Psychological Association at the age of thirty-five, succeeding William James in that post.

**DEWEY, JOHN** (1859-1952). Generally considered the most significant educational philosopher of the twentieth century, Dewey regarded the division of the elements of human reflexes into sensory, brain, and motor processes as inaccurate and misleading. He contended that there is a stream of behavior and that human reflexes are part of a coordinated system that cannot be viewed as anything but a unified whole. Dewey accepted the inevitability of social change but believed that it could be influenced favorably by proper planning. He is considered the father of progressive education.

**DOLLARD, JOHN** (1900-1980). The frustration-aggression hypothesis of Dollard and his partner Neil E. Miller departs from the explanations of Sigmund Freud and Konrad Lorenz, which are essentially biological. Miller and Dollard place considerable emphasis on explanations that have to do with social learning and environmental factors. They collaborated on *Frustrations and Aggression* (1963).

**DIX, DOROTHEA LYNDE** (1802-1887). While teaching inmates in a Boston prison, Dix concluded that many of the women confined as criminals were really mentally ill. She began a campaign to publicize and improve the treatment of the mentally ill in the United States and later in Europe. When she began her crusade in 1841, only 15 percent of people needing care received it. By 1890, that proportion had increased to 70 percent.

**EBBINGHAUS, HERMANN** (1850-1909). Ebbinghaus is best remembered for his systematic study of learning and memory, which flew in the face of Wilhelm Wundt's proclamation that the higher mental processes could not be studied experimentally. A rationalist, Ebbinghaus conducted experiments based on learning out-of-context groups of syllables from a pool of 2,300 that he had devised. His chief interests were in such topics as meaning, imagery, and individual differences in cognitive styles.

**EGAS MONIZ, ANTÓNIO** (1874-1955). Egas Moniz was a Portuguese neurologist, who, aware of C. R. Jacobson's experiments in altering the behavior of chimpanzees by the removal of the frontal lobes of their brains, concluded that such procedures would produce similar results in humans. He was a pioneer in the now largely discredited area of psychosurgery. He was awarded the 1949 Nobel Prize in Physiology or Medicine for his discovery of the therapeutic value of leucotomy (lobotomy) in certain psychoses.

**ELLIS, ALBERT** (1913-    ). As a psychoanalyst and sex therapist, Ellis became disenchanted with the methods of psychoanalysis and sought new means of approaching his patients, which he outlined in *New Approaches to Psychotherapy* (1955). He devised a rational-emotive therapy (RET) which was initially scorned by most of his colleagues, many of whom eventually came to see the practical wisdom of this approach. His *Sex Without Guilt* (1958) was widely distributed and influenced much subsequent thinking about sex and sex therapy.

**ERIKSON, ERIK** (1902-1994). In *Childhood and Society* (1950), one of the most influential books on learning theory in the twentieth century, Erikson defined eight developmental stages through which humans pass as they move from infancy to later adulthood. An understanding of these stages, particularly the first five that move from infancy to adolescence, substantially affected learning theory in the United States.

**EYSENCK, HANS** (1916-1997). In his theory of personality, Eysenck related the dimensions of introversion/extroversion and neuroticism/stability to the way the nervous system is constituted. He enumerated the characteristics that distinguish behavior therapy from dynamic psychotherapy.

**FREUD, ANNA** (1895-1982). The youngest child of Sigmund Freud, Freud became, like her father, a psychoanalyst. Her work, exclusively with children, earned her a worldwide reputation as a child psychoanalyst. Following her father's death, she was regarded as the worldwide leader of the Freudian movement in psychology.

**FREUD, SIGMUND** (1856-1939). Perhaps the most renowned figure in the field of psychoanalysis, Freud introduced the free-association technique into that field. From his patients' free associations, Freud realized that psychoanalysts have to determine the structure and nature of their patients' unconscious minds. He identified and named the Oedipus complex, which contends that on the unconscious level a male's mother is the object of his sexual desire, thereby setting up his father as a competitor. Freud also identified the id, the ego, and the superego as cornerstones of the human psyche.

**FROMM, ERICH** (1900-1980). In his most renowned book, *Escape from Freedom* (1941), Fromm speculated that freedom is a frightening thing to many people and that when they recognize that they are free, they immediately attempt to affiliate themselves with people or organizations that will reduce or totally eliminate their choices. He concluded that being free places an enormous responsibility upon people, who are often willing to trade freedom for the security of having a structure and direction provided by an external force.

**GILLIGAN, CAROL** (1936-    ). Gilligan served as chief investigator for a number of studies of the development of girls and women. Her major research interests were in adolescence, moral reasoning, and conflict resolution, with particular emphasis on the contributions women's thinking have made to psychological theory. She pursued her studies because of the lack of attention women and girls received in most psychological research. She uncovered a "deep sense of outrage and despair" over the disconnection women feel because they believe their feelings have been ignored. Her books *In a Different Voice: Psychological Theory and Women's Development* (1982) and *Meeting at the Crossroads: Women's Psychology And Girls' Development* (co-authored with Lyn M. Brown, 1992) have gained widespread recognition among psychologists concerned with matters of gender.

**HALL, G. STANLEY** (1844-1924). A man of diverse talents, Hall was an antistructuralist who embraced the evolutionary theories of Charles Darwin and adapted them to psychology, particularly in his recapitulation theory, which hypothesized that every child from the embryonic stage to maturity recapitulates, first quite rapidly and later more slowly, every stage of development through which the human race has passed from its earliest, prehistoric beginnings. As president of Clark University in Worcester, Massachusetts, for thirty-one years (1888-1919), Hall made the university a major center for the study of psychology. He was the first person in the United States to call for sex education in public schools.

**HORNEY, KAREN** (1885-1952). A physician, Horney denied that Sigmund Freud's theories on biological motivation were relevant for the people of her day. For her, social and cultural influences were preeminent. She contended that psychological problems grow out of disturbed human relationships, particularly those between children and their parents. Her essays about the psychology of women are cogent and were compiled in *Feminine Psychology* (1967).

**JAMES, WILLIAM** (1842-1910). James's ideas sowed early seeds in psychological thought that eventually germinated into the school of functionalism. Wrestling with the implications of German materialism, Charles Darwin's theory of evolution—from which freedom of choice seemed to be absent—and predetermination, James finally, after reading an essay on free will by Charles Renouvier (1815-1903), moved in new directions that led to the pragmatism for which he is most remembered. His recognition of the importance of stream of consciousness led away from generalizing about humans and their psychological constituents and led to a theory that emphasized the individuality and instinctuality of humans.

**JOHNSON, VIRGINIA E.** (1925-    ). Johnson, along with her partner William H. Masters, was among the leading sexual therapists in the United States. They gathered scientific data relating to sex by means of electroencephalography, electrocardiography, and the use of color monitors. They worked with 694 volunteers, photographed in various modes of sexual stimulation, carefully protecting their subjects' identities and privacy. They classified four stages of sexual arousal. Their work, especially *Human Sexual Response* (1966) and *Human Sexual Inadequacy* (1970), helped to spark the sexual revolution of the late 1960's and the 1970's.

**JUNG, CARL** (1875-1961). Noted for his word-association research, Jung was essentially Freudian in his formative years as a psychologist, although his thinking began to diverge from that of Sigmund Freud beginning in 1909. Jung employed Freud's notions of the preconscious and unconscious minds to arrive at the concept of the personal unconscious. This led him to his renowned theory of the collective unconscious that drew on common experience of people through the ages. Jung contended that predispositions of the human mind are inherited and that in the collective unconscious there exist archetypes, so that at birth the mind is not the blank slate postulated by John Locke (1632-1704) but rather that it contains structures inherited from previous spans of human existence.

**KELLY, GEORGE A.** (1905-1967). Notably iconoclastic, Kelly eschewed much of the theoretical psychology of his day, including a great deal of Sigmund Freud's. In dealing with subjects, Kelly concluded that whether a person has a psychological problem depends largely on how that person views life. While scientists create theories that help them to predict future events, the general public creates systems constructs to make similar predictions. His two-volume work *The Psychology of Personal Constructs* (1955) explains in great detail how nonscientists create their systems constructs.

**KINSEY, ALFRED** (1894-1956). Kinsey had a distinguished career as a zoologist at Indiana University, where his early work dealt with the life cycle, evolution, geographic distribution, and speciation of the gall wasp. He gained his greatest renown, however, for his extensive studies of human sexual behavior, begun in the late 1930's. They culminated in the publication of his landmark study, *Sexual Behavior in the Human Male* (1948), which was followed by a similar study on the human female in 1953. At the time of his death, he was the founding director of the Institute for Sex Research of Bloomington, Indiana.

**KOHLBERG, LAWRENCE** (1927-1987). Kohlberg's greatest contribution was his research on the moral development of children and adolescents. Kohlberg ran an extensive longitudinal study in which he recorded the responses of boys aged seven through adolescence to hypothetical moral dilemmas. He concluded that children and adults pass through six identifiable stages in their moral development, which stems from cognitive development. Older children shape their responses on increasingly broad and abstract ethical standards. Kohlberg detected an evolution from self-interest to more principled, selfless behavior and developed a chronological hierarchy of moral development.

**KRAEPELIN, EMIL** (1856-1926). Kraepelin's chief contribution to psychology was his formulation of a comprehensive list of mental disorders published in 1883. It was used worldwide for more than a century until, in 1952, the *Diagnostic and Statistical Manual of Mental Disorders* (DSM) was published by the American Psychological Association. Kraepelin identified the mental condition of dementia praecox and demonstrated that it was treatable and manageable. He renamed the condition schizophrenia, which means "a splitting of the personality."

**LACAN, JACQUES** (1901-1961). Lacan was trained as a psychiatrist. In the 1930's and 1940's he worked with psychotic patients. In the 1950's, he began to develop his own version of psychoanalysis, based on the ideas he found in structuralist linguistics and anthropology. He questioned Sigmund Freud's notion of the unconscious. Whereas Freud believed that by bringing the contents of the unconscious into consciousness he could minimize repression and neurosis, Lacan contended that the ego can not replace the unconscious or control it. For Lacan, the ego or "I" self is only an illusion, a product of the unconscious itself, and the unconscious is the center of all being.

**LEWIN, KURT** (1890-1947). An early apostle of Gestalt psychology, Lewin applied Gestalt principles to such areas as motivation, personality, and particularly group dynamics. For Lewin, many psychologists clung too tenaciously to the notion that the inner determinants of behavior are foremost in shaping human events. This Aristotelian view was contrary to the Galilean view that how organisms behave depends upon the totality of forces acting upon them at any given time. For Lewin, human behavior can be understood only in the light of the many complex, dynamic forces acting upon a person. He viewed groups as physical systems comparable to the brain. He detected an interdependence within members of groups that dynamically affected their functioning.

**MASLOW, ABRAHAM** (1908-1970). Maslow made humanistic psychology a recognized branch of the field. His early experimental work with monkeys led him to conclude that physical strength had less to do with dominance than the inner confidence of animals, although as he matured, he saw little value in studying nonhuman animals. His emphasis was on studying individuals rather than groups and using subjective reality as the most effective key to understanding human behavior. Maslow's hierarchy of needs led to his concept of self-actualization, for which he is best known.

**MASTERS, WILLIAM H.** (1915-2001). Masters, along with his partner Virginia E. Johnson, was among the leading sexual therapists in the United States. They gathered scientific data relating to sex by means of electroencephalography, electrocardiography, and the use of color monitors. They worked with 694 volunteers, photographed in various modes of sexual stimulation, carefully protecting their subjects' identities and privacy. Masters and Johnson classified four stages of sexual arousal. Their work, especially *Human Sexual Response* (1966) and *Human Sexual Inadequacy* (1970), helped to spark the sexual revolution of the late 1960's and the 1970's.

**MEICHENBAUM, DONALD** (1940-    ). Meichenbaum, a founder of the "cognitive revolution" in psychotherapy, advocated the constructivist perspective. Professor of psychology at the University of Waterloo in Ontario, Canada, he has been a prolific writer, researcher, and lecturer. Meichenbaum wrote the influential book *Cognitive Behavior Modification: An Integrative Approach* (1977). His *Clinical Handbook/Treatment Manual for PTSD* (1994) is an impressive summary of information for clinicians and researchers working with persons suffering the effects of traumatic stress.

**MILLER, NEAL E.** (1909-2002). The frustration-aggression hypothesis of Miller and his partner John Dollard departs from the explanations of Sigmund Freud and Konrad Lorenz, which are essentially biological. Miller and Dollard place considerable emphasis on explanations that have to do with social learning and environmental factors. They collaborated on *Frustrations and Aggression* (1963).

**MISCHEL, WALTER** (1929-    ). Mischel refused to acknowledge that there exist stable characteristics of personality, contending that behavior depends upon specific situations. He questioned the validity of personality inventories and the data obtained from them. For Mischel, the assessment of personality based upon traits is specious because it overgeneralizes. Mischel's most notable works on personality are *Personality and Assessment* (1968) and *Introduction to Personality* (1971; rev. ed., 1981).

**MURRAY, HENRY A.** (1893-1988) Murray had a background in a variety of disciplines, including psychology, chemistry, and biology. He taught at Harvard University from 1927 to 1968 and helped to establish the Boston Psychoanalytic Society. He drew his theory of personality from both Freudian and Jungian psychoanalysis, postulating an elaborate system of basic motivational forces. Murray developed the Thematic Apperception Test (TAT), widely used for assessing personality.

**PAVLOV, IVAN PETROVICH** (1849-1936). Pavlov gained his reputation for his work on conditioned and unconditioned responses. Using dogs that were fed after a bell sounded, he accustomed the dogs to associating the sound of the bell with food. Once they had made this association, Pavlov found that sounding the bell caused them to salivate even though no food was forthcoming. Pavlov was a positivist whose life was centered on his laboratory work. He had a low opinion of psychology, not because of its emphasis on consciousness but because of its use of introspection.

PIAGET, JEAN (1896-1980). Piaget was a central figure in the study of human development. His theory of genetic epistemology links the development of intellectual ability to biological maturity and experience. He contended that when an experience fits a child's cognitive structure, assimilation takes place. When such an experience does not fit its cognitive structure, the cognitive structure is adjusted, by a process that Piaget called accommodation, so that it can be assimilated. His stages of intellectual development have been instrumental in teacher education.

PINEL, PHILIPPE (1745-1826). Pinel's book *Philosophy of Madness* (1793) changed the way that many physicians viewed mental illness. Pinel was appalled at the treatment of mental patients, many of whom were chained and abused. He demonstrated that violent behavior among patients who were chained often disappeared when their chains were removed. Pinel also called for a cessation of the blood-letting that was a common means of treatment in his day.

ROGERS, CARL (1902-1987). Renowned for his client-centered approach to psychotherapy, Rogers outlined his methods in his widely used book, *Client-Centered Therapy: Its Current Practice, Implications, and Theory* (1951). Rogers's nondirective approach was unique and was based on his belief that therapists function most productively when they seek to understand and accept their patients' subjective reality. His complex theory of personality is clearly articulated in *Client-Centered Therapy.*

RORSCHACH, HERMANN (1884-1922). As a small child, Rorschach loved an activity called *Klecksography,* a way of making pictures by using ink blots. This enthusiasm led to his life's work. Undecided about whether to study medicine or art, he finally opted for medicine, but his continuing interest in inkblots caused him to devise a way to use them in exploring the human psyche. Rorschach began showing inkblots to schoolchildren, whose reactions he noted and analyzed. After receiving his medical degree in 1912, he tested three hundred patients and one hundred "normal" people, using inkblots to analyze their unconscious minds. In 1921, he published *Psychodiagnostics: A Diagnostic Test Based on Perception,* which fully described his unique diagnostic method.

RUSH, BENJAMIN (1745-1813). Sometimes referred to as the first psychiatrist in the United States, Rush published *Diseases of the Mind* in 1812. He complained that mentally ill people were treated criminally and urged that their shackles be removed. He said that such patients should never be put on display for the amusement of others. Despite his revolutionary views, Rush nevertheless accepted bloodletting as a viable treatment for mental disorders, as well as rotating patients to relieve their confused minds and strapping them in tranquilizing chairs in order to calm those who were agitated.

**SELYE, HANS** (1907-1982). Selye demonstrated how environmental stress and anxiety could lead to the release of hormones that, over time, could produce a number of the biochemical and physiological disorders common in industrial societies of the twentieth century. Selye's theory greatly affected popular views of stress. In *The Stress of Life* (1978), he reduced the research on stress to terms the public could understand and appreciate.

**SIMON, THÉODORE** (1873-1961). In 1904, Simon, an intern in a French institution for mentally retarded children, worked with Alfred Binet to create tests that would quantify intelligence, differentiating intellectually normal children from those who were intellectually deficient. Together, Simon and Binet in 1905 produced the Binet-Simon Scale of Intelligence, which led to the development of a broad range of tests to measure people's intelligence quotient (IQ).

**SKINNER, B. F.** (1904-1990). Skinner's belief that behavior is controlled by environmental reinforcement mechanisms gave him reason to think that understanding such mechanisms can help to solve many of society's problems. In his view, it is more pressing to understand the environment rather than the mind or the inner self. His method was to manipulate environmental factors and note the effect that such alterations had on behavior. His approach has been designated "descriptive behaviorism."

**SPENCER, HERBERT** (1820-1903). Spencer applied the concept of evolution to the human mind and to human societies. For him, everything in the universe begins as an undifferentiated whole. Evolution leads to differentiation so that systems become increasingly complex. After Charles Darwin's *On the Origin of Species* (1859) appeared, Spencer shifted his emphasis from acquired characteristics to natural selection. He coined the term "survival of the fittest," which is widely associated with Darwinian thought.

**SULLIVAN, HARRY STACK** (1892-1949). An American psychiatrist, Sullivan, along with his teacher William Alanson White (1870-1937), extended Freudian psychoanalysis to the treatment of patients with severe mental disorders, particularly schizophrenia. Sullivan argued that schizophrenics were curable, blaming cultural forces for the condition of many such patients. His writing, especially *Schizophrenia as a Human Process* (1962), greatly altered the views of many psychiatrists.

**TERMAN, LEWIS M.** (1877-1956). Working in the field of psychological testing and measurements, Terman abbreviated the term "intelligence quotient" to IQ. He modified William Stern's method of measuring IQ by adding one element to it. Once mental age had been divided by chronological age, he multiplied the result by one hundred so that it could be expressed as a whole number rather than as one with a decimal point.

**THORNDIKE, EDWARD L.** (1874-1949). A pioneer in the field of learning theory, Thorndike was also intrigued by and wrote in such fields as verbal behavior, transfer of training, the measurement of sociological events, educational methodology, and comparative psychology. Well known for his theories of the Law of Effect and the Law of Exercise, he subdivided the latter into the Law of Use and the Law of Disuse. The former stated that if an association led to a feeling of satisfaction, it would be strengthened, whereas if it led to an unsatisfying feeling, it would be weakened. He later repudiated these theories. In time, the functionalism that he espoused was absorbed into mainstream psychology.

**Titchener, Edward** (1867-1927). British-born psychologist Titchener spent thirty-five years at Cornell University as director of its psychological laboratory, creating there the largest psychology doctoral program in the United States. Convinced that there was little value in applied psychology, Titchener dogmatically insisted that the field, in order to be truly scientific, must deal with pure knowledge. Despite his close relationship with John B. Watson, Titchener eschewed behaviorism and became the founder of the structuralist school of psychology, which opposed not only behaviorism but also such other schools of psychology as functionalism and faculty psychology.

**Watson, John B.** (1878-1958). A major researcher in animal psychology, Watson was the founder of the behaviorist school of psychology. His academic career ended precipitously in 1920 when he was found to be having an adulterous affair with a research assistant. He began to write for the popular press and in 1921 joined the J. Walter Thompson Company, a leading advertising company, of which he became vice president in 1924, remaining there for the rest of his working life. Watson continued his interest and writing in psychology and had a significant effect upon the behaviorists who followed him.

**Wundt, Wilhelm** (1832-1920). One of the most prolific writers in the field of psychology, Wundt held that psychology was a scientific field and that it had become an experimental science. Whereas the other sciences were based on what Wundt termed "mediate experiences," psychology was based on "immediate experiences." He sought to use experimental psychology to discover the basic components of thought and to understand how mental elements combine into complex mental experiences. His method was based largely on introspection, or self-observation and analysis.

*R. Baird Shuman*

# WEB SITE DIRECTORY

## AAASP ONLINE: ASSOCIATION FOR THE ADVANCEMENT OF APPLIED SPORT PSYCHOLOGY

http://www.aaasponline.org

Offers valuable background information that explains the nature of sport psychology, the growing variety and number of people who use it, the services provided by sport psychologists, and how to find a qualified sport psychology professional. Other features include a consultant finder, a list of AAASP publications, a section on how to become an AAASP certified consultant, and links to other sport psychology sites.

## ALL ABOUT DEPRESSION

http://www.allaboutdepression.com

This small but attractive and well-designed site is maintained by Prentiss Price, a Ph.D. in counseling psychology who works for a college counseling center. The site's major sections are overview of depression, causes, diagnosis, treatment, medication, and resources (contact information or links for organizations). Each topic's page has a table of contents along the left edge and a "professional recommendations" section highlighting the most important advice.

## AMERICAN ACADEMY OF CHILD AND ADOLESCENT PSYCHIATRY (AACAP)

www.aacap.org

This organization hopes its site will aid the treatment and understanding of children and youths with behavioral, mental, or developmental disorders. Particularly useful are the fact sheets for family members and other caregivers. The Facts for Families series of more than fifty texts includes discussions of alcohol, bed-wetting, divorce, guns, lying, pregnancy, talking about sex, and violent behavior. The site also provides a glossary of symptoms and mental illnesses that might affect teenagers, policy statements on topics such as juvenile death sentences and psychoactive medications for children and youth, and information for professionals.

## AMERICAN ASSOCIATION OF SUICIDOLOGY (AAS)

http://www.suicidology.org

This site's sections include a detailed outline for understanding and helping someone who is suicidal; an online bookstore, with resources grouped by topic and audience; recent suicide news; crisis centers or support groups searchable by state and city; guidance on obtaining AAS certification; and a resource page, listing suicide statistics, school guidelines, specifics on suicide among youth and the elderly, and more.

## AMERICAN PSYCHOLOGICAL ASSOCIATION (APA)

http://www.apa.org

This extensive site, from the world's largest professional association for psychologists, offers a wide range of information for a variety of audiences. Though content-rich and detailed, the site is clearly organized and easy to navigate. The main page has sections providing recent news, classified ads, portals for psychologists, students, and the public, membership information, and more. Resources for the public include full text reports from APA's news site, links to information pages on twelve topics (including aging, children, depression, mind-body health, parenting and family, women, and violence), and links to help pages. Also includes resources for psychologists.

## ASSOCIATION FOR THE STUDY OF DREAMS

http://www.asdreams.org/index.htm

This international nonprofit organization's site features selected articles from the association's magazine, *Dream Time*, and its journal, *Dreaming*; educational pages, with answers to common questions about dreams and nightmares, and a science project file; and a classified list of dream-related and dream-sharing Web sites and e-mail lists.

## BIRTH PSYCHOLOGY

http://www.birthpsychology.com

This site is provided by the Association for Pre- and Perinatal Psychology and Health (APPAH). Its sections include life before birth (fetal senses, sound, prebirth communication, and prenatal memory and learning); birth and the origins of violence; the birth scene (obstetrics, circumcision, and more); healing of prenatal and perinatal trauma; abstracts and index for APPAH's Journal of Prenatal and Perinatal Psychology and Health; a bibliography of books, videos, and journals; and a current list of practitioners and programs.

## C. G. JUNG PAGE

http://www.cgjungpage.org

This full-featured site aids novice readers with an introduction to Jungian psychology in the form of a Jung Lexicon. The resources page includes links to the Web sites of institutes and societies offering Jungian training. There are also links to the bibliography of the Journal of Analytical Psychology; links to numerous full-text analytical psychology articles; and film commentaries, book reviews, and literary articles employing Jungian criticism.

## CENTER FOR THE STUDY OF AUTISM

http://www.autism.org

The center, located in Salem, Oregon, conducts research on autism therapies and provides information for parents and care providers. Sections include a detailed overview of autism; texts on subgroups and related disorders; about twenty topical issues, including auditory processing problems, self-injurious behavior, and how to determine whether a treatment has helped; interventions (more than thirty, including music therapy, the hug machine, and nutrition); the sibling center; interviews with autism experts; and a detailed page of autism links.

### CLASSICS IN THE HISTORY OF PSYCHOLOGY

http://psychclassics.yorku.ca

This site collects important public-domain scholarly texts from psychology and related fields. There are more than 150 articles and 25 books, as well as links to more than 200 related works on other sites. Some texts are accompanied by introductory essays written for the site. The texts can be accessed by author or by topic (including behaviorism, intelligence testing, psychoanalysis and psychotherapy, cognition, and women in psychology). Users can search the site by keyword.

### COMMUNITY PSYCHOLOGY NET

http://www.communitypsychology.net

This site provides comprehensive information on community psychology. The introductory page defines the topic, distinguishing it from sociology, social work, and public health. The site's organizing metaphor is the university campus. The library provides a classified grouping of links. The lecture hall has course syllabi and reading lists. The admissions office has links to forty universities offering graduate programs. The career planning center lists job ads.

### CONSUMER PSYCHOLOGY

http://www.wansink.com/index.html

This small but effective site has two sections, both related to consumerism and food. The food psychology section covers nine topics (including "Do larger packages increase usage?" and "Measuring ad effects on brand usage"). For each topic, the site provides a one-paragraph overview, a more detailed research brief, and usually a link to a PDF file for a journal article on the topic, written by the site editor. There are also lesson plans suitable for ages twelve to adult.

### CRIMINAL PROFILING RESEARCH

http://www.criminalprofiling.ch

This Swiss site focuses on presenting the results of scientific research. Besides a detailed, referenced introduction to the topic of criminal profiling, it offers brief accounts of how profiling is used in the United States and Europe, a case analysis page, bibliographies of books and journal articles, links to sites explaining how profiling is done, and a FAQ section which includes information on profiling as a career.

**DEPRESSEDTEENS.COM**

http://www.depressedteens.com/indexnf.html

This site strives to help teenagers and their parents and teachers recognize and understand the symptoms of adolescent depression and ensure that depressed teenagers get help. An essential part of the site is information about, and a preview of, the twenty-six-minute video *Day for Night: Recognizing Teenage Depression*. Includes, among other areas, a fact sheet on adolescent depression.

**DOTCOMSENSE**

http://helping.apa.org/dotcomsense

This small site, based on a brochure produced by the American Psychological Association, guides Web users in protecting their privacy on bulletin boards, chat rooms, and Web sites (particularly on those dealing with mental health) that ask for personal information or use cookies. Also gives helpful guidelines for assessing the credibility and accuracy of sites providing mental health information. It lists other Web sites devoted to evaluation of online information.

**EATING DISORDER REFERRAL AND INFORMATION CENTER (EDRIC)**

http://www.edreferral.com

EDRIC provides information for friends and family members as well as treatment referrals for individuals with eating disorders. Sections include a search form for therapists or treatment centers, lists of job openings at treatment centers, treatment scholarships, and recommended books and Web sites. Also examines movement therapy, causes, assessment, treatment, consequences, body image, introductory information on specific disorders, and eating disorders among males, athletes, and pregnant women.

**ECT.ORG: INFORMATION ABOUT ELECTROCONVULSIVE THERAPY**

http://ECT.org

This site aims to be the Web's most comprehensive source of electroconvulsive therapy (ECT) information. Juli Lawrence, the site's creator, had ECT in 1994 and hopes her site, which discusses all aspects of the topic, will help others considering ECT in making an informed decision. The site provides attractive, clearly arranged links (with annotations) to information on these topics: effects (memory loss and, possibly, brain damage); resources (studies, statistics, and official statements from organizations); news; self-help (alternatives to ECT); message boards and event calendars; and the Hall of Shame ("the very worst ECT practitioners and researchers").

**ENCYCLOPEDIA OF PSYCHOLOGY**

http://www.psychology.org

"Intended to facilitate browsing in any area of psychology," this site provides access to more than two thousand Web sites. Categories of topics include careers, environment behavior relationships (with forty-five subcategories and more than one thousand links), organizations, paradigms and theories, people and history, publications, and resources. All categories are divided into subtopics. The Web page for each subtopic includes links to texts and to Web sites. An annotation for each site (usually detailed and often noting the level of user for whom it is appropriate) is generally provided.

## EXPLORATIONS IN LEARNING AND INSTRUCTION:
### THE THEORY INTO PRACTICE DATABASE
http://tip.psychology.org

Provides brief but detailed summaries of fifty major theories of human learning and instruction, all of which have extensive scientific support. The summaries include the name of the theory's originator, an overview of the theory, its principles and application, an example, references for further study, and sometimes a video clip or Web site links. The theories include adult learning, andragogy, cognitive dissonance, Criterion Referenced Instruction, experiential learning, lateral thinking, multiple intelligences, operant conditioning, and more.

## FREUD NET
http://psychoanalysis.org

The site of the New York Psychoanalytic Institute's Abraham A. Brill Library. The library maintains what might be the world's largest collection of information on psychoanalysis. Provides a helpful page of selected links about Sigmund Freud: museum, exhibition, and library sites; links to texts of Freud's writings (with a warning that most of his works are still under copyright, so only the earlier, inferior translations are in the public domain); and writings about Freud.

## GREAT IDEAS IN PERSONALITY
http://www.personalityresearch.org

This sites deals with scientific research in personality psychology. It provides detailed information on personality theories, grouping them into twelve sections, including behaviorism, evolutionary psychology, attachment theory, basic emotions, personality disorders, interpersonal theory, and more. The page describing each theory includes a brief description, names of the theorists involved, references to published works, and links to additional Web sources. The site also features sections on personality in general, practical information for psychology students, links to personality journal sites, and links to personality courses sites for professors.

## HEALTH EMOTIONS RESEARCH INSTITUTE
http://www.healthemotions.org

This clear, attractive site of the University of Wisconsin's Health Emotions Research Institute provides information on studies of positive emotions, their influence on the body, and the implications of this research for preventing disease, affecting definitions of health, and fostering resilience. The site explains the institute's mission and its current projects—including biological consequences of meditation, biological substrates of resilience, and biological bases of positive affective styles.

## THE HUMOR PROJECT, INC.

http://www.humorproject.com

The Humor Project, founded in 1977, focuses on the positive power of humor by training individuals and organizations (through its lectures, workshops, conferences, and publications) to use humor and creativity. The site's playful spirit is immediately apparent in the visitor counter, with its constantly whirling numbers. Includes descriptions of program offerings, the annual workshop, and the international humor conference; an online bookstore; a daily article, interview, and reader's "di-jest"; a spotlight column; and "Today's Laffirmation."

## INTERNET MENTAL HEALTH

http://www.mentalhealth.com

This award-winning site, established in 1995, is intended for both professionals and the public. It functions as an encyclopedia for more than fifty common mental disorders. For each disorder, the site gives both the American and European descriptions, treatment information, research information, booklets prepared by professional organizations and support groups, and magazine articles. The site has links to online diagnostic programs for personality, anxiety, mood, eating, and substance abuse disorders as well as for schizophrenia and attention-deficit hyperactivity disorder (ADHD). It also provides encyclopedic information on common psychiatric medications, a mental health magazine, and links to popular mental health sites.

## MEMORY AND REALITY: WEBSITE OF THE FALSE MEMORY SYNDROME FOUNDATION

http://fmsonline.org

This foundation works to prevent False Memory Syndrome, investigate reasons for its spread, and help families affected by it. Includes a detailed FAQ section; the current newsletter; a searchable archive of newsletter issues back to 1992; a document explaining hypnosis, hypnotic susceptibility, and their role in creating false memories; information about USA v. Peterson, Seward, Mueck, Keraga, and Davis, the first criminal trial to bring charges against therapists regarding false memories; a detailed page dealing with retractors; and discussions of scientific studies.

## MHN: MENTAL HELP NET
http://mentalhelp.net

Developed in 1994, this award-winning site strives "to catalog, review, and make available to everyone all online mental health resources as they become available." Groups the sites into subject categories, which are divided into two lists: issues and disorders, and information. For each topic, the page might include basic information (summarized from DSM-IV); links categorized by type; and news, book reviews, self-help groups, and resources (such as treatment facilities, therapists, professional conferences, and clinical job openings). The site also contains a daily mental health news section and a professional area.

## NAMI: THE NATION'S VOICE ON MENTAL ILLNESS
http://www.nami.org

This site represents the National Alliance for the Mentally Ill (NAMI), a support and advocacy organization for friends and family of people with severe mental illnesses—and for the individuals themselves. It contains a search form for locating NAMI affiliate organizations; information about the NAMI helpline; fact sheets on specific illnesses, treatments, and medications; purchase information for NAMI's books, videos, brochures, and newsmagazines; public policy information and statements; and a links to NAMI research reports.

## NATIONAL ASSOCIATION FOR SELF-ESTEEM (NASE)
www.self-esteem-nase.org

This association works to integrate self-esteem into American society and thus enhance the personal happiness of every individual. The site provides a review of research on self-esteem, relating it to problems such as substance abuse, violence, crime, teenage pregnancy, and suicide. There are also articles from NASE's newsletter, a categorized reading list, a list of published self-esteem educational programs, and a description of NASE's Parent Link Network for raising socially responsible children.

## POSITIVE PSYCHOLOGY
http://psych.upenn.edu/seligman/pospsy.htm

This content-rich site is maintained by Martin Seligman, past president of the American Psychological Association and a researcher on positive psychology, optimism, and learned helplessness. The site offers several articles, columns, and book chapters by Seligman that define and explore the parameters of positive psychology. There are also professional summaries, a concept paper for a network of positive psychology scholars, an e-mail directory of researchers, questionnaires (some downloadable) that researchers can use, and a grouping of essays, units, syllabi, and reading lists for teaching positive psychology.

## PROCRASTINATION RESEARCH GROUP (PRG)

http://www.carleton.ca/~tpychyl

This clear, attractive site is provided by a university learning group at Carleton University's psychology department (Ottawa, Canada) and collects research and information on procrastination worldwide. The Research Resources section includes a featured journal article, summaries of student papers (undergraduate through doctoral levels) written by the PRG, and a comprehensive procrastination bibliography. The site also has a useful self-help page. The latter includes a brief outline of signs of procrastination, suggested strategies for reducing it, a list of recommended readings, and a concise grouping of links to other sites.

## PSYCH CENTRAL: DR. GROHOL'S MENTAL HEALTH PAGE

http://psychcentral.com/grohol.htm

This site provides links to more than 1,700 Web sites that have been reviewed by the author. Its main access point is the resources section, which consists of thirty categories (some as specific as "Bipolar" and "Attack on America," others as broad as "Professional Psychology Resources"). Each category is further subdivided into topics or formats (such as books or support groups). The page for each of the 1,700 Web sites gives a brief but usually detailed description of the site, the date last updated, the number of hits it has received from Psych Central, and its rating by Psych Central users. Besides the Web site links, the site provides concise descriptions of symptoms and treatments for mental disorders, "Have I Got?" quizzes for several disorders, live chat, book reviews, essays, and psychology and mental health news.

## PSYCHOLOGY

http://psychology.about.com/mbody.htm

This content-rich site's main organization is its thirty "essentials" categories (including adult development, cognitive psychology, dreams, love, industrial/organizational psychology, sport psychology, and more). Each topic has additional sections. Another access method, by subject, includes the essentials but adds about seventy additional categories.

## PSYCHOLOGY INFORMATION ONLINE

http://www.psychologyinfo.com

Provides a wide range of information (aimed at consumers, college students, and psychologists) on the practice of psychology. The information falls into these categories: psychotherapy and counseling, diagnosis and disorders, psychological testing and evaluation, other forms of treatment, behavior therapy, forensic psychiatry, and psychological consultations for legal situations. There are separate access points for the three categories of users. In addition, users can consult the navigation guide, the list of links, or the alphabetical subject index for each category.

## PSYCHOLOGY VIRTUAL LIBRARY

http://www.clas.ufl.edu/users/gthursby/psi

This clear, attractive site is part of the World Wide Web Virtual Library, which evaluates each site it includes. The seventeen categories include academic psychology, books, journals, university psychology departments, clinical social work, directories of psychology sites, mental health, history of psychology, and more. Each category has its own subsections. The Stress Virtual Library includes, for example, links for books and publishers, e-mail lists and news groups, mental health resources, professional organizations, stress management, and commercial products. The links on each page are annotated.

## RxLIST: THE INTERNET DRUG INDEX

http://www.rxlist.com

This site, founded in 1995, is maintained by Neil Sandow, a licensed, experienced California pharmacist. The site's primary content includes FAQ sections on more than 4,500 popular drugs, 1,000 professional monographs, and 1,500 patient-oriented monographs. Visitors can search for drugs by brand name, generic name, ID Imprint code, or NDC code. Each FAQ section explains the purpose of the drug, who should not use it, how to take it, potential problems, and what to do in case of missed doses or overdoses. Other features include a search page for alternatives (such as homeopathies or herbal remedies) and a list of the top two hundred prescriptions filled in each of the last six years.

## SCHIZOPHRENIA.COM

http://www.schizophrenia.com

This site was established in 1996 by Brian Chiko in memory of his brother, a schizophrenia patient who committed suicide. Its purpose is to provide, free of charge, accurate information for those who have the disease or whose lives have been affected by it. The site's introduction to schizophrenia is clear and well organized. Other topics covered include causes, diagnosis, medication, managing depression, preventing suicide, getting financial assistance, and assisted or involuntary treatment.

## THE SHYNESS HOME PAGE

http://www.shyness.com

This small site is sponsored by the Shyness Institute in Palo Alto, California. It provides information on upcoming shyness workshops and an e-mail link enabling visitors to ask the institute questions. Also provides links to, or contact information for, a wide range of other shyness resources: newsgroups; shyness clinics; brochures and articles; organizations offering classes, workshops, and coaching; reading lists; and research papers.

**SLEEPNET.COM**
http://www.sleepnet.com
Provides information (not medical advice) to improve sleep and links to other noncommercial sleep information sites. Sections include information on a wide range of sleep disorders and sleep-related topics (sleep apnea, insomnia, narcolepsy, restless legs, shift work, and circadian rhythms), a glossary, a categorized list of links to news articles, public sleep forums, and an e-mail newsletter.

**SOCIAL PHOBIA/SOCIAL ANXIETY ASSOCIATION HOME PAGE**
http://www.socialphobia.org
The site explains that social phobia, a frequently misdiagnosed condition, is the world's third largest mental health problem. It provides definitions and background information, a weekly mailing list, a link to the Social Anxiety Institute's page (offering a variety of therapy programs), and other social phobia links, including personal testimonies and reading lists.

**SOCIAL SCIENCE INFORMATION GATEWAY: PSYCHOLOGY**
http://sosig.esrc.bris.ac.uk/psychology
Lists and describes high-quality Web sites and texts, arranged into eighteen subcategories. Users can search by keyword or browse within the subcategories—including mental health, general psychology, consumer psychology, animal psychology, psychological disorders, developmental psychology, sport psychology, and more. Each subcategory contains further groupings by subject and by type of site. The latter might include books, bibliographies, journals, educational materials, e-mail lists and discussion groups, organizations, research projects, and resource guides. The page describing each Web site gives a descriptive summary, keywords, and the site administrator's e-mail address.

**SOCIETY FOR LIGHT TREATMENT AND BIOLOGICAL RHYTHMS**
http://www.sltbr.org
This society supports those with research or clinical interests in biological rhythm disorders—including those caused by seasonal affective disorder, sleep disorders, jet lag, shift work, and premenstrual syndrome—and therapies for those conditions. The information for the general public includes a detailed "Questions and Answers About Seasonal Affective Disorder and Light Therapy" page as well as links to other Web articles and sites about seasonal affective disorder, sleep disorders, melatonin, and circadian rhythms.

**STRESS INC.—THE COMMERCE OF COPING**
http://stress.jrn.columbia.edu/site/index.html
This creative, attractive site depicts ways in which society has moved from the 1950's, when stress was primarily an engineering term, to the present day. Sections of the site (representing the commerce of stress) include pub-

lishing, advertising, fitness (focusing on yoga), toys, consulting, ergonomics, and yoga. In addition, the site provides a brief history of stress, a stress quiz, information on fringe stress-relief techniques, and tension-breakers.

### TRAFFIC PSYCHOLOGY AT THE UNIVERSITY OF HAWAII
http://www.soc.hawaii.edu/leonj/leonj/leonpsy/traffic/tpintro.html

This site, maintained by Dr. Leon James, a psychology professor at the University of Hawaii, has extensive texts and references on the origins and theories of traffic psychology. James provides an inventory of driving behavior and the psychological aspects of traffic flow, a comprehensive bibliography on driving psychology, a self-test for individuals to determine how they would operate within the nine zones of the driving personality, and a twenty-year overview of what James has learned from teaching his traffic psychology course.

### THE WHOLE BRAIN ATLAS
http://www.med.harvard.edu/AANLIB

Sections of this award-winning site cover the normal brain (with images of normal aging), cerebrovascular disease, brain tumors, degenerative disorders (such as Alzheimer's and Huntington's diseases), and inflammatory or infectious diseases (such as multiple sclerosis, AIDS dementia, Lyme disease, and herpes).

### WHOLEFAMILY
http://www.wholefamily.com/index.html

This site offers problem-solving texts (written by credentialed professionals) about situations encountered within family relationships. The site's main portals are its centers for marriage, parents, seniors, and teens. "What's New" adds sections on additional topics. There are also questions and answers. The site provides chat rooms, topical discussion-forums, "real life dramas," the editor's column, a family soap opera, and a site newsletter.

*Glenn Ellen Starr Stilling*

# INDEXES

# CATEGORIZED LIST OF ENTRIES

Imprinting
Nervous System
Psychosurgery
Thirst

**EXPERIMENTATION**
Animal Experimentation
Behaviorism
Experimentation: Independent,
    Dependent, and Control
    Variables
Survey Research: Questionnaires
    and Interviews

**GROUP PROCESSES**
Crowd Behavior
Groups
Helping
Industrial/Organizational
    Psychology
Support Groups

**HUMANISTIC-PHENOMENOLOGICAL
    MODELS**
Abnormality: Psychological
    Models
Analytic Psychology:
    Jacques Lacan
Humanistic Trait Models:
    Gordon Allport
Personology: Henry A. Murray
Psychoanalysis
Social Psychological Models:
    Erich Fromm

**INTELLIGENCE**
Aging: Cognitive Changes
Creativity and Intelligence
Giftedness
Intelligence
Intelligence Tests
Memory
Mental Retardation
Race and Intelligence

**LANGUAGE**
Language
Nervous System
Speech Disorders

**LEARNING**
Aging: Cognitive Changes
Behaviorism
Brain Structure
Conditioning
Habituation and Sensitization
Imprinting
Learned Helplessness
Learning
Learning Disorders
Memory
Memory: Animal Research
Motivation
Nervous System
Pavlovian Conditioning
Race and Intelligence
Senses
Social Learning: Albert Bandura

**MEMORY**
Aging: Cognitive Changes
Alzheimer's Disease
Dementia
Imprinting
Memory
Memory: Animal Research
Motivation
Nervous System
Senses

**METHODOLOGY**
Animal Experimentation
Behaviorism
Case-Study Methodologies
Diagnosis
Experimentation: Independent,
    Dependent, and Control
    Variables
Motivation
Psychoanalysis

# INDEX